Natalie Livingstone is the author of the *Sunday Times* bestseller, *The Mistresses of Cliveden: Three Centuries of Power, Intrigue and Scandal*. She lives in London with her husband and three children.

Praise for *The Women of Rothschild*

'In this scintillating family saga, Natalie Livingstone reveals that the Rothschild ladies were, if anything, even more extraordinary than their fathers, brothers and husbands . . . With consummate skill, she weaves together . . . the dark as well as the light, and the result is both thrilling and moving' *Mail on Sunday*

'Livingstone marshals a huge cast of characters, spanning two centuries and moving with ease from the Jewish ghetto to the grandest houses in England. She describes the Rothschild women as an "overlooked source of power, strength and imagination", and in this absorbing book she has brought them out of the shadows' *Daily Mail*

'In this gripping biography, Natalie Livingstone shows that Rothschild women were the velvet gloves guiding the iron fists of their male relatives' Hannah Rothschild, author of *The Improbability of Love*

D1342613

The Women of Rothschild

The Untold Story of the World's Most Famous Dynasty

NATALIE LIVINGSTONE

JOHN MURRAY

First published in Great Britain in 2021 by John Murray (Publishers)
An Hachette UK company

This paperback edition published in 2022

1

Copyright © Natalie Livingstone 2021

The right of Natalie Livingstone to be identified as the
Author of the Work has been asserted by her in accordance with
the Copyright, Designs and Patents Act 1988.

Text design by Nicky Barneby, Barneby Ltd

A CIP catalogue record for this title is available from the British Library

Paperback ISBN 978-1-529-36673-0
eBook ISBN 978-1-529-36674-7

Typeset in in Adobe Caslon by Barneby Ltd

Printed and bound by Bell and Bain Ltd, Glasgow

John Murray policy is to use papers that are natural, renewable
and recyclable products and made from wood grown in sustainable forests.
The logging and manufacturing processes are expected to conform
to the environmental regulations of the country of origin.

To my parents Ann and Howard, with love

Contents

Family Tree   x

Introduction   1

PART I
Gutle, Hannah, Henriette

1. The Mother of the Business   11
2. 'Merely a Machine'   20
3. Inventing the Family   28
4. The Husband Hunt   37
5. Madame Montefiore   44
6. A Healthier Climate   49
7. *Concordia, Integritas, Industria*   56
8. Betrayal   67
9. The Financial Prowess of Mrs Rothschild   73
10. A Wedding and a Funeral   81

PART II
Charlotte, Hannah Mayer, Louisa

11. 'This World of Fog and Cares'   95
12. Marrying Out   102
13. Marrying In   108
14. 'The Management of Infancy'   113
15. A Muse   127
16. 'Surely We Do Not Deserve So Much Hatred'   127
17. The Great Abyss   134

18. Loopholes and Legacies   145
19. Living in Hotels   154
20. A Mother's Lesson   164

PART III
Constance, Emma, Hannah, Blanche

21. Flirtations   175
22. Heirs and Graces   184
23. The Rose and the Lion   190
24. Maiden Speeches   197
25. Blanche in Bohemia   204
26. The Royal Seal   213
27. Rescue and Prevention   222
28. Elevations   230
29. 'Big Guns Arrived during the Night'   240

PART IV
Rózsika, Dolly, Miriam, Nica, Rosie

30. Crossing the Border   253
31. Enlisting   259
32. Reconstruction   272
33. Vocations   279
34. Before the Bombs   285
35. Sisters in Arms   292
36. Echoes   306
37. The Baroness, the Bird and the Monk   319
38. The Queen of Fleas   327
39. Spare Rib and the Subversive Stitch   338
40. 'A Glorious Indian Summer'   348
41. Mothers and Daughters   357

Acknowledgements   367
Picture Credits   369
Notes   371
Index   423

Mayer Amschel's five sons were ennobled by the Austrian Emperor in 1822 and granted the right to use the nobiliary particle 'von' in their names. The branches of the family in Frankfurt and Vienna adopted this convention, whereas those in Paris and Naples adapted this to the French 'de'. In England, even though Nathan Mayer originally eschewed his foreign title, many of his descendants began to use 'de' in their names. As will become clear, these honorific titles have not always been included in the text.

Rothschild
Family Tree

The family tree follows several lines of descent that would not appear on a traditional genealogy. As well as Rothschilds by birth and by marriage, the tree includes the offspring of women who were born Rothschild but took another name on marriage (and in some cases their offspring).

There was widespread cousin marriage in the nineteenth-century Rothschild family, therefore some subjects appear on the tree twice – by birth and again by marriage. In these cases, dotted lines have been used to connect them to the offspring listed under their marital entries.

Owing to constraints of space, only figures mentioned in the book are included. Main subjects are shown in **bold type**.

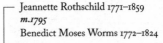

Jeannette Rothschild 1771–1859
m.1795
Benedict Moses Worms 1772–1824

Amschel Mayer von Rothschild 1773–1855
m.1796
Eva Hanau 1779–1848

Salomon Mayer von Rothschild 1774–1855
m.1800 →
Caroline Stern 1782–1854

Nathan Mayer Rothschild 1777–1836
m.1806 →
Hannah Barent Cohen 1783–1850

Gutle Schnapper 1753–1849
m.1770 ——————
Mayer Amschel Rothschild 1744–1812

Isabella Rothschild 1781–1861
m.1802
Bernhard Juda Sichel 1780–1862

Babette Rothschild 1784–1869
m.1808
Siegmund Leopold Beyfus 1786–1845

Carl Mayer von Rothschild 1788–1855
m.1818 →
Adelheid Herz 1800–53

Julie Rothschild 1790–1815
m.1811
Meyer Levin Beyfus 1790–1860

Henriette Rothschild 1791–1866
m.1815 →
Abraham Montefiore 1788–1824

James Mayer de Rothschild 1792–1868
m.1824 →
Betty von Rothschild 1805–86

Anselm Salomon von Rothschild 1803–74
m.1826
Chilly (Charlotte de) Rothschild 1807–59

Betty von Rothschild 1805–86
m.1824
James Mayer de Rothschild 1792–1868

Lionel Nathan de Rothschild 1808–79
m.1836
Charlotte von Rothschild 1819–84

Nat (Nathaniel de) Rothschild 1812–70
m.1842
Charlotte de Rothschild 1825–99

Mayer Amschel de Rothschild 1818–74
m.1850
Juliana Cohen 1831–77

Charlotte von Rothschild 1819–84
m.1836
Lionel Nathan de Rothschild 1808–79

Joseph Mayer Montefiore 1816–80
m.1860
Henrietta Francisca Sichel 1837–1915

Adolphe Carl von Rothschild 1823–1900
m.1850
Caroline Julie Anselme von Rothschild 1830–1907

Charlotte Montefiore 1818–54
m.1847
Horatio Joseph Montefiore 1798–1867

Anselm Alexander Carl von Rothschild 1835–54

Nathaniel Montefiore 1819–83
m.1850
Emma Goldsmid 1819–1902

Alphonse (Mayer Alphonse de) Rothschild 1827–1905
m.1857
Leonora de Rothschild 1837–1911

Louisa Montefiore 1821–1910
m.1840
Anthony Nathan de
Rothschild 1810–76

Salomon James de Rothschild 1835–64
m.1862
Adèle Hannah Charlotte von Rothschild 1843–1922

Chilly (Charlotte de) Rothschild 1807–59
m.1826
Anselm Salomon von Rothschild 1803–74

Anthony Nathan de Rothschild 1810–76
m.1840
Louisa Montefiore 1821–1910

Hannah Mayer de Rothschild 1815–64
m.1839
Henry FitzRoy 1807–59

Lou (Louise de) Rothschild 1820–94
m.1842
Mayer Carl von Rothschild 1820–86

Mayer Carl von Rothschild 1820–86
m.1842
Lou (Louise de) Rothschild 1820–94

Willy (Wilhelm Carl von) Rothschild 1828–1901
m.1849
Mathilde (Hannah Mathilde von) Rothschild 1832–1924

Charlotte de Rothschild 1825–99
m.1842
Nat (Nathaniel de) Rothschild 1812–70

Gustave Samuel James de Rothschild 1829–1911
m.1859
Cécile Anspach 1840–1912

Edmond James de Rothschild 1845–1934
m.1877
Adelheid von Rothschild 1853–1935

Julie (Caroline Julie Anselme von) Rothschild 1830–1907
m.1850
Adolphe Carl von Rothschild 1823–1900

Mathilde (Hannah Mathilde von) Rothschild 1832–1924
m.1849
Willy (Wilhelm Carl von) Rothschild 1828–1901

Puggy (Nathaniel Mayer von) Rothschild 1836–1905

Ferdinand James Anselm de Rothschild 1839–98
m.1865
Evelina de Rothschild 1839–66

Salomon Albert Anselm von Rothschild 1844–1911
m.1876
Bettina Caroline de Rothschild 1858–92

Alice Charlotte de Rothschild 1847–1922

and two other offspring

Constance de Rothschild 1843–1931
m.1877
Cyril Flower, Lord Battersea 1843–1907

Annie Henriette de Rothschild 1844–1926
m.1873
Eliot Constantine Yorke 1843–78

Arthur Frederick FitzRoy 1842–58

Blanche (Caroline Blanche Elizabeth) FitzRoy 1844–1912
m.1864
Coutts Lindsay 1824–1913

Hannah de Rothschild 1851–90
m.1878
Archibald Philip Primrose, 5th Earl of Rosebery 1847–1929

Adèle Hannah Charlotte von Rothschild 1843–1922
m.1862
Salomon James de Rothschild 1835–64

Emma Louisa von Rothschild 1844–1935
m.1867
Natty (Nathaniel Mayer de) Rothschild, 1st Lord Rothschild 1840–1915

and five other offspring

Adelheid von Rothschild 1853–1935
m.1877
Edmond James de Rothschild 1845–1934

and two other offspring

Leonora de Rothschild 1837–1911
m.1857
Alphonse (Mayer Alphonse de) Rothschild 1827–1905

Evelina de Rothschild 1839–66
m.1865
Ferdinand James Anselm de Rothschild 1839–98

Natty (Nathaniel Mayer de) Rothschild, 1st Lord Rothschild 1840–1915
m.1867
Emma Louisa von Rothschild 1844–1935

Alfred Charles de Rothschild 1842–1918
alleged affair with
Marie 'Mina' Wombwell c.1846–1913

Leopold de Rothschild 1845–1917
m.1881
Marie Perugia 1862–1937

Bettina Caroline de Rothschild 1858–92
m.1876
Salomon Albert Anselm von Rothschild 1844–1911

Lionel James Mayer René de Rothschild 1861–61

Charlotte Béatrice de Rothschild 1864–1934
m.1883
Maurice Ephrussi, Baron 1849–1916

Edouard Alphonse James de Rothschild 1868–1949
m.1905
Germaine Alice Halphen 1884–1975

James Armand de Rothschild 1878–1957
m.1913
Dorothy Mathilde Pinto 1895–1988

Maurice Edmond Charles de Rothschild 1881–1957
m.1909
Noémie Claire Alice Palmyre Halphen 1888–1968

Alexandrine (Miriam Caroline Alexandrine) de Rothschild 1884–1965
m.1910
Albert Max von Goldschmidt-Rothschild 1879–1941

Walter (Lionel Walter) Rothschild,
2nd Lord Rothschild 1868–1937

Evelina (Charlotte Louise Adela Evelina) Rothschild 1873–1947
m.1899
Clive Behrens 1871–1935

Charles (Nathaniel Charles) Rothschild 1877–1923
m.1907
Rózsika von Wertheimstein 1870–1940

Almina Wombwell 1876–1969
m.1. 1895
George Herbert, 5th Earl of
Carnarvon, 1866–1923
m.2 1923
Ian Onslow Dennistoun, 1879–1938

Lionel Nathan de Rothschild 1882–1942
m.1912
Marie-Louise Eugénie Beer 1892–1975

Evelyn Achille de Rothschild 1886–1917

Anthony Gustav de Rothschild 1887–1961
m.1926
Lydia Louise Yvonne Cahen d'Anvers 1899–1977

Effie (Harriet Euphemia Susan)
Lindsay 1865–1946

Helen (Anne Helen) Lindsay 1868–1955

Sybil Myra Caroline Primrose 1879–1955
m.1903
Charles John Cecil Grant 1877–1950

Peggy (Margaret Etrenne Hannah)
Primrose 1881–1967
m.1899
m. Robert Crewe-Milnes, 1st Marquess
of Crewe 1858–1945

Harry Mayer Archibald Primrose,
6th Earl of Rosebery 1882–1974
m.1 1909
Dorothy Alice Margaret Augusta Grosvenor
1890–1966
m.2 1924
Eva Isabel Marian Strutt (née Bruce) 1892–1987

Edmond Adolphe Maurice Jules
Jacques de Rothschild 1926–97
m.1 1958
Veselinka Vladova Gueorguieva, b.1927
m.2 1963
Nadine Nelly Jeannette
Lhopitalier b.1932

Neil James Archibald Primrose 1882–1917
m.1915
Lady Victoria Alice Louise Stanley 1892–1927

SIXTH GENERATION	SEVENTH GENERATION	EIGHTH GENERATION

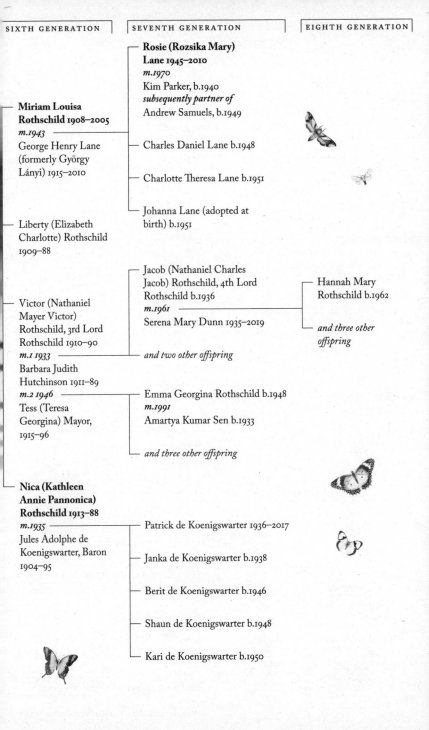

Miriam Louisa Rothschild 1908–2005
m.1943
George Henry Lane (formerly György Lányi) 1915–2010

— **Rosie (Rozsika Mary) Lane 1945–2010**
m.1970
Kim Parker, b.1940
subsequently partner of
Andrew Samuels, b.1949

— Charles Daniel Lane b.1948

— Charlotte Theresa Lane b.1951

— Johanna Lane (adopted at birth) b.1951

— Liberty (Elizabeth Charlotte) Rothschild 1909–88

— Victor (Nathaniel Mayer Victor) Rothschild, 3rd Lord Rothschild 1910–90
m.1 1933
Barbara Judith Hutchinson 1911–89
m.2 1946
Tess (Teresa Georgina) Mayor, 1915–96

— Jacob (Nathaniel Charles Jacob) Rothschild, 4th Lord Rothschild b.1936
m.1961
Serena Mary Dunn 1935–2019

— Hannah Mary Rothschild b.1962

— *and three other offspring*

— *and two other offspring*

— Emma Georgina Rothschild b.1948
m.1991
Amartya Kumar Sen b.1933

— *and three other offspring*

— **Nica (Kathleen Annie Pannonica) Rothschild 1913–88**
m.1935
Jules Adolphe de Koenigswarter, Baron 1904–95

— Patrick de Koenigswarter 1936–2017

— Janka de Koenigswarter b.1938

— Berit de Koenigswarter b.1946

— Shaun de Koenigswarter b.1948

— Kari de Koenigswarter b.1950

Introduction

ROTHSCHILD. A NAME that evokes wealth and power. A dynastic thread, strung with grand houses and gilded lifestyles. A bank whose backing was sought by sovereigns and statesmen, whose decisions could move markets, and whose prominence endured two centuries of breakneck historical change. The Rothschilds' swift and dramatic rise from the cramped world of the Frankfurt ghetto to the capitals of Europe has been the subject of numerous books, as well as countless insidious conspiracy theories. There are few studies of modern Judaism, of nineteenth-century finance, or of the foundation of Israel in which Rothschilds do not appear; European history has the dynasty woven so deeply into its fabric that the Rothschilds have been described as the 'first European Economic Community'; and modern Jewish history is so closely entwined with that of the Rothschilds that they have been referred to as the 'first family of Judaism' or even the 'Jewish royal family'. But what appears at first to be one of history's most heavily chronicled, widely known and deeply mythologised dynasties is really nothing of the sort. Half of the Rothschilds, the women, remain virtually unknown.

Almost everything about the Rothschilds – all the books and articles, the calumnies and myths, the films and plays – concern only the Rothschild men. Mayer Amschel Rothschild is routinely described as a 'founding father', as if the dynasty sprang from him alone. And while his and his wife Gutle's five sons are famous, few could name a single one of their five daughters. Even books that purport to be about the family as a whole are really about the men. Count Corti's *The Rise and Reign of the House of Rothschild* comprises two volumes and 34,140 lines of text, of which 34,000 focus on the men.[1] Even Niall Ferguson's history of the house of Rothschild, a more recent work that makes use of the women's archives, still contains more than five times as many references to the men of the family as to the women.[2]

The root of this exclusion is clear: the world of nineteenth-century finance, in which the family rose to prominence, was a male one. But the Rothschilds were never a banking business alone. They have always been a dynasty whose influence was grounded in banking but whose significance was much broader, reaching into literature and education and religion, into sport, science, horticulture, music and politics. That the women of the family were involved in these pursuits and in many of their own besides is clear from merely a glance at the historical record: their names crop up in contemporary newspaper articles, memoirs and subscription lists; their likenesses appear in cartoons, photographs and family portraits. But they remain silent, their stories untold. Works focusing exclusively on the women of the Rothschild family amount to a handful of essays and a few single-subject biographies, most of them written by female descendants curious at the exclusion of their ancestors from the historical record.

A few years ago I came across one of these works. 'Rothschild Women', by Miriam Rothschild, began life as a catalogue essay for a 1994 exhibition at Frankfurt's Jewish Museum.[3] The life of the author, who died in 2005, was itself a startling indication that the Rothschild women had been unjustly overlooked. Miriam, I discovered, was a twentieth-century polymath: a brilliant zoologist who worked at Bletchley Park, played a pioneering role in the environmental movement, supported important research into schizophrenia, transformed horticulture, sat as the first female trustee of the Natural History Museum, and became known as The Queen of Fleas for her expertise on the wingless insects. 'It is impossible to prepare for a meeting with Miriam Rothschild,' wrote one interviewer. 'Imagine Beatrix Potter on amphetamines and you come close.'[4] Through Miriam's essay, I began to learn about a whole line of Rothschild women, each of them unique in their talents and character and pursuits, and yet each shaped by the singular circumstances of their family.

Miriam began her essay with a quote from the literary critic and scholar of Jewish history, Naomi Shepherd: 'In all the historical literature produced since the end of the eighteenth century, women are a footnote to the story of Jewish survival.' Nowhere was this truth starker, I realised, than in the story of the Rothschild women. Inspired by Miriam's essay, I began my own investigation into these most fascinating 'footnotes'. The story of the Rothschild women begins with an exclusion: the will of the bank's founder, Mayer Amschel Rothschild, explicitly forbade his female descendants or the wives of any male descendants from having any share in the bank's wealth, or in its decision-making processes. So I had not expected the story of the Rothschild women to echo that of the men. But I had no idea of just how different it would be, or how intriguing.

At the root of it all stood the mother of the business, Gutle, who provided her husband with essential business capital through her dowry, managed the Rothschild household, and played an integral role in the early years of the bank. In the following generation, as the family's operations expanded rapidly, two figures – one married into the family, one born into it – forged very different models of Rothschild womanhood for the nineteenth century. Hannah Rothschild (née Cohen) became an indispensable advisor to the founder of the English bank in private, while also fashioning the family's public image. Meanwhile, her sister-in-law, Henriette Rothschild, provided a more daring model of what a Rothschild woman might be. After thwarting her brothers' attempts to marry her off to an unsuitable husband, Henriette moved to London, married a man that most of her relatives had never met, and helped him build up his own business in competition with her birth family. Later, during her long widowhood, she would win renown for her lively Mayfair dinner parties and her 'great fund of the racy old Jewish humour'.

The third generation of Rothschild women, the first to be born into great wealth, both built on and subverted the possibilities established by their mothers and aunts. Hannah Mayer Rothschild scandalised the family by marrying a Christian and renouncing Judaism. Louisa de Rothschild absorbed herself in the study of literature and religion. Charlotte von Rothschild would step into the public-facing role developed by Hannah, soon earning a reputation as one of the most influential hostesses of Victorian London. Late in the nineteenth century a fourth generation of Rothschild women would go on to even more varied pursuits, testing and sometimes breaking family mores as they carved out roles for themselves in art and politics. The influential Grosvenor Gallery, a centre for late Victorian painters excluded from the more conservative Royal Academy, was co-founded by the Rothschild descendant, Blanche Lindsay. Under the title of Lady Rosebery, the woman born Hannah Rothschild would cultivate a significant political influence, turning her London home into 'the social headquarters of Liberalism', and setting her husband on course to become prime minister. Horrified by the social

problems of late Victorian London, Constance Rothschild would throw
herself into social reform work and become a driving force in the late
nineteenth-century women's movement. In the background to all this,
Emma, Lady Rothschild, would make profound personal sacrifices as
she adapted the traditional role of a Rothschild matriarch to survive the
pressures and upheavals of *fin de siècle* Britain.

The early twentieth-century family was dominated by two women
who married into the name 'Rothschild': Rózsika, née Wertheimstein,
was a rakish Hungarian intellectual with a passion for ice skating and
Proust, while Dolly, née Pinto, was a privileged, sharp-witted young
woman betrothed to an older Rothschild man before she was out of
her teens. Thrust into positions of enormous political responsibility
during the First World War, the women would prove themselves to be
talented diplomats and lobbyists, playing hitherto under-recognised
roles in the foreign policy debates that resulted in the Balfour
Declaration (by which the British government committed itself to
the creation of a Jewish homeland in Palestine). In the sixth generation, Rózsika's daughters forged for themselves lives that would have
been inconceivable just a generation earlier, Miriam as a polymath and
scientist, and Nica as friend and patron to some of the most important
jazz musicians of the century. And nor did the story end there: the
lines of inspiration and influence that began in the late eighteenth
century could, I learnt, be traced all the way to the seventh and eighth
generations, and to Rothschild women who had made their mark as
feminists, economists, writers and film-makers.

The more I investigated, the more I was astounded by the range
and scale of the Rothschild women's achievements. They had choreographed electoral campaigns, witnessed revolutions, and traded on the
Stock Exchange. They had advised prime ministers, played a pivotal
role in the civil rights campaign that led to the election of Britain's
first Jewish MP, and written landmark works of feminist art criticism.
One scandalised the world of women's tennis by introducing the over-
arm serve; one shocked her own family by becoming rather too deeply
involved in the mid-century demimonde of Manhattan jazz cafes and
nightclubs; one reared foxes and kept fleas in bags on the end her bedposts, describing the pleasure of examining them under a microscope
as 'better than marijuana'. The Rothschild women had recorded their
thoughts and experiences in newspaper columns and in memoirs, in
sparkling letters, short stories and painfully honest private journals.

They had their own archives, their own culture and community, their own achievements. They were not just a female counterpart to a male line of Rothschilds: they were a dynasty of their own.

The story of that dynasty begins, like that of the male one, in Frankfurt's Jewish ghetto, and plays out across the banking capitals of Europe. But it is not the same story. From the beginning, the women's experience was markedly different from that of their brothers, fathers and husbands. Close enough to touch power but unable to embrace it; informed and talented enough to write books, but not free to publish under their own names; members of the world's wealthiest family, but with little or no disposable income of their own. Yet with intelligence, determination and sheer bloody-mindedness, they shaped history. The family's own past was marshalled against them, as a way of reinforcing expectations. During her later life, Gutle, the founding Rothschild matriarch, came to be mythologised as a pious, frugal, self-sacrificing woman who refused to leave the family home on the Judengasse – her 'humble hut' – despite the wealth and power of her sons. It was a myth deliberately shaped by the male line, who sought to turn their ancestor into an ideal of Rothschild womanhood: industrious, dutiful and fertile.

Up to a point, the women of the family fulfilled this role. Rarely did they rebel outright against the expectations that accompanied their position. As Miriam observed in her essay, 'there was no Rosa Luxemburg, Emma Goldman, Golda Meir or even Lily Montefiore among them'. As German Jews in a Christian society and women within a fiercely patriarchal family, they trod with care. Quietly, cautiously, across the generations, they managed to build new paths, expanding for their daughters and granddaughters the range of pursuits, attitudes and life choices available to a Rothschild woman. Theirs is not a story of outright conflict and contention, but of delicate and sometimes difficult negotiations – between creativity and conformity, defiance and compromise, between family responsibility and the fulfilment of personal potential.

Their wealth could not shield them from the full scope of human suffering. Illness, heartbreak and persecution are leitmotifs in many of their lives, as were other injustices familiar from the biographies of most remarkable women: achievements overlooked, ideas uncredited and potential untapped. The very name 'Rothschild' was a source of anxiety. Some lost it through marriage, but retained a strong identification with their birth family; others were born without it, but obliged by marriage to construct themselves a life and identity as a Rothschild.

Women who married outside of the name found themselves suddenly cut off from their birth family and distrusted as potential business competitors. Those whose name was protected through an arranged marriage with a Rothschild cousin were often shipped off to another branch of the family, in another country, where they had to learn a new language and culture. Some thrived in such conditions: Charlotte de Rothschild, who spent her childhood between Frankfurt and Naples, became a figurehead of the English Rothschild family after her marriage to her cousin Lionel, and a Victorian hostess whose invitations were said to be more popular than the Queen's. Others struggled. Identity is never clear-cut or binary, and the lives explored in the following chapters contain many fraught and fascinating identities, complicated by name and nationality, by gender and sexuality and religion.

In the nineteenth century Rothschild women were doubly isolated: from Christian society, as Jews; and from the male culture of their own family, as women. So they socialised together, and often arranged their lives so that they could live near one another. They wrote endless letters. 'We Rothschilds are inveterate scribblers,' wrote one.[5] Any historian who has spent time looking through the family papers will agree: the archive of one of the family's most enthusiastic letter writers includes hundreds of letters every year through the mid Victorian period, and that of its most prolific diarist includes tens of volumes spanning more than fifty years, each one crammed with minuscule script. Such writing gives a fascinating insight into who the women were and what drove them, and shows the process by which they came to form the community that Miriam Rothschild called 'a parallel but separate little world'.

Any attempt to write a comprehensive history of that 'little world' would be doomed from the start. Such an undertaking would be doomed from the start. Everywhere the family established banks – in the five cities of Paris, Vienna, Naples, Frankfurt and London – there were communities of Rothschild women, and within each of those communities there were many different friendships, cliques and families. During the twentieth century, as the bank's wealth and its authority within the family declined, the women moved further afield and pursued an even broader range of lives.

This book plots a course through one line of Rothschild women within the English branch of the family, from the dawn of the nineteenth century to the early years of the twenty-first. Even focusing on this single branch of the family, there are still many women whom I regret not being able to include because of limitations of space or source material (many of the women's archives have been depleted by loss or purposeful destruction). I can only hope that hearing the extraordinary tales of this selection of Rothschild women will inspire further historians to retrieve some of the many other Rothschild lives that are yet to receive their due.

Though the women in this book were all defined by their connection to the English branch of the family, their story stretches far beyond England. It spans from the East End of London to the eastern seaboard of the United States, from Spitalfields to Scottish castles, from Bletchley Park to Buchenwald, and from the Vatican to Palestine. The cast embraces Rossini and Mendelssohn, Disraeli, Gladstone and Chaim Weizmann; it includes amphetamine dealers, Queen Victoria, temperance campaigners and Albert Einstein. The lives of the subjects span vastly different times and places. Mayer Amschel's will of 1812, forbidding any female involvement in the banking business, bore little relation to his twentieth-century descendants, when Nica Rothschild flew planes, fought with the Free French and drag-raced Miles Davis across Manhattan.

The Rothschild women tell a history of art, culture, politics and money in Europe as seen by people who were in the room but who themselves often went unseen. Theirs is not a story of angels or martyrs. Alongside acts marked by bravery, imagination and intelligence are those marred by deceit, ignorance and entitlement. They were misfits and conformists, conservatives and idealists, performers and introverts. But they were bound by the name, by a set of expectations as well as privileges, and by a profound sense of exclusion from the male and Christian world around them. By drawing attention to them, I hope both to help illuminate some of the overlooked sources of power, strength and imagination in European history, and to give these complicated, privileged and gifted women a little of the prominence they have so long deserved.

PART I

Gutle, Hannah, Henriette

I

The Mother of
the Business

THE MOTHER OF the Rothschild dynasty was born in a dark and crowded ghetto in 1753. For centuries prior to Gutle Schnapper's birth, the Jews of Frankfurt had been confined to a strip of land that curved around the edge of the city's eastern fortifications.[1] This was the Judengasse, or 'Jews' Lane', and Gutle could expect to live her life within its confines. Frankfurt Jews were born among the Judengasse's densely packed houses, they worshipped in its *shul* and shopped at its market; they studied, worked and died there.

The boundaries of their world had been rigidly fixed by the city council centuries before, and were unresponsive to the ghetto's growing population. Over the centuries, with nowhere else to go, the buildings had been forced upwards, and cantilevered overhangs had been constructed to maximise living space on the same small footprint.[2] By the time Gutle was old enough to walk along the lane, the slice of sky visible above her would have been no wider than a pair of outstretched arms. There was so little daylight that visitors were struck by how pale the Jews looked. The dense, smoky air and the open sewers made it hard to breathe.

During the nightly curfew, and on Christian holidays, the gates at the end of the Judengasse were closed, and the Jewish population entirely confined. At other times Jews venturing outside the ghetto were subject to an array of threatening and humiliating regulations. If they visited any of the Gentiles' streets and markets, Jews were forbidden to touch fruit and vegetables. If anyone, even a child, said '*Jud, mach mores!*' ('Jew, do your duty!'), they were obliged to raise their hat and step aside.[3] Unsurprisingly, some chose to remain within the confines of the Judengasse. On the outside of the ghetto gates hung the sign of the imperial eagle, symbolising that the Jews lived under

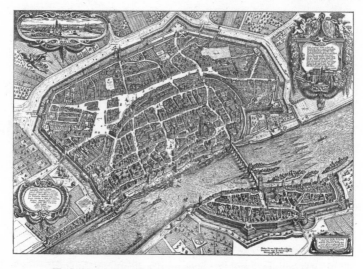

*The Judengasse occupies the north-eastern quarter of the curved
street that begins near the top of the bridge over the Main. It was constructed
along the outside of the old (inner) city wall.*

the protection of the Holy Roman Emperor. The Jews living in the lane were under no illusions: this was not a refuge, but a prison.

The houses of the Judengasse were not numbered. Instead, each was named after the shield that hung above the entrance: Red Shield, the Lion, the Lantern, the Cat. Gutle's family, the Schnappers, lived in the Eule (Owl), just inside the ghetto's gates and within earshot of the slaughterhouse. Built into the backyard of an older house, the Eule was not accessed from the street, but through an alley and a yard. Like most houses, it was occupied by more than one family: during Gutle's childhood, the Schnappers had lived at the Eule along with the Geigers and the Scheyers.[4]

In relative terms, Gutle was fortunate. Since 1179, Christians had been banned from lending money at interest. Some of the city's Jews, who were banned from many other lines of work, ended up establishing their own financial operations, banks catering to the needs of Christian and Jewish merchants alike.[5] For several generations, the Schnappers had run one such business. When Gutle's father, Wolf Salomon Schnapper, married Bella Gans in 1752, the Schnapper bank was doing well enough for the couple to be able to relocate from the ancestral Schnapper home at the Leuchte (Lantern), to the Eule. By the time Bella gave birth to Gutle – their first child – on 23 August 1753, Wolf Salomon had a number of illustrious clients, and his work would eventually earn him a banking pass, which allowed him to leave the ghetto at times when the rest of the population was locked inside.[6] None of that meant the Schnapper family was immune to the perils – of fire and violence and disease – that haunted the lives of all Frankfurt Jews: Gutle's mother Bella died when Gutle was only six. Desperate to keep the broader family and the alliance with his in-laws intact, her father soon arranged a new match, with his sister-in-law. Gutle's aunt became her stepmother.[7]

The Schnappers were not the wealthiest or most prestigious family in the ghetto, but with their small business and a lineage that could be traced to one of the original ghetto families – the Gelhausers – they were highly reputable, and more prosperous than most.[8] The Eule doubled up as the headquarters of the Schnappers' operation, so Gutle spent her early years surrounded by the paraphernalia of a small eighteenth-century banking business. Wolf expected his first child to master basic literacy and numeracy, so that she could help in

The Judengasse, c.1865.

the family firm. In years to come, he knew, such abilities would allow Gutle to aid a future husband in his own work. Many businessmen in the Judengasse depended on their wives as a key source of unpaid labour, and Wolf Schnapper must have foreseen that Gutle's competence in the business of a bank would aid her chances of finding a good husband in the ghetto. He could never have imagined the scale and significance of the dynasty that would spring from his first daughter's marriage. At the root of the Rothschild empire is the figure of a small girl, fighting for air in the cramped world of the Frankfurt ghetto.

The systems of physical and legal oppression confronted by the young Gutle had deep roots. Even before the physical walls of the ghetto were erected, the city's Jews had been confined by harassment, hostility, legal disabilities and violence. Before the establishment of the ghetto, participation of Jews in the city's financial life meant that the underlying hostility of the Christian population was periodically inflamed by business-related resentments, and for centuries periods of fragile tolerance were punctuated by massacres.[9] In the pogrom of 1241, for example, more than three-quarters of the city's Jewish community was killed. A century later, a wave of anti-Jewish violence swept through Europe in the wake of the Black Death, and Christians burnt the Jewish quarter to the ground.[10]

As Frankfurt continued to prosper on the world stage, the status of Jews was kept firmly in check. In 1372 a set of laws, the *Stättigkeit*, began to formalise various forms of discrimination, imposing strict rules and prohibitions on Jewish work, taxes and residential rights. Jews were accorded limited recognition well short of citizenship. In return they were encumbered by levies and obligations, including a 2,000-gulden 'protection tax' and a 250-gulden annual rent for their burial ground.[11]

The forced resettlement of the Jewish community became a serious prospect in 1431, when the Council of Basel, a general council of the Roman Catholic Church, ordered that Jews should only live in designated areas, away from other houses and places of Christian worship.[12] Frankfurt's Christian merchants had other, more pragmatic, reasons for wanting to expel their Jewish competitors from the commercial and trading centre of the city. The area chosen for Jewish resettlement was a narrow strip of land curving along the side of the city's eastern fortifications: the *Wallgraben*, or moat. Construction of buildings began in 1460. Two years later Jews were herded into what became the first legally mandated ghetto in Europe.[13]

By 1610 nearly three thousand people were crowded into two hundred houses.[14] New houses were built in the plots between old ones, then in the backyards of existing structures, or in the alleyways between them.[15] When those spaces became scarce, non-residential structures such as stables were converted into human dwellings, existing buildings divided to accommodate multiple families, and further storeys were added. As buildings were subdivided, so were names: a house known as the Guldener Löwe (Golden Lion), for instance, became seven different residences, each with their own sign, among them the Löwenneck (Lion's Corner) and the Löwengrube (Lion's Den).[16] Stagnant water and waste sat in the courtyards and passages, and the remains of the old moat ran with putrid sewage.

In the Christian parts of the city, the loathing felt for the Jewish population was shamelessly displayed in public 'art'. One mural on the *Brückenturm*, an imposing tower that stood sentinel at the riverside entrance to Frankfurt, depicted a group of Jews dressed in traditional rabbinical clothing devouring the faeces of a pig, incited by the devil.[17] Another, directly above it, showed a dead infant, his body punctured by stab wounds. The child was the victim of a 'ritual murder', a fictional practice whereby Jews allegedly slaughtered Christian children to use their blood in unleavened bread. Normally a tower would be a show of force to warn off external enemies. In Frankfurt, Jews were considered the enemies within.

Against this backdrop of claustrophobia and repression, the community into which Gutle was born had developed its own distinct politics and culture. Frankfurt's Jews spoke their own dialect, *Judendeutsch* – a fusion of idiomatic German and Hebrew – and had their own governors, the *Baumeister*, who were every bit as susceptible to corruption and overreach as the Christian city authorities.[18] Despite a legal ban on printing presses in the ghetto, the Frankfurt Jews published Hebrew commentaries, secular texts, manuals of religious observance and the popular ballads that became the soundtrack to Gutle's childhood.[19] The *shul* and *mikveh* were the first structures to be rebuilt and repaired after fires swept through the ghetto's narrow streets in 1711 and 1721.[20] A dynasty of rabbis dating back to the thirteenth century drew scholars from all over the Continent to the *yeshiva*, and visitors marvelled at 'richly decorated' stone arches, 'tall windows' and 'fine copper ornament' in the synagogue.[21] Dotted among the communal buildings were wine and beer taverns and coffee houses. While the *Stättigkeit* forbade card games, dice games and roulette, other forms of gambling were allowed, so long as the stakes were no higher than a copper kreutzer.[22]

Inevitably, the ghetto had its own hierarchies.[23] There were variations in legal status between those who'd been admitted to the rudimentary rights granted by the *Stättigkeit*, and others, such as visiting students and domestic servants.[24] There were divisions in reputation, between esteemed figures such as doctors and rabbinic scholars, and those such as publicans and nightwatchmen whose occupations were thought of as lowly, and sometimes tainted by an association with criminality.[25] There were divisions in wealth, between the destitute and the wealthy merchants or bankers, including those – the so-called 'Court Jews' – who held appointments as moneylenders or financiers to rulers of the patchwork territories that made up the Holy Roman Empire.

The men of the Frankfurt ghetto – by focusing on their business, their internal politics and their religious observances – had built a world of relative liberty within the severe limits of the Judengasse and the *Stättigkeit*. As a Jewess, however, Gutle Schnapper lacked access to even this limited freedom. On Friday evenings, after the start of the Shabbat, she was forbidden to walk in the city – women, it was thought, would 'gather in groups' and 'bother people' – and if she contravened this regulation, she could have been 'pelted with faeces' by the community wardens.[26] Only married women could attend synagogue on Shabbat morning, and only women married to men born in the Judengasse were eligible for the *Stättigkeit* and the rights of residence that it conferred.[27] Marriages had to be made quickly, and tactically. Only twelve were permitted each year in the ghetto.[28]

In 1770 Gutle was one of the lucky ones: Wolf Schnapper secured his daughter a match.[29] On 29 August, after eight days of ritual confinement in her family home, she made her way along the Judengasse to the courtyard of the Great Synagogue. The man who stood waiting for her had a calm gaze and 'eyes that reflected his sanity and good sense'.[30] He wore the bridegroom's prayer shawl, the *tallit*, over a hooded cloak. She was just seventeen years old.

Mayer Amschel Rothschild, Gutle's husband and founder of the Rothschild bank.

His family was less wealthy than hers, and had a reputation for piety. Yet the man Gutle was to marry was not rabbinic or scholarly. He had spent the last few years as an apprentice in a bank at Hanover, and since his return to the ghetto had been developing a small business of his own.

His name was Mayer Amschel Rothschild.

'Rothschild' derived from the name of a house in the Judengasse: the Rotes Schild, or Red Shield, had been built by an ancestor of Mayer Amschel's in around 1567.[31] At the time, '*zum Roten Schild*' – 'of the red shield' – had been only a moniker, but over the years it became the name by which the family that lived in the house was known. By the time Mayer Amschel's great-great-grandfather moved from the Rotes Schild to the Hinterpfann in the mid seventeenth century, the association between the family and their old house was strong enough for the name to move with them. The Rothschild family had come into being.[32]

The Rothschilds were still living at the Hinterpfann three generations later, when, in 1744, Mayer Amschel was born to Amschel Moses Rothschild and his wife Schönche. When Mayer Amschel's parents both died within a year of each other, his studies at the famous *yeshiva* at Fürth were interrupted.[33] His brothers sent him to Hamburg, to serve an apprenticeship in the bank of Jacob Oppenheim. Here, in the rare coin department, he was able to feed his fascination with numismatics – the study of coins.[34] Collectors of antique coins were predominantly aristocratic, so by the time he returned to Frankfurt, aged eighteen, he had not only become an adept coin dealer but had formed a significant business network.[35] In September 1769 one client in that network, the voracious coin collector William, crown prince of Hesse, granted Mayer Amschel the title of *Hoffaktor* (court agent).[36] The title was an important sign that Mayer Amschel was on the ascent, and there is little doubt that this recent aristocratic patronage won over Wolf Schnapper.[37]

Mayer Amschel had everything to gain from the match. The Schnappers were a reputable family with which to ally, and Gutle's ample dowry of 2,400 gulden was crucial capital for his growing business, which was diversifying from coin trading into antiques and textiles, and would soon come to specialise in another field: banking.[38]

The union of two such prominent families was an important community event, performed in front of a large crowd that included the chief rabbi, the heads of the community and legal scholars.[39] During the ceremony, Gutle and Mayer Amschel stood side by side to take their vows, their wedding girdles hooked together with metal eyelets as a symbol of their union.[40] As the ceremony concluded, the couple threw a wine glass against the synagogue wall to signify the destruction of the ancient Temple as related in the Torah.

Gutle and Mayer Amschel's first marital home was the Hinterpfann, where Mayer Amschel had spent his childhood and where his two brothers, Moses and Carl, still lived. Meaning 'back of the pan', it was less poetically named than the Owl – and a less poetic property. The narrow, cramped house was wedged against the ghetto wall and could only be reached by a tight alley between the buildings in front of it.[41] Though the house backed onto the ghetto's eastern wall and the tree-lined avenue of *der lange Gang*, many windows looking out of the ghetto from the upper floors of houses had been bricked up in order to save Christians the 'indignity' of being overlooked by Jews. As the poet Ludwig Börne said of a similar house on the Judengasse: 'the sunlight seemed never to enter the narrow walls with their low ceilings'.[42]

It was within such gloomy walls that Gutle started her family: Jeannette was born in August 1771. She was followed by Amschel Mayer

(1773), then Salomon Mayer (1774), Nathan Mayer (1777), Isabella (1781) and Babette (1784).[43] Even by the standards of the period, the frequency of Gutle's pregnancies was unusual; she would be pregnant at least nineteen times. Some pregnancies did not go full-term, and some of her children died in infancy. Ten would survive to adulthood.[44]

But Gutle was not just producing and nurturing the next generation of Rothschilds. During this period of steady financial growth, Mayer Amschel needed all the help he could get, particularly with cashing and issuing bills.[45] Raised in a similar environment at the Eule, Gutle brought experience and commercial acumen to the bank's *Kontor* (counting house), as well as to the management of household finances. She economised ruthlessly, despite the family's burgeoning wealth, allocating just a small proportion of their income to the household expenses.[46] She was the epitome of a thrifty matriarch, who, according to a close friend, 'spent nothing, always saved'.[47] In the cramped, overcrowded space of the Hinterpfann, Gutle was constantly on the move, tending to her ever-increasing brood of children, overseeing the domestic accounts, cooking and cleaning – all the while pumping money back into the business.

Gutle's practical contributions remained largely unappreciated by the family's men. One of her sons, Carl, would later write a letter to his older brother Salomon, in which he caustically stated that women make 'bad cashiers'.[48] Much like the Jews of Frankfurt themselves, the women of the Rothschild business tirelessly turned the wheels of industry, and were often rewarded with contempt.

2

'Merely a Machine'

I N NOVEMBER 1786 a thriving business meant that Gutle and Mayer Amschel could move out of the Hinterpfann and buy a house of their own. Situated roughly half-way along the Judengasse, the Grünes Schild (Green Shield) faced west, along a small alley that led to the ghetto's middle gate, the only one that entered directly into the old city. Thanks to the break in the houses opposite, and the unusual width of the lane in front of the house, the Grünes Schild was better ventilated and lighter than almost any other on the street.[1] The staircase to the first floor, though steep and narrow, was adorned with 'beautiful iron handrails' rather than dirty ropes. At the front of the first floor was the *gute Stube*, or 'better living room', where, for a short precious time in the evening, sunlight would pour through the gap in the houses opposite, and through the mullioned windows.[2] Besides being one of the most recognisable houses on the street, it was also one of the best-appointed. It had its own well in the cellar, and a hand-pump to draw water up to the kitchen.[3]

The Grünes Schild was a bustling and chaotic household, cluttered with catalogues, coins, and an expanding range of other stock that Mayer Amschel had accumulated as his business diversified into antiques: woodcarvings, rare stones and medals. There was also a growing cohort of children, four of whom were born in the years after the move: Carl (1788), Julie (1790), Henriette (1791) and James (1792).[4] Later, when the house had become famous for the dynasty that sprang from it and was redesigned for visitors, the *Kontor* – which occupied a narrow outbuilding at the back of the house – would be neatly furnished with a money chest or *Geldkiste*, a stand-up desk with a high stool, and a cupboard for ledgers.[5] The late eighteenth-century reality was a hectic, disorderly place in which cupboard doors hung

The Grünes Schild, where Gutle and Mayer Amschel lived from 1786.

open, papers were left out, few things were locked, and clients and family members came and went constantly.[6] The one place that was truly secure was a second 'secret' cellar, which was accessible through a trapdoor under the stairs.[7]

In autumn 1792, a few short months after the birth of Gutle's youngest son James, the French Revolutionary Wars reached Frankfurt and the Judengasse. French forces stormed the city. By October the Tricolour was fluttering over the arsenal outside the northern gate leading to the Judengasse.[8] Frankfurt's Jews remained largely unmoved by the force's rhetoric of *liberté, égalité, fraternité*: such words did little to alleviate the day-to-day thefts, humiliations and outrages of the occupation, the burden of which fell disproportionately on the residents of the Judengasse.[9] Besides, there was no reason to think that the French occupation would last. Indeed, French forces ceded the city to Prussian and Hessian troops, who in turn capitulated to the Austrians. When the French advanced again in July 1796, they did so to devastating effect, with a ferocious bombardment. In the Judengasse, a fire ignited by shelling spread quickly. The Grünes Schild survived, but 119 houses – about half of the houses on the lane – were destroyed.[10]

From the ashes of this latest devastation, hope would grow for residents of the ghetto. Given the sheer scale of destruction, the Frankfurt city council had little choice but to relax the regulations and allow Jews who had been made homeless to temporarily rent accommodation in the city. In April 1798 it gave permission for Jews to leave the ghetto on Sundays and Christian holidays – in exchange for a yearly payment.[11] Though the city's new policy of defortification was motivated largely by military rather than moral considerations – the fortifications had only intensified the onslaught to which Frankfurt was subjected by advancing armies – it would have significant benefits for the Jewish community: as part of the programme, the bridge tower or *Brückenturm* was torn down, along with the infamous murals, against which Frankfurt's Jews had protested for many years. In 1803, after considerable debate, it was finally agreed that the gates and main wall of the Judengasse would be destroyed, and the lane widened.[12]

The trauma of occupation had begun when Gutle's youngest children were still infants and her eldest were embarking on apprenticeships, business engagements and marriages. Soon after the birth of her last child, James, in 1792, Gutle's eldest daughter Jeannette married Benedict Moses Worms. Her dowry (5,000 gulden) and the legacy promised to her (10,000 gulden) attest to the rapid rise in the family's fortunes during this period.[13] Gutle was used to the idea that her sons might travel to other German towns for work, education and training. But as the business grew, her sons moved farther afield. In 1798, when her third son, Nathan, left the Continent and sailed for England, it was an unprecedented wrench. At the Grünes Schild, Gutle had to endure weeks, sometimes months, without word from Nathan. Their only means of communication was an erratic postal system.[14]

Gutle's maternal instincts and her frugality ran deep. Even as Nathan began to amass his own fortune abroad, she was still keen to send food and clothing.[15] Just to the west of the ghetto walls, next to the Jewish cemetery, was the community's *Bleichgarten*, or bleaching ground. Here Gutle arrayed her resources, allotting different pieces of fabric to be made into tablecloths, shirts, scarves and other items, which were transported to England by trusted associates. 'I sent with Kassel and Reiss 6 shirts,' she wrote to Nathan in a rare surviving letter, 'and with Israel Reiss also 6 shirts, 2 scarfs, and with Michael Bing you will get 2 tablecloths. If you write the length and width, I shall send you more.'[16] In letters to Nathan and Carl, she wrote that 'not a day goes by' without her thinking of her absent sons.[17] As further children moved away from the Grünes Schild, this feeling intensified. Her experience of the emptying house is captured in a later letter, written to Gutle's eldest son Amschel by his wife Eva, while the former was away travelling: 'Tonight, I will certainly feel as your mother did all the time, and shall have to cry at the table.'[18]

While Gutle worried about her sons abroad, trouble was about to erupt closer to home. On an ordinary May morning in 1808, Mayer Amschel and his two sons Salomon and James were bent over their work in the dim light of the *Kontor*, when there was a commotion outside. The men had barely stood up from their chairs when police stormed through the courtyard and into the outbuilding, where they 'sealed all the cupboards containing correspondence and account books with a police seal'.[19] The man leading the search was Frankfurt's director of police, von Itzstein. Accompanying him was a ruthless and intelligent French detective called Savagner, chief of police in the nearby state of Westphalia, where he had been investigating the finances behind a recent armed rebellion. This was no speculative visit, but a raid.[20]

Mayer Amschel, Salomon and James were all arrested. Mayer Amschel was held in the main house by Savagner, while his sons were kept in the *Kontor* under the surveillance of two policemen.[21] In Westphalia, Savagner's methods were notoriously brutal: earlier in the same investigation that had led him to the Grünes Schild, he had questioned the sister of a suspect with a loaded gun held to her head. This, however, was von Itzstein's patch, and the Westphalian chief had to operate with an unaccustomed degree of propriety. Savagner sat Mayer Amschel down and shot questions at him: What were the names of his children? What were their current whereabouts? What role did his sons have in his business? What about the one in England, Nathan?[22] It was the beginning of an investigation that would continue for several days and nights. Over that time, the *Kontor* would be searched repeatedly and the interrogation broadened from the family's sons to its daughters and finally to its matriarch, Gutle.

The origins of the May raid on the Grünes Schild lay deep in the European upheavals of the previous two decades. In 1803 – the same year that Mayer Amschel's old patron, the coin-collecting William, became prince elector of Hesse – France and England went to war. The elector's attempts to play the two sides off against each other backfired horribly, and in the summer of 1806 Napoleonic troops swept into Hesse-Kassel, absorbing it into the new French-aligned Kingdom of Westphalia. William fled, leaving behind medals, coins, financial documents and rare books. In return for a hefty bribe, the French official overseeing the occupation of William's castle turned a blind eye as chests of these possessions were smuggled out. A trusted official, Carl Buderus, was put in charge of hiding documents relating to 27 million gulden of assets.[23] Some of these he sent to Mayer Amschel Rothschild in Frankfurt. They were stashed away at the Grünes Schild, possibly in the hidden cellar.[24]

Mayer Asmchel's loyalty to his old client went beyond hiding chests of documents. He was a frequent visitor to William in exile in Schleswig-Holstein, and when William moved down to Prague the Rothschild bank continued to work energetically on his behalf.[25] 'Whenever I enter the Elector's quarters, I always find Rothschild there,' read one police report.[26] After a rebellion took place against the French-aligned authorities in Westphalia, the police, led by Savagner, deepened their investigations into the network of the exiled elector.[27] Before searching the Grünes Schild, Savagner sought a warrant from Karl Theodor von Dalberg, the prince-primate of the Confederation of the Rhine. But Dalberg was a long-time client of Mayer Amschel, who had realised early on the importance of maintaining clients on both sides of the Napoleonic conflict.[28] That policy was about to pay off.

Equally adept at keeping his options open, Dalberg authorised the search requested by Savagner – and at the same time sent a warning to the Grünes Schild.[29] By the time Savagner's men tramped into the *Kontor*, every scrap of incriminating material had already been hidden in the secret cellar, along with the elector's crates. If, as historians have speculated, the bank kept two sets of accounts in this period – one complete set, and one doctored for official consumption – then the doctored set would have been in the cupboards.[30] The Rothschilds were ready.

After interrogating Mayer Amschel, Savagner turned to Salomon, pressing him on the connection between his father's business and the exiled elector.[31] Savagner knew that Mayer Amschel had visited the elector 'every two to three days' from Hamburg, and that Salomon's brother Amschel had been making frequent trips to Vienna since the elector moved there.[32] In response, Salomon mixed concession with evasion and outright denial. But when Savagner pressed James, who was only fourteen, the boy revealed something significant: his father, he said, 'does not have a cashier, this business is carried out by his sisters, who, like the wife of his brother Amschel [Eva], pay off the money'.[33] When further pressed, James continued: 'Afterward, they give a small piece of paper with the amount to the *Kontor* so that the clerks can write this amount into the books.'

James's answer prompted Savagner to seek out the Rothschild women of Grünes Schild. First came Salomon's wife Caroline, the intelligent and perceptive daughter of a Frankfurt merchant. Savagner asked her if she 'paid off money, with the help of her sisters, in the *Kontor* of her father-in-law'.[34] Caroline said that she 'sometimes' did. And yet when Savagner followed up his initial question by asking whether she remembered making any payments to Buderus, it turned out that Caroline and her sisters-in-law could not remember as they made payments 'to many different people'. The memory of Eva turned out to be similarly vague.[35]

Next in turn was Henriette. By 1808, with her older sisters married into other families, sixteen-year-old Henriette was the only girl working in the *Kontor* who was a Rothschild by birth. Given her relative youth, and the fact that she had no husband to brief her, Savagner might have expected her to be an easier target than the previous two. But already, in her mid teens, Henriette was headstrong and tenacious. She made no secret of the fact that she worked in the *Kontor*, paying out bills of exchange to the servants of local merchants.[36] But beyond that, she gave away nothing.[37] And while Caroline and Eva had excused their answers with claims of forgetfulness, Henriette was more direct. Faced with armed men interrogating her in her own home, she denied everything: she had not made payments to Buderus, nor made any payments at his request; she had not seen Buderus in the *Kontor*; she did not know why her brother Amschel had visited Prague and Vienna. She was, she said, 'merely a machine' in the counting house.[38] It was a statement of ignorance that belied her active, daily engagement with the business.

Gutle was the last of the women to be called for questioning. After fruitless interviews with the rest of the family, the exasperated

*Gutle Rothschild, the mother
of the Rothschild dynasty.*

Frenchman asked the fifty-nine-year-old mother of ten only two questions.[39] First, for what kind of business had her son Amschel 'travelled to Prague and Vienna'? Second, how long ago was it that 'Mr Buderus from Hanau' had visited her husband? To the first question, Gutle responded that she knew 'nothing at all', and did not 'concern herself with business'. To the second, she denied having seen him, once again claiming she only dealt with 'her household'.

Of course, it is inconceivable that Gutle knew 'nothing at all'. With Mayer Amschel and his sons so often away from Frankfurt, Gutle and the other Rothschild women at the Grünes Schild reliably managed their affairs. If there were chests in the secret cellar, they would have known about them. If there were accounts doctored for official consumption, they would have known what was missing from them – they may even have drawn them up. Savagner had realised this. He and the policemen came back the next day and the day after, to ask further questions. But it was a lost cause: the Rothschild women's pretence of ignorance presented an insurmountable obstacle to the investigation. The authorities had been stonewalled.[40]

Gutle had not been entirely untruthful: she did concern herself a great deal with the running of the household. The family's improved financial circumstances meant she could employ staff to assist her.[41] After years performing domestic work alone, she must have been glad to be able to pay for the extra labour. But she was also a stern, outspoken employer unafraid of holding others to her own punishingly high standards. When a girl was late to deliver a batch of sackcloth shirts on account of having just got engaged, Gutle 'quarrelled with her thoroughly'.[42] She had also recently hired a tutor for her younger children. Compared to the conventional religious education at the local *cheder*, Michael Hess (a disciple of the renowned philosopher Moses Mendelssohn) would provide a note of Enlightenment secularism.[43] This was an ambitious, outward-looking move by Gutle, whose vision for the family now stretched far beyond the narrow horizons of her upbringing.

She had reason to feel optimistic about her children's futures. In 1810 Dalberg had been elevated to Grand Duke of Frankfurt, and introduced a constitution that declared all citizens equal.[44] Like previous liberalisations, this one came at a cost: the city's Jews were expected to compensate the city to the tune of 440,000 gulden for its loss of 'protection taxes'. Mayer Amschel raised as much as 290,000 by discounting bonds.[45] It was a signal act of a family that increasingly saw itself as bound to represent, and to some extent bankroll, the wider Jewish community.

It would also prove to be one of the Rothschilds' best investments. In December 1811 Dalberg signed the decree granting equality of civil rights to the Jews of Frankfurt. The Judengasse was no longer a separate part of the city, and Jews were free to live where they liked. Mayer Amschel and Gutle were among the first group of Jews to register in the 'civic register' (*Bürgerbuch*) of the city and take the 'civic oath' (*Bürgereid*) before the mayor in February 1812.[46] Their sons Amschel and Salomon, together with their wives Eva and Adelheid, belonged to the second group.[47]

The gates of the ghetto had finally opened. But even as her nest emptied, and her sons and daughters moved across Europe, setting up homes and businesses in London, Paris, Naples and beyond, Gutle remained in the house of the Green Shield. It was her home, and the Judengasse was her community: she would never leave.

3

Inventing the Family

WHEN NATHAN ROTHSCHILD appeared on the doorstep of her London home in 1798, Hannah Barent Cohen was fifteen, but seemed much older. The 'very beautiful blue eyes . . . fine brow, and a straight Grecian nose' that would strike those who knew her in adulthood, and a childhood spent socialising with her father's staff and respectable business contacts, made her seem unusually adult.[1] Like other wealthy young ladies of the time, she and her younger sisters Judith and Jessie were brought up to be good musicians, artists, horsewomen and linguists: Hannah was not only fluent in English and German, but also spoke French, Italian and Hebrew.[2] The contrast between her and her father's new apprentice from Frankfurt could not have been more pronounced. Hannah's first impression of her future husband was of a man badly dressed, uncultured and emphatically foreign.

Like Nathan, Hannah's father had come to England from the Continent in his twenties.[3] Working for his uncle, a member of the established and successful Goldsmid family, Levi Barent Cohen had rapidly been initiated into 1770s Anglo-Jewry. He and his wife Lydia had eleven children who lived to maturity, of whom Hannah (b. 1783) was the eldest. At a time when many English Jews were turning away from their religion, the Cohens were committed to raising their children as observant Jews, and Hannah's education had been characterised by the mixture of secular education and traditional Jewish teaching extolled by Moses Mendelssohn.[4] From his home and business premises in Angel Court, London, Hannah's father dealt with merchants from across the Continent. Among them was Mayer Amschel Rothschild, who during the closing years of the eighteenth century had become involved in the textile trade, importing, printing and dyeing fabrics for a European market hungry for novel colour, style and pattern.

Like most apprentices at the time, Nathan moved in with his host family.

The spirit of the Cohen home – a 'happy combination of the religious idealism of Judaea, and the refinement of the best Gentile society' – would have been alien to Nathan, whose young life in the Frankfurt ghetto had been characterised by enclosure, exclusion and war.[5] He must have been struck immediately by the self-confidence, gentility and cosmopolitanism of Levi Barent Cohen's daughter. Fleeting encounters during these early months would have been interrupted by the bustle of household and business, and any communication stilted by differences of language and habit: Nathan spoke no English, only German, and even that was not the courtly *Hochdeutsch* (High German), but the distinctive *Judendeutsch* (Western Yiddish) of the ghetto.[6] He had a pronounced lack of interest in the music and art that Hannah had been trained to appreciate.

If there was any chemistry between Nathan and Hannah during these early months, it was cut short when Nathan finished his apprenticeship and moved to Manchester in May 1799, to consolidate his family's textile interests.[7] Hannah might have caught glimpses of her father's ex-apprentice during his brief visits to the capital: Harman & Co., where Nathan could draw on his father's credit, were based in Adam Court, just across Throgmorton Street from Angel Court, and Nathan's London office was a short distance further south, on Cornhill.[8] It is likely she would have heard of Nathan's progress through her father, who continued to do business with Mayer Amschel in Frankfurt, and through the circle of merchants who frequented Angel Court, many of whom – such as Lyon de Symons and Daniel Mocatta – had been persuaded to discount bills for the upstart Frankfurter.

The reports would not all have been favourable. Already, Nathan was gaining a reputation as a haphazard and confrontational figure whose recklessness was occasionally damaging to the Rothschild family name. In 1800 Harman & Co. refused to extend Mayer Amschel's credit because payments were in arrears, 'owing to his son's laxity'.[9] Other Rothschild clients had accused Nathan of overcharging, sending incorrect orders, marking orders wrongly or not sending anything at all. His own father sent frequent, crotchety letters complaining of mix-ups, counter-orders, bad bookkeeping and lacklustre correspondence. And yet Nathan's business was growing, and he was gradually taking root in the unfamiliar country.[10] By August 1802 he was complaining to one of his brothers that their letters were written in 'such very bad English that it is impossible to ascertain the true meaning of what you write'.[11] To an educated native speaker like Hannah, such a claim would have seemed comical, for Nathan's own written English remained imperfect, and his accent was always strong. But Nathan's confidence, and his willingness to take great risks, led him back to Angel Court in 1805, to ask Levi Barent Cohen for permission to marry his daughter.

With his daughter's refined upbringing and sharp intelligence, Levi might have hoped for an altogether more dazzling and cultured match – a Montefiore, perhaps, or a Goldsmid.[12] But Nathan's success had not escaped Levi's attention.[13] He hired a broker to examine the suitor's books and ensure he was worth at least £10,000.[14] Satisfied that he was, but keen to safeguard Hannah from any future fluctuations in Nathan's business, Levi also set up a trust of £3,248 intended solely for Hannah's use.[15] The men who administered the trust included Hannah's brothers and Nathan himself, so this was not a completely independent endowment, but it was a great advance on a simple wedding dowry, the sum of which could have been absorbed into Nathan's burgeoning wealth.[16] The trust provided annual dividends for Hannah, protected her from Nathan's debts, guaranteed her a £3,000 share of his estate, and reserved her effective ownership of clothes and jewellery.

The Frankfurt Rothschilds, who had been following developments keenly, were overjoyed at the prospect of a match with a merchant family as prominent and respectable as the Cohens. In December 1805 Nathan's younger brother Carl wrote to congratulate him on his 'promise with Miss Cohn [sic]', and in January, Nathan's father put aside his usual upbraiding tone to enquire after the terms of Nathan's proposed marriage contract.[17] Shortly afterwards, Mayer Amschel sent Nathan £16,000, making Nathan a man of substantial means in his own right.[18] Social and business contacts, too, were enthusiastic. In December 1805 one noted amiably: 'I have learned from several good friends, that you are going to become engaged and I should like to convey my very best congratulations for you; also I know your fiancée's family very well, being most respectable people.'[19] Another wrote: 'I had the pleasure of seeing your fiancée yesterday ... You have good taste. I am completely enamoured of her.'[20]

On 22 October 1806 twenty-nine-year-old Nathan Mayer Rothschild married twenty-three-year-old Hannah Barent Cohen in London, and the couple moved to Manchester.[21] It was a city on the make: the cotton industry was flourishing and new developments were springing up amid the haphazard streets of the old town. Where once there had been scumbled brickwork, there was now runcorn stone and sandstone ashlar; where once there had been timber frames, there were now porticos and loggias.[22] 'Perhaps no town in the United Kingdom has had such rapid improvements,' wrote local historian Joseph Aston, surveying the city a few years later.[23] Nathan and Hannah's first home was on Mosley Street, one of the city's most fashionable addresses. In order to give it the elegance she was used to at Angel Court, Hannah ordered luxurious furnishings from London, including card tables, decorative fire screens, mirrors, chairs of mahogany upholstered in Morocco leather and a matching chaise longue.[24]

As grand as Hannah's new residence may have been, Manchester was still an industrial city. The French wars and the tumult of the labour market had made feelings towards those deemed 'foreign' particularly volatile, and while the population of the city had swollen to well over a hundred thousand, the Jewish community consisted of no more than fifteen families.[25] To a young woman like Hannah, used to the assured and cosmopolitan life of London's Anglo-Jewish elite, this must have made Manchester seem like a rather isolated and even intimidating place. She sought comfort in the Jewish traditions of her upbringing, arranging for kosher meals to be delivered to Nathan's warehouse every day.[26] Meanwhile, she cultivated a role for herself in Nathan's business, winning the respect of his colleagues and 'mothering' it in the same way that Gutle had done, even though the two women had yet to meet. On 10 August 1807, less than a year after her arrival in Manchester, she gave birth to her first child: Charlotte, nicknamed 'Chilly'. The first English Rothschild was a girl.

During Nathan's absences, Hannah moved from an auxiliary to a managerial role. Her husband's associates respected her authority and directed letters to her attention when he was away.[27] Hannah developed a great rapport with the merchants of Manchester. Pete Fawcett, a dyer who worked closely with Nathan, addressed her in fond terms, and sent bills he owed to the business to her directly.[28] Even in letters that were addressed to Nathan, Hannah often earned an affectionate postscript. The effect of this on Nathan's business relationships was palpable. When he was working by himself, Nathan's relationship with the eminent Reiss family had become so bad that one of his brothers had been forced to intervene; now Nathan's letters from J.L. Reiss in Glasgow came replete with warm notes to Hannah, commenting on business management, politics and society news.[29] In a business culture in which 'character' counted for everything, the note of polite sociability struck by Hannah in her dealings with Nathan's clients was invaluable.

Hannah's letters to Angel Court encompassed both business and family matters, and were a lifeline to the world of her childhood and the familiarities of London life. In the postscript to a letter dated 12 August 1807, two days after Hannah had given birth, her father's clerk Abraham Hertz wished Hannah 'joy with all my heart', and wrote that 'I will not trouble you today'.[30] The warmth of the notes, and the familiarity with which Hertz addressed Hannah, gives an insight into how well known and highly regarded she was within the family business, but just as telling is the fact that when Hertz had a complaint against Nathan, it was Hannah he trusted to sort things out. 'I don't think you attend to your business as usual,' he once wrote to Nathan, 'and I am afraid I shall be obliged to Mrs Rothschild to correct you a little.'[31] Hannah's loyalty was now primarily to Nathan, not to Hertz or anyone else at her father's business. This was a tension that even Hannah's enormous reserves of charm and geniality would soon prove insufficient to resolve.

Just as Mayer Amschel had detected opportunities amid the turmoil of Europe at war, so too had Nathan and his in-laws. Two years after Hannah's marriage to Nathan, the Rothschilds (represented by Nathan) and the Cohens (represented by Hannah's half-brother, Solomon) became jointly involved in a smuggling project to bypass the blockade on British imports to territories under the control of Napoleonic France.[32] From the outset, Nathan's reckless nature and aversion to planning clashed with Solomon's prudence and attention to detail, and after a number of mishaps, including an attempted takeover by Nathan, the project ended with a slow and acrimonious carving up of the disappointing profits.[33] Solomon's fury would eventually lead to the sacrificing of another, more intimate relationship – that of Hannah with her father.

By February 1808, Levi Barent Cohen had fallen ill. Though Solomon had taken over the practical running of Levi's business, and was perfectly positioned to inherit the concern from his father, the transfer of a business from one generation to the next was always liable to be disrupted by manoeuvring in the wider family circle.[34] The arrogance and imperiousness shown by Nathan during the smuggling operation had alarmed Solomon, who feared that his brother-in-law would come down to London and try to take over part of the Barent Cohen business if he discovered Levi was on his deathbed. Solomon's solution to this problem combined a certain vengefulness towards his brother-in-law with a cruel indifference towards his sister: he would not send news to Manchester about Levi Barent Cohen's illness.

The first Hannah heard of her father's poor health was on 11 March 1808. In a letter to Nathan, the clerk Abraham Hertz thanked him for turkeys that he had sent to his in-laws for Purim, and mentioned that Levi Barent Cohen was very ill.[35] That was a dramatic understatement. Levi had been fading for a while, and died later that day.[36] When news of the death and burial reached Manchester, Hannah was distraught. Nathan, furious on her behalf, fired off a series of letters to his brother-in-law. 'You say Hannah is angry that we did not tell her about the state of our father's health,' Solomon replied.[37] 'We did not want to worry her. We also hoped that he would stay among us ... Console Hannah as much as you can. We all lost a good father and friend.' A separate note enclosed for Hannah was more conciliatory in tone – perhaps indicating the guilt Solomon felt for keeping her in the dark. 'He was receding all the last four weeks, but still we consoled ourselves with the hope of his recovering, and unfortunately were disappointed,' he wrote.[38] 'We did did not wish to alarm you and therefore thought best not to mention it. We must all however console each other, and thank God, that he has been and pray to the Almighty for his further protection.' He signed the letter 'your sincere and affectionate brother'.

Almost immediately, Hannah and Nathan made the decision to relocate to London.[39] They moved first to 12 Great St Helen's, Bishopsgate, and then – after the birth of a son, Lionel – to a larger house at 2 New Court, St Swithin's Lane.[40] New Court stood in the shadow of the triumvirate of landmarks which defined the City of London: the Lord Mayor's residence at Mansion House, the Royal Exchange and the Bank of England, which under the architectural direction of John Soane had grown into a vast neoclassical labyrinth covering three and a half acres between Threadneedle Street and Lothbury.[41] But the grandeur of these three great edifices was an anomaly in the cramped, bustling Square Mile, which at this point was still dominated by aged structures of 'smoke black'd brick', their lower storeys 'bespattered freely from the gutters' by the wheels of passing coaches, their murky windows emitting a 'miserable glow' of oil lamps and tallow candles.[42] One visitor expressed amazement that 'the most opulent bankers in the world have chosen this narrow, dark, uncomfortable street as a place to do business'.[43]

Although the move to London did not immediately spell the end of operations in Manchester, Nathan's involvement in the textiles trade began to dwindle as he deepened his involvement in a line of work with which he had long been peripherally engaged: finance.[44] In 1812 alone, the value of the bills of exchange he received in return for the coins, gold and silver that he sent to the Continent was at least £2,500,000.[45] To a certain degree Nathan owed his success to extraordinarily good luck: between 1808 and 1810, many of those who would have been competitors in this area had been swept away by death, export bubbles or the devastating crash of the Amsterdam market.[46] But he was also supremely talented and opportunistic. His brash, domineering business character, which had frequently imperilled his textiles operation, now came into its own.[47] He bulldozed brokers and bargained aggressively. With his brothers, he embarked on a new smuggling operation, transporting gold bullion from France to England in violation of the Continental blockade; Nathan was code-named 'Langbein', London 'Jerusalem', and the shipments 'Rabbi Moses' or 'Rabbi Moshe'.[48]

The renewed smuggling operations would bring Nathan to the attention of the British establishment – and in a far more favourable way than might have been expected.[49] In 1812, as part of the ongoing Napoleonic Wars, an army under the command of Lieutenant General Sir Arthur Wellesley (soon to become Duke of Wellington) had embarked on a new campaign against the French in Spain. John Charles Herries, a talented young official, was faced with the challenge of keeping Wellesley supplied with coin to pay for his army. An experienced smuggler such as Nathan, who was well connected in both English and Continental markets, was the natural choice. Not only did the deal struck with Herries provide Nathan with a substantial two per cent commission on all coin delivered to Wellesley but it also brought him into contact with top government officials and, eventually, the Prime Minister, Lord Liverpool.[50] This sort of access engendered further trust, and further commissions, and when the government needed a banker to make payments to their allies on the Continent, it was Rothschild, rather than more established figures such as Baring or Reid, who was best placed to win the contract.

Between 1811 and 1815 the Rothschilds were responsible for buying up more than 12.6 million francs in France, for transfers to the Continent made on behalf of the British government.[51] Nathan was, wrote the Prime Minister, Lord Liverpool, a 'very useful friend'. 'I do not know what we should have done without him last year,' he wrote in 1815.

Back in New Court, Hannah was now central to an extremely prosperous commercial network. It was, unsurprisingly, a house that rarely slept, with clerks and couriers arriving day and night, dispatch riders' horses clattering up St Swithin's Lane, and the crash of bullion being unloaded from the mail coach continuing long after the driver had retired to the taproom on the corner.[52] Amid this din, young Chilly and Lionel were joined by Anthony (b.1810), Nat (b.1812) and Hannah Mayer (b. 1815). Like the Rothschilds in the Frankfurt Grünes Schild before them, Nathan and Hannah witnessed their business and family grow side by side.

Only months after the birth of Nat, the London Rothschilds were hit by tragic news of the death of Mayer Amschel at the age of sixty-eight. On Yom Kippur he had spent the day standing and fasting in the Synagogue, and appeared for the last time in the Frankfurt Juden-gasse. He died just two days later, on 19 September.[53]

His will, signed 17 September 1812, marked a turning point for the Rothschild sons and daughters – in radically different directions.[54] All of his children were instructed to 'treat each other with constant mutual love and amity, and to behave towards the orders of my well-intentioned and conscientious paternal disposition with childish obedience'. The Rothschild sons were ordered to maintain among themselves an 'unbreakable unity'. Such unity required not only closeness and cooperation between those on the inside of the banking operation, but also the complete exclusion of outsiders.

As for the daughters, their fate was set out in a clause that was to cast a shadow over the women of the Rothschild family for the next two hundred years:

I will and ordain that my daughters and sons-in-law and their heirs have no share in the trading business existing under the firm of Mayer Amschel Rothschild and Sons ... and [that it] belong to my sons exclusively. None of my daughters, sons-in-law and their heirs is therefore entitled to demand sight of business transactions ... I would never be able to forgive any of my children if, contrary to these my paternal wishes, it should be allowed to happen that my sons were upset in the peaceful possession and prosecution of their business interests.

Not only were his wife, daughters, daughters-in-law and sons-in-law forbidden from holding a stake in the business, they were also barred from having any access to business papers and documents. The Rothschild bank – its wealth, its information and its governance – was entrusted exclusively to Mayer Amschel's sons. Though such a gendered exclusion was by no means unusual in wills of the period, it represented a harsh repudiation of the Rothschild women's involvement in the business thus far, and reinforced the exclusion of those Rothschild daughters who had married into other families. While the wife of a male Rothschild would become an adjunct to the business, a female Rothschild would become an adjunct to the business of her husband. Although Gutle had been left the Grünes Schild and 70,000 of Mayer Amschel's estimated 90,000 gulden fortune, the money was to be kept in the family business empire, under the control of her sons and their male heirs. Gutle, so crucial in the Rothschild bank's foundation and success, had been written out of its future – as had all of her female successors.

4

The Husband Hunt

THE SECTIONS OF Mayer Amschel's will relating to marriage had a particular significance for one Rothschild daughter. Feisty, vivacious Henriette, who had successfully joined her sisters-in-law Eva and Caroline and her mother Gutle in stonewalling the French interrogators in 1809, was the only one who remained unwed. Mayer Amschel's will promised Henriette a substantial dowry of 33,000 gulden, and appointed the eldest sons Amschel and Salomon as 'special advisors and guardians, together with the natural guardianship of her mother' to secure a suitable match. The twenty-one-year-old was now of central interest to the male Rothschild heirs as they sought to honour their father's wishes and the stipulations in his will.

Technically, the will allowed for Henriette to choose her own suitor, and for her brothers and mother only to give or withhold their consent, but in reality she would have little say. Nor would the 'natural guardianship' of Henriette's mother count for much, once marriage negotiations were underway. The marrying of Henriette was a business matter, and decisions about it would be reached via ill-tempered letters, sent between the brothers alone.

Like most young women in the Judengasse, Henriette had been brought up to expect that marriage was about far more, and far less, than romance. That had not stopped her from pursuing affairs of her own: prior to her twenty-first birthday she had had at least one significant attachment, to a Frankfurt man called Kaufmann, with whom she may even have been in love. Her recent romantic history was of little concern to her brothers, who trusted that their own preferred candidate – a man from Hamburg known as Hollaender, or 'the Dutchman' – could be installed in Kaufmann's place. In June 1814 Gutle's eldest son delegated to his younger brother James the task of sounding out this suitor. 'If your business takes you to Hamburg,' he wrote, 'will you find out whether Hollaender wants to marry?'[1] Hollaender did – though he had a wildly high expectation for a dowry. So eager was Amschel to honour his late father's wishes and find a match for his sister, that he 'did what I was told to do in order to make our [Henriette] happy' and 'offered [Hollaender] a dowry of 100,000 Gulden'.[2] At more than three times the amount that Mayer Amschel had stipulated in his will, the scale of the dowry discomfited Henriette, who 'could not believe' this kind of money was being offered in order to attract her a husband.[3] But it proved effective: the Dutchman was sufficiently interested that in September 1814 he arrived in Frankfurt.[4] With the older Rothschild brothers spread across the Continent, it fell to Carl to preside over the negotiations.

To the twenty-six-year-old, who knew that his negotiating skills were greatly inferior to those of his brothers, this was an onerous brief.[5] Still, on Hollaender's arrival Carl had the presence of mind to take him to the theatre.[6] It would have been a sound opening move – if they had been able to get seats. He awkwardly escorted Hollaender back home. At the door to the Grünes Schild, Hollaender finally built up the courage to announce that 'he wished to speak to one of the girls'. Not wanting to 'draw too much attention to the affair by arranging it all at my place', Carl invited Hollaender and Henriette instead to the houses of some of the in-laws: first to lunch at the Beyfuses, the family his sisters Babette and Julie had married into, and then, for tea, to the Sichels, the marital family of his sister Isabella. This was a slow and cautious introduction to the family circle, and reflected Carl's inexperience in matchmaking. It was, as he wrote to his brother Salomon, 'difficult for [him] to find out how things stand'.

The difficulty was soon compounded by the reappearance of Kaufmann, who was now determined to challenge Hollaender's suit. The brothers' opinions of Henriette's old flame had, if possible, deteriorated since they opened negotiations with their preferred candidate. In their letters, Kaufmann was was now referred to as a 'crook', and was said to owe considerable debts in London.[7] And yet his relationship with Henriette had been sufficiently serious that if news of it spread, it could scandalise or scare off other potential husbands.[8] Mentions in their letters of 'hush money' and 'keeping quiet' indicate the brothers' willingness to do whatever was necessary in order to secure Kaufmann's cooperation.[9] But it appeared the troublesome ex was not interested in bribes: he was interested in Henriette. Once it became clear that he was not likely to win the brothers' support for his suit, he instead got to work on the marriage broker who was assisting Carl, a man named Ellisen. Returning to Frankfurt after a weekend with Kaufmann at the nearby spa complex of Wilhelmsbad, Ellisen suddenly became 'most outspoken' to Carl on the virtues of love matches.

While the brothers attempted to fend off Kaufmann, they faced an equally distasteful issue with their preferred suitor. A 'stranger' to Frankfurt, the young man Hollaender had since his arrival fallen in with 'a horrible crowd' who spent their days 'having a wild time drinking and amusing themselves all the time'.[10] Carl had invested too much time and energy in Hollaender to be deterred by such youthful indiscretion, and redoubled his efforts to secure the match, arranging morning horse rides for Hollaender and Henriette. The stress and anxiety of reeling Hollaender in, while at the same time keeping the despised Kaufmann out, had sent Carl into a downward spiral of anger and depression, and his letters to the other brothers became increasingly bleak, doom-laden, and chauvinistic.[11] On 18 September 1814 Carl finally snapped: he spoke to Hollaender and told him to 'make up his mind'.[12] Hollaender promised to write to his mother in Leipzig for permission to marry.[13] He told Carl that it should be eight days before she granted her blessing and the saga could draw to a close.[14] In the end, they did not have to wait that long before the reply came. It was a resounding and devastating no.[15]

Carl had no doubt that cliques hostile to the family – including the 'Loebb-Reiss coterie' and the 'gang' that had coalesced around the irrepressible Kaufmann – had somehow played a part in the rejection.[16] There were many people speaking about things in a manner that had 'caused much harm', he wrote. Still, a mother's refusal was a hitch, not an insurmountable problem. And while the luckless Carl may not have excelled in the softer arts of polite courtship, strong-arming was something he could do. 'I shall now force him to give me another answer,' he wrote to Salomon and James.[17] Hollaender soon fled Frankfurt, but he remained the first choice for the Rothschild sons. The older brothers rallied around Carl in seeking to secure the marriage as soon as possible. Salomon wrote to his cantankerous brother Nathan in London, urging him to 'be kind' to Hollaender's brother-in-law, who was visiting the city, as the marriage matter was 'not settled yet'.[18] Meanwhile, Kaufmann refused to leave the scene and more suitors – a Fraenkel, a Goldsmid – threw their hats into the ring, complicating the scenario even further.[19]

Henriette herself was well aware of the toll the question of her betrothal was taking on her brothers, and wrote gratefully to Salomon.[20] But she reserved just as much gratitude – if not more – for Salomon's wife, Caroline. 'I cannot describe in words how much trouble your wife is taking over this matter,' wrote Henriette.[21] 'I am really forgetting the fact she is only a sister-in-law, as I see in her a real sister. If she thinks of something during the night and believes it to be a good idea, she gets up in the morning and tells Carl about it.' Not only did Caroline have an emotional intelligence that far outstripped Carl's, she also had with Henriette a singular, sisterly bond.

As far as Carl was concerned, none of these assets mattered. Any attempt by the women of the family to assist with negotiations was evidence only of impatience and gossipmongering. '[Henriette] runs to see [Caroline], [Caroline] in turn comes to see me,' wrote Carl to Salomon: '"what did he say, what did you say", that is how it goes on continuously.'[22] When one of the young Rothschild women made a mistake in the *Kontor*, he saw it as further evidence of the weakness and financial incompetence of the entire sex. The unfortunate thing for the brothers, he wrote, was that '[their] women' were 'just typical women'.[23] Women were 'bad cashiers'; some were not very healthy, he said, and not very strong. You had to know 'how to handle them'.

The gratitude in Henriette's letter to Salomon should not be misread for passivity. On the contrary; at the end of her letter, Henriette reminded her brothers that they, as Rothschilds, had the right to be every bit as 'proud' as the truculent Hollaenders.[24] Though there is no doubt that the young Rothschild sister's family pride was authentic, here it was being deployed tactically. Henriette had never been particularly fond of Hollaender, and the preservation of pride, in the current situation, meant pursuing him less keenly. It was just the latest in a series of tactical obstructions she had devised. Transparent as it may have been, Henriette's invocation of family pride hit home. Rather than 'chase' after the bridegroom's family, the brothers adopted a more circuitous approach.[25] In November 1814 James, who was in Hamburg again on business, managed to 'bump into' Hollaender at the Stock Exchange.[26] Hollaender behaved politely and appropriately, inviting James to his house for dinner 'so as to find out how things stand'.[27] But it seems the youngest Rothschild brother either played it too cool or lacked the nerve to bring up the issue in conversation. In a letter sent weeks later, Carl expressed his shock that James 'did not dare talk to Hollaender'.[28] After all the months of energy that Carl had put into it, the Hollaender project had fallen apart – and not because of a conclusive (paternal) refusal, but because the youngest brother had lost his nerve.

Failures like this came at a cost: news of abortive matches spread quickly through the marriage market, damaging a woman's future prospects. The Rothschilds had to regroup. The brothers decided that it would be best to send Henriette to London or Amsterdam, where news of the Hollaender disaster would weigh less heavily on people's thoughts, and she would be further from the nefarious influence of Kaufmann.[29]

The widowed matriarch, Gutle, hated the idea of her last unmarried daughter leaving the family home at the Grünes Schild, but feared that Henriette was 'getting grey' with all the delays: if they did not find a match soon, the twenty-three-year-old would become an old maid.[30] Reluctantly, Gutle consented to the idea of her daughter leaving. That Henriette was not so easily persuaded should not come as a surprise. As an unmarried woman of the ghetto, she had not travelled far from Frankfurt before. Now she was being asked to leave her home and her network of close relatives – including her mother, her sisters and her beloved older brother Amschel – and travel abroad, putting her faith in a set of matchmaking skills that had so far proven to be woefully inadequate. The very least she would need were funds with which she could support herself if the new set of negotiations went the way of the old ones. Eventually, Amschel stepped in and paid Henriette 'a large amount of money' to persuade her to leave the ghetto and travel to Amsterdam, to join her brother Salomon.[31] It may be that there were other marital prospects to be pursued in the city. If so, they came to nothing, and Amsterdam became a brief stop on a bigger journey. In the spring of 1815 Henriette crossed the North Sea, bound to join her older brother, Nathan, in England.

While the Continental Rothschilds were embroiled in the matchmaking drama with Henriette and Hollaender, Nathan and Hannah had been settling into family life at no. 2 New Court. In June 1812 Hannah's younger sister Judith Barent Cohen had married the Jewish broker Moses Montefiore (uniting two prominent British Jewish families from the Ashkenazi and Sephardic diasporas at a time when inter-denominational marriages were rare), and the couple had moved in next door, at no. 4.[32] The move not only brought sister and sister into close proximity, it also created a lasting business bond between their husbands, Nathan and Moses.[33]

The two men were a study in contrast.[34] Where Nathan was im-pulsive, reckless and irritable, Moses was considered, cautious and cultured. Nathan was still the Frankfurt newcomer, while Moses was from a longer-established London Jewish family. Their differences were the basis of an unexpected and near instant friendship, and of a thriving business partnership. The Cohen sisters, who had been close since childhood, were central to this deepening tie between the fam-ilies.[35] When they were in the same city, Hannah and Judith were frequent visitors at each other's houses, where they took meals, had intimate discussions and played a somewhat old-fashioned card game called 'commerce' or the more fashionable whist. When away, travel-ling with their husbands, they wrote to each other frequently: when Moses told Judith that a longer stay in Paris would be 'unprofitable', it was the subject of wry comment between the sisters.[36]

This was the sort of close family bond that the very best early nineteenth-century business partnerships were built upon, and the ideal match for Henriette would be one that performed the same function, consolidating a valuable and trusted connection as a basis for commercial as well as domestic success. Nathan, true to his reputation for haughty detachment, had given very little to the negotiations in their initial phase, and the other four brothers were probably glad to have a reason to force him to do his bit. 'Now let us talk about Henri-ette,' wrote Salomon to Nathan.[37] Hannah and Nathan were in luck: it just so happened that Moses had a brother.

Abraham Montefiore had begun his career with a brief stint in the silk trade before moving on to the Exchange, where Jewish traders had their own allocated corner, as did the other 'nations'.[38] Dashing, intelligent and ambitious, the young Montefiore had seemed, like his brother, to have a promising career ahead of him. But in 1812 his life took a scandalous turn when he married Mary Hall, the daughter of a Christian stockbroker.[39] Regency England was a relatively tol-erant place for a Jew to live compared to Frankfurt, but social and professional segregation was nevertheless still enforced by a number of strong taboos. As a result of his marriage to Mary, Abraham lost his job on the Exchange, and the couple were shunned by both their Jewish and Christian circles. In a society in which success depended on reputation and the support of others, such marginalisation was sure to entail ruin. The couple moved to 'obscure lodgings' in Islington, and Mary gave birth to a child, but tragedy followed when she died shortly afterwards.[40]

Cast out and in mourning, Abraham's situation looked bleak. In 1812, however, his older brother Moses made a rescue attempt, bringing him into a new business partnership and negotiating his re-entry to the Exchange.[41] It was the beginning of a rehabilitation, but only the beginning: to ease Abraham back into the community he had so badly offended would require a respectable Jewish marriage. In 1815, right on cue, an eligible Rothschild daughter arrived in London. A marriage between the pair was a neat solution that tied up the vexing matter of Henriette's marriage within Nathan's immediate business circle, and helped Moses at the same time. Abraham, meanwhile, would presumably have been grateful for any match that restored to him social acceptability and offered the prospect of a brighter, more financially secure future – something he now wanted not only for himself but also for his infant daughter, who'd been named Mary after her mother.

The wedding took place in London on 23 August 1815.[42] It was a marriage of convenience rather than romance. Hannah, Judith, Nathan and Moses could have had little idea, as they celebrated the partnership, that this match would end up destroying the alliance it had been designed to cement. The toxic legacy of the marriage is perhaps best summarised by a note made by Moses Montefiore years later, on the death of Nathan in 1836: 'NMR [Nathan] was a great & honored friend to Jud & I until Henrietta arrived in England & married Abraham.'[43] The couple, he wrote, had 'destroyed the kind feeling which precedingly subsisted'.

5

Madame Montefiore

ALTHOUGH NATHAN HAD acquiesced in his brothers' request to help with Henriette's match, he had done so in a characteristically presumptuous fashion, conducting all of the negotiations himself, and rushing ahead without keeping the rest of the family informed. In what must have seemed like a pointed dismissal of her other brother's three-year-long matchmaking project, Henriette had gone along with his and Hannah's wishes, and taken the bold step of getting married without informing her Frankfurt family. News of Nathan's meteoric success in England would have been the talk of the ghetto, and Henriette clearly nurtured a distant, younger-sisterly veneration of him. But her decision to rush ahead with the marriage was also a sign of her personal ambition to leave behind her ghetto youth and make the best she could out of her new situation. Nowhere was that ambition stated more clearly than in her and Abraham's first address: the couple established themselves not in one of the densely populated districts east of the City, nor in one of the City courts such as the one in which Hannah, Nathan, Judith and Moses now lived, but on Great Stanhope Street, in the fashionable West End.

To her family in Frankfurt, the speed of these developments and lack of communication must have seemed like a pointed snub. Amschel, Henriette's doting eldest brother, was particularly hurt. He wrote to her numerous times, but his letters went unanswered. Smarting, he turned to Nathan, raging that Henriette's silence was a sure sign that she did not wish to be Henriette Rothschild any more, but only 'Madame Montefiore'. Nathan must have addressed the subject with Henriette who, within a month, had written a joint letter to Gutle and Amschel. The letter disproved Amschel's theory that Henriette wanted to reinvent herself. Far from spurning her

'Rothschild' identity, Henriette was realigning herself away from the patronage and friendship of Amschel, the brother she had grown up with, to that of Nathan, the brother she barely knew. Virtually all the praise in Henriette's missive is reserved for Nathan and his wife Hannah. It was with Nathan that she and Abraham went on holiday and 'enjoyed every minute'; it was Hannah whose 'charm' was beyond description.

If that was not enough to prompt jealousy and defensiveness in Frankfurt, Henriette had a further pronouncement to make: 'Hannah has become a second mother to me. She continuously looks after me, comes and sees me every day and does not want to go to the country until I have had my baby.' Nowhere is Amschel's injured affection captured more clearly than in his stumbling attempt to articulate his disquiet: what upset him, he explained, was Henriette's inability to 'let her family participate in her happiness'. Perhaps such resentment would have been eased if he had actually been able to communicate with his new brother-in-law, but Amschel did not know English and Abraham did not speak German, nor could he write in Hebrew.

From the perspective of her relatives in the Judengasse, Henriette's new life in the West End must have seemed enviably privileged, and in many ways it was. And yet despite the ostensible glamour of her new life, Henriette had not completely escaped the ghetto. The Jewish population in London was not confined by physical walls, but there was a long legacy of other, less obvious forms of discrimination to overcome.

There had been a Jewish presence in England since at least 1066. As in Frankfurt, prohibitions on Christians being involved in usury, and restrictions on Jewish access to other professions, meant that many English Jews turned to moneylending. In 1290 growing hostility to the Jewish population – exhibited in blood libels, popular ballads and the introduction of a 'Jew badge' – culminated in the official expulsion of England's several-thousand-strong Jewish population by Edward I.[1] Following the 'readmission' of Jews by Oliver Cromwell in the mid seventeenth century, the small community of crypto-Jews who had worshipped covertly during the latter years of the expulsion were gradually joined by immigrant Sephardim and, later, by some Ashkenazim from eastern Europe.[2] Though the legal environment in eighteenth-century England was more favourable to Jews than it was in many other European countries (some Jews, such as the boxer

Daniel Mendoza, even became national celebrities), old prejudices still remained.[3] English Jews were the victims of routine discrimination and humiliation, and occasional antisemitic violence.[4] Legally, immigrant Jews were confined to the limited rights of 'aliens'; an attempt to change this situation in the Jewish Naturalisation Act of 1753 provoked a backlash that resulted in the Act being repealed the following year, and that would deter the leaders of the Anglo-Jewish community from engaging in similar campaigns for decades to come.

London's Jewish population was concentrated around the eastern fringe of the City of London, in an area stretching from Spitalfields, through Houndsditch and Aldgate, down to Rosemary Lane in the south.[5] It was here that most Jews made a living – often precariously, peddling goods or reselling old clothes and waste fabric in the area's markets.[6] The Jewish East End did not have the density or – at least, until the 1890s – the homogeneity of a ghetto. By the late eighteenth century the area had developed its own pockets of wealth, as successful Jewish merchants and bankers bought up town houses in the grander corners: Devonshire Square, Finsbury Square, Goodman's Fields. For the most part, however, this was still an area of abject poverty, and the descriptions left by Christian visitors are strikingly similar to those of the Frankfurt ghetto. The streets were 'unpaved and full of filth' and most of them 'so narrow that a carriage cannot get by'. 'There is no air,' wrote one horrified visitor, 'one cannot breathe.'[7]

Though the streets around Henriette's new London home were a world away from the cramped and insanitary conditions of much of the East End, the luxuriousness and relative freedom of her new life only further antagonised the brothers who felt cheated by her hasty London marriage. By May 1817 Salomon and James had joined Amschel in the chorus of animosity towards Henriette and Abraham, writing from Paris to express their horror at the discourtesy with which they were routinely treated by the couple on their visits to London.[8] Their sense of grievance had certainly outgrown the details, which were rather trivial: Henriette and Abraham had, it appears, not bothered to buy Salomon a tinted lens with which he could observe the solar eclipse during their recent visit. '[O]ur sister and her husband should learn ... next time to sacrifice a shilling and to offer her brother

a piece of blackened glass for the occasion of the eclipse of the sun,'
fumed Salomon.

Clearly there was more to the brothers' grievances. For years,
Nathan's brothers had been suspicious of his English alliances,
and now their suspicions intensified. 'Nathan was on his own too
long and has attached himself too closely to others,' wrote Carl to
James and Salomon a few months after the wedding.[9] James was more
direct: 'Where is your profit?' he asked, after Nathan made a big stock
purchase, 'or are you working for Montefiore?'[10]

Either in ignorance or defiance of such sensitivities, Abraham set
about making the most of his connection with the Rothschild business, attempting to join their lucrative speculations in European financial markets.[11] Henriette, who was perhaps even more ambitious
for her husband than he was for himself, did what she could to help.
Both had experienced vulnerability and deprivation in their recent
past, and were desperate to make their own money in any way they
could. Such energetic attempts to make use of another family's business networks would have come across as brazen; to the Rothschild
brothers, already anxious at the prospect that their family unity might
be eroded by distance and foreign in-laws, it was nothing short of an
outrage. As far as the business was concerned, the marriage had made
Henriette a Montefiore, not Abraham a Rothschild.

Attempting to save his own business relationships by distancing
himself from his brother, Moses dissolved the business partnership he
had set up to rescue Abraham in 1812. 'God grant it may prove fortunate for us both,' he wrote in November 1816.[12] While the end of the
partnership may have salvaged something of Moses's own reputation
with the Rothschilds, it did little to thwart Abraham and Henriette's
aspirations. In the spring of 1817 the pair travelled to Paris with the
express intention of profiting from James's involvement in French
government securities, or *rentes*, the value of which had been rising
sharply.[13] James, however, was not about to provide Abraham with
discounted financial services just because he had married his sister,
and Abraham and Henriette returned to London empty-handed.

Seemingly under the spell of his charming younger sister,
Nathan wrote to James to argue their case. James remained intransi-
gent: the couple were 'arse-lickers' who will 'fall away like blood suckers
when they have drunk too much blood'.[14] His words are particularly
damning given how much, intentionally or otherwise, they echoed

racist tropes about Jews. For months, he mounted a sustained assault on the young Montefiore couple. 'With good wishes,' he signed off one letter, 'from your loving brother who, like all brothers, is the one person you can rely on and whose loyalty and righteousness is more proven than that of a brother-in-law already counting on our brother Amschel's inheritance and working out the quickest way to join us.'[15] After the Paris debacle, Nathan's sympathy for Henriette and Abraham began to wane.

The tone of James's and Salomon's letters indicate that they would have been happy to see Henriette cut off from the family entirely, if it meant being rid of the irksome and venal Abraham. Amschel worried about his favourite sister; in 1817 he wrote to Nathan, urging him to remember that the brothers had decided to place Henriette 'under your protection' when they sent her to London, and that he needed to 'give her support without being drawn [into] women's intrigues'.[16] Early in 1818, Amschel's fears were realised. As Nathan swung into line behind James and Salomon, Abraham and Henriette were decisively relegated to the ranks of business outsiders, and the bond between Henriette and her sister-in-law and mother figure Hannah was consequently weakened.[17]

In the space of two years Henriette and Abraham had married, become a threat to Rothschild unity and been thrown back on their own resources. Together, they turned their energy and attention to the buoyant stock market, with Henriette joining the other women of the Montefiore family in 'speculating as bulls'.[18] In the family home on Stanhope Street, business filled every room, and most of Henriette's waking hours. Abraham's mother was deterred from calling on her son by the thought that in a house so full of business, 'the visits of an Old Woman must be intruding'.[19] If Henriette and Abraham were no longer welcome to share in the success of the Rothschild family, they would make their own.

6

A Healthier Climate

WHILE THE ROTHSCHILD brothers sought a suitable husband for Henriette, Hannah and Nathan's family had been growing. Hannah's home, New Court, may have been perfect for the developing business, but it was not the most tranquil or healthy environment in which to raise children. Previously, Hannah had sent her older children to Margate, Kent, to spend the summer in the care of a Mrs Brashin.[1] But with five children to cater for, she needed permanent access to a more spacious retreat. In the mid 1810s, as Nathan's business thrived on the back of his wartime contracts, they began looking for a base outside the City.

The countryside beyond the northern fringes of London presented Nathan and Hannah with a scattering of well-established Jewish communities, as well as clean air and easy access to the City along the Great North and Old North Roads.[2] First they took out a short lease on a house in Highgate in 1814, then another on a house in Clapton, before turning to nearby Stamford Hill, where they bought the lease on a three-storey brick villa just thirty years old and situated within eight acres.[3] The villa, known as Stamford Hill House, was located near the village of Stoke Newington, just north of the arched brick bridge that carried the Old North Road over the Hackney Brook. To the west, meadows stretched towards Canonbury, and to the east, the fields alongside the brook were thick with watercress.[4] The parkland and orchards around Stoke Newington were popular with city fruiterers, who used them to grow pears, apples, cherries, walnuts and gooseberries.[5] Years later, Hannah wrote to a friend: 'We find this situation more agreeable than in the streets of London; we do not have any benefit from our national friend, the fog.'[6]

Far from being a withdrawal to an isolated country retreat, the Rothschilds' move to Stamford Hill brought them into close proximity to other prominent Anglo-Jewish families who had purchased property in the area, including some Hannah had yet to meet, such as the D'Israelis, and others to whom she had close links, such as the Montefiores and the Goldsmids.[7] After the isolation of Manchester, she found herself thriving among a group of Anglo-Jewish families who had been successful in a whole range of trades and professions, including finance, textiles, law, and the tea and coffee trade. Within a few years she was approached to host the weddings of nieces and nephews from the Samuel, Cohen, Salomons and Worms branches of the family, several of whom had country houses nearby. Her social grace had become a subject of comment even between the Rothschild brothers, and she had a rare ability to combine Jewish tradition with the trappings of the Gentile elite.[8] At weddings hosted by Hannah, there was the crunch of glass under the heel, but also waltzes.[9] There was the *chuppah*, but also a marquee in which Weippert's band played 'till a late hour'.[10]

Hannah's curious fusion of religious tradition with secular glamour, and the growing role of the Rothschilds in national finances, made the weddings a subject of interest for the non-Jewish press. Her parties elicited all the usual clichés in the society columns of the *Morning Post*, where her tables 'groaned under the massive service & profusion of every delicacy', and the 'melodious strains' of a quadrille were 'wafted by a gentle breeze into the drawing rooms'.[11]

In 1818 two familiar faces appeared in Stamford Hill. The energy with which Henriette and Abraham applied themselves to business pursuits after their exclusion from the Rothschild network had paid dividends, and they too were looking for a rural retreat. Among local landowners, it was rumoured that they were worth £700,000.[12] For a woman who had once seemed to her brothers unmarriable, and a man who had languished in 'obscure lodgings', it was quite an ascent. Happily for Hannah and Nathan, the Montefiores' move was not another inflammatory attempt to inveigle themselves into the family business.[13] The birth of Henriette's first two children, Joseph (1816) and Charlotte (1818), had made her want to salvage some Rothschild family relationships, and the growing clan of Montefiore children in the following years – Nathaniel was born in 1819 and Louisa in 1821 – would grow up playing in a garden next to their Rothschild cousins.[14]

These Rothschild cousins were also becoming more numerous. After three sons between 1808 and 1812, in 1815 Hannah gave birth to her second daughter, whom the couple named Hannah Mayer. In the years immediately after the move to Stamford Hill, a son Mayer Amschel (1818) and daughter Lou (1820) followed.[15] The two eldest sons – Lionel and Anthony – were sent to school at Garcia's Academy, a boarding school in Peckham.[16] This had been established to cater for wealthy Sephardim dissatisfied with the teaching at Hurwitz's Academy in Highgate, where the schoolmaster wore a top hat and paced the classroom with a cane jutting from the top of his boots, and Hannah's preference for the new school indicated a progressive educational outlook as well as an interdenominational mindset.[17] After Garcia's, the boys would have a secular education from a neighbour in Stamford Hill, the Reverend Dr Schwabe.[18]

When, years later, the time came to prepare the younger boys for university, Hannah and Nathan looked further afield and hired a German tutor, Fritz Schlemmer. Despite his experiences tutoring the children of French aristocrats, Schlemmer was little prepared for the luxurious trappings of his new job: waking up in a Dover hotel after crossing the Channel, he found 'a superb four-horse carriage' waiting outside his window.[19] 'I asked [a] boy who this carriage belonged to,' Schlemmer recalled in his memoir. It was, of course, his.

Nat, Schlemmer later described, was 'of rapid perception, a firm will, and a great energy', while the younger brother, Mayer, was 'heavily and strongly built for his age [with] no interior inclination for spiritual efforts [and] of a passive and slow perception'. By contrast, in his hours spent teaching Lou and Hannah Mayer he 'found rest'.[20] Alongside their lessons with Schlemmer, the Rothschild daughters received tuition in dancing, music and art. Some of these lessons were conducted outside of the house, at larger academies and conservatoires, the relative merits of which was a subject of endless discussion and disagreement between upper-class mothers. When it came to dancing, Hannah was for Mr D'Egville's Academy, while Henriette preferred Madame Michou's.[21] The boys, too, were initiated into the traditional leisure activities of the English elite. Lionel and Anthony were already, in their early to mid teens, shooting and horse riding.[22]

Nathan had less time than Hannah for cultural or intellectual pursuits, and continued to cut a far less refined figure than his wife. More than one visitor to his office was surprised to find him half-dressed or ill-tempered, and many commented on the enduring imperfections of his English. Hermann von Pückler-Muskau, a Prussian prince who was introduced to Nathan in the mid 1820s, described his speech as 'quite peculiar to himself, half English, half German – the English part with a broad German accent', and the whole thing spoken 'with the imposing confidence of a man who feels such trifles to be beneath his attention'.[23] Anecdotes of his philistinism are scattered across diaries and memoirs of the period.[24] Nathan was quite aware of his reputation for cultural immaturity, and appears to have played up to it rather, perhaps on the grounds that it's better to say something out loud yourself, than risk having other people say it behind your back. As he wrote to his brothers: 'I do not read books, I do not play cards, I do not go to the theatre, my only pleasure is my business.'[25]

In Hannah and Nathan's case, a sharp contrast in background and personality produced complement rather than conflict, and their family life appears to have been generally happy. A stony-faced businessman at New Court, at Stamford Hill Nathan was a devoted, even doting figure. He bought a small goat-drawn carriage in which the children could drive around the grounds of the house, and also let them 'make their equestrian exercises on his back' – once horsing around so enthusiastically that he ended up dislocating his shoulder.[26] Playfulness came easily to Nathan when he was in the company of his family, and was encouraged by Hannah. 'It has always been my aim', she wrote to Nathan, 'that our dear children should not conceal from us their true, innermost feelings.' Such pronouncements were in vogue: both the German *Bildung* and the late eighteenth-century cult of 'sensibility' had conspired to make intimate and informal parent–child relationships very fashionable, and there were doubtless many 'innermost feelings' that Hannah would have been shocked to hear from her children.[27]

But her desire for intimacy and affection was real enough. Letters reporting on her interaction with the younger generation refer to games of Lotto, pony rides in the garden and walks along beaches to gather shells.[28] Such relaxed domesticity was an aspect of family life Hannah and Nathan were keen to share with the general public. A full-size portrait commissioned from William Armfield Hobday and completed in 1821 promoted an image of the family as spirited and informal, with one daughter reaching for a letter in her father's hand and another sitting in her dress on the floor, while the sons appear to be on the verge of leaving the frame, to play with the family dog.

To Henriette and Abraham, such artful domesticity had come at a cost. By the early 1820s they too had built a successful business and a large family, also centred on a home in Stamford Hill. And yet Abraham's frantic application to business matters and social competitiveness had exhausted him, and worn away at his health.[29] For over a decade he had struggled with recurring bouts of tuberculosis, and in 1823 his condition deteriorated dramatically. In a desperate attempt to save Abraham's life, Henriette recruited the Quaker doctor Thomas Hodgkin, who had experience of treating consumptive patients, to accompany him on a journey to Italy.[30]

Hodgkin's parents were worried about his prospective employer. They asked the Stamford Hill neighbours about the family, and were told that Abraham's manners were 'very agreeable'.[31] His wife Henriette, however, was described tactfully as 'rather eloquent', and it was to be hoped that if Hodgkin travelled with the family, she would not be 'of the party'. Anyone who knew Henriette well would have known the hope was futile. She and Abraham were inseparable, practised at setting themselves against the outside world, and there was no chance of her letting him travel across the Continent without her. In fact, the whole family would come: seven-year-old Joseph, six-year-old Charlotte, five-year-old Nathaniel and the cherubic Louisa, a 'dainty' two-year-old with 'auburn wavy hair and a delicate complexion'.[32] The party travelled to Paris at the beginning of September, and left the city on the 16th, Henriette travelling in a coach with Abraham, the children in a second coach, and Hodgkin – who was far more at ease than the rest of the family – riding alongside, stopping now and then to admire the scenery and to take observations on interesting medical phenomena.[33]

In Paris, Hodgkin had found Henriette far less trouble than he had anticipated.[34] He had enjoyed the company of those family members who joined them in the city – especially Moses and Judith – and was impressed by Henriette's devotion to her husband.[35] But as the journey progressed from Nice to Pisa, and from Pisa on towards Rome, Henriette's intensity and her devotion to Abraham, began to trouble Hodgkin, and a note of dread crept into the character sketches he sent home. 'I have never seen anyone more affectionate than she,' he wrote. 'She looks after him almost by herself ... she does without food and sleep, survives the cold and chill. She tolerates all this with almost superhuman vigour.'[36]

There was something in this that frightened him.

If her nature seems scarcely human she does not at all incline to the nature of angels for most of all I think she has got a most unfortunate and accursed power of causing trouble for other people ... In no way do I need a poetic imagination to conjure up a Medusa and the hair styles which she loves to affect is just like snakes ...[37]

Not only was Henriette confronting the possibility that her spouse would soon die, but she had also become pregnant during the trip, and, while maintaining her cold and sleepless vigils at Abraham's side, was struggling with additional exhaustion and discomfort of her own. It should have come as no surprise to Hodgkin that her nerves were shot.

While Hodgkin's treatment of Abraham had emphasised the importance of climate and exercise, the physicians employed by the family in Rome advocated a more interventionist approach that included a series of blisterings and bleedings.[38] Henriette was convinced of the benefits of this, and banned Hodgkin from Abraham's sickroom at the Villa Paolozzi. In January 1824 Hodgkin was formally dismissed: he spent the rest of his time in Rome sightseeing with members of the extended Montefiore and Rothschild families, many of whom were only too happy to stoke his grievances against his Gorgon of an ex-employer.[39]

The strain of round-the-clock care for her dying husband had drained Henriette, who at some point during the spring suffered a miscarriage.[40] With Abraham terribly weak, the couple decided to put aside a plan hastily conceived by Moses to ship his brother for convalescence in the Holy Land, and instead took advantage of the summer weather to head back towards England.[41] In August 1824 they reached Lyon, and it was there that Abraham finally succumbed to his illness.[42] At the age of thirty-three, devoted Henriette, only recently traumatised by the loss of her baby, became a widow. A boat was hired to bring her and the body across the Channel to Dover, where members of the extended family – including Hannah's children and Abraham's mother – gathered to meet her. Hannah herself decided that she would sail across to Calais, so that Henriette would have some support during the crossing. 'It will be some consolation to Henriette under her extreme affliction,' she wrote to Nathan.[43]

Henriette's ordeal was not over. In his final hours, Abraham attempted to write a new, radically simplified will, in which he left almost everything to her.[44] As in his previous wills, the bounty came with conditions, for Abraham also made a final request of his wife

– that she never remarry, for the sake of the children. Once the new will had been drawn up, Abraham was raised in bed in order to sign the papers, but had only managed to scrawl 'I w', before succumbing to violent convulsions, and died before he could sign the document properly. Back in England, Henriette was forced to take legal action to seek probate of the will, which meant bringing a case against the three men named as executors of an earlier signed will: Moses Mocatta, Daniel Mocatta and her own brother Nathan Mayer Rothschild.[45]

The case advanced by Henriette's counsel placed strong emphasis on the mutual high regard between Abraham and his wife: '[n]othing could be more obvious that the unbounded, and doubtless well-merited, confidence which the deceased reposed in his lady'.[46] The opposing case focused on the formal inadequacies of Abraham's final will, and suggested that he was not of sound mind when he wrote it. The will's favourability towards Henriette was construed as evidence. It failed to meet the 'evident intentions of the deceased', because 'it was not likely he meant to reduce the portions of his children, or to give an enormous residue to his wife'.

In the end, the burden of proof that fell on Henriette's lawyers was too great, and the legal inadequacies of the Lyon document too significant, and the court granted probate of a will of 1820.[47] For Henriette, the difference was not life-changing: either would have made her extremely rich. At last, after a year in which she had travelled thousands of miles, suffered constant anxiety, and lost both a husband and an unborn child, she could retreat to Stamford Hill and find some peace.

Henriette Rothschild, 1791–1866.
The youngest daughter of Gutle and
Mayer Amschel, known for her tenacity,
wit and determination. In later life
she was famed for her 'great fund of the
racy old Jewish humour'.

7

Concordia, Integritas, Industria

THE WIDESPREAD INTEREST in Henriette's court case was a small symptom of a very big development: the public appetite for information about the Rothschilds was growing. As early as spring 1816, Carl had written to his brother James: 'We are getting very famous.' From the first, the veracity of information about the family was rarely a matter of particular concern among those who produced, disseminated or consumed it. The family was 'every day in the news', and 'gossip and miraculous stories' took hold whenever one of the brothers arrived on business in a European city.[1]

Along with this fame came the possibility of official recognition, and rumours that Nathan was to be offered a knighthood had already begun to circulate. Hannah understood that by entering the British social hierarchy, Jewish dignity and achievement could find validation. Nathan retained the prickliness and suspicion of the outsider. He made it clear that he would not accept the honour. The other Rothschild brothers, who felt that such a title was 'a mark of distinction for our [Jewish] nation', called upon Hannah to intervene.[2]

'[I]f one Jew is a Baron every Jew is a Baron,' Carl wrote to his brothers.[3] Communal integrity and survival for the Jewish 'nation' as a whole were at stake. At the time, one of the only ways that Jews could escape the legal disabilities attached to their faith was to convert to Christianity, but by demonstrating what could be achieved without conversion and accepting a noble title, the Rothschild family could show that spiritual integrity was compatible with worldly success.

Nathan could not be persuaded, yet. But Hannah's convictions would have a creeping effect on her husband's outlook. In the spring of 1820 he was appointed Austrian consul in London, a position for which he had actively solicited.[4] Carl described his appointment as a 'lucky thing for the Jews', and Amschel wrote to Nathan saying that '[t]hough it may mean nothing to you, it serves the Jewish interest'.[5] By this point, Nathan had come to see the merit in such arguments, and even appears to have developed a pride in the trappings of official honour – albeit one streaked with a sense of absurdity. After being persuaded, during a boozy dinner at Stamford Hill, to try on the consular uniform sent by 'his friend' Klemens von Metternich, he 'tried to assume the various bendings and bowings, and the light and gracious air, of a courtier'.[6]

In 1822, Francis I, emperor of Austria, recognised the service of Salomon's Vienna branch of the Rothschild bank by elevating all of the five brothers, scattered across Europe, to the title of *Freiherr*, or Baron. The family took a crest in which the five sons of Mayer Amschel were symbolised by five arrows, and a Latin motto that emphasised, among other virtues, the unity proclaimed in their father's will: *Concordia, Integritas, Industria* (Harmony, Integrity, Diligence).

Since a previous elevation in 1816 (when the original version of the coat of arms had been devised), the brothers had been allowed to use the particle 'von' or 'de' before 'Rothschild' in their name. Amschel Mayer in Frankfurt became Amschel Mayer von Rothschild; James in Paris became James de Rothschild.[7] Nathan had been unmoved, and was happy to remain 'Mr Rothschild'.[8] Following the elevation to the more significant barony in 1822, however, he was persuaded to apply to the Royal College of Arms for the registration of his Austrian title. It is unlikely, given his previous attitudes on the subject, that he was disappointed when the application failed.[9] Hannah was sufficiently dismayed that she decided to bypass protocol, and began referring to herself as Baroness Rothschild, without official sanction.[10]

In England, the growing public fascination with the Rothschilds found visual expression in the many images produced by political cartoonists. During the late eighteenth and early nineteenth centuries, artists had developed a new, energetic and confrontational idiom for visual satire, doing away with niceties such as anonymity and misdirection, and producing instead scabrous depictions of public figures clearly recognisable to the news-reading middle classes.[11] Jewish subjects were particularly vulnerable to vicious stereotyping.[12] Nathan's business connections to the Tory Duke of Wellington, and to the authoritarian Holy Alliance on the Continent, had earned him a reputation as a reactionary.[13] He was depicted as a rag seller, or as the shadowy puppeteer of national and international affairs.[14]

Among the family on the Continent, who had to deal with a more overt and oppressive antisemitism, complaints about caricatures received short shrift. If anything, it was seen as a sign of prestige and renown: 'We are not going to cry on learning that you have been caricatured,' Salomon and James wrote to Nathan in October 1817.[15] 'As you say, Dick, Tom and Harry are never caricatured but Kings and Emperors are. May God grant us never any greater worry. My [son] Anselm and your [son] Lionel may also be caricatured, as soon, please God, they will become well known in this world.' Such a response underestimated how fine the line was between demonising depictions and actual violence: in 1821 Nathan would receive a death threat for his involvement with governments that had 'designs . . . against the liberties of Europe'.[16]

Hannah appeared in cartoons much less frequently than her husband, but in Alfred Crowquill's satirical 1826 cartoon 'Beauties of Brighton' she was portrayed, fat and floridly dressed, promenading past the Brighton Pavilion where King George IV held court.[17] Compared to other satirical portraits of prominent Jewish figures at the time, this was not particularly vicious, and for someone so concerned with the trappings of social recognition, to be shown parading in front of a fashionable royal venue alongside figures such as Sir Augustus Frederick d'Este and the Duke of York was no bad thing. It was, however, emblematic of the family's growing prominence. By the early 1820s the days when she could travel abroad discreetly, or come and go from town unscrutinised, were long gone; her movements now featured in the 'arrivals and departures' columns of *The Times*.[18]

In June 1824, the newspapers reported Hannah's departure from Dover to the Continent. The family was Frankfurt-bound to celebrate the marriage of Nathan's thirty-two-year-old brother James to nineteen-year-old Betty von Rothschild, daughter of Nathan and James's older brother Salomon. Cousin-marriage, and to a lesser extent the marriage of uncles and nieces, was a minority practice among upper-class families of nineteenth-century Europe. Its popularity declined only very slowly over the course of the century, due both to concerns about consanguinity and an increase in social mobility amongst women. The Rothschilds, however, embraced the practice more consistently and assiduously than most. Not only did endogamous matches enforce the unity instructed in Mayer Amschel's will, they also served to keep wealth within the family. Out of twenty-one Rothschild marriages between 1824 and 1877, fifteen would take place between direct descendants of Gutle and Mayer Amschel.

Nathan chaperoned Hannah and three of their sons – Lionel, Anthony and Nat – across the English Channel to Calais on the steamboat *The Monarch*, before turning around and returning (a rather romantic convention referred to by Hannah as 're-crossing').[19] When Hannah and her sons arrived in Frankfurt for the wedding, it was not towards the Grünes Schild and the Judengasse that they made their way. By 1824, only seventy-year-old Gutle still lived in the Grünes Schild in the old Frankfurt ghetto, and the Rothschild sons had established branches of the bank across Europe: Nathan in London, Salomon in Vienna, Carl in Naples, and James in Paris. Henriette was unusual, among the daughters of the family, for having travelled as far as her brothers. Most of the sisters remained in Frankfurt, living outside the old ghetto but close enough that they could still visit their aged mother frequently. Only the eldest son, Amschel, remained in Frankfurt. It was at his home that Hannah and the children would stay during their visit. They were met on arrival by Hannah's eldest daughter, sixteen-year-old Chilly, who had gone ahead of her mother and brothers to Frankfurt, charged with the task of calming the nervous bride.[20]

Life in Frankfurt beyond the Judengasse remained the same mix of bustling affluence as it had been in the Rothschild brothers' youth, yet in comparison to London, which by the 1830s was the most populous city in the world, it seemed like something of a backwater. Walking through the centre of Frankfurt, the diarist Dorothy Wordsworth had been struck by just how unfashionable the women's hats were, remarking of one that it could have 'belonged to her great grandmother's grandmother'.[21] There was a similar hauteur in the attitudes of the English Rothschilds. To fifteen-year-old Lionel, who had been brought up visiting the Royal Exchange in London, the exchange in Frankfurt was not much to rhapsodise about: 'It is a very small place & it seemed to me that there was very little business doing, in comparison with that of London,' he wrote home, after visiting it with his uncle Amschel.[22]

Hannah was steeped in European language and culture, but the cosmopolitanism of her background had not prepared her for the bleak realities of the post-Napoleonic Continent. While Amschel's house was luxurious, his recent turn towards strict orthodoxy – a development much lamented by the brothers – was unlikely to have put her at ease, and elsewhere she faced the daunting prospect of having to navigate the convoluted politics of her in-laws, without any assistance from Nathan. She found herself waking up before six, and writing letters in which she fondly imagined Stamford Hill: the hushed morning, with the family enjoying a 'second sleep'; her daughter Hannah Mayer making Nathan breakfast; Allard, the cook, baking cakes to send to Mayer at school.[23]

The rest of the day was taken up with the flurry of festivities connected to the wedding. During her eighteen years of marriage to Nathan, Hannah had caught some of his obsession with business, and in her letters, fragments of news and analysis about the markets or politics sat alongside anecdotes about friends and family. Her visitors in Frankfurt included European aristocracy, heads of rival banks and prominent politicians such as the Austrian chancellor, Prince Metternich. 'I find that you have again had some reports of a warlike nature which has had an influence upon the funds which I hope will soon recover to their original price', began one of Hannah's letters home.[24] The wedding took place on Sunday, 11 July. As with previous Rothschild marriages, James and Betty's union was governed by a detailed legal prenuptial agreement stipulating the claims of each party to the property of the other.[25]

After their marriage, Betty and James returned to Paris, and moved to no. 19 rue d'Artois, where Betty quickly earned a reputation as one of Paris's most stylish hostesses.[26] One guest at the couple's Boulogne-sur-Seine mansion found the table dominated by an immense silver candelabra-like sculpture of platters; another noted that the gravies cooked by the prodigious chef Antonin Carême had been made 'with chemical precision', the cooked vegetables still carried their 'shade of verdure', and that the mayonnaise was 'fried in ice'.[27] Her emergence as a society hostess should not be misunderstood as evidence of a precocious independence, however. Years before the marriage, James had complained that his lack of a wife was preventing him from competing with other Parisian bankers. 'I have no house where to receive,' he wrote. 'A house without a wife is like a ship without a captain.'[28] Just months after his and Betty's marriage, he wrote to Nathan that '[t]o deprive oneself of one's wife is difficult. I could not deprive myself of mine. She is an essential piece of furniture.'[29]

Though it's hard to imagine Nathan speaking about Hannah in such stark and cold terms, she undertook the same vital work for the

English branch of the business that Betty did for the French one, and in the mid 1820s this work was expanding dramatically, following Nathan's purchase of the lease on a new house in Piccadilly, in the West End. This district had once been an outlying area of the city, but it had been transformed by the construction of mansions, shopping streets and grand entertainments such as William Bullock's Egyptian Hall Museum, where Napoleon's captured carriage had recently drawn huge crowds for several months.[30] The buildings were more elegant and spacious than in the City, the shopping was better, and it was close to Hyde Park, which still retained an air of exclusivity from its time as a royal hunting ground.[31] In the years since Henriette and Abraham moved there, a stream of Jewish families had followed them, and in the same year that Hannah and Nathan took up residence at no. 107 Piccadilly, Hannah's sister Judith and her husband Moses Montefiore moved in round the corner, to Green Street, off Park Lane.[32]

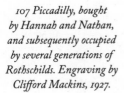

107 Piccadilly, bought by Hannah and Nathan, and subsequently occupied by several generations of Rothschilds. Engraving by Clifford Mackins, 1927.

Although Hannah and Nathan still retained New Court for business, and Stamford Hill for the children, Hannah quickly adjusted to the distinctly upper-class environment of Piccadilly. Writing to Lionel and Anthony in Göttingen on the eve of her first night in the house in January 1826, she excitedly declared that the building and furniture looked 'exceeding well'. The staircase had been rebuilt, the ceilings raised, and a 'very pretty Billiard Room and Table' had been fitted.[33] Not everything was done, but Hannah had been busy at Stamford Hill and at New Court, and generally found it 'impossible to get things completed' until she was on site herself, to supervise the works.

The new house allowed for entertaining on a different scale to Stamford Hill, and Hannah, now in her early forties, rose to the task. While a typical event at Stamford Hill had fewer than a hundred guests, over three hundred people might pass through the doors of no. 107 during a single night.[34] The house would be transformed for the occasion: orange and lemon trees 'in full bearing', as well as 'a profusion of rare plants', were brought to line the inner hall, staircase and anterooms.[35] Dancing generally began at eleven o'clock, paused at one o'clock in the morning, when supper was served and then resumed, often not winding down until the flames of Piccadilly's new gas lamps were paling against the dawn.

Gastronomy was a contemporary obsession, and fascinated the English Rothschilds. In their letters, foodstuffs are described with curiosity, glee and gourmand-like obsession: partridges, quails and ortolans; truffled and Strasbourg pies; apples, peaches, pears; sweetmeats and glaces. Sending food was almost as common within the family as sending letters, and Rothschild couriers were often given treats such as grapes and sugar plums to transport across Europe. But food was also part of a gift economy, a way of treating family friends, acquaintances and allies. 'I sent it to the Duchess of Gloucester,' wrote Hannah, on the subject of a 'very large and extremely beautiful Pine Apple'; 'It came very opportune, she having the same day a large dinner party.'[36]

The refreshment room was a focal point of Hannah's events. She engaged the services of the confectioner Robert Gunter, who had worked for her at Stamford Hill, and also of William Jarrin, who had worked for Napoleon before moving to England and becoming one of London's most innovative chefs.[37] Jarrin represented a virtuosic Continental tradition: he could make flowers and fruit from candy, or spin an animal from sugar.[38] Alongside reliable favourites such as champagne ices and pyramids of strawberries, Jarrin was famous for odder creations: brown-bread ice cream, vinegar drops and chocolate harlequin pistachios.[39] By the 1820s the Rothschild family across Europe were known for such luxurious spreads, and the need constantly to better themselves must have been exhausting. At a Christian aristocratic or upper-class banquet, grandeur was commendable, but among a parvenu Jewish family, the appreciation of it was often tinged with distaste. One guest at a ball thrown by James de Rothschild joked sarcastically and antisemitically that tickets changed hands at a premium after it emerged that diamonds and brooches would be given out, and every lady in attendance entered into a prize draw.

Although famously lavish, Hannah's parties were as much about business as pleasure. Important political contacts were a mainstay of her guest lists, which during these years were dominated by the political right. The Tory politician and Master of the Mint, John Charles Herries, was a frequent guest, as was the Duke of Wellington.[40] These were international affairs too: at one ball, Hannah's guests included the 'Swedish, Bavarian, Wurtemberg [sic], Mexican, Neapolitan, Sardinian, and Saxon Ministers' as well as Baron de Neumann (the first secretary at the Austrian Embassy) and Prince and Princess Esterházy (the Austrian ambassador and his wife).[41]

The entertainment, like the food, was decidedly European.[42] Each London season brought a new cohort of musicians, some of whom came speculatively, some on the recommendation of more established figures, and some under contract to companies such as the Italian Opera.[43] A hostess like Hannah was obliged to navigate an obstacle course of impresarios, agents, performance contracts and rival hostesses in order to secure the services of the most coveted performers. She had already hosted several concerts at Stamford Hill, where the celebrated pianist Ignaz Moscheles had played to a gathering of foreign ministers and Rossini had once performed alongside his wife.[44] At Piccadilly, she hired musicians for both 'select musical entertainments' and larger parties. By the season of 1828, she had come to find the work of booking each performer too complex and burdensome, and contracted the work out to Moscheles, who spent £167 – 'a pretty little sum according to our German notions' – hiring the services of Madame Stockhausen, Monsieur de Beriot and himself.[45] The following season, Moscheles' preferred performers included a nineteen-year-old German-Jewish student of his from Paris: Felix Mendelssohn.[46]

While Hannah's engagements were necessarily in keeping with current fashions, her commitment to musical patronage was enduring, and concerts became a genuine love.[47] Many of the virtuosos who came to Piccadilly to perform in the evenings also visited during the day as teachers: her daughters' tutors included Mendelssohn, the German virtuoso Louis Spohr and the Italian composers Vincenzo Bellini and Gioachino Rossini.[48] The piano on which the girls learnt, an Érard, had been selected after consultation with Moscheles. He insisted that the decision was down to Hannah's own good ear. 'Now that she has heard an Érard,' wrote Moscheles, 'she wants one.'[49] In reality, the choice was probably not quite so impartial as that: a few years earlier, Érard had effectively recruited Moscheles as a sort of brand ambassador, providing him with a concert piano worth 160 guineas, and arranging for it to be transported around with him on tour. It is likely that his fondness for the instrument – which, despite being a little dry on the top notes, had a light touch and a quick repeat – played as large a part in the sale as Hannah's own discernment.

Charity fundraisers of the period often followed a similar pattern to society balls, featuring the same musicians, guests and chefs, and Hannah was careful to give to what were generally thought of as 'Christian' causes.[50] She donated to the London Hospital, to the distressed silk manufacturers of Spitalfields, to Spanish refugees, the Irish poor, and victims of a calamitous balcony collapse in the Brunswick Theatre.[51] But the most significant of her charitable relationships was with the Jews' Free School on Bell Lane, in the East End of London.

The Jews' Free School (JFS) began life as a Talmud Torah attached to the Great Synagogue in Duke's Place, offering religious teaching to a small number of boys.[52] In 1817 it reopened as the Free School for German Jews, teaching an expanded curriculum of religious and secular subjects, and a few years later, when it moved to the East End, it began to admit girls.[53] '[T]he complete amelioration of society', the governors had decided, 'could not possibly be effected unless females ... were likewise initiated into those duties, which if known and practised, must invariably ensure individual happiness and general prosperity.'[54] The girls' curriculum would focus on domestic skills, including needlework, dressmaking, knitting, cleaning and cooking – but the argument for any kind of formal schooling of girls must have resonated with Hannah, given the relative breadth of her own education. The new girls' school opened with 170 students, soon increasing to 230.[55]

Hannah donated £10 to the JFS in 1819 – a substantial amount, with only two other benefactors that year giving more – and another £15 in 1820 to help with the move to Bell Lane.[56] The school quickly became her favourite cause, and in a general meeting in July 1822 her commitment was recognised with a nomination for life governorship.[57] Although there had been female governors at the school before, Hannah was one of the first women to be appointed since the school began accepting female pupils. As a governor, she took it upon herself to provide uniforms for all the pupils, and helped establish a permanent endowment, which secured the future of the school.[58] The link in the public mind between Hannah and the Free School was strong: in the 1840s, the French socialist traveller and writer Flora Tristan would visit London and misdescribe Hannah as its founder.[59]

Hannah's social and charitable activities, as well as her husband's extraordinary wealth, were of growing interest to the press. Early in 1828, when a tussle between George IV and his ministers led to public scrutiny of Nathan's close relationship with the Tories, cartoons emerged drawing on the usual racial stereotypes, including one by George Cruikshank that depicted Nathan as a ragman, calling in a debt from the Prime Minister, the Duke of Wellington (who was depicted playing Britannia's shield like a fiddle).[60] Hannah was drawn into the fray. A tongue-in-cheek article in the newspaper *The Age* promised a fantasy 'list of Ladies who are to form a female administration'.[61] Hannah was to be 'Mistress of the Mint' – an allusion not only to the family's private wealth but also to their close friendship with the real Master of the Mint: Herries.

At the turn of the nineteenth century the name 'Rothschild' had been virtually unknown in England. By the middle of the 1820s it was recognised more than any other name of Anglo-Jewry. In the mind of the Gentile public there was increasingly little distinction between the Rothschild family and the Jewish community at large. It was becoming vital to control the public image of the Rothschild family, both in England and beyond. The English family had already experimented in this area: the enormous family portrait commissioned from Hobday, showing the family as sturdy, affectionate and very English, had been exhibited at the Royal Academy in 1821.

Salomon, meanwhile, commissioned the journalist Friedrich von Gentz to write an encyclopedia entry about the Rothschilds, published in F.A. Brockhaus's *Allgemeine Deutsche Real-Encyklopädie für die ge-bildeten Stände* (*General German Encyclopedia for the Educated Classes*) in 1827.[62] The article was a counter-blast to the hostile and sometimes scurrilous accounts of the family in the press, but it was also a foundational act of Rothschild self-styling. Gentz's article was preoccupied with family unity. What was remarkable about the brothers, he wrote, was the way in which they had obeyed 'with great conscientiousness' the deathbed injunction of their father to remain united.[63]

8

Betrayal

BY THE 1820s Rothschild funding of the great monarchist powers of Austria, Prussia and Russia had earned the family a reputation, in some quarters, as the bankers of European reaction. That reputation was unfair on Nathan, who counted abolitionists and Quakers among his closest associates, but the inaccuracy of it was particularly jarring to Hannah, whose politics were more liberal than those of her husband.[1] As early as the 1810s, her progressive inclinations had led her to develop connections with writers and campaigners whose aims would flourish, over the following decade, into the defining causes of the period: the abolition of slavery, social reform, and civil rights for religious minorities.

One of her most influential associates was the Welsh textile manufacturer and utopian socialist Robert Owen, who since 1800 had been engaged in a paternalistic-utopian experiment at his New Lanark mill in Lanarkshire, Scotland. In *A New View of Society*, Owen had argued that if his innovations at New Lanark – which included educational facilities, improved housing and welfare programmes – were replicated on a wider scale, Britain would witness unprecedented moral regeneration.[2] Hannah Rothschild was an avid follower and supporter of his political agenda, and Owen's underlying belief that environment could shape character and life prospects was influential on her work at the Jews' Free School. Writing years later in his autobiography, Owen remembered 'the truly good and excellent Madame Rothschild' as one of the people who had taken 'a lively interest in aiding my measures' after the publication of *A New View* in 1813.[3]

In 1824 Owen went to America, and invested the bulk of his industrial wealth into the utopian community of New Harmony, Indiana, with little success. When he resettled in London four years later, he did so as an activist and campaigner with somewhat more radical aims than he had previously espoused. His letters to Hannah, which had previously been warm and appreciative, now took on a more foreboding and prophetic quality, warning her of 'sudden revolutions in all the states of Europe which may now any day take place'.[4] Any doubts she had about this new, more ominous Owen would have been exacerbated by his comments on religion. Hannah, he advised, ought to become 'emancipated from religious and national prejudices'. Judaism was at the time conceived of as both a religion and a nation, and there is no mistaking which 'prejudices' Owen is referring to. What interested Hannah was not emancipation from her religion, but the emancipation of it. Hannah felt keenly the communal responsibility that came with her family's singular economic position. To help the Jewish 'nation' was not just a desirable goal; it was a God-given responsibility.

The legal situation of the Jewish community in England remained almost exactly as it had been after the repeal of the Naturalisation Act in the mid eighteenth century.[5] Jewish men such as Nathan, who had migrated to the country, could in theory apply to become a denizen (a stage short of being a citizen). But the thousands of Jews who did not have the funds to pursue the costly process of denization remained deprived of basic civil rights, including the right to vote or bequeath property, on account of being 'aliens'.[6] Other legislation excluded non-Anglicans from public office. The late seventeenth-century Test and Corporation Acts stipulated that anyone who wished to hold civil, military or municipal office had to take communion in the Church of England and swear the oaths of Supremacy and Abjuration (which included the phrase 'on the true faith of a Christian').[7]

This did not stop Hannah from pursuing her political agenda at home, in Piccadilly. Westminster was short of places where politicians could mingle across party lines or between the front and back benches, and hostesses like Hannah presided over some of the few places where politicians could meet informally, to negotiate and strategise. At her parties in the West End, she learned to exercise the soft power that came with her family's social prestige, and to lobby effectively for causes close to her heart.

The political climate was already changing, thanks to the Catholic Association, which agitated for legislative change by sponsoring pro-emancipation and Catholic parliamentary candidates.[8] By the late 1820s the movement had a vast following in Ireland, and their leader –

the charismatic lawyer Daniel O'Connell – was internationally famous. The fight for Catholic emancipation had a catalysing effect on related causes, both because of the shift it appeared to signal in public mood, and because the exclusion of many different groups all arose from the same pieces of legislation.[9] The Sacramental Test Act of 1828 repealed those parts of the Test and Corporation Acts that prevented Catholics and Dissenters from taking public office, including the stipulation that government officials had to take communion in the Church of England. In its original form, the 1828 Act would have removed limitations on Jews too, but a last-minute amendment in the Lords reinserted the phrase 'on the true faith of a Christian' into the oath required of office holders.[10] Britain's Jews needed their own strategy.[11]

The first flush of Anglo-Jewish activism would be centred around a neglected communal body, the Board of Deputies of British Jews, which had not met since 1820 but was now revived under the leadership of Nathan, Moses Montefiore and Isaac Lyon Goldsmid, with the intention that it would serve a more active lobbying role.[12] Before long, however, it would be Hannah who emerged as the driving force behind the campaign. In February 1829 Judith and Moses Montefiore went 'to see Hannah Rothschild and her husband', with whom they 'had a long conversation on the subject of liberty for the Jews'.[13] The Board of Deputies had spent many months in discussion with allies from the Catholic and Dissenting communities, and the time had now come to translate some of the campaign's momentum, through the Rothschilds' governmental connections, into a parliamentary petition or preferably a bill. Moses's description of the meeting at Piccadilly continues: '[Nathan] said he would shortly go to the Lord Chancellor and consult him on the matter. Hannah said if he did not, she would.' Moses was struck by the 'brief but impressive' language that Hannah employed.

Hannah's threat to visit the Lord Chancellor, Lord Lyndhurst, continued to hang over Nathan throughout March and April 1829, as his repeated attempts to secure a meeting were repeatedly brushed off.[14] A Catholic Relief Bill had just reached the Commons, and Lord Lyndhurst had no scruples about using the progress of one emancipation to obstruct another. He responded to Nathan and Moses by saying that with all 'the Catholic business', they could 'attend to nothing else'.[15] Hannah did what she could to maintain momentum elsewhere. At Piccadilly she brought together Daniel O'Connell, Dissenters such as the Quaker Gurney family, and influential MPs and aristocrats.[16]

At one such event, after listening to Moscheles accompany a song by Hannah's daughter Hannah Mayer, Moses Montefiore stayed until midnight, and left no. 107 Piccadilly 'highly gratified with the result of the conversations he had with several influential noblemen on the subject he had so much to heart'.[17]

On 13 April the Catholic Relief Act, which gave Catholics the right to sit in the Commons, was passed, and Lord Lyndhurst's excuse of preoccupation expired. The campaigners had prepared a petition, the phrasing of which had been approved by both Hannah and Nathan.[18] In late April, Lyndhurst met Nathan, Isaac and Moses, and recommended that Lord Bexley be chosen to introduce the petition to the Lords: if its introduction did not cause too much upset, they might follow it up with a bill.[19] What was needed now was a concerted campaign to ensure the petition met with a good reception. The evening after meeting with Lord Lyndhurst, Moses Montefiore dined with Hannah.[20]

In June and July Hannah held two legendary parties.[21] The hall was decorated with the usual grove of orange and lemon trees, and William Jarrin, who had become something of a stalwart, had provided ices and fruits. 'The dancing did not stop till half-past five in the morning,' claimed the *Morning Post*, in a breathless report that also commented on the 'gold plate', which was 'very massive' and 'richly chased'. But it was the talking that really mattered: snatches of conversations about the emancipation project could be heard on the landings and in the hallways, amidst the scent of citrus trees. The Prime Minister, the Duke of Wellington, who during these months was doing everything he could to avoid making any concrete commitments on the subject of a Jewish relief bill, was notable by his absence. Hannah decided that this was something that needed to be addressed. Wellington, after all, owed the Rothschilds a great deal: it was Nathan who had arranged, during the Peninsular Campaign, for the supplies of money that Wellington himself had described as 'very ample', and without which his army would have floundered. A petition from a Rothschild, Hannah reasoned, was likely to be taken very seriously. She urged Nathan to address the subject of Jewish emancipation with the Prime Minister himself.

He raised it at the end of a discussion on other, financial matters. 'God has given your grace the power to do good,' Nathan beseeched him. 'I would entreat you to do something for the Jews.'[22] The Prime

Minister remained non-committal. This was not such a bad sign: Nathan knew that the passage of Catholic emancipation had left the Duke at the head of a divided party, and that actively to support Jewish emancipation would put him in a precarious position. For Wellington merely to not oppose a 'Jew bill' might have been all the campaigners needed to get a bill through the Lords.[23] Hannah began to feel the first sense of real hope for a cause which now obsessed her.

First, though, a bill would have to pass through the Commons, where Sir Robert Grant had agreed to introduce one. With connections to both the abolitionist circle of William Wilberforce and to Robert Owen, Grant was typical of the Liberals and reformers that Hannah had cultivated during the preceding years.[24] He brought the 'Bill for the Relief of His Majesty's Subjects Professing the Jewish Religion' before the Commons on 5 April 1830. Daniel O'Connell – known as 'the Emancipator' for his role in the Catholic campaign – was one of its fiercest advocates. An elated Moses Montefiore rushed to tell Hannah and Nathan that the bill had passed its first reading – something of a formality, but nevertheless a landmark for the campaign.[25] But the success of the bill stoked intense reactionary sentiment, and when it came to the second reading, the number of MPs who voted against it was larger than the total number of MPs who had voted on either side in the first.[26] The bill was defeated by a vote of 228 to 165.

It was April 1833 before a second, successful attempt was made to get the bill through the Commons, and August by the time it was introduced to the Lords. Among those gathered in the White Chamber, beneath tapestries depicting the defeat of the Spanish Armada, was the man who had made himself so scarce during the preceding campaign: the Duke of Wellington. Though the Duke had been succeeded as prime minister by Earl Grey, his views still held considerable sway in the Lords. Rising to his feet, the hopes of the Jewish community on his shoulders, he delivered a devastating claim. 'This is a Christian country and a Christian legislature,' he said, 'and the effect of this measure would be to remove that peculiar character.'[27] His speech drew heavily on the notion that had haunted the emancipation campaigners since the passage of the Test and Corporation repeal in 1828: that 'there is a material difference between the cases of the Dissenters and the Roman Catholics, and the Jews'.

The bill was defeated in the Lords by a majority of 104 to 54. Hannah most likely learnt of the result the same night, but did not

know the details of Wellington's speech until she saw it in the newspapers the next morning. She read it with a rising mixture of shock and
fury. The man whose political endeavours her husband had supported,
whose campaigns against Napoleon the Rothschilds had helped to
finance, the man whom she herself had welcomed to Piccadilly, had
stood in the House of Lords and denounced all Jews as unworthy
aliens.

All of the Rothschild family had 'political objects', warned Wellington in a letter to Sir Robert Peel, but 'particularly the old lady
[Hannah]'. She and Lionel had 'long been anxious for support to the
petitions of the Jews for concessions of political privileges.'[28] During
the late 1820s and early 1830s, hosting events at Piccadilly had been
one of the most useful campaigning tools. Despite Wellington's betrayal, Hannah remained steadfast in her ambitions. The Rothschild
tutor, Schlemmer, recorded that the curriculum he taught Hannah's
sons – which included political economy and constitutional history –
was tailored towards the goal possessed by 'every Englishman of a rich
family', namely 'to become a member of St Stephen's Chapel, and to
be able to have his name followed by the letters MP'.[29]

9

The Financial Prowess
of Mrs Rothschild

To BE A good hostess was – so far as the Rothschild brothers were concerned – among the most important duties of a wife, and Hannah's success at Piccadilly was something that Nathan could be proud of. But there was another dimension to his and Hannah's relationship that was far less acceptable to the family culture: Nathan valued Hannah's contribution to his business affairs. He sought her opinion frequently, depended on her assistance, and was so convinced of his wife's good judgement that he sought legal advice in 1824 on how to protect Hannah's interests in the event of his death.[1] Among the wider family, such confidences had to be concealed. Nowhere was this more the case than during the summits the Rothschild brothers held every few years, in the city of their birth.

Since 1810, the Rothschild brothers had gathered regularly in Frankfurt to discuss the finances of the five branches of the family and renew the terms of their partnership agreement.[2] In August 1828 Hannah travelled with Nathan and the family once more across Europe, to the palatial home of Amschel and Eva, in the suburbs of Frankfurt. This year's negotiations, explained Hannah in a letter home, were 'held in the Tower in the Garden' and were 'perfectly secret'.[3] The tower was an elaborate stone folly, closed off from the house and grounds alike. With the dramatic setting and the emphatic secrecy of the deliberations that occurred there, the meeting turned Mayer Amschel's injunction against the women's participation into a sort of theatre.

While they were excluded from the summit, Hannah's younger sons were welcomed to the male socialising that accompanied it. With a swagger that showed they knew their time in the tower would come, Nat and Anthony joined their father and uncles on shooting trips.[4]

Hannah, who at this point still had more direct experience of the business than any of her sons, was expected instead to attend the usual round of tea parties, dinners and balls. She wrote to Lionel (who had remained behind in London), asking him to run an errand to a plumber in Frith Street, and to make the journey out to Stamford Hill to check that the maids were keeping the place well and that 'the red beds' had been moved up to the front bedroom, where she wanted them on her return. She heard little from Nathan about the meeting, but knew enough to speculate that discussions were being held up by a delay in the English house's accounts arriving from London.[5]

Hannah's father's will had ensured her some property rights, by creating for her benefit a trust that included, among other things, various stocks and shares. This sort of arrangement was fairly common among the upper classes, and nor was it unusual for a woman to be involved in trading the shares held in trust for her.[6] Henriette's speculation in the buoyant stock market was just one of several instances of Rothschild and Montefiore women analysing the markets and making investments. Judith Montefiore had speculated in the Omnium, a British government bearer bond, and Salomon's wife Caroline followed the price of Consols so closely that they continued to rise and fall in her dreams, where, one night in August 1816, they ticked as high as 86.[7] Hannah's opportunity for direct engagement with the stock market would come two years after the August 1828 summit, during a trip to Paris.

Just before the Frankfurt summit, Chilly and Anselm lost their first child, one-year-old Mayer Anselm Léon. By late 1829 Chilly was pregnant again, and this time Hannah insisted on being present at the birth. Once she reached the French capital, however, it was not the imminent arrival of a new grandchild that would command her attention.

It was a tumultuous time to be Paris-bound. On 25 July Charles X, the reactionary French king, had suspended press freedoms and dissolved parliament, provoking mass protests.[8] Arriving in the city for an internship with his uncle James, Hannah's son Lionel had found the shops closed, and gendarmes outside ministers' houses and newspaper offices; passing the Palais-Royal, he saw a skirmish break out as a man who was attempting to sell papers was seized by soldiers, and a crowd came to his defence.[9] Lionel hurried to join his sister and her husband, Anselm, at their family's mansion in Suresnes, to the west of the city. On 30 July he wrote to assure his parents that he was 'perfectly well, & completely out of danger'.[10]

The fear of disorder spreading out of Paris became so intense that Lionel and his uncle had spent the day hiding 'all the bonds &c.' in the garden at the Château de Suresnes.[11] By the following day, however, Charles's soldiers had fled his palace at Saint-Cloud to surrender their arms, and a new ministry had been installed under the duc d'Orléans. With the threat of violence abating, Lionel was able to return to the city, and witness the aftermath of the revolutionary violence that had taken place during what would become known as the July Days or 'three glorious days'. In the streets, he told his parents, 'fine large trees' had been cut down and 'the pavement taken up & piled against them & broken doors &c.', to make 'barricades, as they call them'. His optimism about the outcome of the revolution is indicative of the liberal outlook that Hannah had imparted to her children. The events of the week had been 'glorious', he thought, and the removal of the overreaching king represented 'a good lesson for other governments'.

When Hannah reached Paris in mid August, the new government was still establishing itself. The markets were unpredictable, and prices of securities – including that of the usually reliable *rente*, a French government bond with no maturity – fluctuated wildly. The Rothschild brothers' counting house on the rue d'Artois had become a forum for anyone with something at stake in the market's fluctuations, whether brokers, petitioners, other bankers or politicians. Even under normal conditions, visitors to the counting house found it to be a place of 'deafening and unceasing cacophony' that possessed an 'air akin to the Tower of Babel' on account of 'all the tongues of the world' being spoken there, 'including Hebrew'.[12]

Hannah saw the potential advantage. On 24 August, having paid a brief visit to the pregnant Chilly at Suresnes, she travelled through 'eerily quiet' Paris, and into the din of the rue d'Artois.[13] '[W]e are all assembled to hear the various prices of the rentes,' she wrote excitedly to her husband in London.[14] The oscillations were 'tremendous', with substantial variations every half hour. Hannah set about trying to ascertain the underlying factors that would determine the course of the *rente* in the longer term. Despite pockets of working-class protest, Paris was quiet, and the new Orléanist regime had established itself on a firm footing, with the duc d'Orléans being proclaimed King Louis-Philippe I by the Chamber of Deputies. Although there was 'some little agitation' among the working classes, that was because they were 'out of employ', and not because of any lasting volatility following the removal of the Bourbons. James, who like his brothers had spent years cultivating relationships with politicians and civil servants, had suggested that the bank was finding ways to support the new regime. She could only conclude that the recent falls in the value of the *rente*, which she knew would cause alarm in England, were in fact a result of short-term financial fluctuations rather than an expression of any underlying political problems. Given this, she thought it would be a better idea to hold onto *rentes*, and wait for the prices to recover, rather than sell. 'You must look at it coolly, dear Rothschild,' she wrote to Nathan, '[i]t will blow over.'[15] To her son Anthony, whom she knew would be 'very surprised at this tremendous fluctuation', she added: 'There have [been] such panics before – patience.'

In the eighteenth century female investors were usually depicted as aggressive intruders in a male sphere.[16] More recently, prejudice had coalesced in the form of a new stock character, the 'doe in the city' – a wealthy, naive woman, more pitiable than blameworthy, who left herself vulnerable to the commercial instincts of men.[17] Hannah's sister Judith downplayed her purchase of bonds as a 'trifling transaction', intended 'merely to amuse', and even then cautioned herself: 'I should be sorry to apply my whole time to the idea of increasing my fortune, as I have a protector whom I rely upon to use his utmost endeavour to support me.'[18]

Hannah, with her quiet self-confidence, was far less influenced than her sister by the popular conception of women's role in finance. When she began buying *rentes* in Paris, she bought 10,000, and did so without consulting Nathan.[19] The profit on them, she hoped, would at least cover the cost of her voyages to and from the city. Her position was vindicated: by the time she was signing off her letter, the *rentes* had risen. It was the first of several speculations she would make that summer. Sometimes, Hannah's interest in the movements of the Bourse seemed to have outstripped her interest in the profit she might make from them. She was mesmerised by the febrile markets, determined to see through the apparently random rises and falls to the patterns beneath.

Hannah's updates on Chilly's pregnancy as the birth grew nearer became increasingly brief and sporadic, often tagged on to the end of letters or sandwiched between financial intelligence.[20] '[Chilly] still remains well,' she wrote in one letter, after three substantial paragraphs of financial news and advice, 'I think she may [be] a day or two more but no longer. I will now conclude.' Hannah arrived at the rue d'Artois early, before the first prices had come from the Bourse, and often did not leave until trading closed. 'Our attention is so engrossed with the funds that I can dwell upon nothing else,' she wrote to Nathan.[21]

In the hours before trading opened, when political figures often visited the counting house hoping to avoid the crowds, she scoured the newspapers and observed the comings and goings of politicians and brokers, looking for business opportunities. Among the visitors one morning was the secretary to the duc d'Angoulême, the former Bourbon heir to the throne who had gone into exile in England with his father, Charles X.[22] The secretary needed 300,000 francs transferred out of France to his exiled employer. Moments after the secretary had left, Hannah wrote to Nathan, suggesting that he 'offer to transact [the duc d'Angoulême's] money affairs'.[23] '[Y]ou would very likely obtain their business,' she wrote, which 'would be of some consequence.' At a time when the Rothschild bank was beginning to engage with the new regime, doing business with the old one was risky, and there was something of Mayer Amschel's daring in Hannah's proposal.

When, on Tuesday, 31 August 1830, Chilly showed signs of going into labour, Hannah still insisted on returning to the centre of the city, and it was only on Thursday, 2 September, when Chilly gave birth to Caroline Julie Anselm Rothschild, that she finally abandoned the counting house.[24] In the long term, what would remain with Hannah from that summer in Paris was not the revolution, nor even the birth of her granddaughter, but her first-hand experience of the *rentes* crisis. It instilled in her the fervent and liberating belief that, rather than remaining a financial auxiliary, she could be an agent in her own right.

In the winter of 1830–1 Chilly visited England with her new baby.[25] Hannah arranged to take them to Brighton, along with Hannah Mayer and Mayer Amschel, who were now both in their teens, and eleven-year-old Lou. As the children got older, their experience of the family's favourite seaside resort had shifted. Out went the childish seaside Brighton of playing on the beach and accompanied strolls; in came coach trips to Worthing, mud-based beauty treatments, visits to the Pavilion, and parties in grand houses and hotel rooms, where they danced, played cards and indulged in 'round games'.[26] For all Hannah's talk of 'speculations', the family distaste for 'gambling' still held strong, and Lou was keen to emphasise to her father that five shillings had been the largest win at the card table. Such entertainments were rudely interrupted when, in the wake of a sudden market crash, Nathan requested his wife to join him in London. 'Mamma is going to leave us tomorrow,' Hannah Mayer wrote, as Hannah prepared to join the throng of businessmen in their carriages up from the south coast back to the capital.[27] Hannah was only too happy to make the journey: after her experiences in Paris, she was craving stakes a little higher than five shillings.

In contrast with the fast pace and analytic bent of her work advising Nathan, the niceties of upper-class social engagements seemed to Hannah increasingly superficial and tiring. Following the death of King George IV the previous summer, William IV ascended to the throne. In February 1831 his wife Queen Adelaide held a 'birthday drawing room' – her first such gathering since becoming queen – and invited Hannah and Chilly to attend.[28] The *London Courier*, which included both Hannah and Chilly in its 'list of most distinguished dresses', described 'Baroness Rothschild' as wearing a 'dress of white tissue, embroidered in silver', a 'train of lilac satin, richly embroidered with silver' and a 'head-dress [with] feathers'. Chilly was described as appearing in a 'rich dress of white crape, trimmed with gold lama, worn over a white satin slip', a 'train of white terre velvet, trimmed with gold lama', and a similar feathered headdress.

There was a time when Hannah would have taken enormous pleasure in such an occasion and the social validation that it represented, but as the failed struggle for Jewish emancipation had shown, Rothschilds were still seen primarily as Jews who belonged on the periphery. These events were crucial to the maintenance of her family's status and reputation, so she still attended, but she did so dutifully, and with a growing irritation at the drawn-out process: the discomfort of being trussed up in a 'distinguished dress', the inevitable delay in the jam of coaches around the palace, the slow shuffle through crammed anterooms as guests awaited their turn to be received. When the presentation finally took place, it was over in a flash: a name, a curtsey.

Hannah Rothschild. Portrait by Sir William Beechey, 1825.

Left: Hannah and Nathan Rothschild captured shortly after their marriage in 1806.

Below: Hannah and Nathan Rothschild, with their children Charlotte, Lionel, Anthony, Nathaniel, Hannah Mayer, Mayer Amschel and baby Lou. Portrait by William Armfield Hobday, 1821.

Charlotte von Rothschild. Portrait by Moritz Daniel Oppenheim, 1836.

Evelina de Rothschild by Samuel Bellin.

A young Constance Rothschild, later Constance Flower, Lady Battersea.

Cyril Flower, 1st Baron Battersea.

Waddesdon Manor in Buckinghamshire, built for Ferdinand de Rothschild, widower of Evelina.

Queen Victoria planting a tree during a visit to Waddesdon in 1890.

Rózsika Rothschild.

*Miriam Rothschild photographed in 1929, the year she was awarded a
table at the Naples Marine Biological Station.*

Compared with the thrill of trading *rentes*, such ceremonies felt dull and unimportant. Everywhere she went that summer, Hannah found her thoughts drifting back to the financial markets, and their tangled relationship with European politics. When in London, she visited New Court frequently, assisting Nathan and gathering news. When on holiday near Windsor, she found herself absorbed by reports in the *Courier*, about Dutch rule being overthrown in Belgium. This was important enough news in itself, but what really interested Hannah was the possible ramifications for the prices of securities. If the new French National Congress could agree on a constitution, she thought, the markets were likely to rise. She wrote to Nathan in London, instructing him to buy her 20,000 government securities if the price rose above 83½.[29]

In late summer 1831 Hannah returned to Paris, to find further instability in the markets and ongoing political disorder. There was a new, more direct and authoritative tone to the letters she wrote to her husband. 'If there is any fall [in the markets] I would not sell,' she wrote, 'but should the funds remain the same [and] you can sell French rentes well I think you would be doing right.'[30] She also made her own purchases: 3,000 ducats, the gold and silver coins traded across Europe at the time, and 60,000 *rentes*. 'I must wait a little for the advantage,' she wrote to her son Anthony, 'but the prospects are good.'[31]

Hannah stayed in the French capital for another month, through summer into early autumn, and over Rosh Hashanah. When she wrote to Nathan again, her predictions for the Bourse had a more reflective and expansive quality than usual. 'The state of things is better but we must not be led away by good appearances but keep in mind what has occurred which have so changed the interests of so many thousands,' she wrote. 'Nations revolutionized and new plans made by the ambitious.'[32]

In September the markets rose, and Hannah's 60,000 *rentes* increased in value. She was sufficiently experienced to read this sort of rise, and recognised that the ascent was not likely to continue much beyond the current price. '[N]othing can be done in the way of a spec[ulation] when the rentes have risen above 61,' she wrote to Nathan, 'for they open each day higher and I cannot think it prudent to enter into any purchase after so great a rise.'[33] Her cautious, enquiring approach could not have been less like that of the 'doe', who bought into markets credulously, taking a rise as a sign of a further rise, and failing to investigate the underlying prospects.

Nathan's few recorded pronouncements on the role of women in the banking business – including, notoriously, that they were 'fit only to be archivists and book keepers' – belied the true nature of his partnership with Hannah. They had achieved that rarest of relationships, in which each was the other's chief counsel, a colleague in commerce and a partner in life.

10

A Wedding and
a Funeral

THOUGH THE ROTHSCHILDS had risen from a family of the ghetto to an international dynasty, Frankfurt remained their spiritual and geographic base. Regular pilgrimages were made to visit Gutle, who was now well into her eighties and had steadfastly stayed put in the Grünes Schild. Her resolve to remain in the Judengasse was rooted in a sentimental attachment to a house which held so many memories, as well as in practicality; while her sons had gravitated towards the wealthy suburbs, several of her daughters still lived in the defunct ghetto, or on the nearby Zeil, and the Judengasse remained the centre of Jewish cultural and spiritual life in the city. Rightly or wrongly, some contemporaries also detected in Gutle's attachment to the house a degree of superstition – a belief that her sons' extraordinary success must somehow still be tied to her continued residence at their childhood home.

The humble nature of her locale aside, Gutle in her dotage had become quite the *bon vivant*, developing an appreciation for the trappings of her sons' wealth. She enjoyed visiting Amschel's landscaped garden in the suburbs; she went frequently to the opera and the theatre; she travelled by private carriage and sedan chair, and enjoyed having French romances read to her by her maid.[1] She was showered with gifts by her sons, who 'ordered jewellery and caps, made with costly laces and decorated with pale red roses' from Paris, and a visitor in 1840 found her to be 'very old but gaily attired with artificial flowers ... ribbons &c.'[2] In one letter, she thanked her son Salomon for the 'earrings and brooch' he sent, which she had worn to the bar mitzvah of a family friend: 'everybody who saw them, admired them'.[3]

The disparity between the modest house and the wealth of the dynasty that sprang from it attracted tourists, who included the old ghetto on their itineraries.[4] Although Gutle had made some improvements to the interior, travellers who passed by the Grünes Schild remarked that it was 'miserable-looking' and 'not a bit better' than any other house on the street.[5] Elizabeth Gurney, who was touring Europe with her aunt, the prison reformer Elizabeth Fry, remarked with interest that Gutle 'prefers living in the Jews' street in a miserable house tho' from the immense wealth of the family she might reside in a palace. It was a very interesting sight.'[6] A few years later the diarist Charles Greville was one of a small crowd that gathered to watch with fascination as the door of the Grünes Schild opened to reveal Gutle being helped by her daughter-in-law Adelheid down a 'dark narrow staircase', and making the short walk to her carriage, which could not fit down the lane.[7] He had never seen a 'more curious and striking contrast' than 'the dress of the ladies, both the old and the young one, and their equipages and liveries, with the dilapidated locality in which the old woman persists in remaining'.

In the spring of 1836 the extended Rothschild family again convened in Frankfurt. This time, the focus was twenty-seven-year-old Lionel. The eldest of Hannah's sons was not only set to become a full partner in the family firm, but was also engaged to marry his sixteen-year-old cousin Charlotte von Rothschild, daughter of Carl. The idea for this match between cousins had first been set in motion by Lionel's older sister Chilly, in a letter sent to her mother almost five years previously. Carl's then twelve-year-old daughter, she wrote, had 'improved very much the last few months. She is dark but will I think be much admired ...'[8] A few weeks later Chilly wrote again, telling her mother: 'I want Lionel to make a certain young Lady's acquaintance.'[9] In 1832 Lionel's aunt Henriette visited the town she had departed seventeen years previously. 'Without saying one word too much in her praise, [Charlotte] is an extremely pretty, well behaved and elegant girl,' reported Henriette, who had 'no doubt that if Lionel were to meet her and not knowing who she was ... he would make love to [i.e. court] her'.[10] Coming from Henriette, who Hannah knew from bitter experience was unafraid to speak her mind on sensitive issues, this sort of recommendation counted for a great deal.

Despite the matchmaking of his sister and aunt, Lionel was in no hurry. As in other upper-class families at the time, Rothschild women were generally married off before they had even made it through puberty, while the Rothschild men were afforded bachelor lives, and sexual licence, and only encouraged to marry later on. In letters to one another, their comments about women veered between adolescent innuendo and boasts of conquest. When the men were eventually forced to consider marriage, they generally did so in a resigned and unsentimental fashion. In March 1835 Lionel wrote to his brother Anthony, who was shortly due to visit him in Madrid: 'I have no particular fancy to get married just immediately. A few weeks later or earlier makes no difference ... You must therefore be so good as to settle it amongst yourselves, and whatever is agreed upon I shall be happy to do.'[11] It was only when advising on the prospects for premarital flirtations that his letter became more energetic. He advised his brother to come via Bordeaux, and to 'bring as many little nice things for ladies as you can': in Madrid he would 'find lots to accept them'.

Later in 1835, Lionel finally made the trip to Frankfurt, where he met Charlotte and the engagement was made official. Negotiations were conducted in the tone of affectionate formality that had grown up around such endogamous matches. Hannah sent her niece a pearl necklace, and wrote that the 'very amiable moment' Charlotte consented to the union with Lionel had 'heighten[ed] considerably our satisfaction'.[12] The idea that genuine affection could arise from a match brokered tactically between families was familiar to Hannah. 'I am persuaded that you entirely engross Lionel's time and attention,' she wrote to Charlotte, before asking her to remind Lionel to write home.[13] Hannah knew how isolating and nerve-racking it was to be married off at a young age to a man you hardly knew, and she reassured Charlotte that she had her fiancé's affection and respect, while also reminding her of her right – her duty, even – to influence and instruct him.

On 1 June 1836 Hannah, Nathan, Lou and Hannah Mayer endured a choppy Channel crossing during which 'all experienced to a great extent the effects of the sea'.[14] Hannah arrived in Calais shaken and drained. 'I cannot tell you a word that is interesting,' she wrote to her son Nat, who had been left behind to manage family affairs in London. The morning after the English family's arrival in Frankfurt, the social merry-go-round of family festivities began. By far the most important of the early engagements was the visit from Charlotte to Hannah and Nathan's hotel. The family had met Charlotte before, but Hannah had not seen her for many years. With her cascading dark hair and cavernous eyes, Charlotte was, Hannah wrote back to

London, as beautiful as they had been led to believe.[15] She also possessed an 'agreeable' and 'easy' manner – quite an accomplishment for the young bride, given how unnerving it must have been to experience so much attention from the extended family.

For Nathan, the meeting with the niece who would soon be his daughter-in-law was overshadowed by physical discomfort. During the long journey he had received a 'most unpleasant visitor' in a 'most inconvenient place' – a boil on his backside.[16] This was something of a recurring problem, but for one to appear in so unmentionable an area, in the middle of a long coach ride across the Continent, was particularly cruel. In Frankfurt, he was confined to his bedroom at the Römischer Kaiser hotel, where the discussion of matters crucially important to the future of the Rothschild family business – including arrangements for Lionel to become a fully-fledged partner, and for Anthony and Nat to follow when they came of age – took place around his sickbed.[17] His condition cast a pall over the festivities, making everyone 'melancholy and uncomfortable', and yet preparations for the nuptials could not wait.[18] Amschel hosted dinner, and the mother of the bride, Adelheid, held a grand ball at her and Carl's town house in Frankfurt. Hannah and the family attended only briefly, eager to return to Nathan's bedside.[19]

Eventually, on 13 June, Nathan was forced to undergo the lancing of the boil by Professor Maximilian Chelius, a renowned surgeon at Heidelberg University.[20] By the morning of the wedding, two days later, his discomfort was a little less than it had been, and he was able to walk the short distance from the hotel to Carl and Adelheid's, where the ceremony was to take place.[21] In view of his condition, proceedings were kept as brief as possible. 'The ceremony lasted but half an hour and was very solemn,' Lionel reported with relief to his brothers, Anthony and Nat. 'I am happy to say it went off very well.' After a dinner for eighty at Carl and Adelheid's home, the bride and groom left Frankfurt in 'a splendid travelling carriage with 4 post horses', heading along the River Main to Wilhelmsbad, where they were to spend their honeymoon.[22]

After the wedding Hannah transferred the family from the hotel to Chilly's Frankfurt house, where Nathan underwent further surgical interventions.[23] Chilly was seven months pregnant, and Hannah had some misgivings about imposing on her, but the hotel was no fit place to continue Nathan's treatment. Dr Chelius, who had other work commitments, had to hurry back to Heidelberg for several days at a time, leaving Nathan in the care of the local doctor and surgeon.[24] Though these men were 'thought clever' by the locals, Hannah was used to dealing with experts, and she could not help viewing the local doctors with a degree of distrust. Eventually, she wrote to London with queries for Dr Travers, who had lived next door to the family in New Court, and eventually he set off to join them.[25]

The situation was becoming more complex and concerning. 'The gatherings and swellings have so rapidly succeeded each other that we cannot speak with certainty about them,' wrote Hannah.[26] The lancing of the boil, which quite sensibly attempted to drain the abscess, had caused Nathan terrible pain and created a serious risk of infection, while failing to effect any real improvements. As July progressed and the symptoms of blood poisoning set in, she began to confront the fact that her husband was a dying man, and to shift her attention to palliative care. She wrote to London with requests for fruit to be shipped over by steamboat; Lionel wrote, ordering soda water, lavender water and 'good oranges'.[27] Ensconced in her daughter's home, Hannah maintained a round-the-clock vigil at Nathan's bedside. 'I hardly quit Papa's room,' she wrote to Nat on 27 June.[28] The *London Evening Standard* would later report that during the two-month duration of her husband's illness, Hannah scarcely ever left his sickbed.[29]

Throughout his illness Nathan continued to give business orders, with Hannah and Lionel acting as his deputies and amanuenses. By 25 July Nathan's instructions had become increasingly ill-considered. When writing to London with instructions to sell various stocks and shares, he apparently did not mind a loss of 'one or two percent' and instructed the sale of '£20,000 India Stock more'.[30] 'I do not know if I misunderstood him,' wrote Lionel to Nat, 'but I did not like to ask for an explanation.' The following day, Hannah and Lionel began to take over some of his responsibilities, writing to London with instructions and advice of their own. Though it was Lionel who had just been admitted to the business partnership, Hannah had the most extensive knowledge of the day-to-day running of the bank. 'Mamma thinks it necessary that two persons should sign,' Lionel wrote to Nat, in response to a query about a bill of procuration, 'Mamma mentioned Ben [Cohen] and J[ohn] Helbert.'[31] At the time, with attention focused on the feverish Nathan, these hurried instructions may have seemed insignificant, but in fact they were momentous: Hannah and Lionel were rehearsing a new arrangement of power, for a family that would imminently lose its patriarch.

The trusted London doctor, Benjamin Travers, arrived in Frankfurt on 26 July and came straight to Chilly's house. His assessment of the situation was not optimistic: the next day, Nathan signed a new will.[32] In enjoining the English Rothschild sons to 'harmony, constant love, and close unity', Nathan's will purposefully evoked his father's.[33] His command was enforced by an annexe to the recently redrawn Rothschild partnership agreement – Nathan's role in the partnership was to devolve jointly upon his four sons, with 'the sons together acting as a unit with one vote in the partnership'.[34] Mayer Amschel's original principle had been adapted for a new generation.

But there was one significant modification. 'My dear wife Hannah', continued the will, 'is to co-operate with my sons on all important occasions and to have a vote upon all consultations. It is my express desire that they shall not embark on any transaction of importance without having previously demanded her motherly advice.'[35] Nathan's annexe to the partnership agreement conformed to Mayer Amschel's vision, dividing up Nathan's vote in the partnership between his four sons, and making no mention of his three daughters. But his will made clear that when his sons voted as sub-partners, they were also bound to give weight to Hannah's opinion. Quietly, tactically, and in a way that likely went unnoticed by his own brothers, Nathan had smuggled the opinion of his wife into the decision-making structure of the family business. He had come as close as he possibly could to making Hannah, who was now in her mid fifties, a partner in the Rothschild bank.

On 28 July Nathan's older brother, Amschel, asked him to say his prayers, which he did, and his family joined him.[36] Nathan Mayer Rothschild then kissed his wife and said 'good night' quite distinctly. At five o'clock he passed away with little struggle. According to Jewish tradition, the burial should have taken place within a day of his passing, but Nathan had requested that he be interred in England.[37] A family conference confirmed the choice, and so his wife and children began the long journey home with the body. Because of the distance, Nathan's body was transported in a lead-lined coffin in place of the traditional wood.[38] An oak breastplate bore the Rothschild family arms, granted to the brothers in Vienna: a lion grasping five arrows in its right forepaw.

For several days while the family was still in Frankfurt, news reports in London had been conflicting and confused. Some papers reported that Nathan had died; others denied it; several pinned their hopes on the figure of Dr Travers, who was 'awaited in Frankfort with great anxiety'.[39] The uncertainty sent financial markets plunging, and by 3 August, when *The Times* carried a conclusive confirmation of Nathan's death, the end to the uncertainty that had plagued trading for the past few days was enough to make the markets rally a little.[40] To the family, the rise would have been reassuring, for it represented market confidence that, as *The Times* put it, 'his business, under the management of his sons, will go on as usual'.

The arrival of conclusive news that Nathan had died did not end the rumour and fabrication that had filled the columns of certain papers during late July and early August. Immediately, hacks began to brush up the story of Nathan's life and death in order to add a dramatic, moral or ideological slant. Though the first news of Nathan's death to arrive in the capital almost certainly came with the redoubtable Dr Schlemmer, who had been bundled into a post-chaise and sent home ahead of the body, it was the carrier pigeon that arrived two days later, carrying the gnomic message '*il est mort*', upon which most accounts of the death would fixate.[41]

Within weeks, much greater and more concerning liberties were being taken by writers. In one account, which recalled the early Rothschild years in the ghetto, the Elector's documents and medals that had been stored in the cellar in the Grünes Schild became 'treasure' that had been 'buried' in the corner of a 'little garden'.[42] In another, it was said that Nathan's success had been down to a 'talisman' he had received from a 'phantom' – and that his death had occurred because he betrayed the contract with the phantom when, instead of 're-establishing Judah's kingdom', he settled for a title and a 'petty English Emancipation Bill'.[43] It was in the aftermath of Nathan's death, too, that one of the most enduring myths about the Rothschilds – that Nathan had made a fortune by playing the Stock Exchange in the aftermath of Napoleon's defeat at Waterloo – would begin to circulate, appearing first in veiled form in Honoré de Balzac's 1838 novel *The Firm of Nucingen* (in which the gambling banker resembles James more than Nathan), and then, nine years later, in the slanderous pamphlet, *The Edifying and Curious History of Rothschild I, King of the Jews* (1846). In fact, the end of the Napoleonic Wars had initiated a period of crisis for the English Rothschild bank, but that did not matter: after his death, Nathan's image had become public property, for people to do with as they wished.

For the most part, in the days and weeks after her return to England, Hannah must have been struck by how fondly the image of her husband was used. By the mid 1830s, she was accustomed to the newspapers and cartoons, but the brooches, commemorative medals and scarves on sale all over London were new.[44] On each was an image of her husband: Nathan laurelled, like a Roman. Nathan's shadow, against a column at the exchange. Nathan in characteristic top-hatted profile. Nathan stood with four keys behind his back (an allusion to the succession of his four sons).[45] She saw her husband on stalls, in shops, waved about in the hands of hawkers, tossed over shoulders and hanging from chests. What this represented was overwhelmingly positive. Finally, now that he had died and the effects had registered so legibly in the financial markets, people were beginning to realise what a pillar Nathan had been, not only to the City but also to the nation's government. And so in death he began to earn some of the public fondness that had eluded him during his life. It was a sign of this growing warmth towards Hannah's husband that the obituary published in *The Times* and syndicated in many other papers was not written by a critic, but by a 'friend well acquainted with the subject'.[46] Just as the 1821 Hobday family portrait had done, the obituary stressed Nathan's 'domestic happiness', which 'identified him so honourably with English morality'.

Before Nathan died, he and Hannah had commissioned several paintings of their sons from Moritz Daniel Oppenheim, who, though he may not have been a particularly fashionable painter, was capable of painting their family in the light they desired, with a feeling for both Jewish tradition and modern aristocratic appearances. Oppenheim's paintings of 1835 took their cue from portraits of civil servants and diplomats common in the nineteenth century, using national uniforms and insignia to suggest – just as Nathan's obituarist had done, with his references to 'English morality' – that the brothers' loyalty to a Jewish European financial family was compatible with patriotism to their respective countries.[47] The portraits were copied for each branch of the family and used as the basis for a print advertising the bank under its new leadership.

At one o'clock on 8 August, Nathan's body was driven at the head of a cortège from New Court, through the City and the East End, to the burial ground of the New Synagogue in Whitechapel. Among the seventy-five carriages that followed the hearse were those belonging to 'numerous branches of the Goldsmid, Cohen, Samuel and Levi families', the Lord Mayor's carriage, and 'a line of foreign ambassadors' and noblemen's carriages'.[48] Many shops were closed, and newspapers reported that ten thousand people lined the roads. As the cortège passed the church of St Mary Matfelon, Whitechapel, it was joined by children from the Bell Lane schools and the Jews' Hospital. In keeping with orthodox tradition, Hannah did not see any of this, but sat *shivah* at home with the other women of the family.[49] After the funeral, she went into deep mourning, preferring to bear her loss away from the bustle of London, 'at home and grieving only'.[50]

She moved into a rented house at Roehampton, near Gunnersbury, where, in the summer of the previous year, she and Nathan had completed the purchase of a new country estate.[51] Gunnersbury Park had been the site of a royal retreat used by George II's daughter, Princess Amelia.[52] With seventy-five acres of park and farmland, a conservatory, coach houses, a dairy, a brewhouse, an icehouse and an orchard, it was a country house on a far grander scale than Stamford Hill.[53] They had bought it for £17,000. Princess Amelia's residence had been demolished in 1800, and the current house dated to shortly afterwards.[54] This suited Hannah's purposes: whereas Stamford Hill had attracted them for the homeliness of its existing proportions, Gunnersbury appealed to her as a blank canvas. Soon after purchasing the estate, they had commissioned the architect Sydney Smirke to come up with plans for a substantial remodelling and extension.[55]

During the terrible weeks in Frankfurt, Hannah had sought comfort – or at least, distraction – in thoughts of her new country home. 'I long to see Gunnersbury,' she wrote.[56] She corresponded with Anthony, who was in Paris, about 'vases and other marbles' for the house, and sent instructions for the grounds to Nat in London: 'I should like dear Nat that the fruit and other things might be properly disposed of ... I should like to see plenty of chicken reared – the butter might be salted and barrelled and put in tubs it would do for cooking and the fruit preserved.' The fact of having planned the house with Nathan in the months before his untimely death appears to have invested the estate with a special significance. During the autumn she made frequent coach trips out of Roehampton and over the toll bridge at Kew, to check on the progress of the works.[57] But as Nathan's will had recognised, it was Hannah who was most familiar with the workings of the London house, and her responsibility to the bank soon tore her away

from the riverside peace of the south-western suburbs. She made long
and frequent stays in Piccadilly, from where she could easily travel
in to New Court. 'We are again in this bustling place,' she wrote to
Mayer in the late spring of 1837.[58]

At Gunnersbury Smirke added a parlour and, on the south-west
side, a dining room, with a vast cellar of cast-iron columns that indicated Hannah's ambitions for the house as a place of entertainments
even grander than those at Piccadilly.[59] The outside of the property
was a lesson in restraint – the Doric columns and bow windows would
not have looked entirely out of place at the more modest Stamford
Hill House – but the interior was executed in an opulent, Franco-
phile style later used by Smirke in London clubs. In the main drawing room, there was a ceiling painting commissioned from Edmund
Thomas Parris, who would paint Queen Victoria's coronation the following year.

In 1838, two years after Nathan's death, Lionel was finally granted
a royal licence for him and his family to bear the Austrian title they
had been given over two decades previously. The matriarch who retired
to Gunnersbury, then, really was Hannah de Rothschild: the baroness

Gunnersbury House, a centre of English Rothschild life
throughout the nineteenth century.

she had long claimed to be. After all of the homes that she had lived in during her marriage to Nathan – the fashionable Mosley Street house in Manchester, and noisy no. 4 New Court in London, the bucolic rural retreat of Stamford Hill and glamorous no. 107 Piccadilly – it was Gunnersbury that became her court and her haven. If Gutle's continued residence at the Grünes Schild served to moor a family who were striking out into new countries and cultures, Hannah's at Gunnersbury would tether the younger women of the English family during the turmoil of the Victorian age.

PART II

Charlotte,
Hannah Mayer,
Louisa

II

'This World of Fog and Cares'

DURING HER WEDDING ceremony on 15 June 1836, Charlotte Rothschild – dark-eyed, slim and pale with nerves – was required to circle her husband seven times, symbolising her duty to make him the centre of her world.[1] It was a responsibility that she felt all too acutely. Two days earlier, on the evening of her seventeenth birthday, the doors of her childhood home had been thrown open to celebrate her impending marriage to her cousin Lionel Rothschild. For Charlotte, the occasion had been too much. She spent most of the party hiding upstairs in her bedroom.[2]

In the months of Charlotte and Lionel's courtship, the flurry of letters crossing the Continent had seemed to Hannah to be proof of the pair's burning feelings, but a closer look at the correspondence shows that they barely knew each other. Lionel was a man equally worldly in business and sex. Charlotte, ten years his junior, was a dreamy, naive teenager whose knowledge of life had been gleaned mostly from books. She fretted over the sincerity of her future husband, and worried about the gossip she had heard concerning his bachelor liaisons. There were moments in which Lionel's affection seemed reassuringly genuine – when, expecting the arrival of a bridal portrait, he described himself tearing open parcels 'with my heart beating quicker than usual' – but there were also moments when it became disconcertingly stilted.[3] Asked by Charlotte whether he loved her, Lionel replied:

If you could see me, you would be better able to answer the question you so often made to me, than I ever was able now that I am separated, I only know the meaning of the word and am only able to judge of my love of my entirely devoted love for you Dear Charlotte.[4]

Charlotte was desperate for romantic reassurance, and deeply conscious of the weight of dynastic expectation that rested on the union. In short, she was terrified.

It was not until nightfall on the day of the wedding, as the couple departed Frankfurt in a 'splendid travelling carriage with 4 post horses', heading east along the Main to the spa town of Wilhelmsbad, that the young bride found herself alone with her new husband for the first time.[5] The honeymoon did not go as planned. Lionel, writing two days later to his brother Anthony, sheepishly stated that

[t]ill now there is not much to relate as you well know that the fright has generally such an effect upon the young ladies that they are immediately troubled with some thing that pays them very often a visit. I can only say that she is a most beautiful person in every respect.[6]

If Lionel's letter tiptoed around the subject, a letter Anthony sent to Nat was far more pungently euphemistic: 'The fright brought on the flowers,' he wrote. 'Poor fellow – he will be obliged to cool his passion for a few days.'[7]

Could Lionel's version of events – that 'fright' at the prospect of consummating their marriage had brought on Charlotte's period – be true? Another explanation is that a panicked Charlotte decided to pretend that she was menstruating; the rules of the *niddah* forbade sexual contact between husband and wife during her period. In any case, the couple's honeymoon was brought to an abrupt, unconsummated end only one day after they arrived when they were summoned back to Frankfurt on account of Nathan's deteriorating condition. In Frankfurt, they spent nights at the Russischer Hof hotel, days with Nathan and Hannah, and evenings with Charlotte's mother in her house on Neue Mainzer Straße. For Lionel, who had been yearning for weeks now to escape with his new bride, this was crushing news. But to Charlotte, it came as a relief.[8] The move back to the city brought her once more within the reassuring family environment, from which she had been so suddenly and completely severed.

Charlotte never lived in the Frankfurt ghetto: by the time of her birth, on 13 June 1819, her father Carl and mother Adelheid had moved to a spacious town house at 33 Neue Mainzer Straße.[9] But she was accustomed to visiting her grandmother at the Grünes Schild. In 1821, when the Holy Alliance occupied Naples, Carl established a new branch of the Rothschild business in southern Italy. Charlotte, her mother and siblings shuttled between Frankfurt and Naples, where the family lived in a seafront suburb of gardens and palaces, stretching out along the headland to the west of the old town.

The area's beauty and good climate, as well as its political import-ance within the Kingdom of the Two Sicilies, made Naples a des-tination for aristocrats and diplomats, and Charlotte grew up among a shifting cast of powerful guests from across Europe.[10] Though her family would move back to Frankfurt when she was eight years old, Naples left an indelible mark on her imagination: years later she would describe with burning nostalgia her father's Neapolitan mansion, the Villa Pignatelli, as 'a paradise upon earth'.[11]

The Jewish community in Naples was far smaller and less estab-lished than that of Frankfurt.[12] When it came to finding someone to teach Charlotte's younger brother Willy, Carl and Adelheid were unable to find a suitable Jewish tutor in the city, and ended up engag-ing a rabbi who worked in the Vatican, to whom they had been in-troduced by the family's favoured painter, Oppenheim.[13] However, it soon became evident that the rabbi was committed to a rather stricter orthodox education than Carl wanted for his children. According to Oppenheim, the couple were so alarmed at Willy's veer towards or-thodoxy that they packed Charlotte and her brothers off to Frankfurt again, to be educated there instead.

Charlotte did not have to grapple with physics, chemistry, biol-ogy and astronomy, as her three younger brothers did.[14] Instead, her studies were concentrated on languages: German, French, Italian and English.[15] Her fluency in English would make the adjustment to her marital family easier for her than it had been for her uncle Nathan and aunt Henriette. Within days of the wedding she was charming her mother-in-law, Hannah, who described her as 'simple and amiable in her manner'. Hannah could not help noting 'by the bye' in her letters to Nat in London that Lionel's new bride 'complains of feeling a little sickness'.[16] 'I must tell you this is a symptom,' she said. The intense scrutiny was misplaced – by late July it was apparent that Charlotte was not pregnant. After Nathan's death, Charlotte made the journey back to London with Lionel and his family, feeling keenly the burden of her mother-in-law's expectation.

Upon Charlotte's arrival, no. 107 Piccadilly was far from the vibrant place where Hannah had hosted balls in years gone by. The family home was consumed by the rituals of *shivah*. For seven days of mourning, mirrors were covered, portraits turned to face the wall and curtains drawn, as mourners arrived in sombre lines to pay their respects to the Rothschilds. Once the cycle of prayers and eulogies had come to a close, Charlotte retired from the family mansion to no. 10 Hill Street, Mayfair, the house that Lionel had selected for them before the wedding.[17] Thrust into the role of managing the English bank, Lionel was, she later wrote in her journal, 'never with me between the hours of ten in the morning & 6 in the evening'.[18] Even Hannah, whose intense grief had daunted Charlotte in the weeks after she moved to London, might have been welcome company, but Hannah, too, was now often at New Court, guiding her son as he learnt his way around the management of the family firm.

Charlotte was left to a lonely house, in the middle of an unfamiliar city. Her knowledge of English language and literature did nothing to ameliorate her feeling of isolation, and she felt keenly that she remained a child of the Continental family.[19] Accustomed to 'the bright skies' of her childhood Naples, she felt weighed down by the 'dense atmosphere of the metropolis'.[20] She would later wish that she had 'ardently and assiduously' thrown herself into reading, so that she might have distracted herself, 'dried [her] tears and made [her] thoughts into pleasant and profitable channels'.[21] At the time, however, Charlotte had found it impossible to summon the will to do anything. Newly wed, cut off from her close-knit family and friends, and transplanted into an unfamiliar city, she was clearly immobilised with depression.

For all the unsettling nature of her early days in London, Charlotte's romantic feelings for Lionel, which before the wedding had been dampened by fear and apprehension, were kindled in the time they managed to snatch for themselves at Hill Street. 'There is many a fond look and kiss from dimpled lips and brilliant eye' between the couple, Hannah noted.[22] In December 1836 Charlotte gave her mother-in-law the news she had been longing for: she and Lionel were expecting a baby.[23] Hannah would be there for her daughter-in-law as she began her journey towards motherhood – offering advice, wisdom and the use of Gunnersbury Park, where Charlotte found solace amid the frequent headaches and the fatigue of pregnancy.[24]

Charlotte's first child, a daughter named Leonora, or 'Laury', was born on 25 August 1837, and acted as an instant cure for the melancholy that had dogged Charlotte since her move to London. Like many upper-class mothers influenced by ideas about 'natural' parenting that had become increasingly fashionable since the middle of the previous century, Charlotte opted to breastfeed Leonora rather than employing a wet-nurse.[25] She began a diary in which she recorded observations, thoughts, fears and dreams relating to her young daughter. The birth was a 'bliss so unexpectedly great, that the moments which followed her appearance in this world of fog & cares, swept away at once the recollection of past sufferings, of moral anxiety and anguish, of physical pain & fatigue'.[26] Charlotte had an easy way with words, and the tone that emerged in her diary was one for which she would become famous within the family: witty, concise and sophisticated.

Hannah remained an invaluable support. She had sent Charlotte items for her toilet, and a quilt carefully chosen for the late summer heat. Soon after the birth, she began to introduce her daughter-in-law

148 Piccadilly, following renovation by Charlotte and Lionel Rothschild in the early 1860s.

to the concerts and balls of the *haut ton*. In February 1838 Benjamin Disraeli, then a young politician who had won his seat in Parliament a year earlier, wrote to his sister about a recent concert he had attended. Among the Rothschilds, who formed the 'most picturesque group', he noticed Charlotte in particular: 'the young bride, or rather wife, from Frankfort' was 'universally admired, tall, graceful, dark, and clear, picturesquely dressed ... quite a Murillo'.[27] Hannah, who had a soft spot for the Spanish Baroque painter, would have been proud of the comparison.[28]

By the summer, Charlotte and Lionel were making their own way, attending balls hosted by the Duke and Duchess of Cambridge, and by Countess Stroganoff.[29] The couple had taken up residence in no. 148 Piccadilly, on the edge of Hyde Park, and almost next door to the Duke of Wellington's magnificent Apsley House.

Soon after the move, Hannah arranged a social engagement for Charlotte that would confirm her entry to the highest rank of London society: an invitation to meet the new queen at St James's Palace. Victoria was the same age as Charlotte, and had also been thrust into a position of great responsibility at a time when her peers were thinking about parties and flirtations. In her case, it had happened on 20 June 1837, when she was woken by her mother and informed, while still in her dressing gown, that her uncle William IV had died and she had acceded to the throne. A year later, Charlotte dressed carefully in the rich, white watered-silk tablier gown she had had made for the occasion, with an elaborate headdress of silver-blonde fabric, diamonds and feather plumes.[30] As she took her place in the Throne Room, Victoria was stunned by the sheer number of guests waiting to be presented. '[A]n immense Drawing-room, the fullest I ever witnessed,' she commented in her diary later that evening.[31]

A week later, the area around Charlotte's mansion filled up with workmen assembling barriers and walkways and banks of seating. Timber was strewn across the pavement, the air rang with 'hammering and knocking', and 'falling fragments stunned the ears and threatened the head'. Once preparations were completed, London descended on Piccadilly: 'not a mob here and there, but the town all mob, thronging, bustling, gaping, and gazing'.[32] In nearby Hyde Park, tents and illuminations sprang up until it resembled 'one vast encampment'. People had come to catch a glimpse of the new queen as she made her way from Buckingham Palace to Westminster Abbey for the coronation.

Next door to Lionel and Charlotte, at Apsley House, the Duke of Wellington had filled his balcony with chairs for his guests. Lionel, meanwhile, had worked with his other neighbours to erect a giant gallery in front of their three houses, with grand, ascending seats set against a crimson cloth.[33] As Victoria's gilded coach passed beneath the gallery at no. 148 Piccadilly, horses hooves struck against the macadam, ringing out the changes for a new era in British history.

12

Marrying Out

LIKE CHARLOTTE AND all young Rothschild women, Nathan and Hannah's fifth child, Hannah Mayer, had been raised to blend in among the Christian upper classes. In her early years she had been demure and reserved, and her fledgling musical abilities pampered. She was bought a tiny harp supposedly made entirely of gold, and counted among her many tutors the Italian composer Gioachino Rossini and the English harpist Elias Parish Alvars.[1] As she grew up, her musical ability and classic beauty were accompanied by exactly the sort of personality that young upper-class women were encouraged to cultivate: mild-mannered, amiable and attentive. In letters to the family, her mother wrote that Hannah Mayer was a 'very good girl', if one 'of rather quiet habits'.[2] With hindsight, Hannah Mayer's fall from grace seems almost inevitable.

In finding a match for her 'very good girl', Hannah Mayer's mother had help from close quarters. Henriette Montefiore had met the challenge of her husband Abraham's death in 1824 with the same resolve and inventiveness she had called upon so often during their marriage, settling into a life of grand widowhood split between her three houses – the country estate at Worth Park Farm in Sussex, the old family home in Stamford Hill, and her London residence in fashionable Stanhope Street. In all of these places, but especially in the last, she threw frequent parties and soirées.[3] With her pronounced German accent and 'great fund of the racy old Jewish humour', she stood apart from the restrained, genteel and thoroughly English hostesses who held sway in Mayfair at the time.[4] Her dinners, remarked Disraeli, were 'frequent and have renown'.[5]

Henriette was determined that her children would not experience the same dislocation that she had suffered when she had been forced to leave the familiarity of the ghetto and travel to London to find a husband. The Rothschild tradition of marrying cousins gave her the opportunity to ensure her children – who had grown up in Stamford Hill, playing with their cousins in the neighbouring garden – returned to the heart of the family. In 1836, before the family gathered in Frankfurt for the wedding of Charlotte and Lionel, she had conceived of a double plan: to marry her eldest son, Joseph, to Hannah Mayer, and her youngest daughter, Louisa, to Nathan and Hannah's second son, Anthony. With Louisa barely fifteen and Anthony in Paris, that part of her scheme would have to wait. In Frankfurt, during Charlotte and Lionel's wedding festivities, she concentrated on kindling an affection between Hannah Mayer and Joseph Montefiore.[6]

It was a more difficult task than she might have hoped. Joseph, it seems, failed to relieve Hannah Mayer's frustration with the 'dreadful tedious long dinners' that took place every day in Frankfurt.[7] She was, as her mother saw it, 'so very distant with a certain gentleman, that he feels himself repulsed, and will not make any advances'.[8] Back in London, Hannah realised that she would have to look elsewhere for her daughter, just as Henriette would for her son. No doubt Hannah would have found someone appropriate, in due course. But, distracted by the grief and business concerns surrounding Nathan's death, she failed to act quickly enough. In the churn of the London social scene, with hordes of nobility and gentry packing into ballrooms and around dinner tables every night, the increasingly headstrong Hannah Mayer would soon find someone for herself. And the man who swept Hannah Mayer off her feet was not a member of the family, nor even a 'co-religionist', but a Christian MP.

Henry FitzRoy was the dashing second son of a prominent aristocratic family that traced their ancestry back to the 1st Duke of Grafton, the illegitimate son of Charles II and his mistress Barbara Villiers.[9] The passage of two centuries had given a patina of respectability to the family's illicit royal connection, and, in spite of their descent from a dukedom to a more modest barony, the FitzRoys had shored up their wealth through marriages to military and colonialist families. Elected MP for Lewes at the young age of thirty, FitzRoy appeared to have a promising political career ahead of him. As both were very much part of the narrow London elite, Hannah Mayer and FitzRoy would have been at many of the same dinners, opera premieres and dances; Hannah Rothschild even invited FitzRoy to attend a party at her Piccadilly home in the spring of 1838.[10] By the time the young Queen Victoria made her way past Piccadilly and Hyde Park on her coronation day, the Rothschild daughter and FitzRoy son were in love.

While FitzRoy's family disliked the prospect of a Jewish bride from a 'mercantile' background, the Rothschilds were truly horrified. The family's efforts to blend in with Christian upper-class society did not in any way signal an acceptance of 'marrying out', which was still considered to be a grave betrayal, an assault on an identity that for centuries had been under threat. This was not the first time there had been trouble with Hannah Mayer. Aged eighteen, during a stay in Paris, she had been thrown a ball by her aunt Betty. The sight of the young English Rothschild, wearing a white satin dress cut narrow at the skirt and trimmed with small red roses, was enough to attract the attention of the Austrian Prince Edmond de Clary. After the ball, the Prince travelled to London and sought the family's permission to marry her, only to be told by an enraged Nathan: 'I will never allow my daughter to marry a Christian.'[11] This time, with FitzRoy, more radical avoiding action was required.

In August 1838 FitzRoy was asked to leave the country for six months, to let things cool off.[12] He eventually agreed, but with a card up his lordly sleeve: he had persuaded Nat, Hannah Mayer's sympathetic brother, to act as a go-between during his exile. Just before FitzRoy crossed the Channel bound for Hamburg, Nat brought him a letter from Hannah Mayer, in which she reaffirmed her love and promised to wait for him. FitzRoy's reply, via Nat, included an itinerary of the places in Europe he was planning to visit, so that she might write to him.

In Hamburg, FitzRoy took a stroll around the old ramparts, in 'the most glorious moonlight'. 'To walk on such a night with her whom my soul loves, would be worth whole years of other enjoyment without her,' he confided in his diary.[13] Things did not improve in Berlin, where FitzRoy went to see *Norma* at the opera, and was reminded of Hannah Mayer by 'every scene'.[14] 'Give me a small cosy home with Hannah,' he wrote, 'and I never wish again to move.'[15] His words would have struck a chill into Rothschild hearts. To write and dispatch love letters was hard for Hannah Mayer, who had to smuggle them past her family with the assistance of Nat. For FitzRoy, living in love-struck idleness, every day without communication brought new anxieties, and during October, after several days without a letter, he began to fear that Hannah Mayer had 'at last yielded to annoying remonstrances and determined to give me up to her family prejudices'.[16] But she never did: by early 1839, when FitzRoy returned to England, Hannah Mayer loved him more than ever.[17]

Behind the back of his disapproving mother, Nat continued to act as the primary go-between. He visited FitzRoy and reported to him that Hannah was 'pining and has not slept all night or eaten a crumb of bread'.[18] Then he visited Hannah and told her that when he had arrived FitzRoy had been tucking into a 'large beef-steak' for breakfast, and 'did not look as though he were dying for love!' The Rothschilds now saw that they had played their hand and failed.[19] Meetings were arranged between FitzRoy and Hannah Mayer's eldest brother Lionel. It would be imperative for the Rothschilds to control the financial arrangements of the marriage. According to the strict stipulations in Nathan's will, should Hannah Mayer or her younger sister, Lou, choose to marry 'contrary to the will of her mother and brothers', they risked losing their inheritance and dowry.[20] Hannah and her sons had reluctantly acquiesced to the love match with FitzRoy rather than let it provoke an outright conflict in the English family, so whether the marriage was 'contrary to their will' was a moot point, but Hannah Mayer had already been bequeathed a significant amount during Nathan's lifetime, and in the immediate aftermath of his death.[21]

In the months that followed the widowed Hannah – who had initially been so hostile to the match – was 'won over by the charm and goodness' of her daughter's fiancé.[22] Committed as she was to defending the family's Jewish identity, Hannah also had a pragmatic streak. Relations between her and her daughter's family would never be as warm or uninhibited as they might have been with an approved Rothschild partner, but they were not hostile. The Rothschilds across the Channel took a different approach. For James, 'nothing could possibly be more disastrous for our family, for our continued well-being, for our good name and for our honour than such a decision, God forbid'.[23] In February 1839 he resolved to visit England and try to persuade his niece out of her marital plans. Privately, he acknowledged that Hannah Mayer was unlikely to 'take any notice of our well-meaning advice' and that 'in view of this girl's independent character we are more likely to exasperate her even more than convince her to abandon this ill-starred love affair'.[24] And yet the expectation of failure was not enough to deter him. This was about honour.

As it happened, James never reached London. Struck down by a heavy illness, he was forced to go to Switzerland to convalesce. Even from his sickbed, James wrote to Hannah suggesting she bring her wilful daughter to visit him in Switzerland as a way to divert or delay the wedding. He was too late. On 29 April 1839, the day after he sent this desperate, final plea, wedding bells rang out at St George's church in Hanover Square, tolling an unprecedented rupture in the Rothschild family.

The wedding was a rather sombre affair, the congregation hunkered down among tall-backed oak pews, beneath the forbidding canopied pulpit.[25] In order to be able to marry a Christian in church, Hannah Mayer was required to publicly declare that she had desired to become a Christian since the age of fifteen. Hannah resolved to support her daughter as much as she could bring herself to, accompanying the bride in a carriage to the church – but even her strong maternal love could not draw her beyond the church's austere portico. Nat was the only family member to attend the wedding. During the silence that followed the signing of the register, he strode over to his sister and kissed her on the forehead, then turned to his new brother-in-law and enthusiastically shook his hand. The gesture went only so far in softening the harsh reality Hannah Mayer now faced, excluded from her own family and unwelcome within her husband's.

The news of Hannah Mayer's match attracted attention far beyond the Rothschild family. A month before the wedding, at dinner on 28 March 1839, Queen Victoria discussed Christian–Jewish matches with her prime minister and confidant, Lord Melbourne. The Queen later recorded that he had observed, 'Jewesses "All are round eyed, hook nosed", and he don't admire them'; the day after the wedding, Melbourne expressed surprise that Hannah Mayer had gone against her family's wishes and married FitzRoy.[26] Hannah Mayer's conversion was 'the first instance of a member of the Rothschild family abandoning the faith of their fathers', noted The Times, coyly adding: 'it is said that the bride's uncles are by no means pleased with a match which renders a change of religion necessary.'[27]

Still convalescing in Switzerland, James raged in a letter to Nat that the marriage had 'made me quite ill … She robbed our whole family of its pride.'[28] The family would have to 'forget her and cut her out of our memory', he decreed. 'As long as I live I shall not wish to see her, nor will anyone in our family.' When Nat challenged this excommunication, James simply doubled down, writing in July: 'My dear Nat, both as your friend and Uncle I want to give you my very frank and honest opinion ... We are determined that, as long as the Almighty grants us good health, neither we nor my children will again come into contact with Hannah Mayer.'[29] She would be made an example of, showing other young Rothschilds what they risked by failing to toe the family line. Two months later, when Nat's older brother Anthony visited James in Paris, all the conversation was still about Hannah Mayer, and he advised his brothers for the sake of 'the union amongst us – not to receive H.M. for the present'.[30]

The sense that family unity was under threat made further, author-ised marriages among the younger generation an urgent priority.[31] Henriette's daughters Louisa and Charlotte were both now in their late teens. A match between one of them and a Rothschild son would serve to strengthen Henriette's position in the dynasty – her offspring would take the Rothschild name and at last be reintegrated into her birth family – but the vast family wealth left from her and Abraham's time in business would make the match attractive to Hannah's family too. The most obvious and immediate course of action was to hasten a union between Louisa Montefiore and Anthony Rothschild.

13

Marrying In

LOUISA MONTEFIORE WAS proof that privilege cannot buy happiness. Her mother Henriette had spent her formative years trapped in the Frankfurt ghetto, working alongside her father in the *Kontor*, and by her mid teens had become a lively, headstrong young woman capable of resisting Napoleonic interrogators. Louisa's own childhood had been spent in bucolic Stamford Hill, with leisured spells in Germany and Italy, and had produced a young woman crippled by shame and self-doubt. In her earliest diary entries at the end of July 1837, a few months after her sixteenth birthday, Louisa surveyed her short life with a pessimistic, puritanical eye: 'I have now been sixteen years in the world. It may be that half my career is already passed.'[1] She pledged to devote the next year 'to the service of the Almighty ... studying as well my own foibles and faults'. Looking back a year later, she assessed her performance unblinkingly: 'I have fulfilled none of those promises I made to my Creator.'[2]

Yet in public, Louisa made a striking impression. Benjamin Disraeli, attending a lavish dinner at Henriette's just weeks before Louisa's eighteenth birthday in March 1839, found his hostess's daughter to be 'fair and young just out and something like the Queen, only prettier, very charming, perfectly bred, clever, highly educated and apparently in voice, pronunc[iat]ion and appearance, thoroughly English. I like her very much.'[3] Disraeli had been observed to spend most of his time at Henriette's casting amorous glances at another of Henriette's regular guests, the widowed Mary Anne Wyndham Lewis, and the romantic haze that descended over his evenings at Stanhope Street may have caused him to overstate himself here. Though she was indeed 'thoroughly English', and may well have been prettier than Queen Victoria, Louisa was not beautiful by nineteenth-century standards.[4]

But, as the Hannah Mayer debacle had shown, there was the risk of attracting the wrong suitor. Henriette was not going to let her daughter make the same mistake. Louisa simply had to marry a Rothschild, whether she liked it or not.

Anthony, known as Billy to his family, was the undisputed playboy of his generation of Rothschilds, a louche young man with a fondness for gambling, sport and sex. In Paris, in early 1839, he hired the London-born prize fighter Owen Swift to give him boxing lessons, and later the same year he established his own racing stables.[5] Along with his younger brother, Nat, Anthony belonged to the French Jockey Club, where high-stake card games were common and debts easily accumulated. His sexual appetites were prodigious. On one European tour, he took with him what his younger brother, Mayer, described as 'an enormous store of bonnets [condoms]', and years later he was still the go-to Rothschild for advice on Parisian prostitutes: in 1844 his cousin, Joseph Montefiore, wrote asking him to 'send me a good address or two, [of] some old Lady who can procure a young one'.[6]

What worried James and Amschel, the self-appointed keepers of the family line, was not the quantity of wild oats being sown across Europe by their wayward nephew – such behaviour was tolerated, and even discreetly encouraged, among the family's young men – but rather that he showed no sign of forming a lasting and appropriate attachment. In 1829 Anthony, then nineteen, had been summoned home early from a trip to Frankfurt by his furious father, after word reached Nathan that his second son was pursuing a woman considered unsuitable for a young Rothschild.[7] Ten years later, Anthony was once again showing signs of pursuing a rogue relationship in Paris. This time the news fell on even more sensitive ears, following as it did on Hannah Mayer's conversion, when the family was feeling particularly raw about marital matters. The pose of toughness struck by the boxing lessons had done nothing to disguise an underlying feebleness of character. Anthony was, wrote James, 'rather a weak man', who had no serious intention of resisting the family's marital plans.[8] This would not be a struggle, as it had been for Hannah Mayer. It would be a pushover.

James was right. In the summer of 1839, when Amschel probed him on the subject of marriage, Anthony 'told him quite short that if aunt Henrietta would cash up that I was ready'.[9] A match with either of Henriette's daughters – Louisa or Charlotte – would bring him a sizeable dowry from their late father's bequests, and get Uncle James to simmer down. In his euphoria that the family had avoided another scandal, James displayed a rare glimpse of humour. 'Dear Anthony I am glad that your feeling for Louisa Montefiore is such a deep one,' he wrote to his nephew in November 1839, adding, 'I only hope that love will not make you lose too much weight …'[10] Anthony's indulgent lifestyle had taken its toll, and by the late 1830s his tailors at Stultz & Housley could no longer disguise his growing girth with their furs and black frock coats.[11] As his waistband expanded so his hairline had receded, and what was left to grey, had greyed.[12]

Before the end of the year Anthony was working in Paris again, and his relationship with Louisa unfolded by post. From her point of view, that was no bad thing. Louisa's shyness was less a problem in writing than it was in person, and she easily mastered the type of letter that was required of Rothschild fiancées: glassily affectionate, with a strong practical undercurrent that tugged towards the matter of houses, work arrangements and children. Her puritanical streak had developed into a witty and sometimes biting frankness.[13] Even when confronted with interests that were foreign to her – horse racing, hunting, boxing – she was able to navigate the subjects deftly. Romance was something of which she was less capable, but her understatement in this area turned out to be a strength, for it nudged her fiancé into the role that she and the family needed him to inhabit: that of the devoted suitor. In Paris Anthony set about buying Louisa gifts, among them 'a hat, a cap, and ring … also three very beautiful handkerchiefs', as well as 'a bracelet which I am sure will be very much admired'.[14]

As Louisa maintained her reserve, Anthony became looser, more courtly, more cumbersomely affectionate. He soon started addressing her as 'my dearest, best, most amiable and most charming Louisa'; to Louisa, he was just 'my dear Anthony'.[15] Her letters to him were consistently more intelligent, witty and succinct than his to her.[16] Yet Louisa knew the role she would be expected to play as a Rothschild wife. When Anthony told her to keep quiet about something, Louisa 'scrupulously bridled' her tongue; when he told her to take a walk, she 'studiously followed your injunction'.[17] When her fiancé implied that she had failed to send him something he had requested, she wrote back hoping that her 'dear Anthony' would 'not again have so little confidence in me as to think that I shall not immediately do whatever you ask me'.[18]

When their letters turned to practical questions, Louisa advanced her own opinion with a subtle stubbornness. One of the subjects that the couple discussed frequently was where they were going to live after they were married. Would they be in Paris or in London? Should they take a country pile or a town house? Paris had few attractions for Louisa, who was shy and detached enough without having to start again in a strange place, in an unfamiliar language, and besides, would have been wary of settling in a city where the sites of Anthony's bachelordom – the racetracks, the brothels – were within such easy reach. If they were to stay in England, her preference was for a country house. This was not so much because of the fog and gloom that had so depressed Charlotte; Louisa had grown up partly in London, and was wryly matter-of-fact about these things: 'a dense, genuine, yellow, London fog conceals most effectually the brightest sun or the darkest clouds.'[19] What put her off were the 'petty agitations, jealousies and vexations' of London society. Much better, she told her betrothed, to seek a country life, which had 'more charms than any other'.

Anthony's commitments to the family bank meant that, even if they did wish to live in the country, it would only ever be as a complement to a London base. He broached the subject in his letters, explaining that 'the family are complete slaves to business'.[20] That was not something Louisa needed to be told: her own father had worked himself to an early grave trying to compete with them. She knew that the dream of a country house might take years to realise, while finding the right 'town residence' had to be done before they married. With Anthony still in Paris, Louisa enlisted the house-hunting experience of her future mother-in-law, Hannah. It must have been a good opportunity for the two women to get to know each other on equal terms: while Louisa had grown up loving and esteeming her powerful aunt, it had always been as a lesser relative, not as the daughter she would soon become. But just as the house-hunting was gathering pace, the engaged couple's plans were 'very much changed by circumstances' when it became clear that Anthony would, after all, need to assist his uncle James.[21] Louisa would spend the first few years of her married life not in London or the English countryside, but in Paris.[22]

On 30 March 1840, less than a year after Hannah Mayer's wedding had threatened to tear the London Rothschilds apart, the marriage between Anthony Rothschild and Louisa Montefiore reunited them. Unlike Hannah Mayer's union, this was not a love match. Louisa found it hard to imagine how she would maintain a warm, workable relationship with a husband who had been thrust upon her by the family, and with whom she had little intellectual affinity. The night before their wedding, she once again wrote a series of promises to herself and to God. She endeavoured 'to pray earnestly, to act piously', and to ensure that she made her husband happy by fulfilling all his desires.[23] Like resolutions she had recorded as a younger teenager, they were much easier to make than they were to honour. 'I am not yet gentle and affectionate towards Anthony,' she wrote a year later. '[O]ne of my chief endeavours ought to be to please him.'[24]

Though it must have felt to Louisa that she faced this challenge alone, the three London Rothschild women of the 1830s all struggled to cope with being a Rothschild wife. Charlotte had been lucky enough to be paired with a man who was right both in the family's eyes, and, for the most part, in her own. With Hannah Mayer and Louisa it was hard to see which choice had caused more pain: marrying out, for love – or, loveless, marrying in.

14

'The Management of Infancy'

BY THE END of the 1830s Charlotte Rothschild had turned twenty, and was failing in her dynastic duties. Two years exactly after the birth of Leonora, she had produced a second child, but once again it was a daughter. They named her Evelina, or Evy. Writing later in life, Charlotte recalled that Lionel 'was neither glad nor sorry to hear of the arrival', and thought his daughter was 'rather plain than otherwise when he condescended to look at her tiny face'.[1] This joyless reception of girls was not unique to the Rothschilds at the time, but that did not mean the women of the family accepted it unquestioningly. Charlotte was acutely aware of the chauvinism. 'As she was my second child & only a girl,' she wrote, 'no one thought much of her, and she passed through the earlier months & years of infancy unnoticed except by me.'

Under such pressure to provide a son, it is hardly surprising that Charlotte became pregnant again before Evelina was even six months old. On 8 November 1840 Lionel and the rest of the Rothschild men finally got what they wanted. Nathaniel Mayer Rothschild – Natty, as he would come to be known – entered the world a sickly baby. For the men this hardly mattered, so long as he survived to carry the Rothschild name. Lionel was overjoyed. His happiness – so conspicuously absent at Evelina's arrival the previous year – provoked Charlotte against her son. 'He was a thin ugly baby,' she wrote, but this illness 'did not signify. He was a boy and as such most welcome to his father and the whole family.'[2] Unlike her husband, Charlotte admitted that 'I could never prefer [Natty] to his sisters'. It was not long before she produced another son, Alfred; at just twenty-three, she was a mother of four.

Hannah Mayer's controversial marriage would add an extra layer of difficulty to her experience of pregnancy and motherhood. For the first few years of her marriage, she waited for the ripples of the scandal to fade away. Among her close family, the ostracism had never been complete – there were plenty of letters and visits – and in December 1842, when Arthur Frederick FitzRoy was born, the family's pretence of observing James's excommunication slipped even further.[3] In the summer of 1843, during a holiday through Europe, Hannah Mayer, Henry and baby Arthur stopped in Mainz, a short distance from Frankfurt. Assuming that he would be unwelcome in the city that was still the heart of the Rothschild family empire, FitzRoy stayed in Mainz while, somewhat apprehensively, Hannah Mayer travelled on to visit her relatives. It was not long before she was back in Mainz, accompanied by two nephews and her older sister Chilly, who persuaded FitzRoy to come to Frankfurt and dine with them.[4]

Hannah Mayer remained in close contact with her younger sister Lou, who had moved to Frankfurt the previous year to marry Charlotte's brother Mayer Carl. Hannah Mayer repaid the affection heartily, sending from London a 'wonderful' book 'on the management of infancy' – Andrew Combe's *Treatise on the Physiological and Moral Management of Infancy* (2nd edition, 1840) – to help Lou with the rearing of her first child.[5]

Louisa, who was pregnant and living in Paris with Anthony at the end of 1842, would have relished an opportunity to trade advice and share concerns about childbirth with her sister-in-law Hannah Mayer, but she knew better than to welcome the FitzRoys to her temporary home in a Parisian hotel while James's fury still burned so fiercely. Instead, she received Hannah Mayer's recommendations second hand from her other sister-in-law Lou, who heartily recommended Combe's *Treatise*.

By the spring of 1843, Louisa was back in the familiar surroundings of London, and heavily pregnant. 'Have you formed your own opinion as to its being a son or a daughter?' wrote Lou, from Frankfurt.[6] 'As for me I have been so entirely out in my prophecies that in future I do not intend making any.' It was a daughter: Constance. Charlotte, who was in Paris with Lionel at the time, heard the news in a missive from Hannah, who reported that Louisa had 'an excellent time' throughout the birth on 29 April, and 'fully maintained her character for quiet and placidity'.[7] Anthony, who had joined the other men in the family by mocking Lionel when his first two children were girls, soon forgot this earlier condescension when he laid eyes on his own and, brimming with pride, told anyone who would listen that the small baby was 'the picture of himself'.

Louisa's outward composure during labour masked the fear and panic that had gripped her before the birth. Days before she went into labour she had written a letter to her husband, marking it to be read on the event of her death in childbirth.[8] She told him 'to take care of our dear little child if it survives me, speak to it sometimes of its Mamma and give it a good and religious education'.[9] She also implored Anthony to read the green book that lay on her desk – her precious diary, with all its chastising reflections and sacred resolutions – and to make sure that it would be given to the couple's child on its sixteenth birthday.

In the 1840s mothers risked their lives with every child they bore. Hannah Mayer's daughter, Blanche Elizabeth, was born in good health in 1844, but Hannah Mayer – who had gone through labour without the support of mother and sisters – suffered severe complications that left her physically and mentally ill for months.[10] Charlotte and Louisa observed their sister-in-law's plight with a mixture of sympathy and terror. Louisa was six months pregnant when Hannah Mayer was laid low by the difficult birth, and Charlotte remembered Natty's sickliness in his early days.

In December 1844 the birth of Louisa's second daughter went smoothly. She was named Annie Henriette. But Hannah Mayer's problems disturbed Charlotte. By the time Charlotte became pregnant for the fifth time, in the spring of 1845, she was haunted by the idea that something terrible would befall her or her child. While outwardly presenting a strong face for her husband, children and wider London society, Charlotte spent the summer of 1845 in inner turmoil, obsessing over these fears; later she wrote of how she was rendered 'morally, mentally & bodily ill' by the morbid conviction that 'I could not escape unhurt'.[11] Keeping this desperation hidden from the family, she employed a personal *accoucheur*, Sir Charles Locock, to help her through childbirth. Locock had already helped the young Queen Victoria through the birth of four children.

As Charlotte entered the final months of her pregnancy, she received news that Hannah Mayer was finally showing signs of recovery. After a year in bed, suffering emotional and physical trauma, Mrs

FitzRoy had turned a corner and was heading back to health and normality. Charlotte wrote to Louisa in Paris: 'Of H.M. I can forward the most satisfactory accounts; On Saturday she took her first drive, and this morning she was to have left town for her husband's manor in Norfolk, where she expects to be dreadfully, hopelessly dull [i.e. bored].'[12] With Hannah Mayer's recovery underway and Locock tending to her needs and fears, some of Charlotte's dread began to abate. Leopold Rothschild was born on 22 November 1845; when the Queen's physician declared him in perfect health, Charlotte burst into tears of gratitude.[13] Unlike the coolness she had felt towards Natty, which had built up in response to the pressure on her to produce an heir, she felt only love towards her third son, who always seemed an unexpected gift after that summer of quiet dread and obsession.

15

A Muse

'YOU ASK, DEAR husband, if I am going to Mentmore,' Charlotte wrote testily to Lionel in 1848.[1] Mentmore was the grand country house built by Lionel's brother Mayer and his wife Juliana. Most guests marvelled at the modernity of the fittings and the vaulted glass ceiling, the grandeur of the Jacobethan architecture and the exquisite collection of antique furniture, but for Charlotte, visits to the mansion were more about matrimonial duty than personal pleasure. Her letter continued:

[A]s your mother wishes to go there for a few days, I have no choice but to go with her. Ever since I became your wife, I have got to do what others want, never what I would like to do. Pray, that I shall be compensated when in Heaven.

It was a rare outburst against a fact she generally accepted in silence: that being a Rothschild wife was stressful and thankless work.

The burden of that work could be overwhelming. Charlotte found herself constantly preparing for dinner parties at short notice, or rushing between family engagements. Calling cards, left by those seeking a meeting, were addressed to the women of the house, and at Piccadilly they piled up daily. As the family's reputation grew so did expectations for the scale and variety of their Piccadilly House functions. In his memoir, the impresario P.T. Barnum recalled being summoned by Charlotte soon after his arrival in London with the celebrated performing dwarf Tom Thumb. 'Her mansion was a noble structure in Piccadilly, surrounded by a high wall, through the gate of which our carriage was driven, and brought up in front of the main entrance.' At the door to the mansion, he and his performer were 'received by half

*General Tom Thumb (right),
posing with his manager
P. T. Barnum, c.1850.*

a dozen servants', and shown up a sweeping marble staircase to the drawing room, where, surrounded by 'a party of twenty or more ladies and gentlemen', Tom Thumb embarked on his routine – dancing a sailor's hornpipe, impersonating Napoleon, singing 'Lucy Long' and 'Oh! I Should Like to Marry'.[2] Barnum knew that success at Piccadilly House augured well for success in London society at large.

Charlotte's hostessing was an essential part of Lionel's business operation: successful salons like the one at which Tom Thumb appeared were a forum for news to be shared and even made. John Thadeus Delane, the editor of *The Times*, often slipped by no. 148 Piccadilly, or 'Piccadilly House' as it became known, on the way to Printing House Square in the evenings, and again in the mornings, after the edition had gone to press; Charlotte's guest lists ensured that he gathered just as much news as he contributed.[3] While some other hostesses defined themselves by the political allegiances of their gatherings – Lady Palmerston's banquets were redoubtably Whiggish, and the Tory Lady Jersey was known to be aligned with the Duke of Wellington – hospitality at no. 148 Piccadilly crossed party-political lines. Charlotte hosted Tories, Whigs, Radicals and Peelites; diplomats, peers and journalists.[4] She did not like them all, but that did not matter.

For all the diversity in their political views, the guests at Piccadilly House were overwhelmingly upper class, and Christian. A family story had it that when Lionel's mother Hannah was a girl and some Christian gentleman walked in on her at Angel Court, when she was dressed in mourning attire and reciting the lamentations of Jeremiah on occasion of Tisha B'Av, she had become flustered and embarrassed, and shied away from explaining what she was doing.[5] Charlotte suffered no such flashes of self-consciousness and shame in connection with her religion, but she had embraced English Christian fashions in food and music and art, and there was a tendency for her and Lionel's own religious and cultural traditions to be pushed into the background at their social events. There was, however, at least one frequent guest around whom the family would have felt no pressure to conceal or downplay their Jewish identity.

Though Benjamin D'Israeli had been born into a Jewish family, his father Isaac had severed most of his ties with the city's Jewish community. When Benjamin's grandfather died, Isaac abandoned the last vestiges of religious observance by having his four children baptised as Anglicans.[6] This transformed Benjamin's prospects, making him eligible at a stroke for the highest positions in politics and law. At eighteen, Benjamin decided to drop the apostrophe from his surname, and to decapitalise the 'I'.[7] By 1840 he was a rising star of the Commons and married to the widowed Mary Anne Lewis, with whom he had often dined at Henriette Montefiore's.[8] Mary Anne, the eccentric and warm-hearted daughter of a Welsh naval commander, was an enthusiast for Jewish culture, proudly describing herself as half Jewish by marriage, and Benjamin too had developed a fascination for the heritage from which his father's decisions, as well as his own, had distanced him.

Through Henriette, the Disraelis became acquainted with Hannah, and they were among the guests at a lavish *fête champêtre* hosted by Nathan's widow at Gunnersbury in 1843.[9] After admiring Charlotte's beauty from afar, Benjamin's first meeting with her and Lionel, which most likely took place that day, appears to have been understated enough to lose out in his letters to Hannah's 'temples and illuminated walks', the impressive military band, and the excellent turtle soup that he was brought by a former servant of his.[10] Subsequent meetings felt intimate and precociously familiar, as if they had been friends for years already. Frequently, and especially on Sunday evenings, a 'quiet family party' would be expanded by the arrival of the 'Disis', into what Charlotte called the 'magic circle'.[11]

In 1841, after being passed over by Peel for a cabinet position, Disraeli had begun to think in more critical ways about the Prime Minister and his Conservative Party elite. Now in his late thirties and consigned to the back benches, he became the figurehead and driving force of a new political clique. The 'Young Englanders' were appalled by what they saw as the amorality and atomisation of modern, industrialised society, and found in a romanticised idea of Britain's feudal past a vague model for national renewal.[12] Though the Young Englanders did occasionally influence parliamentary business, their project was more fully articulated in literature than in legislation. In 1844, just months after first meeting Charlotte and Lionel, Disraeli published *Coningsby*, the first of three novels that would come to be known as his 'Young England' series.

Coningsby was a *Bildungsroman* about the youth and political education of Henry Coningsby, an orphaned grandson of a marquess. Disinherited by his grandfather, Lord Monmouth, Coningsby manages, through integrity and hard work, to establish himself as an MP. Much of the novel – the swipes at Peelites and Utilitarians, and the depiction of a Britain smothered by Whig misrule – would have been familiar to readers of Disraeli's previous works. What came as a greater surprise – and attracted most comment – was the novel's treatment of Jews and Judaism. Among the novel's characters was a Jewish banker named Sidonia. Contemporary readers were struck by the similarities between Sidonia and two real Jewish bankers, Lionel and his late father, Nathan. Reviewing the book, the *Morning Post* commented: 'Many of the characters are portraits, which no person acquainted with the circles in which the originals move, can fail to detect. Lord Monmouth and his creature, Mr Rigby, who writes "slashing" articles in the reviews – Milbank, the cotton lord – Sidonia, the great Jew capitalist, who holds all the Courts of Europe in his cheque-book . . . none of the them can be mistaken.'[13]

In his conversations with the young Coningsby, Sidonia argues that Jews have been responsible for every great intellectual movement in European history, and that English culture and history are grounded not in Teutonism – as many contemporaries wished to believe – but in Hebraism.[14] Such a boldly revisionist account of Jewish and English history had obvious implications for debates about emancipation and civil disabilities: Sidonia, for instance, was shut out from universities and schools 'which were indebted for their first knowledge of ancient philosophy to the learning and enterprise of his ancestors'.[15] Disraeli also had Sidonia reflect on the position of Jews within the commonplace racial taxonomies of the time, which, following the German physician and anthropologist Johann Friedrich Blumenbach, often divided humanity into five groups: the Caucasian, Mongolian, Malayan, American and Ethiopian. Sidonia considers the Jews to be a Caucasian race, and not only that, but the only Caucasian race that had not intermarried, and therefore the only 'pure Caucasians'.[16] This view of Jewish ethnic identity – a view which Disraeli himself believed and defended, in letters to the *Morning Post* and other newspapers – was one that daringly revised the position of Jews within nineteenth-century racial hierarchies.[17]

Writing to Disraeli in late spring 1844, twenty-four-year-old Charlotte announced her intention to 'close my doors to all intruders and devote this day wholly and solely to the agreeable visitor [*Coningsby*] whose presence I owe to your flattering recollection of me'.[18] Charlotte found much to admire in the novel, and particularly in the arguments that Disraeli made through Sidonia. She started using the adjective 'Caucasian' in her writing, for 'Jewish'. Soon her letters were full of references to Caucasian and non-Caucasian guests, to Caucasian children at the Jews' Free School in Bell Lane, Caucasian facial features, and Caucasian 'casts of countenance'.[19] The English family's observance of the *kashrut* had become distinctly flexible as they cultivated an appreciation of the upper-class Christian penchant for delicacies such as turtle soup, but when kosher food was mentioned – most often in connection with religious festivals or the visits of more orthodox family members – Charlotte now sometimes described them as 'Caucasian provisions'. It was a small nomenclatural shift, and usually delivered with an air of drollery, but it also made a serious point: in a cultural world that still tended to depict Jews according to a handful of age-old stereotypes, Disraeli's bold claim had come as a revelation, and furnished an opportunity to express cultural pride.

As a well-known friend of Mary Anne and Benjamin, and a practised hostess, Charlotte was soon approached for introductions. She arranged private soirées in Piccadilly, where admirers of *Coningsby* could meet its author.[20] Such events were mutually beneficial: her reputation as a hostess of relevance grew, while he, by associating himself with the Rothschilds, gained good company, political intelligence, credit, excellent food and a new, powerful following.[21] Soon enough, Benjamin was using events thrown by Charlotte to manoeuvre against the Tory front bench. At a 'grand entertainment' in June 1844, the 'pride and pattern of the new generation' tried to persuade Whig MPs to administer a *coup de grâce* to the ailing Peel government, by attempting to form their own administration.[22] His confidence grew; by March 1845 he was attacking Peel openly in the House of Commons.[23] Charlotte had played a key role in Disraeli's transformation from disappointed Peelite to leader-in-waiting.

Mary Anne, who was twelve years Benjamin's senior and almost three decades older than Charlotte, was just as devoted to the new family friends as her husband. '[B]oth of them are in love with Baron Lionel and his fair wife,' reported Nat in 1845, after a dinner with the Disraelis in Paris.[24] In her youth Mary Anne had been charmingly unconventional, but as she got older she was becoming increasingly outlandish and idiosyncratic. She wore ribbons on everything and, partly thanks to her obsession with Judaism, often made extraordinary remarks.[25] After Charlotte gave birth to Leopold in late November 1845, Mary Anne pronounced the 'beautiful baby' to be 'the future Messiah'.[26]

As 'Mrs Dis', 'Mrs Disi' or 'Mrs Dizzy', Mary Anne became a frequent cameo in Charlotte's letters, where her mercurial moods and impulsive behaviour provided endless comic material: she appeared in 'high glee' and low spirits, and 'rattled away famously' over tea; she requested 'amusing French books' for her bed-bound husband, spoke 'with rapture' about her recent invitations, held forth loudly about 'the young men of the present day', and reported 'with horrible loquacity' on the illness of an aristocrat.[27] Her toilette and clothing were a subject of particular fascination. In one letter, she appeared wearing a wreath of red feathers, 'like the savages'; in another, she was 'a regular Gayina with a cap covered with pearl drops on her head, and a Turkish jacket embroidered with gold on her shoulders, and artificial eyebrows and eyelashes'.[28] Her colourful comments and non sequiturs entered family folklore. For years to come, Leo would be known to his cousins as 'the little Messiah'.[29]

In September 1845 Charlotte had a particularly good vignette of Mary Anne to report. 'I'll tell you a secret that will astonish you, if aught relating to our excellent and eccentric friend Mrs Disraeli can possibly produce an impression, a feeling of that kind,' she wrote.[30] Early in the evening of an autumn Friday, Charlotte heard a 'violent ringing and pulling of the bell', after which, suddenly 'into my reluctant arms rushed Mrs. Disy'. Tearful and agitated, Mary Anne breathlessly announced that she was about to go abroad and had an ominous feeling that she would not return. Reaching into her pocket, she pulled out a piece of paper and, with a flourish, declared: 'This is my will and you must read it, show it to the dear Baron [Lionel], and take care of it for me.' Despite Charlotte's attempts to calm her, Mary Anne carried on. 'In the event of my beloved husband preceding me to the grave, I leave and bequeath to Evelina de Rothschild ... all my personal property ... I love the Jews. I have attached myself to your children, and [Evelina] is my favorite.' The next day, perplexed and somewhat amused by the display, Charlotte went to see the Disraelis and – politely yet firmly – returned the will.

On this occasion there may have been another motive behind Mary Anne's seemingly bizarre behaviour. A few weeks earlier, in August 1845, Lionel had ridden to the rescue of the Disraeli family's investments. Benjamin Disraeli had never been good with money. Within a few years of their marriage the couple had soon spent Mary Anne's inheritance from her father and first husband – and plenty more besides.[31] Lionel had managed to bail the pair out of terrible debt. The will, which named Lionel and Charlotte's daughter Evelina as sole beneficiary of whatever little was left, had only been written on 5 September 1845 and could easily have been the Disraelis' attempt to repay an immense debt to their friend and financial saviour. Charlotte was unaware of the financial dealings that lay behind the friendship; to her the episode seemed comically incomprehensible.

That year, Disraeli published the second novel in his Young England trilogy. *Sybil* reprised his concern with religious and cultural conflict, but added to this a new concern with the relationship between the 'Two Nations' of the Rich and the Poor. The 'Condition of England' question was not guaranteed to chime with the Rothschild women in the same way that Disi's reflections on Jewish history had done: but there was one for whom it struck a deep chord. Soon after the publication of *Coningsby*, Disraeli's Young England colleague George Smythe had confided to Mary Anne his belief that 'Mrs Anthony de Rothschild ... will understand Coningsby better than any of the family Rothschild. She has more brains than all the others together.'[32] Louisa certainly had more of a head for books; but it was Disraeli's second novel rather than his first that struck her most powerfully. *Sybil*'s focus on the ills of industrial society, and the possibility of alleviating them, resonated with her. Her natural shyness was particularly pronounced in her dealings with Disraeli, whom she remembered from her youth when he was a charismatic guest at her mother's Stanhope Street dining table. But after reading *Sybil*, she forced herself to overcome this reserve. She wrote praising the novel's 'glorious pages' and 'eloquence for reforming humanity'.[33]

The role of literature in social reform preoccupied her. In 1840 Louisa and her sister Charlotte Montefiore had founded the Cheap Jewish Library (CJL), an ambitious project aimed at producing affordable, engaging books for working-class Jews.[34] The need for literature that explained, celebrated and defended Jewish religion and culture was particularly pressing among working-class Jewish communities, which were often targeted by Christian proselytes: during the 1820s and 1830s pamphlets and novels exhorting Jews to accept the 'true Messiah' had poured from English presses.[35]

Between 1841 and 1849, under the mentorship of David Aaron de Sola, a rabbi and author, the sisters produced ten serial stories issued across eighteen booklets.[36] The prejudice against female authors was still strong, and the project was veiled in secrecy. 'I beg of you to remember that our project is a secret from every one even from my brothers,' wrote Charlotte Montefiore to de Sola.[37] Even Grace Aguilar, the rising star of Anglo-Jewish letters, was not allowed to know who her editors and publishers were at the CJL: the sisters corresponded with her only through de Sola.[38] The sole person who knew about Louisa and Charlotte Montefiore's involvement in the project, beyond de Sola and themselves, was their mother, Henriette.

Perhaps the most successful of the works published by the CJL was one written by Charlotte Montefiore herself. Set in a poverty-stricken district of London, *Caleb Asher* romanticised loyalty to Judaism, depicting principled, impoverished Jewish characters being nourished by their religion and refusing to sacrifice their faith for social and monetary gain.[39] For Louisa, the superiority of spiritual integrity to wealth, which Charlotte dramatised in the book, would become a guiding principle. Following the success of *Caleb Asher* – which was published in a single volume in both Britain and America – the reputation of the series spread.[40] It must have been with great pride that the sisters read comments in the *Jewish Chronicle* emphasising that literature and education, as much as parliamentary reform, would be responsible for improving the condition of Jews in England, and for challenging prejudice: it was 'not a seat in Parliament alone' that would 'elevate the Jews in England', opined the newspaper, but 'the mental cultivation of the working classes, and Jewish emancipation within'.[41]

Having served as a champion for *Coningsby*, Charlotte Rothschild became a close companion of 'Mr Disi'. The pair lent each other books, visited and wrote to each other frequently, and had many discussions about Judaism. As Disraeli hurried to complete the final part of his trilogy, Charlotte was kept updated on its progress by a breathless Mary Anne. 'The first proofs of Tancred are now on the table,' she wrote on 19 April 1847.[42] 'How much I hope you will be here when [it] is presented to the public.' In *Tancred*, the ideas about Judaism that had existed in the background of the previous two novels became a central feature of the plot. The protagonist – Tancred, Lord Montacute – has been brought up in a claustrophobic and evangelical Christian household. To his family's alarm, he decides he is fed up with society, and resolves to visit the Holy Land to better understand the origins of his religion. There, he falls in with a family of Jewish bankers and begins an intellectual and spiritually enlightening relationship with their daughter, Eva.

Once the action shifts to the Holy Land, the plot of the novel becomes outlandish and rickety, unfolding through a series of adventures, battles and abductions, but the mainstay of it is Tancred's relationship with Eva, who, with wit and piercing intelligence, gradually teaches him to see the Hebraic roots of his own religion, and corrects the bigoted excesses of his Protestantism. Even if it were not for the physical similarities between Eva and Charlotte – Eva is described as having 'a noble forehead', a 'small, slightly elevated' nose, and a 'round chin, polished as a statue' – Eva's opinions and her manner alone would be sufficient to make it clear that the character drew heavily on Disraeli's muse.[43] Charlotte was a passionate supporter of Jewish emancipation, and would certainly have recognised her own opinions in Eva Besso's trenchant defence of Jewish civil rights, and Tancred's unfolding romantic relationship with Eva quite clearly echoes Disraeli's strong connection with Charlotte. Within the world of fiction he was free to explore the adoration that simmered beneath their friendship.

After the publication of *Tancred*, Disraeli turned his attention back to formal politics. Now that he had articulated something of his political vision in his 'Young England' novels, and the patronage of Charlotte Rothschild had helped him gain key social and political traction, he was in a much stronger position than he had been at the start of the 1840s. Charlotte was too admiring of Mr Disi to doubt whether he would be an effective advocate for the family's cause in Parliament, and it fell to the ever-astute Louisa to sound a note of caution about their family friend. In November 1847 Louisa and Anthony Rothschild hosted the Disraelis together with Charlotte and Lionel for dinner. Throughout the course of the evening, wrote Louisa, Mary Anne was 'as usual an odd mixture of good sense and non sense, of amusing humour and gaiety and of no less amusing absurdity'.[44] As for Disraeli: 'He spoke of the Jew's life in his strange, Tancredian strain, saying we must ask for our rights and privileges, not for concessions and liberty of conscience.' What she really wanted to know was whether 'he will have the courage to speak to the [H]ouse in this manner'. High-minded literary reverence for Judaism was one thing – practical political support another. Once Disraeli's ego, Mary Anne's eccentricity, Charlotte's youthful infatuation and Lionel's ambition were all taken into account, Louisa may have been the only one who could see things clearly.

16

'Surely We Do Not Deserve
So Much Hatred'

O N A MIDSUMMER'S day in 1847, John Thadeus Delane, editor of
The Times, called 'by appointment' at no. 148 Piccadilly.[1] This was
not one of his customary morning visits on the way to or from the
newspaper's offices. A general election was looming. The conversation
focused on whether Lionel could drum up sufficient support to stand
on the Liberal slate of candidates for the City of London. If successful,
this would position a Rothschild to become the first Jewish Member
of Parliament and, Charlotte hoped, would exert critical pressure on
the Christian oath that served to bar Jews from the Commons and
Lords. For the first time in more than a decade, a breakthrough on
Jewish emancipation once again seemed possible.

In order to stand a chance, Lionel first had to win a place on the
party's slate by writing an address which laid out his political platform
for the City Liberals, who had the final say on the selection of the constituency candidates. A few days ahead of the crucial meeting, Delane
returned to Piccadilly to help fine-tune Lionel's manifesto.[2] Later in
the evening, Charlotte, Anthony and Louisa arrived back from the
opera, and, before even getting changed out of their finery, offered
their own opinions on the address.[3] Once it was written, Delane sent
it to the Prime Minister, Lord John Russell, who was one of the four
sitting Liberal representatives for the City of London. Two days later,
on the eve of the selection meeting, Russell returned the draft with
some suggested amendments, and Delane spent another evening with
Lionel and Charlotte, finalising the speech. Their persistence paid off.
At a meeting on 29 June 1847, Lionel was unanimously approved as
one of the Liberal candidates.[4]

With this first hurdle cleared, Lionel now faced the task of
convincing the voters. The following day, Delane published Lionel's

letter 'to the electors of the City of London' on the front page of *The Times*, emphasising his business expertise and downplaying the fact that his election would invite a constitutional confrontation.[5] The Jewish Association for the Removal of Civil and Religious Disabilities, a group hurriedly set up by the Board of Deputies to support the parliamentary campaigns of Lionel and the several other Jewish men campaigning for election, had no such caution. They plastered the walls of the City of London with posters, calling on 'friends and fellow citizens' to overturn the 'grievous disabilities which you have it in your power to remove'.[6] It was not long before the the City Tories mounted a vicious counteroffensive. They attempted to drum up fear and intolerance, claiming that Lionel intended to take his seat 'by force and compulsion', and even 'by storm'.[7]

Charlotte and Louisa embarked on a campaign of their own, taking to the streets of the City of London to meet voters and win them over one by one. July 1847 was a sticky, stifling month, and electioneering was exhausting work. While Louisa was 'rather amused' by the novelty of canvassing, she remained reserved and quiet.[8] Charlotte meanwhile was in her element, canvassing confidently and passionately in what was turning out to be a 'hard fight against hatred, envy and intolerance'.[9] Though it was occasionally explicit, most prejudice lurked in the background, unspoken: 'not one would express with their lips the intolerance which still lies concealed in their hearts,' wrote Charlotte after one trip to the City.[10]

Unable to canvass on the streets as energetically as Louisa and Charlotte, Hannah worked to support her son Lionel in her own way. In the years since Wellington's betrayal in the early 1830s, Hannah had remained focused on achieving forms of advancement and distinction for her sons.[11] Her efforts had culminated in Lionel being offered a baronetcy in 1846.[12] Lionel had rejected the offer – a barony was the least he deserved – and the title had passed to Anthony.[13] At the time, Hannah had been enraged by her elder son's decision, and her usually restrained tone had evaporated in a letter 'concerning the offer by her majesty', which she thought it was 'not in good taste for you to refuse'.[14] In hindsight, however, she could see the benefit of his petulance. Unrestrained by a title, Lionel could focus on achieving a place in the Commons.

She knew that a successful campaign would require more than the votes of Jewish electors – who were concentrated in the Portsoken,

Aldgate, Billingsgate and Tower wards – and devoted herself to winning the support of other important figures in the constituency. 'I enclose you the names of persons of respectability who have promised their votes which you may rely upon and hope to obtain more,' she wrote to Lionel.[15] It must have occurred to Hannah that this latest bid for emancipation could end the same way as her previous campaigns, with betrayal, defeat and more years in the wilderness. There were, however, reasons for cautious optimism. In response to the accusation that Lionel planned to take his seat 'by force and compulsion', Lord John Russell spoke out at a hustings, claiming that 'there is no man in this country who would take care to obey the law more implicitly than my friend Baron Rothschild'. Hannah found such words of support 'highly gratifying and complimentary'.[16]

On the day of the vote, Louisa and Charlotte made their way to the Guildhall in the heart of the City. At eight in the morning, when they arrived, the hall was already packed, and the atmosphere tense. Louisa later recalled 'an anxious, agitating, but highly interesting day, during which everyone exerted herself to the utmost'.[17] By the end of the first hour of voting all the Liberal candidates had pulled ahead, with over two hundred votes separating the last of them from their nearest Tory rival.[18] In response, the Tory lobbyists shifted their tack, urging their supporters to concentrate votes on a single candidate, the Peelite John Masterman, who they believed offered their best chance to defeat the most vulnerable of the Liberal candidates, Lionel Rothschild.

After the close of polls, Louisa and Charlotte retired to the gallery.[19] Rumours swirled around the crammed Guildhall that the Tories had edged ahead. If this was the case, the women knew that Lionel's prospects were bleak. Yet as the results were chalked up on the blackboard at the front of the hall, the name Charlotte, Louisa and Hannah were praying for appeared in vivid white. Lionel Rothschild had won 6,792 votes of the 13,500 cast in the constituency, beating his Tory rival John Masterman, and securing one of the constituency's four seats by a margin of 73 votes.[20] Charlotte watched with pride as her husband took to the stage. Once the rapturous applause had died down, Lionel thanked the electors. He 'could not find words' to express the value of their support, or the service that they had 'rendered to the cause of civil and religious liberty'.[21] Later that evening, when he dropped by no. 148 Piccadilly, Delane found Charlotte 'in a state of almost frenzied delight and gratitude'.[22]

As the results came in from other seats, it became clear that Lionel would be the lone standard-bearer for this cause. The defeat of other Jewish candidates – including Lionel's brother Mayer, who had stood in Folkestone – failed to dent the mood in the family: it had only taken one O'Connell, after all, to break the ban on Catholics sitting as MPs.[23] Congratulatory letters poured in from Rothschild women across the Continent. Betty found herself carried away with a rare bout of revolutionary excitement: 'The breach has been made, the obstacle of imputation, prejudice and intolerance is distinctly foundering. Hope is lifting up all of Europe and from every corner the echo resounds, carrying far the seed of this new era now approaching on a wider horizon of civilization.'[24] The wife of Lionel's younger brother Nat echoed this hope when she wrote: 'This day will be the beginning of a new era for the Jewish Nation, having a most distinguished champion like you.'[25] Despite this excitement, all were still aware of the major obstacle that Lionel faced before he could properly occupy the position to which he had been elected. 'I trust that but little difficulty will be met with in taking your seat in Parliament,' added Lionel's sister Lou, attempting to strike an optimistic note.[26]

The extended Rothschild family was staying at Gunnersbury when, on 16 December 1847, Lord John Russell brought forward a parliamentary resolution on Jewish emancipation. While Louisa decided to 'remain quietly, comfortably' at the family's estate, Hannah hurried to the Commons, where she took a seat in the gallery.[27] Russell's line of reasoning was clear: 'Every Englishman, born in the country, is entitled to all the honours and advantages of the British constitution.'[28] In an attempt to make this palatable to those who still rejected the idea of Jewish representation, he dressed his argument up with tactical disclaimers, insisting that the Jewish population was so small that the bill would make little difference, and stressing that the current arrangement was flawed and inconsistent as it had allowed those such as Edward Gibbon, who constantly 'sneered' at Christianity, to take the oath in bad faith, while truly pious individuals who professed the Jewish religion were excluded. The Prime Minister's resolution was opposed by Sir Robert Inglis, speaking on behalf of the Ultra-Tories, who had vigorously opposed similar bills in the early 1830s.[29] Far more significant to the Rothschilds, however, was the speech of another Tory who rose to speak at this first debate: Benjamin Disraeli.

Tactically, Disraeli was in a tricky position. At the end of June 1846 he and his ally Lord George Bentinck had defeated Peel, in the

A PARCEL OF OLD ——— FRIGHTENED AT A NASTY!
GREAT! UGLY! JEW BILL.

An 1849 cartoon from Punch, *satirising the response in the House of
Lords to Lionel Rothschild's attempt to take his seat in the
Commons. Assorted Lords stand up on the benches with their robes lifted
in horror at the Bill – depicted as a stick insect – with one raising
the ceremonial mace in readiness to squash it.*

process splitting the Tory party between the Peelites and their own faction, the Protectionists. Both Bentinck and Disraeli were supporters of emancipation, and yet most reactionary Protectionists were opposed to it, and there was a risk that the issue would further fracture their Commons base. Given that the December debate was not yet on a concrete bill but rather on the question of whether the House should establish a select committee to discuss the removal of Jewish disabilities, Disraeli still felt confident to stand up and speak on emancipation as a matter of conscience. '[T]he peril is not so imminent,' he had written to his erstwhile Young England ally, Lord John Manners, '& the battle will not be fought until next year.'[30]

As readers of his Young England series might have expected, Disraeli's argument was a fairly eccentric and 'Tancredian' one, grounded in established arguments for religious liberty rather than in an interpretation of 'religious truth'. In a move that was calculated to rile the Anglican Tories on his own benches, Disraeli argued that Jews were 'humanly speaking, the authors of your religion'. 'The very reason for admitting the Jews', he argued, 'is because they can show so near an affinity to you. Where is your Christianity, if you do not believe in their Judaism[?]'[31] Charlotte read Disraeli's speech in the papers the next morning with a great sense of relief. Later, reflecting on the December debate in conversation with Delane, she did nothing to hide her admiration: 'it was not possible', she said, 'to express oneself with greater intelligence . . . power, wit or originality than our friend, Disraeli.'[32]

At last, on Thursday, 25 May 1848, a new Jewish Disabilities Bill graduated to the Lords. On this occasion, Charlotte and Louisa were persuaded to stay away from Parliament by their husbands, who feared a hostile atmosphere.[33] Hannah, however, was not to be dissuaded. She and her sister, Judith Montefiore, joined Lionel and his brothers in the Strangers' Gallery to watch the first vote. For a Jewish family who had done so much to assimilate themselves at the highest level of English society, it was a stomach-churning experience. The Lords launched unencumbered into arguments against 'diluting' a 'Christian parliament', with Samuel Wilberforce – the Bishop of Oxford and son of the famous abolitionist – claiming that Jews were 'haters of Christianity' and another speaker claiming that Jewish MPs would spell the end of Britain's 'greatness' as a nation.[34]

The debate lasted until half past one in the morning, and was, according to Moses Montefiore, 'a painful excitement'.[35] The majority against the bill was thirty-five. A devastated Hannah retired to no. 107 Piccadilly, while Lionel, Anthony and Mayer returned to no. 148, where Louisa and Charlotte had waited up anxiously for the news.[36] Lionel, whose self-control was legendary, was the only one smiling: Anthony and Mayer were 'crimson in the face'.[37] While a defeat might have been foreseeable – Disraeli himself had been pessimistic – the majority against the bill, or, as Moses Montefiore tellingly put it, 'against us', was 'much greater than expected'.[38] Charlotte took to her diary to process the blow. 'I went to sleep at 5 and woke again at 6; I had dreamt that a huge vampire was greedily sucking my blood,' she wrote.[39] 'Apparently, when the result of the vote was declared, a loud, enthusiastic roar of approval resounded . . . through the House. Surely we do not deserve so much hatred. I spent all day Friday weeping and sobbing.'

The defeat itself, and the ferocity of the bigotry voiced in the Lords, enraged even the less excitable Louisa. She had disregarded the men's advice not to read the 'scandalous' speeches in the newspapers, even though doing so made her feel ill.[40] 'The speeches against the admission of Jews into Parliament were intolerant and bigoted and calumnious,' she seethed in her diary. 'The Bishop of Oxford, in particular, spoke like a fiery, zealous, unscrupulous, party man, and not in the least like a clerical one. I was quite sorry that Wilberforce's son should have made such a display.' Then a letter from Lionel's younger brother Nat – who was working for his uncle in France – brought equally dismal news. Since February that year, when King Louis Philippe was overthrown and the Second Republic declared, an uneasy peace had reigned in the French capital. Now, in June, that peace had been shattered, and 'the worst revolution . . . that ever happened' had erupted in Paris.[41]

17

The Great Abyss

IN THE 'DEAD of night' on Saturday, 26 February 1848 young Constance Rothschild was shaken from her sleep and carried downstairs to the hallway of her London home.[1] There, the four-year-old daughter of Louisa and Anthony found her aunt Betty and three of her Parisian cousins, their cheeks flushed from the biting cold outside. Louisa was 'astonished' at the women 'having the courage to leave the gentlemen' in the French capital, and to travel alone to England.[2] The news they brought with them was bleak. As Louisa wrote in her diary two days later: 'a revolution in Paris, the citizen king, the monarch of the people [Louis Philippe] forced to abdicate, fly, France declared for the second time a republic! . . . Our age seemed a sober quiet one, we thought we should never [see] such heart-stirring scenes.'[3]

The Paris revolution was one of many that would sweep through Europe in the Springtime of the Peoples in 1848, toppling long-established regimes and dynasties, and in the process shaking the foundations of the Rothschilds' empire. In January a revolt that had started in Palermo quickly spread to Naples, where the Bourbon rulers of the Kingdom of the Two Sicilies had been forced to grant a constitution. In March uprisings spread across German states and the Habsburg Empire. In Vienna, where Betty's father Salomon Mayer had established his branch of the family, the conservative State Chancellor Prince Metternich was overthrown. In May 1848 the first freely elected German parliament was held in Frankfurt, the family's original seat, where Gutle and her eldest son Amschel still resided.

On that cold February night at Grosvenor Place, Louisa hurried about preparing rooms and beds for relatives who had fled the Continent. It helped to keep busy: among the Rothschild men still in Paris when the revolution broke out was her husband Anthony, who had been working there with his uncle James and brother Nat. For months, the revolution was the only subject of conversation in the Rothschild family. Betty soon became the fiercest and most vocal Rothschild opponent of the revolutionary regimes, writing to her sons angry letters in which she attacked the 'red republic' in France and celebrated the blows dealt against liberal and radical causes as reactionary forces gained ground during the spring.[4] When, in November 1848, she heard her four-year-old nephew declare, 'If I had the money, I would buy a gun to shoot the republic and the republicans', she commented, approvingly, that this was a 'child of [the] reaction'.[5]

Betty's trenchant views did not chime with the English Rothschild women. For Louisa, the revolutionary developments were 'Strange & wonderful'.[6] Still fired by the spiritual ideas that had guided so much writing in the Cheap Jewish Library, she was not concerned about the impact of revolution on the family fortunes. She found herself revisiting Psalm 29, whose subject is the vanity of earthly riches and success: 'How strangely applicable ... to the events of the last most eventful week.'[7] The revolutions, although complicated and painful, exemplified important spiritual truths. They might also bring benefits for the family's cause. Further civil rights for the Jews of the new France could spark changes in Britain.

For Charlotte, the convening of a National Assembly in Frankfurt had evoked the possibility of a 'prosperous, powerful, united and free' Germany.[8] She also admired those on the republican left in France. Writing in her diary in March, she praised Alexandre Ledru-Rollin, the firebrand defender of working-class rights, as having 'honest intentions for France ... at this time of general turmoil'. '[O]f all the members of the administration', it was Ledru-Rollin who was, in her opinion, 'capable of taking action as a leader'.[9] Charlotte's approval was expressly for his honest intentions and capabilities rather than for his policies. But it is striking that for a woman of her position – who stood to lose so much – she could see objectively enough to admire a man on the left of the revolutionary assembly.

As reports from the Continent grew increasingly dire, however, the Rothschild women began to feel more uneasy. During the spring, London had witnessed numerous mass demonstrations in support of Chartism, a radical political movement with demands including universal suffrage for men, the secret ballot and annual elections.[10]

The Chartist gathering scheduled for 10 April looked set to be the biggest yet: a 'monster demonstration' on Kennington Common followed by a march to Parliament and the delivery of a petition demanding universal male suffrage and other democratic reforms.[11] The government steeled itself for massive confrontation. Now that the threat was so much closer to home, some of Louisa's earlier admiration and idealism evaporated. The evening before the demonstration, she dined at Piccadilly, where they worried about the impending rally and the 'preparations and warlike demonstrations' of the army and police.[12] These, Louisa hoped, 'will have alarmed the mob'. Briefly, the relationship between the Continental and London branches of the family was reversed. Now it was the former who waited for news at a distance. 'I hope your Chartist meeting will pass over without fighting,' Nat wrote from Paris apprehensively, the day before the demonstration. 'Where will it remain quiet if in England the ... people intend playing the same game as here[?]'[13]

Against most expectations, remain quiet it did. Heavy rain dampened the crowd's enthusiasm, the attempt to confine protesters to the south side of the Thames was successful, and the petition gained far fewer genuine signatures than was estimated. 'The stirring wind of revolution that destroys old injustices', wrote Charlotte, 'did not blow in England.'[14] However, with branches of the family bank struggling on mainland Europe, it was undeniable that the 1848 revolutions had shaken the Rothschilds.[15] In mid April Charlotte had to contend with the taunts of the Austrian ambassador, who spent an evening as a guest at no. 148 Piccadilly making mocking comments about her family's bleak financial future. Prevented by diplomatic considerations from speaking her mind, Charlotte saved her retort for her diary. The power of the Rothschild house in Europe '[d]oes not lie in our wealth alone', she wrote, 'and God the Almighty will not withdraw his protecting from us. Amen!'[16]

By July 1848 the situation in Germany appeared to have stabilised somewhat, and Louisa travelled with her daughters to the Rothschild ancestral home in Frankfurt. Here she found the black, red and gold of the newly adopted German flag festooning public buildings and fluttering from the tower of the imposing Paulskirche, where the new

German National Assembly was meeting. Even Nathan and Henriette's older brother, the venerable and conservative Uncle Amschel, had hung nationalist flags from his windows, albeit only to satisfy crowds of protesters.[17] His wife Eva had recently died, and he was mourning, but Louisa knew enough about her uncle to doubt this situation would last long. Amschel would 'soon be consoled', she wrote, and Eva 'forgotten'.[18]

Although life among the Frankfurt family felt less lively and engrossing than usual, Louisa kept herself occupied by exploring the new democratic hub of the fledgling German nation. On 8 August she and Chilly made their way to the Paulskirche, to watch a sitting of the National Assembly.[19] Crowds of people had squeezed into seats beneath the huge rotunda, so that by the time Louisa and Chilly arrived there was little space and 'half the pleasure was lost'. The morning's discussions included a 'very stormy' debate about the use of Hebrew as a language in the Assembly. As Louisa had hoped, the revolutionary fervour of 1848 was providing a fertile ground for Jewish advancement.

Soon, however, Frankfurt lost its political charm for her, and she slipped once more into melancholy. It was a relief when, on 14 August, she and her daughters boarded a river boat on the Rhine to begin the long journey home. As they steamed up the river under the 'bright sun and blue sky', Louisa observed a country gripped by patriotic fervour.[20] Every riverside village and boat they passed was 'crowded with holiday folks and decked with flags of all the different German states'. She saw 'processions of National Guards with moving banners ... gliding from romantic glens and marching on the banks of their national river, and every now and then, above the drums and the fife, sounded a salute of canons or of guns'. And yet the day's most lasting memory would not be of the glens, or the sound of drums, but of an unlikely friendship forged with another passenger.

The author William Makepeace Thackeray had spent the previous few weeks holidaying with a French duke and duchess in Spa when, on an impulse, he decided to take a boat ride. 'What if I were to pay my bill and go off this minute to the Rhine?' he wrote. 'Who knows, by setting off at twelve o'clock, something may happen to alter the course of my whole life? Perhaps I may meet with some beautiful creature ...'[21] Louisa was probably not the figure he had in mind. On meeting her aboard the steamer, he would have had reason to feel abashed: he had never held back when it came to parodying the Rothschilds in his writing, and the caricatures of Nathan Rothschild in his earlier works verged on bigoted. His recent depiction of the fictional 'Scharlachschild' banking family (the barest of disguises) in the satirical articles collected in *The Book of Snobs* (1848) had been more grudgingly admiring, but he had not gone entirely soft on them. One of his latest pieces had been a spoof news article for *Punch*, in which he imagined James de Rothschild fleeing revolutionary Paris for London, escaping 'in a water butt as far as Amiens, whence he went on in a coffin'.[22]

With the image of Betty's portly husband stuffed into a barrel no doubt lurking in their minds, Thackeray and Louisa struck up a conversation. The friendship was as immediate as it was unlikely. 'We talked of literature, drawings, Jews, of whom he has a bad opinion, politics, etc., and we parted very good friends – at least I fancy so,' Louisa wrote that first evening.[23] Despite the 'bad opinion' which Thackeray clearly made no attempt to hide, Louisa concluded that he 'seems a good and an honest man, with a kind heart, notwithstanding a large fund of satire'.

Back in London in the autumn of 1848, the surprising new friendship temporarily receded into the background while Louisa was occupied with a visit from Anthony's younger sister, Lou. Both women were pious, widely read and intellectually ambitious, and both shared the conviction that the other was the only person in the extended family who truly understood them. In the weeks after Lou's departure in mid November, that conviction struck Louisa with renewed force. This was only brought into sharper contrast when Louisa hosted Charlotte for a few days in December. Afterwards, Louisa confided to her diary that it had been 'rather slow work', for, although Charlotte was 'clever and amiable', Lou had helped the hours pass at a much quicker pace, and left behind a 'far more agreeable reminiscence'.[24] Hoping to keep this sense of isolation at bay, Louisa turned to her budding friendship with Thackeray. She hosted him for 'good natured and amiable' chats at Grosvenor Place, and made timid claims on his attention at parties.[25]

Like Charlotte's relationship with Mr Disi, Louisa's with Thackeray soon led to a wider friendship with the extended Rothschild family. In February 1849 the writer was lent a box at the opera by 'my friend Jim Rothschild', and in London he attended a 'grand dinner in Jewry', at which Henriette and others were present.[26] While some of Thackeray's dubious views on Jews and Judaism persisted, in his novel

Pendennis Louisa made an appearance, rendered as an angelic 'Jewish lady ... with a child at her knee', in the act of dispensing bonbons.[27] In the first edition the scene was accompanied by a woodcut depicting a simply dressed gentlewoman untainted by any of the usual bigoted shorthands that still so often identified figures as Jewish in cartoons.

During Louisa's visit to Frankfurt in 1848, her grandmother Gutle had remained bed-bound in her Judengasse home. The woman who started it all, the daughter of the ghetto who went on to give birth to the greatest banking dynasty the world has ever seen, was in her mid nineties. Her decision to remain in the house had gone from being a matter of curiosity to one of legend when Hans Christian Andersen wrote a short tale about it, attributing her decision to remain there to the belief that if she left 'the despised street and the little house', her sons' good fortune might desert them.[28] Her great age, too, was a subject of fascination, especially when combined with her reputation for having a quick, dry wit.[29] One popular story from the 1840s had a physician responding to Gutle's growing list of health complaints by saying '*Que voulez-vous madame*? Unfortunately we cannot make you younger,' and Gutle replying: 'You mistake me, doctor. I do not ask you to make me younger. It is older I wish to become.'[30]

But even Gutle could not live forever. On 7 May 1849 the end came. She was ninety-five, an extraordinary age for the time, and the family must have known that her time was limited, and yet the scale of the loss still left the family reeling – Louisa described life without Gutle as a 'great blank' , and Betty called it a 'great abyss'.[31] In this time of confusion and grief, old grudges began to look inconsequential. In March Betty and James finally lifted their stubborn embargo against Hannah Mayer and the FitzRoys, hosting them for two weeks in Paris. 'You may be surprised to hear, dear son,' Betty wrote magnanimously to her son Alphonse, 'that I have made my peace with HM ... I took my courage in both hands and agreed to forget our difference.'[32]

As they had done in previous periods of uncertainty and loss, the family gathered in Frankfurt, to broker further matches and plan a wedding. It was just over ten years since Charlotte had married in Frankfurt: now it was her brother Willy's turn. He was engaged to marry Mathilde, the daughter of Chilly and Anselm. The wedding date was set for October 1849. Seeking distraction from the bruising defeat of the Emancipation Bill, the family travelled to Europe in July, and spent the summer weeks in a series of German spas.

At the end of July 1849 Charlotte arrived in a Frankfurt transformed not only by the death of her grandmother but also by political reaction. The previous month Prussian troops had entered the city, and the National Assembly had fled to Stuttgart, where it was soon dissolved. The Tricolour flags that had fluttered around the city were gone, and with them the atmosphere of democratic optimism. Writing to Louisa on 1 August, Charlotte described Frankfurt as 'full of shabby dirty-looking Prussian soldiers, and people say that what remains of German unity and its representatives is to be removed'.[33] The 'dirty, crumbling' synagogue was 'packed to suffocation', and the sermon was filled with the type of political allusions that she thought should 'be entirely banished from a place of worship'.[34] This, then, was the new Frankfurt: churned up by a reversed revolution, and bereft of the matriarch who, to the members of the Rothschild family, had defined it as home.

As Louisa predicted, Amschel had quickly recovered from the loss of his wife, and with all the talk of weddings in the air, his main regret now was that Eva had not died ten years earlier so that he could have remarried more easily. In honour of Charlotte's visit, Amschel held a dinner to which he invited various members of the Frankfurt branch of the family, including Chilly and her daughters, Mathilde and Julie.[35] The girls had just shed the mourning clothes they had worn in tribute to their great-grandmother, and now appeared in 'light summer dresses with long bright-coloured sashes and flowing ribbons and undulating flounces and airy lace scarfs'. During the meal, Amschel stunned his guests by announcing that he was to remarry. Not only that, but his bride would be Julie – his eighteen-year-old great-niece who was sitting right there at dinner.

It had not slipped Amschel's attention that over half a century separated him and his great-niece in age. Speaking calmly and strategically, he conceded that he might face some stiff competition from Louisa's brother, the young and still unmarried Joseph Montefiore, who was due to arrive in Frankfurt imminently. Clearly, though, he trusted that his position at the head of the family would outweigh his advanced years. The women thought differently. Each time the match was mentioned, Charlotte looked across the table and observed Julie's mother, Chilly, blushing with discomfort. As for Julie, 'the person most deeply interested in the question on which the felicity of her whole life depends', she remained, in Charlotte's words, 'motionless and impenetrable like a sphinx'.[36] The fact that the aged Amschel was in a position to stake this outrageous claim to a teenager and be met only with silence and blushes speaks to the disturbing power of the Rothschild men over the women of the family, and especially of the most senior ones.

Charlotte's concern was both for her niece, Julie, who would spend her youth at the side – and in the bed – of her great-uncle, and for the family's wider reputation. Such a marriage, she wrote to Louisa, would be 'a misfortune, an indelible stain on our escutcheon and on her fair fame, eternal disgrace'.[37] When she visited Betty and James in a spa town just outside Frankfurt, she was determined to broach the subject of the scandalous match. 'Betty tells me she has no doubt whatsoever that Uncle A. will lead Julie to the altar,' Charlotte relayed to Louisa.[38] 'The lady has no objection to wed her aged relative, and he is overjoyed at the idea of having made the conquest of his niece.' Julie may have had 'no objection', but she had her terms. 'The lady is to be at liberty to travel all over the world whenever she pleases,' reported Charlotte, 'to dine out, and eat forbidden fruit or meat whenever she thinks fit', and to receive an enormous cash payment 'for every kiss she bestows upon her aged spouse'. According to Charlotte, Amschel had 'cheerfully' agreed to all three conditions. The teenage Julie understood only too well that marriage in this family was a business deal, and she had struck one that would, albeit in very different circumstances, have made the men of the family proud.

In the event it was Charlotte's younger brother, Mayer Carl, who managed to knock some sense into the family. 'I am told that he will not hear of Julie's union with her almost octogenarian uncle,' reported Charlotte, who had been anxiously hoping that something or someone would stand in the way of the plan.[39] Her own protests would have been futile, but now that one of the men had objected, the plan was dropped. The whole drama had rather stolen the limelight from Willy and Mathilde, whose own wedding kept being postponed by various technical hitches. The strictly observant Willy was busy building a *mikveh* for his bride – something that attracted bewildered comment from Charlotte.[40] By late October, Charlotte could not wait any longer, and took her family back to London.[41] While disappointed to miss the celebrations, she was relieved to leave Frankfurt behind. Without Gutle at its heart, life in the city had seemed gloomy, strange and very off-kilter.

As well as stretching the patience of the family visiting Frankfurt, the postponement of the wedding had the unexpected consequence of depleting what little patience and trust survived between Louisa and Charlotte. Ongoing delays meant the window in which to buy wedding presents was extended, and throughout the autumn Louisa repeatedly found herself having to dash out from the 'little abode' she was renting in Paris, to purchase gifts on Charlotte's behalf.[42] In addition to a diamond wreath and headdress, 'a pretty watch attached to an elegant chain or chatelaine, a fan, a gold or enamelled comb, and a small corbeille de mariage' were all added to the shopping list.[43] Though such requests were routine among the family, Louisa was experiencing another bad bout of anxiety and nerves, and resented the imposition. Charlotte apologised for sending orders 'at a time when you were so little able to bear fatigue'.[44] Coming from anyone else it might have sounded genuine, but the outgoing and energetic Charlotte sometimes struggled to find sympathy for her pained, plaintive sister-in-law.

If there was a whiff of sarcasm to Charlotte's note, Louisa would have been the first to detect it. Increasingly, she had been reading her cousin's letters with a critical eye. With their polished descriptions, witty asides and elaborate set pieces, they struck Louisa as being more about performance than communication. 'Received what I call a vain letter from C, written evidently to be shown,' she wrote, after one especially theatrical missive.[45] And the faltering relationship was about to receive another blow. For over ten years now, Louisa's brother Joseph had been fishing about the Anglo-Jewish elite for an appropriate wife, and for a while it looked as if he had hooked a suitable candidate in Juliana Cohen. It was a bad enough blow when the deal fell through at the eleventh hour. But then it turned out that Juliana had not simply got cold feet. She intended to pursue a better prospective match, with Charlotte's brother-in-law, Mayer. Joseph Montefiore had been gazumped by the Rothschilds.[46]

For several months, bad feelings simmered between the women. In early March Louisa wrote a note to Charlotte 'expressing my sentiments', but rather than drawing the poison, that only seemed to inflame things.[47] While hosting the Cohens, she could not 'bear the idea of being friendly' to those who had 'behaved so ill towards my brother', and when Lionel and Mayer visited, she felt 'vexed and uncomfortable'.[48] In April 1851, after a year of barely concealed anger and seething diary entries, the storm broke: 'Yesterday was an eventful day for my quiet life, for I had a quarrel with Charlotte,' Louisa wrote. 'I must say it was quite unprovoked on my part . . .'[49]

While the subject of the quarrel was ostensibly the 'everlasting one of Juliana', really the tension between the sisters-in-law had been brewing for many years.[50] In 1847, when they had taken to the streets to help door to door with Lionel's political campaign, Louisa had confessed in her diary 'feelings of envy & discontent' as she trailed around in the shadow of the charismatic Charlotte.[51] As the years wore on, she had come to see in Charlotte's beauty and social grace evidence of a peacockish vanity, while Charlotte took Louisa's shyness and self-scrutiny for a wallowing sense of victimhood. Superficially, the two women reconciled within two weeks of their argument. But the root cause of the friction, the discrepancy in their characters, was not so easily solved.

The women's misfortunes were dwarfed by those that had recently struck their sister-in-law, Hannah Mayer. In 1848 her young son Arthur was out riding with his groom on Upper Grosvenor Street when his pony shied and threw him onto a pile of flints stacked up in preparation for road repairs.[52] The fall left him paralysed, and despite various, painful attempts at rehabilitation he remained an invalid.[53] Ten years later, at the age of only fifteen, he died.[54] While emotionally devastating for both parents, the death of Arthur crucified Henry Fitz-Roy. The dashing, big-hearted Gentile who had swept Hannah Mayer off her feet in the summer of 1838 developed a series of illnesses as he mourned his son's death.[55] On 17 December 1859, at the age of fifty-two, he died of a fever, leaving Hannah Mayer and young Blanche Elizabeth to fend for themselves.[56]

Though the formal exclusion against Hannah Mayer had relaxed somewhat in the aftermath of Gutle's death, it was still striking to many in the family that her plague of misfortunes – the postnatal complications, her son's painful accident, the premature loss of a husband and a child – had all begun with her marriage to a Christian. To the younger generation, who grew up grappling with the knowledge that there was something different and tainted about their aunt, this bad luck would take on a supernatural aspect: 'I cannot help thinking that all the misfortune and distress which have overwhelmed poor Aunt Hannah Mayer have been a punishment for having deserted the faith of her fathers,' wrote Constance, 'and for having married without her mother's consent.'[57] This was the sort of interpretation that developed over time, as family stories calcified into myth. To Charlotte and Louisa, who remained on affectionate terms with their black sheep of a sister-in-law, Hannah Mayer's suffering seemed not like divine retribution, but the result of multiple, terrible misfortunes that merited sympathy.

18

Loopholes and Legacies

WHILE TENSION AND suspicion simmered among the younger generation, Hannah remained unswerving in her commitment to the emancipation cause. In July 1849, when Lionel sought to restate his claim to his Commons seat by triggering a by-election, she defied her increasingly fragile health by returning to full-scale hosting, throwing open the doors of Piccadilly to politicians from both main parties. It was as if she sensed this was her last chance.

Lionel won his seat again, this time by a landslide.[1] He began working on a plan inspired by a Quaker MP, who had been able to take his seat by swearing an amended oath.[2] On 26 July 1850 Charlotte accompanied Lionel to the Commons, and watched from the public gallery as, amid applause from his allies, he approached the Speaker's table and was offered a copy of the Bible by the clerk.[3] 'I desire to be sworn upon the Old Testament,' Lionel announced. The chamber erupted, and Lionel was forced to bow out – but he had thrown down the gauntlet. The following Monday, when questioned in the Commons about why he had called for the Old Testament, Lionel explained: 'that is the form of swearing that I declare to be most binding on my conscience.'[4] That afternoon, in a stunning turn of events, MPs voted by a majority of fifty-four that Lionel be granted his wish.[5] The only obstacle that now remained was the phrase 'upon the true faith of a Christian'.[6] When the family returned the following day to the House, Lionel followed the instructions of the clerk but stopped short at this phrase, explaining: 'I omit those words as not binding on my conscience.' Placing his hat firmly on his head, he bowed to kiss the Old Testament, declaring: 'So help me, God.' There were loud calls to take his seat from friendly MPs, but Lionel had no intention of taking his seat 'by storm', as his Tory opponents had claimed he would: he obeyed the order to withdraw.[7]

The following month, when a vote to change the wording of the oath was debated in the House, only Disraeli and his colleague Lord George Bentinck broke ranks with the Protectionists to vote in favour of it, and what little progress the Rothschilds had made in the summer of 1850 was obstructed once again. The news hit Hannah hard. With the discovery of the loophole it must have seemed to her, briefly, as if emancipation would be achieved within her lifetime. It was not to be. Only a few weeks after the decisive defeat of the oath proposal in the Commons, while playing with Charlotte's daughters in the garden at Gunnersbury, Hannah collapsed.[8] The family held vigil by her bed for two weeks.[9] In comparison to this new family crisis, the resentment between Louisa and Charlotte over Juliana's marriage shrank into insignificance, and at Gunnersbury the women stood together alongside their anxious husbands. On 5 September 1850, Hannah Rothschild, widow of Nathan and matriarch of the English house, breathed her last. She was sixty-seven.

The death shattered the English family. 'Poor, dear aunt!' wrote Louisa.[10] 'If good and charitable deeds meet with their reward after death, surely you must be happy now. Few ever performed more acts of true beneficence than you did, nor I think ever possessed nobler and more generous feelings.' There was one final act of generosity yet to be discovered. Under the terms of Nathan's will, women who married against the wishes of the family were to be excluded from any Rothschild inheritance. In keeping with this edict, Hannah should have written Hannah Mayer out of her own will. Wishing neither to defy the conditions set by her dead husband nor to exclude her daughter, the ever-innovative Hannah had found her own loophole. She had not written a will at all. Having died intestate, her estate was divided equally between her children, with Hannah Mayer FitzRoy receiving the same share as her siblings.[11] It was the ultimate parting gift from a mother who, despite the family rift, had always loved her wayward daughter.

In May 1851 another Emancipation Bill died in the Commons, the only consolation being that Hannah was not around to see it. Louisa and Charlotte tried, in vain, to distract themselves with a visit to the wonders of the Great Exhibition, in Hyde Park's 'Crystal Palace'. Hannah was on their minds that day: with her hearty patriotism and enthusiasm for new technology, she would, Louisa commented, have been 'proud and pleased . . . to witness such a day for English intelligence, art, order, and loyalty'.[12] But after a trip through the medical and chemical departments – where they could learn about things as varied as the extraction of iodine from seaweed and the manufacture of gunpowder – even the pacifying thought of her 'poor Aunt' was not enough to soften Louisa's feelings towards Charlotte, which had hardened again since Hannah's death.[13] 'I am sure Charlotte remembered all she saw much better than I did,' she wrote. 'Her love of names, facts and what I should call tangible knowledge is infinitely greater than mine.'[14] There is no mistaking the damning faintness of her praise. The following afternoon, Louisa's friend Thackeray gave the first in a series of lectures on eighteenth-century literature. This was more her sort of thing: 'instructive talks' that dealt not with 'facts or deeds' but with 'original thoughts'.[15]

Her continued resentment towards Charlotte led to a cooling off in Louisa's support for Lionel's emancipation drive. 'Circumstances', she wrote, 'have made me less zealous and warm in favour of the representative of that cause.'[16] Though she wished Lionel 'every success', and still followed his progress keenly, she continued to struggle with the memory of his and Charlotte's betrayal in the matter of Joseph's engagement. Having stepped back from the campaign, she began to notice how much work there was to be done outside of Parliament, if emancipation was to be meaningful. Her work for the Cheap Jewish Library had given her a glimpse of the hardships under which most Jews laboured, and she had come to think that while Lionel's campaign might have been important to the likes of the Rothschilds, Montefiores and Salomons, winning civil rights would mean nothing to the vast majority of Jews, who were barely scratching a living.[17] Like the previous generation of Rothschilds, Louisa was convinced that the Jews of London's East End would only achieve security and employment as they became more English, and like the previous generation, the best vehicle she had for promoting such anglicisation was the Jews' Free School.

Louisa's husband, Anthony, had recently been appointed president of the board of governors of the Jews' Free School – the same institution that his mother, Hannah, had championed so passionately. Louisa's fear that her husband would be 'too busy with the elections' to make good on his promise to alleviate the 'misery of the Jews of the City' turned out to be well founded, and she soon realised that if she wanted to make a difference, she would have to take matters

*Louisa de Rothschild, mother of
Constance and Annie.*

into her own rather more diligent hands.[18] She started visiting regularly and resolved to 'take a real time interest in the free school & hope to be of some use there'.[19] She was 'anxious to go about among the poor and lighten a little their heavy burdens', but there was self-interest here too. Her relationship with Charlotte was just one of several that had faltered during a period of deep and depressive unsociability. At one low point, recorded in her diary, she had found herself sitting in a 'smart room' awaiting her 'smart guests' and had been assailed by the thought: 'what a fuss for poor creatures who will soon be food for worms'.[20] The 'active occupation' of going to help at the Free School became the 'best cure' for what Louisa described as her 'shy & miserable ... unsocial feelings'.[21]

The school was in the throes of transformation. In the late 1840s a change in funding arrangements meant that the JFS had its first government inspection. The inspector responsible for the Spitalfields area – the young poet and Oxford fellow, Matthew Arnold – had been impressed by the standard of teaching, but had pointed out that six classrooms (two for boys, two for girls, and two for the Talmud Torah) were insufficient for the nearly two thousand students now in attendance.[22] In the 1850s four thousand pounds would be spent on renovating the site, and on decorating what had hitherto been austerely simple classrooms of bare brick.[23] Arnold was so impressed with the changes at the school that he selected the JFS as the location for the general examination of pupil-teachers in London, and used his next report to praise the management.[24] Such praise meant a great deal to Louisa, who, as well as being reassured that her work at the JFS was having some effect, was developing an enormous personal respect and affection for Arnold; over the coming years he would become a 'dear, kind, genial friend'.[25]

Arnold's endorsement also boosted the school's wider reputation, and within a short time the JFS had begun to attract the attention of educationalists, journalists and well-intentioned upper-class sight-seers. Annie Thackeray, daughter of William Makepeace, wrote an article on the school for the *Cornhill Magazine*, and a reporter for the *Weekly Dispatch*, who had been sent to the school's annual dinner, praised the institution's achievements in shaping a generation of honest, educated and very English children.[26] In case the relevance of this praise to the ongoing emancipation debates was not clear enough already, the author made it explicit:

Bah! To think of the cant and trash that contrive to keep Baron Rothschild at the threshold of the Commons, when any wiseacre with eyes in his head might see the distinctions between Jew and Gentile, at all times the result of external circumstances, are daily becoming less as the conditions that surround them are becoming identical.

Further opportunities for Louisa to take the educational 'cure' would soon arise from unexpected quarters. In 1852 she and Anthony finally obtained the country house she longed for when they took on Aston Clinton, an estate near Aylesbury that had been in the family's property portfolio for several years.[27] The following May, Louisa visited with her daughters and her mother, Henriette, and commented cautiously that '[t]he place looked pretty enough to make me like it'.[28] Come August, she and her family were 'quietly established in our own little country house'.[29] A 'ten years' dream' had been realised; 'and am I happy at its realization?' she asked. Louisa had a romantic idea of life in the country based on idealised memories of her childhood at her mother's house in Worth.[30] A property that had been bought by the family as an investment was not likely to satisfy such nostalgic cravings. She tried to convince herself of her affection for the place by praising it as 'unpretentious' and 'comfortable', but the fact remained: 'Aston Clinton is not the country house that I dreamt of.'[31]

A short distance away from Aston Clinton, Mayer and his wife Juliana were in the process of completing work on their own Buckinghamshire mansion. On 31 December 1851, along with their six-month-old daughter Hannah, they laid the foundation stone for the family's future home. When construction was completed in 1854, Mentmore had twenty-six bedrooms, hot running water and a huge glass-roofed hall designed by Joseph Paxton himself. It was decorated with lanterns made for the Doge of Venice, a series of tapestries by Gobelin, and a large collection of antique furniture from sixteenth-century Italy and eighteenth-century France.[32] It was, wrote one visitor, a 'Venetian villa' in the middle of Buckinghamshire – 'rather palace than villa', in fact.[33] Louisa, who became a frequent visitor to the house, was not immune to its attractions, and admitted to feeling 'a slight pang of jealousy or envy rather' when she compared it to her own country house.[34] There was only one thing for it: renovation. She and Anthony commissioned George Henry Stokes, an assistant of Joseph Paxton, to draw up designs for a remodelled Aston Clinton.[35]

Stokes's plans would take several years to realise. In the meantime, what began to win her over to Aston Clinton was not any alteration or improvement, but the pleasure that the place brought to her children. Even before they moved in, Louisa wrote in her diary that ten-year-old Constance and eight-year-old Annie had 'declared they were so happy they did not know how to contain their joy!'[36]

While work in the East End had given Louisa a passing acquaintance with urban poverty, the scale of rural deprivation around her new home came as a shock. 'The country was delightful, so quiet, fresh and green, but alas, how much misery and sorrow exist in those tranquil shades and daisied meadows where all looks so bright and peaceful,' she wrote in June.[37] The only day school in Aston Clinton was, as Constance later recalled, 'kept by a drunken schoolmaster, who had about thirty miserable dejected-looking male scholars', and the only alternative to this 'disgracefully bad' school was the 'plaiting school', where old working-women taught children how to plait straw – an important cottage industry in the area.[38] During her youth, Louisa and her sister had worked with a local parish priest to set up a new, improved village school in Worth.[39] She became determined to combine the lessons she had learnt there about rural Christian education with her more recent experience from the Jews' Free School in London, to make real improvements in the Buckinghamshire schools.

She must have talked about it at home, for as she started developing ideas for the improvement of the local schools, Constance and Annie began their own acts of educational vigilantism. Armed with 'some lesson books', they went down to the plaiting school and 'proceeded to instruct the little "plaiters"'.[40] It became a regular engagement, and the girls were enthused enough that they went 'further afield to another school of the same sort in our village'. When, on one 'damp, warm afternoon in autumn', Louisa found her girls engaged in their favourite pastime, she was horrified at the haphazard arrangement and the insalubrious conditions, and forbade any further teaching.

Determined to show her girls that their 'youthful attempts at instruction should give place to some method of real education', Louisa persuaded Anthony to fund the construction of a girls' school for Aston Clinton.[41] To Constance and Annie, this was enormously exciting. They made frequent visits to the building site, Constance testing the growth of the walls by 'going each day to jump over them, until my efforts were out-distanced by the masons' work'. Once the school was built, the 'real good' could begin.[42] Within a few terms, Matthew Arnold was invited up from London, to make the first of what would become regular inspections.[43]

Then, in the summer of 1854, tragedy struck. Just one week after giving birth, Louisa's sister Charlotte Montefiore died from postnatal complications. 'My best, my dearest friend gone for ever – for ever from this earth I mean, for I cannot believe that a pure, active, loving spirit is destroyed,' Louisa wrote.[44] As she grieved, Louisa resolved to honour her sister's memory by redoubling her efforts to improve educational opportunities in both Buckinghamshire and the East End. At the end of September, she wrote in her diary:

The poor at Aston Clinton and Halton must now claim my care and our own poor Jewish brethren. It was [my sister] Charlotte's greatest wish to improve their moral and intellectual condition, I must both for her sake and theirs try to follow in her wake and do all I can to raise them.[45]

Pain and loss had only confirmed Louisa in her newfound vocation.

While Louisa focused on her charitable work in Buckinghamshire, Rothschild life in London continued to revolve around emancipation. Still unable to take his seat, Lionel spent the 1850s acting as a kind of external lobbyist – an MP without a seat – on Jewish issues.[46] Charlotte too had changed tack, joining Louisa's efforts to help students at the JFS achieve what the *Jewish Chronicle* had referred to as 'emancipation within' – the emancipation of literacy, of employability, and of cultural and religious knowledge.[47] Charlotte began writing her own religious addresses.[48] Sometimes she travelled to Bell Lane to give her 'poor sermons' herself; sometimes her daughters, Leonora and Evelina, delivered the addresses she had written.[49]

By the time of the 1857 general election, emancipation had become a prominent political issue, debated in constituencies far beyond Lionel's. In 1857 Viscount Chelsea, a High-Church Tory, had declared his intention to stand in the seat of Middlesex, within which Gunnersbury was situated.[50] The seat had been dominated by the Liberals for the last few decades, but Chelsea's candidacy – which represented the arrival of a new, rabidly reactionary voice – appeared to be riding high on local Tory support. Undeterred by heavy rain, Lionel and Charlotte travelled up from Gunnersbury to attend the hustings. Flanked by twenty menacing militiamen, Chelsea did his best to whip up antisemitic sentiment.[51] Should a Jew take a seat in Parliament, he ranted, 'they would feel compelled to do all in their power to put down the Christian nation'.[52] Channelling his anger and shock, Lionel put himself forward to speak and, after a show of hands in his favour, was allowed to take the platform, where he launched into a rousing speech decrying Chelsea. Charlotte, meanwhile, stood in stunned silence.

Back at Gunnersbury, she wrote to Chelsea. 'My Lord,' she began. 'I have no words sufficiently vivid to express my astonishment to your speech of the 1st of April.' Jews, she explained, in her precise but biting prose, 'never try to make proselytes. Faithful to their own creed, they do not, either directly or indirectly, endeavour to undermine the religious opinions of others.' Jews 'respect all religions and all varieties of religious belief'.[53] Charlotte, like Louisa, had spent much of the 1850s not in parliamentary intrigues and Commons spectatorship, but out among the Jewish population at grass-roots level, teaching and reading and writing. Her letter to Chelsea represented the culmination of that communal work, with its emphasis on Jewish identity and dignity rather than on legal freedoms. She sent the letter anonymously: the point was not to speak with the authority of the Rothschild name, but to let the argument speak for itself. In the election, a few days later, Chelsea was defeated. Over in the City, Lionel himself was elected once again.[54]

Everything was political. The March 1857 nuptials of Charlotte's daughter Leonora to James and Betty's son Alphonse were choreographed to illustrate the family's blending of Jewish tradition with English respectability, and were favourably reported in newspaper stories, which also reflected on the family's 'enterprise, prudence and industry'.[55] The wedding was only the beginning of a much larger social offensive: in March Charlotte hosted a 'grand juvenile ball' at Gunnersbury for over a hundred children, was at Carlton House for a dinner thrown by the prodigious hostess Lady Waldegrave, attended by a range of sitting lords, and, on the 21st, brought together Benjamin and Mary Anne Disraeli for dinner with Lord John Russell, the former prime minister and long-standing Liberal champion of emancipation.[56]

Russell had been instrumental in devising a new plan to break the parliamentary deadlock. Lionel, he suggested, should be voted onto a Commons committee, to contribute to a report on the reform of oaths. For Charlotte, it was, she wrote to her husband, 'breaking my heart not to see you take your seat', and among the wider family, hopes ran high. 'Pray tell Papa he must not make his maiden speech until we arrive,' wrote Leonora to her mother, from Paris.[57] This time, the optimism was not misplaced. The committee published a report recommending that Jewish members should be allowed to omit the phrase 'on the true faith of a Christian' if the house in which they were seeking a seat allowed it.[58] The Commons had cut themselves free from the Lords' objections. On Monday, 26 July 1858 – eight years to the day after his first dramatic march into the Commons – Lionel once again entered the House, and stated that he had a conscientious objection to the prescribed oath. Lord John Russell proposed a new oath, to be sworn on the Old Testament, omitting the 'true faith of a Christian' phrase. The resolution was passed by a majority of thirty-two. Lionel could at last take his seat.[59]

19

Living in Hotels

SUMMERS IN LONDON could be unbearable: the heat exacerbated the stench of the horse manure that piled up in the streets, and of the untreated waste that – with the city's new sewage system yet to be completed – still drained through channels intended for rainwater, towards the River Thames. Those who could do so, escaped the city – to the countryside or to Europe. For Charlotte in the early 1860s there was an extra reason to leave London: no. 148 Piccadilly was undergoing extensive renovations, and although the family's temporary base at Kingston House in Kensington was pleasant enough, it was not home. So in August 1861 she travelled up to Grasmere, in the Lake District.

The hotel she stayed in had been built in the mid 1850s to cater to the tourist trade that burgeoned on the back of Romantic interest in the Lakes.[1] A recent visit from the heir to the throne had drawn it to the attention of high society, and the owner, Mr Edward Brown, had attempted to capitalise on this attention by renaming what had been the Lakes Hotel the Prince of Wales.[2] When Charlotte arrived, however, the social circle at the hotel was 'tiny', and the gentlemen 'chiefly reverends'; in the coffee room there were stifled sniggers when the waiter collided with the lemonade urn. It would – Charlotte reported to her children with astonishment – take a whole five days for a letter sent from Frankfurt to reach the hotel. She continued to conduct her London affairs remotely, writing to Leo with instructions to make payments, collect birthday presents and call on dressmakers.[3] It took the arrival of Natty and his tutor Mr Wright, who had come equipped with immense iron-pronged Alpine stocks, to draw her attention away from her correspondence and into the glorious outdoors.[4]

She was better practised at wry social commentary than she was at describing the natural world, but after Lionel arrived, she tried her hand at the latter, writing about an excursion to Patterdale through scenery 'wild in the superlative degree', with 'mountain streams rolling over boulders' and 'the animal kingdom represented by lean sheep, noisy crows, ugly dogs and non-beautiful tourists'.[5] Back at the hotel, Mr Brown had installed a cannon on the terrace, 'to wake the echoes that slumber among the surrounding mountains'. 'You can have no idea of the magical effect,' wrote Charlotte to her daughter Evelina. The next day she went out in a boat with Natty, to experience the echoes at a closer range. Convention was to call out the names of loved ones, but mother and son, whose names appeared frequently in the newspapers, were shy about such a public display, and instead shouted the names of characters in *Great Expectations*, which they had just been reading in serialised form.

August in London was the off-season, and would usually have struck Charlotte as 'dull and empty', but after the seclusion of the Lakes, even the deserted capital seemed 'wonderfully animated' when she returned.[6] Charlotte met with Louisa and gossiped about a family engagement. At Grosvenor Place, she bumped into Constance and Annie, arriving home in their silver-grey riding habits after a gallop round Hyde Park. But it was only a few weeks before she was off again, this time across the Channel to the French capital.

In Paris, the fog – a murky white to London's yellow, Charlotte noted – swirled around the streets and squares, concealing the top of Napoleon's column in the Place Vendôme.[7] Like Hannah before her, Charlotte was determined to be present when her daughters gave birth. This time she had come to the side of her heavily pregnant eldest, Leonora, who had moved to Paris following her marriage to Betty and James's son Alphonse. Charlotte had barely settled into her hotel, the Bristol, when she was summoned to welcome her grandson into the world. The baby spent two days drifting in and out of sleep, staring up at visitors with his dark blue eyes, and barely crying.[8] He was plump enough, wrote Charlotte, to invite comparisons with 'the quails and ortolans upon which your sister feasted con amore, while the traveller was on his journey into the world'.[9] In keeping with French upper-class custom, Leonora was confined to her bed for several weeks after the birth, and forbidden from reading, writing or working.[10] Her eating was closely regulated: the first step towards a normal diet came a full six days after the birth, when she was allowed hot chocolate for breakfast and a chicken wing at dinner.[11] The stuffiness of the

Parisian postnatal rituals grated with Charlotte, who reported to Leo that his older sister was bearing 'the ennui of her imprisonment as well as can be expected'.[12]

Lionel arrived in Paris on 17 October, and the family went to the *mairie* to inscribe the infant's name in the register: Lionel James Mayer René de Rothschild.[13] Even by Rothschild standards this was a mouthful, and in a letter home Charlotte wryly inserted commas between each of the names. Leonora's husband, Alphonse, had decided that the child would be known as René; Charlotte did not care for the alliteration of 'René Rothschild', commenting that her son-in-law's ears were 'not very musical'.[14] She thought the circumcision operation had been borne 'admirably well' by the baby, but within a few days René became feverish and broke out in a rash. Charlotte wrote home reporting that 'our dear baby had been suddenly seized with erysipelas' – an acute disease caused by bacterial infection.[15] The doctor prescribed an ointment of belladonna and poultices made of corn starch.

In order not to impede Leonora's recovery, and in the hope that the infection would pass, Charlotte and Alphonse decided not to share the news about René's illness with her. It was all Charlotte could do to 'ardently hope and trust and pray' that by the time her daughter was allowed out of her bedroom a few days later, René's condition would have improved.[16] Her prayers went unanswered. After emerging from her room, Leonora still spent most of the day on the sofa, and although it might have been possible to conceal the desperate operation of tending to the baby, René was now in such a critical condition that recovery no longer seemed likely. On 31 October Leonora was finally told the full extent of her son's illness.[17] Three days later René died. Charlotte could not bring herself to write anything.

At the Bristol and the rue Saint-Georges, endless 'melancholy conversations' turned on the same subject: 'the irrevocable past, the causes of our darling's illness, and its fatal termination'.[18] The possibility that the infection had happened as a result of the ritual circumcision was painful to consider in private, and very sensitive in its public aspect. If illness or death had arisen from the operation, it would provide ammunition to antisemites desperate to depict the *brit milah* as abusive or dangerous. Sensitive to that risk, most of the family were angry at the doctors for maintaining and repeating 'throughout Paris' that the fatal infection was the result of the operation.[19] Charlotte, who would normally have understood such concern, was numbed by grief into not caring. '[W]hy should they conceal it?' she wrote of the doctors. 'I never saw a more perfect baby, or a more healthy one before the terrible day.' Soon she was reaching even more drastic conclusions. 'I wish the ceremony could be abolished,' she wrote to her son Leo.[20]

Following her bereavement, Leonora was again confined to her bedroom and it was several days before she could bring herself to be carried down to the drawing room.[21] Alphonse took his meals by her side.[22] Having previously been depicted in letters to England as soppy and tone deaf, Charlotte's son-in-law began to win her esteem through his devotion. His most pressing task, the whole family agreed, was to help Leonora escape the tragic associations of the rue Saint-Georges, by finding them a new house.[23] It was a bad time to be house-hunting in Paris. Old districts were being demolished and 'endless distractions and constructions were going on simultaneously' along the new network of boulevards, where old mansions were being pulled down to make room for new apartment blocks that rose like 'towers of Babel, eight stories high'.[24] There were few suitable houses available and the rent on those that were had become 'fabulously dear'.[25] Eventually, they reconciled themselves to moving into one of James's existing properties by the Place de la Concorde.

Back in London, Prince Albert had died, and the city was shrouded in black – banners, rosettes and clothes.[26] The children's painting teacher, Mr Corbould, told the Rothschilds of the tense time his more famous brother – one of Queen Victoria's favourite painters – was having at Windsor, where he was attempting to capture the monarch's 'very red eyes'.[27] Early in 1862, while mourning for the Prince was still evident around the city, the Rothschilds were dealt yet another blow. Charlotte's son Alfred fell seriously ill, and was forced to come home from university in Cambridge to Kingston House.[28]

As summer set in, and Alfred's condition stabilised, Charlotte made arrangements for a restorative trip to the seaside at Folkestone.[29] The day the family set off, the main roads east through the city were so clogged with traffic that they were forced to divert through backstreets.[30] Charlotte stared through the carriage window at the 'unwashed children all in rags and tatters', and reflected on the enormous poverty that lay 'in the background of the great prosperity and wealth' in the capital.[31] This glimpse of another world seems to have acted as a wake-up call for her, and the remainder of the journey to Folkestone

– including the special invalid carriage that was added at London Bridge for Alfred – was documented in her letters with a new sense of gratitude for all the comfort and luxury that her son had access to in the midst of his illness.

Alfred soon recovered. After a few weeks of rest in the Hotel Pavilion, he was looking a 'picture of health' – indeed 'fat', Charlotte noted with happy relief, 'very fat'.[32] He chatted with passing aristocrats through the window of his hotel room, and was transported in a little donkey carriage to one of the squares along the cliff, to hear a band play. The music in Folkestone was almost continuous, wafting in six days a week from the green sward outside the hotel and the bandstands along the cliff: 'soul-stirring strains' from a Scottish regimental band as well as by an 'aetheopian' group whose songs were 'really very funny ... and some of them extremely melodious'.[33] Holidaying in a resort town like Folkestone, where there were, Charlotte wrote, 'no Jews', was both a deeply acculturated act and also one that intensified her sense of distance from the Christian world surrounding her. She noted with renewed attention the atmosphere of Sundays, 'being the strictly kept Sabbath of the English world', when the music ceased and 'all the co-quettish, funny little hats disappear', replaced by plainer bonnets.[34]

There were minor stresses and strains. Matilda, the orthodox wife of Charlotte's brother Willy, had announced her intention to join the family for a fortnight, and for several days Charlotte was absorbed in the task of finding someone who could provide her 'pious relative' with strictly kosher meals.[35] A contact in the Dover congregation could send kosher provisions and a Christian cook was 'used to jewish meals', but Charlotte suspected that Matilda would 'fly from the sin of such an arrangement', and so resorted to telegramming contacts in the 'orthodox portions of London' to find a cook. It had been years since she and her family loosened their dietary observances, and she found herself depending on more orthodox friends for advice on 'the best Jewish restaurant' in the West End. 'It is to be hoped', she wrote, 'that within the last ten or eleven years, the orthodox cuisine has improved in London.'[36]

No sooner had the *cordon bleu* been identified and summoned, than new and more worrying problems presented themselves. As he entered his fifties, Lionel had been increasingly afflicted by rheumatic gout – a complaint that would persist, causing him great pain during the final decades of his life. In Folkestone, the gout flared up, his feet swelling until they no longer fitted in his boots, and his knees requiring endless applications of soothing chestnut oil. But in the midst of it all, Charlotte retained some of the perspective she had earned on the miserable journey through London's backstreets. Leonora and Leo, who were currently travelling around Europe, sent a letter to Charlotte complaining of the ugliness of people in the mountains. 'My dear Laurie,' Charlotte replied, 'while you are surrounded by the grandest scenery on earth ... and ugly specimens of humanity, we are domiciled in a most uninteresting spot, unhallowed by art, science, history, or the beauty of nature, but literally teeming with human loveliness.'[37] It was an optimism she had to work hard to sustain through the ensuing winter season, which was spent – this time with Lionel's rather than Alfred's health in mind – in the dowdier surroundings of Torquay society. Living in hotels and buffeted by illness and mortality, Charlotte had become keenly aware of the most important ingredient in her happiness: not landscape, or luxury, but other people.

On her eventual return to London, Charlotte's energy was absorbed by the Piccadilly building project. The shell of the rebuilt no. 148 Piccadilly had been completed early in 1862, accompanied by a burst of publicity in the newspapers and building journals.[38] The *Builder* reported breathlessly on the concrete foundations and Portland stone exterior as well as the servants' halls, pantries, wine cellars, strongrooms, columned galleries, first-floor reception rooms, eight-foot-wide marble staircase and vast upper hinterland of bedrooms.[39] But for all the publicity, the building was still far from finished, and Charlotte spent her first months back in London checking on the progress of the remaining works.[40] On 3 November 1863 she saw the roof lit up with new gaslighting, with the effect 'good but improvable'; in April the following year she had to shake the dust and plaster from the folds of her skirt after a visit to what was still, unmistakably and expensively, a building site.[41]

In late May the place was finally habitable, and Lionel was able to ride between the floors on the Otis Brothers safety lift. (Thanks to an innovative locking mechanism that dramatically reduced the chance of accidents, Otis Brothers had transformed the lifts into a high-tech feature of hotels and mansions.) The bleak admission implied by the purchase of the lift – that Lionel's gout was not going to get better any time soon – was forgotten in the pleasure of riding it to the top floor, to watch a military parade in Hyde Park.[42]

The West End was still the centre of English Rothschild life, and a return to Piccadilly meant a resumption of the usual dramas of family life: the friendships, deaths, fallouts and marriages. The biggest recent development was the engagement of Hannah Mayer's daughter, Blanche. Her talent at drawing and painting had been evident from a young age, and she had fallen in with an artistic set at Little Holland House, where she had met a baronet called Sir Coutts Lindsay – a tall, distinguished, silver-haired man. Though he was related to the Coutts banking family, it was through his mother, and Sir Coutts had pursued a military career, before becoming a patron of the visual arts.[43] Lionel had given his support to the match, and Charlotte was overjoyed. Coutts, in her opinion, was 'excellent and admirable in every relation of life . . . and the most accomplished of men, good and clever, full of talent and highly cultivated, in short perfection'.[44] The fact that he was not Jewish was relatively unimportant – Hannah Mayer's apostasy meant that any child of hers was considered an outsider to the family, and their marriage exempt from the usual strict terms.

Hannah Mayer had been confined to her bed by a long and painful illness, and when Charlotte visited her sister-in-law after returning from Torquay, she had been forced to disguise her horror on seeing a growth 'as prominent as the hump of a camel' that had developed on Hannah's back.[45] Charlotte hoped that the news of the engagement would have provided a momentary reprieve from the illness, and so was surprised, on her arrival at Upper Grosvenor Street, to find that Hannah Mayer had 'been crying and sobbing indeed almost shrieking'.[46] 'The congratulations', Charlotte wrote, 'died on my lips.'

Although Hannah Mayer had acquiesced in the proposal, it turned out that Coutts Lindsay had not satisfied her high standards. The baronet was far too old, she explained to Charlotte, and his title was not as high as she had hoped for in a son-in-law. Hannah Mayer's high opinion of her daughter was legendary. As Charlotte wrote two years previously: 'Aunt HM has always been convinced that Blanchy's dazzling beauty causes all continentals to stare her out of countenance on rail-roads and high roads and by-roads, on steamers and at hotels.'[47] So a match anything less than perfect was bound to cause distress. But Charlotte suspected there was more at play here than disappointment. Blanche's 'rapturous' happiness had brought home to Hannah Mayer the bleakness of her own situation, imprisoned in bed and crippled with pain.

Hannah Mayer's anxieties struck Charlotte as overblown, but they would soon turn out to have been justified. Over the following weeks, Blanche became so absorbed by her relationship that she barely visited her mother. She and Coutts arranged to spend August in Scotland and then the winter in Rome.[48] Initially, Charlotte tried to persuade herself that what seemed from the outside to be cruel disregard was just romantically induced blindness – that Blanche was 'in a sort of paradise' and 'cannot know how ill her mother is'.[49] However, when Blanche continued to spurn her mother after the wedding, Charlotte's patience expired.[50] 'What a horrible humbug and heartless hypocrite Blanche, Lady L. is,' she wrote to Leo.[51] She continued her regular visits to Upper Grosvenor Street. When Hannah Mayer was not in extreme pain, she was drowsy from codeine, and when neither in pain nor drugged, she raged 'against every body and every thing'– except her own daughter, against whom she was incapable of bearing a grudge.[52] Charlotte bore the brunt of Hannah Mayer's fury with a stoic calm, but came away from her vigils feeling thoroughly depressed.

In August 1864 Charlotte and her family retreated to Gunnersbury. It was another sweltering summer. In the city, hostesses struggled in vain to limit the damage – 'the wines warm, the water tepid, the cream turned' – and at their estate to the west of London, the family found the grass scorched brown, the flower beds 'burnt up' and a group of old beech trees 'sinking into an untimely grave'.[53] These would be soporific months, filled with reading in the shade and gambols with the growing menagerie of pets, which now included dogs, a monkey and a new macaw that Evelina had taught to say the word 'Mamma' in a way that greatly unnerved Charlotte.[54] Leonora was pregnant once more and, in September 1864, Charlotte left for Paris. A telegram sent to Gunnersbury at eleven p.m. narrowly missed her, so it was only as she was passing through Amiens the following day that she received news of Leonora's confinement. This time, there were no dramas. From Paris, Charlotte wrote describing 'a little beauty, with a quiet temper, and very pretty features'.[55] As if hedging their bets after the recent tragedy of Lionel James Mayer René's death, Leonora and Alphonse gave the new arrival only two names: Charlotte Beatrice, to be known as Beatrice.

Back in London, Blanche's self-absorbed behaviour had contin-ued during Charlotte's absence. In letters to Leo, Charlotte described her niece as an 'unnatural daughter', 'that heartless, incomprehensible woman' and a 'heartless serpent' who was too 'immensely happy at being Lady Lindsay . . . to feel deep anxiety for her suffering and per-haps dying mother'.[56] Sometimes she was simply 'the icicle'.[57] When, in mid November, Blanche became pregnant and was incapacitated with morning sickness, Charlotte and Louisa paid a dutiful visit to Grosvenor Square, and found Blanche 'giggling and simpering' on a sofa.[58] Scattered evidence of Blanche's continued indulgence in music and art, and the way she 'asked after her dying mother as if the poor sufferer had had a mere cold', pushed Charlotte's opinion of her niece to a new low. Blanche, she thought, might be 'a monster'.[59]

In December Charlotte visited Upper Grosvenor Street to find Hannah Mayer lying 'speechless, motionless, as cold as ice, with eyes wide open'.[60] The attending doctor told her that she ought to 'send quickly for Lady Lindsay'. Hannah Mayer repeatedly kissed and blessed her daughter, asked her when the baby would be born, begged that her grandchild would be given a pretty name, and, after this brief and fevered reconciliation, lapsed into a painful decline. She died later that evening. With the exception of seven hundred pounds left 'to the poor', and some small bequests to her staff, she had left everything to Blanche.[61] It was a bitter reminder of the unequal relationship be-tween mother and daughter. But in one way it came as a relief: with no Rothschilds named in the will or appointed as executors, there would be no 'pretext for disagreement' and no grim legal proceedings to accompany the death.

Hannah Mayer had been terrified of being buried alive and, as insurance against this, had requested that her body lie for a week in an open coffin at Upper Grosvenor Street before being interred.[62] This request was alien and frightening, and when a waiting woman at Upper Grosvenor Street asked Charlotte if she would visit the body again, five days after death, to observe how well Hannah Mayer's last wishes had been honoured, she agreed with trepidation, fearing a 'painful change' in the body's appearance.[63] But the waiting woman was right. The body had been prepared 'well and tenderly and care-fully' and 'there was not the slightest alteration' in Hannah Mayer's appearance: 'calm and smiling she lay in her coffin'. After this unusual farewell, Charlotte steeled herself and made the short trip to see her bereaved niece. Blanche, it turned out, was on the point of leaving London for the Lindsay family estate at Lockinge in Berkshire. 'Not until after the last mournful ceremony,' Charlotte exclaimed, stunned that Blanche would miss her own mother's funeral. 'Oh! Yes!' Blanche responded; 'I cannot be of any use – Coutts wishes me to go, the Doctor insists upon it.' Charlotte left in disgust.

On the day of the funeral, Charlotte and Louisa sat with Hannah Mayer's body in Upper Grosvenor Street and mused on the 'long martyrdom' that was their cousin's life. The daughter of Hannah and Nathan Rothschild had suffered ostracism, tragic accidents and multiple bereavements. But most painful of all for Charlotte to witness had been that final cruelty – a daughter's neglect of a mother in need.

20

A Mother's Lesson

EVELINA DE ROTHSCHILD had grown up in the shadow of her older sister, Leonora. In the eyes of society, she was the lesser of the two: less beautiful, less talented, less eligible. It was a judgement that Charlotte was not prepared to swallow. During the late 1840s, before Evelina even reached her teens, Charlotte made numerous attempts to improve her daughter's complexion with diets, lotions and visits to specialist doctors. She kept a wary eye on her figure, which, at the age of ten, was already deemed too 'tall and stout for her age' and 'somewhat less graceful' than it had been.[1] The wrong kind of look could attract the wrong kind of man. In 1851, when Evelina was just twelve, Charlotte had been bemused by a romantic approach made by a civil engineer called Frederick Glass who, after spotting Evelina at the Great Exhibition, had written to ask for her hand in marriage. It was a notion so absurd that Lionel took the request to be a hoax. But the fact that Evelina was attracting people her parents considered to be little more than glorified mechanics confirmed everything Charlotte feared.

If Evelina shared her mother's concerns, she managed to hide it behind a carefree and joyous demeanour. It was this lightness of spirit that attracted her cousin, Ferdinand de Rothschild, who proposed on 19 January 1865.[2] Ferdinand, Chilly's younger son, had grown up in Frankfurt, but had always felt a keen affinity with England and his English cousins. A few summers previously, he had flirted with Constance, Louisa's daughter, and later exchanged letters with her.[3] But it amounted to nothing. Further visits to England had drawn him closer to Charlotte's family, with whom his warmth, wit and artistic instincts made him a great favourite.[4] Both Charlotte and Evelina were thrilled by the match. At the end of February, Ferdinand joined the family for dinner at Piccadilly House, where he boasted lovingly that he wanted Evelina's wedding jewels to be more beautiful and tasteful than any others that had been worn in the family.[5] The couple decided to settle in England, and chose a mansion at no. 143 Piccadilly, just a few doors down from Evelina's childhood home.

The sumptuous wedding was held at the new no. 148, Piccadilly House. After being walked into the ballroom, Ferdinand stood under a velvet canopy borne by his four *garçons d'honneur*.[6] Evelina descended the stairs to the ballroom wearing a Parisian lace and satin white gown adorned with orange flowers, and followed by fourteen bridesmaids, among them Constance and Annie. The ceremony was conducted in Hebrew by the chief rabbi, Dr Adler, and at the grand banquet that followed Benjamin Disraeli proposed a toast. Having fretted and fussed over her daughter's attractiveness and eligibility, it seemed – at this point – that Charlotte had achieved a fairy-tale ending.

Shortly before Evelina and Ferdinand's wedding, John Thadeus Delane, the family's friend and editor of *The Times*, had come to Piccadilly House to dine with Charlotte and discuss a question that would dominate politics during the mid 1860s: the potential enlargement of the franchise.[7] Long experience of campaigning for reform had taught Charlotte something about the shoddiness of arguments used to prop up the current parliamentary system against outsiders, and she was convinced that Parliament had to change with the times. The first step, she believed, was to make a small adjustment in the franchise to include the artisan classes: the artisans of the 1860s were, after all, 'infinitely better educated' than the ten-pound householders had been thirty years earlier, when they were lifted into the existing franchise.[8] The morning after her meeting with Delane, Charlotte's views would be reproduced in the leader column of Delane's newspaper.[9]

In late 1865 Prime Minister Lord Palmerston died suddenly, and Lord John Russell – now Earl Russell – formed a government for the second time. The Parliament that opened in February 1866 had three Rothschild men sitting as MPs: Lionel; his younger brother, Mayer; and his son, Natty, who had just been elected for Aylesbury. Charlotte visited the Lords to watch the Queen's Speech. Of the speech itself she heard little: Chancellor of the Exchequer, William Gladstone, who delivered it, 'mumbled ... quite, quite inaudibly', and anyway she, like most people present, was preoccupied with the sight of the Queen, who was appearing in an official capacity for the first time since Albert's death.[10] Still stricken with grief, Victoria sat on her throne 'as motionless, if not as white as a marble statue'. It was only when Charlotte got home and read the speech in the papers, that she took in one of its elements: 'I have directed that information should be procured in reference to the rights of voting in the election of members to serve [P]arliament.'[11] Charlotte would not have been fooled by the cautious wording. Russell was a committed reformer, and electoral reform was going to be the defining issue of this Parliament.

Since the emancipation debates, when Gladstone had made a 'fine, silver-toned' speech 'in our favour', both Charlotte and Louisa had admired him from a distance.[12] Within weeks of the opening of Parliament, the new Chancellor began appearing on guest lists at Piccadilly House.[13] Though Charlotte was obviously attracted by Gladstone's views on reform, she remained a distinctly cross-party hostess, and he sat down with guests of various political persuasions. In times of deep political division like this one, hosting required care and tact. Breadth of opinion was desirable, but a guest list that included sworn political enemies was not. A practised hostess would not invite Gladstone to dine with Robert Lowe, who belonged to the anti-reform faction in his own party, and certainly not with his arch-rival, Benjamin Disraeli.[14]

Not all political animosity could be reckoned in terms of belief. Personal rifts were the hardest to navigate. Delane held a grudge against Earl Russell, and from the moment Russell took over as leader of the Liberals ran an energetic campaign against the pro-reform ministry. Even Disraeli – a main beneficiary of this campaign – admitted privately to the Rothschilds that 'Mr Delane has been absurd in his attacks upon Lord Russell'.[15] Delane refrained from discussing the details of the disagreement with Charlotte, who he knew broadly supported Russell's proposed reforms, but he discussed them with Evelina and Ferdinand, who reported back to Piccadilly House. Delane, Charlotte noted disapprovingly, was 'bent upon being Argus, and keeping ninety-eight eyes open to discover nine hundred thousand faults in Earl Russell and Co.'[16]

On 19 February, shortly after the opening of the new Parliament, Henriette Montefiore, the doughty and uncompromising daughter of the Frankfurt ghetto and the first Rothschild woman to venture to London, had died.[17] Over the following days, Louisa had 'wept incessantly', and at the funeral the wrench of seeing her lively, eccentric grandmother being carried from the house caused Constance to dissolve into violent hysterics.[18] It was at the same time as trying to hold the family together after this terrible loss that Charlotte began following through Parliament the new reform bill aimed at enfranchising the 'respectable' working and artisan class.[19] The weekend before a crucial Commons vote, however, her concern for the bill was eclipsed by 'selfish terrors', when she realised she was expecting Gladstone and Disraeli for dinner on consecutive nights.[20] On Saturday, the night of Gladstone, spirits ran high; the 'great man' was 'quite inexpressibly delightful'.[21] The following night, as if detecting the recent social success of his rival at the same table, Disraeli appeared glum and 'out of sorts'.

No doubt Disraeli's gloom lifted when Gladstone's high spirits turned out to be those of a politician heading for 'glorious defeat' rather than victory: the reform bill was voted down, Lord Russell's government fell, and the Conservatives formed an administration under Lord Derby.[22] When Delane swaggered into the dining room at no. 148 Piccadilly on 20 July, puffed up with his defeat of Russell and 'boasting of his intimacy with great personages' – presumably, Derby himself – Charlotte had to exercise all her self-control not to snap at him.[23] 'I kept my temper,' she wrote to Leo, 'but was not very gracious to the turncoat Editor.'

Supporters of reform planned a rally in Hyde Park for 24 July 1866. Although Derby's Home Secretary, Spencer Walpole, outlawed the rally and had the gates of Hyde Park shut, crowds still gathered in defiance of the ban. The railings gave way under the crush, and protesters poured into the park. Charlotte's support for the reformers inclined her to think of them as reasonable people with a serious grievance, and she had advised her family that 'there is no harm done by peaceful demonstrations'.[24] The residents of no. 143, where Evelina was now four months pregnant, did not share her equanimity. Terrified at the sight of the mob, Evelina and Ferdinand abandoned a plan to join the Duchess of Newcastle at the opera, and instead hid at home, where the Sèvres vases had been carefully packed away.[25]

Charlotte's attitude was vindicated, at least where her home was concerned. As the protesters passed by no. 148, they cheered, and Natty and Alfred were received enthusiastically among the crowd.[26]

In contrast, Disraeli's house had ten windows broken.[27] When Natty defended the reformers during a debate at his gentleman's club, one fellow member, a Tory, said he was 'sorry all our windows had not been smashed'. Natty's retort earned a proud mention in Charlotte's letters: 'We were perfectly safe,' said Natty, 'as the crowd knew us to be their friends.'[28]

A few smashed windows were nothing compared to the upheavals occurring elsewhere in Europe, and London remained a favoured destination for Rothschilds seeking sanctuary from violence and conflict in their home countries. In the summer of 1866 the ongoing power struggle between Austria and Prussia in the troubled German Confederation escalated into war. Among the Rothschild women and children who fled Frankfurt was Emma Rothschild, Lou's daughter and a close friend of her cousins Constance and Annie. Emma was now twenty-two, a remarkable intellect who had not only excelled at the family's standard 'feminine' curriculum – five languages, art and music – but also in pursuits generally deemed suitable only for the men such as maths and physics, even teaching herself Morse code. Charlotte found her niece 'well and blooming, and smiling', in marked contrast to her mother, who was deeply distressed at the situation on the Continent.[29] Charlotte embraced the pair, and brought them to stay at Gunnersbury.

It was during these months that Emma and Natty fell in love, and by the end of the summer they told their parents of their intention to marry.[30] Though it was not a match their mothers had planned, it was a respectable combination, and there was a romantic intensity between them that was rare among Rothschild cousins.[31] Permissions were given and wedding details arranged hurriedly, before Emma and Lou left England at the end of September. Everything had proceeded at such a pace that when Emma arrived back in Frankfurt – which had, as expected, been taken by the Prussians – she was embarrassed at the thought that she had been insufficiently grateful towards her future mother-in-law, and wrote explaining that her heart had been 'too full, when at Gunnersbury, to permit me to express all the deep thankfulness I felt for your affectionate welcome'.[32] She could only hope to show her gratitude in due course, through her 'filial devotion' as a daughter-in-law.

After so much bad news, the match between Natty and Emma had a transformative effect on the London family. Natty, who was usually such a practical and austere young man, had been extravagant and absent-minded as he shopped for jewels and awaited love letters from Germany. 'Now he can no longer laugh at me,' wrote Evelina, who had suffered no end of teasing from Natty during her courtship with Ferdinand, 'as he himself is very spoony.'[33]

Ferdinand was currently in Austria, and although Evelina got 'grumpy' when a day passed without a letter from him, she had otherwise managed the final few months of her pregnancy with characteristic energy and resilience.[34] At the end of November, with the baby expected in weeks, she was still dragging her mother Charlotte on carriage rides and social visits, taking walks in the garden, and dining at no. 148 in 'wonderful spirits'.[35] 'So blithe and merry was she,' Charlotte wrote to Leo, 'that dear Papa prophesied the infant would be ushered into the world between two peals of laughter.' Charlotte could have no idea how horribly inaccurate this prophecy would prove to be.[36]

On 4 December 1866 Evelina went into labour. During the early stages she was gripped by violent convulsions. Before the stunned doctors could act, Evelina and her child were dead.[37]

'O shocking sad day! It seems almost impossible to write about it.'[38] The day after Evelina's death, Constance travelled to no. 143 Piccadilly, where the nursery, 'that gay bright room', decorated with rose-coloured chintz on which storks delivered newborns, now hosted 'the motionless form on the bed, with the poor tiny baby in the case'.[39] Ferdinand was 'so crushed with grief that he cannot speak at all'.[40] He had, he wrote, loved Evelina 'ever since childhood', and had been 'so intensely happy' during their short married life.[41] Henceforth, his life would be 'wrought with sorrow and with anguish and with bitter longings' for a loss which 'years can not repair, nor any accidental circumstances relieve'. He holed himself up at no. 143, unable to receive further visitors.

Charlotte, too, found that seeing people was unbearable. At the turn of the year, when her son-in-law, Alphonse, was talking politics at Gunnersbury, she answered him 'like an automaton wound up, like a piece of machinery'.[42] When Ferdinand's sister, Alice, announced that she wanted to visit, Charlotte asked her son: 'How could I say, or

write to the young girl: "don't come".[43] She missed Evelina desperately – her conversation, laughter, jokes.[44] She had depended on her
daughter to 'brighten the house with her mither' for so long that she
did not know how to do those things alone.[45]

On the second day of 1867 a snowstorm gripped Gunnersbury.[46]
Hundreds of letters of condolence began to arrive. Even the 'strange
and far fetched' ones – such as Delane's, in which he clumsily described
Evelina as dying 'in the noblest office of her sex' – demanded the cour-
tesy of a reply, and Charlotte trudged on through the pile on her desk.[47]
'I have answered two hundred and sixteen, nay eighteen letters, and
might hope to write about twelve today,' she wrote to Leo.[48] Reminders
of Evelina came in sudden stabs, such as when she observed her granddaughter Bettina 'shrieking with delight at the curious movements' of
servants who were skating on the frozen pond, and was reminded of her
daughter's fits of uncontrollable laughter.[49]

It was unthinkable that either Lionel or Charlotte would attend
wedding festivities when they were so deep in mourning. At the end
of January Natty departed for his wedding in Frankfurt alone. For
weeks, Charlotte had been looking at everything in connection with
the wedding with a sort of double vision: how it would have been if
Evelina were still alive, and how it actually was.[50]

Dr Kalisch, the family's tutor, gently suggested to Charlotte that
she try writing a tribute to Evelina.[51] For several days in January,
Charlotte circled the task, simultaneously drawn to it by the prospect
of preserving Evelina's memory, and repelled by the thought that she
would 'never be able to do justice to the much-beloved'.[52] Eventually
she produced a character sketch, which would replace the existing
preface in the new edition of Charlotte's book of 'sermons'.[53] The
sketch had been a necessary exercise, raw and urgent, but Charlotte
thought it 'faint and feeble – miserably poor', and as the months
stretched into years, she continued to work on short stories, parables
and vignettes in which she reckoned with her daughter's life and
death.[54] In 1873 she published *From January to December*, a selection
of pieces for each month of the year, along with twelve introductions
full of monthly miscellanies.[55] Though Charlotte would publish the
book anonymously, anybody who knew her would have been able to
identify the author from its preoccupations and settings. One story in
the December portion of the collection stood out as having particular
autobiographical significance.

'The Precious Jewel' was a story about a queen and her daughter, Nonbella, to whom fairies give an amulet to consult whenever she is in emotional difficulty. The amulet makes Nonbella exquisitely kind – she is pained by the sight of worms writhing on anglers' hooks, and determined to 'improve the condition' of 'poor neglected children' – but she is also distressed by her own 'plainness'.[56] At the end of the story, Nonbella meets Prince Carissimo, who asks her to marry him. Nonbella struggles to believe that the Prince would select a bride so 'burdened with ugliness'.[57] The Prince replies that Nonbella's amulet is 'the most valuable of possessions', and makes her beautiful: it 'gleams in your smiles, it shines in your eyes'. Charlotte finished the story with the message: 'Gentle young readers, you have, no doubt, guessed long ago that the precious jewel was Nonbella's own good heart.'[58] The story was both Charlotte's tribute to her daughter and an attempt to alleviate the guilt she felt at the way she had fixated, for so many years, on Evelina's appearance.[59] Charlotte must have prayed that Evelina's marriage to Ferdinand had given her the reassurance Carissimo gives to Nonbella, and that she had died knowing how deeply she was loved.

PART III

Constance, Emma,
Hannah, Blanche

21

Flirtations

'MAY I INDULGE in a flirtation!' wrote Constance in her diary.[1] By the turn of 1865, Louisa's older daughter had blossomed into a restless romantic with an oval face and thick dark hair that she had the habit of wearing in neat plaits, as an example to the children at the Aston Clinton school. She had inherited both the melancholy self-scrutiny of her mother Louisa and the ebullience of her *bon vivant* father, and her diaries reveal a personality marked by sudden movement between these two tendencies: between ecstatic optimism and depressive self-criticism, frantic activity and prolonged stasis. Her energy and intelligence had caught the attention of many young upper-class men, and at the age of twenty-two she had no shortage of potential husbands. It seemed just a matter of taking her pick.

Constance had started to give serious thought to her romantic prospects seven years earlier, in the late 1850s, when Louisa had taken her and Annie to Germany for the summer. They had stayed with Louisa's cousin, Lou, and her daughters, Adèle and Emma, on their Günthersburg estate, north-west of Frankfurt. Constance, who had turned fifteen in the spring, brought with her a small diary, and the early entries are soaked in the sunshine of that 1858 holiday. She recorded swims in the nearby baths, shopping trips into town and perambulations around Lou's farm in a little trap, to see the animals and gorge on cherries.[2]

Swimming was one of their favourite pastimes – and not just for the sport. The pool became a favourite place for meeting male cousins, especially Chilly's sons Puggy (Nathaniel), who was twenty-one, and Ferdinand, three years his junior. The young men teased the girls, who clearly enjoyed the attention, and on the evening before Louisa's daughters left Frankfurt, there was a flirtatious exchange of compliments and handwritten verses between Constance and Ferdinand.[3]

But it was Ferdinand's older brother who arrived in London a few months later, and embarked upon a more determined courtship with his cousin. At the beginning of August 1858 Constance went on a 'very pleasant ride' with Puggy in Hyde Park.[4] That alone was enough to get Annie 'talk[ing] absurd nonsense' about marriage.[5]

A week later, Constance was lounging listlessly in her room after a heavy day of German, Hebrew and history lessons when the doorbell rang. Puggy's excuse for turning up was to visit Louisa, but on hearing that his aunt was absent, he made himself comfortable in an armchair and chatted to Annie and Constance. Before he left, he asked Constance if he could kiss her hand.[6] Constance 'would not let him', but her interest was clearly piqued. 'I wonder when I shall see him again!' she wrote in her diary.

Egged on by the younger members of the family, Puggy pressed his suit further. Just two days later, when Constance came downstairs to say goodnight to her father, she hesitated outside the door to the green room because she 'did not like to go into the room where all the gentlemen were'.[7] Puggy appeared in the hall and stopped to talk. Within minutes he was imploring her to take a trip to Alsace with him. When she demurred and retreated upstairs, Puggy called out for her to 'dream of me'. 'At that moment,' Constance recorded in her diary, 'a dream so exactly like the present scene that it was quite startling flashed before me and with burning cheeks and flashing eyes I ran up stairs and went to bed' – where she did indeed dream of him. A few weeks later, when Constance retired from the dinner table with the intention of heading to bed, Puggy followed her up the stairs and 'did the greatest absurdities running after me and looking up under my petticoats'.[8] When her beating heart settled, Constance must have regretted recording this event in ink, as she crossed out 'up under my petticoats' and substituted 'at my feet'. Such self-censorship was perhaps motivated by caution rather than disapproval of Puggy's actions: when he left London in mid September, she begged him to send photographs from the Continent.[9]

Within a few months, however, Constance was also in correspondence with Ferdinand – who sent her a photographic portrait of himself from Frankfurt.[10] Louisa was becoming suspicious, and started supervising her daughters' correspondence. On Christmas Day 1858, after Annie had refused to let her mother see a letter she was sending to her cousin, Emma, the girls' mother looked 'very angry' and 'said that we ought to have no secrets from her'.[11] Later that day, Louisa instituted new rules: from now on, she would read all outgoing letters to the Frankfurt cousins.[12]

Constance was not to be deterred. From her diary, it becomes clear that she was developing a new crush – on her London cousin Natty, whom she admired for his 'lively and conversational' nature.[13] Over the years that followed she spent much time and ink weighing up the relative merits of her German and English cousins. Ferdinand was 'sympathetic', with admirable artistic talents, but dreamy and impractical; Natty was optimistic and more intellectually engaging, but he could be 'somewhat stuck up'.[14] By the early 1860s the incessant comparison and prevarication in her diaries begin to look less like the preamble to a decision. Whatever the reason, the moment seemed to have passed for her to make a match in keeping with the family's habit of intermarriage.

The flirtation that Constance contemplated in her diary several years later, in 1865, was not such an appropriate one for a Rothschild woman. Maynard Wodehouse Currie was a Whig, and not only a Christian but also the curate at Mentmore.[15] In the past, this might have given Constance pause for thought, but by 1865, when it was announced that Currie was set to accompany Constance and her sister to a ball and Constance made her giddy comment about considering a 'flirtation', such obvious inappropriateness seems to have become part of the fun. Two days later, Mr Currie, she recorded, 'pressed my hand in the hall'; in the tearoom, he pressed it again 'so tenderly I felt he was making love to me'.[16] Early in February, in the carriage on the way back from Halton, he squeezed her fingers then grabbed her hand. 'A thrill ran thro me,' wrote Constance in her diary.[17]

But Constance was as mercurial as she was romantic, and such feelings turned out to be transferable. 'Lord Henry is the kindest most good-natured of mortals,' she wrote the following month, having arrived in Torquay on holiday with her family.[18] 'I feel quite fond of him & sh[ould] like to see as much of him as possible.' Lord Henry Lennox was a Tory MP in his mid forties and the third son of the Duke of Richmond. After a week of mild flirtations and simmering jealousies, Lord Henry asked Constance to accompany him on a Sunday walk and began to unburden himself, speaking with 'feeling & tenderness & devotion'.[19] The conversation left Constance feeling disquieted. Hand-holding, even the sort that felt like love-making, came with no explicit promise. Romantic conversations were a different matter altogether, and ill-advised.[20]

If she had thrown cold water on the relationship there and then, the damage might have been limited. Instead, she let things drag on until April, when she finally pulled Lord Henry aside at Grosvenor Place.[21] He was 'frantically angry', and the nervous excitement of the confrontation would linger in Constance's mind for days. Nor was that the end of it, for this was in the heat of the London season, and they were bound to see each other again. At Stafford House in May, they quarrelled and Lord Henry got so angry that 'he turned his back & would not speak' to her.[22] Two days later he bounced back with a direct proposal at the Eustasy ball: '[he] proposed,' wrote Constance, 'how shocking I was horrified I shall never forget it, proposed directly.'[23] After witnessing the scene at Stafford House, Ferdinand took the opportunity to 'lecture' Constance on her 'misdeeds'.[24] The older generation, too, had noticed that something was going on: Lionel waded in, advising Anthony that 'any other man' would be 'more appropriate' for Constance 'than that ugly, world-worn beau'.[25]

Anthony and Louisa did not need to be warned off Lord Henry. They were in the midst of discussions with their own preferred – and somewhat surprising – alternative, Alfred Seymour, yet another Christian, who had also pursued Constance in Torquay. Seymour had been even more forthright than Lord Henry in declaring his love, and had been rejected more decisively by Constance, who found his attentions cloying.[26] But Seymour was already acquainted with Anthony and Louisa, and was able to make a more conventional approach, visiting them and asking for Constance's hand.[27] On this, the one occasion when Constance might have been grateful for the strict Rothschild marriage policy, her father, who liked Seymour, announced he was willing to countenance a Christian match. Backed into a corner, Constance rejected the idea of a match with Seymour so ferociously that she was 'considered a cold-blooded monster' by her parents.[28] After brief reflection, however, the upside to the situation became apparent. Anthony's willingness to support a suit by a Christian suggested that, in religious terms, '[w]e may marry whoever we like there is no limit put upon us we are quite free like every other girl'.[29]

That summer, the family were rocked by the news that David Davidson – a relative of the Rothschilds by marriage through the Cohens – had shot himself on Hampstead Heath. Although the official conclusion was that impending surgery had terrified him into taking his life, it was widely suspected that Davidson's enormous debts had driven him over the edge.[30] 'O God to think what love of money leads to,' wrote Constance.[31] Suddenly, the glitz of London balls and aristocratic courtship seemed not only frivolous but somehow menacing, and when, at the end of the year, she attended a small local wedding in Aston Clinton, she could not help but feel jealous of the bride and groom, who only had a handful of other witnesses present. 'It is just a nice quiet way of being married without absurd fuss or pomp or show,' she wrote.[32] 'I wish that I might be married like that.'

Victor Yorke was a godson of Queen Victoria and close in age to Constance and Annie. He had served with the Horse Artillery in Canada, where he suffered a blow to the back of the head.[33] Despite causing him occasional pain, his injury had not prevented him from leading a lively and accomplished life back in England. His father, Charles Yorke, the 4th Earl of Hardwicke, knew Anthony through business, and during the late 1860s Victor spent a lot of time at Aston Clinton, where both Constance and Annie became besotted with him. 'I like Victor Yorke extremely,' wrote Constance in November 1867, '& what is more I feel that I cld love him.'[34]

Yet only the following month, disaster struck. Victor was at Aston Clinton for a weekend party. On the Sunday, Constance reported him being in 'tearing spirits never leaving us alone for a moment'.[35] He distracted her from work, but made her 'perfectly happy' with his diversions. The next day he and Constance and Annie, 'full of fun and in high spirits', drove up to Aston Clinton school, where Victor had volunteered to do a reading.[36] Among the pieces he read that evening was Tennyson's 'The Grandmother'. 'Willy my beauty, my eldest-born, the flower of the flock,' he read, 'Never a man could fling him, for Willy stood like a rock' – on which line he suffered a stroke and dropped forwards off the front of the stage. He was carried unconscious to the schoolteacher's house, where he was attended by two doctors, but died later that night without regaining consciousness.[37] He was just twenty-five.

Following this tragedy, the Rothschild and Yorke families formed a bond as strong and mutual as one of marriage. 'The tenderness and sympathy shown by Sir Anthony and Lady de Rothschild on this occasion made a deep impression on our bereaved hearts,' Victor's sister Elizabeth later wrote.[38] 'It was quite beyond words.' Over time, Constance formed a particularly close friendship with Victor's brother, Alick, with whom she had long and intimate discussions about interfaith marriage, and whether a Christian could ever convert to Judaism upon marriage, rather than the other way around.[39] Alick began to learn Hebrew. Perhaps stoked by the intensity of the shock and trauma over Victor, an unspoken attraction seemed to grow between the two. Annie, meanwhile, began a courtship with the third Yorke brother, Eliot, an energetic and theatrical man with a large store of anecdotes – many of them gathered during his time working as a royal equerry.[40] By the autumn of 1872, Constance had taken on the role of chief negotiator, meeting Eliot, discussing the romance with her cousins, then having 'long, long' talks with Annie, late into the night.[41] The job of intermediary could in itself be surprisingly intense, and on occasion Constance's role seems to teeter between matchmaker and love rival: 'stayed at home in the afternoon to receive E[liot]. He came sat down cried, took my hands kissed them. I kissed his forehead, he raised his lips & touched mine how I wld go through fire & water for him. I love him so much.'[42]

Whether the ever-impulsive Constance was harbouring secret feelings for Eliot or simply overjoyed at the love he felt for her sister, she pressed on with organising the match. In October she judged it time to involve the parents. But matters failed to go as she had hoped. Louisa, who had become deeply attached to an earlier suitor, 'was miserable' at the news, and became 'ill & white & trembling & sad' whenever Constance tried to broach the subject over the following days.[43] But Constance's mother would have to accommodate herself quickly to the new situation: two weeks later Eliot proposed. Anthony, who liked Eliot's father, was in favour of the match, despite Eliot's Christianity.[44]

Others in the family were less enthusiastic. With the exception of a few close family members, including Constance and Louisa, most of the Rothschilds stayed away from the church where the celebratory service was held (the wedding itself took place in a Mayfair registry office).[45] When Constance travelled to the Continent later that year, she found support among her cousins in Vienna, where Albert 'gave vent to his feelings about the family and their ridiculous marriages' in a diatribe that left her saying 'amen to every word'.[46] In Paris, things were chillier. 'With the exception of Laurie none of them asked after Annie,' recorded Constance, 'rude idiots!!'[47] The spectre of Hannah Mayer and Henry FitzRoy hung over the match. And yet Annie and Eliot's partnership would be different in one important respect: neither would convert.

Constance's own prospects had thinned out since the early 1860s. After a fiery few weeks, her tie with Maynard Currie had mellowed into a friendship; the tempestuous relationship with Lord Henry Lennox had blown over; Alfred Seymour had married someone else. Now that he was unavailable, Seymour became incredibly attractive to Constance, who lamented in 1869: 'O how he loved me and I really shld have married him had it not been for Lord Henry. I hate myself. I am miserable.'[48] Seeking distraction in a fresh romance, Constance turned her attention to another young man who moved in the Rothschild circles: Cyril Flower, a friend of Leo's from university.

She had first met Cyril in 1864, when he and Leo had ridden over from Mentmore, and the three of them had 'played, or pretended to play, a game of billiards, knocking balls about, laughing and chaffing'.[49] Constance was struck by Cyril's 'fine features, bright dancing eyes, mass of waving golden hair and ruddy complexion', all of which produced 'a picture of youth, vigorous health, and bright activity such as one seldom sees'.[50] She was not the only one who found him physically attractive – during his student days, Cyril had a reputation for being the most beautiful man at Cambridge.[51] His beauty, as well as his supposed 'genius' for male friendship, provoked suspicion among the older members of the Rothschild family. Charlotte was unsettled by how much time Leo spent with Cyril, and a later Rothschild relative would capture the family's attitude when she wrote that Cyril was 'far too beautiful – decked out in a wine coloured velvet coat – and several of his male friends were also endowed with an undesirable type of good looks'.[52]

It does not take a modern sensibility to understand what they were implying, but Constance appears, initially at least, to have been unaware of Cyril's rumoured relationships with men. When he appeared in her diaries during the early 1870s he did so unproblematically, as a 'nice bright jolly host'.[53] Cyril had been called to the bar in 1870, but had been forced to change his career when his father died and bequeathed to him the management of the family's estate in suburban Battersea.[54] New work as a property developer had given Cyril the freedom to manage his business affairs remotely and to indulge his significant appetite for socialising. During the early 1870s Constance saw him at Rothschild houses in Buckinghamshire, and in the Albert Mansions apartment in London that he had had lavishly decorated by his friend Thomas Jeckyll.[55]

The romantic dimension of their relationship burst into view in the summer of 1874, in St Moritz. Constance had come to join her cousins Leo and Leonora, who were on holiday with Cyril. Soon after Constance's arrival, Leo took her aside and told her that Cyril loved her. 'I cannot forget it,' wrote Constance, 'it seems like a dream, at times I cannot believe in the reality of such a thing.'[56] On Sunday, 23 August she 'requested an interview with C.F.'.[57] As they sat together on the grass under a scorching sun, Cyril began to cry. Constance 'felt weak & comforted him'. Cyril 'took me in his arms and kissed me and pressed me and loved me & I felt the passion of his love'.

Constance was torn. Her ongoing need for a passionate relationship had been ignited by Cyril's apparent ardour – but after what had happened with Annie and Eliot, she suspected this was not an arrangement her parents would endorse. 'I felt excited & half mad,' she wrote two days later.[58] 'Do I love him or not reason says no passion says yes & then I know that he is good & devoted he adores me. I feel that Mamma is very much against it. I can hardly read or write or occupy myself.' The rest of the week was turbulent, with Constance 'giving Cyril up' one day, and fighting an urge to tell him that she loved him the next.[59] But the memory of the initial interview, 'that heavenly morning', held fast.[60]

Over the next two years family suspicion about Cyril impeded the courtship. And then, at the beginning of 1876, Constance's father Anthony died. The demise of a Rothschild patriarch always caused disturbance and insecurity for the women they left behind, but it also led to some new freedoms. In September 1877 Louisa consented to a marriage between Constance and Cyril, giving a seal of approval to the second of her daughters to marry out of the faith.[61] Writing in her diary shortly after the engagement, Constance declared that she was 'radiantly happy. I love and am beloved.'[62] But this outpouring of joy only tells part of the story. Diary entries covering the months of courtship leading up to the engagement, as well as entries covering the marriage itself, have been cut from the diary, either by Constance herself or by a vigilant executor. Similar aggressive excisions and redactions appear in Constance's diaries throughout her married life. When ink has been used, the original entries – or fragments of them – can sometimes still be made out, but even when the original text is irretrievable, the bouts of self-censorship themselves tell of the unhappiness, distress and soul-searching that punctuated their marriage.

A few days after news of the engagement was made public, the *Jewish Chronicle* published an editorial decrying the recent trend of Rothschild women marrying non-Jews.[63] It was no longer about conversion, but about the spiritual integrity of European Jewry, and the responsibility of the Rothschilds to provide an example to those from less prestigious families. 'The rabbinical query is on every lip,' asserted the editorial, "'If the flame seized on the cedars, how will fare the hyssop on the wall: if the leviathan is brought up with a hook, how will the minnows escape?'"

22

Heirs and Graces

In the weeks after her marriage to Natty Rothschild in 1867 – while Constance and Annie were still dancing at balls and dallying with suitors – Emma Rothschild let go of her youthful pleasures, of her piano playing, painting, swimming, and her trick of walking up stairs on stilts, and dedicated herself to the task of reinventing herself as a banker's wife.[1] Although her spoken English was good, she had yet to learn lightness and wit in the language of her adoptive country. Her letters, with their distinct Germanic syntax, seem clumsy when read alongside the sparkling prose of her mother-in-law, Charlotte.[2]

Nor was there the luxury of time to settle into London as a young bride. On 8 February 1868, barely nine months after marrying Natty, Emma gave birth to their first child, Walter. His birth – and the glow of new hope that it brought – was timely, especially for his grandmother, Charlotte, who was still grieving Evelina's death. In September 1869 Charlotte wrote to Leo that both Emma and Walter were 'flourishing' and, a year later, that the baby was 'rosy and . . . merry'.[3] But she was seeing what she wanted. Emma, always considerate of the feelings of others, had concealed, perhaps partly to herself, too, her young son's frailties of health. It soon became apparent that he had speech problems and difficulties with motor control. From December 1870 and throughout the following year, he suffered repeated seizures.[4]

The demands of caring for a sickly infant meant that Emma had little time to see her English cousins. 'Emmy is quite estranged now!' Constance observed wistfully in her diary.[5] Natty and Emma had not yet settled in a permanent home, and it was Constance – still living at Aston Clinton – who encouraged them to consider buying the estate at Tring Park. The location and setting of the extravagant mansion was perfect, nestled at the foot of the Chiltern Hills with Mentmore

Tring Park, home of Emma and Natty. Emma adored Tring,
describing it to her mother-in-law as 'fairy land'.

a short distance to the north, the town of Aylesbury (which Natty represented in Parliament) a few miles west and, crucially for Constance, Aston Clinton under an hour's walk away.[6] 'Great news,' she wrote in 1872, 'Tring Pk is bought & will belong to Emmy.'[7] That was not quite accurate: Tring had been bought by Lionel and Charlotte, who lent it to the young couple, but only after they had renovated it in a style they considered appropriate. Emma, who was pregnant once again by late 1872, was not even permitted to choose how the nursery would be decorated for the new baby.[8]

She was not resentful, however: she knew that such lack of control would accompany her marriage to Natty. 'I am so bewildered by all I see that I cannot find words to express to you how much I admire this beautiful house & its perfect arrangements,' she wrote to her mother-in-law, soon after moving in.[9] From the writing desk in her bedroom, she made a hurried tour of everything she most admired in the house: the hanging of pictures in the dining room, the fashionable Chinese and Indian ornaments, the wallpaper and chintz that Charlotte had selected for the 'blue room'. She had 'often longed to possess the carpet which is described in an Arabian Night & to be transported to fairy land but I have obtained that end without the carpet for Tring is indeed quite fairy land'. She thanked Charlotte and Lionel for their 'g[rea]t kindness in allowing us to live here'. When the baby arrived in 1873, it was a daughter. Born the year that Charlotte published *From January to December*, she was named Charlotte Louise Adela Evelina. To her grandmother's joy, she came to be known as Evelina.

Emma's appreciation of Tring Park was not feigned for Charlotte's benefit. She fell deeply in love with the surrounding countryside, and developed a genuine affection for the estate workers: the carpenter Haystaff, the dairymaid Miss Lawrence, and Mrs Gutteridge in the stables, who reared shire horses. In the following years Emma developed a system whereby anybody who lived or worked at Tring could pay £1 a year in return for free medical attention and access to a newly built nursing home.[10] Her efforts marked a shift in family attitudes, away from the moralistic philanthropy of Louisa and her daughters in Aston Clinton, and towards a more paternalistic model that Emma's granddaughter, looking back from the post-war period, would describe as a 'miniature welfare state'.[11]

Although Walter recovered from the worst of his health difficulties, he remained a fragile child who spoke slowly and with difficulty.[12] Emma wrapped him up in the cotton-wool fairyland of Tring, with its rolling parkland and ancient woods. He loved the natural world and developed a precocious ability to recognise insects, birds and flora.[13] In response, Emma and Natty established a quirky menagerie which soon included tame partridges and pheasants, parrots and white-crested cockatoos.[14] Whenever Charlotte visited, she found Walter 'lively' and 'talkative', and eager to show off his creatures.[15] At six years old, he was already helping to prepare daily puddings of rice, currants, potatoes and eggs for the more delicate birds. Charlotte got on well with Emma, but her stated purpose in visiting Tring was, as she put it, 'to embrace the children'.[16] Her phrasing may have been pointed: Emma was averse to demonstrations of physical affection, barely exchanging a hug or kiss with her children, and Charlotte, whose own style of parenting was more tactile, felt the lack of it.

In other respects, Emma was quickly learning the ways of the English family. Her letters offered snatches of political intelligence, tied up in droll anecdotes, and descriptions worthy of Charlotte herself. In one letter, Lady Suffield – wearing sober colours, a big hat and 'almost a total absence of crinoline' – was described as looking 'exactly like a large living mushroom', while the Suffield daughter, who had a purse, pencil case and other implements hanging from her fashionable leather belt, was an 'elegant pedlar'.[17] As a hostess, Emma was grand and meticulous, employing one of the finest chefs in Europe (Grosstephen Senior, whose annual bill for fish alone ran to over £5,000) and inviting people from all political backgrounds.[18] It was a style of entertaining appropriate to the family circumstances, for Emma was emerging as a hostess at precisely the time that the Rothschilds' old tribal loyalty to the Liberal Party was giving way to a mosaic of new allegiances.

The ultimate social prize was still to host royalty. With the death of Prince Albert in 1861, the Rothschilds had lost their closest royal champion, and feelings towards the family at court had cooled. '[W]hen the poor Prince was alive, dear [Lionel] used to apply to him – when forgotten or omitted,' wrote Charlotte, but 'now one would not like to trouble the Queen.'[19] The antisemitic feeling held by powerful courtiers, such as Lord Sydney, was becoming obvious, and nor was Queen Victoria shy of expressing her own prejudices. As late as 1869, when Gladstone proposed making Lionel a peer, she expressed 'a strong feeling' on the subject: 'To make a Jew a peer', recorded Lord Granville, was 'a step she c[oul]d not consent to'.[20]

When members of the family were invited to court, they had to swallow antisemitic jibes: Charlotte reported an incident in which Natty was introduced by Lord Sydney, 'fine gentleman and jew-hater that he is' as 'Roshil'.[21] Arthur Hardinge, the Queen's equerry, took a visiting Russian royal to Westminster Abbey 'as a corrective' following a Rothschild dinner 'resplendent with Hebrew gold'.[22] Such views had not, mercifully, been inherited by younger members of the royal family. When Lord Spencer advised Victoria's son, Albert 'Bertie' Edward, Prince of Wales, that he ought not to attend a Rothschild ball because the family were 'very worthy people but they essentially hold their position from wealth and perhaps the accidental beauty of the first daughter they brought out in the world', Bertie ignored him.[23] Both Natty and his brother Alfred had met Bertie while studying at Cambridge. Nominally, their friendship had been forged over a shared passion for drag hunting, but all of Bertie's passions came with a substantial garnish of cigars, womanising, practical jokes and debts. It was 'perhaps better to say as little as possible about the festivities here', Natty had written to his parents, as his friendship with the heir to the throne blossomed.[24]

Following his marriage to Princess Alexandra of Denmark in 1863, Bertie and his wife took up residence at Marlborough House, and Natty and Alfred graduated into the quasi-courtly 'Marlborough House Set', who lived fast and loose and made a sport of antagonising the Windsor court. They were at odds with the royal establishment politically – Bertie's crowd were pro-Danish, anti-Prussian – and culturally, for adultery, gambling and smoking were all acceptable, not to say encouraged. In 1868 Bertie publicly signalled his connection to the Rothschild family for the first time, travelling down from Euston to stay at Mayer and Juliana's Jacobethan mansion, Mentmore.[25] He was accompanied by an entourage of four, including the uninvited Lord Alfred Paget, whom Mayer suspected of spying for the Queen.

After Bertie's visit, Juliana complained that Annie and Constance had 'steadily refus[ed] to join our company'.[26] Louisa's daughters were not the only Rothschild women who regarded the family's new friend with circumspection. Reports of Bertie's practical jokes – one time he picked up a dead starling and served it to Lord Shrewsbury as a quail, another time he secretly stuffed Dr Quin's pockets with silver spoons and had him arrested by a real policeman – were relayed by Charlotte and Louisa with chilly displeasure.[27] Emma, who had grown up amid the comparative conservatism and religious orthodoxy of the Frankfurt family and stood out from the English family for her strait-laced attitudes towards money and sex, was even less disposed to like Bertie. But she knew that the friendship between the heir to the throne and the heir to the Rothschild fortune was one that had to be not only tolerated but cultivated. In 1873, when Bertie visited Natty at Tring, Emma spared no expense in decorating the mansion for his arrival, even having ceremonial arches erected along the drive up to the house.[28]

What worried her more than the Prince's high jinks was seeing the behavioural norms of Marlborough House take hold within her own family. In the early 1870s Emma's brother-in-law Alfred embarked upon an 'open liaison' with Marie Wombwell, known as Mina, the beautiful French wife of a British Army officer.[29] Marie's second child, born in 1876, was a daughter named Almina. That the name was a portmanteau of 'Alfred' and 'Mina' did not go unnoticed by contemporaries, and it was an open secret that Alfred was the father. Emma took a stand, refusing to entertain her brother-in-law's mistress.[30] This decision infuriated Alfred, who took every opportunity to paint Emma as a prude. 'All Emma's children must have been conceived under protest,' he liked to say.[31] At one dinner party he finished a particularly blue anecdote by adding, with heavy sarcasm: 'Emmie told me that one.'

Though they may not have recognised it, such feuds only made the Rothschilds more similar to the royals whose social attentions they were courting. In 1879 Emily Francis Pattison (later Emilia Dilke), the writer and activist, went to stay with Louisa and her daughters at Aston

Clinton. She quickly picked up on the simmering tensions: Louisa and Natty were still at odds with one another over Natty's brief attempt to commandeer Aston Clinton after Anthony's death, and Louisa had been further enraged by the Marlborough House culture that Emma was forced to endure. 'Sir Nathaniel de Rothschild and his wife came to dinner,' wrote Pattison, 'and well knowing as I did two other members of the family I could see how strongly like a Royal Family the Rothschilds are in one respect, namely that they all hate one another but are united as against the world.'[32]

Following the death of Mayer in 1874 and Anthony two years later, Lionel was the last surviving son of Nathan and Hannah, and the only remaining Rothschild man of his generation in the London branch of the family. His health was as unpredictable as ever, and flare-ups of gout meant he increasingly came to rely on his sons, Natty and Leo, for help in running the business. Even Charlotte, who had always been at her husband's side when poor health had struck in previous years, was starting to feel the ravages of age. She had developed a cyst on her eye, which impaired her vision, and felt 'spasms' in her chest, which were a source of concern for the family doctors.[33]

In May 1877 Charlotte saw another grandchild enter the world when Emma gave birth to a second son, Charles. But she did not have much time to enjoy her newest family member: that summer she suffered a debilitating stroke.[34] Years later, Natty deemed it necessary to burn a large quantity of papers relating to Charlotte's health, and all that is left from the difficult months following the stroke are brief vignettes in Leo's letters, describing his mother's slow and painful demise.[35] For all the English family, Lionel's and Charlotte's illnesses were alarming. For Emma, they were also a stark reminder of the future that awaited her, as heir to the English Rothschild matriarchy.

23

The Rose and
the Lion

WHEN BERTIE, PRINCE of Wales, arrived in the grand porte cochère at Mentmore Towers in 1868, he was greeted not by the mistress of the house, Juliana, but by her sixteen-year-old daughter Hannah, 'white and pink and plump and merry'. Among the women of the younger generation of Rothschilds, life at the palatial Mentmore had a reputation for vanity, vacuity and dissipation. Hannah was seen as a product of that world: a 'petted' and 'spoilt' young woman whose parents had sheltered her from the harsh realities of 'sickness and sorrow' beyond the walls of their mansion, and whose gentle, talkative nature had disintegrated, due to a lack of serious education, into vacuousness.[1]

This picture of Hannah was not entirely accurate – from an early age she had sat in on her mother's salons and had learnt much, at least in theory, about politics and art.[2] But it is true that Hannah, even by Rothschild standards, was a pampered and isolated child. Her youth appears to have been singularly carefree: she was, wrote her aunt Charlotte, 'gay as a lark, plump as a partridge, and as ruddy as a little red-breast'.[3] In family letters, she appears being tended to by portraitists and pored over by doctors – who were strictly not supposed to be mentioned in the family correspondence, so sensitive were her parents to any mention of their daughter's health.

Hannah's youth ended abruptly in February 1874, when her father Mayer died. At the age of just twenty-two she inherited in excess of £2 million, as well as numerous properties, including no. 107 Piccadilly and Mentmore, one of the greatest houses built in the Victorian era.[4] With this legacy came the responsibility of managing her phenomenal wealth. Initially, Hannah at least had her mother to help her – but Juliana's own managerial experience was limited, and she was already suffering from an illness that would kill her three years later.[5] At twenty-five, Hannah found herself orphaned, unmarried and unprepared for the future.

Mayer had loved racing – he owned a stud farm and was a member of the Jockey Club – and, fittingly enough, it may well have been at Newmarket that Hannah had her biggest stroke of luck: meeting Archibald Primrose, Lord Rosebery.[6] Later in life he painted a romantic picture of their first meeting, describing himself leaping from his carriage after it collided with hers, catching the teenage Hannah as she fell, and taking her to recover in a nearby house, where Benjamin Disraeli, a mutual friend, formally introduced them.[7] Rosebery may well have added some romantic garnish in hindsight, but the couple certainly met in the mid 1860s, and Newmarket is not an entirely implausible location. Soon Archibald had become a familiar figure in Hannah's family. His dashing demeanour, sharp-witted conversation and love of sport had made him popular with Mayer and Juliana.[8] A decade later, soon after Mayer's death, there were rumours that Hannah and Rosebery had agreed a secret match. But it was not until after her mother died that Hannah felt bold enough to confide her feelings for Rosebery in a mutual friend of theirs, Sir James Lacaita, who soon turned marriage broker.[9]

On 3 January 1878, with a 'sapphire locket in hand', Archibald arrived at Mentmore and duly proposed.[10] Hannah accepted immediately. 'Remember, darling, I have no one on earth but you,' she wrote; and then, a few weeks later: 'I cannot be thankful enough for the absence of the terrible loneliness.'[11]

Once again, a Rothschild was marrying 'out'. It was something to which the family were having to get accustomed, and Hannah – partly because her parents were no longer around – escaped much of the censure. The same could not be said of Archibald. Though his mother, the Duchess of Cleveland, stopped short of attempting to forbid the marriage, she made clear her dismay that her daughter-in-law would not have 'the faith and hope of Christ'.[12] Although she promised to receive Hannah 'with all the kindness & consideration that are her due', she asked, for the moment, to be spared 'any agitating interviews', which she was sure would make her 'physically ill'.

Distressed as she was at the Duchess's response, Hannah had no plans to convert. 'If my religion is in your way, don't marry me,' she wrote to Archibald at the end of January.[13] 'It would break my heart but I could not face to be a hindrance.' He reassured her that he had no intention of giving her up, whatever his mother might think. Days later, Hannah wrote back, explaining away her moment of doubt: 'Do you know I seem to freeze occasionally,' she told Archibald.[14] 'I have been so long without much affection that it takes a long time to break through the stiffness which you see.' The iciness that had built up during her strange and solitary Mentmore childhood would take time and love to melt. In Archibald, though, she seemed to have found a man with the patience to try.

Hannah's immense wealth meant that news of the engagement spread far. Across the Atlantic, *Harper's Bazaar* offered its American readers 'an excellent portrait' of the future Lady Rosebery, and commented that the match 'excited a degree of public interest scarcely second to that of the Duke of Norfolk's marriage'.[15] Not all of the coverage was positive. The scale of Hannah's fortune was enough, predictably, to cast doubt on Lord Rosebery's motivations. Millicent, Duchess of Sutherland, was probably not the only one to think that Rosebery had 'married Hannah Rothschild for her money'.[16] It would later become received wisdom that Rosebery had decided at a young age on his life's three ambitions: to marry an heiress, win the Epsom Derby, and become prime minister. With Hannah he had secured the first; with her inheritance – the Mentmore stud farm and the Rothschild money and influence – he would be well positioned to achieve the remaining two. This sort of attention cannot have been welcome to someone like Hannah, but at least one feature of the coverage came as a relief. As Constance noted, 'times do change; there has not been an ill-natured article in the *Jewish Chronicle*.'[17]

The couple married with much pomp in London in March 1878.[18] Hannah was given away by Benjamin Disraeli, currently midway through his second term as prime minister, and among the assembled guests was the Prince of Wales.[19] The male Rothschilds refused to attend the wedding, but such gestures of opposition were now futile. After the marriages of Annie and Constance in the 1870s, this was the third marriage to a non-Jewish man in a single generation of English cousins, and the family's endogamous marriage policy was in tatters.

The couple's London base was Lansdowne House off Berkeley Square, and on racing weekends they were often to be found at the Durdans, Mayer's old bachelor box in Epsom, where Gainsboroughs and Watteaus hung on the walls alongside old sporting pictures.[20] The novelist Henry James, a frequent guest, found the cosy book-lined rooms much more to his taste than stiff and splendid Mentmore, with its Gobelin tapestries and sixteenth-century Italian furniture. Nevertheless, he eagerly accepted invitations to the mansion when he was offered them: in 1880 he wrote to his mother from the 'huge modern palace', reporting that he had walked down to the stables with John Everett Millais, 'to see three winners of the Derby trotted out in succession'.[21] The hospitality Hannah showed James at both houses failed to earn his affection. In his letters home, she appeared as 'large, fat, ugly, good-natured, sensible and kind', and then, as the last trace of his sympathy ebbed, as 'large, coarse, Hebrew-looking, with hair of no particular colour and personally unattractive'.[22]

Archibald had travelled widely before his marriage to Hannah, and James was just one of a large social circle that included many Americans and Europeans. Hannah's early years at Mentmore had given her some experience of what it took to be a salonnière – a job as much as a lifestyle – but it would have been inadequate preparation for the level and scale on which she now found herself hosting. Even Constance, who rarely had a good thing to say about her cousin, admitted that it was impressive. 'She went cheerfully through an amount of entertaining in London and in the country such as rarely falls to the lot of any woman.'[23]

Unlike other contemporary Rothschild circles, whose social networks included a broad range of political figures, Hannah's was a strictly partisan affair. Rosebery was a close ally of William Gladstone, and Lansdowne House soon acquired a reputation as being the 'social headquarters of Liberalism'.[24] Constance's husband, the beautiful Cyril Flower, was considering a move into Liberal politics, and Constance was forced to swallow her disdain of Hannah in order to support her husband's ambitions. The couple soon found themselves gravitating towards the Rosebery dinner table, where Gladstone was often present.[25] Talking to him in 1879, Constance found the once and future prime minister to be 'quiet, impressive, earnest and full of interest . . . a human being as well as a great statesman', and made no secret of her belief that his intellect and sincerity were lost on her cousin.[26]

Gladstone had resigned the Liberal leadership five years earlier, after being ousted from office by Benjamin Disraeli. In 1876 he began a comeback, publishing a pamphlet attacking what he saw as Disraeli's bloody and immoral imperial policy. But he needed to do more to capture the public's attention. By the late 1870s, when he came into Hannah's life, he had decided that the way to do this was through an electoral campaign. His onslaught against Disraeli had incited a fierce backlash in the capital, where jingoistic feeling ran high. He decided to give up his seat in Greenwich, leave London behind, and seek a nomination as a Liberal candidate in the county seat of Midlothian, sometimes known as 'Edinburghshire'.

The Roseberys were perfectly placed to help. Archibald's ancestral home, the turreted Dalmeny House, sat at the western edge of the constituency, on the Firth of Forth. When Rosebery returned from Paris at the beginning of 1878 it had not primarily been to propose to Hannah – though he grabbed the opportunity to do so – but to attend a meeting of the Midlothian Association, where Gladstone had just been confirmed as the Liberal candidate. Once they were married, however, it was clear that Hannah would be an asset. On the couple's first visit to Scotland, crowds gathered at Waverley Station to see them arrive, and 250 local dignitaries attended a banquet at Dalmeny.[27] Rosebery addressed the crowd, saying: 'My wife, as you know, is a Jewess by race, an Englishwoman by birth and today, by adoption, you have made her a Scotswoman.' They were at Dalmeny when Hannah gave birth to her first child, a daughter that she and Archibald named Sybil, after Disraeli's heroine.[28] Such a decision might have appeared somewhat off-message on the eve of a campaign that, in its national aspect, intended to unseat Disraeli. But the choice was strangely congruous. In his novel, Disraeli articulated the need to alleviate conflict between classes with social and political reform, a crusade that was, in Hannah and Archibald's view, now being carried forward by Gladstone's Liberals.[29]

Sybil's birth did nothing to diminish Hannah's role in the nascent political campaign. In late November 1879 Gladstone with his wife Catherine and his daughter Mary travelled to Dalmeny, where they were greeted with 'torches and fireworks and bonfires'.[30] At the end of Gladstone's first week there, Hannah organised an 'at home', to introduce him to some of the locals whom supportive newspapers were already referring to as his 'future constituents'.[31] Gladstone felt as safe in Hannah's hands at Dalmeny as he did in Rosebery's when out and about in the constituency. His dependence on her presence later became a subject of wry comment in *Punch*, where it was alluded to in a spoof piece called the 'Essence of Midlothianism', purporting to be Gladstone's campaign diary.[32] 'Whenever I go to strange house, or strange town,' wrote *Punch*'s pseudo-Gladstone, 'I want no better welcome than a look from Lady Rosebery's kindly face.'

Whether Hannah realised she commanded this confidence is un-certain. '[F]or God's sake don't leave me running behind after politics,' she had written to Archibald, shortly after their engagement.[33] That he would not fully initiate her into his political life was a constant fear of Hannah's, stemming both from an awareness of her educational shortcomings and from Archibald's reserved nature. Determined not to let her husband down, she sought out tuition in Scottish literature and history, and soon developed a reputation as an energetic and out-spoken campaigner.[34] The traditional expectation that peers and peer-esses should remain aloof from political campaigning persisted, but the couple evidently regarded this convention to be outdated, and responded to any criticism with good humour. When Hannah's name won cheers from the crowd during a speech Archibald made at a banquet of the Scot-tish Liberal Club, he responded, with more than a touch of dryness: 'I am afraid that my wife is a little apt to go beyond the rules prescribed for the inanimate nature of peers in her sympathy with the Liberal party.'[35]

On 28 November the Gladstones and the Roseberys travelled to Edinburgh for an evening of rallies. Gladstone spoke at the Corn Exchange and then at Waverley Vegetable Market, in front of an im-mense crowd. Hannah took a seat behind a barricade in the reporters' area, along with Gladstone's wife and daughter.[36] Behind her were as many as twenty thousand people, a large proportion of whom had been waiting for three hours. According to a favourable account writ-ten close to the time, the crowd was packed in so densely that 'men went down under pressure and were picked up breathless', and the roof was so low that 'the heat of the gas' from the lights was 'over-powering'.[37] When people collapsed, the only thing to do was bundle them overhead, and 'at every moment somebody with a white face and rigid body' was handed over the barricade to the relative safety of the press enclosure. Hannah was on the receiving line, providing tumblers of water and administering sniffs of her 'vinaigrette' – a bottle or box charged with revivifying salts – to those who had fainted.[38]

As well as orchestrating and funding many of these rallies, Archibald frequently appeared on stage, speaking alongside his political mentor. Hannah had never before seen her husband make a political speech in public. His eloquence and popularity came as a revelation. 'I wish you could have seen the control Archibald exercised over the dense masses of the people,' she wrote to her sister-in-law after one speech.[39] Situations that only months previously would have alarmed her were now reported with relish. 'The audience show him great affection at their political meetings,' she wrote, 'and they patted me on the back till my shoulders were sensitive.' The campaign awakened Hannah's ambition for her husband, and made her believe that he could be a statesman of serious standing in his own right.

It was not long before the flashy new campaign machine would be deployed in the context of a general election. In early March 1880 Disraeli was persuaded by a Tory by-election victory that his party was riding high against the Liberals, and called for a dissolution of Parliament, hoping to be returned with an increased majority. It was far from perfect timing for the Roseberys: Archibald was recovering from scarlet fever. But this was what they and Gladstone had been waiting for, and there was no time to lose. By half past nine in the morning on the day of the Gladstone and Rosebery families' departure from King's Cross, 'the crowd on the platform had swelled to such vast proportions that barriers had to be formed by seats in order to keep a passage clear for those proceeding by train'.[40] When Hannah and Archibald arrived, the crowd 'became musical', bursting into a rendition of 'Auld Lang Syne' 'to the whistling accompaniment of the engines'.[41] The Flying Scotsman steamed out of the station to wild cheers of 'God speed!' from the crowd. The Liberal lion was back, and with Rosebery and a Rothschild woman at his side, the election campaign of 1880 had begun in earnest.

24

Maiden Speeches

A FEW DAYS BEFORE Hannah set off from King's Cross with the Gladstones to campaign in Scotland, Constance had taken the train from Euston station to Brecon in Wales, where Cyril was fighting his own election battle. Constance may have considered Hannah's education inadequate, and disapproved of the culture at Mentmore, but there were more similarities than she cared to admit between her life and her cousin's. Both were daughters of Rothschild families with no male heirs, and both were married to non-Jewish men with expensive political ambitions. Cyril's looked set to be a close race: although Brecon was currently a Tory seat, it was vulnerable to the Liberals.[1] Though he had no deep connection to the area, Cyril knew that a close-fought constituency contest offered an excellent chance for him to prove his worth to his superiors in the Liberal Party, and perhaps to win a seat in Parliament in the process. When the candidacy was offered, he had jumped at it.

The couple had made their first trip to Brecon in December 1878. To Constance, the journey from London had seemed endless.[2] When they arrived, she found the weather cold and damp, and the Wellington Hotel – where Cyril was due to speak to Liberal Party supporters – unattractive. Cyril's speech was an ornate thing that ended with a humorous misquotation from Joseph Addison's *Cato*. It is not hard to imagine how the Flowers would have appeared to the people of Brecon – flamboyant Cyril, with his golden locks and lofty rhetoric, and Constance, whose contact with people of lower social classes, well-meaning as it may have been, was limited to cottages on land owned by her family, and classrooms in schools funded by them. But what Constance lacked in experience she made up for in courage. When opposition to Cyril began to spread, and Constance was warned off from going to Conservative strongholds such as the county tennis club or the annual agricultural show ball – where no one, she was told, would dance with her – she ignored the advice.[3] At the ball she found herself snubbed by everyone except one man, a notorious drunk, who invited her to dance. Clearly this was not going to be an easy fight.

By the time electioneering began in March 1880, the couple were settled in a rented home two miles from town. The Regency house at Ffrwdgrech was no beauty, but its situation at the foot of a wooded hill, and the 'rippling stream' of its name, appealed to Constance's romantic nature.[4] With her literary interests, she might have been best equipped to advise Cyril on his speeches, but an early attempt at this had made him 'very angry', and she had backed off, instead focusing on stitching together a network of supporters, guides and allies in the constituency.[5] Among her first calling points was the 'charming and picturesque home' of Liberal supporter Mrs Morgan and her daughter Fanny. The pair had moved to Brecon in the late 1860s, after the death of Mrs Morgan's curate husband. Fanny, in her early thirties, was just over ten years Constance's junior, but Constance's initial impression of Fanny, as a 'young girl' whose 'fine brow, direct steady gaze, healthy complexion and golden hair' made a 'pleasing picture', would be complicated as she learnt about her new friend's fierce views on politics and temperance.[6]

The Morgans helped to target key groups of electors: railwaymen, who were invited to Ffrwdgrech to be driven round the grounds by the Flowers' coachman; the town's 'very poor'; and 'wealthier trades people', such as the Protheroes, who owned a timber yard.[7] The relationship between the women, forged 'in those difficult times of my first acquaintance with the Brecon voters', would last for decades, and Fanny would be a profound influence on Constance's subsequent campaigning interests, which included temperance and women's rights. '[M]orally and intellectually,' Constance would later comment, 'she stands in the front rank of women.'[8]

Campaigning alongside Fanny Morgan in the narrow lanes of the old town, Constance was forced to abandon her preferred coach-and-four and travel instead by donkey or by foot in order to reach her electors: '[I]l faut s[o]uffrir pour idée belle,' she wrote to her mother.[9] She soon became familiar with the town's main venues – the Wellington Hotel, the Castle Hotel and the Town Hall – but steered well clear of the pubs.[10] In December 1878 Constance's sister Annie had been suddenly widowed, and had subsequently thrown herself into campaigning for temperance, a burgeoning movement that was closely associated with Liberal politics, the Church and women's rights campaigns; Constance had followed her sister into the temperance movement. In Brecon, that made enemies of the publicans but won the support of the middle classes, many of whom were dissenting Protestants who regarded alcohol as a social evil. During one hustings at the Town Hall, the chair was taken by a dissenting minister, Puritan songs were sung, and 'the whole audience congregated around the door' to cheer Constance and Cyril on their way.[11]

As sympathies began to swing and it became clear that Cyril posed a real threat to the incumbent MP, James Gwynne-Holford, the Tory gloves came off. Thugs hired by Lord Tredegar and Lord Camden arrived in Brecon and marauded through the town, 'bullying & threatening the poor little people in a manner quite scandalous'.[12] Where threats failed, bungs were offered: 'Alas!' wrote Constance to her mother, 'the enemy is bribing.'[13] Constance entreated her husband to 'send for a good London detective' who would be able to root out any foul play among the opposition, but Cyril preferred a local solution, hiring a twenty-four-hour watch – six people during the night, six during the day – to keep an eye on the Tory campaigners. Gwynne-Holford responded by hiring his own watchers and, when they found nothing incriminating, trying to lure Cyril into traps, sending beggars to the door of Ffrwdgrech, and a watcher to lurk nearby.[14]

Soon the whole town seemed full of spies. '[E]very body is watching every other body,' wrote Constance; 'there are mysterious groups in the streets, little ominous bands of people who dart into the houses when we pass.'[15] Meanwhile, campaigning tactics were becoming increasingly chaotic. Both political parties attached their colours to goats, releasing the animals into the town's narrow streets strung with ribbons and rosettes: the Liberal goat in blue and the Tory one in red. In hostile windows, red shawls were displayed at Constance as she passed, and red posters appeared, bearing the name of the Rothschilds' family friend, Benjamin Disraeli, Lord Beaconsfield. The Liberals held a parade; the Tories held one mocking them, marching through the town with signs that proclaimed 'Last Week of the Circus'.

Soon after this, the Liberals held a rally at the Town Hall. With the 'beer ... flowing', tensions running high, and the opposition evidently willing to engage in skulduggery, Cyril and Constance had been nervous about the rally, and were braced for 'interruptions, hooting, and even free fighting'.[16] It came as a surprise when they were received instead by 'perfect order and the greatest possible attention'. Constance watched from the gallery as the eight-hundred-strong crowd cheered in all the right places – including at any mention of Gladstone – and remained respectfully silent in between. At the end of the event, the hall rose to their feet to applaud first Cyril, then Constance, who, stunned and nervous, stood up to receive the applause. A bow was all she intended, but as she rose the hall fell silent. 'What could I do?' she wrote to her mother. Mustering her courage, Constance called out, as loudly as her nerves allowed: 'Gentlemen I thank you for the kind reception you have given my husband. I am glad and proud to be here and I am growing very fond of Wales.' It was a brief speech, and the pressure of making it turned her 'white as a sheet', but it would turn out to be the beginning of something much bigger. In the years to come she would 'learn how to conquer my terrible shyness, or rather nervousness, when speaking in public', and would go on to speak in support of her own causes.[17]

Cyril spent the night before polling day at a hotel in Brecon, but Constance had been warned that the town might be unsafe, and instead retired to Ffrwdgrech. On the morning of the election, dressed in blue – the campaigning colour of the Liberals – and accompanied by Fanny Morgan, Constance drove into town to arrive 'amidst cheering and awful hooting'.[18] If the trade in blue flowers was anything to go by, their chances of success were high: '500 bunches of artificial forget-me-nots had been sold in one morning!' From a room in the Wellington Hotel (which was decked out in blue flags) the women watched the carnage of democracy in action. Gwynne-Holford passed beneath their window, leading to the polls an assortment of Tory labourers who had walked to town; fights broke out between crowds of opposing supporters; a gang of 'Irish female "blues"' turned up, offering to 'fight any male Tory who would like to have a turn'. The experience did nothing to lessen Constance's fear of the new working-class electorate, and she would leave Brecon convinced that the franchise was 'as much too low' in the boroughs as it was 'too high for the Counties'.[19]

After the polls closed, Constance and Fanny drank 'endless cups of tea' and then stood with a visiting temperance preacher in the portico of the Wellington, begging the crowds 'to go to the Coffee Tavern and not to the publics'.[20] Their entreaties largely fell on deaf ears and soon 'the drunkenness was awful!' Constance retreated into the hotel. The first sign of good news came around seven in the evening, when one of Cyril's allies noted that a Liberal agent had 'turned his hat towards us from the window of the Town Hall – a preconcerted sign that you had polled enough votes to have won'. The victory was confirmed twenty minutes later, when the agent himself ran across to the hotel screaming that Cyril had won by a majority of fifty-nine votes, and Constance's servant burst into the hotel room at the head of a celebrating crowd. Constance 'seized a flag and waved it enthusiastically' from a window while Cyril clambered out onto the roof and, 'grasping a point to keep himself steady', delivered a speech to the crowd below. He had learned the word for 'victory' in Welsh: *buddugoliaeth*.[21]

Over the following days, letters and telegrams poured in. Matthew Arnold wrote that he had heard of Constance 'dazzling in bright blue, and winning everybody's good will', while Helen Gladstone expressed her 'delight at the victory'.[22] Constance was not the only Rothschild woman with cause to celebrate. Emma's husband Natty had been returned again as an MP for Aylesbury, and Hannah and Archibald had helped Gladstone to win a seat in Midlothian.[23] In recognition of the role played by Gladstone in the nationwide renewal of Liberal fortunes, the two men who had headed the party during the election campaign, Lord Hartington and Lord Granville, stepped aside when Queen Victoria asked them to form a government. Gladstone assumed the office of prime minister for a second time.

Constance was no stranger to the 'evils of intemperance'. As a child, she had observed that heavy drinking was common among both rich and poor, and more recently she had seen the effects of alcohol abuse first-hand in Hamble and Netley, in Hampshire, while campaigning with her sister Annie. And yet the scale of the drunkenness she had seen in Brecon, as well as the pernicious role she perceived it to have had in the election there, was new and shocking to her. After returning from Brecon, Constance committed herself to a project she had been contemplating for a while: the establishment of a new coffee house, the Swan, in Aston Clinton.[24]

The various temperance groups with which Constance was involved – including the Church of England Temperance Society and the Band of Hope movement – were Christian in character, and some of them staged meetings that were highly emotional, enthusiastic events, rather like revivalist church services.[25] Although she had not abandoned her Judaism when she married Cyril, Constance found herself stirred by the atmosphere of the temperance meetings, and by the sermons of the speakers. 'I enjoyed it to the full and felt the true spirit of God was with him,' she wrote, after listening to Canon Wilberforce preach on temperance at Aston Clinton.[26] 'How cold and soulless is our Jewish church ... How different is the Xtian church and oh! How I long to belong to it.' In London, she attended a service held by the famous American evangelist Dwight L. Moody, and scribbled with amazement her impressions of the gathering: 'the crowd, the upturned faces, the singing, the earnestness, the enthusiasm'.[27] Before long, she had begun to conceive of her past struggles with Judaism not as hurdles on the way to a reinvigorated Jewish faith, but rather as steps on a road towards Christianity. Writing on Rosh Hashanah, Constance commented:

One of our old holydays – its return brings back the remembrance of past days; of the time when I clung to Judaism, when I wanted it to be the pattern for all other faiths, when I longed to purify & revive it, when I wished to lead a Crusade in favour of it.[28]

Paradoxically, though, as she inched closer to Christianity, her religious differences with the nominally Christian Cyril became greater. In the early years of their marriage, Cyril's reluctance to attend church had struck Constance as neglectful of his duty as a good Anglican. But as she became more 'advanced' in her admiration for Christianity, she began to see his indifference to church as indicative of a deeper spiritual malaise. It must have been frustrating for Constance to feel that while her own religious inheritance prevented her from making a public, formal conversion to Christianity, Cyril, who'd been born into the cradle of Anglicanism, rejected it out of hand. '[A]nnoyed at Cyril's persistently remaining away from church,' she wrote in November 1881, and then, when he did finally attend a service one week later: 'Cyril actually went to church.'[29] She prayed that attendance would make him more peaceable and spiritual, yet the effect always seemed to be the opposite: 'Church going attended with the usual results, that of making Cyril intensely cross and irritable.'[30]

The blottings out and excisions in Constance's diaries covering this period speak volumes about their relationship. Between the hasty redactions, there are oblique references to blazing rows, sullen silences and to her increasing discomfort at the amount of time her husband spent in the company of men. In March 1881, when Cyril brought two men to Aston Clinton, she described them in her diary as a 'disturbing element'.[31] In June she described Cyril being 'as usual rough & unkind', and the following year she inked out a passage in which she described him loving her 'in such a cold halfhearted way that at times it frightens me'.[32] By the spring of 1882 she seemed to have given up on the idea of deep love or even understanding developing between them, and had fallen back on the hope that Cyril might at least improve himself, ethically and spiritually. 'He will never love me with passion,' she wrote, 'that is not in him, but he might love goodness and holiness with passion.'[33] Spurned by her husband, the romanticism of Constance's youth had been channelled into a new love: of Christianity.

25

Blanche in Bohemia

THE SENSE OF freedom that Blanche felt as she left the home of her mother Hannah Mayer was not as enduring as she had hoped. To the world outside, the Lindsays had it all – fame, fortune and success – but among the Rothschilds there were whispered rumours of strife and betrayal. Constance had never been apprised of the details, noting vaguely in her diaries that her cousin was in a 'low and miserable state' and 'most unhappy in her married life'.[1] Then, in October 1882, Blanche appeared at Surrey House, determined to tell her cousin everything.[2] Without her adoring mother, or any other immediate family, she was in desperate need of someone to talk to. Her marriage to Coutts was on the verge of collapse. She 'threw herself down on the sofa', wrote Constance, and 'told me all the sad story'.[3]

Blanche and Coutts's Scottish estate, Balcarres, was only a short distance across the Firth of Forth from Rosebery's at Dalmeny, but it was worlds away in terms of culture. Arriving guests passed through elaborate bright blue and 'lavishly gilt' wrought-iron gates, which had been shipped over from Italy, and up through terraces of walled gardens that one visitor remembered being 'well adapted to lovers' meetings'.[4] If the presiding spirit at Dalmeny was politics, here it was art. It was at Balcarres in the early 1880s that Louise Jopling, one of the pre-eminent Victorian women artists, painted a portrait of Blanche, *Looking Back*, which captured her essence: a woman 'with hair of rich brown colouring' and 'beautiful blue eyes' who shunned the stuffiness of upper-class society and instead established a reputation for frivolity and bohemianism.[5]

Blanche was a prolific performer and composer, and although her output was not particularly daring or innovative, she (as composer) and Coutts (as lyricist) were adept at turning out the kind of sentimental and humorous pieces for piano and voice that fuelled late nineteenth-century weekend parties: 'Waft Me on a Wandering Dream', 'Honest Heart', 'A Farewell Song', 'Raindrops'. At Balcarres, there were frequent fancy-dress balls and drawing-room theatricals, the *dramatis personae* of which invariably reflected the rustic or exotic obsessions of the avant-garde art circles in which the Lindsays moved – fishermen, peasants and 'Turks'. Blanche herself, according to Jopling, looked 'scrumptiously handsome' as a 'gipsy girl'.[6]

The frivolity of these weekend parties of the late 1870s and early 1880s would not have diminished Charlotte's suspicion of Blanche (which had already been stoked by Blanche's attempt, soon after Hannah Mayer's death, to auction off portraits of her grandparents, Hannah and Nathan).[7] But Blanche was a far more complicated figure than the 'serpent' of Charlotte's imagination. She had lost her brother, her father and her mother, all before turning twenty-one. As the offspring of a Christian marriage, she was regarded by the wider family as tainted by apostasy. However close she was to her cousins, aunts and uncles, she knew that she would always be considered an outsider. Her marriage to Coutts, her attempt to sell the portraits of her grandparents, and even her rejection of crinolines in favour of the long and flowing gowns made popular by the Pre-Raphaelites, were part of an attempt to carve out for herself what her parentage had prevented her from obtaining within her extended family: a sense of cultural belonging.

If Blanche had hoped that life with Coutts would help her to escape the tragedies of her youth, she was to be disappointed. Before their marriage, Coutts had fathered two illegitimate children with a woman called Lizzie Chambers. Although Lizzie had largely faded from his life by the late 1850s, she still sent Coutts the occasional letter, and the Lindsays sometimes glimpsed her at the opera.[8] Blanche almost certainly knew about the children before she married him. The beginning of their relationship had been passionate, and she had no reason to fear that what had happened with Lizzie was the beginning of a pattern. And yet soon after their marriage, Coutts took up with a new mistress, Kate Madley (née Burfield), who was in her late teens and worked as a model for London painters. Blanche gave birth to a daughter, Euphemia, in May 1865, and a second, Helen, at the end of 1868; less than a year after that, Coutts fathered a third illegitimate son, Arthur Harris Burfield Madley.[9]

Blanche did not have the temperament to turn a blind eye to such behaviour. She was, as her cousin Constance later recalled, 'cast in the heroic mould ... firm of purpose, relentless where wrong had been inflicted, very generous, but also determined'.[10] She remonstrated with her husband, demanding that he stay away from other women. Only a few sources survive to illuminate these stormy years. In May 1872, after visiting her brother, Coutts's sister Minnie wrote that there had been 'one or two regular "blow ups" with Blanche' during her visit, and that she had heard her brother speaking with unwonted bitterness.[11] Coutts, in whom a soldier's machismo and an artist's vanity had combined to produce a sense of entitlement, stood his ground against Blanche's objections, insisting on his right to 'take his own way'. Although Minnie was sympathetic to Blanche's situation, she was also resigned to women being subordinate to their husbands' whims. The important thing, for her, was to keep the pair together, regardless of her brother's cruel misbehaviour. 'She had a difficult part to play at first to gain her husband to herself,' wrote Minnie to her mother.[12] '[O]ur part is to try and love Blanche and bring him nearer along with her.'

*Blanche, Lady Lindsay,
and her husband
Sir Coutts Lindsay.*

Whatever marital turbulence they were going through, the Lindsays were determined to maintain the carefree face they had cultivated as patrons of an emerging art scene. Among the many artists, performers and impresarios who passed through the blue and gold gates of Balcarres during the 1870s was the painter Charles Hallé. In the summer of 1875, talking with Coutts during a break between partridge shooting and evening charades, Hallé bemoaned the failings of the Royal Academy in London.[13] Not only were the paintings in the Academy's shows crowded together in a jumbled and outdated fashion, but the jurors who evaluated the submissions were held in such low esteem by younger and more experimental artists that some of the more famous among them – including Dante Gabriel Rossetti, Edward Burne-Jones and William Holman Hunt – had been 'kept ... away from exhibiting altogether'. That winter, in collaboration with Hallé, Coutts and Blanche started making plans to set up a gallery to rival the Royal Academy.[14] Unable to find a suitable gallery to rent in London, the Lindsays decided to build one from scratch, in a plot they had found for sale on the west side of Bond Street. Blanche and Coutts would each invest half of the money necessary for the new 'Grosvenor Gallery'.[15]

By the summer of 1876 builders were at work on the Bond Street site, and Blanche turned her attention to securing exhibitors. She soon discovered, however, that dissatisfaction with the Royal Academy did not always equate with support for the Grosvenor – especially when fragile artistic egos were involved. Angry that he had not been consulted about the venture at an earlier stage, Ford Madox Brown declined the invitation to exhibit, as did Rossetti. 'It was a lesson on the sensitive nature of painters,' recalled Hallé, 'and how warily they must be dealt with.'[16] Blanche began to cultivate a circle of favoured artists at her London home, where they were met at the door with some circumspection by her butler, Gates.[17] One evening, Gates came into the smoking room to inform Hallé and Coutts that there was a gentleman on the doorstep wearing no tie, but with a feather on his head. The feather, it turned out, was a spray of white hair that would immediately have identified the guest to the cognoscenti as James McNeill Whistler, who had rejected formal attire as 'the badge of the Philistine'. By the spring of 1877 the artists who had signed up to exhibit at the Grosvenor included Whistler, the Pre-Raphaelites John Millais and Holman Hunt, and French Symbolist Gustave Moreau – as well as Hallé, Coutts and Blanche herself.[18]

At the Royal Academy's Burlington House works were hung densely with little or no space between them, and covered the walls all the way up to the ceiling which meant that only those paintings at eye level – on 'the line' – could be properly appreciated. Other works, particularly those with which the jurors took issue, could be 'skyed' – hung at the very top of the wall, effectively out of sight. At the Grosvenor, these conventions were discarded.[19] All works were exhibited at a visible height, with six to twelve inches of wall space between each frame. 'In this way,' wrote Burne-Jones, 'the usual patch-work quilt effect of an exhibition was avoided, and people could take breath before passing from one work to another.'[20] What's more, each artist had their works grouped together, in a way that gave greater authority to the individual painter. It was the beginning of a new way of looking at art – and at artists.

During the night of 29 April 1877 gallery technicians worked by lamplight to get all the paintings up in time for the 'private view', an innovative opening event at which select guests would be able to enjoy the show before general admission began.[21] The following day, when invitees poured through the doors from Bond Street, the innovative hang attracted enthusiastic comment. Constance later recalled how 'pictures were exhibited to the very best advantage, beautifully hung with an artistic background, never overcrowded or badly placed', and Louise Jopling praised the way each painting was permitted to 'reign alone, without being spoilt by the close juxtaposition of another work entirely out of harmony with it'.[22] The art itself was harder to as-sess. No single school was being represented, but rather a mix of late Pre-Raphaelitism, Romanticism and Neoclassicism, and many pieces that would later be thought of as belonging to the Aesthetic Move-ment. After writing at some length about the furniture in the gallery, a baffled critic for *The Times* devoted only a few lines to the paintings, which were explained away as 'unaccountable freaks of individual ec-centricity' and 'strange and unwholesome fruits of hopeless wander-ings in the mazes of mysticism and medievalism'.[23] Others were even more direct in their criticism: John Ruskin precipitated a famous libel case when he accused Whistler, whose *Nocturne in Black and Gold – The Falling Rocket* was a prize exhibit, of being 'a coxcomb [asking] two hundred guineas for flinging a pot of paint in the public's face'.[24]

Blanche attempted to capitalise on such publicity, hosting a series of dinner parties and Sunday afternoon salons at the Grosvenor. At the first of these, on 7 May 1877, guests included the Prince of Wales, Princess Louise and Princess Mary of Teck. The task of hanging the pictures was, Hallé later recalled, 'far less bother' than working out the proper order in which the profusion of titled guests should be brought in for dinner.[25] Flowers were shipped down from Balcarres, and by the cartful from the Rothschild estates at Gunnersbury and Mentmore; the family were clearly keen to support their bold cousin.[26] To begin with, the stuffiness and formality of the occasion must have felt rather oppressive to Blanche – whose 'greatest pleasure' was to 'appear foolish' – but everything was, improbably, put to rights when the Prince of Wales spilt a glass of champagne over her, prompting a relieved burst of laughter.[27]

Blanche's Sunday salons became a regular fixture in successive seasons, drawing aristocrats, Rothschild relatives, writers such as George Eliot, and luminaries of the new Aesthetic Movement, including Oscar

*The Grosvenor Gallery on Bond Street, established by
Blanche and her husband Coutts Lindsay.*

Wilde.[28] When Henry James was charged with the responsibility of launching two American visitors – Mr and Mrs Henry Adams – into London life, one of the first things he did was to ask Blanche to send them a card for a Grosvenor salon.[29] Depending on who was present, the events could either be restrained or veer towards the playfulness favoured by Blanche: 'After the Royalties had had supper and gone,' recalled Jopling of one gathering, 'I (chiefly) got up a dance. [Alberto] Randegger played, and we had three rounds.'[30] If success could be measured in column inches, then the Grosvenor was booming. The incomprehensibility of its paintings and the limp, forlorn appearance cultivated by the gallery regulars were ripe for lampoon in *Punch*, and the Grosvenor 'look' also received a nod in Gilbert and Sullivan's *Patience* (1881), in which the 'fleshly poet' Reginald Bunthorne described himself as a 'Greenery-yallery, Grosvenor Gallery / foot-in-the-grave young man!'[31]

Unfortunately, this outward success did not mirror an improvement in the Lindsays' private affairs. Coutts was still in regular contact with Kate Madley, the mother of his son Arthur, and Blanche had given birth to no further children, meaning that the couple had no male heir. For Coutts, as for any man with substantial wealth and a hereditary title, this was a problem, and though he evidently needed no excuse to nurture his extramarital relationships, Blanche's 'failure' to provide him with a son gave him one. In the late 1870s the young Arthur Madley took a new name, 'James Lindsay'.[32] It was a sign, Blanche realised, that her husband's illegitimate son was being positioned ahead of their two daughters as heir to Balcarres. In the autumn of 1882 her patience broke. Though it would take a while for her to leave Coutts, she began to talk more openly about the matter with her friends and family.

In the aftermath of Blanche's breakdown at Surrey House in October 1882, Constance increasingly found herself taking on the role of counsellor and mediator. Coutts came to see her to press his side of the argument: 'a miserable and depressing interview', commented Constance.[33] His sister May Holford, by contrast, talked 'so nobly and so well' of the crisis that Constance was left wondering why Blanche had bothered with the company of her 'bohemian friends', when she had such a remarkable woman for a sister-in-law. For all the meetings, the chances of reconciliation between the Lindsays seemed slim. The only thing that had kept the marriage going for so long was their joint commitment to the Grosvenor, which tethered them together socially, professionally and financially. But when it became clear that Coutts was not going to give up his mistress and son, even those ties were insufficient. In November 1882 Blanche walked out on Coutts, taking her two daughters with her.[34]

After seeing news of the Lindsays' split in the *Washington Tribune* in December, Marian Adams wrote to a friend that the separation would 'be a great blow to one set in London, as their Sunday teas at Grosvenor Gallery were very entertaining'.[35] Blanche herself had rather more pressing concerns. She prudently sent her daughter, Helen, on an embassy to New Court, where her Rothschild relatives and their lawyers worked their magic, securing Blanche's dowry and leaving Coutts considerably worse off.[36] He retreated to Rome, where he holed himself up in the studio of the American sculptor William Wetmore Story and emerged three months later with a painting that depicted 'an entirely naked man, and a girl sitting near him mending a net'. 'Nobody could imagine', wrote another British resident of the city, 'why the man had no clothes on.'[37]

Blanche moved out of the family home and rented in Kensington while her new house in Hans Place was being renovated. Though Constance continued in her role of confidante and counsellor, her initial sympathy began to wane as she came to think that her cousin was 'too egotistical' and unable to talk of anything except 'herself & sad affairs'.[38] Although Coutts was clearly more to blame for the split, societal norms and customs were arranged in favour of the husband retaining his social circle and standing when couples separated, and Blanche knew that she would have to be proactive in order to maintain friendships and links with the art world. She wrote to Robert Browning, commenting that he 'must have heard by this time of all the sorrows that . . . made me resolve not to live any more in my husband's house', and inviting him to visit her in Kensington.[39]

It worked: Browning remained a friend, as did the singer Amelia Chambers, Arthur Sullivan and the Burne-Joneses – Edward and his wife Georgiana – who provided Blanche with studio space at their house and invited her regularly for dinner.[40] With the space to think and work, Blanche became more productive as a painter. The Royal Academy would not admit female painters until 1922, so in the absence of the Grosvenor as a place in which to exhibit, she turned towards the Society of Lady Artists, exhibiting at their 1887 show at the Egyptian Hall on Piccadilly. Her paintings were of no great merit, and certainly not in the same league as those of her friend Louise Jopling, but by exhibiting them with the society she earned herself a minor place in a much bigger campaign, for the better representation of women in the arts.

Settled in Hans Place, with a goldfinch for company and a view over the Cadogan Estate for inspiration, Blanche turned away from the visual arts and towards literature. She would go on to have a patchy career as a poet and writer, producing several autobiographical novels and then a number of poetry collections, the first of which was published in 1890.[41] Her poetry would win over readers with its blend of whimsy and sentiment, and briefly her writer's garret at the top of the Hans Place house was a destination for journalists writing fawning profiles of the poet at work. Her novels received a more mixed response. Oscar Wilde, who had been introduced to Blanche during her time at the Grosvenor, wrote in *Woman's World* that Blanche's autobiographical novel *Caroline* was 'full of esprit and wit' and 'written in a very clever modern style', but those commenting from a greater social distance were uniformly less polite.[42] A critic for the *Graphic* admitted that Blanche showed a degree of skill; but then, 'the material is so thin that it required skill to make anything out of it at all'.[43] Blanche's real contribution to art lay behind her, in the brief and influential decade of the Grosvenor Gallery.

If she was diminished without the Grosvenor, so was the Grosvenor without her. In loyalty to Blanche, a number of artists, critics and associates began to distance themselves from the gallery. Effie Millais, the wife of John Everett, was one of Blanche's strongest advocates, and when Hallé approached her for some help with an exhibition of her husband's works that the Grosvenor was putting together, he did so in the full – and correct – expectation that he would be rebuffed.[44] Such defections, combined with the loss of Blanche's money and her talents as a gallery manager, hit the Grosvenor hard, and worsened internal tensions over management and money. As Hallé later recalled: 'the departure of Lady Lindsay sounded the death-knell of the Grosvenor Gallery.'[45]

26

The Royal Seal

OVER THE FIRST few years of the 1880s Charlotte had become ever weaker, and, in the spring of 1884, she suffered another stroke. Nearly half a century had passed since the nervous, pale-faced teenager from Frankfurt married her English cousin. On receiving news of her stroke, the family hastened to Gunnersbury. In the early hours of the morning of 13 March she died, surrounded by her sons and their wives. Constance received 'the dread telegram' at eight thirty a.m. and, with Cyril, arrived at Gunnersbury just after her mother, Louisa.[1] They paid their respects to the woman who now lay 'like a beautiful marble statue in her bed, with a little bunch of violets on her pillow', her mouth in 'sculptural repose, her broad high brow in all the dignity of rest'.

The funeral cortège left Gunnersbury at ten o'clock on 16 March, making its way along Ealing Road and Harrow Road to Willesden Cemetery, where the path was crowded with pupils and students from the Jewish schools Charlotte had done so much to support.[2] She was buried next to Lionel, who had died five years before her, in June 1879.

Just days away from her fortieth birthday, Charlotte's daughter-in-law, Emma, found herself stepping into the role of the English family's matriarch. It would not be long before her responsibilities and privileges were expanded beyond those Charlotte had known. Back in 1869, Queen Victoria had vehemently opposed Gladstone's idea of making 'a Jew a peer' by raising Lionel to a barony, but when Gladstone again pushed for the elevation in the mid 1880s, she raised no objections. On 9 July 1885, with one hand on the Hebrew Old Testament, Natty was sworn into the House of Lords; Emma became Lady Rothschild of Tring.[3]

She was not the only Rothschild woman to benefit from shifts in royal favour. Just a few months earlier, in May 1885, Queen Victoria recorded in her journal that Lady Rosebery had visited with her 'four nice children' – Sybil had been joined by Peggy (b. 1881), Harry (January 1882) and Neil (December 1882).[4] Ever since Gladstone's Midlothian campaign, Hannah had worked tirelessly to advance her husband's ambitions, dedicating herself to them above more conventional maternal duties. Edward Hamilton, Gladstone's private secretary, was one of her closest contacts, and the two corresponded frequently during the early 1880s, passing on political intelligence and sharing assessments of Archibald's latest speeches.[5] Hannah, as her cousin Constance later recalled, 'made an admirable, unselfish, loving wife', but was 'a less fond and devoted mother; tho she deeply loved the children'.[6] Politics, and Archibald's political career in particular, had become everything to her.

In late 1885 a Conservative government under Lord Salisbury was on the verge of collapse, and Gladstone – whose second ministry had crashed from office earlier that same year – began trying to piece together a Liberal ministry that could plausibly form a government if or when Salisbury fell. Hamilton, a close and trusted contact of Gladstone's, ran ideas for appointments past Hannah before he consulted Archibald. His respect for her was grounded in personal affection. 'I went with Lady Rosebery, who is very kind to me,' he wrote in his diary, after a trip to the theatre to see Oliver Goldsmith's *She Stoops to Conquer*.[7] Over the years, and in the course of many trips to her Liberal salon at Lansdowne House, his appreciation of her kindness had grown into an admiration of her political judgement that bordered on reverence. 'You can rely upon my secrecy,' Hannah wrote to Hamilton at the end of January, having received from him a list of possible ministers in a minority cabinet.[8] 'I will do nothing to betray your confidence ... I have merely glanced at your document. I will study it tonight. I will not show it to Archie till you let me.' These were highly sensitive discussions, and the pair used code names for the prospective ministers. Hannah's excitement at the fine and quick judgement required by such political manoeuvring is palpable in her letters: 'I still believe I am right, and [Gladstone] will secure a good staff. But the working of it!'[9]

It was with great diplomacy that she responded to the suggestion that Archibald might be appointed Foreign Secretary. 'I do not in the least anticipate such a position,' she wrote to Hamilton.[10] Her attempt at surprise rings false – it seems unlikely that she would have forgotten

Hamilton's trip to Mentmore some months earlier, when the assembled group had played at putting together their ideal cabinets, and he had placed Rosebery in the Foreign Office.[11] The matter, however, required delicate handling: at thirty-eight, Archibald was very young for the post, and Gladstone, who was prone to bouts of suspicion towards his protégé, had also been considering Lord Spencer and Lord Granville. Hannah insisted that Hamilton not press too hard for Archibald's appointment, at the same time making it clear that he would not refuse the post.[12] The offer was made, and with some trepidation, Archibald accepted. For all her restraint during the lobbying process, Hannah's letter of thanks to Hamilton reveals how much she had wanted the appointment. 'Gratitude I feel to you,' she wrote.[13] 'It is a word very seldom used by me and it comes from my heart . . . You are a real friend. Remember I can be likewise.'

Earlier in the 1880s, Edward Hamilton had detected some hostility in the Queen's behaviour towards Lady Rosebery: 'though H[er] M[ajesty] invited all the Tory notabilities, male and female, to break bread with her,' he wrote after one court event, 'she never asked Lady Rosebery to accompany her husband to dinner.'[14] But as Archibald's political star ascended, Hannah's presence could no longer be prevented, and both Roseberys became frequent visitors to court. Queen Victoria was impressed by Archibald's conduct in the office, and by the skill and tact with which Hannah discharged her duties as the wife of a secretary of state, which included accompanying the wife of the Chinese ambassador for an audience with the Queen and attending a reception of 'Colonials, Indians, & Home Commissioners'.[15] Soon Hannah was being invited to social occasions, including dinners at Windsor, and although Gladstone's minority government would fall at the end of July 1886, the Queen's favour would endure. Later that summer, Hannah and Archibald were invited to join her for a banquet at Holyrood House.[16]

Princess Louise was Victoria's sixth child and fourth daughter. Born in 1848, as Europe was erupting with revolutions, she grew into a fiery and artistic young woman whose prickly demeanour, rakishness and attraction to the bohemian milieu of London's nineteenth-century art world would lead her to stretch the conventions of royal propriety. During family gatherings at Balmoral and Osborne, she had been known to flirt inappropriately with the Private Secretary to the Queen, and it was widely rumoured that she was conducting an affair with the Queen's Sculptor in Ordinary, Sir Joseph Edgar Boehm. When Boehm died, in 1890, she was present at his house on the Fulham Road – it was claimed by some that he died *in flagrante*.[17]

On the surface, moralistic Constance Rothschild and wild Princess Louise were not obvious soulmates, but the public's preoccupation with the princess's peccadilloes obscured the full character of an independent-minded woman engaged with a number of campaigns in which Constance played a role.[18] One night Princess Louise attended a meeting, hosted by Constance and Cyril at Surrey House, on a new scheme to remedy the lack of accessible recreational facilities open on Sundays.[19] The princess arrived as an 'interested member of the audience', and left as a friend.

Unlike her older brother, Bertie – who, as heir to the throne, had both the motivation and the resources to establish his own power base – Princess Louise remained firmly in her mother's orbit. It was natural, then, that as the friendship developed, she should invite Constance down to Windsor. In May 1886 Constance arrived in Windsor for a weekend stay. In an excitable diary entry, she recorded arriving to find that the chestnut trees of Windsor Park were in 'magnificent bloom' and the 'whole place redolent of spring'.[20] On the Sunday morning she ate breakfast with the household, then wandered the castle's famous Long Gallery, amusing herself 'by a study of the interesting portraits and pictures'. She asked Princess Louise to take her to the Wolsey Chapel to visit the tomb of the Duke of Albany, Queen Victoria's youngest son, who had died a couple of years earlier.

Constance's relationship to Hannah Primrose, and her tender gesture of visiting the chapel, provoked the Queen's interest. On the Sunday night she was invited to dine with Her Majesty. Bedecked in diamonds and emeralds, Constance gathered in the Long Gallery with the other dinner guests. Eventually a royal functionary called out 'The Queen!', a door opened, and Constance saw a 'short but stately figure in black advancing towards me with the greatest dignity and solemnity'.[21] Constance had met Queen Victoria once, many years before. But that had been a fleeting moment in a royal drawing room, where she barely had time to peck the Queen's hand before she was 'hurried on, my train hastily gathered up and thrust under my unwilling arm'.[22] At first, the Windsor meeting looked as if it might play out in a similar fashion: Constance curtsied so low she 'felt as if the carpet were going to swallow me up', and the guests were ushered through to dinner, where the talk was so hushed that several times she felt 'much inclined to scream'. Afterwards, however, once the company had retired to the gallery, the Queen beckoned Constance to her. For the first time, the women had a conversation.

Victoria began by telling Constance about the time she saw her Rothschild great-grandfather, Mayer Amschel, when she was visiting Frankfurt as a child. Constance gently reminded the Queen that Mayer Amschel had died in 1812, seven years before the monarch's birth.[23] The Queen waved away the suggestion that the Rothschild she had seen might instead have been Constance's great-uncle Amschel, maintaining that 'it surely must have been the husband of that wonderful old Frau Rothschild [Gutle]'. They went on to discuss other members of Constance's family, including her mother, Louisa, and her great-uncle, Moses Montefiore, who had died the previous year, at the age of 100. Constance recalled for Victoria 'how my venerable uncle used to drink [her] health every day in a glass of port, removing the small skull-cap which he habitually wore, and saying most fervently, "God bless the Queen"'.

Over the following years there were further trips down to Windsor for Constance, and more meetings with the Queen, including one in the White Drawing Room, where the explorer Henry Morton Stanley gave a lecture.[24] Princess Louise also went to stay at Constance and Cyril's new coastal home in Overstrand, Norfolk, where she would settle in with her paintbox, brushes and sketchbooks. 'Princess Louise actually took her tea on the wee lawn and nobody turned their heads to look at her,' reported Clement Scott, whose gossipy book *Poppyland* did much to popularise the north Norfolk coast among late nineteenth-century metropolitans.[25] 'That the fishermen's wives hung their washing up in full view ... and the royal visitor bought her own stamps at the shop and strolled unattended on the sands – this seems incredible.' The princess loved the simplicity of Norfolk life. 'Let me thank you both again so very much for my delightful little stay at Overstrand,' she wrote to Constance and Cyril, after her visit, 'you were both so very very kind to me, & I did enjoy myself so much – It did me real good ... I quite delighted in the place, & the dear pretty little house so cosy, with such a charming hostess & host.'[26] Princess

Louise's letters now came addressed to 'my dear Constance' and were signed, 'ever yours affectionately, Louise'.

In 1890 the Queen gave a very public seal of approval to the Rothschild family by visiting Ferdinand's Waddesdon Manor in Buckinghamshire. Evelina's widower, who had not remarried, had begun work on the house in 1874, but it was only in 1883 that his spectacular Renaissance Revival mansion was completed. The Queen was greeted at Waddesdon by Ferdinand's sister, Alice, while Constance waited patiently in the inner hall, alongside other family members, including her husband, her mother and the Roseberys.[27] After eating lunch in private and having what Constance referred to as 'her snooze', the monarch was given a pony carriage tour of the grounds, and planted the obligatory commemorative tree.[28] Constance's husband Cyril, who had a further social engagement in the capital that evening, became impatient as the day drew on, and slipped off in the late afternoon to catch a train back to London.

Hannah was determined that the Liberal Party being out of office would not hamper Archibald's political career, and after a trip to India during which she managed to ignore the British political news for a while, she returned to Liberal politics with renewed energy. By 1889 she was giving speeches on his behalf at charity events in Glasgow, and that year she attended a football match at Ibrox Park, where she was cheered enthusiastically.[29] In February she was elated by Archibald's election as the first Chairman of the London County Council.[30] Even after being struck by an exhausting illness early in 1890, she continued to read the newspapers, write letters and, when she was capable of leaving bed, attend important events, such as Queen Victoria's visit to Waddesdon. She was, wrote Edward Hamilton, 'a very bad patient. She is quite conscious of being by no means strong; but she will not follow Doctor's instructions.'[31] In the summer, when her condition improved for a short while, Hannah was able to devote time to reading and writing on two of the biggest political questions in Scotland: the disestablishment of the Church, and Scottish home rule (both of which she considered to be inevitable).[32] It would have been a remarkably productive year for someone in full health, let alone for someone who was, it transpired in October, beset with typhoid fever.

Gladstone had a campaigning trip to Midlothian planned for the autumn, and it had been intended that Dalmeny would, as usual, serve as his base and political headquarters. Instead, it was closed off for Hannah's convalescence. Her absence would, Hamilton recorded, 'take a good deal of the gilt ... off the coming campaign'.[33] In the autumn Hannah's condition deteriorated badly; the prognosis was dire. Archibald wrote a note to Mrs Gladstone, who was staying in Edinburgh with her husband, asking if she might arrange for prayers to be said for his wife at the cathedral. 'I do not know who to ask at the cathedral,' he wrote, 'or whether they will pray for a Jewess.'[34] Hannah held on into November, clinging to life as determinedly as she had supported her husband. In their most optimistic moments, she and Archibald planned convalescent breaks to Torquay and Corfu. As they tried to face up to the worst, they remembered the best. 'No one could have made me so happy as you,' she told him.[35] 'I sometimes have felt it was wrong that I thought of the children so little in comparison to you. I will try to live for you.'

On 19 November Edward Hamilton wrote in his diary of the children Hannah felt she had wronged; that 'dear little quartet' had been 'left motherless'.[36] The draft of his funeral eulogy is covered with inserts, adjustments and crossings-out – the editorial twitching of a man struggling to capture in words the significance of his friend, and fearful of not doing her justice.[37] Hamilton's tribute is a rare account of Hannah from someone who saw her goodness: her shrewd judgement, her 'high sense of duty', and above all, the loyalty she showed to those she loved.

By comparison, the reaction to Hannah's death in the wider Rothschild family was muted. Many still thought of her as the pampered young woman of her Mentmore youth, and as an outsider to the family culture. Louisa did not pick up her diary to record the death. Constance was surprised by the strength of feeling she observed among mourners at the Roseberys' Berkeley Square home, and was stopped short by the sight of the coffin, the carpet around it strewn with flowers. With distance, however, her thoughts became franker and more critical. 'I admired her heroic qualities but I did not love her dearly, she was not one of my dearest friends,' she wrote, later commenting that 'much of the very marked outburst of affection' for her death was a result of 'the prominent place her husband holds. She would not have been what she was, had it not been for him.'[38]

Among the guests at the funeral was the courtier Sir Henry
Ponsonby, who arrived with a 'wreath of laurel, interspersed with Cape
Everlasting flowers' and a note which read that it was a 'mark of sin-
cere regard from Victoria R.I.'[39]

In the spring of 1891 Constance and Princess Louise travelled to
France together. Writing home to her mother, Constance painted an
intimate portrait of the princess, who was 'desperately conversational
– oh: how she talks!! Quite as much as I do', and made light of her
shambolic style of travelling: '[she] dresses & undresses in the train,
undoes her bag, opens her parcels, straps up her shawls (very well too),
puts on her gaiters – ties on her veil, over & over again.'[40]

The pair were headed for Grasse, on the French Riviera, where
Princess Louise's mother would also be spending the spring. Queen
Victoria would be staying in a hotel, while Constance and Princess
Louise would stay with Constance's cousin – Ferdinand's sister – Alice
de Rothschild, in the Villa Rothschild, the mansion Alice had built on
her 135-acre estate. When Constance and Princess Louise arrived at
the villa, the mistral was whistling, and Alice was hurrying around in
an anxious panic, pasting up doors and windows against the grit and
sand.[41] For weeks leading up to the royal arrival, she had been operating
in what Constance dubbed her 'Napoleon' mode, issuing instructions
to the inspector of police, preparing her garden and supervising the
creation of an identity card system for security reasons. She even had
a mountain road levelled and widened in order to create a new vista
for the Queen, an undertaking that involved 'building up small walls,
picking out huge stones, covering the smaller ones with macadam &
turning a stream'.

Even after the Queen had arrived, the ongoing business of choreo-
graphing an enormous team of police, gardeners and Provençal workers left Alice with little time for the usual graces of hostessing: it fell
to Constance to 'do the amiable to the Queen's household', with visits,
strolls and polite conversation.[42] The Queen was 'quite amaze[d]' by
Alice's energy and 'much touched' by the arrangements, but also appears to have been tickled by the mock-aristocratic grandeur of Alice's
life in Grasse. She was 'much amuse[d]' by the costume of Alice's
workers, who wore bright blue blouses, coloured caps (blue, scarlet

or yellow depending on their job), and matching stockings. When Constance let slip that Alice was remodelling the mountain road as a surprise, the Queen responded with 'a smile and a twinkle, like a child who thinks that the great fun of a secret is in divulging it'.[43]

At the end of March, Constance was invited by the Queen to join her in watching the town's famous Bataille de Fleurs from her hotel balcony. The Queen 'enjoyed herself immensely', throwing over the balcony nearly all the flowers that Alice had provided, and then, 'like Oliver Twist', asking for more.[44] There had been an outbreak of small-pox in the town, and everyone's arms were still aching from the inocu-lations given by the court physician, but Victoria was enjoying herself too much to worry about the possibility of infection, and happily re-ceived further flowers brought up from the street. 'These may be full of infection,' she said to Constance, her eyes twinkling, 'what would y[ou]r Cousin say to this?' Constance's social graces appealed to the Queen, who soon issued her daughter's friend with another invitation to the royal apartments.

On her next visit, Constance found 'H[er] M[ajesty] sitting in a low arm chair' and Princess Beatrice 'strumming away on the piano' while Princess Marie turned the pages of the music; Lady Church-ill's 'thin form' stood nearby.[45] Initially, the conversation was about the recently deceased Hannah, Lady Rosebery, but later, following a reception of local notables and a dinner, the Empress of India grew 'quite learned', talking about 'Hindostani and Hebrew'.[46] From then on, 'it was almost daily that I had the privilege of seeing, and often of speaking with, the Queen, who seemed to be fully enjoying the beauties of the South'.[47]

Now that she was on such intimate terms with the monarch, Con-stance started to find Alice's panicked stiffness around her 'really very funny'. In a letter home, she reported an occasion on which Alice, encountering the Queen unexpectedly, had 'walked backward, thro her room, for some yards, until the Queen was able to pass her'.[48] She was also becoming less tolerant of Princess Louise's frustrating char-acteristics – her tardiness, her showy informality and her short temper. Though Constance, now in her late forties, was Princess Louise's elder by only five years, she increasingly wrote about her friend with the impatience of someone from an older generation commenting on the antics of a child. After sitting through several spats between Prin-cess Louise and her sisters, Constance felt herself pitying the 'poor old Queen', who was 'made quite miserable' by the 'battle royales'.[49] Victoria was 'always gracious & kind', she wrote to her mother, '& I wish she would let me drive or sit with her for I am sure I could amuse her. But there is a hedge of etiquette around HM & I do not think that the Princesses wish one to see her very frequently or in a more intimate fashion.'

On her last day in Grasse, she somehow forgot to let the Queen know that she was leaving town: 'I like a goose did not inform her that I was going to depart.'[50] Thankfully, the mutual regard that had been established during the holiday in Grasse was resilient enough to withstand this breach of etiquette. It may also have helped that Alice had renamed her mansion in commemoration of the Queen's visit: the Villa Rothschild became the Villa Victoria.

27

Rescue and Prevention

ONE NIGHT IN 1885 a surprise visitor appeared at Constance and Cyril's London mansion, Surrey House, 'somewhat weary and agitated'.[1] Miss Pigott was a friend of Constance's from Norfolk, and a fellow temperance campaigner, who had recently been working in an East End Mission house, supporting 'streetwalkers who sought rest and refreshment'. One evening, two young Jewish girls had turned up. When the Christian volunteers talked to them, they discovered that the girls had no other way to earn money but to work in the 'unhappy sisterhood', and that they lacked any source of support. 'Our own people disown us,' they explained, because 'their Law forbids them to receive us again,' and the girls would 'not enter a Christian Home.' Miss Pigott needed Constance's advice, and her help.

Through the work of the social reformer Josephine Butler, Constance was aware of so-called 'white slavery', in which young and vulnerable women were forced into sex work. While many among the Anglo-Jewish elite were privately aware that there were Jewish women among those unfortunates, they were prevented from admitting it publicly out of fear that it would damage the reputation of the wider Jewish community. Institutions such as the Jewish Board of Guardians had 'tacitly ignored' the worsening situation, and the taboo had become so complete that even someone like Constance, who had an active interest in identifying and alleviating social problems of this kind, had found it possible to believe that the crisis affecting poor East End women had somehow bypassed those who were Jewish. 'The subject was one I had always avoided,' she later recalled, 'and I had never heard, nor, indeed, did I believe, that any so-called rescue work had been needed amongst the Jewish Community.'[2]

Though Constance had visited the East End plenty of times, it had mostly been to make visits to long-established charity contacts or teach in the family-sponsored school on Bell Lane, and what Pigott was describing initially overwhelmed her. 'Alas, I was hopelessly at sea in the matter!' she later recalled. Daunted, and fearful of breaking the communal taboo about Jewish sex work, she was initially reluctant to act. And yet Pigott managed to make Constance 'ashamed of my lukewarm sympathy', and persuaded her to arrange a meeting between some young Jewish sex workers and members of the Anglo-Jewish establishment.[3] Constance involved her cousin, Claude Montefiore, who was a progressive in terms of politics and religion. A few days later, Montefiore travelled to the Mission, accompanied by a priest and a police officer. The two Jewish girls failed to show up. It was a fitting introduction to the difficulties of the situation: the women they were trying to help were impoverished, not always at liberty to go where they wanted, and often had limited knowledge of London beyond the few streets in which they lived and worked. On top of all that, they had reason to be wary of the authorities.

The trip was not completely wasted. Claude spoke to the volunteers at the Mission, and came up with a plan. 'Mrs. Herbert should be invited to meet a few influential ladies of the Jewish faith, who would hear from her lips a plain and unvarnished account of what she had witnessed during the Mission week.' Constance's sister Annie offered the drawing room of her Curzon Street house as the venue. The meeting that ensued was a turbulent one, with some expressing angry incredulity at what Mrs Herbert had to report, while others 'reddened and wept'.[4] Constance was confident that the outrage and denial would mature into action – and she was right. After Mrs Herbert left, 'complete silence prevailed for a few minutes', and then began the 'warm proffers of personal help'. The women formed an organisation, the Jewish Ladies' Society for Preventive and Rescue Work – which sought to stop women from being forced into sex work, and to 'rescue' those who already had been. Constance was installed as honorary secretary, and Emma, the new Lady Rothschild, promptly accepted an invitation to act as president.[5] Her reputation for piety and modesty – not to say prudishness – would make the work of the society more palatable to those conservative elements still scandalised by even the acknowledgement of Jewish women's participation in the sex trade.

In the early 1880s a wave of pogroms swept across the Pale of Settlement – the western swathe of the Russian Empire in which Jews
were permitted to live – prompting an unprecedented influx of poor
Jewish immigrants to Britain. In 1860 there had been a Jewish population of forty thousand; in the thirty-three years from 1881 to 1914
around a hundred and fifty thousand Jewish immigrants would arrive
on British shores. Most settled near to their port of entry, and, for the
majority, that meant London's East End.[6] The influx of Ashkenazim
from the Russian Empire reinvigorated and diversified the existing Jewish cultures in the area. New synagogues were built, Yiddish
theatre thrived, and on Brick Lane a new bathhouse (Shewzick's)
opened, modelled on the steam baths or *banya* found in the Pale of
Settlement.[7] Constance had been taught Hebrew, but had little knowledge of Yiddish, which meant she had to rely on 'the kind offices of
some of the neighbours' to translate for her when she was performing
charity visits.[8] Walking around the East End at the beginning of the
society's work, she was struck as much as any outsider by the mezu-
zahs – parchment inscribed with verses from the Torah rolled inside
decorative cases and fixed to the doorposts of Jewish homes – and
the fringes of false hair, or *sheitel*, used by married women to cover
their heads.

The concentration of new arrivals in what was already a poor area
prompted a resurgence of antisemitism, among both those who lived
in the East End and those further afield, who pointed to the area as an
example of social decay. 'Is there any more sordid district in the world
than that part of London which lies to the south of Commercial-
road[?]' asked *Reynolds's Newspaper* at the end of the 1880s.

The air is impregnated with odour of offal. Indescribably offensive matter
litters the streets . . . A teeming population breathes this foetid atmosphere.
The gutters are alive with children . . . One cannot escape here from the
overpowering personality of the Jewish type. It meets one at every turn.[9]

Established Anglo-Jewry had spent decades attempting to assimilate and anglicise poor and working-class Jewry, and to create
a coherent, conformist identity for English Jews: this, after all,
had been one of the main endeavours of the Jews' Free School.
The new influx of migrants threatened to undermine that identity
– and if the motive for the new rescue and prevention charity was

in part an urgent interventionist one, it was also part of an effort to revive the long-standing project of anglicisation, in challenging circumstances.[10]

Constance spent the rest of the spring and summer developing a basic infrastructure for the society. The front line of their operation was the docks, where the society's agents attempted to intercept vulnerable or trafficked women amid scenes of 'indescribable confusion'. Pimps, runners and con artists jostled to reach newcomers before the charity workers did, crowds gathered to mock the 'strange garb and broken accent of the poverty-stricken foreigners', and boatmen argued with migrants unable to pay the landing fee.[11] Once two agents had been appointed (one to do the front-line work, and another to make sure the first did not himself take advantage of the women), Constance focused her energies on establishing the hostels and training centres that would serve as places of refuge for those rescued from the docks. The first was opened in Mile End in August 1885, but the aim was to open a home on the other side of the city, in Shepherd's Bush, where the 'fallen women' would be much further removed from East End traffickers, pimps and clients.[12]

The move out west would cost money, and fundraising was added to Constance's administrative duties. She wrote to the *Jewish Chronicle*, emphasising that, with an annual income of barely £400, the charity was 'sorely in need of a more extensive subscription list'.[13] While charities with long-standing links to the Rothschild family could rely on bountiful donations, individual women did not have a say in the resources of the bank, and, if they wanted to make major donations, often ended up trying to inveigle the support of male relatives. Just an additional £200, Constance pointed out, 'would enable us to move the Home for rescue work into premises admirably suited for our purpose, and which our Committee are anxious to engage'. By the end of 1886 she was able to record with satisfaction in her diary: 'Have moved into Charcroft House which admits 20 girls besides matrons.'[14]

The late Victorian philanthropic mentality tended to view 'fallen' women as minors, and the policies of Charcroft House were in keeping with this attitude. Adult women and teenage girls were given little freedom, and good conduct was rewarded with a system of treats.[15] When the social reformer Laura Ormiston Chant visited in 1887, she suggested that the women's emotional outbursts should be considered pathological events, and treated with sedatives; the same year, a new fence was constructed around the house's grounds to prevent women from running away.[16] Constance operated at some distance from the day-to-day struggles of managing the home, but the difficulties of maintaining discipline, hiring staff and winning the cooperation of the women did not pass her by. She was involved in the search for capable Jewish matrons (lack of similar pre-existing Jewish facilities meant there were few suitable candidates), and became familiar with some of the residents, which inevitably exposed her to 'heart-breaking disappointments' when 'rescue' attempts failed.[17]

Constance attributed such failures to the character of 'Jewish girls', who 'may be easy to touch for the moment' but were 'generally emotional, excitable, and often full of real true feeling', and so 'difficult to influence for any long period of time'.[18] In retrospect, and to many radical critics at the time, the failure was clearly less to do with character than with the failure of the home's methods to address the grinding imbalances of power and wealth that produced the problem of 'white slavery'. Among Constance's friends and close family, however, the most common criticism of her philanthropic work was a more straightforward and snobbish one. 'The fact is I am sulky,' wrote one guest at Overstrand, the lawyer and socialite Raymond Asquith.[19] 'The house is reeking with the gross and human odours which ever cling about the skirts of philanthropy: one sits down to dinner with a rabble of small shopkeepers from Balham and Battersea.'

As the years drew on, the scale of the problem in the East End only grew. Dispirited with the lack of progress being made through the Society, Constance began spending more time at the Hanway Street Sabbath classes, one of the few educational institutions aimed at helping East End Jewish women. She had become aware of the lack of amenities for women on Friday nights and identified this as an area in which she could make a significant difference.[20] The result, set up with the help of her mother Louisa and various social workers, was the West Central Friday Night Club, Britain's first working girls' club for Jewish immigrants. Attendees could sign up for training in technical trades, art, languages and public affairs, as well as receiving instruction on their labour rights and how to join trade unions.[21]

There was a logic to this shift in focus, because Constance was convinced that better social and educational amenities would save many Jewish women from falling victim to sexual exploitation. And yet the jumping between projects was becoming something of a pattern –

from temperance, to Rescue and Prevention, to the Friday Night Club. Beatrice Webb, a critical but by no means hostile commentator, once observed that Constance was 'good natured and quite intelligent', but 'like all these "Society Dames" quite incapable of anything but chit-chat, flying from point to point'.[22] That flitting, distractible quality marked Constance's charitable enterprises just as much as her conversation, and her endeavours suffered as a result. Within months the combination of residual society commitments with the new demands of the Friday Night Club was, Constance confided in her diary, 'more work than I can possibly manage',[23] and an increasing amount of work in both organisations was handed over to other social workers.

The situation at the Friday Night Club was not made any easier by attacks on the club from conservative voices in the Jewish community, who regarded the institution as drawing women away from their responsibilities as domestic workers and mothers on the most important night of the week, and were further alarmed by the club being based in Soho.[24] Though Constance disagreed with such objections, she did what she could to manage them, maintaining a 'semi-religious' element in the club's curriculum and moving its premises to Dean Street when it transpired that the Frith Street classrooms were next to a 'bad house' of the kind that the club campaigned against.[25]

Constance's new line of work was also causing controversy at home. Two months after the society was established, the *Pall Mall Gazette* carried a series of reports on sexual exploitation and trafficking in London: 'The Maiden Tribute of Modern Babylon'.[26] The articles, written by the paper's editor, W.T. Stead, were forerunners of modern scandal journalism, combining moral outrage with titillating detail. The combination of their shocking content, and Stead's tactics – he had actually purchased a young girl, Eliza Armstrong, for the price of five pounds – electrified public discussion on the sexual exploitation of women. Cyril appears to have regarded Stead's work as part of a moral panic and an attack on men in general, and saw Constance's rescue and prevention endeavour as part of the same project. He made no attempts to hide his feelings from Constance or her mother. 'Rather stormy discussions with Cyril about Women's Rights, Stead etc.,' Louisa wrote in her diary after one evening at Aston Clinton.[27]

There was a personal dimension to these arguments, too. In the summer of 1885 Charles Dilke – a Liberal MP and close friend of Cyril's, as well as of other Rothschilds – was accused of seducing his brother's sister-in-law, the nineteen-year-old Virginia Crawford. In any period, such a case would have piqued the public interest. But at a time when sexual exploitation was coming under renewed scrutiny, it was dynamite. Cyril was, Constance noted, 'determined to pull [Dilke] thro whether he has done right or wrong'.[28] When the case came to trial, he was one of the friends who put on a public display of support by accompanying Dilke to the court.[29]

In February 1886 the case returned a paradoxical verdict consistent with the double standards of the day: Virginia had been guilty of adultery with Dilke, but there was insufficient evidence to show that Dilke had been guilty of adultery with Virginia. Stead responded to this by launching a campaign against Dilke, whom he regarded as the more culpable party. Constance shared Stead's outrage at the court's decision. In public, she had a role to play as a loyal and supportive wife, but privately she recorded her belief that Cyril 'seems ... to lose his proper judgement in such cases'.[30] She was determined, however hard or unpleasant it was, to 'stick to what I think right'. After a visit from the Dilkes, she took to her diary to vent her true feelings on the situation: 'He looked very uncomfortable, she excited & tearful. I believe him to be guilty.'

28

Elevations

DURING THE EARLY 1880s Gladstone's support for home rule and his failure to speak out against antisemitic pogroms in the Russian Empire had lost him the support of many Anglo-Jewish Liberals – Natty among them – but Cyril remained a dogged ally.[1] His loyalty was rewarded: after his Brecon constituency was abolished in 1885, he was ushered into the new seat of Luton. 'I am delighted that he has not lost his favourite occupation,' wrote Louisa, who had been to Luton to see Cyril's victory declared.[2] In early 1886 Gladstone offered him the role of Liberal Chief Whip and Lord of the Treasury, and in 1892 he was offered a barony. Constance had managed to suppress her misgivings about the role of whip – it was, she thought, an unprincipled role that made one 'slave to the House' and 'tyrant of the numbers' – but when it came to the barony, she could not help airing her doubts.[3] By the early 1890s the Lords was coming to be seen by Liberals as a constitutionally problematic house, and Constance was convinced that the Commons was the place for 'real' political work.[4] On the way back from the opera festival in Bayreuth, Constance wrote to Cyril to express her misgivings. After a couple of days, having seen how much the title meant to him, she dropped her opposition and wrote supportively about his chosen name, which was 'Lord Battersea', after the estates he had inherited from his father. But Cyril had been 'hurt and vexed' by the initial letter, and would, she feared, 'never quite forget it'.[5]

If he did, it was only because this falling-out was dwarfed by a cataclysmic dispute over another role, offered to him less than a year later. Arriving at Surrey House one afternoon in January 1893, Constance saw a telegram addressed to Cyril lying on the table.[6] It was from Lord Ripon – a loyal Gladstonian and Secretary of State for the

Colonies. She waited nervously for Cyril's return. He arrived in a celebratory mood. 'I have good news for you,' he said, flinging himself into
a chair. 'I have been offered the governorship of New South Wales.'
The Australian territory was one of the more prestigious colonial gov-
ernorships – and one of the furthest away. The posting would be for
five years, meaning that should Cyril take the position, Constance
might never again see her mother Louisa, who was in her seventies.
The news, Constance wrote, 'struck me like a knife'.[7]

That evening she sat distractedly through a play at the Haymar-
ket Theatre, before spending a sleepless night at Surrey House. The
next day, following a Rescue and Prevention committee meeting, she
went to see Lord Ripon herself. Depleted by sleeplessness, she 'broke
down & cried my heart out'. Lord Ripon was 'so kind', but by this
point things were beyond his control.[8] Annie acted as a go-between,
travelling to and fro between Cyril, at the House of Lords, and Surrey
House, where her sister was feeling 'more and more wretched'. At the
heart of the matter was her relationship with her mother. 'The idea
of leaving my mother ... and going to the other end of the world appeared to me like committing a sin,' Constance later recalled.[9]

When he was not at the Lords, Cyril had been out and about,
consulting his family members and friends. Opinion was uniformly in
favour of him taking the job. Worse, he had anticipated the objection
relating to Louisa, and had devised a solution: she could come to New
South Wales with them.[10] Backed into a corner, Constance agreed to
go with her sister to Aston Clinton to seek counsel from their mother,
who had not yet been told anything about the offer.[11] They took with
them a sealed letter from Cyril.

Though Louisa immediately noticed how careworn her daughters
appeared when they arrived at Aston Clinton – Annie looked 'grave
and concerning' and Constance positively 'ill' – she was still stunned
by the letter presented to her after lunch.[12] The governorship, Cyril
had written, was 'my life long ambition but an ideal I never hoped
to realise', a 'one in a million' opportunity that he 'could under no
combination of circumstances be offered again'.[13] In a manipulative
final flourish, he had enclosed two letters, both addressed to Lord
Ripon. One accepted the post, the other rejected it. He had arranged
with Constance that a messenger would take the chosen reply to the
Colonial Office on Tuesday. Writing her memoirs nearly thirty years
later, Constance remembered the days that followed as some of the

most miserable of her life.[14] Eventually, the women came to a decision, and sent their chosen letter by courier to the desk of Lord Ripon. It explained that Cyril had 'discussed the question with my wife & her mother' and that 'both are against it': he would therefore have to 'decline the service which it would have been a delight to me to have rendered the govm't and the country'.

After the refusal had been forwarded to Lord Ripon, Constance picked up her pen to compose a much harder letter: to Cyril. 'I really do not know how to write to you to day,' she began.[15] 'I feel so shaken with what we have all been going thro!' Desperate to explain herself, she emphasised that the decision had been made purely for the sake of her ageing mother.

If you could have seen dear Mamma's state of alarm, & anxiety; if you could have heard her emphatic declaration that she could not join us, & her heartbroken words that she would never see us again, & if you could have caught the loving way in which she spoke about you, I feel sure you would have been deeply moved.

And yet in her diary, Louisa claimed to have acted for Constance's benefit alone. 'If I had imagined for a moment that it could have conduced to dear Connie's happiness,' she wrote, 'I should not have put myself in the way.'[16]

Cyril resented all three women. A week after the refusal had been sent, he came down to Aston Clinton with some friends. It was the type of small weekend gathering that usually gave Louisa pleasure, but on this occasion Cyril's 'disappointment and anger about the New South Wales appointment' hung over him like a black cloud, making her feel 'most uncomfortable!'[17] Cyril's bitterness infected her mood: 'Feel low and sad – whatever I am doing, my thoughts refer to the events of last week and to the terrible offer and Cyril's wish to accept it.' In the immediate aftermath of the refusal, all three women sent letters to Cyril to explain, excuse and defend their decision, with Annie and Louisa taking pains to stress that Constance had behaved 'quite impartially' throughout the process.[18] It was a rearguard action against a resentment that threatened to take a devastating toll on Constance and Cyril's marriage.

Cyril began to detach himself from his wife's family, making fewer and fewer visits to Aston Clinton, and spending time instead at the

The Pleasaunce, Constance and Cyril's country house in Overstrand, Norfolk.

couple's Overstrand property, the Pleasaunce, which became a sump for his frustrated energies. The architect Edwin Lutyens, then in the early years of his career, was hired, and, under Cyril's whimsical instruction, embarked on what would be a long and confused programme of renovations and additions.[19] Some cloisters were added, a clock tower sprang up; on one occasion, Constance arrived from London to find a wall being built across one of her favourite views, and she began pulling it down, brick by brick. Lutyens's compliance towards his client belied his own private frustrations with Cyril, who, he wrote, 'murders and alters everything I design'.[20] When Cyril was not planning new alterations, he was rethinking the gardens, taking photographs, or playing tennis, cricket or golf.[21] Constance watched with dismay as her husband's interest in serious political work, once his 'favourite occupation', evaporated. 'Feel so disappointed about Cyril,' she wrote a year after the New South Wales incident, 'he has entirely thrown his chances away, leads an idle and cut-up life, alas! I feel I have been seriously to blame.'[22]

Shut out by Cyril, Constance felt obliged to make the best she could of the English life that had been purchased at such a cost. Along with the expansion of her Rescue and Prevention homes, a more explicitly political strand was developing in her charity portfolio. The late 1880s and early 1890s had seen the founding of several councils and congresses that united, across the lines of religious and political affiliation, those campaigning on 'women's issues' – a broad term that included sex work, unequal pay, temperance and votes for women. In 1892 her friend from Brecon, Fanny Morgan, invited her to a conference on 'women's work' in Bristol. The idea of the conference was, as the *Woman's Herald* put it, that women of 'all shades of creed and opinion', involved in all kinds of fragmented but interrelated endeavours, could 'meet together, and in perfect peace and amity discuss some of the most important questions of the day with regard to their own sex'.[23]

Constance was prominent among the three hundred delegates – she 'always sat on the platform' and received a vote of thanks for her contribution.[24] But none of that was enough to quell the paralysing self-doubt that tended to assail her at events like this, surrounded by so many other women who she feared were working with more energy, insight or effectiveness than her. She later wrote in her diary: 'Oh! How weak and ignorant I am.'[25] Her insecurity was exacerbated by the sneering coverage in newspapers and journals. *Punch*'s report on the event, written in the form of a letter from a lonely and disgruntled male reader – 'An Old Bachelor, The Growleries, Lostbuttonbury, Singleton' – had a veneer of irony to it, but there was no mistaking that the satire, which mocked the mixed metaphors in Constance's speech, was intended to wound.[26]

Thankfully, the conference provided Constance with more than enough support and inspiration to make up for the snide press coverage, and over the following years her 'women's work' would only expand. In 1894 – during the brief premiership of Hannah's widower, Archibald, Lord Rosebery – she was appointed to the Board of Prison Visitors. The inmates of the purpose-built women's prison at Woking (the only facility of its kind in England) had just been moved to a much older jail in Aylesbury, not far from Aston Clinton. During her childhood, Constance had felt a chill as she passed Aylesbury prison, which then housed male inmates: she imagined the gatehouse to be haunted by the last man hanged there.[27] One 'gloomy afternoon' in December 1894, at the age of fifty-one, she steeled herself against her childhood fears and made her first visit, chaperoned by the civil

servant Sir Algernon West. There was, she discovered, 'nothing particularly striking or tragic' about the inmates themselves, and yet the
conditions of the place – cold, unfurnished, 'clothed in gloom and
shrouded in silence', and staffed by female wardens 'dressed severely
in black' – were haunting.

This first visit left Constance doubting whether she could have
any meaningful impact on the lives of the inmates, and it took some
encouragement from Sir Algernon before she was persuaded to try.[28]
Over the course of several years and many more prison visits, she
started to believe that she could make some positive changes. Her
list of small victories grew: a 'qualified nurse for the Infirmary'; better clothing, nightdresses and shoes; toothbrushes; better books and
educational opportunities; 'strips of carpet for the patients by the side
of their beds in the winter months'; and numerous other little improvements that highlight just how bad the conditions were: 'Oh,
how rejoiced I was when I first caught sight of a real chair!'[29] The
work helped to reinforce Constance's existing opinions on a number
of social issues, especially on the subject of alcohol. In a speech given
in June 1897, she recalled asking one returning inmate why she was
in prison again, and being struck by the response: 'Why are there so
many public houses in Marylebone?'[30]

Soon after her prison visiting began, Constance was appointed
one of ten vice-presidents to the National Union of Women Workers
(NUWW), an organisation affiliated to the International Council of
Women (ICW). It was in her role as vice-president that Constance
attended the ICW's quinquennial meeting, which in the summer of
1899 drew to London over two thousand campaigners from across
the globe.[31] The popularity of the congress took the organisers by
surprise. Even after the 'public meeting of welcome' was moved
from Westminster Town Hall to the much larger Convocation Hall
of Church House, the reporter for *The Times* found an 'overflowing
attendance'.[32] The crowd erupted in cheers as Lady Aberdeen, president of the International Council of Women, delivered her opening
address. Constance occupied a prominent place in the crowd. She
was not just one attendee among many: Mrs Booth, president of the
National Union of Women Workers and a delegate for Great Britain
and Ireland, had been forced to withdraw from the congress at the
last minute due to ill health, and had nominated the fifty-six-year-old
Lady Battersea to stand in for her.

The breadth of the ICW was both a strength and a weakness. Many member organisations, from many countries, had to approve the council's programme, with the effect that more radical and divisive voices – such as those advocating the 'New Woman' ideas of divorce reform and female suffrage – were often excluded from the agenda.[33] That is precisely what happened at the 1899 conference, where more moderate demands (such as for equal pay and state-paid maternity maintenance) dominated the agenda and the question of suffrage was avoided.[34] This time, however, the Council had underestimated the strength of some delegates' feelings on the vote. In protest at no debate being scheduled on women's suffrage, there were several high-profile resignations.[35]

Lady Aberdeen, who was more sympathetic to the suffragist cause than the NUWW contingent of which Constance was a part, sought to smuggle the topic back onto the agenda by organising a special panel away from official congress proceedings.[36] The 29 June meeting – chaired by Millicent Fawcett – was a packed, fiery affair that inspired discomfort in the NUWW. 'To the well-bred and conventional ladies that dominate it,' observed Beatrice Webb, 'the "screeching sisterhood" demanding their rights represents all that is detestable.' Constance was bound to the conservative NUWW clique both by her role as a proxy for Mrs Booth and by her own conservative political instincts. Throughout the Congress she worked in support of the Union's preferred approach, which was for 'decorous' meetings on topics that were 'practical, even technical in character'.[37] Her loyalty won the approval of her colleagues in the Union, and would, within a few years, lead her to positions of greater responsibility.

On the evening of 22 January 1901 the nation was shocked to a standstill by news from the Isle of Wight: the Queen was dead. In London, the shop windows were suddenly full of black garments, and cab drivers wore bows of crêpe on their whips; at the women's prison at Aylesbury, some of the convicts pulled 'small pieces off their boot-laces' and pinned them to the front of their gowns in black bows, in order to 'show some mark of respect to the memory of their Sovereign'.[38] Constance had seen less of the Queen during the 1890s, catching only fleeting glimpses of her in drawing rooms and at garden parties. It was her sister Annie, who lived at Hamble just over the water from Osborne, who had the most contact with the monarch in the years preceding her death. '[T]he Queen asked a great deal after you and Constance,' she had written to her mother, after a trip to Osborne in 1898.[39] Annie received a card of admission to the chapel where the Queen's body lay, and saw the casket, startlingly small among the flowers and wreaths. 'The Ancien Régime saying farewell!' she wrote to her mother.[40]

The Queen would be buried in Windsor alongside Albert, but her coffin would pass through London in a military cortège from Victoria station (where it arrived from the south coast) to Paddington (from where it left for Windsor). Once the route was announced, high society responded with a grim mirror image of the sociability that went on during a monarch's lifetime. Hostesses sent out invitations on black-bordered paper, competing to offer the best window or balcony for a view of the coffin, and the best refreshments to go with the view.[41] Annie was persuaded to join Emma at no. 148 Piccadilly, while Constance chose to host her own guests at Surrey House. Cyril's official duties required him to meet the funerary train on its arrival from Portsmouth.[42]

On the morning of the procession, Constance drew up the blinds of her room overlooking Hyde Park and saw 'with astonishment' that 'lines of black-clothed women had already taken their places'.[43] Horse-drawn night trams had brought the first grieving Londoners into the city centre before the sun was up. Many of those visiting from elsewhere in the country had arrived at the main-line stations in the middle of the night, and had wandered the streets for hours, trying to keep warm.[44] Even the houses, Constance thought, 'seemed to have put on mourning', draped as they were in hangings of black or – the Queen's preferred colour – violet.[45] Constance was stunned by the 'extraordinary hush' which hung over the usually raucous thoroughfare. Later that day she sat waiting at the window 'in a state of trembling excitement'.[46] All of a sudden, the procession came into view. 'The coffin reposing on the gun-carriage and covered with the Union Jack looked strangely small and un-regal.'

That evening the synagogue was packed, with 'every seat taken'.[47] It was a disappointing service: over-long, 'all read, no chanting', with a 'prayer for the R[oyal] F[amily] in English', and an 'affected sermon affectedly given'. Outside, in spite of the crowds left milling around after the procession, London felt deserted. 'The emptiness of the great city without the feeling of the Queen's living presence in Her Empire & the sensation of universal change haunted me more than any other sensation,' wrote Constance. To her mother, who had stood in the gallery of St James's Palace more than sixty years earlier and watched the Queen as 'a radiantly happy young bride, beautiful from happiness', the death seemed 'ominous of many things to come'.[48]

Upon the death of his mother, the Prince of Wales ascended to the throne as King Edward VII, and his counter-court became the court proper. For the Rothschild men, this was transformative: never before had they had such a close and trusting relationship with a reigning monarch. Within a few years of his accession, Edward VII had dined with Alfred, hosted Emma and Natty at Windsor, and been hosted by them at no. 148 Piccadilly.[49] The culture of the new court was still unmistakably one that had so offended the Rothschild women decades earlier, during its incubation at Marlborough House. Alice Keppel, the King's mistress, was even given an official seat in the side gallery at the coronation.[50]

The brazen positioning of Mrs Keppel would have pained Emma in particular. Since the 1880s Natty had been conducting his own affair, with Lady Gosford, an attractive woman fifteen years his junior. Lady Gosford was, like Emma, something of a bluestocking – Natty had once written to a friend, looking for a copy of Schopenhauer for her to take on holiday – but she was less prudish than Emma, and more deeply connected to the world of Liberal politics in which Natty had made his name.[51] Even more conveniently, Lady Gosford's husband held an official position at the new court, making it easy for Natty to bring his mistress to social events. Lady Gosford's friendship with various family members, including Leo and his wife Marie, meant she was also a frequent attendee at Rothschild parties. Emma, who was intensely loyal to Natty, endured the situation in silence. As her daughter-in-law would later tell one of Emma's grandchildren: 'your grandmother is not the complaining sort'.[52]

In the year that Victoria died, Constance was offered – and reluctantly accepted – the post of president of the NUWW. Although she continued to have a nagging fear that she lacked 'quickness and brainpower' compared to her fellow campaigners, her first term in office allayed some of her self-doubt.[53] The following year, at a conference in Edinburgh, she was re-elected to the same post. To those who appointed her, she must have seemed a safe pair of hands to shepherd the organisation through the early Edwardian years. And yet, for all of Constance's skills and diplomacy, and her unblemished record of moral probity, some things lay beyond her control. One of these was the private life of her husband.

29

'Big Guns Arrived during
the Night'

EVEN AS A young girl and a novice diarist, Constance had always
been careful about what she wrote. She would often have second thoughts, and return to her prose to ink out a strong emotion or
embarrassing event – as she did after her cousin Puggy peeked under
her petticoats. Sometimes she did so out of fear at how future readers
might judge her, and at other times because she could not bear to
accept the truth of what she had written. The diary entries covering
the days after her re-election as president of the NUWW are almost
obscured by these heavy redactions, but it is still possible to piece
together what happened, if not the full extent of its emotional effect
on her.

Constance was still in Edinburgh when she received some news
about Cyril that left her feeling 'nervous, anxious, uncomfortable'.[1]
She returned to London as soon as she could. Cyril had retreated to
Overstrand, complaining of congestion of the lungs.[2] Although his
ailment seems to have been real enough, he was escaping more than
the London pollution. From the fragments that remain of Constance's
diary entry covering her arrival at Overstrand, it appears that Cyril
found it impossible to look his wife in the eye.

That same day, the *Sunday Special* printed a brief – yet tantalis-
ing – article entitled 'Rumoured Society Scandal: A Peer's Flight'.
'There are persistent rumours in society circles', ran the report, 'that
a well-known peer has been compelled to leave the country in order
to escape prosecution on a criminal charge of a most serious character. Sensational developments may be expected.'[3] Over the following
days the story was picked up by newspapers up and down the country,
from the *Bournemouth Daily Echo* to the *Dundee Evening Telegraph*,
the *Gloucestershire Echo* to the *Sunderland Echo and Shipping Gazette*.[4]

The incident they were skirting round was a homosexual sex scandal at court. Sex between men had been illegal for hundreds of years under the statute against sodomy. In 1885, amid a rising moral panic, the new and broader offence of 'gross indecency' had ushered in decades during which surveillance of male sexuality intensified and prosecutions – most notoriously that of Oscar Wilde in 1895 – became more frequent and severe. The *Sunday Special* hinted that another such prosecution was imminent.

Though the papers left the disgraced peer unnamed, the timing of Cyril's sudden retreat to Norfolk did nothing to stop the rumours. Amid the intense gossip surrounding the sexuality of prominent men, Cyril's name had often been mentioned. The social campaigner Josephine Butler had written to her son seven years previously, in 1895, about 'the Oscar Wilde madness' which was, according to her, 'spread like a plague thro' London fashionable & artistic society', saying that she had heard a 'dreadful account' of Cyril being 'led astray' by his friend, the psychical researcher Frederic William Henry Myers.[5] Tethered to him by loyalty, Constance must have turned a blind eye to what was obvious to so many around her for so long.

In November 1902, after Cyril's retreat to Overstrand, the diarist George Ives – who was an early campaigner for gay rights and well informed about the scandals and legal threats that affected men in London – noted in his diary:

it has been said in several papers that a certain peer well known in financial circles has been charged with offenses against morality & held to bail in £5,000. Rumour & information ... said it was Lord B[attersea] & that he was safe across the water. But ... my Lord B[attersea] is reported to be ill at his country place, & there is profound silence: I wonder what it means?[6]

After receiving further information, Ives went back to his diary and added a postscript. 'It probably was [Lord Battersea]. King Edward is said to have squashed the whole thing tho it was quite well known.'

Cyril remained at Overstrand for the following month, barely venturing from his room.[7] When they encountered him at all, guests found him to be sullen and distant. During a visit to Overstrand in January 1903, Beatrice Webb found her host to be a 'distinctly objectionable' man 'without either intellect or character' (perhaps influenced by the recent rumours, she suspected he had 'many bad habits of body and mind'). In striking contrast with Raymond Asquith, who thought Constance's charitable work ruined the atmosphere at the Pleasaunce, Webb regarded it as one of the house's few redeeming features. 'They live in a gorgeous villa overflowing with objects of virtue and art, with no individuality or taste. There are no children. He has no public spirit. They are both overfed. If it were not for her genuine kind-heartedness and good intention the household would be positively repulsive.'[8]

Just months after Beatrice Webb's visit, Cyril would travel to a sanatorium on the Continent, where he would spend lengths of time, on and off, for several years. At the end of the year Constance recorded in her diary that 1902 had stood out for 'three significant reasons, or rather, events'. One of these was 'national', one 'individual', and one 'conjugal'.[9] The national event was the coronation of Edward VII and the individual her work in the NUWW, especially her re-election as president in Edinburgh. As for the conjugal event, the pages recording it have been cleanly cut away.[10]

Although the scandal surrounding Cyril did not have an immediate impact on Constance's leadership of the NUWW, she chose to stand down the following year.[11] When she attended the next meeting of the ICW, in Berlin in 1904, she did so as a veteran rather than as president. This time a debate on the female franchise was part of the official programme, and a pro-suffrage resolution was passed, although there remained a substantial anti-suffrage presence within the organisation.[12] Constance stayed relatively aloof from such controversies. She delivered her paper on temperance, attended the usual rounds of concerts and picnics, and took motor rides through the woods at a 'terrific pace' with her friend Frau Deutsch.[13]

Constance's personal views were now firmly in favour of female suffrage, at least for local elections. In 1907, following the defeat of a bill that would have allowed women to vote for and serve in local government, she and other prominent campaigners, including Lady Aberdeen and Millicent Fawcett, signed a letter that was sent to the Prime Minister, Henry Campbell-Bannerman, demanding urgent change. They were successful: the Qualification of Women Act 1907 asserted (against a background of varied exclusions, up and down the country) the right of women to serve on county and borough councils in England and Wales. Later, one of the many women to take advantage of the new right was Constance's old friend from Brecon, Fanny Morgan, who had campaigned so ardently with her during the 1880 election. Fanny became the first woman to sit on a borough council in Wales, and, in 1910, the first woman to sit as mayor of a Welsh borough.

Following Cyril's return from the Continent, the couple spent an increasing amount of time at Overstrand, where Cyril purchased the lease to a nearby farm, and developed an obsession with motoring.[14] Constance stood by her husband, spending more and more time at the Pleasaunce. Her attempts to seek out local causes to occupy her while in Norfolk offended against Cyril's wish to keep the Pleasaunce as a place of private leisure, and he objected vociferously to her being involved locally in educational institutions or philanthropic projects. 'It is difficult, Cyril does not like my being on the school Board or taking any prominent part in anything,' she wrote.

The cracks in the marriage were becoming crevasses that even weekend guests could not ignore. The novelist Rhoda Broughton commented that 'the more I go up in Lady Battersea's estimation, the more I go down in Lord Battersea's'.[15] When Raymond Asquith complained to Cyril about the 'gross and human odours' of the 'rabble' at Overstrand, 'the poor man agreed with me: he suffers terribly from his wife, who is full of philanthropy and temperance and all that sort of nonsense.'[16] Increasingly, the life choices of husband and wife seemed incompatible. As Constance commented in a diary entry of January 1905: 'life here is not easy'.[17]

She took refuge, as she had before, in religious reflection. The emergence of a new school of progressive Jewish thought, Liberal Judaism, had given her hope that she might find a way out of the no-man's-land in which she had so long felt trapped, like her mother before her, cut off 'from much of Judaism' but unable to pass beyond 'the very outer gates of Christianity'.[18] The pioneer of Liberal Judaism was Constance's cousin, Claude Montefiore, who had helped with the 'fallen' Jewish women in East London some years before. Much of his thinking – including his universalist social ethics, his interest in the New Testament, his feminist critique of the Talmud, and his tendency to mysticism – echoed Constance's own. The reformed Liberal Jewish service was also much more appealing to her: many traditional rituals were discarded, elements of 'church-like' worship were introduced, and men and women sat together.[19] In 1902 Lily Montagu – who had worked with Constance to expand the West End Friday Night Club during the 1890s – established the Jewish Religious Union (JRU) to promote Montefiore's new vision for Judaism.[20] After her retreat to Overstrand, Constance continued to follow Claude and Lily's work closely. 'The Jewish question seems to meet me at every turn,' she wrote, 'I am enormously interested in the development of the J.R.U. also in Claude & his work.'[21]

During the spring and summer months Cyril decamped from Norfolk to the German spa town of Karlsbad. Constance joined him for short periods in the summers, when she adopted her own mild health regimen of massages, motor rides and afternoons reading Schiller. Karlsbad had once been a favourite resort among the Rothschilds, but either the town or the family's expectations had changed, because these days it struck Constance as a drab place, full of 'fat, heavy Germans with enormous stomachs protruding', 'Polish Jews in long coats, with light corkscrew curls', and 'Jewish women with wigs, some looking very poor'.[22] It was the same distaste that many Rothschild women had felt in the East End, where they were confronted by co-religionists whose orthodoxy, subsistence lifestyle and conspicuously foreign – or 'oriental' – character would, they thought, reflect badly on their own meticulously crafted example of an acculturated Jewishness. But not everything German was bad – at the same time as disdaining the German visitors, she wrote adoringly of the wooded Germanic landscape, and of German language and culture. In Berlin, she had delivered a paper in German. Now, in Karlsbad, she wrote in her diary that German increasingly felt like her mother tongue: 'I think in German.'[23]

Meanwhile, Cyril's health was getting worse. On top of his pulmonary congestion, he had been diagnosed with diabetes, and by 1905 he had a developed a recurring eye problem that impaired his vision and disrupted his sleep.[24] On her arrival in Karlsbad at the beginning of June 1906, Constance was 'shocked' by Cyril's appearance and by his depressed spirits.[25] Back in London, Cyril's condition remained unstable. Constance had to cancel her usual visit to Aston Clinton for Yom Kippur so that she could remain in Norfolk, where she did not attempt to fast, but by October Cyril was well enough for her to attend the NUWW conference in Manchester.[26] When they reunited in London, she was again horrified at his deterioration: 'Cyril arrived in his car looking wretchedly ill.'[27] The pair stayed at Surrey House for the night, and the following day Cyril drove on through a dense November fog to the south coast and the Isle of Wight, where, at the Pier Hotel, he was struck down with pneumonia. On Friday, Constance rushed to Ryde to join him. The following Wednesday, 27 November, Cyril Flower, the first and only Baron Battersea, died at the age of sixty-four.[28]

Cyril's death precipitated a period of painful introspection for Constance. Ten pages have been cut from her diaries for November and December 1907, and our sparse record of Cyril's burial in Overstrand comes instead from her mother Louisa: 'Dear Cyril's funeral takes place today!'[29] The entry on Cyril's funeral was the last she ever wrote.

Though Constance and Cyril's marriage had been riddled by deception and misunderstanding for many years, there were periods further back when it had been more rewarding, and Cyril's death awakened in Constance a nostalgia and craving for those happier days. '[I] long for his love,' she wrote.[30] 'If only he could know it now. Does he? I cannot find his short one line diaries & he has left nothing of written importance. Oh! if I could but have had one line.' Frederic Myers, Cyril's university friend and possible lover, had maintained to Constance that, despite some mediums being charlatans, others may also have authentic access to the spirit realm. Desperate for contact with her late husband, Constance was struck by this recollection, and decided to give it a try.[31] That spring, after staying at Grasse with Alice, she visited the coastal town of Valescure, for a session of 'automatic writing' with the medium, Miss Wingfield.[32] Miss Wingfield's spirit guides warned Constance that Cyril would not be able to communicate with her 'until he has got over every drawing towards earth & can look at everything & hear everything & see everything without pain', but reassured her that 'you need have no fear about him, for he is absolutely happy'.

Still in a daze, Constance returned to Overstrand where, at the end of April 1908, she found Cyril's diaries and papers. He had kept every single one of her letters, stretching back to the early days of their courtship.[33] The discovery was the sign that she had so desperately wanted – that there had been something loving amidst all the torment of their relationship – and gave her the impetus to set in motion a memorial she had been planning: a botanical and horticultural library, in his old room at the Pleasaunce.[34] On the first anniversary of Cyril's death, she went to the churchyard at Overstrand with wreaths sent by her mother and sister: 'The sun shining gloriously upon the grave, so beautiful, so peaceful, my heart felt quiet and grateful.'[35]

It was one of many goodbyes over four short and troubled years. Alick Yorke, Annie's brother-in-law and the Yorke brother to whom Constance had been closest in the 1860s, died in 1911, as did seventy-three-year-old Leonora, whose body was brought back across the Channel under the icy January rain, and laid to rest in Willesden Cemetery near her mother and father, Charlotte and Lionel. Other friends and relatives followed. For months on end, Constance's diary was reduced to a register of deaths.

Most painfully for both Constance and Annie, their mother Louisa died in September 1910, eight months shy of her ninetieth birthday.[36] Constance sought consolation in reading old letters, and recalling the Rothschild and Montefiore relatives who had made such an impression during her youth. The 'nice gossipy letters' of grandmother Henriette captured 'a bright & amusing woman, of the world & worldly, but with a good heart & devoted to her family', and made the letters of her paternal grandmother, Hannah, appear 'rather dull & commonplace'.[37] Most 'heart rending' of all were the letters of Louisa. 'Dear dear blessed mother,' exclaimed Constance in her diary afterwards. 'How I miss you, how I long for you! How changed is my life without you!'

In the summer of 1911 Constance and Annie sought some respite. Accompanied by two of Annie's nieces, they crossed the North Sea to Stavanger in Norway, where they boarded Annie's 300-ton steam yacht, the *Garland*.[38] Annie had been introduced to sailing during her marriage to Eliot, and Constance had many vivid memories of time spent on the *Garland* with her sister and parents: days spent quarantined with chickenpox on Venice's Grand Canal; nights in Madrid moored alongside the *Thistle*, the yacht of Empress Eugenie, widow of Napoleon III; a sun-drenched summer evening on the deck outside Salerno; a campaigning tour of England's south coast with Gladstone.[39] Cyril's preference had been for the Mediterranean, but now that the choice was their own, the sisters opted for 'northern shores' and a summer's cruising in the fjords.[40]

It appeared they had made the right decision. Norway was, wrote Constance, 'the country par excellence to visit in one's floating castle'. However, as the yacht began its journey along the coast, Constance found herself struck repeatedly by the same ominous sight: German warships, 'disporting themselves in the northern waters'.[41] Since late in the previous century, Kaiser Wilhelm II's Germany had been constructing a battle fleet that was intended to rival that of the British Royal Navy. Although the naval arms race had abated somewhat in the last two years, ships still circulated in the waters of northern Europe. There was hardly a fjord where the *Garland* was not anchored alongside a German vessel, and hardly a town where Constance's party did not come across 'the very trim and active members of their crews'.[42] Even high up in the mountains, they were unable to escape the German military presence. Arriving at a hotel for lunch after a morning's hike, Constance was startled to hear 'strains of music'. A full naval band had carried their instruments up the mountain, and were sat in the bar playing spirited Germanic tunes.

On their return to the *Garland*, Constance and Annie were told by the skipper that the *Hohenzollern*, Kaiser Wilhelm's yacht, had recently arrived on the coast.[43] The daughters of a less European family might have been reluctant to seek contact with the German Emperor, but the sisters wasted no time in having the *Garland* steam to the picturesque fjord of Balholm, where the Kaiser was moored. Having anchored so near to the *Hohenzollern* that they could hear the commands being shouted out by the ship's crew and the strains of the band on deck, it was not long before their presence was recognised.[44] On 20 July Constance and Annie received an invitation to lunch. Kaiser Wilhelm greeted them 'in the undress of an Admiral' – he was shorter than Constance had expected, but with 'oh! what a clever face & what piercing eyes'.[45]

Luncheon was served on deck, the Kaiser sitting on a raised chair at the middle of the table and using – on account of his withered arm – a peculiar instrument that served as both knife and fork.[46] Constance happily chatted with him on subjects that included music, pensions policy, smoking (in spite of her early experiments, she had now decided she was 'too early Victorian' for it) and Lloyd George's National Insurance Bill. After eating, she and Annie were led admiringly on a tour of the yacht, with its electric lighting, fitted telephones and linoleum deck. The Kaiser struck her as a 'very brilliant, distinguished personage', and she even found herself wishing that 'he could have known dear Cyril'.[47] But she had not missed the note of threat that entered the conversation whenever they strayed to the subject of international politics. 'I know in England I have been called a "damned German",' the Kaiser had said to her.[48] At one point, after insisting on the friendship that Germany was capable of showing Britain, he added: 'But we do not like to have our toes trodden upon, and we can tread back ...' Back aboard the *Garland*, Constance turned over the events of the day in her diary. 'I wonder whether I shall ever see him again,' she mused.[49] 'I hope never as our conqueror.'

The return to England was a return to melancholy. Shortly after Cyril's death, Constance had relinquished the lease on Surrey House and, when Louisa died, she and Annie stripped Grosvenor Place of all the personal effects and furniture so that it, too, could be sold.[50] The house she returned to was one that she had bought with Alfred's help, at 10 Connaught Place.[51] The transformation of her English life made her value the handful of old family relationships all the more, but also motivated her to seek new friendships among the younger generation: Rózsika von Wertheimstein, who had married Emma and Natty's younger son, Charles; Dorothy 'Dolly' Pinto, who had married James Armand, the grandson of James; and Sybil, the eldest Rosebery daughter.[52]

Then, on 28 June 1914, the assassination in Sarajevo of the Archduke Franz Ferdinand ignited European politics. Successive declarations of war followed one another so rapidly that several of Constance's close friends found themselves caught behind enemy lines. Charles and his wife Rózsika had been visiting family in Hungary when war broke out and were forced to flee back west, in the hope of reaching England before borders became impassable. Annie was aboard the *Garland* in Bergen. 'Well, all this is a most unprecedented and unexpected dilemma,' she wrote, but 'one must not think of any little discomfort one may have in the face of the awful tragedy of a European war!'[53] In Overstrand, where Constance arrived in late July, the outbreak of war felt only half real – 'weather glorious, summer like peace here' – but as her summer guests dispersed, and the newspapers began to report 'carnage and bloodshed' on the Continent, she began preparations for the inevitable irruption of war.[54] She attended Red Cross meetings in Norwich, and organised the Pleasaunce for use as a hospital.[55]

By late autumn the eerily tranquil atmosphere of the summer had evaporated, and the jingoism that Kaiser Wilhelm had commented on back in 1911 was given full expression as a wave of anti-German feeling swept Britain. Neither Constance's own background nor her close identification with Germany in recent years gave her immunity from such sentiments; she looked on with awe at the 'truly wonderful' rate of recruiting, wrote in horror at German 'cruelty', and, in late September, drove down to Aston Clinton to offer the house to the 21st Division, one of six divisions created as part of Kitchener's Third New Army.[56] Amid the tub-thumping patriotism, fear was growing, and Zeppelin raids were anticipated. In London, the men of the Rothschild family were making haphazard attempts to fortify New Court against twentieth-century weaponry. Sandbags were piled into the Dividend Office gallery in an attempt to protect the Bullion Room, which lay beneath it, and Alfred built himself a personal shelter in the corner of the Drawn Bond Department.[57]

At Overstrand, the militarisation of the coast proceeded apace: 'some big guns arrived during the night' and a squadron was deployed to Sandringham.[58] In November, Constance gave permission for all the serving staff at the Pleasaunce to leave, and began preparations to transport her collection of paintings to the inland safety of Aston Clinton. Writing to Annie, she confessed: 'There is so much talk of a raid here that I am thinking of leaving tomorrow (Wednesday) by car for AC.'[59] She would meet Annie at Aston Clinton, in the hope of returning to the coast once the threat of air raids had abated.

Constance was right to be apprehensive. The war would be unrecognisable from the conflicts that her Rothschild ancestors had weathered, and would bring to Europe destruction on an unprecedented scale. In time, it would shatter old assumptions, creating opportunities unthinkable to previous generations of Jewish women. But first, it would usher in a period of terror and trauma that dwarfed anything Constance could possibly have imagined.

PART IV

Rózsika,
Dolly, Miriam,
Nica, Rosie

30

Crossing the Border

In the high summer heat of 1914, Nagyvárad train station seethed with tension. On the platform was Charles Rothschild, son of Lord Natty and Lady Emma, together with his wife Rózsika and two of their daughters. To reach their train, the beleaguered Rothschilds had to battle their way through crowds of soldiers, tourists and refugees. For those in Austria–Hungary eager to avenge the assassination of Archduke Franz Ferdinand in Sarajevo, news that war had been declared against Serbia had struck a chord of nationalistic fervour; but for those caught on the wrong side of the burgeoning conflict, the only concern was to escape to friendly territory before the Continent descended into gunfire and bloodshed. A peaceful holiday to visit Rózsika's family home was about to end in a race for life and liberty.

They had packed at speed, failing to bring enough of the basic necessities. The two Rothschild children were used to the 'germless immunity of Pullman coaches' and had never experienced hunger in their short, privileged lives. Now they sat in a packed carriage, and had to make do with a small ration of cake.[1] At one frontier, the whole family had to 'get out and walk for ½ an hour in pitch darkness with some drunken reservists', and according to family lore, their mother was eventually reduced to asking a fellow passenger for a cash loan.[2] 'This is the proudest moment of my life,' the fellow passenger is said to have replied. 'Never did I think that I should be asked to lend money to a Rothschild!' By the time the family reached Ostend in Belgium for the Channel crossing, they had been travelling for almost a week and were 'in absolute rags'. Mercifully, the fear which gripped Charles and Rózsika had not filtered through to their children. At one point during the journey, Miriam began singing a few of her favourite German songs, and Rózsika was forced to hush her. This was not the occasion to flaunt the Germanic inheritance and pan-European ties that had defined the Rothschilds for generations. For Hungarian-born Rózsika, arrival in England would not be the straightforward escape that it was to her husband and children.

Rózsika von Wertheimstein had been born into a European Jewish family with an even longer pedigree than the Rothschilds. Her great-grandfather had been raised to the Austrian nobility in 1792, making the Wertheimsteins the third Jewish family to be ennobled in the Holy Roman Empire.[3] In the late 1850s her father Alfred bought an estate at Cséhtelek, around forty miles from Nagyvárad in what is now western Romania. It was at Cséhtelek that he raised his family with his wife Marie. The family were not, as the Rothschilds had it, 'as poor as the proverbial church mice', but it's nevertheless true that by the time Rózsika was born, in 1870, their wealth had been depleted by several generations of heavy spenders, and they relied on the patina of their name.[4] Rózsika enjoyed a rich upbringing nevertheless. Living so close to cosmopolitan Nagyvárad meant that her childhood was infused by a mixture of Jewish and Hungarian culture. Though her home education did not extend much beyond basic literacy, it was decidedly cosmopolitan – she spoke English, German, French and Hungarian fluently – and a youthful friendship with two erudite young aristocrats, the Ritok sisters, had extended her education beyond the classroom, introducing her to literature, politics and philosophy. What was most striking about the young woman, however, was the reckless *joie de vivre* she displayed in sports, vaulting over barrels on ice rinks and taking over seventy falls while perfecting her loop-change-loop jump. In summer she played tennis, sending shockwaves through *fin de siècle* society when she introduced the overhand serve to the Hungarian women's game – and subsequently using it to win the national women's championship.[5]

After her mother's death in 1904, and well into her thirties, Rózsika remained resolutely unmarried, continuing to live at Cséhtelek with her father and siblings. Later in life, she would joke that if she had not married then she would have become postmistress at Nagyvárad – but the world of aristocratic matchmaking had other plans for her. In 1906 the Hungarian writer and suffragist Countess Iska Teleki invited Rózsika to a resort in the Carpathian Mountains with the intention of introducing her to another friend of hers – the second son of the Lord and Lady Rothschild of Tring. Charles Rothschild was travelling to the Carpathians on a butterfly-hunting expedition with his friend, the composer Ralph Vaughan Williams.[6] He hoped for a fleeting moment of relief from the monotony and depression of his life in England, where, given the frailty and incompetence of his older brother Walter, he was de facto heir to the Rothschild banking business. He could not have anticipated what was waiting for him. Over several days spent together in the Carpathian Mountains, Rózsika and Charles fell in love. Just months later, around Christmas of 1906, Charles visited Rózsika's family at Cséhtelek to propose.[7] What he found there was a lively, informal family: the antidote to everything he had found oppressive about Rothschild life.

The wedding took place two months later, in Vienna. Rózsika, still lively and athletic at thirty-six, only met her new in-laws the day before the ceremony. Natty, Lord Rothschild, was gruff and aloof; Walter was silent and embarrassed and seemingly much more at home among exhibits than people, slinking off to the Museum of Natural History as soon as he got the chance.[8] Nor can the Wertheimstein family have come across to the Rothschilds as entirely conventional. For a while, it seemed that Rózsika's brother Victor would be late for his duties as usher thanks to a rapier duel he was fighting on the morning of the wedding.[9] Just before Rózsika left for the synagogue, her other brother Heinrich arrived with the 'good' news that, although Victor had sliced off his opponent's ear, he was himself unharmed, so would still be able to attend.

Arriving in Tring after a honeymoon in Venice, Rózsika soon discerned that the family eccentricities she had glimpsed in Vienna were part of a much more onerous and complex psychodrama. Emma's overprotective mothering of Walter (itself a response to her son's ill health in childhood) had provoked an intense jealousy in Charles, who had sent his mother no fewer than twenty letters during his and Rózsika's three-week honeymoon.[10] Lord Rothschild, well into his sixties by this point, had long since given up on his first-born Walter as a suitable heir and turned his attention to Charles. This had placed on Charles's slight shoulders an unbearable weight of expectation that neither he nor his father seriously thought he could fulfil: Charles had neither the charisma, nor the devotion to Judaism, nor the conservative political instincts that had generally been expected of heads of the family.

In 1907 the pressure on Charles intensified when Walter brought scandal to the family. He had two mistresses, one of whom had just borne him a child; worse still, a peeress with whom he had once had an affair was blackmailing him. After two years of avoidance, during which Walter hid the threatening missives in a laundry basket, one of the mistresses arrived at Tring in person, demanding to speak with Walter's mother. Although mistress-keeping had been common among Rothschild men of the late Victorian and Edwardian periods, it had never been managed quite as badly, or with such a disastrous result. If Walter had been an asset to the bank, then such a catastrophic episode might have been hushed up and forgiven. But he was a financial liability: through a series of woeful choices in the stock market, he was rumoured to have racked up debts in excess of £750,000.[11] In late January 1908, less than a year after Rózsika arrived at Tring, Walter was ignominiously removed from the family business, his desk at New Court cleared, his allowance capped, and his name shrouded in shame.[12] Were it not for the devotion of his mother Emma, he might also have been evicted from Tring. However, he remained living in his old apartment, and, supported by covert funding from Charles, he built up the Tring Museum of insects and birds. Natty refused to speak to his son, and even when they were in the same room, comments were relayed through other family members.[13]

Rózsika was thrust into a tangled and intimidating situation. Fortunately, like generations of Rothschild wives before her, she was able to develop a strong and enduring friendship with her mother-in-law, to whom she soon gave grandchildren: Miriam in the August of 1908 was followed by Liberty in November 1909, Victor in October 1910 and Pannonica ('Nica') – named after a rare moth – in December 1913. During the children's early years, Charles spent his weeks at the family's London residence, Arundel House, and supposedly worked dutiful eighteen-hour days at New Court.[14] At Tring, Rózsika read Proust, gardened, and cultivated an interest in contemporary politics – in later years she would subscribe to newspapers in four different languages, turning the pages with distinctive suddenness and an accompanying short, sharp smoker's cough.[15] The children were raised at arm's length. Nica's earliest memories were not of her mother and father, but of domestic staff, 'a regiment of nurses, governesses, tutors, footmen, valets, chauffeurs and grooms'.[16] When she did appear in the nursery, Rózsika struck the children as a forbidding presence. Nica was terrified of her as a child, and Victor remembered his mother removing a copy of *Alice in Wonderland* from the nursery, 'because [she] had read Freud'.[17] With an intellectually inaccessible mother, a frequently absent father, and a large cohort of domestic staff operating between parents and children, the situation at Tring was hardly a paragon of family warmth.

Initially, Charles's marriage had brought him a degree of happiness. 'I am so glad', he wrote to a friend, 'that [your] "blues" are getting less. Marry as I have done and you won't have any at all ... My wife is a real treasure. I wish you knew her better.'[18] But this had been only a temporary respite from a lifetime struggle with crippling depression. After the birth of Nica in 1913, Charles became increasingly insular and unsociable. The lighter moments – for him, and so for the family as a whole – came on family trips to Ashton Wold in Northampton-shire, which Charles had fallen in love with during his bachelor years, and remodelled as a Tudor-style manor house. At Ashton Wold, with the burden of Tring family tensions lifted, Charles became the parent whose memory the children would cling to during their adult lives: jocular, approachable, enthusiastic.[19] He played records on the gramo-phone, introducing his children to Debussy and Stravinsky as well as to young American artists like Scott Joplin, and used his scientific studies as a means of communicating with his children rather than escaping from them.

Trips to Rózsika's family in Cséhtelek represented an even more complete escape from the pressures of wider Rothschild life. There, Charles felt blissfully removed from the stresses of the bank, and he and Rózsika could relax. The children sensed the shift in mood, and relished their Hungarian holidays. It was in Cséhtelek that the eldest daughter Miriam first began to indulge the enthusiasm for nature that she had inherited from her father, counting the spots of ladybirds and learning to tell the difference between a comma butterfly and a small tortoiseshell.[20] The thrill of such pursuits, and the palpable improve-ments in her father's mood, gave Miriam's memories of Cséhtelek an idyllic air. These were, she later wrote, 'some of the happiest times of my life as a child'.[21] That idyll was shattered by the family's frantic flight across Europe in the summer of 1914. As they arrived back in England after the gruelling journey across the Continent, Miriam understood that a chapter of her childhood was already over.

Once war broke out, Natty's position as Lord Lieutenant of Buckinghamshire obliged him to raise funds and help with recruitment. Tring itself was given over to the Royal Northumberland Fusiliers, and Rózsika and the children watched from the windows of the house as miners in civilian clothes were drilled by a single officer in uniform.[22] None of this was enough to ease the suspicions which now clung to any family with ties to the other side of the growing conflict. After someone put up on the wall at New Court a *Daily Mail* poster that declared 'Intern them All', Charles and the other family bankers resolved that they should no longer converse in German during their lunch breaks.[23] To Rózsika's children, her Hungarian accent was a bountiful source of fascination and comedy, but in public it now marked her out as an enemy alien, someone to be watched closely and perhaps distrusted. Suspicion was not limited to strangers: Constance wrote in 1915 that while she viewed Rózsika as 'a remarkable woman', she did find her 'German proclivities' a source for concern.[24]

To make matters worse, Charles's health was deteriorating – possibly as the result of a bad strain of influenza – and as it did so, his underlying depression flared up. Rózsika fell back on the time-honoured solution to intractable illness by planning a trip to a sanatorium in neutral Switzerland, but eventually the plan was abandoned – not least because of the risk that, as a Hungarian, Rózsika would be denied re-entry to Britain on their return.[25] Instead, she spent most of her time in Tring, helping to look after her husband, her children and her father-in-law (whose health was also deteriorating), and assisting Emma in the management of the wartime household. Occasionally she travelled to London, where she ran banking errands at New Court, made social calls on her new family – Lady Rosebery's youngest daughter Peggy was becoming a close friend – and made visits to the Jewish East End. 'Today I have a hard day,' she wrote during a trip in March 1915, 'as I have to visit the free-meal restaurants and in the afternoon I must go to Houndsditch!! to see one of my poorer patients.'[26]

There was also one more unusual meeting scheduled for her March visit. A close family member had recently put her in touch with Chaim Weizmann, a chemist at the University of Manchester and a figure of rising importance within the Zionist Federation. On 17 March, Weizmann and Rózsika would meet in person for the first time. It was a meeting that would change the course of Jewish history.

31

Enlisting

DOROTHY PINTO BEGAN life as a disappointment. On the day of her birth, 7 March 1895, her father, 'walking dispiritedly in . . . Regent's Park, was halted by a neighbour who offered congratulations on the event. "Thank you," said Mr Pinto, "but it's only a girl."'[1]

She was a child of the city. Her brother worked in the Stock Exchange, and her father had investments in the cinemas that were spreading across the capital during her youth; her mother had grown up in Kensington. From the window of the schoolroom in her family home on Carlton Gardens, Dolly could see the Foreign Office. The little experience she had of rural life had come with her riding lessons, but even those had taken second place to her education in the suburban pursuits of the Edwardian leisured class: lawn tennis and golf, bridge and bezique.[2]

Like Rózsika, Dolly found a genuine freedom and excitement in the sporting activities made accessible to her in her youth. It may have been her enthusiasm for such pursuits that brought her into contact with James Armand 'Jimmy' de Rothschild, son of Edmond and Adelheid (and grandson of James Mayer, the youngest of Gutle and Amschel's children). James Armand had been born in Paris in 1878, but had come to England to study and had remained in the country, where he acquired a reputation as a 'popular sportsman' first and foremost, and a banker a distant second.[3] Though the exact time and nature of their first encounter is obscure (family lore suggests that it took place on a golf course), we know that Dolly was barely out of childhood when James proposed to her, since she had only just been 'promoted by my parents to dine with them at 7.45'.[4] The first reports of James's romance to reach his Parisian family were somewhat mangled at the hands of Alfred, who, having been

Dolly de Rothschild with her husband James Armand de Rothschild.

asked by James's parents to find out more about their prospective daughter-in-law, confidently reported that she was a star of musical comedies and recent lead in the West End revue show *Hullo, Ragtime!* That was Dorothy Minto. The discovery that James's romance was in fact with a respectable Anglo-Jewish woman with no connections to the stage must have come as a relief to Edmond and Adelheid; and the discovery that the surname Pinto (which meant little to the French family) concealed a matrilineal connection to the Cohens (which meant a lot) cannot have hurt Dolly's chances either. The Parisian Rothschilds gave their blessing for her to wed thirty-five-year-old Jimmy, and the couple were married in February 1913 at the Central Synagogue on Great Portland Street, just weeks before Dolly's eighteenth birthday.[5]

The couple planned to split their married life between homes on Park Street in Mayfair and the Champs Élysées in Paris, but their hopes for this were short-lived. Dolly was in Hove on the south coast when news crossed the Channel that France had entered the war.[6] James, meanwhile, was at the bank in Paris, and enlisted in the French Army at once. Dolly and James's marriage was marked by an ardour rare between Rothschild spouses, and the prospect of a long separation was difficult. 'God bless you my darling,' wrote James to Dolly soon after war was declared, 'I love you more than I can tell.'[7] 'I kiss you my darling,' replied Dolly. 'You know I love you.'

In the circumstances, even such adoring letters as these seemed insufficient, and in August Dolly travelled to London, hoping to get through to James on the telephone. She was one among many Rothschild women arriving in the capital.[8] Germaine de Rothschild – the French daughter-in-law of Leonora and Alphonse – had taken up residence at Claridge's; Marie – wife of Charlotte and Lionel's youngest son Leopold – had also managed to make it back from the Continent; Rózsika's family were just returning from behind enemy lines. 'You cannot imagine how nice they have all been to me,' Dolly wrote to James on 5 August, as she prepared to decamp to Gunnersbury.[9]

Many of the family's young men – Leopold and Marie's sons Evelyn and Anthony, as well as Hannah and Archibald's sons Harry and Neil Primrose – were in the process of enlisting. 'It does give one a pang to see them in khaki,' wrote Dolly to James.[10] James's replies from Europe raised worrying questions about what awaited them. Despite his early reassurances that he would only be working as a driver, James was soon asking Dolly to buy him a revolver (the gunsmiths in France had been cleared out), and by September was writing from the Western Front, describing the 'stacks of corpses' lying amidst roads and fields 'ploughed up by shells'.[11] By the time of the Jewish New Year and Day of Atonement in September, James replied to his wife's letter wishing her 'every happiness' but admitting that, in the chaos of the war in France, it was 'quite impossible for one to realise it is Yom Kippur'.[12]

The usual wartime occupations of upper-class women had little appeal to single-minded Dolly. After one first aid class in which she encountered the dancer Lady Constance Stewart-Richardson 'playing the bright pupil' in a 'turban, flowing robe, bare legs and tapestry sandals', she dismissed the whole endeavour as a 'typical society woman's occupation' and 'quite useless'.[13] Instead, she devoted herself to managing her absent husband's concerns. Some of the work was fairly routine, at least for a Rothschild wife – there were charitable commitments to be maintained, functions to attend, and financial affairs to be monitored. One part of it, however, was highly unusual. In early November 1914 an unassuming letter postmarked Manchester arrived at Gunnersbury, addressed to Dolly.

'Madame le Baronne, Please forgive these lines and I hope you won't consider me an intruder ...'[14] It was with these words that

Chaim Weizmann – the future first president of Israel – began his campaign to enlist Dolly in the cause to which James, like his father Edmond, had signalled his commitment before the outbreak of war. Dolly agreed to a meeting with Weizmann, in which she listened, increasingly captivated, as the young bearded intellectual spoke passionately about the threat of antisemitism and his dream of establishing a Jewish homeland in Palestine.

Although they all sought to revive the Jewish connection to the Holy Land, the precise aims of early twentieth-century Zionists were myriad. 'Political' Zionists like Theodor Herzl sought to establish in Palestine an internationally recognised homeland for the Jewish diaspora; 'practical' Zionists preferred to emphasise Jewish emigration to the Holy Land over the goal of statehood; 'cultural' Zionists, meanwhile, prioritised the creation of cultural and educational institutions in the Holy Land, as a way of supporting and preserving a Jewish identity that risked being eroded across the diaspora.[15] All three approaches were united by fear of the antisemitic violence that had swept across Europe as the nineteenth century drew to a close, convincing some that Jews would never achieve safety and civil rights within European nations.

Chaim Weizmann had grown up in the Russian Pale of Settlement, and although he had gone on to study at university and to lecture at Manchester, he wore his *shtetl* background proudly in his accent and manners. Supporters emphasised his *folks-mensch* credentials: to his friend and secretary Israel Sieff, he was 'a man of the people, of the masses, not of the elite, a leader in whose breast beat[s] the common heart of man'.[16] It was a reputation that drew him a devoted following, and in the early 1900s Weizmann emerged as leader of the radical Democratic Fraction of Zionists. His was a 'synthetic' approach, combing the three strands of late nineteenth-century Zionism.

Historically, the Rothschild family had – with a few minor exceptions – been opposed to all forms of Zionism. Through their own self-invention, religious reforms, civil rights campaigns and institutions such as the Jews' Free School, the family had for generations encouraged the anglicisation of immigrant Jews, and attempted to carve out a space for them in the civic and cultural life of Britain.

The creation of a strengthened, alternative, ethno-religious citizen-ship threatened to undermine their achievements. Such anxieties were reinforced by class-based condescension: support for Zionist move-ments was particularly strong within working-class and middle-class immigrant Jewish communities, and grander Anglo-Jewish families often perceived the movement as being lower class, uneducated and uncouth.[17]

The years leading up to the outbreak of war had seen a small but significant shift in the opinions of some members of the Anglo-Jewish upper classes. Natty had met with the 'practical' Zionist Israel Zang-will in 1905 and pledged some money to an emigration fund; Dolly's father-in-law Edmond de Rothschild had taken a more active role, funding the development of Jewish agricultural settlements.[18] Now that Britain was at war with the Ottoman Empire and the future of Palestine was unclear, Weizmann sought to capitalise on the advances he had made among the Rothschilds. While Dolly, just nineteen years old and only recently initiated into the Rothschild family, could not answer Weizmann's questions about what Natty, Lord Rothschild, thought of the project, she promised to sound out other potential supporters in the family.

James wrote to Dolly from France, eagerly asking after 'the result of your intervention' and reassuring her that he was 'particularly glad' she had fielded Weizmann's letter 'without going to New Court'.[19] But his enthusiasm quickly flared into frustration when he read that Weizmann seemed to be harassing Dolly for an update: 'you can tell him that insistence & persistence are two different things altogether & that he had better not forget [this] when dealing with high officials – ministers of the crown & yourself,' he scribbled furiously from the front.[20] It was a shift that would come to be typical of the relation-ships between the Rothschilds and Weizmann, who swung, in the family's estimations, between visionary and upstart.

When Dolly wrote back to Weizmann on 19 November, it was with the encouraging news that she had spoken casually with Rózsika's husband Charles, as well as Lord Crewe, the husband of Hannah and Archibald's daughter Peggy, and leader of the House of Lords.[21] Charles, she assured Weizmann, 'thoroughly approved of the idea' of settling Jews in Palestine, while Lord Crewe thought 'our compatriots would not be unwelcome in Palestine ... if by some chance it became British'. There was good reason for Lord Crewe's cautious phrasing: he knew that Lord Kitchener had recently approached Hussein bin Ali, Sharif of Mecca, promising that if there was a rebellion against the Ottoman Empore, Britain would support an independent Arab state in the eastern Mediterranean. Dolly and Weizmann were unaware of these complications, and they saw what Lord Crewe said as a ringing endorsement of the scheme.

As November 1914 drew on, Weizmann became more dramatic, telling Dolly tales of his own encounters with antisemitic violence. 'We defended the Jewish quarter with revolvers in our hands,' he wrote of his experience during the Kishinev massacre, a vicious anti-semitic episode of April 1903 in which forty-nine Jews were killed and scores of women raped.[22] While the pogrom at Kishinev was very real, Weizmann had not been present in the town during the massacre, and his experience of it was pure fiction, designed to shock a young woman into fighting for his cause.[23] In that respect it succeeded: such stories resonated with Dolly, whose husband was fighting his own battle for survival on the French front. At the end of the month, James returned from France for four days of leave, and immediately contacted Weizmann to arrange a meeting.[24]

The next step, they agreed, was to win over – or, failing that, drown out – the most vocal anti-Zionist members of the Anglo-Jewish establishment, among them Leo and Marie Rothschild and Claude Montefiore. James suggested the historian Sir Philip Magnus as an important anti-Zionist figure to target for persuasion.[25] Weizmann developed a more ambitious plan. The most influential person to win over to the Zionist cause – the one whose support was most likely to convince or silence voices of dissent within the Anglo-Jewish community – was undoubtedly Natty, Lord Rothschild himself. Dolly could not arrange a meeting with Natty, nor with his taciturn heir, Walter. But she could arrange a meeting with Walter's headstrong Hungarian sister-in-law. And so she had written to Rózsika, proposing the meeting of March 1915.[26]

Chaim Weizmann's passionate conviction often won him instant re-spect, and even devotion. Israel Sieff, an Anglo-Jewish businessman, wrote of his first meeting with Weizmann that his 'longing to be well thought of by him, [and his] impulsive urge to be of service to him, could not be contained'.[27] From a letter sent by Rózsika, after the meeting in March, it is evident that Weizmann had a similarly powerful impact on her. At a time when so much contemporary discourse had taken on a jingoistic, Anglocentric tone, Rózsika relished the chance to talk with another intelligent and internationally minded figure. She found his arguments persuasive and his vision impressive. Unlike many other Rothschild women, she was excited rather than frightened by Weizmann's zealous and uncompromising approach. 'Fanatics and idealists have always a great attraction for me,' she wrote to Dolly, 'and W. is both'.[28]

Rózsika had left the meeting pledging to seek the support not only of her husband and father-in-law but also of the Foreign Secretary, Sir Edward Grey, who was a frequent guest at Tring. Although Grey was not an instinctive Zionist, he was willing to adopt Zionist policies if persuaded that they supported British geopolitical interests.[29] In government circles, there was a growing feeling that they might: a recent cabinet memorandum entitled 'The Future of Palestine' had argued for post-war Palestine becoming a British protectorate in which Jews could claim citizenship. Natty seemed to find the memo persuasive, and was moving ever closer to the Zionist position. And yet Natty's health, which just weeks prior to Rózsika's meeting with Weizmann had appeared to be on the mend, was now deteriorating fast. Shortly after Rózsika came to London, he was transported down to no. 148 Piccadilly for a prostatectomy. In the early hours of 31 March 1915, four days after his operation, the first Lord Rothschild died.[30]

Natty left Emma the family house at no. 148 Piccadilly and a small fortune.[31] Though his title of Lord Rothschild devolved to his disgraced son Walter, it was Rózsika's husband Charles who received most of the rest of the family estate and the share in the family business. The normal rules of primogeniture had been bypassed, and Rózsika had come into a position of influence that she would not, as wife to the family's second son, have necessarily expected when she first met Charles. With Emma retreating from public life in her widowhood, Rózsika stepped into a more prominent role within the family.[32] That suited Weizmann.

In mid August Rózsika organised a conversation between the Zionist campaigner and Lord Robert Cecil, the Under-Secretary of State for Foreign Affairs. Although Cecil was struck by the 'rather repellent and even sordid exterior' of Weizmann, he was nonetheless impressed and convinced by the arguments put forward about Palestine.[33] Via Dolly and Rózsika, Weizmann was able to confirm this positive outcome, writing in a letter to fellow Zionist Harry Sacher: 'I met Mrs. James [Dolly] yesterday who saw Mrs. Charles [Rózsika], who saw Lord Cecil after the interview. Cecil told her that he does not remember ever having had such an important and interesting conversation.'[34] Charles committed to support the cause in early summer 1915, and was arranging meetings with Weizmann by the end of the year.[35]

Meanwhile, Rózsika had got to work on her reclusive brother-in-law Walter and his overprotective mother Emma at Tring. Her campaign made rapid headway. Peggy, Lady Crewe, had been alarmed at an initial meeting with Weizmann by the man's unrelenting focus on bloody, antisemitic violence. 'Instead of emphasizing the nobility of the task that lies before one in the venture he expatiates on the evils,' wrote an exasperated James.[36] 'It annoyed me when I first saw him in London last November and I can quite well believe that it displeased Peggy.' But such was the wave of Zionist feeling sweeping the family that even she was now among the converts. At a March 1916 dinner hosted by the Crewes at their Curzon Street home, Dolly overheard Peggy tell Lord Cecil: 'we all in this house are Weizmannites'.[37]

Peggy was precisely the sort of political hostess who could help Weizmann win over the political establishment. With Dolly and Rózsika, she subsequently set up an unofficial three-woman advisory group to coach Weizmann on his lobbying technique – so as to avoid the tactical mistakes he had made on his first approach to her.[38] Under the women's tutelage, Weizmann learned the intricacies and mores of lobbying among London's political class: who would be susceptible to his ideas, and who would be resistant; what kind of story was suitable for the dinner table, and what for the drawing room. He learnt to tone down his *folks-mensch* image in a way that would make him and his cause more palatable to the conservative political tastes of Anglo-Jewry. Less than a year after Peggy had recoiled from Weizmann's first approach, her salon at Curzon Street had become the unofficial headquarters of his insurgent campaign.[39]

As the Zionist movement flourished, so Rózsika's personal life took a tragic turn. The few reports she received from Hungary painted an unremittingly bleak picture. Her father was in his seventies and, with the war entering its third year, she knew that she might never see him again. Her brother was now a cavalryman in the Austro-Hungarian Army. Meanwhile, Charles's depression had become so overwhelming that Rózsika, as well as his close friend Theo Russell, had begun to fear for his life. 'My husband often says he is sorry to have lived to see, or more, to know all this,' she reported to Weizmann.[40] Rózsika returned to the challenge of getting her husband to Switzerland for help. What would eventually make that possible was an offer from Charles's friend, the Tring entomological curator Karl Jordan, to accompany Charles to a Swiss sanatorium.[41] It was an act of major sacrifice: Dr Jordan was German-born, and knew that he might not be allowed back into England.

Despite, or perhaps in response to, these familial crises at home and abroad, Rózsika threw herself into facilitating Zionist negotiations. In the autumn of 1916 she managed what Weizmann had long hoped to achieve, when she finally recruited Lord Rothschild – now the wayward Walter rather than his father Natty – to the campaign.[42] Lord Rothschild's name would come to eclipse most others in its association with the Zionist breakthrough, but Dolly and Rózsika had been lobbying long before Walter's name first appears in the papers of Weizmann or of his ally, Nahum Sokolow.[43]

It does so in connection with a lunch held by Emma Rothschild at Tring, on Thursday, 16 November 1916. Among those in attendance were Rózsika, Dolly, Charles and Walter. 'It will be a Zionist lunch,' Weizmann wrote to Sokolow.[44] The guests drafted a Zionist memorandum, which was circulated through the family in the weeks that followed.[45] James approved, with Weizmann happily noting that his feedback was only 'very superficial and related to matters of style and presentation'. With Charles still in poor health and preparing to depart for the Continent, Rózsika read the draft in his stead and offered comments at the end of November.

Although some Rothschild family members were helping Weizmann, others remained implacably opposed to his programme. The fears of the anti-Zionists were deeply felt. Many, like Marie, believed that if Zionists had their way and achieved the new state then antisemitism would increase, as all Jews outside of Palestine would be viewed as aliens in the countries where they had built their lives.[46] During the summer and autumn of 1916, Marie had become more outspoken in her opposition to Weizmann. Events reached a head when she overheard a conversation between Rózsika and Peggy about Zionism during a lunch at Ascott, Marie and Leopold's country house.[47] Marie, Rózsika told Dolly, had first viewed the conversation 'with suspicious eyes', then 'pounced down on me'. Rózsika was lambasted for a whole range of issues relating to the Zionist campaign – among them 'our underhand methods', 'my ignorance' and 'East End Russians' – until she simply 'apologised for being alive at all'. By the time she arrived back at Tring, her indignation at the ambush had grown, and she sat down to write Marie an eight-page letter, defending the Zionist campaign and making clear that she and Peggy should not be made to feel like 'illicit lovers', simply because they represented a new kind of political view within the family. 'It was a masterpiece,' she told Dolly.

The winds changed for the Zionists in December 1916, when David Lloyd George became prime minister. Lloyd George was far more supportive of Zionism than his predecessor, Herbert Asquith, and his government included two further supporters of Zionism, both of whom had already been in contact with Weizmann: Arthur Balfour, the new Foreign Secretary; and Lord Milner, who served as Minister Without Portfolio in the five-person war cabinet. In July 1917 they were joined by a new Minister for Munitions, Winston Churchill, who was also sympathetic to Zionism. As political opinion shifted in favour of the Zionist movement, the need for private lobbying receded, and the three Rothschild women, who had so effectively created a platform for Weizmann, now found themselves marginalised. On 28 January 1917 Chaim Weizmann met with Sir Mark Sykes, the government's leading advisor on Middle Eastern policy; a 'blur of small conferences' followed.[48]

Perhaps sensing this groundswell of support, the anti-Zionist Conjoint Committee wrote a statement to *The Times* and the *Jewish Chronicle*, objecting to 'any proposals which implied the idea of nationality for the Jews in Palestine, or the granting of privileges detrimental to the other inhabitants'.[49] Walter, enraged by this committee's decision to drag the dispute into the public eye, wrote to *The Times* in response.[50] The acrimonious disagreement within the Anglo-Jewish community, and indeed within the Rothschild family, had suddenly become public. Seventy-four-year-old Constance, Lady Battersea, ever the eager recorder of familial strife, took to her diary: 'Marie somewhat vexed with Walter on account of letters in the *Times* concerning Zionism'.[51] The same day that Constance noted this, however, Marie's husband Leopold died – fatally depleting the anti-Zionist position within the family. *The Times* published a new lead article in support of the Zionist position, and a vote in the Anglo-Jewish Association was narrowly won by opponents of the Conjoint Committee. The balance of communal opinion had tipped in favour of the Zionists.[52]

When Walter met with Balfour on 19 June, the Foreign Secretary informed him that he was convinced of the need for a British protectorate, and persuaded Walter and Weizmann to submit a declaration for the cabinet to consider.[53] Walter discussed a draft declaration with Rózsika over the following weeks, and at the end of October the cabinet authorised Balfour to make a public declaration of sympathy with Zionist aspirations.[54] He did so in a letter that Walter received on 2 November, and which was published in the national press a week later, on 9 November:

Dear Lord Rothschild,

I have much pleasure in conveying to you, on behalf of His Majesty's Government, the following declaration of sympathy with Jewish Zionist aspirations which has been submitted to, and approved by, the Cabinet:

'His Majesty's Government view with favour the establishment in Palestine of a national home for the Jewish people, and will use their best endeavours to facilitate the achievement of this object, it being clearly understood that nothing shall be done which may prejudice the civil and religious rights of existing non-Jewish communities in Palestine, or the rights and political status enjoyed by Jews in any other country.'

I should be grateful if you would bring this declaration to the knowledge of the Zionist Federation.

Yours sincerely

Arthur James Balfour[55]

Such an emphatic statement threatened to exacerbate existing divisions within the family, and it was telling that the 'Weizmannite' women responded by immediately seeking to mend family bridges. Circumstances made this all the more important: on 19 November 1917 news reached the English Rothschilds that both Evelyn de Rothschild and Neil Primrose had died fighting in Palestine.[56]

The death of Evelyn, just days after the declaration that his mother Marie had fought so hard to prevent, needed to be handled sensitively, not only out of respect for his grieving family but also for the sake of family unity. A letter was sent to the World Zionist Organization, urging them not to politicise the death of Evelyn by making it seem as if the son of one of the most ardently anti-Zionist Rothschild couples had died fighting for a new Jewish homeland. Many, including Weizmann himself in his autobiography, have attributed the authorship of the letter to the grieving Marie.[57] But it was in fact Rózsika who wrote this letter to Weizmann. With the political momentum clearly behind the Zionist cause, she had stepped back from her political role into the role of family mediator and matriarch, in which capacity she would serve as an ally and defender of Marie, despite their previous disagreements.[58]

On 2 December, Zionists held a 'Great Thanksgiving Meeting' at the Royal Opera House in Covent Garden.[59] Both Rózsika and Dolly were on the platform, along with Walter, James, Robert Cecil, Mark Sykes, Herbert Samuel and, of course, Chaim Weizmann. Speeches were effusive and emotional, with Robert Cecil speaking about 'Judea for the Jews' and Herbert Samuel ending his speech with the Passover exhortation: 'Next year in Jerusalem!' Over breakfast the following day, Rózsika's nine-year-old daughter Miriam 'was all agog to hear the news'. Rózsika told her daughter how, with the crowd inside whipped up by the unaccustomed zeal of supportive politicians, and a crowd in the street pressing to get inside to hear, the meeting descended into chaos. She told her how Uncle Walter – usually so reserved and quiet and incapable of dealing with people – had risen from his chair and bellowed for silence, and got it.

It was an off-the-cuff story, told to delight the younger generation. Yet it contained the seed of a narrative that would grow over the years. The journey to the Balfour Declaration had had as much to do with the women of the family as with the men, but within days the narrative was being restructured around the improbable, awkward man to whom the document was addressed. Writing much later in her life, Miriam reflected on the story told to her over breakfast that morning in 1917. Her mother had been on the stage, as had her aunt Dolly, and yet somehow she, 'while scooping out the bottom of her boiled egg, got the impression – an impression dispelled only years later – that, after all, only ONE person had been there – Uncle Walter'.[60]

32

Reconstruction

CONSTANCE'S COUNTRY HOUSES, like so many across the country, were adapted for wartime use. Aston Clinton began the war as the staff base for an infantry division; Overstrand would house Belgian refugees and, later, soldiers recovering from physical and psychological wounds of war. In December 1915 Constance wrote to Annie about the three latest arrivals to the hospital at Overstrand: 'One frost bitten feet, one a broken ankle & one who has been shot thro' the lung'.[1] Annie was a frequent visitor to the hospital at Hamble, and in their letters the sisters discussed treatment, recreation and rehabilitation. In March 1916 Constance praised the advantages of art therapy and occupational therapy, telling her sister how her convalescents busied themselves with bookbinding and carpentry.[2]

For the most part, the women of the Rothschild family remained phlegmatic. Writing to James, Dolly had dismissed the threat of German invasion as 'a rumour', insisting that, regardless, people were 'quite prepared'. Rózsika, meanwhile, found the stockpiling of respirators and anti-incendiary sand 'most amusing', and Annie made frequent trips to her Curzon Street home through the summer of 1916, despite warnings that the West End was likely to suffer from further Zeppelin raids.[3] Whether it was the exposed easterly position of her Norfolk home, or simply a matter of character, Constance was far less sanguine about bombing and invasion than many of her relatives were. The first Zeppelin raid, in January 1915, had aimed for Humberside, but winds had driven the airships south, and they had released their payloads along the Norfolk coast.[4] From that point onwards, Constance was haunted by fear: 'a thick fog hangs over the sea wh. makes me think of invasions & raids & other horrors!!' she wrote to Annie in March 1916.[5] In Overstrand, she worried about the inadequacy of the defences on the cliff ('we have the most ridiculous little guns'), and when she had to be in London, she slept with her pearls on and a fur cloak at the foot of her bed, so that she could make a hasty retreat to the stillroom if her butler announced that the Zeppelins were on their way.[6]

Fear and anxiety drained her of energy and induced 'a great deadness of the soul'.[7] The hobbies and commitments that had occupied her over previous decades fell away one by one. During the war her school visits became infrequent, she resigned from the executive of the National Union of Women Workers, and she began to take a far less active role in prison visiting.[8] She became bleakly fixated on the horrors of the war, and on the global upheavals that were throwing off the certainties of the Victorian era she had known so well: the Easter Rising in Ireland, and then the Bolshevik Revolution in Russia. When Lloyd George became prime minister at the end of 1916, she could find no cause for optimism, predicting further 'insensate warfare'.[9] While other women in the family were reluctant to renounce cultural and familial connections with 'the other side', Constance was all too happy to sever ties with a Germany that had recently felt so close, but that she had now come to see as brutal and militaristic. After the royal family changed their name from 'Saxe-Coburg and Gotha' to 'Windsor' in mid 1917, Constance and her sister agreed that in future Rothschild men should 'select their wives from English Jewish families'.[10] Though she still observed major festivals and made occasional trips to the synagogue, Constance's engagement with her Jewish heritage was now minimal, and she generally steered clear of the Zionism debate that had threatened to tear apart friendships between other Rothschild women.

More than anything else, it was the deaths of the three sons of Lionel and Charlotte – Natty in 1915, Leopold in 1917, and then Alfred in 1918 – that impressed on Constance the fact of her own generation fading away.[11] That realisation, as well as her confinement while recovering from diphtheria, gave her 'a mad desire to write', and she began drafting her memoirs.[12] She had only spent a few months on the project when her writing was interrupted by the news she thought would never come: the Kaiser had abdicated, and it seemed likely the war would soon end. On the day the armistice was announced, Constance had a 'little school meeting' in Overstrand. Later, she reflected in her diary: 'how cld any one attend to such a small parochial matter when thrones were tottering, rulers abdicating.' News of the peace had made everything seem 'transfigured'.

Peace after 4 years & a half, after the slaughter of 20 millions of human beings, after the destruction of beautiful cities, churches, libraries, homes, after the most inhuman, monstrous, abominable deeds, peace at last. Almost impossible to believe this to be true. And yet so it was![13]

Charles was still at the sanatorium in Switzerland, and Rózsika had remained determined to manage his treatment without involving the broader family. To Dolly, her one Rothschild confidante, she emphasised the importance of blanket reassurance. 'Don't mention about Charlie's health except that he is really much better to the family, as you know letters will be showered upon me from various aunts etc.'[14] Like Dolly, she had been thrust into the position of having to manage her husband's business. In Rózsika's case, this meant frequent trips to New Court, where she became her husband's representative. The banking office had never been a very welcoming place to the women of the family, and following the deaths of the three Rothschild brothers in quick succession between 1915 and January 1918, Rózsika found herself with the unenviable task of having to represent Charles in discussions about the reshaped partnership.

The responsibility came at a fraught time. The First World War had taken a serious toll on the Rothschild bank. Old international alliances on which the bank's success was built had been fractured, the failure of the Rothschilds to establish a satisfactory operation in America meant that they were excluded from the transatlantic banking contracts that came to define the period, and the turn towards progressive tax systems meant that the family found themselves paying substantial tax bills on their income and inheritances for the first time. Even without all these difficulties, it is doubtful whether the operation at New Court would have continued to thrive in the new century; the bank Rózsika visited was a slow, conservative organisation, riven with Victorian hierarchies and hobbled by dated, cumbersome banking practices. The partners had their own panelled office, and retired at lunch to their own dining room, where Rózsika 'partook of some egg dish with mushrooms' that gave her 'appalling tummy-aches'.[15] Visits to the bank brought her face to face with the difficulties that were in part responsible for Charles's ill health. 'I am afraid I will have a stiff fight before it is all over,' she wrote to Dolly after a gruelling negotiation lasting three and a half hours. 'They are very shrewd, no doubt about it. I wish you were here, you would open your eyes and ears if I could tell you all.'

Rózsika worried constantly about the situation in the Austro-Hungarian Empire, where the rest of her family remained. In September she learnt from her sister Sarolta that their father had fallen victim to the influenza pandemic that was ravaging Europe.[16] One day soon afterwards, just before boarding a train down from Tring to London, she received an unexpected telegram: 'Most sorry to inform you, your father much weaker, hope to send better news soon.' She told herself that it was a 'badly worded wire', and on her arrival in London tried to distract herself with visits to the dressmakers, then the Foreign Office. But when she reached Arundel House she found another telegram, confirming the worst: her father had died.

Later, in a letter to Dolly, Rózsika would describe the terror of that night, during which she dared not lie down for fear that she would 'suffocate', and instead paced up and down 'for hours'.[17] In October 1918 her grief and confusion were exacerbated by events in Hungary, where, in the aftermath of a social-democratic revolution, Prime Minister István Tisza – a 'dear friend' of hers – was assassinated.[18] Following the upheavals in Hungary, Rózsika became fearful of the 'violent and Bolshevik tendencies' in the politics of Chaim Weizmann, and yet her commitment to Zionism was becoming even stronger. Recent violence against Jews in Poland and Galicia, and the threat of further pogroms within the collapsing Austro-Hungarian Empire, had made her determined 'more than ever' that a 'Jewish Palestine will be necessary'.

But Rózsika's energies were needed for Charles's homecoming. On the day he returned from the sanatorium, his children waited excitedly in the hallway of their home to greet a father who some of them – especially Nica, who had just turned five a few weeks earlier – barely knew.[19] Charles stepped out of the car and walked upstairs to his room, passing by his children as if they were invisible – an event that burnt itself on the memory of his daughter Miriam. Rózsika was determined to cocoon her family and focus on supporting Charles, whose underlying depression, the family would later realise, was worsened by a case of encephalitis lethargica or 'sleeping sickness'.[20] She apologised to Peggy Crewe for not making a visit, writing that 'Charlie can't spare me at all and wild horses won't drag him away from the children over a weekend.'[21] On 23 December Rózsika confided in

Dolly her fear that Charles would never return to how he had been before the illness had first taken hold.[22]

Her thoughts were constantly being pulled towards her homeland. In Hungary, social democracy had given way to a brief spell of Communist rule, and then to the counter-revolutionary regime of Miklós Horthy. Under Horthy, a brutal so-called White Terror was instigated against those who were thought 'to have supported the Soviet government. Among the peasants, students, workers and intellectuals killed were a large number of Jews. People were, Rózsika wrote to Dolly, 'being exterminated and hunted to death systematically'.[23] Britain had been broadly supportive of the new regime, and Rózsika's attempts to influence foreign policy on this matter came to nothing.[24] Less politically fraught were her efforts to help ameliorate the post-war situation in Austria, where material shortages were widespread and the threat of famine loomed. In mid December 1919 Rózsika fitted in her festive preparations around the task of writing statements and giving speeches on the Austrian situation. '[A]t one [meeting] I spoke for nearly 2½ hours, with press-people present,' she reported to Dolly.[25] 'Then I had to write long statements for Lord Bryce, Bole, Sir Hedley Le Bas, the *Daily Express* etc. all these were done <u>at night</u>, sometimes I was up to 2–3 a.m.'[26]

Rózsika's experience of lobbying for Zionism had given her the confidence and appetite to speak out on political causes she believed in. By 1920, when the situation in Hungary was stabilised somewhat by the Treaty of Trianon, she had become well known as a leading advocate on Hungarian issues in London. When the Hungarian politician János Teleszky arrived in London in the spring of 1922, it was Rózsika he approached for letters of introduction, and when the new Hungarian ambassador and his wife arrived in the city, they wasted no time in asking Rózsika 'to help them settle down, give advice etc.'[27] In the course of the 1920s Rózsika would negotiate the issuing of three loans from New Court to her native country: one of nearly £8 million, and two further loans of approximately £1 million each.[28] Throughout this period her husband remained stuck in the depths of his illness. Even a move back to Ashton Wold, where he was surrounded by his beloved butterflies and children, failed to lift his depression.[29] By the autumn of 1923 Charles was sinking out of reach again – and this time he would not recover.

Liberated from her fear of Zeppelins, Constance's spirits were further buoyed up by the approach of polling day. The general election of December 1918 would be the first in which some women (those over thirty years old, who owned property worth at least £5 rent per annum) were allowed to vote. Given her past work in the women's movement, it comes as no surprise that Constance had become an enthusiastic supporter of the franchise being extended. On 5 December she attended a meeting of women in Overstrand 're. the vote', and complained in her diary that there were 'too few present'; on polling day she recorded excitedly in her diary that she had 'voted!!!'[30] In other letters and diary entries, however, her excitement at the extended franchise was overshadowed by fears about radicalism. 'I do hope that the women will vote for order,' she wrote apprehensively.[31] She was mostly encouraged when Lloyd George's coalition government was returned with a healthy majority – though Sinn Fein's victory in Ireland gave her cause for worry.

Two years after embarking on her memoirs, her ambitions for the project had grown, and she now hoped to publish for a wide audience. Although others in the family, such as her aunt Charlotte, had published as a way to deal with the traumas of losing family members, these publications had been cloaked in poetic and fictional licence. Constance's memoirs promised to be far more direct in their description of the family's life and culture. Even those who had been supportive of the project – such as Hannah's widower Archibald, Lord Rosebery, who loved the 'intimate touches of Disraeli and Gladstone' – were horrified by the idea of general publication, and some readers outside the family were just as adamant in their opposition. 'I think you are wise not to publish your reminiscences,' wrote Princess Louise in 1921, '& particularly not just now.'[32] Though this reply forced Constance into a temporary retreat, by October she sent a draft of a chapter on family history to Lucien Wolf, the eminent Anglo-Jewish historian.[33] Wolf praised the 'delightful little glimpses of Gutle', and corrected several myths that Constance had repeated in her book, including the one about the Elector's treasure, and one about Nathan playing the stock market after Waterloo. (It's telling of the potency of these myths that they also circulated within the family.) The following year, Constance signed a contract with Sir Frederick Macmillan for publication.[34]

When *Reminiscences* was published in November 1922, Constance was 'quite amazed' by the positive reviews: *The Times* described it as a 'tender and fragrant piece of writing', which was 'neither egoistical

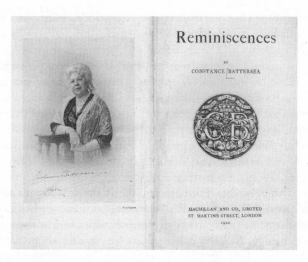

Reminiscences, *the memoir of Constance, Lady Battersea,*
first published in 1922.

nor ill-natured'.[35] The book's cosy and intimate portrait of the Victorian era – including, of course, details of Constance's interaction
with Queen Victoria herself – provided comfort for this generation
of post-war readers trying to rebuild their worldview by finding solace
in nostalgia. It sold all 1,500 copies of its first print run in a fortnight,
and was in its second impression by New Year.[36] Having spent most
of her years being funded by the wealth of her ancestors and then of
her husband, Constance found herself in the novel position of making
money. One morning, when a royalty cheque arrived at Overstrand,
she could not control her excitement: she ran up to the bedroom of her
guest, the Bishop of Norwich, and 'flung the long envelope at him'.[37]
The bishop read the figure – £597 – and 'congratulated me'. For the
first time in many years, Constance felt real energy and optimism.

In the autumn of 1923 news reached Overstrand of a 'tragic awful
death'. Only two months later, returning to the event in her round-up
of the year, did Constance bring herself to add a crucial further detail –
'self-inflicted'.[38] On 12 October Charles Rothschild had locked himself in his bathroom, picked up a shaving razor, and cut his throat.[39]
Rózsika was left alone with their son, Victor, and three daughters,
Miriam, Liberty and Nica.

33

Vocations

A DEAD FROG CHANGED Miriam's life. In the years after Charles's suicide, she had retreated from the zoological study and exploration that she associated with her father. Her time at home had been geared towards literature, and to traditional sporting pursuits: the *Daily Mirror* profiled her as 'sport-loving, fond of hunting and a keen follower of the Whaddon Chase'.[1] Then, during a school holiday in the mid 1920s, Victor returned home from Harrow and entreated his older sister for help with a homework task. 'I've got to dissect a frog,' he told her.[2] The two ventured over to the Tring zoological laboratory, a place they had barely visited since their father's suicide. In the lab, the siblings chloroformed the frog and began to pick its body apart. As she gazed in awe at the 'incredible beauty of the blood system and the arteries and veins' laid out in front of her, Miriam knew that her attempts to distance herself from her father's zoological passions were futile. 'My whole life was changed,' she later recalled. With the new academic year just weeks away, she hastily enrolled for evening classes in zoology at Chelsea Polytechnic.

Although they would soon dominate her thoughts, the zoology classes constituted a secondary course of study, chosen to fit in around her main lessons in literature. These took place at Bedford College, University of London, where she soon fell in with a crowd of young literary enthusiasts and writers. The Scrap Club, as they called themselves, included Patrick Balfour, Paul Robeson and Evelyn Waugh.[3] With the freedoms of living in the capital for the first time, Miriam soon led a double life. From one perspective, she was the consummate model of what a Rothschild woman might look like in the twentieth century: literary-minded, well-known socially, and a frequent attendee of what she would still remember, half a century later, as 'marvellous parties'. But on the nights she was not at parties or balls or theatrical performances, she was in the library or the laboratory, engrossed in zoological pursuits that lay far beyond the range of endeavours traditionally considered acceptable by her family.

An early interest in molluscs soon gave way to a fascination with the parasitic worms that lived inside them; then, after a chance encounter with the conchologist G.C. Robson in the library of the Natural History Museum, she found herself being offered a research table at the Naples Marine Biological Station.[4] There she began studying the life cycle of a genus of mollusc that lived independently before taking up residence inside a fish and eventually, when that host was eaten by a bird, in the predator's kidneys. Miriam forged a good rapport with the team of scientists at the research station – when an eruption of Vesuvius caused a small island to appear in the bay of Naples, they named it Monte Miriam – and the director of the centre, Reinhard Dohrn, was a 'magical personality' who became an inspiration and mentor.[5]

Back in England, aged twenty-two, she continued her mollusc research with a visit to the Marine Biological Association laboratory in Plymouth.[6] She spent her days between the laboratory and the research station's boat, 'otter-trawling and plankton netting' to retrieve specimens for study. In 1932 her studies at Chelsea Polytechnic ended, and she was given her own bench at the Marine Biological Association. In Plymouth, she began research on the parasites of *Hydrobia ulvae*, a snail found on tidal mud and salt marshes.

While Miriam dealt with her father's death by emulating him, her younger sisters developed their own coping mechanisms. During her teens, Nica became deeply interested in the jazz to which Charles had introduced her at a young age.[7] While Charles's interest in the new music emerging from America had been genteel and somewhat scholarly, Nica's appreciation was raucous, and part of a wider, wilder pattern of behaviour. In her early teens she was already terrorising her mother with a practice known as 'corridor creeping'. Between two and five a.m, after Rózsika had gone to bed and before the servants woke, she would summon her siblings and any visiting friends downstairs, where she would play them jazz records and ply them with wine from the family's superlative cellar.[8]

At a loss as to what to do with her wayward daughter, Rózsika turned to her friends, one of whom suggested a finishing school in Paris.[9] Nica and her nineteen-year-old sister Liberty were duly sent to France. While it failed to provide Rózsika with the prim and polite girls she hoped for, the school provided Nica with plenty of fodder for anecdotes: later in life, she would regale friends with stories about how the school was run by 'three lesbian sisters' who wore outlandish wigs, gave lessons in how to apply lipstick, and made occasional passes at their charges.[10] After a year in Paris, Nica and Liberty set off on a tour of the Continent, staying with cousins and other members of the extended family. When their letters home were insufficient, Rózsika followed her daughters' progress in the society columns of the foreign-language newspapers she still studied daily at Tring.

Liberty and Nica had won medals in the annual children's competitions staged by the Royal Drawing Society, and the same newspaper article that described Miriam as 'sport-loving' had emphasised Liberty's 'artistic and musical tastes'.[11] So it was in high spirits that they reached Germany, where they enrolled for classes at the Munich Academy of Fine Arts. And yet from the beginning, their time in Bavaria was marked by an unease they struggled to pinpoint. This was a Germany where the impact of the financial crash was fuelling the rise of support for Adolf Hitler and his National Socialist Party. 'It was during Hitler's rise,' Nica said later in life, 'but we weren't aware of what was going on, until it finally occurred to us that the people who were behaving boorishly were those who knew we were Jewish.'[12]

On the sisters' return to London in 1931, Rózsika set about arranging Nica's debutante season. Presentation to the reigning monarchs – currently George V and Queen Mary – was still part of the 'coming out' festivities of any upper-class young woman. Nica's took place in June 1932, and was followed a few weeks later by a grand party at no. 148 Piccadilly, where society journalists marvelled at the 'huge marble halls . . . vast fireplaces, gigantic chandeliers and colossal mirrors', and the older guests were put in mind of 'pre-war functions in Vienna and Berlin'.[13] But it was in the new nightclubs and music venues of the West End and Fitzrovia that Nica really felt at home – the Café de Paris, the Kit-Kat Club. Decades later, when she talked to her great-niece Hannah about her first love, the bandleader Jack Harris, it was not just his performances in the clubs she could remember; she still recalled his phone number and the way he liked his eggs in the morning.[14]

Her sister Liberty, meanwhile, was struggling with a far more troubling legacy from their father. Even before the European tour in 1931, it was clear that she was suffering from symptoms of mental ill health similar to those that had dogged Charles throughout his life.[15] Though Miriam had taken her sister to doctors in France and Switzerland, it had been to no avail, and eventually Rózsika decided that a prolonged hiatus from London life might help. In 1933 she arranged for Liberty to stay in New York, where she would study painting under the Hungarian portraitist and family friend, Maria de Kammerer.[16] The family hoped it might give her a chance against the despair which had devoured her father.

Nica remained in London. Her brother had managed to secure tuition from the swing pianist Teddy Wilson, and Nica sat in on the lessons. Soon she forged her own bond with Wilson, who fed her burgeoning musical obsession by recommending record shops, venues and innovative artists. As she became more deeply involved in the London jazz scene, Nica met the saxophonist Bob Wise, who in addition to his musical prowess was also a qualified pilot. Thus a passion for jazz gave rise to a new passion: flying.[17] Through the early 1930s Nica trained for a pilot's licence, with her short flights extending in length as her confidence grew.[18] In the summer of 1935 one of these flights took her across the Channel to Le Touquet, for a lunch that some Rothschild cousins had arranged. It was at this lunch that Nica met Jules de Koenigswarter, a widower who, at the age of thirty-three, was ten years her senior. Jules was suave, handsome, and the son of an ennobled Austrian-Jewish family.[19]

Jules's first wife had died three years before, but he had no wish to wait before falling in love again. After lunch, he whisked Nica off to the local aerodrome and took the young Rothschild up in his Leopard Moth plane. The following months were a whirlwind romance for the two pilots. As summer turned to autumn, the pair flew across the breadth of Europe, stopping in Deauville, Salzburg, Vienna, Budapest, Venice and Monte Carlo.[20] It seemed inevitable that this courtship was leading to a marriage proposal, but when it came Nica panicked. In September 1935 she booked a passage to New York, ostensibly to visit Liberty and to sample the American jazz scene first hand, but really hoping to find some space and time to think. Her hopes were dashed when Jules arrived in hot pursuit and, on 7 October, proposed again. This time Nica said yes, and the two married barely a week later, on 15 October, at the New York Municipal Building.[21] Liberty was the only other family member there, and the chief bridesmaid.

Having courted in Europe and married in North America, the couple flew down to Panama, then to Los Angeles, then onwards to the Far East. From smoking opium in Peking to crash-landing their plane and hitch-hiking in rural China, to buying souvenir musical sex toys in the Japanese city of Kobe, theirs was a honeymoon unlike any other in Rothschild family history.[22] After months of travelling, Jules and Nica settled in Paris and began house hunting. In the evenings Nica immersed herself in the bustling jazz scene of Montmartre and the more bohemian Montparnasse. She returned to London in July 1936 and gave birth to her first child, Patrick, in the same London mansion where she herself had been born.

The couple would continue to flit between London and Paris in the years that followed, as further children came. In London, the society papers carried photographs of them standing on runways with their aeroplane, and reported with excitement on their adventurous honeymoon. In Paris, however, the couple were increasingly reverting to convention, purchasing a grand suburban estate, the Château d'Abondant, where they gathered around them the usual household staff and collection of priceless art.[23] Rothschild cousins who visited the young family commented on how quickly Nica seemed to have reverted to the role of traditional Rothschild matriarch. What they did not see was her simmering frustration at this new, chateau-bound existence. In quieter historical circumstances, such a frustration might have simmered for years, or even decades, without being acted upon. But these were not quiet historical circumstances, and events would soon give Nica the opportunity to break out of a situation that had, in the mid 1930s, begun to feel like a trap.

The frustrations of her sister Liberty, aggravated by mental ill health, would surface more quickly and dramatically. Shortly after Nica and Jules had left New York for their honeymoon, Liberty attended a grand dinner party in the city. Guests were shocked as she declined the food, instead devouring the table decoration, an arrangement of roses.[24] Rózsika brought Liberty home and placed her in the care of a family friend, the psychiatrist Dr Freudenberg, who had fled Germany during Hitler's rise to power and taken up a job at Moorcroft House, a private psychiatric hospital in Hillingdon. There, he was known for his experimental techniques, such as the injection of insulin as a potential treatment for schizophrenia.[25] That Liberty was subjected to such hazardous and generally ineffective interventions is quite likely but impossible to confirm either way. Over the coming years, as her sisters emerged into the public eye, she would recede further from view, her name disappearing from newspapers and memoirs, her private records destroyed, and her experiences muffled beneath the same blanket of silence that had descended on the family in the wake of Charles's suicide.

34

Before the Bombs

O N SUNDAY, 22 NOVEMBER 1931 – the fifty-fourth anniversary of her marriage to Cyril Flower – Constance, Lady Battersea died at home in Overstrand. She was eighty-seven, and in her later years had done what no other family member had dared, putting their grand and gilded lives on public view. In an article that stressed Constance's mixture of hosting and charitable work, *The Times* praised the 'Liberal Hostess and "Grand Dame"' and described her mother Louisa as 'one of the most remarkable ladies of the house of Rothschild'.[1] Other newspapers emphasised the roll-call of famous Victorians she had known, with one reporting the death of a 'Friend of Gladstone', and another describing Constance as a 'friend of three Sovereigns and eight Prime Ministers'. That overstated things slightly – she had been friends with three prime ministers, and her relationships with royals had been warm acquaintances rather than friendships – but the fact that the newspapers were echoing the grandiose claims of her own memoirs was proof of how successfully her *Reminiscences* had shaped public perceptions of her life.

One by one, the Rothschild figureheads of the late Victorian period were departing the stage. Among the Tring branch of the family, two deaths were particularly hard. In January 1935 Emma Rothschild ended her twenty-year widowhood when she died aged ninety, and in late August 1937 Walter died in his sleep. Victor, now the third Lord Rothschild, inherited the bulk of his uncle's art and property, but much of Walter's zoological legacy would go to Miriam, including a share of his collection of moths and butterflies, and the editorship of the Tring Museum journal, *Novitates Zoologicae*. The museum at Tring and its entire contents – including 144 giant land tortoises, 2 great auk eggs and a library of 25,000 volumes – were left to the British

Museum's Natural History Department (later the Natural History Museum), with the proviso that if the collections could not be left intact and *in situ*, then they too should go to Miriam.[2] The terms were entirely reasonable but had within them the seeds of an acrimony that would grow between Miriam and her brother. For while Miriam resented the way in which her brother disposed of the property and art he had inherited from Walter, Victor would struggle to reconcile himself to the fact that it was his sister, rather than him, who was the more original intellect of their generation.

The prominence of Miriam in her uncle's will shows that Walter had appreciated her steps towards a scientific career. One of her earliest papers was accepted in the same journal that she would later inherit, *Novitates Zoologicae*, and the first article arising from her Plymouth research – a piece on the life histories of trematode flatworms – had been published in 1936, in the *Journal of the Marine Biological Association*. Her scholarly writing was lucid and bright with fascination. Describing a trematode larva in 1938, she wrote: 'The cystophorous cercariae ... are among the most extraordinary and beautiful of all known cercariae, and have never failed to excite the enthusiasm of those helminthologists fortunate enough to discover them.'[3] Later in life, the way in which she communicated her enthusiasm would become freer still. Looking at fleas under a microscope, she would say, was even more enjoyable than smoking marijuana.[4]

From the first, her experiments were conducted with an adventurous and unorthodox attitude. When, during her study of trematodes, she came to need gulls that were not already hosting parasites, she had no hesitation in pursuing what seemed to her like the obvious solution: buying gulls' eggs intended for eating from 'Mr James Campbell and Mr Thomas Jeffryes' at Leadenhall Market, and hatching them herself.[5] Frequently, the resources, confidence and expertise of her Rothschild upbringing were repurposed to scientific ends. Early on in her investigation into the change of pelage in stoats, she discovered there was a consensus among scientists that keeping stoats in captivity was an 'exceedingly difficult proposition'.[6] And yet, she wrote, 'a perusal of the advertisement columns of *The Gamekeeper* and similar periodicals shows this is frequently accomplished in less scientific circles'. Among the acknowledgements in her paper on changes of pelage was one to Mr Fred Young, who worked at Ashton Wold, for 'the enormous trouble he took with the management of the stoats'.[7]

In the summer of 1933 Miriam had the opportunity to turn her zoological attention from snails, gulls and stoats to a group of young human beings. During his time at Cambridge, Victor had cultivated a circle of friends who had a reputation for being mildly and faddishly left wing, but were in fact deeply so: several were Communists, and two – Guy Burgess and Anthony Blunt – would later become members of the Cambridge Spy Ring. In celebration of Burgess finishing his exams, the friends rented a villa near Nice. Miriam joined them and, after a day or so of observing the group, wrote home to Dolly, describing the villa as a hive full of different types of bee: the queen bee was the aristocratic socialite Venetia Montagu; the leftish Anthony Blunt was a worker bee; and the two gay men in the group, Arthur 'Arty' Marshall and Guy Burgess, were bumble bees.[8] Victor was 'Bee' pure and simple, though his engagement to Barbara Hutchinson was, Miriam suspected, a 'double double bluff', for she was sure her brother had 'leanings towards Bumble bay'.

By October, Miriam and Victor had moved on to another, more conventional Rothschild gathering in Merano, South Tyrol, where a couple of romantic suitors – or, as Miriam preferred to call them, 'erotic appendages' – joined the family at the Hotel Savoy: Barbara Hutchinson for Victor and Tony Lambert for Miriam.[9] Though Lambert had once been Rózsika's choice, his recent rejection from the Foreign Office meant that his marital candidacy had been put on ice, and he found himself tagging along a little awkwardly on trips out to collect fleas or to the local synagogue. Though not particularly enamoured of Lambert, Miriam found it 'a fascinating idea' that 'a Rothschild must wait until their prospective spouse gets a job'. Romantically, she was much more interested in John Foster, a lawyer and fellow of All Souls, Oxford, who had been staying at the villa with Victor and his friends.

In England, Miriam and her siblings turned their minds to more serious matters. Their mother's proud and uncomplicated relationship with her own Jewish heritage gave the younger Rothschilds a strong sense of their responsibility to help German Jews. In May 1934 they attended a film screening at the Tivoli on the Strand to raise funds for German-Jewish women and children.[10] The film was *The House of Rothschild*, an American drama offering a somewhat rose-tinted version of the family's history, albeit one that perpetuated the myth of Nathan Rothschild's Waterloo profiteering. Such romanticising was necessary: the family was inevitably the focus for some of the Nazi regime's most malicious antisemitic propaganda, culminating in 1940 with Erich Waschneck's film *Die Rothschilds*, in which the myth of the Waterloo profiteering was deployed to show Mayer Amschel's five sons as part of a Europe-wide Jewish capitalist conspiracy.[11]

Miriam, like her brother Victor, spent much of the late thirties writing, speaking and fundraising in support of German Jewry. By 1938 her research commitments had become a secondary consideration: 'I am sorry to say that I am terribly busy,' she wrote to Karl Jordan at the Tring Museum; 'it is this question of refugees. Since the Anschluss I have been unable to do my scientific work, and I am afraid, that for the next number of *Novitates*, there will only be about 4 very short papers from me.'[12] She spoke to congregations in London and Plymouth, organised fundraising events, and worked alongside John Foster to help Jews seeking refuge in the UK.[13] She was, as she told the Plymouth Hebrew Congregation, 'in daily contact, with the heart-rending problem of the refugees'.

Later, she would claim that her charity work and her frequent trips to Switzerland during this period had made her 'absolutely certain . . . that the Germans were going to declare war', yet letters she wrote at the time suggest that the outbreak of hostilities came as something of a surprise to her.[14] In August 1939 she made a trip across the Atlantic, to stay at the Waldorf Astoria in New York. Only once she was there, and read the headlines on the other side of the ocean, did she realise how bad the situation had become. 'One is peculiarly stupid really,' she wrote to Dolly on 26 August, 'as I did not believe in such a bad crisis as this, & had consequently not weighed up the price one paid if there was one!'[15] Seeking respite, she visited the American Museum of Natural History, where the only staff member present was a 'charming young ornithologist from Plymouth!' With the desperation born of mutual isolation, the two clung to each other, travelling back to Miriam's hotel where 'we talked about British finches till midnight'. The ornithologist was, she wrote to Dolly, 'a rather plain short, fair haired gentle schoolmaster – the type I am most unattracted by, and I could have positively k i s s e d him. I think the same was true of him.' A week later, on 3 September 1939, Britain declared war on Hitler's Germany.

By this point, John Foster had come to join Miriam in New York. Now a practising lawyer, he was pressed into service by the British

Embassy as First Secretary, in which role he advised on the fraught matter of ensuring that wartime deals between the countries protected American neutrality. Miriam and John relocated to Washington, where they 'defied the conventions of the world's most conventional society' by moving into a house together.[16] 'Who cares?' wrote Miriam to Dolly, on the potential for their cohabitation to provoke scandal. 'Not me anyway . . .' If there was any romantic element in her relationship with her 'companion' – as she referred rather cryptically to John during this period – it was not much in evidence during those fraught weeks in the American capital: John dined out most nights during the week and was away most weekends. '[I]t would be difficult to imagine a more lonely life really – short of a German Refugee!!' wrote Miriam to Dolly in late October.[17] 'Yet I would wish for no other and only dread the moment when I must leave – for that is inevitable.'

Late in the autumn she travelled on an Italian boat to Genoa, and onwards to Britain from there.[18] Though the Ashton Wold estate was marked as accommodation for evacuated German-Jewish children, Miriam found that the staff had been 'obstructionist' about the changes necessary – 'and to be frank Mummy was a little bit also'.[19] She took over the management of the scheme, and soon began receiving children at the estate, taking 'first come, no discussion'.[20] She had received a letter from the government informing her that she was, as a scientist, in a 'reserve profession', and should carry on with her current work until reassigned. She therefore continued to spend most of her weeks at Plymouth – where she began a 'patriotic sideline' producing chicken food from seaweed – and travelled up to Ashton as often as she could.

It was during one of Miriam's visits, in June 1940, that Rózsika suffered a fatal heart attack. 'She actually died having lunch with me,' Miriam would say.[21] 'We were sitting at the table having lunch when she had a heart attack and died.' It was a particularly cruel time for Rózsika to die: just as European conflict was again breaking out, and with much of the Continent in the clutches of the Nazis. It was a cruel time, too, for Miriam, who due to the war was cut off from the Wertheimstein relatives of her mother's who had meant so much to her during her childhood and youth. 'Things got very much worse,' she later recalled, 'because . . . you lost all possibility of contact with the people you knew and loved and I had lots of people in Hungary I was devoted to. Among them of course my mother's sisters and her brothers.'[22]

Miriam inherited most of her mother's fortune.[23] Along with the property and capital came a responsibility to continue the allowances of certain staff members and to look after Ashton. It was a managerial role that several generations of Rothschild women had held before her, and one that she would fill capably – in her own distinctive way.

In the year after Rózsika's death, two bombing raids changed the course of Miriam's war. The first was in London, on the morning of 9 September 1940, when the Natural History Museum was hit by two incendiaries and an oil bomb. In the aftermath of the bombing, Miriam went to the site, and found the director, Clive Forster-Cooper, wandering through the rubble, 'collecting bits of bombs'.[24] Though Forster-Cooper was rather too dazed at that moment to consider Miriam's offer to house the helminthological collection, the offer was eventually accepted.[25] On 8 November Dr Bayliss, who was responsible for the helminths, visited Ashton Wold to inspect the facilities. Shortly after that, removals began, vans shuttling up to Northamptonshire carrying the slides of trematodes and the catalogues that went with them. Dr Bayliss moved with the collections, bringing his family in tow. Bayliss was 'very nice', as was his daughter, but Miriam found his wife 'tiresome', and resented her refusal to chip in with the garden work of clearing ground and planting war supplies. Part of the main house had been turned over for use as a hospital, and between this and the museum collections, Miriam was left with only a couple of rooms to herself. Feeling claustrophobic, and still 'in despair about my mother's death', she moved to a cottage in Ashton village. It was the village that would be her base, whenever she was in Ashton, for the rest of the war and some years afterwards.[26]

A few months later, in March 1941, Miriam was working in her laboratory in Plymouth when she heard the chilling wail of the air-raid sirens.[27] As the laboratory where she was working had no proper air-raid shelter, the occupants of the lab took cover in the tunnel leading to the boathouse for the duration of the night. Through an open space in the roof of the tunnel Miriam could make out a purple patch of sky with 'silver pencils of the searchlights sweeping across it'. They staggered out at four a.m. to find a thick pall of smoke over the dawn city and a 'soft, licking, sobbing murmur' coming from the Turnchapel oil tanks, which had been set ablaze during the raid. After a few hours' trying to snatch sleep in a deckchair, Miriam made her way back to the laboratory to assess the damage in the light of day. The door had been blown off, and the interior was a giant pile of shattered glass.[28] The sole survivor of her research was one of her birds, a tame sandpiper, which picked its way across the glass before lying down and dying. There was no sign of her notebooks, her drawings or the hundreds of snails she had so painstakingly infected and isolated; there were no microscopes, watch glasses, finger bowls, shelves or jars. 'Gone,' she later wrote. 'Seven years' work had vanished, pulverized with a ton of glass.'

The loss affected her physically. She took to her bed, suffering from a pain in her back as intense as if someone had hit her. But three days after the bombing, she woke with a sudden realisation. She had been so intensely gripped by her work at Plymouth that she no longer felt herself: she had become merely 'an appendage of the experiment'.[29] The 'wretched Luftwaffe had really freed me'.

35

Sisters in Arms

B EFORE LEAVING TO join his regiment in September 1939, Jules handed Nica a map. Pointing at a marker, he told her: 'If the Germans get to this point, take the children and escape any way you can to your family in England.'[1] Nica claimed that she could 'count the times in my life when I cried'.[2] The day of Jules's call-up was one of them. 'I remember we had this enormous lawn . . . and walking and running and crying [and I] couldn't stop.' Through the autumn and into the winter Nica remained at the chateau with her three-year-old son Patrick and infant daughter Janka, her mother-in-law, stepson Louis and a whole host of household staff. In May 1940 German forces began their advance into France, and by the end of the month the British Expeditionary Force and the broken French Army would be forced to evacuate from Dunkirk. Jules, leading his troops in retreat in the Somme valley, managed to send a note to Nica, imploring her to pack up and leave as soon as possible.[3]

Yet her mother-in-law Jeanne refused to leave the chateau, and rather than joining the throngs of refugees passing by her gates, Nica opened the doors of the house and offered people beds. By the time she reconciled herself to fleeing in late May, her options were severely restricted. There was no possibility that she would be able to find fuel to fly her plane across the Channel, and there were no more commercial ships. What was usually a ten-hour train journey to the coast took two days, but they were lucky to reach the port at all – theirs was one of the last trains to do so before escape routes were cut off by the German advance.[4] After a two-day wait, Nica and her children managed to get on a ship to England, where she arrived in a state of superhuman calm – 'as if she came from a picnic', commented Rózsika.[5] The reunion between Nica and her ailing mother Rózsika at Ashton Wold was brief: at Jules's request, Nica, her nanny and her two children boarded a ship in Liverpool on 11 June 1940. Three days into the Atlantic voyage, Paris fell. On Saturday, 22 July Nica wired her mother to tell her that she had arrived safely in New York; just over a week later, she would receive a message back from England bearing news of her mother's death.[6]

Determined to return to Europe as soon as possible, Nica desperately sought a family who would take in her children for the duration of the war. She worried that the children would not be considered legitimate refugees and would struggle to find a home. But she was in luck: a wealthy family in Long Island were having a complementary dilemma.[7] The family was that of Harry Frank Guggenheim and his third wife Alicia. Though a number of Guggenheim properties had been turned over to housing European refugee children, Harry and Alicia had been reluctant to look after refugee children in a private capacity, worrying that it would be potentially damaging for children whose experiences had been incalculably remote from Guggenheim splendour. The couple were put in touch with Nica by Miriam's 'companion' John Foster, and came to New York to meet their potential wards. 'They came and met the children at the Waldorf,' Nica recalled. 'They fell right in love with them.' Arrangements were made for the children, along with their British nanny Miss Davenport, to take up residence with Harry and Alicia. Any doubts the Guggenheims had as to the suitability of their refugees was presumably allayed by the response of Nica's son Patrick, as they pulled up at Falaise, the family's *faux* Norman mansion on Long Island: 'Oh, what a nice little house.'

Reassured that her children would be safe and comfortable, Nica rented an apartment on the Upper East Side and began working out how she might join her husband at war.[8] Jules had managed to escape France after the fall of Paris, and had reached England in time to attend Rózsika's funeral on 4 July. In London, he had signed up with the newly formed Free French, and by the end of the summer he had been posted to French Equatorial Africa. Through the late summer and autumn of 1940 Nica worked in New York with the American organisation France Forever, preparing provisions and medical supplies for West Africa.[9] When the supplies were shipped in December 1940 aboard a Norwegian freighter, Nica made sure that she and her lady's maid were also aboard.

Jules was understandably shocked by his wife's sudden appearance, but both he and his commanding officer were glad for any extra support. Nica was put to work decoding messages and driving troops, officers and supplies.[10] She had a lot to learn about how people lived in wartime. Her decision to bring a maid with her across the Atlantic stunned local society, and meant that the local servant and cook who worked in her quarters had to be moved elsewhere, to make room – wartime billets were not fitted out for the kind of entourages with which Rothschild women preferred to travel. Nonetheless, Nica proved herself capable of adapting quickly. Within a short time she had been formally inducted into the Free French as a private second class.[11]

Late in 1942 Nica's work with the Free French was suddenly disrupted when she contracted malaria. On the last day of 1942 she boarded the SS *Santa Paula* at Lagos in Nigeria, and set sail again for New York City. Since she shipped out, the United States had joined the war, and during her return journey, her boat was attacked twice within six hours by submarines.[12] The first torpedo missed by twenty feet; the second, even more narrowly. For Nica and the other passengers on board, safety was not assured until they finally reached New York on 24 January 1943. This arrival would bring Nica some respite and a chance to reunite with her children. Predictably, though, it would not be long before she itched to return to the action.

Before the bombs destroyed her Plymouth laboratory, Miriam had been asked to fill in a questionnaire. Slipped between mundane questions about her height and health were more searching queries, about the nature of her research, and how many languages she spoke.[13] At the end of 1941 the outcome of this questionnaire finally arrived in the form of a call-up for Miriam to work at a secret government facility in Buckinghamshire. For a while, it was referred to as Station X, and then by the official acronym of GC & CS; staff jokingly called it the Golf Club and Chess Society.[14] Later, it would come to be known as one of the most crucial government facilities in the British war effort, and the real meaning of the official acronym – the Government Code and Cypher School – would be eclipsed in the public mind by the name of the estate where the school was based: Bletchley Park.

Miriam worked for the Naval Section, translating German messages on night shifts that ran from four in the afternoon until eight the following morning. She was constantly nervous about the secrecy surrounding the institution, and even in interviews conducted many decades later, she would still reveal very little about the precise nature of her work there.[15] It certainly had a Rothschild twist, however. While most workers at Bletchley slept in dormitories on the estate, Miriam jumped into her car after each shift, and drove the twelve miles south to Mentmore, where the Roseberys' eldest son Harry, the sixth Lord Rosebery, provided her with her own apartment and housekeeper.[16]

Nevertheless, Miriam was miserable at Bletchley Park. The anxiety surrounding her work, combined with the all-night hours, meant that she slept poorly in the two years she was stationed there.[17] Adding to her worries was the condition of her sister Liberty, who was still under the care of Dr Freudenberg, now at Springfield House in Hillingdon. On Boxing Day 1941 the nurse Annie Gray wrote a letter reporting on her patient's behaviour.[18] 'I am sorry to say that Miss Liberty was not very good on Christmas morning,' she began, before describing how Liberty had pulled to pieces a book sent by a friend as a present. By the evening, when Annie judged it safe to give her the rest of her presents – including books and records from Miriam and chocolates from James and Dolly – Liberty was 'much happier', but yearning for her family.

The Christmas gathering at Liberty's childhood home was not one she would have recognised. With Rózsika gone, Victor taken up with counter-sabotage work (taking apart exploding Nazi chocolate bars) for the Special Operations Executive (SOE), and Nica away with the Free French, Miriam was the only member of the immediate family present among a crowd that included the curator of the Natural History Museum's helminthological collection and fifty child refugees.[19] The house itself was still occupied by a Red Cross military hospital, and the grounds were being used by the Army, Air Corps and Ordnance Corps. The most difficult guests were the last, who torched trees to get rabbits out, detonated practice bombs, and stole rifles in order to cull the swans on the lake.[20] Miriam knew that worse things were happening elsewhere, and remained calm in the face of such chaos. 'Damaging the property isn't quite the right word,' she said, looking back on the period, 'but their form of occupation was not very delicate.'

In June 1942 the airbase adjacent to the estate, RAF Polebrook, was turned over to the United States Army Air Forces, and the first of over five thousand American servicemen arrived. At her cottage in the village, Miriam kept an open house, hosting servicemen and members of the US Bomber Command.[21] Among her guests was the film star Clark Gable, who, alongside flying his own combat missions, was shooting a recruitment film for aircraft gunners. Miriam found him to be 'very conceited' and lacking 'all sense of humour', but his exceptional good looks made him a pleasant companion when shooting the rooks that had begun to overrun the estate.[22] As Miriam later put it to an interviewer: 'I like good-looking people.'

Another good-looking man arrived at Ashton Wold in 1943. Captain György Lányi was a Hungarian-born Jew who went by 'George Lane', a name that would become official when he was naturalised as a British subject in 1946. Athletic and adventurous, George had trained with the Hungarian Olympic water polo team in the early 1930s, before moving to England in the years before the war, to work as a journalist. In that capacity, he had written an account of some Hungarian refugees arriving on the east coast of England in the late 1930s. Rózsika had read it eagerly and invited George to Ashton Wold.[23] The war had disrupted this plan – George was recruited for the Special Operations Executive, for whom he undertook a number of risky secret missions. 'I had to go into Germany and crack a safe which contained secret documents,' he recalled long after the war. 'A convicted safe cracker was released from Dartmoor prison to teach me. We met in a safe house on the Isle of Wight and on the condition that I never use it in peace time, he taught me everything he knew.' At one point, he was parachuted into France with a case of carrier pigeons: 'It was pitch dark and I had to jump 400 ft into enemy territory. I landed in a field with the pigeons in a small cage strapped onto my chest. The goal was for them to deliver a secret message.'[24] During one such mission, George broke his arm; he was sent to Ashton Wold to recuperate.

Arriving at the hospital, he recognised the address and asked a matron if he might meet Rózsika. The matron explained to him that Rózsika had died, and that the estate was now run by her daughter – who happened to be coming home for the weekend from Bletchley. Miriam arrived exhausted, and had no interest in exchanging pleasantries with a strange soldier who had wanted to speak with her mother.[25] 'But,' replied the matron, with a twinkle in her eye, 'he's awfully good looking.'

Miriam and George Lane were married on 14 August 1943 to very little fanfare. The marriage to a Hungarian national concerned her superiors at Bletchley Park, who considered George a security risk despite all the bravery he had displayed fighting for the British SOE. Although the authorities would later renege on this view, Miriam seized the opportunity to leave the work she hated, and turned them down when they asked her to stay on.[26] Instead, she began a new programme of research for the government, looking into whether bovine tuberculosis was being spread by bird parasites.[27] When George's arm had recovered, he was deployed with a new Commando regiment to Aberdovey in Wales. Miriam went with him, wood pigeons in tow.

Early in 1944 their life together was suddenly curtailed when George's secretive 'X troop' of No. 10 Commando – a troop made up almost entirely of German-speaking Jewish refugees – was engaged on a mission that required them to live and train in isolation.[28] The aim of 'Operation Tarbrush' was to obtain details of German mines and other defences that had been laid across the French coast, in order to help prepare for Allied landings in June. Preparations were so secret that Miriam was not even allowed to know where her husband was stationed – though a rogue postal stamp on one of his letters revealed that he was in Exbury, which enabled the couple to orchestrate a surreptitious meeting in the village church.[29]

On his third mission for X Troop, George was sent to Calais to investigate a new type of German landmine.[30] He and a comrade were captured by a German patrol boat, interrogated for several days, then blindfolded and loaded onto a truck. When George's blindfold was removed, he found himself standing beneath 'a most extraordinary castle built against a rock'. This was La Roche-Guyon, the headquarters of Field Marshal Erwin Rommel. While in captivity at the castle, George was subjected to further gruelling interrogations, and taken to Rommel for an eerily friendly meeting.[31] Throughout the ordeal he adopted as convincing a Welsh accent as he could muster, hoping that by doing so he could mask his Jewish-Hungarian heritage. Instead of being executed, as they had feared, the two men were sent on to further prisons: first to Fresnes, near Paris, then to the POW camp at Spangenberg Castle, Oflag IX-A/H. All Miriam knew was that her husband had gone missing in action. After a frantic search, she discovered that he was being held as a prisoner of war.

In the summer of 1943, after six months with her children in New York, Nica returned to Africa. Jules was now on the move, and she found herself hopping across West and then North Africa with him in a small plane, from Brazzaville to Bangui, and eventually to Cairo, from where British North African operations were being directed. Soon after their arrival, Jules was summoned to Tunis, to take charge of several thousand prisoners of war, and Nica remained behind in the city.[32] Her day job was to organise Free French supplies and equipment – but day jobs were only a small part of life in Cairo. A long history of colonial occupation had left the city with a substantial infrastructure for pleasure-seeking European visitors, including restaurants, night-clubs, cabarets and rooftop dance floors. Rothschild family lore would later have it that an American soldier, searching for the source of the wonderful music drifting down the hallway in his hotel, would find it came from a gramophone in the room of a 'beautiful woman with long dark hair': Nica, who invited him inside and promptly seduced him.[33]

When Jules's regiment crossed to Naples to join the Italian offensive which had started the previous autumn, Nica followed. Once in Italy, she began working for the War Graves Commission, driving ambulances and helping to retrieve and identify the bodies of soldiers. That her husband was not among the corpses was a matter of good luck: during fighting along the Garigliano River he narrowly escaped death when a mortar exploded a foot away from his head, leaving him temporarily blind and deaf.[34] Rome was captured on 4 June 1944, just two days before the D-Day landings in Normandy. In September the couple arrived in recently liberated Paris, where they spent a brief period of leave staying in a Rothschild property that was already partly occupied by an American army unit. That suited Nica just fine. After overhearing a sergeant playing a piano downstairs to entertain his comrades, she invited him to her apartment, to dose him with Courvoisier and unleash him on the Pleyel Grand.[35]

After the fall of Hitler, Nica retired from active service with the rank of lieutenant. She was awarded the *Médaille commémorative des services volontaires dans la France libre*, while Jules received the prestigious *Ordre de la Libération*. The horrors of war had somehow brought them into what looked, at times, like a productive and admiring partnership. But many of Jules's family, including his mother, had been murdered in Nazi death camps. He was doubtless traumatised, as was everyone else, whether they knew it or not. Character traits

enlarged and abetted by the war – Jules had been a ferocious commander, who sometimes had his men beat up insubordinate soldiers in
front of the whole regiment – would sit uneasily with the attempted
return to peacetime, and to domesticity.[36]

Miriam too had a bittersweet experience of the peace that came in
1945. When her husband returned from his camp in the late spring,
she found him to be a completely different person: remote and quick-
tempered, with 'an unfortunate habit of knocking men down in night-
clubs'.[37] Nevertheless, she clung to the hope that she and George
might be able to build a semblance of normal life together. The couple
had tragically lost a child at the beginning of their marriage, but with
George back from the war, Miriam was soon pregnant again. 'My husband is home from a P.O.W. camp and I am having another attempt
at a family,' she wrote to a contact at the Natural History Museum.[38]
On 27 December Miriam gave birth to their daughter, named Mary
Rózsika after her grandmother. She would be known as Rosie.[39] With
their second child, born in 1948, they followed the same respectful
pattern, calling him Charles after his grandfather.

George had a long-standing interest in breeding show cattle, and
Miriam in growing flowers, so after the departure of the Red Cross
and the military, it seemed sensible to revive Ashton as a working farm
and nursery. Since a young age Miriam had been uneasy at some of
the practices she had seen used on the Ashton livestock: the dehorn-
ing of cattle, castration without local anaesthetic, shelterless pastures
and long journeys to slaughter. On the revived farm, all such practices
would be banned. An advisor was hired to assist with the selection of
modern agricultural machinery. Miriam visited Holland to study the
tulip industry, and Switzerland to learn about floriculture, 'how they
grew their plants in the greenhouses under sunlight in the winter
and all the various dodges'. Keen to save money, and not afraid to get
her hands dirty, she did a great deal of the work herself, planting and
weeding in the cottage garden, and driving crops of flowers down to
London, where, dressed in riding breeches, she sold them straight
from the van.[40]

At the same time, she embarked on a campaign to help Jewish survivors of the war and the Holocaust. In partnership with her old friend
John Foster, who was acting as a legal advisor to General Eisenhower in
occupied Germany, she joined a chorus of voices aiming to highlight the
dangers facing the survivors of concentration and extermination camps,

some of whom had died as a result of thoughtless care and overfeeding post liberation.[41] Miriam began in earnest to write to politicians about the 'unexpected and desperate situation' in which some who had survived the Nazi genocide were dying because of Allied mismanagement.[42] Over the coming months she would make contact with two MPs – the Labour politicians Richard Crossman and Patrick Gordon Walker – to raise the profile of this issue within Parliament. Later in life she tended to exaggerate her own role in movements whose achievements she was proud of, and her own telling of the post-war campaign – which ended with Foster leaving a meeting with Winston Churchill and announcing to Miriam that 'the random freeing of concentration camps by a sympathetic army was now over' – overstated the extent to which this was her and Foster's cause alone. All the same, it's true that Miriam and John Foster played an important role in the broader humanitarian effort to help survivors of the Nazi genocide, and that for both of them, this represented the beginning of a lasting commitment to campaigns on restitution and Jewish welfare.

The expectation that Rothschilds act as spokespeople for Jews nationally and internationally had lessened in recent years: the rise of Zionism had split the family and provided a new generation of non-hereditary leaders, and the decline of the family bank had eroded the material basis of the Rothschilds' pre-eminence. Nevertheless, when Miriam learned that Jews who were considered 'enemy nationals' (because they held citizenship in an Axis country) were being denied access to property seized during the war, she felt obliged to become an advocate for them.[43] Under the terms of international agreements, 'enemy nationals' were able to reclaim such property only if they could prove that they had 'suffered deprivation of liberty under discriminatory legislation'. Baron Ullmann, a Hungarian banker, had endured eight months hiding in a windowless cupboard in the attic of his Christian barber, but because this hiding was 'voluntary', he forfeited his savings of £4,000 in the UK. Miriam's Hungarian aunt Johanna von Wertheimstein, who had made a dramatic escape from imprisonment, was arrested in Budapest in 1944 and imprisoned in a so-called 'Jewish house', awaiting deportation to a death camp. After escaping by faking her own suicide, she sheltered for some time in a cellar and was nearly executed by the invading Soviets – before being denied access to her impounded British assets on the grounds that it was unclear whether there had been a wall around the house in which she had been imprisoned. In many cases, a 'polite' but persistent antisemitism lay behind the apathy of the British establishment. Returning from a meeting with Sir Henry Gregory (the Custodian of Enemy Property), John Foster had told her: 'We will get nowhere. Gregory himself is a purposeful anti-semite.'

Gradually Miriam realised how fortunate she had been to stay safe during the war by an accident of geography. In the aftermath of the Holocaust she found herself drawn with horror, incomprehension and even a degree of misplaced guilt, to the memory of those close relatives who had not had such luck: Élisabeth Rothschild, the estranged wife of Philippe, who perished in Ravensbrück concentration camp; Miriam's favourite Hungarian aunt Aranka, who was beaten to death with meat hooks on arrival at Buchenwald; Nica's mother-in-law, Jeanne de Koenigswarter, who was arrested soon after the Nazis arrived at the Château d'Abondant, and was later killed at Auschwitz.[44]

In 1946 Nica and her family moved to Oslo, where Jules had been posted as part of the French diplomatic service.[45] Jules's pride in the scale and grandeur of the premises leased as the French embassy, the Villa Grande mansion in Bygdøy, concealed another, deeply unsettling fact about the house: the previous occupant had been Vidkun Quisling, the head of Norway's Nazi puppet government and the man responsible for rounding up and deporting the country's Jews to Nazi death camps. Even without this macabre setting, the life of a diplomat's wife would have been intolerable to Nica. The arrival of further children in 1946 and 1947 only pulled her deeper into the stifling boredom of domesticity.

Jules, baulking at Nica's lack of the 'feminine virtues' that ambassador's wives were expected to exhibit, started behaving more autocratically.[46] He installed a light bulb in front of his wife's seat at the dining table, and would turn it on when the time came for her and the ladies to withdraw. As Nica stared into the distance with glazed eyes, he would flick the bulb on and off until she relented and followed his instructions. In 1950 Jules was offered a new role in Mexico City, where his frustration at Nica's lax timekeeping and offbeat cultural tastes began to manifest itself in spite and resentment. He told her that art and music were 'not serious matters', and was embarrassed by Nica's association with black musicians during her increasingly frequent trips to New York. When Nica was late for dinner, as she often was, Jules would smash her beloved records.[47]

At a friend's house in Mexico City, Nica first heard Duke Ellington's 'Black, Brown and Beige'.[48] Against the backdrop of the 'diplomatic life and all the bullshit', she felt the lure of the music more strongly than ever: 'I got the message that I belonged where that music was.' In New York, her brother Victor's former piano tutor Teddy Wilson provided an entrée to the burgeoning jazz scene on Broadway. During one visit, just before she was about to leave, Wilson persuaded her to listen to a record by a pianist called Thelonious Monk, "Round Midnight'. Nearly twenty years later, she would tell club owner Max Gordon: 'The first time I heard Thelonious play "'Round Midnight", I cried.'[49] She remained in New York for a further three months before returning to her family in Mexico City. It would turn out to be a rehearsal for a much bigger separation.

Christmas of 1949 was wretched for Miriam. A month previously, she had endured the unbearable loss of another child just after birth, an event that had left her feeling 'older than I can say', and this Christmas was, she wrote to Dolly, 'the epitome of all sorrows'.[50] She struggled to articulate the loss to her young children. When four-year-old Rosie turned to her mother and asked if God had taken her baby sister back, Miriam replied with a simple yes. There was a long pause, before Rosie asked, 'and is God a nice person?' That, for Miriam, cut to the heart of the matter. While her sense of her own Jewishness had been heightened by the events of the last two decades, so had her certainty of her own atheism. As she later put it: 'I don't believe in God ... I think it's immoral to believe in God.'[51]

Looking back at the lives of her parents, who were also not religious, she would realise that, for them, religious ideals had been replaced by secular ones, of morality, goodwill and public service.[52] Similarly, Miriam's books were 'written as acts of service', and none more so than the one she embarked on after the war: a catalogue of her father's vast collection of fleas, which he had donated to the Natural History Museum. She originally estimated that it would take her seven years; in the end, it would take over three decades. A less imposing publishing project began in 1947, when she was approached by the publisher Collins to write a popular book about parasites for their New Naturalist series. She began writing the book during several days marooned in a 'pock-marked public house' in the ruins of Calais, and continued working on it in snatched moments and at night, while nursing her newborn son, Charles. Miriam's *Fleas, Flukes and Cuckoos* was finally published in 1952.[53] The book was an immediate success, and rapidly went through several editions, becoming a standard introductory text. For years to come, Miriam would meet parasitologists who credited her with having interested them in the field.

By the time *Fleas, Flukes and Cuckoos* was published, it had become clear that Miriam and George's agricultural endeavour at Ashton was failing. Miriam's commitments as a writer, scientist and mother were too great, and George had turned against the idea of a rural life.[54] In the early 1950s he tried to persuade Miriam to relocate their family to the capital. Their marriage, which had enjoyed such a brief honeymoon phase before George's capture in 1944, was in a fragile state. They compromised and instead moved to Elsfield, just outside Oxford: urban life for George, countryside for Miriam, and schools nearby for their children. By the time of the move in 1953, Rosie was eight and Charles six. Miriam had given birth to another daughter, Charlotte, in 1951, and in the same year the couple also adopted at birth a fourth child, Johanna.[55]

Miriam would continue to spend time at Ashton too, and it was here in 1953 that she was reunited with Nica, who was back in the UK after finally separating from Jules. Nica's 1953 visit was timed to coincide with Teddy Wilson's UK tour, during which she would act as a patron and chaperone. In September, when Wilson arrived at London Croydon Airport, it was Nica (along with her teenage daughter Janka and two eager journalists from the *New Musical Express*) who met him off his plane.[56] At some point during the trip, Nica's other children joined from Mexico, and the sisters found themselves and their offspring crammed into the cottage that had remained Miriam's main base at Ashton since the war. 'There were about 7 children there at the cottage,' Miriam remembered, 'and they spread into the laundry.'[57]

Nica would turn forty in December. Her early attempts at getting involved in the London jazz scene – such as the reopening of Studio 51 in Soho, and her patronage of Al Timothy – had been moderately successful, but did not represent the sort of immersive occupation that she needed, and she spent much of her free time in favourite venues such as the Stork Club, drinking heavily. Then she heard from a friend – the jazz pianist Mary Lou Williams – that Thelonious Monk was

Nica and her children Janka, Shaun, Berit and Kari, photographed in 1957.

about to play at the Salle Pleyel, as a last-minute addition to the line-up at that year's Paris Jazz Festival.[58] She flew there straight away.

Monk's performance that night was met in the music press with the bafflement that had become customary at this stage in his career. 'His right hand stabs at the keyboard in a Chico Marx manner, apparently without flexibility,' wrote the critic for *Melody Maker*.[59] 'He hits with a finger and the rest of the hand arches stiffly like a fan. He hammers unrelated chords, while his feet writhe and twist on the floor. His right foot hits the pedal, misses, slips off; it poises, and bangs down sometimes on the pedal, often on the floor.' 'You can't assess Monk,' the critic concluded, 'because there are no set standards by which to judge him.' Nica disagreed: though he had only played two tunes and Nica could tell 'the audience weren't really grasped by it', she was awestruck.[60]

After the gig, Mary Lou Williams introduced the two backstage. Monk was, Nica remembered, 'the most beautiful man I [had] ever seen'. Though Nica 'needed an interpreter to understand what he was saying at the beginning', the two hit it off immediately. They hardly left each other's company for the rest of Monk's time in Paris, and Nica's great-niece and biographer, Hannah Rothschild, has speculated that the days after their meeting were taken up with a whirlwind affair.[61] That seems highly plausible. Certainly they forged a connection that would shape the rest of their lives. By the time they parted ways, Nica had made up her mind: she would move to New York, and 'get in on the jazz scene' there. When she left Europe later that year, it was for good.

36

Echoes

O N 14 MAY 1948 Dolly and James de Rothschild were at home in Buckinghamshire when three and a half decades of lobbying, dreaming and hoping came to fruition, in the birth of the State of Israel. Following the Second World War the United Nations had devised a plan under which the British mandate would be terminated and Palestine partitioned into Arab and Jewish states. The plan had met with fierce resistance from Arab leaders, and ignited a civil war in the region between the Arab and Jewish populations. In May, with the civil war still raging, the leaders of the Jewish population had drawn up a unilateral declaration of independence. Within hours of the declaration ceremony being held – and in no small part due to Weizmann's personal lobbying of President Truman – the United States had recognised Israel.[1] This should have been the apotheosis of Weizmann's dream. But while David Ben-Gurion became the state's first prime minister, it was no secret that Weizmann's role, of president, was largely ceremonial, and given as a token of gratitude. When he asked his friend Moshe Sharett, the new Israeli Foreign Minister, what his duties as president would entail, Sharett replied: 'Oh, just to be a symbol, Dr Weizmann.'[2]

Dolly was acutely aware of Weizmann's frustration with this position. In 1949 her friend Isaiah Berlin, the philosopher, wrote to her from New York, describing the President of Israel – whom he had recently met – as being 'openly libellous about his government'.[3] 'It really is a pathetic sight,' Berlin continued, 'to see a man with a unique appetite for power and a capacity for using it, stripped completely of all traces of it, in a state of impotent fury.' By October 1950, when Dolly received a letter from Weizmann, 'impotent fury' had been tempered by frailty, and had subsided into a melancholic nostalgia for the early days of the Zionist movement:

When I think of our first tentative conversations, and of the various events that have happened in the intermediate period, I am deeply sorry that it is not given to you to take a personal part in the consolidation of the State of Israel, which would have surely given you both great satisfaction. Believe me, it is our loss to be deprived of your invaluable collaboration.[4]

Dolly and James had been unable to play a major role in the lead-up to the 1948 declaration owing to the latter's poor health. The loss of an eye in a 1919 golfing accident, failing sight in his remaining eye and a bad fall during the 1940s combined to make him heavily dependent on Dolly, and meant that travel was difficult.[5] Their lives were centred on Waddesdon Manor, which James had inherited in 1922. Dolly developed a familiar portfolio of work at local schools and hospitals, and like her husband – who served as Liberal MP for Ely between 1929 and 1945 – was actively engaged with Liberal politics. In the 1949 election she was invited to stand as the Liberal candidate for Aylesbury, the local seat previously held by four successive Rothschild men between 1865 and 1923.[6] Dolly declined, but agreed to become president of the Mid-Buckinghamshire Liberal Association.[7] As the next election approached, she wrote letters to local newspapers, valiantly attempting to challenge the narrative of decline that dogged the party during the campaign, and urging people to seriously consider the Liberals' distinctive set of policies, which included electoral reform and devolved parliaments for Scotland and Wales. The election in February 1950 saw the Liberals lose seats, and yet the defeat appears only to have galvanised Dolly's commitment to the 'future strategy' of the party.[8] In April 1950 she won a seat on the county council.

Though they were not yet in a position to visit Israel, Dolly and James had glimpses of life there through correspondence with a broad range of people. Miriam, who visited Israel several times in this period, provided them with opinions on conservation and the performance of scientific and research institutions, as well as on more esoteric matters such as the value of a black bear that the Biblical Zoo in Jerusalem had considered buying.[9] The flavour of a more typical immigrant life in Israel came from regular letters sent by some of the 'Cedars Boys' – the thirty German-Jewish refugees whom James and Dolly had managed to evacuate from Frankfurt to The Cedars, a house on the Waddesdon Estate, in 1939. When the boys arrived in England, they were aged between six and fourteen, and after the war several moved to Israel as young men.[10]

Their gratitude for Dolly and James's wartime refugee work was immense. As one of the boys, Henry Black, later recalled at a 1983 reunion, 'Without [Dolly] all of us here would have been just a statistic of the Nazi death camps.'[11] Hans Bodenheimer wrote every year at Rosh Hashanah, describing the progress in his own small settlement in Israel: 'this week at long last our Road was finally completed'; 'the main sources of income are the gardens, the farm, and our woodwork factory'; 'this year we are concentrating mostly on Potatoes, but also grow Tomatoes, Cucumbers, Marrows, "Peppers", and "Eggplant" which I still remember in the greenhouses in Waddesdon'.[12] Caring for the Cedars Boys was the closest Dolly got to motherhood. Although there are no details in the letters and diaries as to why she and James were unable to have children, we know that they remained childless 'much to their dismay'.[13]

By 1952, James was feeling strong enough for the couple to consider visiting Israel. At the same time, however, the health of their old friend Chaim Weizmann had gone into precipitous decline, and on 9 November that year he died at his home in Rehovot. Letters of condolence to his widow Vera poured in from across the globe, including one from Dolly at Waddesdon. Vera's reply explained that 'even during his long and severe illness, [he] frequently and repeatedly spoke of you, of Jimmy (as he used to call him) and his father who played such an important part in my husband's life and realization of his dreams in Israel'.[14] In early 1953 Vera visited James and Dolly at their London home, and was thrilled to find out that the couple planned to visit the Holy Land the following year.[15]

One of the principal aims of the visit was to honour the final wishes of James's parents. Edmond and Adelheid de Rothschild, both devoted Zionist campaigners, had died in France in 1934 and 1935 respectively. Although they had been interred in Paris's Père Lachaise cemetery, they had always hoped to be finally laid to rest in the Holy Land when this were possible. The disinterment ceremony took place in March 1954, with three thousand Parisian Jews in attendance.[16] In the late nineteenth and early twentieth centuries, Edmond and Adelheid's support for Zionism looked somewhat eccentric, not least to members of their own family. By the 1950s, however, their early championing of agricultural settlements and educational institutions was recognised as having played a pioneering role in the founding of Israel. Their reinterment would command attention across the Jewish diaspora, and would have all the trappings of a major state occasion. The two bodies were accompanied down to Marseille by a group of Israeli sailors from the frigate that would be taking the bodies to Haifa. Dolly and James set off from England by plane, and Dolly was surprised to find how much the experience had improved since she had last flown. 'The aeroplane is pressurised, so there is no need to swallow, blow one's nose or put wax in one's ears!'[17]

On 1 April the couple visited the eighteen-acre burial ground outside Zikhron Ya'aqov. Previously known as Um-el-Alaq, the site had been renamed Ramat Hanadiv, or 'Plataeu of the Benefactor'.[18] The only directions that James's parents had left was that they should be buried 'in rock'. There was no suitable rock at the burial site, and instead a 'cavern had to be made (from rock in the immediate neighbourhood)'.[19] Dolly had known for a long time that James's sight in his remaining eye was getting worse, and yet watching him at the burial site brought home to her just how serious the situation had become: he was only able to get a sense of the stone by putting his nose up against it.[20] For the ceremony itself, he would have to sit in a wheelchair for all but the Kaddish and the very final moment in the crypt. The ceremony was attended by thousands, including the President and Prime Minister, Moshe Sharett, former Prime Minister Ben-Gurion and other members of the Rothschild family.

Dolly and James remained in Israel for some time, long enough to be reminded that they were outsiders in the young nation for which they had done so much to lay the foundations. The cultural differences between elite Anglo-Jewry and most emigrants to Israel – who were on the whole relatively poor, quite religious, and much more likely to speak Yiddish – were conspicuous in the newly established state. Isaiah Berlin noted to Dolly in a letter from an Israel-bound ship in 1950 that his fellow passengers were largely 'the Bronx', with people speaking 'a few perfunctory sentences in quasi-English' before 'dipping into Yiddish'.[21] While he knew these people were 'flesh of my flesh, etc.', without whom there could be 'no Israel', and that in the scheme of things he was 'on their side', he nevertheless felt a nagging sense of distance and incomprehension. 'I embarrass them, and they me, and I chat *sotto voce* with the nice Danes, like a governess accidentally forced into the same waiting room with tipsy tramps.'

Generations of Rothschild women had known that feeling thanks to their work in the East End, where they had encountered the extreme differences of class, language, culture and religiosity that were nonetheless bound together by shared Jewishness. In Israel, they experienced a new variant of this feeling. For Dorothy and James, it was their ignorance of Hebrew, rather than Yiddish, that marked them as outsiders. When, on 7 April, they attended the Knesset to hear a speech delivered in honour of the reinterment by Moshe Sharett, they 'appreciated . . . only its cadence & restrained delivery – just seizing a familiar word here & there'.[22]

Back in England, Dolly returned to work for the local Liberal Party, sent books and other presents to Liberty, and wrote frequently to Miriam. In letters as in person, the pair's communication allowed them to vent the stresses and grievances for which there was no adequate outlet in the life of a Rothschild public figurehead or mother. It was Miriam in whom Dolly confided about James's worsening health, which increasingly kept her at home, and Dolly to whom Miriam sent her most candid letters, describing the strains of mental and physical ill health, and of raising children without her husband.[23]

The compromise of living near Elsfield had simply not been enough to save Miriam and George's marriage. In the mid 1950s George moved to London, while Miriam remained at Elsfield with Rosie, Charles, Charlotte and Johanna. As the children began to attend schools in Oxford, Miriam pressed on with the Herculean task of cataloguing the Rothschild fleas. Though the first volume of the catalogue was published in 1953, the scale of the project kept growing. New flea specimens arrived from colleagues and collectors around the world, and further ones had to be sought from the wild. During a trip to Wengen, Miriam found herself hunting for the nests of snow finches and redstarts, and tracking marmots across a glacier in order to retrieve samples of their parasites.[24] To keep the fleas out of reach of her children, she kept them in plastic bags which she hung from her bedposts or stashed in her car.[25] Once the children were in bed, Miriam would retire to her microscope and work late into the night. Most parents want to keep their children free of fleas; Miriam wanted to keep her fleas free of children.

In October 1953 the flea work acquired a new and unexpected dimension when there was an outbreak of the deadly myxoma virus among wild rabbits in Edenbridge, Kent. About a week afterwards, Miriam received a letter asking if she would take part in an advisory committee on myxomatosis being appointed under the chairmanship of Lord Carrington, who was Parliamentary Secretary to the Minister of Agriculture and Food. Tellingly, what qualified her for membership of the committee was not only her scientific expertise – in press reports, she appeared as an 'eminent parasitologist' – but also her gender, 'as there are certain humanitarian aspects involved and the presence of a woman on the Committee would probably have a reassuring effect on public opinion'.[26] On a committee of sixteen, she would be the only one.[27] Wartime secrecy around government work had become deeply ingrained, and her role was something she hardly mentioned. From the Tring Museum, Dr Smit (who had provided the scientific drawings for the flea catalogues) wrote to Miriam, oblivious of her key contribution. 'A few weeks ago the BBC-newsreel announced that a white-paper has been published on myxomatosis. I wonder whether you have seen this and whether there is anything of importance re rabbitflea in it.'[28] Miriam's secrecy did not equate to a lack of pride in her achievement: 'I helped write it!' she scrawled in the margin of Smit's letter.

It was the first of two government inquiries to which she contributed during the decade. In 1954, following a number of high-profile prosecutions for 'homosexual offences' as well as a growing moral panic about the conspicuousness of prostitution in British cities, a committee was convened under Sir John Wolfenden to consider the current law on both 'homosexual acts' and prostitution. When the committee began to solicit 'expert' opinion on the subject (few prostitutes or gay men were consulted), Miriam played a leading role in bringing together a group of biologists and zoologists – among them herself, Julian Huxley and Sir Ronald Fisher – to assemble a submission on homosexuality and genetics. Her own name would be omitted from the report – possibly because, unlike the other authors, she held no formal qualifications or university post. But her voice and sensibility are abundantly evident in the document, with its lively literary and historical references, and trenchant line of argument. Though parts of it now seem arcane and misguided, in the context of the other evidence given to the committee the report submitted by Miriam's group stands out as highly progressive. The authors maintained that homosexuality had occurred throughout history and across all races and genders and geographies, and that 'the genetic as opposed to environmental component' was predominant. They also asserted that legal prohibitions like those in place in Britain had arisen in large part because 'persecution of minorities gives emotional satisfaction to the majority'. The group's first recommendation to the committee was that 'homosexual acts between consenting adults committed in private should not be classed as a crime'.[29]

At the time of the inquiry, Miriam spoke of being motivated by a desire to end the threat of blackmail that hung over the lives of gay men. Though her surviving papers are elusive on the subject of her partners before and after George Lane, in later life she was openly bisexual, and it seems probable that she was also moved to contribute to the inquiry by her own experience of living in a homophobic society.[30] Sex between women had never been criminalised in the way that male 'homosexual acts' had, but gay and bisexual women had nevertheless suffered the same burden of prejudice and stigma as their male counterparts, and the struggle for legal change was seen as a keystone of the struggle for wider equality in matters of sexual

*Miriam Rothschild in her laboratory with her
children Charlotte, Charles and Johanna.*

orientation. The recommendations of Wolfenden's report were modest
– the decriminalisation of 'homosexual behaviour between consenting
adults in private', with an age of consent set at twenty-one – but they
were a start.[31] Years after they were incorporated into law (which
happened in 1967), Miriam would continue to proudly emphasise
that the Report had 'really adopted quite a lot' of what her panel had
advised.[32]

By the mid 1950s an annual ski trip to Wengen had become a highlight of the year for Miriam and her family. Miriam's chalet above the
town had a view over the Jungfrau – she would later list the sight of
dawn over the mountain as one of her 'seven wonders of the world'.[33]
It became a popular destination for the extended British and French
Rothschild family. Victor's wife Tess visited frequently with her daughters, including the prodigiously intelligent Emma, who learnt to skate
there in the winter of 1956/7. At the heart of Miriam's Wengen social
circle, though, was a friend. Gabrielle Fischer, or 'Gay', and her children
Benjamin and Jane, visited for Christmas five years in a row during the
early 1950s. In letters to Dolly from Wengen, Miriam rarely made distinctions between her children and Gay's: this was one household, run
by two mothers and no fathers.[34] Gay and Miriam's relationship was
affectionate and supportive. It had to be, as Gay had a serious and lasting depression, intense enough for her to have spoken to Miriam about
taking her own life. Gay and her children also spent time with Miriam's
family at Elsfield, where Miriam undertook a lot of the mothering work
that previous generations of Rothschild women would have outsourced
to staff.

As a woman in her late forties with her own absorbing professional
and intellectual interests, and a restlessly critical mind, mothering did
not always come easily to Miriam. It was through conscious effort, as
well as through a deep love of and fascination with children, that she
managed to adapt so impressively to the role. She was an attentive,
open-minded and strikingly modern parent who took a serious interest in the character, aspirations and intellectual development of her
children, while reacting angrily to other more superficial upper-class
mothers who were interested only in their children's 'clothes, their
appearance, their behaviour, their performance, their figures'.[35] '[S]he
has absolutely no interest in [her children] as individuals,' Miriam
wrote to Dolly, about a mutual acquaintance, 'only as her personal
belongings so to speak.'

One of the things Miriam most valued about her father was that he had never talked to her 'as a child', and when Charles was barely six Miriam began including his name on scientific papers towards which he had helped with the research. Through the mid fifties there were numerous articles in the *Entomologist* in which the names of mother and young son appeared side by side: papers on moths at Ashton and Elsfield, notes on 'the brush organs and cervical glands of the ruby tiger [moth]', observations on 'insect migration near Deauville, France', notes on wasps visiting vapour traps, on butterfly migration, and on the change of pelage in stoats. 'Charlie has now become an enthusiastic trapper and as a collector he has the golden touch,' Miriam wrote.[36]

But the echoes of her father also rang out, tragically, elsewhere. Late in April 1955, when Gay and her children were staying at Elsfield, Miriam went away for a few days. When she came back home on Sunday, she found that Gay's room was locked. A handyman used his ladder to climb through the window into the bedroom, where he found Gay slumped on the floor, unconscious. Miriam rushed her friend to the Radcliffe Infirmary in Oxford, but she was pronounced dead on arrival.[37] Suicide was still technically illegal in the UK, and the coroner recorded an open verdict, doing the best he could to provide other explanations: 'I think it is more than probable that this lady was in great discomfort for which she had taken some of these [barbiturate] tablets. She was perhaps beginning to become a little too fond of them, became a little confused and took some more too soon.'

Miriam knew otherwise. This time, at least, she was older, and capable of fighting against the evasiveness, euphemism and silence that had engulfed her family after Charles killed himself in 1923. To close friends, she wrote frankly of the loss. Writing to Dolly from Wengen in January 1956, she confessed that she 'did not realise how difficult it would be for me here without Gay. I have been at Wengen so much on my own I did not realize how our joint holidays here at Xmas over the last five years had left such a mark.'[38] She felt Gay's presence with '[e]very creak in the boards, every piece of tinsel on the tree'. Worse still, Miriam blamed herself for not having acted on the warning signs sooner. 'Death is bad enough on its own, but death with the regrets I have got into the bargain is pretty intolerable.'

Following Gay's death, her children Benjamin and Jane became Miriam's wards. The addition of two further children to the existing four would have been a heavy responsibility at the best of times, but in such troubled circumstances, and with the wounds caused by Gay's death still fresh, it was overwhelming. 'I miss Gay quite unbearably.' Her health suffered under the emotional strain.[39] She tried to mask this with black humour. After being told by her doctor in July 1955 that she was 'on the verge of a nervous breakdown', she wrote to the Keeper of Entomology at the British Museum: 'I have told him that all members of my family are permanently in the state of breaking up or down, and that I feel sure the condition is a normal one!'[40]

But her letters to Dolly were, as ever, franker and more open. Two years after Gay's suicide, another of Miriam's friends also took their own life, intensifying the feelings of guilt that had dogged her since Gay's death. It was, she wrote to Dolly, 'a sad fact I am insensitive or deaf to the S.O.S. even when yelled into my ear . . . I seem to attract lunatics, but I fail to handle them.'[41]

In May 1957 James died. He and Dolly had agreed that on his death, Waddesdon would be transferred to the ownership of the National Trust. In preparation for the handover, two historians came to catalogue the contents of the house, and were led around the extensive collections by Dolly's friend and companion Maria Brassey.[42] The initial plan had been for Dolly to move to the Pavilion at Eythrope, adjacent to the Waddesdon estate, but renovation works there were still ongoing when James died, so Dolly, now in her early sixties, moved temporarily into an apartment in the main house.[43]

In his will, James had bequeathed money for the erection of a new building for the Knesset, Israel's parliament – and, no doubt with Dolly's encouragement, had arranged for the creation of a successor organisation to PICA, the Palestinian Jewish Colonisation Association, which since the 1920s had played a major role in supporting Jewish settlement in agricultural colonies in Palestine. The new organisation was called Hanadiv ('benefactor'), and would sponsor Israeli development by funding science, art and culture. Dolly was its founding president.[44] One of her first acts was to pull together a council, surrounding herself with those she knew she would find most helpful and trustworthy in the management of the organisation's work: Victor's son Jacob, Isaiah Berlin and Maria Brassey.

Along with such formal institutional responsibilities came harder family ones. Though the nineteenth-century system, in which marriages and careers were planned by the older generation, had largely collapsed, the family's new national role in Israel had prompted a revival of dynastic concerns. These were especially sensitive in the branch of the family descended from Edmond and Adelheid, whose role in the creation of Israel had been so potently emphasised in the 1954 reinterment. Soon after their son James's death, it emerged that his nephew Edmond Adolphe was determined to marry Veselinka Vladova Gueorguieva, a Bulgarian Catholic. As Edmond's father was also dead, Dolly carried the responsibility for representing the Rothschild view on the match – both as an aunt and as the president of Hanadiv. How could the family be taken seriously as leaders in Israeli nation-building if their sons and daughters, nieces and nephews, were marrying outside of the faith?

In the autumn of 1958, back in Israel to witness the laying of the foundation stone of the new Knesset building, Dolly had a private conversation with Ben-Gurion, confiding in him her anxieties about Edmond's marital plans. Later, she wrote to him, hoping 'with all my heart that I was unduly pessimistic about my personal family affairs'.[45] To Edmond, she wrote reiterating the scale and importance of family responsibilities, and insisted pointedly that the reverence for his grandfather within Israel stemmed not just from his generosity but from his 'religious & moral status', which had given the state 'the secure basis on which it is founded'.[46] Edmond Adolphe refused to reconsider his choice of bride, and Dolly was forced to concede defeat. In a letter sent before the wedding, however, she administered one last twist of guilt, attempting to turn the now inevitable marriage into a spur to greater communal responsibility on Edmond's part. Precisely because Edmond's marriage did not fulfil the conditions that would have been expected by his grandfather, she wrote, 'your task in safeguarding the trust which is in your keeping, is all the heavier'.

The importance to Israelis of a Rothschild marriage was made clear in a letter to Dolly from Ben-Gurion, relaying a report from his director-general, Teddy Kollek:

'I have met Edmond de Rothschild's fiancée,' [Kollek] writes. 'A charming girl – makes an excellent impression. In a long conversation with her I came to understand the reasons why she does not wish to become converted; there are grounds for her views, which ought to be respected. In the meantime she is studying Jewish history and Jewish things in general, and if only they become firmly attached to Israel, I believe that there is no foundation for Mrs. de Rothschild's concern.'[47]

Dolly wrote back, thanking Ben-Gurion and letting him know that she had, after all, attended the civil ceremony in Paris.[48]

I came back from it greatly heartened by the demeanour and attitude I found there, and full of hope that my new niece would take her responsibilities with true sincerity. If time justifies this view we can be very happy as she has great charm besides firmness of character and purpose, and I hope and believe my apprehensions and misgivings were misplaced.

Dolly de Rothschild with the Israeli politician Kadish Luz at the 1966 inauguration of the Knesset building, funded with a bequest from her husband James.

Back in England, the main renovations at Dolly's new home at Eythrope had been completed, and she began the process of decorating it, sending and receiving a flurry of letters on subjects that included wall hangings, tapestry repairs and upholstery for her bedroom ('the outside of the bed would be entirely in the pink Dauphine chintz with the inside lined pale pink and the edges bound or fringed in green').[49] But her thoughts were increasingly elsewhere. The responsibilities thrust upon her since James died – and especially the task of managing the family's philanthropic endeavours in Israel – had freed her to act decisively and independently in a field with which she had long been concerned. In 1959, when Ben-Gurion's Mapai party won a majority in the Knesset, she was quick to write: 'You must be delighted – it is by no means given to all outstanding statesmen to be recognised in their own day at their true worth and by their own compatriots – and to be recognised by the Israelis is really "something"!'[50] Dolly's trip of October 1958 had invigorated her. She was enthralled by 'the future that lies before us'.[51]

37

The Baroness, the Bird
and the Monk

WITH HER LEOPARD-PRINT coats, her long cigarette holder, her aristocratic drawl and her silver Rolls-Royce, Nica was bound to be noticed when she arrived in New York. Toot Monk, son of Thelonious, the jazz musician who Nica had travelled to Paris to see play earlier in the 1950s, remembered the day on which she first pulled up outside his family's apartment block in the impoverished San Juan Hill area of Manhattan. '[I]t was certainly a sight to see – the whole neighbourhood knew she was there.'[1] It was often well after five in the morning before she returned to her apartment, and her exploits soon became tabloid fodder. By early 1955, a year after Nica's arrival in the city, the gossip columnist Walter Winchell had begun chronicling the antics of 'the Baroness'.[2]

Toot recalled how she would often drive up to Harlem on 'missions of mercy' – bringing food to musicians who needed it, or sourcing instruments for those who had lost theirs. When Coleman Hawkins was taken ill on stage and refused to be hospitalised, she visited him regularly, regaling him with lively anecdotes and restocking his fridge. Another time, when Bud Powell, who Nica knew suffered from depression, disappeared, she combed the length of New York to find him.[3] 'This bitch was so rich,' Hampton Hawes fondly recalled, 'she had permanent tables reserved at all the clubs and a number you could call from anywhere in New York to get a private cab. If I was sick or fucked up I'd call the number and the cab would come and carry me direct to her pad.'[4]

The 'pad' was her suite at the Stanhope Hotel, on the corner of Fifth Avenue and 81st Street. The Stanhope was a quiet, conservative place, where male guests were expected to wear suits, and where racial segregation was strictly enforced: black visitors were allowed to enter only through the service entrance.[5] Nica's friends had to be smuggled into her suite; the bebop pioneer Charlie Parker, known as 'the Yardbird', or simply 'Bird', was a regular. In the early 1950s Bird had struggled with poor mental health and addictions to alcohol and heroin. His health had worsened in the spring of 1954, following the death of his three-year-old daughter Pree, and for a while he was committed to the psychiatric ward of New York's Bellevue Hospital. After his release, Bird spent much time with Nica and her teenage daughter Janka at the Stanhope, playing the board game Pegity with Janka or holding long and meandering conversations with her mother.[6] Among his interests were extrasensory perception, African politics, chess, mysticism and the paintings of Salvador Dalí. But unlike Monk, whose presence dominated the room even when he was silent, Bird was 'a relaxed type of person, and sometimes you hardly knew he was around'.[7]

Early in March 1955 Bird stopped by the Stanhope shortly before he was due to head to Boston for a gig. He had stomach pains, and was exhausted by a 'bandstand fight' between himself and Bud Powell at Birdland – the New York jazz club that had named itself after Parker in an attempt to cash in on his popularity.[8] Nica suspected instantly that her friend was seriously ill, and had her suspicions confirmed when he refused the offer of a drink.[9] Minutes later, he was vomiting blood. Nica summoned her doctor, Robert Freymann, who asked Bird if he was a heavy drinker. Bird managed to summon the energy to wink coyly and reply: 'Sometimes I have a sherry before dinner ...' Freymann diagnosed Bird with advanced cirrhosis and stomach ulcers, and urged them to go to the hospital. He was met with flat resistance: Bird was not going back to any institution. Nica promised she would care for him at the Stanhope.

Over the next few days Nica and Janka took turns to bring Bird endless glasses of water, which he drank thirstily, and sometimes brought straight back up, laced with blood. Dr Freymann visited frequently. Once Nica realised that Freymann was unfamiliar with Bird's work, she made sure to play his records during the doctor's visits, a gesture which momentarily roused Bird from his stupor. On Saturday, 12 March, having been propped up in a chair to watch Tommy Dorsey's *Stage Show* on CBS, Bird started to laugh, then to splutter, then to choke, before slumping unconscious in his chair. He was dead.[10]

It was not long before the same newspapers which had worked up Nica's 'Baroness' persona turned venomously on her. With its prurience, racist overtones and heavy innuendo, Walter Winchell's 17 March gossip column encapsulated the media response to Bird's death: 'We columned about that still-married Baroness and her old fashioned Rolls Royce weeks ago,' wrote Winchell, 'parked in front of midtown places starring Negro stars. A married jazz star died in her hotel ap[artmen]t . . . Figured . . .'[11] After that, the story exploded. The *New York Daily Mirror* ran with the punchy 'Bop King Dies in Baroness's Flat', while the scandal rag *Exposé* wrote: 'Blinded and bedazzled by this luscious, slinky, black-haired, jet-eyed Circe of high society, the Yardbird was a fallen sparrow.'[12] The very notion of an interracial relationship between Bird and Nica was scandalous enough, but the fact that she was a Rothschild gave the story an even bigger frisson.

It was rumoured that Bird had been shot dead, and that Nica had paid off the doctor not to mention the mortal wound in the autopsy report.[13] Others claimed that Nica had abetted Parker's heroin addiction, which led to his downfall. Four years later, the Argentine writer Julio Cortázar would publish a short story called 'The Pursuer', in which an alto saxophonist called Johnny Carter is provided with heroin by his patron and admirer, Tica, aka 'the Countess'. In case these name switches were not clear enough, the story was published with the dedication: '*In Memoriam* Ch. P.'[14] Although Nica had managed to brief her close family about the news storm, she neglected to mention it to Jules, who instead heard of the scandal from Walter Winchell's radio gossip column.[15] Relations between the couple, who were proceeding with a relatively amicable separation prior to Bird's death, came to an abrupt end. Jules set in motion a quick divorce, in which Nica would lose custody of her younger children, retaining a close living arrangement with Janka and her elder son, Patrick.[16]

Nica's Rothschild family, though doubtless mortified by the furore, rallied to her support. Her brother Victor flew out to New York to settle Nica's debts and deal with the Stanhope, which had taken the opportunity to attempt to evict her. A few weeks after Bird's death, Nica and Janka moved into a new apartment at the Bolivar, 230 Central Park West. At the beginning of 1956, Nica took Thelonious Monk to the Steinway showroom in New York to buy a grand piano, which was delivered to the Bolivar on 30 January. On a recording Nica made in her hotel room on a Wollensak reel-to-reel, Monk gave a spoken preamble to the song 'Pannonica', explaining that it was 'named after this beautiful lady here. I think her father gave her that name after a butterfly [*sic*] that he tried to catch. I don't think he caught the butter-fly.'[17] Another song – 'Ba-lue Bolivar Ba-Lues-Are' – was inspired by Nica's battle with the Bolivar management over the late-night musical disturbances.

Nica had always drunk heavily, but in the aftermath of Bird's death her dependence on alcohol grew. Jazz memoirs from the period are strewn with references to her gold and silver hip flasks and the bottles of whisky she hid in her car, in a book with the pages carved out.[18] She would credit Monk with helping her to bring the drinking back under control. But other dependencies went unchecked. Freymann was one of several doctors across New York who offered his patients 'vitamin shots' – vitamin B12, with an amphetamine kicker.[19] Administering amphetamines was not illegal in New York, but the circumstances in which they could be given were increasingly restricted by state and federal law. In 1963 and again in 1964, Dr Freymann was found guilty of administering narcotic drugs to habitual users, who visited mul-tiple 'Speed Doctors' in a single night. 'If you wanted to make a big night of it,' a patient recalled, 'you'd go over to Max's and get a shot and then over to Freymann's and then down to Bishop's. It was just another kind of bar hopping.' Thelonious Monk's son Toot remembers Freymann taking an even more lax approach. He was a 'brilliant guy', Toot recalled, 'a very nice man, but an enabler. So, he would give Nica anything she wanted, including bennies [Benzedrine].'[20]

Although Nica had lost custody of her younger children in the divorce, Janka remained fully engaged in her mother's life in Amer-ica, sharing Nica's hotel suite, friends and, increasingly, her narcotic preferences. In the spring of 1956, just under a year since Parker had died at the Stanhope, eighteen-year-old Janka was travelling back from a Jazz Messengers gig in Philadelphia when a policeman on a motorbike pulled the car over.[21] The passengers were Art Blakey, Horace Silver (drummer and pianist in the Messengers, respectively), Art Blakey's 'band boy' Ahmed and Janka. All the police saw, as Sil-ver later recalled, was 'three black men in a car with a white woman' – and 'that was reason enough for him to stop us'. Blakey, whose car it was, argued with the police officer, who took them to the police station and had the car searched. The police found a loaded gun and a box of shells, for which Art had no permit, and a box of Benzedrine pills belonging to Janka. The police booked all four, threw Art Blakey and Horace Silver in one cell, and took Janka and Ahmed elsewhere.

Horace wanted to call his father to get him to come and try and arrange bail, but Art told him: 'Don't worry your dad. I'll call Nica, and she'll get us out.'[22]

But when he discovered that three of those being held at the station were black, the lawyer Nica had hired 'didn't want to get involved', and it was only Janka who was let out, on a $5,000 bail. The news soon reached Britain, with the *Daily Express* running an article on 9 March under the headline 'Rothschild Niece on Drug Charge'.[23] According to Silver, the court hearing which followed was 'a farce'. Bribes had exchanged hands, he suspected; everyone was acquitted.[24]

A year later Nica, Janka and the Steinway moved again, this time to the Algonquin Hotel in Midtown. Nica later recalled how she had chosen it because she had heard that it was 'broader-minded' and that they 'liked having geniuses there'.[25] Monk, however, 'turned out to be one genius too far for them'. A black man walking around the hotel corridors in a loud red shirt and sunglasses, occasionally knocking on the wrong door, was enough to provoke complaints from the elderly white clientele. When the management responded by telling Nica that 'Mr. Monk is no longer welcome at the Algonquin', she began smuggling her friend in when the night manager's back was turned. It was a ploy that worked well – until they bumped into the night manager in the elevator. Nica found herself in need of a fourth place to stay.

Victor flew over at the end of 1957 to facilitate her buying somewhere more permanent – a 2,600-square-foot modernist pile, perched on a clifftop in Weehawken, on the New Jersey side of the Hudson River.[26] Nica furnished the interior with Monk and his jamming sessions in mind: the Steinway was installed in an upstairs room, and a ping-pong table was ordered for downtime. Shortly after moving, in early 1958, Nica also bought two Siamese cats, a male and a female. Soon, there were enough offspring for the musicians who visited the Weehawken mansion to rename it after the proliferating pets: to Nica as well as her visitors, this would always be the 'Cat House'.[27] The Rolls-Royce was replaced with a new car – the so-called Bebop Bentley – which Hampton Hawes recalled being put through its paces in a late-night drag race against Miles Davis.[28] 'Monk and his wife and Nica and I were driving down 7th Avenue in the Bentley at three or four in the morning – Monk feeling good, turning round to me to say, "look at me, man, I got me a black bitch and a white bitch" – and Miles pulling alongside in the Mercedes, calling through the window in his little hoarse voice cut down by a throat operation, "Want to race?"' In Hawes's recollection Nica nodded, then turned to the passengers and said, in her clipped British accent: 'This time I believe I'm going to beat the motherfucker.'

In October 1958 Nica was driving through Delaware with Monk and his tenor saxophonist, Charlie Rouse. Monk was sweating profusely and was thoroughly miserable. As they drove through Newcastle, he asked: 'Could we stop somewhere for a cold drink, a beer, a glass of water, anything?' Nica pulled over at a motel, and she and Rouse waited in the car while Monk went in.[29] When, after ten minutes, he had not reappeared, Nica started to get worried, and was about to go in after him when a jeep screeched to a halt in the motel parking lot. Two police officers jumped out and ran into the motel. They soon re-emerged, with Monk held between them. Monk had asked the receptionist at the motel for a glass of water. Unable to understand his slurred speech, she had panicked, and called the police.

Having been dragged out onto the forecourt, Monk refused to answer any of the troopers' questions. Nica explained that her friend was unwell, and begged the police to let them go on their way. They relented, and soon the trio were back in their car on the main road. But the ordeal was not over. Just minutes later, the police reappeared and flagged down the car. They had decided to arrest Thelonious over whatever had occurred at the motel. He passively resisted arrest, remaining silent when asked his name, and – in different accounts – either sitting on his hands or taking hold of the car door.[30] The police dragged him from the car and threw him to the ground. Further patrol cars skidded to a halt at the side of the road, and further police officers piled in on him, beating him with their batons.[31] Nica screamed for them to stop but, as she later recalled with horror, could only stand and watch as they 'beat on his hands . . . his pianist's hands'. Thelonious was eventually forced into the back of a squad car. When he refused to bend his legs to allow the police to close the door, he was beaten into submission again. Before they drove off, the officers told Nica to follow them to the local magistrate's office. Here, Monk was charged with disorderly conduct and fined ten dollars. When they found among Nica's possessions a small amount of marijuana, they charged her with 'unauthorised possession of a narcotic drug'.

The trial date did not come around until a year and a half later. At Nica's New Year's Eve party, Monk was on the piano as the clock struck, and broke into the song that had first induced her to seek out a future in New York: ''Round Midnight'. It was increasingly clear to Nica's family back in England how important Monk was to her, so they finally came over to meet him. Feeling intensely nervous, Monk began self-medicating, and when Nica arrived at his apartment to pick him up ahead of meeting Miriam and her son Charles, he was 'high as a kite'.[32] Although Miriam was, as Nica remembered it, 'frankly cool about it' and recognised Monk's 'genius', it was obviously a less than perfect introduction. Things went little better with Victor, who had played such a guardian angel role over Nica's wild years in America. Victor tried to impress his sister and her friend by recording his own performance of one of Monk's compositions. Although Victor was quite pleased with his effort, Monk found it comically amateur, and spoofed it in a new recording of his own.[33] Nica's brother, who had first introduced her to jazz years before, now found himself on the outside, mocked by the friend of his better-connected sister.

Throughout these meetings, Nica's family urged her to flee the country and return to England, so that she could avoid the trial and any possible jail time.[34] She refused, and on 22 March 1960 her day of judgement arrived. She sat outside the church of St Martin in Manhattan, and wrote to her friend Mary Lou Williams in her rapid, impressionistic prose: 'Today is the day upon which my entire future may well depend ... Life ... or approximate Death ... It's simple as that ...'[35] Despite the enormity of the situation she was facing, Monk remained at the forefront of her mind: 'his protection is the root of the whole business ... I have never discussed it with him ... I do not believe he is really aware of it ... I do not want him to be.'

She was found guilty and sentenced to three years in prison, at the end of which she would be permanently expelled from the United States.[36] Nica's defence lawyer lodged an appeal, and her brother Victor once again swooped in, this time to pay the bail of $10,000. The appeal came up in January 1962 at the Superior Court of Delaware. Nica's appeal was based on the illegality of the police search that had found the marijuana: no warrant had been produced, and there was no way Nica could have consented to the search without 'coercion or duress' – she had, after all, just witnessed her friend being repeatedly beaten at the side of the road.[37] This turned out to be crucial. All the evidence acquired in the search – including the drugs themselves – was deemed inadmissible, and the case against Nica collapsed. When news reached Miriam in England, she wrote to Dolly: 'I have information from the States that Nica has triumphed in the law courts. This seems a near miracle!'[38]

With the threat of a jail term lifted, Nica found new reserves of energy to invest in Monk and his music. That year, he signed with Columbia Records, and entered into what would be one of the most successful phases of his career, touring Europe and Japan.[39] He was always accompanied by Nica, or by his wife Nellie. Both women travelled to Japan, where the three of them spent time between concerts shopping for souvenirs and visiting the country's famous jazz cafés. Back in America, Nica continued in her role of high-speed chauffeur, driving Monk and Nellie to the Newport Jazz Festival and to Buffalo for a week of shows at the Royal Arms nightclub – insisting on a detour to Niagara Falls.[40] But the deaths of several friends and idols (including Billie Holiday) in the 1950s had shaken Monk, and in the 1960s further bereavements of family and musical collaborators took an even greater toll on his mental health. When a fan gave him a tab of acid at a gig in 1965, Monk disappeared for a week.

The year 1968 began promisingly. Nica had her children with her for a New Year's party, and adapted Monk's studio at the Cat House into a dormitory. 'Happy happy happy New Year,' she wrote to Mary Lou Williams.[41] 'Have all my kids, even Patrick, here ... craziest Christmas ever!!!' That May, Monk had a short residency booked in San Francisco. On the eve of the trip, he fell to the floor and began foaming at the mouth.[42] He was taken to hospital, where he lay in a coma for several days. When he came round, his humour was undimmed. 'Y'all thought I kicked the bucket,' he said.[43] 'Thought I was going to split. Thought I was gonna cut out. Aint that a bitch.'

38

The Queen of Fleas

A T HOME IN Elsfield, Miriam cut a striking figure. David
Benedictus, a young Oxford graduate who arrived at the house
in 1960 to be interviewed for a job as a live-in tutor for young Charles,
was met by a 'tall' and 'handsome' woman in her early fifties.[1] Miriam
greeted him with a 'beaming, though rather vague smile, the sort one
might bestow on the world in general rather than anyone in particular'. The house, Benedictus noted, had the feeling of being furnished
'for comfort rather than aesthetics', although exquisite paintings – a
Modigliani, a Picasso and an Augustus John – hung on the walls.[2] The
formal part of the job interview was concluded rapidly, and Benedictus
was dispatched to play table tennis with Charles.

Twelve-year-old Charles, Benedictus came to agree with Miriam,
was intellectually brilliant: only by 'furiously studying in advance'
could the tutor 'maintain even the pretence of authority'.[3] Rosie, who
had just turned fifteen, was now described in Miriam's letters as 'one
of the "best sorts" imaginable ... incapable of a mean act or thought
& curiously Victorian in her sense of right and wrong' – but also 'a
great worryier [*sic*] – worries ceaselessly about my health, her work,
her shortcomings, the animals, burglars'.[4] Miriam recognised in Rosie
her own perceptiveness and bluntness as a young woman. One winter,
Miriam announced to her children that she was taking them for 'a
drink at the local' with a couple of young people and some other
adults.[5] 'Is this a drink for duty, fun, or to improve social contacts?'
asked Rosie, witheringly. 'On looking back,' wrote a proud Miriam to
Dolly, 'I think I must have been exactly like Rosie.'

Her relationship with Charles continued to be nourished by a
shared love of science. On a trip to Israel in 1961, the pair brought
a large moth trap with them, and, having managed at length to

persuade customs officials to let the strange device into the country, set it up on the balcony of the Hotel Sharon at Herzliya, hoping to catch a particular species of moth during its migration from the Levant to Europe.[6] On an excursion to Lake Tiberias, mother and son saw hundreds of painted lady butterflies migrating – an event they would later write up for the *Entomologist*.[7]

In other respects it must have been a disturbing trip. The previous May, Adolf Eichmann had been captured by the Mossad in Argentina, and brought to Israel to face justice for his part in the Holocaust. The trial, held at the Beit Ha'Am – or House of the Nation – in Jerusalem, had become a spectacle, broadcast on television and radio, and witnessed live by the few who had managed to get hold of tickets.[8] Over tea and chocolate cake, Vera Weizmann had offered to get seats for Miriam.[9] For anyone, but especially for a Jewish woman, to sit in on such proceedings must have been profoundly troubling. And yet Miriam's only recorded response to the trial takes the form of blackly comic comments, made to Benedictus: that Eichmann looked 'very Jewish' and 'exactly like the Attorney [G]eneral'.[10] The next day, she was moth hunting with Charles again.

Her interest in Israel's insect life was in stark contrast to the work done there by Dolly. The more Miriam saw of Israel in the mid 1960s, the more she came to despair at the ecological devastation that was being wrought by full-throttled industrial, urban and institutional state-building. By 1965 the degradation of the land and wildlife of the country put her in mind of 'biblical folly', and seemed like a form of 'spiritual suicide'.[11] She wrote an angry letter to Dolly, lamenting that 'the Jews, who have won back Israel against such impossible odds, should set about destroying their heritage in a way which puts them in the forefront of ignorant vandals', and describing the building of the Knesset – which had, of course, been funded by a bequest from Dolly's husband James – as 'the building of yet another tower of Babel ... while the flowers, the plants, the quails & the manna from Heaven are destroyed'. In case it was not clear enough that her criticism was aimed at the Rothschild family, and indeed at Dolly's own involvement in the creation of Israel's industrial, educational and governmental infrastructure, Miriam concluded:

I don't think you, personally, or any of us, can realize, also, how spoilt we are living in London but having a quiet country place to come back to if we want to. The refreshing quality of one's private green belt is taken for granted. Israel is too small & the needs of humanity too pressing to [provide] green belts for all.

Miriam's growing environmental concern came hand in hand with a renewed focus on zoological work. Later in life, when he thought back to his time at Elsfield, one of David Benedictus's abiding memories would be of Miriam, dressed in a 'flowing cotton robe and Wellington boots', at the top of the house's staircase, smiling at him and the children as she turned and retreated to her study.[12] In the previous decade, Miriam's attempts to fit in scientific work around her commitments as a mother of six had exhausted her. Now, as the 1960s drew on, she had become far more regimented: she observed the Sabbath and Sunday, and stopped work religiously at five, the same time that the children finished their supplementary lessons with David.[13]

In this way, Miriam found she was able to work far more productively. While doing research on moths and their predators, she became particularly interested in insect aposematism: the development of characteristics – including warning markings, smells or bad tastes – that have the effect of warding off attack. Along with the Nobel laureate Tadeusz Reichstein, she discovered that the monarch butterfly was capable of sequestering toxins found in very low concentrations in its diet during the larval stage, storing them for defensive purposes, to make it unpalatable to would-be predators.[14] This discovery had a wide application, not least in providing some of the theoretical underpinnings for the emerging discipline of chemical ecology.[15] J.B. Harborne, in his preface to the *Introduction to Ecological Biochemistry* (1993), would write that 'by her own pioneering experiments with aposematic insects and equally her encouragements of other scientists', Miriam had 'contributed more than anyone else to this new subject'.[16]

Miriam had never expected to receive such recognition. In spite of her wealth, her connections and the collections inherited from her father and uncle, being a woman without a university degree had always counted against her. But she persisted in her work, coming up with a brave new hypothesis about the close relationship between the hormones of rabbits and the breeding cycles of their parasitic fleas.[17] As Miriam later explained: 'The rabbit flea has turned over the control of its reproductive cycle to the rabbit ... the flea depends not on its own hormones, but on the hormones of the rabbit, to become pregnant.'[18] Initially the idea was 'laughed out of court' by her peers, but in 1960 two government scientists published findings corroborating her theory. She began to be taken seriously. Miriam's reputation in later life as 'The Queen of Fleas' rested not only on unrivalled knowledge but also on the regal self-assurance it had taken to win recognition within a scientific community whose attitude towards a talented female amateur ranged from wariness to downright hostility.

There was one further, more personal element to Miriam's scientific work during this period. For years now, Miriam's sister Liberty had been moved between doctors, psychiatric wards and nursing homes. The specifics of her treatment were a well-kept family secret, but controversial interventions such as electro-shock treatment and lobotomy were common in the mid twentieth century, and it cannot be ruled out that Liberty was subjected to these or other potentially traumatic practices. Towards the end of the 1950s, social and political attitudes towards mental health in Britain had begun to shift. The 1959 Mental Health Act had established the then radical aim of treating mental and physical illnesses in the same way, and the possibility of mental illnesses being treated pharmaceutically – rather than with surgical and shock-therapeutic techniques – was being widely discussed.[19] Liberty had been diagnosed with schizophrenia.[20] Despite being a relatively common diagnosis – it was something of a catch-all term, with a vague definition and countless possible manifestations – funding for schizophrenia research was still severely limited. Moved by the spirit of change, Miriam and her cousin Evelyn used fifty thousand pounds of the family's money to establish the Schizophrenia Research Fund in early 1963.[21] In October that year the fund awarded its first fellowship, and in November 1965 one of the trustees wrote an article in the *New Scientist*, 'Schizophrenia: A Chink in the Armour', in which he reported on initial, encouraging findings in the search for a biochemical basis for schizophrenia. 'I expect I have already sent you the enclosed at least twice,' wrote Miriam to Dolly, with a copy of the article.[22] 'But it's nice to feel one's money is put to good use . . .'

Miriam's work for the fund largely entailed publicity and fundraising rather than lab work. Yet she did follow the science of the field closely, and the more she learnt, the more impatient she became with the inertia of medical and nursing attitudes towards schizophrenic patients. By the mid 1960s Liberty was being looked after in Beaulieu, a residential home in Sandgate, Folkestone. There, the nursing staff

remained adamant that new treatments – such as the use of nico-
tinic acid, which Miriam had read about in the work of the Canadian
psychiatrist Abram Hoffer – would not have any positive impact.[23]
Miriam's complaints about the home's conservative attitude towards
schizophrenia treatment soon degenerated into general irritation at
the way the place was managed and the way in which care was given.
Her letters were strewn with references to disputes with the nurses,
and Johanna became so familiar with her mother's exasperation that
she came up with a new theory, which Miriam reported delightedly
to Dolly: '[Johanna] always maintains that if one is really objective it
is clear that the only sane person at Beaulieu is Liberty.'[24]

Though Johanna and Charlotte were still at home, Miriam's other
children were starting to fly the nest. In 1966 Rosie began studying at
the Courtauld Institute of Art, in London, and in 1967, having already
undertaken several scientific apprenticeships, Charles matriculated
at Cambridge.[25] Their cousins via Miriam's brother Victor were also
moving into higher education: Victor's daughter Emma, who as a girl
had learnt to skate at Wengen, was at the age of fifteen offered a place
at Somerville College, Oxford. 'This has not been done since Isaac
Newton!' wrote Dolly.[26]

The departure of the children freed Miriam to seek out romantic
company for the first time in years. In among her papers, references
appear to new dalliances – in one she refers to the imminent arrival
of 'my lover' and their plans for a weekend 'among the wild geese',
and in another a friend writes that Miriam's 'escapes are manifold –
in your work in love in every thing'.[27] The details of most of these
relationships remain obscure, but surviving letters in the archive of the
Austrian-born painter Marie-Louise von Motesiczky give a glimpse
into one significant, albeit less successful, romantic entanglement of
the late 1960s.

Marie-Louise von Motesiczky had fled Austria after the Anschluss
and moved to England with her mother in 1939. Though she was
modest and even secretive about her painting, through the post-war
years her work received increasing attention, with solo exhibitions
hosted in the Netherlands, Germany, Austria and England. In 1968
Marie-Louise was approached by Alix de Rothschild of the French
Rothschild family. Hoping both to support refugee artists and to celebrate her relative's status as a zoologist, Alix wanted to commission a
portrait of Miriam. 'I hope you will get together somehow although

she is terribly busy,' wrote Alix to Marie-Louise, enclosing Miriam's telephone number in Elsfield. Shortly afterwards, Marie-Louise went to stay at Elsfield, where she embarked on the portrait and took photos from which she would continue work on the canvas in her studio. For Marie-Louise, the trip was one of a growing number of sittings in what was a productive period artistically; for Miriam, it was a revelation. Later, she would write of their chance discovery of each other in grand romantic terms, comparing it to a meteorite grazing the atmosphere of earth as it 'dash[es] through infinity'.[28]

In the spring of 1969, during some time the pair spent together in Israel, the feelings Miriam nurtured for the woman she called 'Madame Mott' blossomed. Though the precise course of events remains hazy, Miriam's memories of the holiday came to be endowed with profound emotional significance. 'Do you remember the drive back to Tel Aviv from Hanadiv?' she wrote to Marie-Louise. 'I recalled it all this summer. As the car drove on I saw yellow anemonies growing in the sand – like little moons shining in the dusk. And I thought: How can this happen to me at 60? How can the desert flower for me at 60?'[29] Though Miriam's pursuit would eventually end in disappointment, during these early months it brought feelings of excitement and liberation. For the first time in years, here was a close relationship that was allowed to grow on its own terms – through effusive letters, trips to Israel and visits to Elsfield – without being crushed by the twin pressures of work and single motherhood.

Without a full cohort of children, however, she knew that her time at Elsfield was coming to an end. Once Charlotte had finished school in 1967, Miriam decided, she would move back to Ashton Wold. Winters were still a whole family affair spent, as they had been for many years, in the chalet in Wengen. It was there, in December 1966, that Rosie celebrated turning twenty-one. She had started to see an American engineer named Kim Howard Parker. Miriam approved of him – though interestingly, given her liberal attitude in most matters of family life, she regretted him not being Jewish.[30]

The new addition brought unexpected benefits for Miriam's scientific work: Kim devised the photographic apparatus that would finally allow her to capture fleas in the act of jumping.[31] Working out the exact muscle mechanism took further study, but the theory that emerged from her investigation – and that was published in 1967 in the *Proceedings of the Royal Entomological Society* – was remarkable.[32]

The jump of the flea was made possible by a pocket of rubber-like protein, resilin, that could be compressed and released to create an enormous propulsive force. The pocket was located on the flea's 'shoulder', which 'used to be the wing hinge ligament of the flea far far back before they evolved this leg mechanism for getting onto the host'. So really the anatomical feature was a 'residual bit of wing', and the flea's jump could be thought of as a sort of vestigial flight. Fleas were, as Miriam put it in the title of her groundbreaking paper on the subject, 'insects that fly with their legs'.

By the late 1960s Miriam's growing stature as a scientist had brought with it a busy schedule of lectureships and public appearances in Britain, Continental Europe and America. She was lecturing in America when, late in 1967, she received shocking news: Charlotte had fallen from a ski lift and fractured her spine.[33] In the immediate aftermath of the incident, she remained optimistic about keeping up with her work commitments – when George Lane flew out to Switzerland, Miriam had him bring the latest volume of the flea catalogue she was working on, in the hope she would be able to write the glossary. As the scale of Charlotte's injury became evident, however, that hope evaporated. Charlotte would have to undergo painful spinal surgery, and to endure at least ten weeks of immobilisation, followed by six months in a plastic jacket.

At the beginning of 1969, Charlotte finally began to recover a degree of mobility. She picked up the final year of further education, which she had postponed after her accident. Charles, who was now at Cambridge, commented to Dolly that the A levels 'do not seem to be keeping [Charlotte] unduly occupied', and that she was largely busy attending 'tea parties'.[34] In fact, he wrote, 'she seems to have become the toast of Oxford. The Pre-Raphaelite must be "in."'

With a growing number of lectures, peer-reviewed papers and striking discoveries to her name, and four volumes of the monumental Rothschild flea catalogue published, Miriam had finally begun to shake off the label of 'dilettante'. She preferred 'amateur' – a term she used with pride, as it was her expert amateurism that allowed her to follow her broad interests, work across subdisciplines, imbue her work with her love of literature and philosophy, and avoid the increasing specialisation that she observed taking place in the academy. Her amateur approach received perhaps its greatest vindication when, in 1967, she became the first woman to serve as a trustee at the Natural History Museum. The following year, the University of Oxford granted her an honorary doctorate of science, and she was appointed visiting professor of biology at the Royal Free Hospital. All three institutions were still overwhelmingly male-dominated, and Miriam's appointments at such places were, as one scientist later put it, 'wrested from the educational establishment by the sheer compelling merit of her research'.[35]

As a trustee and a professor, she entered a working world that was characterised by both casual and codified male chauvinism. At the Natural History Museum, the hostility of the other trustees was often implicit, and expressed in a way that made it hard to distinguish between professional grudges and prejudiced ones. Sometimes, however, and especially in letters sent between hostile male colleagues, sexism reared its head more obviously. 'Thanks for the copies of further correspondence with M.R.,' the ornithologist Arthur Landsborough Thomson wrote to the director in November 1968.[36] 'Did you expect her to play the game to your rules? She can mix the issues much faster than you can sort them! It's too easy; it's done with a whirling motion of the bodkin.'

By the spring of 1969, the portrait Alix had commissioned from Marie-Louise was completed. In it, Miriam sits accompanied by her owl Moesje and her collie Foxi; a magnifying glass in her lap alludes to her entomological expertise.

That Miriam was not impressed by the portrait did nothing to dent her feelings for Marie-Louise, to whom she wrote frequently through 1969. Often Miriam's feelings were close to the surface of her letters: 'Just pack your paints and your canvases (not to forget the brushes), or don't pack anything at all – just c o m e,' she wrote, urging Marie-Louise to join her in Elsfield.[37] Even in a letter on a subject as banal as Marie-Louise's financial accounts – which Miriam had offered to help tidy up – subtext and innuendo proliferated. Miriam pleaded with Marie-Louise not to let her current lover anywhere near 'your banking a/c or your bills', insisting that she instead be 'heroically faithful' to Mr Parkes, an accountant sourced by Miriam. The thought of Marie-Louise's recently reordered finances being destroyed in 'one abandoned afternoon' between Marie-Louise and her lover was, wrote Miriam, 'too much . . . I will have to give in my notice!'[38] Such intense adoration amused others in Marie-Louise's circle. In July 1969, a friend of the painter's sent her a postcard with a rhyme on it: 'M. . . .e-L. . . .e/ Has only to sneeze/ And M. . . .m/ Contracts delirium.'[39]

The relationship was not entirely one-sided. Marie-Louise visited Elsfield and hosted Miriam at her home in Hampstead; she sent replies to Miriam's letters, enclosing poems and pâtés. She did this because she was flattered by Miriam's attentions and enjoyed her company, not because she felt any reciprocal romantic or sexual attraction. When she addressed this disparity head-on in a draft letter, Marie-Louise became convoluted in her reasoning, writing in her idiosyncratic English that while 'part of her' wanted to 'trie' to be a lesbian in order to make Miriam happy, a relationship with Miriam would damage the 'picture' of her held by a former lover, Elias Canetti:

Dear Miriam, I admired you when I got to know you in Oxford. I still do. I put you very highly. Since I have Canetti I did not come across such a person. You are all I am – not. One part of my true nature could say to you: I am not a lespian but if it makes you happy that I should be one I will trie – I will never be such a good one as you, but I will trie my very best. – Smile – but there is an other side of me – I can't and don't want to hurt people I love. I belong to Canetti for 30 years – we did hurt each other of course – but the good things prevailed. Would I only play with the idea that a completely new cind of adventure is in my reach – I would not only destroy the present but all the past as well. I would destroy the picture he has of me for ever.

Later in the same letter, Marie-Louise came closer to the truth of the situation: 'If I hear the words "I fell in love with you", I think I have to say "yes or no", and I say no.'[40]

Around the same time as she wrote the draft letter, Marie-Louise was working on a second painting of Miriam, wildly different from the one commissioned by Alix. In the fantastical double-portrait *Confrontation in the Forest* (*c*.1970) the painter depicts herself holding a palette like a shield and her brushes like a quiver of arrows, as she confronts a hulking figure with the branch of a tree rising between her thighs. By her dress and her characteristic streak of white hair (if not by much else), the antagonist is immediately recognisable as Miriam. Though there are some ambiguities here – Marie-Louise is on her knees as if in awe, and in several ways the painting echoes her joint portrait with Elias Canetti, whom she adored – the overall impression is clear: the painting both enacts and depicts a brutal rejection. Whether or not Miriam ever received a version of Marie-Louise's draft letter or saw *Confrontation* is impossible to know. One way or another she must eventually have come to recognise the painful asymmetry in the relationship. In the letter, Marie-Louise referred to Miriam having insisted she did not need any more friends – 'friendship for going to antique markets and goodness knows what' – but hoped that there might nevertheless be a place for her in Miriam's platonic affections.[41] It appears that there was not. Correspondence between the two dried up around 1970, and would not resume for a decade.

Relations between Miriam and her brother Victor were also deteriorating. Miriam had long ago asserted her independence from her younger brother – something that she suspected offended his patriarchal instincts. In letters to Dolly she traced this insecurity of Victor's back to games of cricket played in childhood: '[W]hat [he] can't stand', she wrote, 'is the knowledge that he backed away from fast bowling in our nursery days & I didn't & that, as I strode ungracefully down the front drive, the servants said: "There goes a better man than Mr V."'[42] The incidents that had damaged their relationship since then would 'fill a book', but the most recent conflict, which had brought their relationship to a nadir, related to a private letter that their mother Rózsika had given Miriam shortly before her death. For some reason, Victor became obsessed with getting his hands on the letter. His approach to the task, Miriam told Dolly in August 1968, 'at best is threatening, at worst savours of blackmail – demanding to see the whole letter which, if I complied, would transgress my mother's last wishes'. Her brother's aggression had filled her not only with 'chagrin' and 'hurt feelings' but also with 'despair about the family genes'. She could only be thankful that her own son had not inherited the 'envy, jealousy, spitefulness, pettiness, peevishness, injustice, [and] ungratefulness' of some other men in the family.

There was, however, one respect in which Miriam was content to stand alongside her brother. In 1969 she learnt that in the latest edition of *Who's Who*, a reference book of prominent people in Britain, she and Victor were the only Rothschilds who received mention. Victor was listed as a scientist, civil servant and 'captain of industry'; Miriam was there as a naturalist.[43] To Miriam, the meaning of this was clear: her and Victor's achievements in science and industry now eclipsed the declining reputation of the Rothschilds as bankers. She had to be careful admitting this pleasure to the family at large, but in Dolly, she expected a sympathetic audience. 'To have edged the partners out of the lime-light', she wrote, 'is a moment of great malicious pleasure to me.'

39

Spare Rib and
the Subversive Stitch

ONE DAY IN the summer of 1972, Miriam's daughter Rosie stumbled across an interview with an editor of a new feminist magazine that had been set up with the intention of 'challeng[ing] traditional perceptions and representations of gender'.[1] This was of great interest. Her degree at the Courtauld had focused exclusively on the canon of great male artists, and when students dared to suggest the syllabus should include the work of women, they were shut down quickly by the tutors.[2] And yet across the Atlantic in Baltimore, where she had studied for her postgraduate degree, theorists, curators, artists and activists were beginning to bring the demands of second-wave feminism to bear on major galleries and institutions. In 1971 Linda Nochlin published her influential essay 'Why Have There Been No Great Women Artists?' and in the same year Baltimore's Walters Art Museum staged an exhibition entitled 'Old Mistresses', in which they exhibited many paintings by women that the gallery had in its collection but hardly ever showed. By the time Rosie returned to London, in 1972, her frustrations of the Courtauld era had been replaced by a steely determination to shift the cultural conversation about art and gender in Britain. All she needed was an opportunity. When she came across the interview, she felt as if it was speaking directly to her.[3]

Spare Rib was named ironically after the biblical account in Genesis of the origin of women. It diverged radically from traditional women's magazines that 'focused on beauty, romance, and the domestic sphere', and saw its readership as including 'women from all backgrounds'.[4] It would be stocked, its editors hoped, in high-street newsagents. 'The concept of Women's Liberation is widely misunderstood, feared and ridiculed,' stated the magazine's founding manifesto. 'Many women remain isolated and unhappy . . . We want to publish *Spare Rib* to try and change this.' On the cover of the first edition was a picture of two women, laughing and make-up free. Articles inside included a feature on suffragettes, a discussion about breast size and a report on a new abortion clinic in Liverpool. In July twenty thousand copies appeared on news stands across the country.

Shortly after the first edition was published, Rosie visited the offices of the magazine, in a decrepit building near Carnaby Street. She found a crowded, bright yellow room, the air clattering with typewriters, the walls covered with copy for the next issue. The open, convivial atmosphere arose from the fact that *Spare Rib* was a collective, where members shared authority and editorial responsibility. Rosie immediately felt at home, and was soon appointed arts editor. 'She wrote and said that her new job is going well,' reported Miriam to Dolly in August, 'but I've no very clear picture of what it is.'[5] Nor did Rosie, necessarily – the collective structure of the publication meant that responsibilities were fluid, with everyone having an equal say in editorial decisions. Editorial meetings were long, the discussions animated just as much by feminist and critical theory as by conventional journalistic considerations.[6] The publication that emerged had a strong identity: *Spare Rib* was the first publication to devote serious attention to Erin Pizzey's pioneering domestic violence shelter in Chiswick, and the first magazine to cover the struggle of workers at the London fashion brand Biba to form a trade union; the magazine's guide on how to get an abortion became a 'kind of handed-on definitive guide for women who don't know where to turn in this situation'.[7]

Rosie's role as arts editor often took her out of the office, to a whole range of mainstream and countercultural spaces. She covered Gallery House – a radical showroom that operated out of an empty mansion next to the German Institute on Exhibition Road – and exhibitions at the South London Women's Centre at 14 Radnor Terrace in Vauxhall, a house at the centre of a large lesbian squatting community.[8] Her reviews were accompanied by deeper and more forensic investigations into the gender politics of the industry – one of her earliest pieces was about the increasing number of women opening commercial art galleries, 'putting an end to the notion that a woman's place is beside the gallery door looking bored and beautiful, selling catalogues'. All her articles were characterised by her trademark interdisciplinary style, which drew simultaneously on history, art, literature, feminist theory and psychoanalysis. As a friend and colleague later observed: 'It was her gift to think across borders.'[9]

By the early seventies the feminist rethinking of art and politics was provoking a backlash from conservative critics. Rosie reported on the ensuing culture war with great care, as well as spirited partiality. A year into her editorship at *Spare Rib*, she investigated the fallout of the controversial exhibition 'Five Women Artists: Images of Womanpower' at Swiss Cottage Library.[10] The show's centrepiece was a work by Monica Sjöö titled *God Giving Birth* (1968) – a large painting of a woman in labour, executed in a heroic realist style. Within days of the show opening, both the police and Camden council had received numerous complaints about the painting, which opponents considered to be 'pornographic'. Scotland Yard's Obscene Publications Squad were sent to inspect the show, and although they took no further action, their visit turned the exhibition into a national talking point.[11] In a church hall near Swiss Cottage, a public meeting was held by supporters of the painting, to discuss gender in the arts. Perhaps inevitably, protesters opposed to the exhibition also turned up, and Rosie's report described the church descending into a 'chaotic variety of behaviour'.[12] But the meeting did have one constructive outcome: it was here that Rosie meet Griselda Pollock, who had also attended the Courtauld, and was committed, like Rosie, to challenging the patriarchal attitudes of the art world.

In the aftermath of the meeting, Rosie and Griselda, along with a group of other artists, critics, art historians and journalists, established the Women's Art History Collective.[13] Part reading group, part discussion forum, part 'consciousness raising group', the collective was soon meeting regularly.[14] The task they had set themselves was a formidable one. As Griselda Pollock later put it: 'We had to create out of nothing a theoretical and critical framework for tackling the structural sexism of the art world, art history and the conventions of art, and the purely masculinist mythologies of the artist.' The discussions fed back into Rosie's journalism. She began writing about the history of embroidery and the way the form had developed over several centuries, from being an art practised by both women and men to being a feminised activity, associated with domesticity and denigrated as a 'craft' rather than an art.[15] Within months, the group had begun to deliver courses at the Holloway Institute, and in 1974 they were involved in curating two all-women exhibitions, at the Arts Meeting Place in Covent Garden and the Almost Free Theatre in Soho.[16]

Given the breadth of her own interests and the collaborative editorial approach of the magazine, it was inevitable that Rosie's work would soon spread far beyond the art pages of *Spare Rib*. Over the first few years she produced articles on eating disorders, abortion and self-defence, and on women's experience of prisons and psychiatric institutions. The belligerent stance that she and other editors at *Spare Rib* took on many issues was inevitably met with ridicule and raised eyebrows in other magazines and newspapers. While admitting that the staff at *Spare Rib* were not 'aggressively anti-men', and that they had addressed double-standards on gender with 'devastating effectiveness', one journalist who visited the office to profile the magazine could not help commenting that the magazine's staff had not 'taken any trouble to beautify themselves ... none of the ladies took time off to arrange her hair or make-up, except for Rosie Parker who just shook her hair. Women!'[17]

Miriam's own response to sexism was generally to laugh it off. Rosie's approach – more combative and more analytical – was foreign to her mother, and yet it did not take Miriam long to see the merit in it. 'It seems to me the younger generation are infinitely nicer, cleverer & more serious than their parents,' wrote Miriam to Dolly.[18] In another letter she encouraged Dolly to consult a copy of *Spare Rib*: 'I think your godchild will impress you!'[19] Her hope had been that Dolly might provide a subsidy to the magazine. Whether that happened or not is unclear – though it's hard not to delight in the idea that cautious and stately Dolly could have ended up funding a combative and notoriously foul-mouthed organ of Women's Lib. At any rate, loans and donations did come in, some of them formal (John Foster helped arrange a meeting with a bank), and some highly informal (one day, a woman in the street stuffed £500 into Rosie's hand).[20] The magazine moved to new offices in Clerkenwell, where the members of the collective shared both editorial duties and the non-editorial tasks that kept the magazine running: the cleaning, the couriering, the trips to the bank and answering the phone (the clicking noise on which was assumed to indicate police surveillance).[21]

In the Clerkenwell office, Rosie became familiar with the whole messy business of producing a magazine: the faintly inky smell of the typeset articles festooning the wall; the blue pencils used to mark up copy, and the scalpels used to cut it; the big boards on which the final edition was pasted together, using cow gum.[22] The night *Spare Rib* went to press was usually a long one. There were protracted waits in the nearby 'Quality Workman's Cafe' while overdue articles trickled in, and final checks and corrections until '1 or 2, or even 3 in the morning', before the boards were lugged over to Euston station for delivery to the printers, and the remaining members of the collective were dropped back home. It was an exhausting, shoestring operation, and one that Rosie loved.

Although the Women's Art History Collective disbanded in 1975, the ideas that grew from it would for years to come inspire the work of its former members, many of whom went on to become successful artists or writers. In 1977 Griselda Pollock took a teaching post at the University of Leeds, but she and Rosie continued to spend weekends together, collaborating on a new book that aimed to capture the ideas they had developed over the course of their time with the collective.[23] While many contemporary American writers and curators had focused on reinstating women artists who had been excluded from the canon, Rosie and Griselda wanted to write about how and why the work of these artists had been ignored and undervalued in the first place.

Old Mistresses: Women, Art, and Ideology was published in 1981, and remains a key theoretical text for art historians and feminists. Among its conclusions was that

women artists only 'disappeared' in the twentieth century, in the moment of modernism, when the first museum of modern art was opened to tell the story of then recent and contemporary art ... when Art History expanded in the universities, when art publishing houses were founded to create and feed a market for knowledge about art.[24]

It was a startlingly original thesis, but also – somewhat unusually, for a book of theory – expressed with a clarity and simplicity that made it accessible to a wide audience. That was largely due to Rosie, whose objection to 'arcane' language was a guiding principle in the writing of the book, as it was in her journalism.

Miriam was just as proud of Rosie's new endeavour as she had been of *Spare Rib*, and wasted no time in recommending it to the painter who had meant more to her than any other, Marie-Louise von Motesiczky. Though the pair had drifted apart during the 1970s, Miriam was prompted to write again in 1981 when she saw that Marie-Louise's former lover, Elias Canetti, had won the Nobel Prize for Literature. 'Here is a voice from the past,' she began. In the same letter, she urged Marie-Louise to 'borrow a book called *Old Mistresses* ... It is a book about women & art history and you will be interested. The author is that fat little girl you will remember at Elsfield (she is now very thin but beautiful!), called Rosie.'[25]

The founding manifesto of *Spare Rib* had declared that this would be a magazine to 'reach out to all women, cutting across material, economic and class barriers, to approach them as individuals in their own right'.[26] And yet on the subject of the barriers created by race, ethnicity and religion, the manifesto had been silent. And while *Spare Rib* had published articles and interviews touching on the experience of women of colour, the editorial collective was overwhelmingly white. During the 1970s a wave of activism by women of colour, and the publication of key works of theory by writers such as Audre Lorde, had focused the attention of feminists both on the ways in which gender intersected with race and the ways in which women of colour had been under-represented in the women's liberation movement.[27] While many of the ensuing debates were about forms of exclusion and oppression particular to women of colour, the shift in thinking also had significant ramifications for Jewish women. In Britain, Jewish women had played a leading role within the women's liberation movement – within the *Spare Rib* collective alone, Rosie was one of three Jewish women – and yet such women had, as one journalist later observed, 'tended to keep their religion in the background'.[28] In 1979 Rosie had resolved to challenge this, and embarked on her first piece of writing in which her Jewish heritage would feature prominently.

'Being Jewish: Anti-Semitism and Jewish Women' was the culmination of numerous interviews with Jewish feminists about 'the ways anti-semitism lives in this society, how it intersects with sexism and shapes their sense of self'.[29] Antisemitism was rarely discussed by Jewish feminists, despite clear evidence that it was on the rise – Rosie gave the example of graves in a north London cemetery, desecrated the previous year with graffiti reading 'Yid Out'. 'The silence', she hypothesised, signifies the effects of anti-semitism. It's not just the old fear that to name it – to make an issue of it – is to inflame it, but on a deeper level it indicates how conflicted and ambiguous are our feelings about our Jewish backgrounds. In different, complex ways the history of anti-semitism has marked our attitudes towards our parents and ourselves, towards other Jews and towards non-Jews.

The article addressed numerous pressing and difficult topics: the use of stereotyped Jewish physical traits in the depiction of Jewish women, the 'excessively self-sacrificing behaviour parodied in the stereotype of "the Jewish Mother"', and the potential significance of the lasting preference Jewish mothers had for their daughters marrying Jewish husbands. Frequently her interpretation was psychoanalytic, seeking to identify the fears and traumas that were shaping, through transference or repression or denial, the nature of Jewish female experience. In taking such an approach, Rosie inevitably ended up drawing from hundreds of years of Jewish history – from medieval antisemitism, the ghetto, *shtetl* life and the Holocaust – to try and understand the present moment. Consciously or not, she was drawing a line of descent between her own experiences and those of Gutle in the Frankfurt ghetto. With humour and perspicacity, she also began to reflect on more immediate family relationships that had not always been easy for her.

My mother's primary responsibility as a Jewish mother was to feed me massively. But she had an unparalleled capacity for double binding, for giving contradictory messages. The classic is saying on the one hand 'Eat Eat' and on the other 'You're too fat'. Good and plentiful food signified survival, security and success – but today so does thinness.

It was the beginning of an investigation into the mother–daughter relationship that would soon also encompass non-Jewish experience, and that would eventually produce some of Rosie's most important and lasting psychoanalytical work.

One Jewish experience that Rosie considered to be passed on from parents in general, rather than the mother specifically, was a deep sense, especially during childhood, of 'outsiderness'. This was an experience universal among the women she spoke to for her article, and one that she recognised immediately from her own childhood.

In their specific ways all our parents saw themselves as members of an 'out group' (whose existence made others feel 'in'), and we grew up with a sense of being different, and with a sense of isolation. How our parents negotiated their situation shaped our sense of outsiderness.

In many ways, her hypothesis sums up the story of the Rothschilds themselves – but she was also addressing many other Jewish women who had hitherto felt there was little place for their experiences within the women's liberation movement.

Along with a Jewish women's workshop held during the 1978 Women's Liberation Conference, Rosie's article for *Spare Rib* has been cited by one historian as marking a turning point for discussions about Jewish womanhood, which thereafter became much more common 'within a feminist public space'. The two pioneering events can be regarded as founding moments in the emergence of the Jewish feminist movement in Britain.[30] In the years following Rosie's article, that movement grew rapidly, and in 1982 it held its first conference. 'In near-Arctic conditions,' reported the *Jewish Chronicle*, '200 women tramped through snow and ice to attend the first Jewish feminist conference, at the Michael Sobell Centre in Golders Green.'[31]

The Jewish feminist movement was a response to a number of concerning trends, the most alarming of which was the recrudescence of antisemitism that Rosie had referred to in her article. Though many antisemites were affiliated with far-right political parties and groups, there was a growing problem with antisemitism across the political spectrum. As Rosie reported in her article: 'Several women described "Leftists standing up in Meetings, starting discussing Zionism and ending up making anti-semitic statements". "Zionism" was increasingly becoming a pejorative term, invoked by those on the political left (who often viewed the policies of the Israeli government through the lens of anti-colonialism) to denote those who supported or justified Israeli military excursions or settlement building.

The new ambiguities in the term were troubling, especially when someone identified themselves as 'anti-Zionist'. In the 1910s members of the Rothschild family like Leopold or Marie had described themselves as 'anti-Zionist' because of their preference for assimilation and citizenship policies. By the early 1980s the term was far more dangerous and loaded. Were anti-Zionists arguing their opposition to a specific set of military policies pursued by the Israeli government, or were they actually questioning the very right of Israel to exist? Could a Jewish person support the existence of Israel without being a 'Zionist' in the new, negative sense of the word? While there was nothing inherently antisemitic in the new ambiguities around 'anti-Zionist', it was certainly exploited by antisemites, and created discursive conditions in which antisemitic attitudes could be concealed within language that purported to be about politics rather than about ethnicity or religion.

These issues would explode into bloody reality in June 1982 when, following escalating exchanges across the Israel–Lebanon border between the Israeli Defence Forces and the Palestinian Liberation Organization, Israeli Prime Minister Menachem Begin ordered a ground invasion of southern Lebanon. The invasion commenced on 6 June, and within eight days Beirut was under siege. Schools and residential blocks were destroyed in the fighting, and the Red Cross estimated as many as fourteen thousand deaths – mostly civilian – in the first two weeks of the war.[32] In August that year, amidst continuing outrage at the invasion, *Spare Rib* member Roisin Boyd wrote an article with the title 'Women Speak Out against Zionism' and the subtitle 'If a Woman Calls Herself Feminist, She Should Consciously Call Herself Anti-Zionist'.[33] Boyd's article included interviews with a Lebanese woman, a Palestinian woman and an 'Israeli anti-Zionist woman' on the subject of Israeli military activity during the recent war, and the implications of this for feminists. In amongst the women's accounts of their experiences and opinions were several outrageous claims, including that Zionism was 'similar to Nazi ideology' and that 'Zionist leaders used to say Jewish people should thank Hitler because without him the state of Israel would never have been created'.

The article, unsurprisingly, provoked many letters, especially from Jewish feminists. Though some of these were supportive, the majority were not. Despite disagreeing with recent Israeli foreign policy, they resented the tone of Boyd's piece.[34] Though the decision was not unanimous, *Spare Rib*'s editorial collective decided not to publish any of the letters of protest. In an editorial, it was explained that 'even if other writers did not declare themselves as Zionist, the substance of their politics was (i.e., even if critical of the present policies of Israel, they still, through silence in this area, negated the oppression and struggles of the Palestinian people)'.[35] 'As a collective we are united in a pro-Palestinian position,' they wrote. The decision laid bare the stance of the editorial majority regarding the ambiguities of the word 'Zionism'. As Rosie's fellow Jewish editor Linda Bellos told a journalist, the unpublished letters 'could not be described as Zionist unless you consider Zionism to be anything which supports the right of Jews to identify with other Jews and to live in Israel. By refusing to publish them, *Spare Rib* accepts this definition and I find that attitude offensive.'[36] Rosie's own opinion on the matter is not recorded, but it seems that she felt similarly: she wrote her last piece for the magazine in November 1982, while the controversy over the article was raging. One of her leaving gifts was from the artist Beryl Weaver, whose embroidery had featured in a number of issues of *Spare Rib*. She had stitched a table runner with a large rose and the words 'We Can't Spare Rosie'.[37]

It would turn out to be an even more fitting gift than Weaver realised. On quitting the magazine, Rosie would begin to devote more time and energy to the work on embroidery that she had first developed during the Women's Art History Group. In 1984 she published *The Subversive Stitch*, in which she emphasised that embroidery had once been a medieval art form with no overall gender orientation.[38] During the Renaissance, she argued, both material changes with the destruction of the guild system and ideological discourses about gender difference had led to embroidery being 'domesticated', and to the belief that women were suited 'by nature' for needlework. Within the home, embroidery was used to inculcate a feminine behavioural ideal of 'obedience and patience', but was also used by women as a vehicle for individual expression and resistance. That duality had continued into the Victorian era, with some critics blaming needlework for domestic unhappiness while others saw it as a solace to women trapped in the domestic sphere. Rosie's history ended in the present day, with the adoption and adaptation of embroidery by radical artists determined to reclaim it from its diminished (and heavily gendered) status as a 'craft' rather than an art. The art historian Victoria Mitchell would later comment that 'the history of embroidery itself heaved a sigh of relief' when *The Subversive Stitch* was first published in 1984.[39] 'Henceforth we could understand that to stitch is to be active, to think, to question, to invent, to subvert, and above all to be heard.'

Spare Rib had been the organ in which Rosie was able to develop a distinctive voice, but it was *The Subversive Stitch*, together with *Old Mistresses*, that earned her recognition as one of the founders of feminist art theory in Britain. A clear and cross-disciplinary thinker in the same mould as her mother, she had refused to partition her various intellectual interests and the different aspects of her identity, and had instead realised her ideas about art, feminism and Jewishness in concert. It was the first stage in an intellectual adventure that would continue for many more decades, much to the pride of her mother. In 1984, the same year that *The Subversive Stitch* was published, Miriam wrote to Dolly comparing Rosie's attitude towards her Jewish heritage with that of her brother Charles: 'she has taken a more active part in Jewish matters ... Do you realise that all the true Jews in our family come via the female lines?'[40]

40

'A Glorious
Indian Summer'

WHEN MIRIAM RETURNED to Ashton Wold in 1970, after nearly twenty years of living just outside Oxford, she had a startling realisation: the Northamptonshire countryside around her childhood home had become as ecologically uneventful as a 'snooker table'.[1] Modern agriculture had 'bulldozed, weed-killed and drained all the flowers out of the fields I'd known as a child'. Miriam had been helpless in the face of runaway development in Israel, yet here, at her family's home, she could do something. Her first step was to stop mowing the grounds.[2] Next, she visited the neighbouring Polebrooke airfield, which had been used as a site for American thermonuclear missiles for a decade and then abandoned for several years before being reincorporated into the Ashton Estate.[3] Neglect had turned it into a haven for wild flowers. Miriam collected seeds and scattered them on patches of ground she had scraped bare, where the tennis court and bowling green used to be.

By 1973 the garden at Ashton was dotted with cowslips and white violets, which transported Miriam back to the remembered country-side of her childhood.[4] Rózsika's taste in gardening had been for the primness of flagstone terraces and rose walks, and Miriam knew that her mother would have been bemused by the sight of Ashton running wild. 'My father on the other hand would have been delighted.'[5] She found that her gardening work also connected her with much more distant Rothschild ancestors. She learned about Gutle's eldest son Amschel, who had been filled with joy at being able to move out of the Frankfurt ghetto and grow flowers in his own garden.[6] She read letters from Amschel's younger brother (her own great-great-grandfather) Nathan, who approved of his brother's dreams, noting that a garden 'can be looked on as a necessity just as much as bread'. She learnt about the mid-nineteenth-century horticulturalists of the family's English branch: about Charlotte's collection of orchids at Gunnersbury, and about Anthony's and Mayer's gardens at Aston Clinton and Mentmore respectively.[7]

Miriam's most abiding family-historical interest, however, was in her uncle Walter. When Rózsika died, Miriam had been scrupulous in burning all the letters and papers she had been ordered to destroy; that destruction had been matched by the British Museum, which, during works at Tring in the late 1960s, had held a bonfire of the papers stored in the basement. Only now did she realise the consequences of such destruction for an historian.[8] Surviving family papers from her mother and Walter's generation amounted to 'a mere handful', and those were full of cryptic and incomplete information. Thanks to one box that 'toppled off the truck on its way to the bonfire and rolled away', a selection of the Tring administrative papers had survived – but personal papers were harder to come by. 'Have you, by any chance, any records yourself of Uncle Walter's pronouncements, or Jimmy's views on Uncle Walter's pronouncements at this period?' Miriam wrote to Dolly, on the subject of the 1910s and Zionism.[9] 'Perhaps I ought to come over and have a talk to you about this some time?'

It would be in 1978 – eight years after she first mentioned the project – that Miriam felt ready to send a draft of her biography of Walter to Dolly. It was a disheartening experience. Dolly had been schooled in the reserve and obsessive privacy that had characterised the family for over a hundred years. Confronted by Miriam's frank investigation into recent Rothschild history, she echoed the objection that had been raised two generations earlier, when Constance was preparing her *Reminiscences*: what did Miriam hope to gain by making private matters public? Miriam replied forcefully:

Whereas writing about butterflies is pure pleasure writing about Tring is profoundly traumatic ... But why does anyone indulge in so called creative activity? Not for pleasure. Not for a masochistic enjoyment of blood & tears. Probably because one cannot cast aside one's heritage & the wandering Jew must fiddle & tell his tale.[10]

As the ghosts of the Rothschilds' recent past gathered around her at Ashton, so did her living family. Her son Charles moved into the top floor, her other children were frequent visitors, and in 1973 Liberty

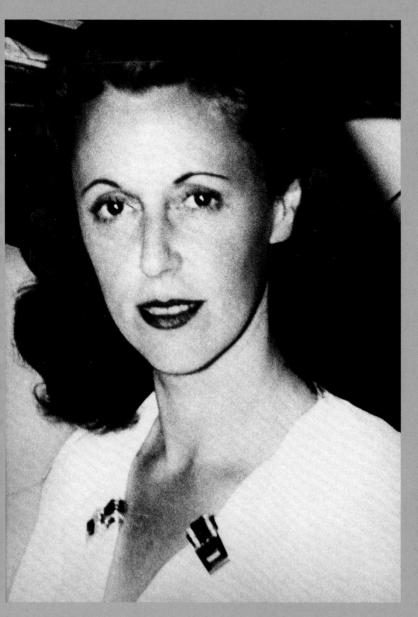

Nica, photographed in Mexico, where her husband Jules worked as a diplomat during the 1950s.

Nica, photographed in 1956.

Nica and Thelonious Monk at the Five Spot Café,
a jazz club in Manhattan.

Miriam Rothschild, *by Marie-Louise von Motesiczky, 1968/9.*

Confrontation in the Forest, *by Marie-Louise von Motesiczky, c.1970.*

Miriam tending to one of her beloved pet owls at Ashton Wold, 1991.

Thelonious Monk and Nica in Central Park, New York, 1956.

Miriam with one of her collies in the grounds of Ashton Wold, 1993.

moved out of institutional care and into a cottage on the estate.[11] That summer, Liberty asked to visit the Waddesdon aviary. For Christmas, she wanted 'a colour TV or one of those very comfortable swinging garden chairs with an awning over it'; 'luxury' books about natural history would also be acceptable, Miriam told Dolly, especially ones 'with young animals'.[12] Liberty had several animals of her own – ponies and donkeys – from which she derived great pleasure.[13] In October 1974 garden furniture arrived as a present from Dolly – perhaps ahead of Liberty's sixty-fifth birthday, which was on 5 November. Liberty thanked 'cousin Dollie' for the 'beautiful chairs' coloured 'like the autumn leaves'.[14] 'I see they were made in Denmark,' she added. 'What a long way to get me things from.'

Years later, in the middle of an interview with a journalist from the *New Yorker*, Miriam was interrupted by Liberty entering the room, playing some passages on the piano 'with great finesse', picking up a cup of tea, and leaving wordlessly.[15] Miriam turned back to the journalist. 'I think lunatics should be allowed to live at home, as part of your community,' she said. 'She really doesn't bother me at all. Oh, sometimes she'll do frightfully annoying things, like letting my butterflies out. Says they should be free.' Among Liberty's regular visitors was Edward Adamson, a pioneer in the practice of art therapy. Though he had been developing his therapeutic practice since the Second World War – largely at Netherne Hospital in Surrey – Adamson's work had come to much wider attention as a result of the wave of deinstitutionalisation in British psychiatric care in the post-war period. By the time he left Netherne in the late 1970s, there was significant enough interest in his work for a trust to be established, with the mission of preserving his vast collection of 'schizophrenic art', and using it to educate the public and professionals about mental illness and therapy.[16] He and Liberty had first met in the late 1940s, and in the 1970s Miriam became one of the trustees of the new Adamson Collection. When finding a suitable gallery space proved difficult, she offered one herself: a 'magnificent thatched medieval barn' at Ashton.[17]

The gallery opened in 1983, and soon became a destination for patients, NHS managers, mental health professionals and interested members of the general public.[18] A few years later, Adamson moved to a cottage on the Ashton estate, where he divided his days between running a programme of gallery events and spending time with Liberty – visiting her at home, taking her to see exhibitions, and even bringing her with him when he repainted the sign of the local pub, the Chequered Skipper.[19] When his book, *Art as Healing*, was published in 1983, he was close enough to the family to send copies not only to Miriam but also to her sister in New York.[20] It was an apt present: Nica had spent the previous decade in a therapeutic struggle of her own.

After being diagnosed with a 'biochemical imbalance' in 1969, Thelonious Monk's mental and physical health had continued to deteriorate. In October 1970 he had suffered a severe manic episode during a tour of California, and spent the next two months undergoing electroshock treatment in San Francisco.[21] This and subsequent hospitalisations severely disrupted his earnings at a time when he was already short of income, and when he moved into the Gracie Square Hospital at the beginning of 1972 it was Nica who paid. Gracie Square was a hospital that specialised in progressive, biochemical treatments. Monk started taking lithium, and the effect was instant. As long as he took his medication and ate healthily, his moods seemed to stabilise, and by early 1973 he was in good enough shape to return home. During his hospital stay, his wife Nellie had become obsessed with an alternative therapy of her own: juices. The couple's apartment had come to resemble a greengrocer's, piled high with carrots, spinach, celery and beets.[22]

Monk had become so dependent on Nellie as an accountant and manager that the new craze left him feeling neglected and resentful. On top of that, the roar of the two juicing machines – so loud that a neighbour had threatened to sue – disrupted the peace he now craved. The situation came to a head in January 1973, when Nica drove Monk back to his and Nellie's apartment after a gig, and he refused to get out of the car.[23] They sat there in stalemate until six in the morning, with Nica flicking the heating on and off so as not to run the battery down. Eventually she persuaded him to go inside. But the victory was short-lived. The next afternoon he rang Nica, asking her to come and pick him up and take him to the Cat House. Nellie sent a friend over to Weehawken to ask for her husband back. Her friend returned with an ultimatum: Thelonious was not coming back until the juicer went. The juicer won.

The side effects of the lithium became more pronounced with time. Monk developed a tremor, significantly impaired memory and creativity, and a passivity that was entirely foreign to his personality. When he first moved to the Cat House, he would wake every morning, get dressed, then spend most of the day lying on his bed watching television. The piano that Nica had bought when she first moved to the house lay dormant. As the pair drove back to Weehawken, after one of Monk's rare trips into Manhattan with Nica, he turned to her and said: 'I am very seriously ill.'[24] One thing the lithium had given him was an occasional and frightening sense of clarity.

Between 1972 and 1976 his income collapsed, and his debt to Columbia Records – who deducted production costs from their artists' earnings – grew. Nica stepped in to cover her friend's shortfall. She was desperate to reignite Monk's artistic spark. In 1975 she and a group of others entered him for a Guggenheim Fellowship, arguing that the support might make it possible for him to start composing again. Monk was one of the 300 recipients of a fellowship in 1976, but while the money was a boon, it did little to help him write; on 4 July that year he gave his last public performance, an impromptu set at a Greenwich Village bar.[25]

The jazz scene he left behind was in the throes of transformation. A younger avant-garde – led by artists like Archie Shepp, Ornette Coleman, Cecil Taylor and John Coltrane – was abandoning traditional bebop forms in favour of a formally daring, Afrocentric and overtly political approach to jazz. Nica, as a wealthy, white, non-musician patron, looked increasingly out of place. The writer Amiri Baraka, a poet and critic who had served as an unofficial spokesperson for the Black Arts Movement during the sixties and early seventies, made no secret of his opinion: Nica was a 'groupie' and a 'wealthy dilettante', he wrote – and 'that is the kindest thing I could say'.[26] By this point, Nica's relationship with Monk was that of friend and carer, rather than patron. She hired a pioneering orthomolecular psychiatrist to give Monk regular check-ups and a masseur to provide weekly Shiatsu massages ('a form of massage like acupuncture without the needles', explained Nica to Mary Lou); she invited the composer Joel Forrester to play piano outside Monk's bedroom door.[27] 'Nica was attempting in a hundred different ways ... to find out whether Thelonious Monk could be brought out of himself,' Forrester later recalled.[28] Forrester himself was, he thought, 'on the level of the witch doctors, massage artists, and others' whom Nica had hired in an attempt 'to figure out whether Monk might respond to some invitation to live in a fuller way'.

Her efforts were in vain. On 5 February 1982 Barry Harris, also in residence, found Monk lying unconscious in his bedroom. He had suffered a stroke, which had been complicated by his hepatitis. For twelve days Monk lay in a coma at Englewood Hospital; on 17 February, just before eight o'clock, he died. Nica had 'cried herself out' so many times in anticipation of Monk's death that when it actually happened, she found she had no tears left. 'I didn't cry when Thelonious died,' she would later tell an acquaintance, 'and I haven't cried since.'[29]

Monk's memorial service drew a thousand mourners, and for two years afterwards Nica was absorbed in the question of how to honour his legacy.[30] In March 1984 Miriam crossed the Atlantic to visit her grieving sister, finding her 'in very good form', though she was 'deaf and she can't stand long'.[31] Soon after Miriam left, Nica was diagnosed with cancer. She began radiotherapy treatment in the summer of 1984, while reading and rereading her new copy of Adamson's book *Art as Healing*.[32] In October she wrote to a friend in England that she was 'feeling fine, though still a little tired from the radiation treatments'.[33] New York was in the 'midst of a glorious Indian summer', she said, and 'the leaves are red + gold outside . . . + sounds of a Chopin Prelude are drifting down from the studio . . .'

It would be another year and a half before Nica made the trip to Ashton Wold to embrace her sisters once again and to see Adamson's gallery in person.[34] In that time, Miriam's various projects – scientific, personal, horticultural – were thriving. Her gardens were wilder, and she had been made a Fellow of the Royal Society in 1985. *Dear Lord Rothschild* had been published in 1983, and despite predictable protests from certain relatives, Miriam was stubbornly proud of the way it fixed Walter's achievements within the context of the broader family, weaving them together with biographies of recent Rothschild women: Emma, Rózsika and Dolly. Writing the book had left her feeling more ambivalent than ever about some of her living relatives. 'I don't know why the present family are so totally devoid of personalities,' she wrote to Dolly.[35] The prodigious Emma, who had been awarded a Kennedy Scholarship after graduating from Oxford at the age of nineteen, 'could become one I suppose, but the rest are really éminences grises of the plumber types'.

Nica spent much of the summer of 1986 with her sisters at Ashton, and Miriam made sure to bring the family's prodigal daughter to various dinners and meetings. 'I hope the idea of adding Nica to your dinner with my brother did not prove disastrous!' she wrote to Dolly in June.[36] 'Nica was keen to see you and I think since Thelonious died she has been lonely (& also ill) & very much wanted to see every one of the family before going back.'

As she entered her seventies, Nica remained as opinionated as ever on the subject of jazz. In the Manhattan clubs, she would judiciously turn her good ear towards artists she liked, and her bad to those she did not. She also had her eyes firmly on the next generation of musicians. Since Monk's death, one of the major beneficiaries of her patronage had been the Jazz Cultural Centre, set up by Barry Harris in Monk's memory.[37] The club's peeling plaster walls did not matter to her, and nor did the paper cups in which drinks were served – Nica shared with Miriam an aristocratic nonchalance towards her surroundings. Although the house in Weehawken was a mansion, Hannah Rothschild, visiting her great-aunt, was struck by the general dilapidation: the 'tired old clothes', the 'frayed carpets' and the lack of 'food and decent wine'.[38]

After a period in the wilderness, bebop was enjoying a resurgent popularity, with interest in the form spilling over from the music itself, into books and cinema. Nica began receiving calls from writers and journalists working on biographies of musicians she had worked with in mid-century New York. In the autumn of 1986 Bertrand Tavernier released *Round Midnight*, a musical drama mash-up of the lives of Bud Powell and Lester Young.[39] Set between Paris and New York, *Round Midnight* was full of references to musicians and venues that Nica had known. Clint Eastwood was at work on *Bird*, based on the memoir of Charlie Parker's widow, Chan. Dirty Harry and the Jazz Baroness met in spring 1988 at the Stanhope. The same hotel that had unceremoniously ejected Nica during the scandal following Bird's death had now capitalised on her legendary stay by renaming their bar 'Nica's'.[40]

The most promising of the jazz film projects, from Nica's point of view, was the documentary about Monk being planned by the film-maker Bruce Ricker. Although Nica expressed a willingness to share her memories with Ricker, he found it hard to pin her down – she missed several interviews, and failed to return a tape recorder he had sent for her to record her recollections on.[41] Her slowness may in part have been due to bad news from Ashton Wold. On 30 March 1988 her sister Liberty had died. The relative happiness and tranquillity of Liberty's final years had compensated somewhat for the years of isolation in homes and psychiatric institutions, and Nica felt some solace in having seen her sister at Ashton Wold cared for by Miriam and Edward Adamson. But the news still came as a blow.

Eventually, when the mood struck her, Nica invited Ricker and the film's director, Charlotte Zwerin, over to the Cat House for an interview, with the instruction to bring a bottle of Scotch. Nica no longer drank – but wanted Ricker to drink for her. They spoke until the bottle of Johnnie Walker Red Label was empty and the sun was rising, at which point Ricker asked Nica if she had any regrets, and Nica alighted on a final, terrible admission. That she had not been able to save Thelonious: 'That is my only regret.'[42]

The film was released in late October 1988. Weeks later, Nica was taken into the Columbia-Presbyterian Medical Center for heart surgery.[43] Clint Eastwood sent an enormous vase of flowers to the hospital and Joel Forrester slipped past the nurses to sit by her bedside.[44] Her children were with her immediately before she was taken to theatre but, during the operation, in the early evening of 30 November 1988, Baroness Nica de Koenigswarter died of heart failure. She was seventy-four. Her children subsequently recalled that the night before her surgery, she had been gripped by the sense that Thelonious Monk and her sister Liberty were with her in the room.[45]

The obituary that appeared in the *New York Times* emphasised the centrality of jazz to her life.[46] On 11 December there was a memorial service at St Peter's Church, Lexington Avenue – the same place Monk's service had taken place nearly seven years before.[47] Nica, unlike Monk, would be cremated. Regarding her ashes, her instructions had been very specific: the family were to hire a boat, and – ''Round Midnight' – scatter her remains into the dark waters of the Hudson River, between the New Jersey shore and the Manhattan skyline.[48]

41

Mothers and Daughters

AFTER NICA LEFT Ashton Wold in summer 1986, Miriam and Liberty often found themselves alone, two ageing sisters in a house of memories stretching back to the far side of the First World War. When Liberty died in March 1988, it was Miriam who managed the task of informing people, clearing out the cottage, and distributing Liberty's few bequests. 'I could hardly comprehend that Liberty had been taken from us,' wrote Edward Adamson.[1] 'As you know I was closer to her than most. But how much more is the loss of a beloved & cherished sister for you ... She was like a delicate gentle butterfly & we shall miss her.' Neither experience as a historian nor as a campaigner for greater openness on the subject of mental illness was enough to prevent Miriam from burning Liberty's papers. Family tradition reasserted itself, and years of medical records and other fragments of the troubled sister's life went up in smoke.

By the end of 1988 Miriam had lost both her sisters, and also her long-time ally and confidante, Dolly. The Zionist campaigner had, well into her nineties, continued her work on philanthropy and on the Rothschild initiatives in Jerusalem. As late as April 1988, she had visited Israel to chair a meeting of the Council of the Open University, of which she remained chancellor until she died, on Saturday, 10 December.[2] By the time of their deaths, both Liberty and Nica had shaken off some of the grandeur that attached to older Rothschilds – Liberty through her illness and obscurity, and Nica through her lifestyle. Dolly's death was another matter entirely. Thanks to her title, her enormous wealth, her seniority at ninety-three, her prominence in Israeli state-building and philanthropy, and her reputation as what the *Jerusalem Post* described as 'a binding force on her powerful, far-flung and sometimes contentious clan', news of her death reverberated equally in Israel and England.[3]

President Herzog cabled his condolences 'on behalf of the people of Israel' at the loss of 'a great lady, a proud Jewess and a remarkable humanitarian'; her memorial service at Bevis Marks was officiated by the Chief Rabbi Lord Jakobovits.[4] She left behind the largest probate estate ever in England at over £94 million, and her will contained a vast list of beneficiaries.[5] But the main private recipient was Victor's son Jacob, who personally received £76 million. The notions of 'patriarch' and 'matriarch' might have felt dated as the end of the millennium approached, but Dolly's decision was a reaffirmation of tradition. The wealth would remain within the British family, and, just as importantly, with its men.

In the years after the publication of *The Subversive Stitch* in 1984, Rosie had retrained as a psychotherapist. In that capacity, she entered the 1990s as busy as she had ever been at *Spare Rib* – working in private practice, for various schools and foundations, and at the Mayo Centre in Islington, where she helped to provide free counselling to women on low incomes.[6] Her marriage to Kim Parker had broken down, but by the end of 1985 she had fallen in love again, with Jungian analyst and social theorist Andrew Samuels, who was Jewish.[7] As Rosie entered her forties, she gave birth to the couple's two children.

By the time she had her children, Rosie had, in her own words, 'accepted childlessness'.[8] The intense gratitude she felt on initially becoming a mother made her all the more sensitive to the subsequent strains of the role, and to the coexistence of feelings of intense love and those of alienation or even 'hate'. At *Spare Rib* she had received 'so many unsolicited manuscripts from women "confessing" to their loneliness and shame that motherhood was not the unalloyed pleasure they expected'. At the time she had known that such confessions were important but had not considered the phenomenon of 'motherly misery' in any great detail. Now she began to consider the emotional experiences of mothers afresh. She began seeking out other women who were willing to talk about their experiences of 'maternal ambivalence', and, through the early 1990s, worked on drawing these testimonies together into a book.

While exploring unspoken difficulties in the mother–child relationship, Rosie made frequent visits to Miriam, who, following the death of Victor in 1990, was the only child of Rózsika and Charles still living, and one of the few surviving members of her generation of Rothschilds more widely. Miriam's new gardening style, which just over a decade earlier had seemed deeply eccentric, was now precipitating something of a 'wild flower renaissance', with major horticultural companies imitating her 'farmer's nightmare' seed mix, and thousands of gardeners endeavouring to create their own 'medieval haymeadows'.[9] It had also led to a friendship with Lady Bird Johnson – the widow of President Lyndon B. – who had led a similar campaign in Texas. The pair made a documentary about their shared obsession, each visiting the other on home turf.[10] For Miriam, that meant a stay at the Johnson ranch in Texas, where she found the standards of housekeeping to be far below those of Emma's Tring, and was astonished at the presence of security guards in the house during the night.[11] For Lady Bird Johnson, it meant a tour through the increasingly ramshackle Ashton glasshouses, and a drive to a nearby A-road embankment, where Miriam had used a bottle of whisky to bribe the maintenance workers into letting the grass run wild.[12] Mrs Johnson was one of numerous visitors who came to enjoy the thriving wild flower meadows around Miriam's Northamptonshire home; the director of Kew Gardens was delighted by his visit, telling Miriam that he had not seen such clouds of butterflies since his childhood.[13]

As ever, Miriam refused to remain rooted in just one project. Having already been involved in several local campaigns against road building during the 1970s and eighties, she threw her weight behind a new generation of ecological campaigners who were opposing the extension of the M3 across Twyford Down in Hampshire.[14] She became vice-president of the Twyford Down Association, and visited Downing Street as part of a delegation from Friends of the Earth, to deliver a letter of protest.[15] At Ashton, she hosted salon-like weekend parties, where friends from the conservation and environmental movement were brought together with scientists, actors, activists, students, musicians and farmers, along with anyone else Miriam happened to have recently met and liked. Visitors recalled impromptu concerts, film screenings on the squash court, tours of the wild flower projects, and long sessions in the Chequered Skipper. Even as her eyesight faded, she could recognise visitors by voice, and would boom from the entrance: 'Welcome to Liberty Hall. Do whatever you like here!'[16]

The Ashton phone rang constantly. A writer who had come to do a profile on Miriam for the *New Yorker* described the series of phone calls she overheard during her weekend visit: 'Allies on the fronts of her various causes; friends in Jerusalem ... or in Zurich or America; friends to meet in town ... or over luncheon back home in the country'.[17] One call was 'a request, for the second time in two days, that [Miriam] provide a home for a fox ... "Tell me," she instructed the caller, firmly taking charge. "Is it tame? What age is it? Is it very nervous?"' At Ashton, several of them stalked the corridors, and would settle down to watch television with their 'mother'. The Duchess of Gloucester, lunching with Miriam one day, was startled to find a fox sitting on the chair next to her.[18] Foxes made up just one part of a menagerie that included collies, owls, rabbits and donkeys. In the mornings and evenings, Miriam left the front door open, so that swallows could swoop in and nest in the hallway.

Her enthusiasm for communicating to a broad public, which had previously been expressed in the wildly popular *Fleas, Flukes and Cuckoos*, found a new lease of life in television. To her 1980s appearances in *Nature Watch* (1988), *After Dark* (1988) and *Women of the Century* (1989) she added *Geoff Hamilton's Paradise Gardens* (1997) and a series called *Seven Wonders* (1995), in which prominent public figures chose their seven wonders of the world.[19] Television was the perfect medium for her. Her trademark uniform of Liberty silks, matching headscarves and rubber boots was visually spectacular and highly recognisable. More importantly, television suited her fondness for jokes and anecdotes, the clarity with which she could express complex zoological and botanical ideas, and the endless bubbling energy of her conversation. On screen,

Miriam debating animal welfare on After Dark.

she spoke about her passions – rewilding, conservation and vegetarianism – with a humour, clarity and intensity that many found startling in a woman in her eighties. As one newspaper profile memorably put it: 'It is impossible to prepare for a meeting with Miriam Rothschild. Imagine Beatrix Potter on amphetamines and you come close.'[20]

Her appearance on *Seven Wonders* drew an unexpected admirer. The actor Sir Alec Guinness wrote, thanking her for the show and particularly for its details about nematode flatworms.[21] 'I was so delighted with your kind words about my choice of the seven wonders,' Miriam replied.[22] 'Delighted and enormously flattered . . . I would love to tell you more about the worm world!' She found an eager audience, with Guinness writing in his diary at the start of 1996:

A pleasing letter this morning from Miriam Rothschild saying that if we encounter each other this year (which I very much hope we may) she will tell me a romantic story about worms. Also she will bring me up to date on the minute creature that lives under the eyelids of the hippopotamus and feeds on its tears. Can't wait.[23]

Theirs was an Indian summer of a friendship. The few meetings they had before Guinness's death in 2000 were enlivened by their shared curiosity in the natural world, as well as by deadpan frustrations at their advancing age.[24] From the early 1990s, when an emergency stop on the A1 gave her whiplash, Miriam had used an electric wheelchair. As the years drew on, she became more and more dependent on it, until she could no longer tackle the stairs at Ashton. She moved in to a large ground-floor room instead. Along with a bed, the room contained the paraphernalia which still defined her life scientific: a workbench with microscopes, and bags of insects.[25] Outside, the rewilding had taken root so fervently that the grounds ran riot. '*Après moi, le déluge*,' she told one journalist.[26] As Miriam crept towards her nineties, the house retreated from view and was engulfed by the greenery.

In February 1994 ninety members of the Rothschild family from across the world gathered in Frankfurt, the city where their story began.[27] The purpose of their visit was to celebrate 250 years since the birth of Mayer Amschel. Like previous Rothschild gatherings, this was an occasion in which the patriarchal obsessions of the family were much in evidence. The various talks and exhibitions scheduled at Frankfurt's Jewish Museum – based in a building that had once been owned by Mayer Carl – were full of references to Mayer Amschel and his five sons, as were the accompanying publications. The women of the family were hardly mentioned.

The Jewish Museum's main exhibition planned to coincide with the anniversary was called 'The Rothschilds: A European Family'. In his address at the museum, German Chancellor Helmut Kohl styled the family as pioneers of European integration: 'For a century, [Mayer Amschel's] descendants have been living the reality we are trying to achieve through the unification of Europe.'[28] The exhibition was also timely in another way, coming at a moment when German institutions were starting to address the country's Nazi past. 'The fact that such an exhibition could not have been shown 20 or 30 years ago was symptomatic of an amnesia based on bad conscience,' the *Frankfurter Allgemeine Zeitung* reported.[29] This emblematic European family were being welcomed back to Germany with remorseful pride.

The eclipsing of the family's banking business by varied new interests had continued apace, and Victor's son Jacob, now the 4th Baron Rothschild, noted that alongside the bankers and philanthropists gathered at Frankfurt were 'an actor, a picture restorer, a horticulturalist, a singer, a scientist, a film maker', as well as 'several, of course, engaged in the business of making wine'.[30] Miriam was neither the 'horticulturalist' nor the 'scientist' – she had not made the trip to Frankfurt. She did, however, contribute a number of exhibits, ranging from photographs to a copy of her flea taxonomy. But perhaps her most significant contribution was to be found in the exhibition catalogue. As the deterioration of her eyesight made work with microscopes more difficult, Miriam had increasingly turned her gaze back into her own life, and the lives of her Rothschild ancestors. 'I have a habit of looking over the past,' she wrote to Marie-Louise Motesiczky.[31] By the 1990s, her family history work reached far beyond her Uncle Walter. For the Frankfurt catalogue Miriam wrote two essays, one titled 'The Rothschilds and the Original EEC, Family Reflections I: The Men', and the other, 'The Silent Members of the First EEC, Family Reflections II: The Women'.[32] The latter began with a quote from Jewish historian Naomi Shepherd: 'In all the historical literature produced since the end of the eighteenth century women are a footnote to the story of

Jewish survival.'[33] Miriam's essay, written in her mid eighties, would be her attempt to draw the women of the family out of the footnotes and into the main text of the family's history.

The women's role had not been entirely forgotten. From a very early age, young Rothschilds of every generation were instructed on the importance of their distant matriarch, Gutle, as well as the patriarch, Mayer Amschel.[34] They knew, from their own mothers, the import-ance of Rothschild women in forging the culture of the family, as well as in doing much of the work on which the family's wealth and success was based. But at the same time, in public as well as in private, the family emphasised success in a way that was decidedly male.[35] Only men were directly involved in the bank, and the family's greatest com-munal achievements were represented by the men: by Lionel taking his seat in the Commons, by the barony, and by Walter receiving the Balfour Declaration.

It was, strangely enough, in writing about her uncle Walter that Miriam's interest in the biographies of her female relatives had been awakened. Walter's story had highlighted the role of women in the family's history – of Walter's mother Emma in creating the culture at Tring; of her own mother Rózsika, with her political enthusiasm and implacable nature; of her friend Dolly's precocious wartime diplomacy with Weizmann. In her essay, Miriam delved further into the history of the family, introducing readers to a remarkable female lineage that ran all the way back to the eighteenth century, and the Frankfurt ghetto. She wrote about the way that Gutle 'coped admir-ably with the police who came to interrogate her about the family business', and drew attention to the foundational exclusion of daugh-ters and wives that Mayer Amschel had declared in his will.[36] She described how Hannah had surreptitiously assumed 'a far more active role in Nathan's affairs than the conventional Jewish wife', and em-phasised that her 'determination and fearlessness' had been a driv-ing force in the campaign for Jewish emancipation.[37] She covered Constance's tireless work on the 'ugly problems connected with the so-called White Slave trade', and paid homage to her indomitable grandmother Emma, who had taught herself physics and Morse code, and taken no fewer than four hundred charities onto her account book when she first moved to Tring.[38]

One of the main themes in Miriam's article on the Rothschild women was the relationship between mothers and their children.

How were ideas, expectations and cultures transmitted from mother to child? What freedom did mothers have in shaping their children's lives, education and attitudes? How did women's experiences of motherhood vary? These were issues that her own daughter Rosie had explored in her writing for *Spare Rib*, and had continued to investigate in the decades since. The year after Miriam published her essay on the Rothschild women, Rosie's investigation of 'maternal ambivalence' would culminate in the publication of *Torn in Two* (1995), which offered an unblinking study of women's true experience of motherhood, and a scrupulous examination of the way in which simplified cultural ideals of mothering – as straightforwardly joyous and loving – generated shame and secrecy around the true and complex feelings of mothers towards their children.

In Miriam's case, as in Rosie's, a revived interest in hidden, matrilineal histories went hand in hand with a renewed curiosity towards her own Jewish heritage. While she had never been religious, Miriam's work in the aftermath of the Holocaust, and her attentiveness to the resurgence of antisemitism in the late twentieth century, had already cemented the importance of Jewishness in her own life. Her research into her family's history had only reinforced that attachment. Regardless of whether a Jewish God existed, she thought, the shared experiences and history of the Jewish community drew them together. 'I don't believe in God,' Miriam once told a journalist.[39] 'But I do believe very strongly in the Jewish community. I don't mind who I say I'm Jewish to.'

Just as Miriam found herself and relaxed into her beliefs, so the rest of the world discovered her, too. On top of her fellowships at St Hugh's College, Oxford, and the Royal Society, Miriam had accumulated eight honorary doctorates.[40] In acknowledgement of her influence on his environmental and horticultural views, Prince Charles commissioned a bust of her for his 'wall of worthies' in his garden at Highgrove. In the New Year Honours list 2000, Miriam became a dame on account of her 'services to nature conservation and biochemical research'.[41] While her male predecessors had used wealth and influence to wrest aristocratic titles from the British establishment, Miriam had, with characteristic verve, defiance and determination, won them on her own merits.

Perhaps it was inevitable, given Miriam's unquenchable spirit, that when the end came, it would come quickly. 'A few days before her death,' a colleague recalled, 'Miriam was still telephoning her ento-mological friends with new proposals for joint work.'[42] In hindsight, colleagues came to think that she had been 'giving us her instructions for our work programme after her death!' On 20 January 2005 Dame Miriam Rothschild died from heart failure at Ashton Wold, where she had been born nearly a hundred years earlier. She had left her mark on an extraordinary range of people and subjects. There were tributes and obituaries in major newspapers in Washington, New York and Toronto, in scientific journals like the *Journal of Parasitology* and *American Entomologist*, in the *Jewish Chronicle*, and in two wildly dif-ferent British staples: *The Economist* and *Country Life*.[43]

Miriam's life had spanned centuries, careers and continents. She had broken codes, reared wild animals, dodged bombs and inspired a generation of scientists and ecologists and curious laypeople. She had written books, appeared on television, and protested loudly against cruelty, injustice and environmental degradation. Latterly, she had shone a spotlight on her female antecedents. In the foreword to a new edition of *Torn in Two*, published in the year of her mother's death, Rosie wrote that the book and the psychotherapeutic work related to it were 'daughters ... of Second Wave Feminism, the feminism that emerged in the 1960s'.[44] Rosie would outlive her mother by five years, dying from pancreatic cancer in 2010 at the age of only sixty-four. She and Miriam had both, in their own ways, come to realise how broad and deep their debts were to the women who had gone before them. Rosie's response had been to focus more intently and honestly on the feelings of women towards their children. Miriam, one of the family's most vocal and inquisitive daughters, had instead reached into her own past, and stirred the voices of her many Rothschild mothers.

Acknowledgements

I T ALL BEGAN in July 2015 over lunch with my dear friend Andrew Roberts. Our conversation turned to the Rothschild family, and the relatively low profile of its women. Andrew suggested I investigate further and, in so doing, introduced me to the characters who would dominate my thoughts for the following five years.

Writing this book has been an honour, unveiling countless surprises and a plethora of gripping stories. The Rothschild dynasty continues to produce a panoply of inspirational women, none more so than Hannah Rothschild. *The Baroness*, her brilliant book about her great-aunt Nica, remains the gold standard of biographies. I only hope I have done her family justice.

There are inexhaustible swathes of source material about the Rothschild family. Attempting to marshal it would have taken more than one lifetime. I am indebted to Dr Will Clement, Dr Rebecca Coll, Dr Daniel Cowling and Dr Jennifer Meyer, who enthusiastically helped me track down and translate letters and diaries from archives from New Jersey, Frankfurt and back to London. My special thanks go to the brilliant Tom Evans: I could not have shaped this book without his help.

I am also indebted to the trustees and staff of The Rothschild Archive in London for their thoughtful introduction to the family papers, and for being so accommodating in the course of a long research process. Tremendous thanks is owed to Sir Evelyn de Rothschild, who during his time as head of the Rothschild bank made the bold and imaginative decision to establish the RAL as a charity open to the public, and to his wife Lynn for the enormous understanding and support that she has shown throughout this project. At Waddesdon, home to the Windmill Hill Archive, the generosity, attentiveness and expert guidance of Catherine Taylor and Pippa Shirley made the archives truly accessible, opened up numerous rewarding avenues of enquiry, and meant that trips to Waddesdon became a real pleasure; that the collections can be consulted in such a peaceful, spacious and art-filled reading room is a tribute to the passion and vision of Jacob, Lord Rothschild.

Kate Weinberg and Charlotte Mendelson have supported me throughout the writing process. I have learned so much from them and could not be more appreciative of their time or their patience. The same is true of my sparkling editor Jocasta Hamilton and my agent Caroline Michel.

Lawrence Bernstein, Laura Hilton, Professor David Reynolds and my uncle Professor Robert Reiner have provided personal insights and wisdom that have helped me challenge ideas and develop key themes. Anna Albright has had the even trickier role of ensuring I retained the sanity to process them.

Writing about another family has made me ever more thankful to my own. My mother Ann, to whom I owe my love of history, and my father Howard who ignited my passion for Jewish studies. My sisters Caroline and Laura who have always been my greatest supporters, as well as my nephews Zachary and Charlie, and my brother-in-law Jonathan. My mother-in-law Gillian continues to move me with her strength and resilience.

I am very grateful to those who have become family along the way, each providing their own brand of wisdom, support and encouragement: Caroline Carr, the font of gracious advice; Richard Dennen, whose belief in this project has sustained me. And my Cliveden Literary Festival co-conspirators: the witty, wise and wonderful Andrew Roberts who gave me the idea for the book, the dazzling Catherine Ostler who has provided constant guidance, reassurance and the warmest friendship, and the inimitable Simon Sebag Montefiore whose writing continues to be the greatest inspiration.

Above all, the family I have created with my husband Ian means everything to me. Nothing would make sense without him and our three daughters Grace, Alice and Elizabeth Rose. Living with me for five years requires a level of endurance at the best of times. Five years with me, plus multiple Rothschild women, must have seemed like a test too far. As ever they all passed with flying colours. I love you all more than you can imagine.

Picture Credits

Insets

Alamy Stock Photos: 3/Artepics, 8/The Natural History Museum, 9/Album, 14/John Glover, 15/Album. Mary Evans Picture Library: 6 above/Francis Frith, 6 below/© Illustrated London News Ltd, 7/The Natural History Museum. Ben Martin/Getty Images: 11. © Marie-Louise von Motesiczky Charitable Trust, 2022: 12/Painting in private collection, 13/Painting in the collection of the Marie-Louise Motesiczky Charitable Trust. © National Portrait Gallery London: 4, 5. Private collection: 2 above. Reproduced with the permission of The Trustees of the Rothschild Archive: 1, 2 below. Shutterstock: 10/Daily Mail. Nick Sinclair/Science Photo Library: 16.

Images within the text

Alamy Stock Photos: 13/Everett Collection, 17/Sueddeutsche Zeitung Photo, 21/Lebrecht Music & Arts, 90/The History Collection, 99/Granger Historical Picture Archive, 118/Archivio GBB, 131/Chronicle. Bildarchiv Pisarek/akg-images: 26. Mary Evans Picture Library: 185, 209/© Illustrated London News Ltd. Future Publishing Ltd: 233. Pridan Moshe/Government Press Office Israel: 317. © National Portrait Gallery London: 148, 206. Open Media Ltd 1998, Creative Commons Attribution-Share Alike CC-BY-SA-3.0: 360. Public domain: 12/map of Frankfurt, 1628, engraving by Matthäus Merian. Reproduced with the permission of The Trustees of the Rothschild Archive: 55. © The Savile Club: 61. Shutterstock: 304/ANL, 312/Carl Mydans/The LIFE Picture Collection. Waddesdon (Rothschild Family) Acc no:135.2005 Lafayette Ltd: 260.

Notes

Introduction

1 Egon Corti, *The Rise of the House of Rothschild*, trans. Brian Lunn and Beatrix Lunn (London: Victor Gollancz, 1928).

2 Niall Ferguson, *The World's Banker* (London: Weidenfeld & Nicolson, 1998).

3 Miriam Rothschild, 'Rothschild Women', *Jewish Women: A Comprehensive Historical Encyclopedia*, 27 February 2009, Jewish Women's Archive. https://jwa.org/encyclopedia/article/rothschild-women.

4 'A Passion for Wild Flowers', *The Times*, 23 January 1999.

5 Charlotte to Leonora and Leopold, 25 August 1874: Rothschild Archive, London (hereafter RAL), 000/84/5.

CHAPTER I:
The Mother of the Business

1 Carl-Ludwig Holtfrerich, *Frankfurt as a Financial Centre: From Medieval Trade Fair to European Banking Centre* (Munich: Verlag C.H. Beck, 1999), 57.

2 Isidor Kracauer, *Die Geschichte der Judengasse in Frankfurt am Main* (Frankfurt: Gebrüder Fey, 1906), 312–13.

3 Niall Ferguson, '"The Caucasian Royal Family": The Rothschilds in National Contexts', in *Two Nations: The Historical Experience of British and German Jews in Comparison*, ed. Michael Brenner et al. (Tübingen: Mohr Siebeck, 1999), 300.

4 Alexander Dietz, *The Jewish Community of Frankfurt: A Genealogical Study*, ed. Isobel Mordy, trans. Frances Martin (Camelford: Vanderher, 1988), 508.

5 Holtfrerich, *Frankfurt*, 59.

6 Dietz, *Jewish Community*, 311, 508.

7 Ibid.

8 Ibid., 310–11.

9 Robert Liberles, 'Introduction: The World of Dietz's Stammbuch: Frankfurt Jewry: 1349–1870', in Dietz, *Jewish Community*, i–xxxii; Ferguson, *World's Banker*, 38.

10 Ruth Gay, *The Jews of Germany: A Historical Portrait* (London: Yale University Press, 1992), 62; Liberles, 'Introduction', i.

11 Gay, *Jews of Germany*, 8; J. Fuchs, 'Preface: Concerning the Jews of Frankfort', in *The Five Frankforters: A Comedy in 3 Acts*, ed. Carl Rössler (New York: Fly, 1913), 17; Kracauer, *Geschichte der Judengasse*, 416–17.

12 Mitchell Duneier, *Ghetto: The Invention of a Place, the History of an Idea* (New York: Farrar, Straus & Giroux, 2016), 42.

13 Gay, *Jews of Germany*, 62.

14 Kracauer, *Geschichte der Judengasse*, 313.

15 Ibid., 312–13.

16 Ibid., 317.

17 Ibid., 246, 369, 373.

18 Ferguson, *World's Banker*, 42; Kracauer, *Geschichte der Judengasse*, 422, 424.

19 Kracauer, *Geschichte der Judengasse*, 336.

20 Ibid., 340–1.

21 Gay, *Jews of Germany*, 70.

22 Kracauer, *Geschichte der Judengasse*, 424. One gulden was worth sixty kreutzer.

23 Gay, *Jews of Germany*, 67–70.

24 Gabriela Schlick, 'Frauen in der Judengasse', in *Frauen in der Stadt – Frankfurt im 18. Jahrhundert*, ed. Gisela Engel, Ursula Kern and Heide Wunder (Königstein/Taunus: Helmer, 2002), 151.

25 Gay, *Jews of Germany*, 74.

26 Kracauer, *Geschichte der Judengasse*, 422–5.

27 Schlick, 'Frauen', 150, 153–4.

28 Fritz Backhaus, *Mayer Amschel Rothschild: Ein biografisches Porträt* (Freiburg: Herder, 2012), 33.

29 Manfred Pohl, 'From Court Agent to State Financier: The Rise of the Rothschilds', in *The Rothschilds: Essays on the History of a European Family*, ed. Georg Heuberger (Woodbridge: Boydell & Brewer, 1994), 56.

30 Isidor Kracauer, *Geschichte der Juden in Frankfurt a. M. (1150–1824)*, vol. 2 (Frankfurt: Kauffman, 1927), 247–8.

31 Dietz, *Jewish Community*, 287.

32 Corti, *Rise of the House of Rothschild*, 3; Dietz, *Jewish Community*, 289.

33 Ferguson, *World's Banker*, 45.

34 Amos Elon, *Founder: Meyer Amschel Rothschild and His Time* (London: Faber, 1996), 34.

35 Ferguson, *World's Banker*, 45; Backhaus, *Mayer Amschel Rothschild*, 39.

36 Christian Wilhelm Berghoeffer, *Meyer Amschel Rothschild: Der Gründer des Rothschildschen Bankhauses*, 3rd edn (Frankfurt: Englert & Schlosser, 1924; reprinted Paderborn: Salzwasser-Verlag, 2012), 8. Citations refer to the Salzwasser-Verlag edition.

37 Elon, *Founder*, 66; Backhaus, *Mayer Amschel Rothschild*, 81.

38 Ferguson, *World's Banker*, 46; Backhaus, *Mayer Amschel Rothschild*, 81.

39 Kracauer, *Geschichte der Juden*, 2:248.

40 Ibid., 2:247.

41 Dietz, *Jewish Community*, 538.

42 Quoted in Kracauer, *Geschichte der Judengasse*, 396–7.

43 Backhaus, *Mayer Amschel Rothschild*, 49.

44 Dietz, *Jewish Community*, 291–2.

45 Elon, *Founder*, 71; Edith Dörken, *Berühmte Frankfurter Frauen* (Frankfurt: Otto Lembeck, 2008), 47.

46 Elon, *Founder*, 71, 112.

47 Maria Belli-Gontard, *Lebens-Erinnerungen* (Frankfurt: Diesterweg, 1872), 283.

48 Carl to Solomon, n.d. 1814: RAL XI/109/1/4/2 (T29/255).

CHAPTER 2:
'Merely a Machine'

1 JL, 'Das Stammhaus der Familie Rothschild', *Frankfurter Nachrichten* (2nd supplement), 13 November 1927.

2 Quoted in Backhaus, *Mayer Amschel Rothschild*, 27.

3 Corti, *Rise of the House of Rothschild*, 18; Ferguson, *World's Banker*, 47.

4 Elon, *Founder*, 93.

5 JL, 'Stammhaus der Familie Rothschild'; Corti, *Rise of the House of Rothschild*, 18; Elon, *Founder*, 80.

6 Ferguson, *World's Banker*, 49.

7 Ibid., 47.

8 Elon, *Founder*, 89.

9 Ferguson, *World's Banker*, 50; Elon, *Founder*, 89–90.

10 Kracauer, *Geschichte der Judengasse*, 428–9.

11 Ibid., 430–1.

12 Yair Mintzker, *The Defortification of the German City, 1689–1866* (Cambridge: Cambridge University Press, 2012), 140–5; Kracauer, *Geschichte der Judengasse*, 434.

13 This was, according to Elon, *Founder*, 92, 'one half of a son's current share in the inheritance'.

14 Ibid., 112.

15 Maria Belli-Gontard visited Gutle at home most weeks and depicts her as a thrifty matriarch, who 'spent nothing, always saved'. See Belli-Gontard, *Lebens-Erinnerungen*, 283.

16 Gutle to Nathan, 12 May 1805: RAL XI/82/10/1/2 (also T27/3).

17 Gutle to Nathan and Kalman, 29 July 1804: RAL XI/82/10/1/1 (also T27/2).

18 Eva Hanau to Amschel, 18 April 1810: RAL XI/82/10/1/7 (also in T[a]9).

19 Process mit Savagné, fo. 11v: RAL Moscow Papers 000/1059 (637-1-4).

20 Ferguson, *World's Banker*, 73.

21 Process mit Savagné, fo. 11v: RAL Moscow Papers 000/1059 (637-1-4).

22 Ibid., fos. 11v–12r.

23 Berghoeffer, *Meyer Amschel Rothschild*, 58–9; Ferguson, *World's Banker*, 70.

24 Ferguson, *World's Banker*, 72.

25 Berghoeffer, *Meyer Amschel Rothschild*, 91, 97, 102; Ferguson, *World's Banker*, 70–1.

26 Quoted Ferguson, *World's Banker*, 75.

27 Ibid., 73.

28 Backhaus, *Mayer Amschel Rothschild*, 102.

29 Ibid.

30 Ferguson, *World's Banker*, 74.

31 Process mit Savagné, fo. 18v: RAL Moscow Papers 000/1059 (637-1-4).

32 Ibid., fo. 14r.

33 Ibid., fo. 24r.

34 Ibid., fo. 25v.

35 Ibid., fo. 26v.

36 Ibid., fo. 28r.

37 Ibid.

38 Ibid.

39 Ibid.

40 Ferguson, *World's Banker*, 73.

41 Backhaus, *Mayer Amschel Rothschild*, 50–1.

42 Gutle to Salomon and Jacob, n.d.: RAL XI/82/10/18 (also in T[a]29).

43 Ferguson, *World's Banker*, 80; a *cheder* is a school for children of pre-*bar mitzvah* age.

44 Kracauer, *Geschichte der Judengasse*, 448; Backhaus, *Mayer Amschel Rothschild*, 116.

45 Ferguson, *World's Banker*, 81.

46 Berghoeffer, *Meyer Amschel Rothschild*, 131.

47 Backhaus, *Mayer Amschel Rothschild*, 119.

CHAPTER 3:
Inventing the Family

1 Constance Battersea, *Reminiscences* (London: Macmillan, 1923), 8.

2 Judith and Sir Moses Montefiore, *Diaries of Sir Moses and Lady Montefiore*, vol. 1, ed. L. Loewe (London: Griffith, Farran, & Co., 1890), 3–4.

3 Herbert Kaplan, *Nathan Mayer Rothschild and the Creation of a Dynasty: The Critical Years, 1806–1816* (Stanford, CA: Stanford University Press, 2006), 6–7.

4 Ibid., 8; Montefiore and Montefiore, *Diaries*, 1: 3–4.

5 Lucien Wolf, 'Lady Montefiore's Honeymoon', in *Essays in Jewish History*, ed. Cecil Roth (London: Jewish Historical Society of England, 1934), 239–40.

6 Sir Thomas Fowell Buxton, *Memoirs of Sir Thomas Fowell Buxton, Baronet. With Selections From His Correspondence*, ed. Charles Buxton (London: John Murray, 1848), 343; Stanley D. Chapman, *N.M. Rothschild, 1777–1836* (London: N.M. Rothschild & Sons, 1977), 5.

7 Bill Williams, 'Nathan Rothschild in Manchester', in *The Life and Times of N.M. Rothschild, 1777–1836*, ed. Victor Gray and Melanie Aspey (London: N.M. Rothschild & Sons, 1998), 36.

8 Richard Davis, *The English Rothschilds* (London: Collins, 1983), 23; Chapman, *N.M. Rothschild*, 8.

9 Kaplan, *Nathan Mayer Rothschild*, 4.

10 Mayer Amschel to Nathan Mayer, 28 June 1809: RAL XI/85/0 (also T5/6).

11 Chapman, *N.M. Rothschild*, 5.

12 Wolf, 'Lady Montefiore's Honeymoon', 235.

13 Buxton, *Memoirs*, 343–4.

14 Lucien Wolf, *Sir Moses Montefiore: A Centennial Biography* (London: John Murray, 1884), 31.

15 Ferguson, *World's Banker*, 62.

16 Kaplan, *Nathan Mayer Rothschild*, 10.

17 Ibid., 9.

18 Davis, *English Rothschilds*, 23.

19 Alex Philipson to N.M. Rothschild, 3 December 1805: RAL XI/114/0 (also T3/271).

20 Kaplan, *Nathan Mayer Rothschild*, 9.

21 'London Sessions: Married', *Morning Chronicle*, 28 October 1806.

22 Joseph Aston, *A Picture of Manchester* (Manchester, 1816), 20.

23 Ibid., 19.

24 George Ireland, *Plutocrats: A Rothschild Inheritance* (London: John Murray, 2007), 30; Bill Williams, *The Making of Manchester Jewry, 1740–1875* (Manchester: Manchester University Press, 1976), 21, 30.

25 Williams, *Making of Manchester Jewry*, 16.

26 *Jewish World*, 7 September 1877, quoted Williams, *Making of Manchester Jewry*, 12.

27 Davis, *English Rothschilds*, 26.

28 Melanie Aspey, 'Mrs Rothschild', in Gray and Aspey, eds., *Life and Times of N.M. Rothschild*, 61; Peter Fawcett to Hannah, 2 October 1808: RAL XI/112/7B.

29 J.L. Reiss to N.M. Rothschild, n.d. 1807: RAL XI/114 (also T3/313).

30 A. Hertz to N.M. Rothschild, 12 August 1807: RAL XI/119 (also T4/23).

31 Ibid., 4 December 1806: RAL XI/112/05.

32 Kaplan, *Nathan Mayer Rothschild*, 11–12.

33 Ibid., 11.

34 Ibid., 22.

35 Ibid., 21.

36 *Morning Post*, 15 March 1808.

37 Selig Cohen to Nathan, 16 March 1808: RAL XI/82/10/1/3 (also T27/13).

38 Selig Cohen to Hannah, Manchester, n.d.: RAL XI/82 (also in T[a]7).

39 Kaplan, *Nathan Mayer Rothschild*, 25.

40 Ibid., 24; Lucien Wolf, 'Rothschildiana', in Roth, ed., *Essays in Jewish History*, 271.

41 David Kynaston, *The City of London: A World of its Own, 1815–1890*, vol. 2

(London: Chatto & Windus, 1994), 32.

42 Ibid., 2: 9–10.

43 C.A.G. Goede, *The Stranger in England; or, Travels in Great Britain* (London: Mathews & Leigh, 1807), 49.

44 Chapman, *N.M. Rothschild*, 19.

45 Kaplan, *Nathan Mayer Rothschild*, 64.

46 Ferguson, *World's Banker*, 91–2.

47 Kaplan, *Nathan Mayer Rothschild*, 52.

48 Ferguson, *World's Banker*, 93.

49 Ibid., 94.

50 Ibid.

51 Ibid., 96.

52 Wolf, 'Rothschildiana', 272.

53 Backhaus, *Mayer Amschel Rothschild*, 154.

54 Berghoeffer, *Meyer Amschel Rothschild*, 171–5.

CHAPTER 4:
The Husband Hunt

1 Amschel to Jacob, 17 June 1814: RAL XI/109/0/1/29 (also T29/11).

2 Gelche to Solomon, 18 September 1814: RAL XI/109/1/2/12 (also T29/232).

3 Carl to [? Amschel], n.d.: RAL T28/37.

4 Amschel Mayer to Nathan Mayer and Salomon Mayer, 24 July 1814: RAL XI/109/0/4/34 (also T29/113).

5 Carl to Solomon, n.d.: RAL XI/109/1/4/2 (also T29/255).

6 Carl to Solomon and Davidsohn, 19 September 1814: RAL XI/109/1/2/14 (also T29/234).

7 James to Nathan, 4 October 1814: RAL XI/109/1/4/10 (also T29/263); Carl to Jacob, 19 October 1814: RAL XI/109/1/5/16 (also T29/288); Carl to Solomon, 22 December 1814: RAL XI/109/1/8/22 (also T29/365).

8 Carl to Solomon and Davidsohn, 19 September 1814: RAL XI/109/1/2/14 (also T29/234).

9 Amschel to Solomon, July 1814: RAL T28/10; Carl to Solomon and Davidsohn, 19 September 1814: RAL XI/109/1/2/14 (also T29/234).

10 Carl to Solomon and Jacob, 18 September 1814: RAL XI/109/1/2/13 (also T29/233); Carl to Solomon and Davidsohn, 19 September 1814: RAL XI/109/1/2/14 (also T29/234).

11 Carl to Solomon and Jacob, 18 September 1814: RAL XI/109/1/2/13 (also T29/233).

12 Ibid.

13 Ibid., 22 September 1814: RAL XI/109/1/2/19 (also T29/239).

14 Carl to [? Amschel], n.d.: RAL T28/37.

15 Carl to Solomon and Jacob, 22 September 1814: RAL XI/109/1/2/19 (also T29/239).

16 Ibid.; Carl to [? Amschel], n.d.: RAL T28/37.

17 Carl to Solomon and Jacob, 22 September 1814: RAL XI/109/1/2/19 (also T29/239).

18 Solomon to Nathan, 24 September 1814: RAL XI/109/1/3/3 (also T29/244).

19 Carl to Solomon and Jacob, 18 September 1814: RAL XI/109/1/2/13, also (T29/233); Carl to Solomon and Jacob, 22 September 1814: RAL XI/109/1/2/19 (also T29/239); Carl to [? Amschel], n.d.: RAL T28/37.

20 Carl to Solomon, 22 December 1814: RAL XI/109/1/8/22 (also T29/365).

21 Jettche to Solomon, 28 September 1814: RAL XI/109/1/3/9 (also T29/250).

22 Carl to Solomon, 26 September 1814: RAL XI/109/1/3/6 (also T29/247).

23 Ibid., n.d.: RAL XI/109/1/4/2 (also T29/255).

24 Jettche to Solomon, 28 September 1814: RAL XI/109/1/3/9 (also T29/250).

25 Amschel to Carl and Gutle, 17 October 1814: RAL XI/109/1/5/11 (also T29/281).

26 Carl, Berlin, to Jacob, 19 October 1814: RAL XI/109/1/5/16 (also T29/288).

27 James to Amschel, 6 November 1814: RAL XI/109/1/7/9 (also T29/316).

28 Carl to Solomon, 22 December 1814: RAL XI/109/1/8/22 (also T29/365).

29 Ibid.

30 Solomon to Nathan, December 1814: RAL XI/109/1/8/46 (also T29/372); Solomon to Nathan, 13 January 1815: RAL XI/109/2/3/21/1 (also in T30).

31 Amschel to unknown, 29 March 1815: RAL XI/109/2/3/51/1 (also in T30).

32 P. L. Cottrell, 'The Business Man and Financier', in *The Century of Moses Montefiore*, ed. Sonia and Vivian D. Lipman (Oxford: Oxford University Press, 1985), 26; Chaim Bermant, *The Cousinhood: The Anglo-Jewish Gentry* (London: Eyre & Spottiswoode, 1971), 15.

33 Montefiore and Montefiore, *Diaries*, I: 19.

34 Sonia Lipman, 'The Making of a Victorian Gentleman', in Lipman and Lipman, eds., *Century of Montefiore*, 14; Abigail Green, 'Brothers-in-Law: The Rothschilds and the Montefiores', *The Rothschild Archive Review of the Year* (2008–2009): 16, https://www.rothschildarchive.org/materials/review_2008_2009_brothers_in_law_1.pdf.

35 Wolf, 'Rothschildiana', 275.

36 Abigail Green, *Moses Montefiore: Jewish Liberator, Imperial Hero* (Cambridge, MA: Harvard University Press, 2010), 35–6.

37 Solomon to Nathan, December 1814: RAL XI/109/1/8/46 (also T29/372).

38 Paul H. Emden, *Jews of Britain: A Series of Biographies* (London: Sampson Low & Co., 1944), 158.

39 Green, *Moses Montefiore*, 28.

40 Wolf, 'Lady Montefiore's Honeymoon', 241n; Lipman, 'Making of a Victorian Gentleman', 8.

41 Green, *Moses Montefiore*, 28.

42 Joseph Valynseele and Henri-Claude Mars, *Le Sang des Rothschild* (Paris: ICC Editions, 2004), 475.

43 Quoted in Green, 'Brothers-in-Law', 20.

CHAPTER 5:
Madame Montefiore

1 Cecil Roth, *A History of the Jews in England* (Oxford: Oxford University Press, 1941), 85; Bernard Glassman, *Anti-Semitic Stereotypes without Jews: Images of the Jews in England, 1290–1700* (Detroit, MI: Wayne State University, 1975), 20; Frank Felsenstein, *Anti-Semitic Stereotypes: A Paradigm of Otherness in English Popular Culture, 1660–1830* (Baltimore, MD: Johns Hopkins University Press, 1995), 29.

2 Roth, *History of the Jews*, 162; Todd Endelman, *The Jews of Georgian England* (Philadelphia: Jewish Publication Society of America, 1979), 174.

3 Elon, *Founder*, 109.

4 Endelman, *Jews of Georgian England*, 115–16.

5 Hilary L. Rubinstein et al., *The Jews in the Modern World: A History since 1750* (London: Edward Arnold, 2002), 64; Jerry White, *London in the Nineteenth Century: An Awful Human Wonder of God* (London: Jonathan Cape, 2007), 154.

6 Rainer Leidtke, 'Nathan Rothschild and London Jewry', in Gray and

Aspey, eds., *Life and Times of N.M. Rothschild*, 52.

7 Flora Tristan, *The London Journal of Flora Tristan, 1842; or, The Aristocracy and the Working Class of England*, trans. Jean Hawkes (London: Virago, 1982), 144–5.

8 Salomon and James to Nathan, 19 May 1817: RAL T27/256.

9 Green, 'Brothers-in-Law', 20.

10 Quoted in Green, *Moses Montefiore*, 37.

11 Green, 'Brothers-in-Law', 20.

12 Montefiore and Montefiore, *Diaries*, 1: 21; Green, 'Brothers-in-Law', 20.

13 Green, 'Brothers-in-Law', 20.

14 Ibid.

15 Ibid., 18.

16 Amschel to Nathan, 18 June 1817: RAL T27/274.

17 Green, 'Brothers-in-Law', 20.

18 Cottrell, 'Business Man', 28.

19 Green, *Moses Montefiore*, 28.

CHAPTER 6:

A Healthier Climate

1 Wolf, 'Lady Montefiore's Honeymoon', 249–50.

2 Vivian D. Lipman, 'The Rise of Jewish Suburbia', *Transactions (Jewish Historical Society of England)*, 21 (1962): 93, www.jstor.org/stable/29777992.

3 Wolf, 'Rothschildiana', 275; Ireland, *Plutocrats*, 49–51.

4 Isobel Watson, *Hackney and Stoke Newington Past* (London: Historical Publications, 1998), 20.

5 A.P. Baggs, Diane K. Bolton and Patricia E.C. Croot, 'Stoke Newington: Economic History', in *A History of the County of Middlesex: Volume 8, Islington and Stoke Newington Parishes*, ed. T.F.T. Baker and C.R. Elrington (London:

Victoria County History, 1985), 184–94. British History Online, http://www.british-history.ac.uk/vch/middx/vol8/pp184-194.

6 Hannah to Lady Carmarthen, 24 November [no year]: RAL T17/72.

7 Malcolm Brown, 'The Jews of Hackney', *Jewish Historical Studies*, 30 (1987): 83.

8 Carl to Salomon and James, 18 May 1817: RAL XI/109/7/22/1 (also in T62).

9 *Weekly Messenger*, 4 November 1827.

10 *Morning Post*, 13 July 1827. A *chuppah* is a ceremonial canopy beneath which marriage ceremonies are conducted.

11 Ibid.

12 Elizabeth and John Hodgkin to Thomas Hodgkin, 1 August 1823: Wellcome Library, London (hereafter WL), PP/HO/D/A269.

13 Battersea, *Reminiscences*, 7–8.

14 Ibid., 8.

15 Lou was more commonly known to her family as Louise, but for clarity the shortened form is used here and throughout.

16 Cecil Roth, 'Lucien Wolf: A Memoir', in Roth, ed., *Essays in Jewish History*, 31.

17 William D. Rubinstein, Michael A. Jolles and Hilary L. Rubinstein, eds., *The Palgrave Dictionary of Anglo-Jewish History* (Basingstoke: Palgrave Macmillan, 2011), 313.

18 Ireland, *Plutocrats*, 51.

19 Souvenirs du Docteur Schlemmer, 3: RAL 000/924/2/8.

20 Ibid., 5–6.

21 Hannah Floretta Cohen, *Changing Faces: A Memoir of Louisa Lady Cohen* (London: Martin Hopkinson, 1937), 36; Hannah to Nathan Mayer, n.d.: RAL 000/10.

22 Ferguson, *World's Banker*, 222.

23 Hermann Fürst von Pückler-Muskau, *Tour in Germany, Holland*

*and England, in the Years 1826, 1827,
& 1828; with Remarks on the Manners
and Customs of the Inhabitants, and
Anecdotes of Distinguished Public
Characters*, trans. Sarah Austin, vol. 3
(London: Effingham Wilson, 1832),
63–4.

24 For the most famous of these
anecdotes, see Louis Spohr, *Louis
Spohr's Autobiography* (London:
Longman, Roberts & Green, 1865),
77–8.

25 Quoted in Kynaston, *City of London*,
2: 6.

26 Wolf, 'Lady Montefiore's
Honeymoon', 239–40; M.B. Kitzinger
Nyjmwegen to Nathan Mayer
Rothschild, 15 October 1832: RAL
T6/113.

27 Joanne Bailey, *Parenting in England
1760–1830: Emotion, Identity and
Generation* (Oxford: Oxford
University Press, 2012), 30–1.

28 Hannah to Lionel, [? September
1846]: RAL 000/10/95; Hannah to
Lionel and Mayer, [? 12] October
1841: RAL 000/10/7; Hannah to
Charlotte, 14 October 1842: RAL
000/10/26.

29 Green, *Moses Montefiore*, 58.

30 Amalie M. Kass, 'Hodgkin, Thomas
(1798–1866), physician and social
reformer', *Oxford Dictionary of
National Biography* (hereafter
ODNB), 23 September 2004.

31 Elizabeth and John Hodgkin to
Thomas Hodgkin, 1 August 1823:
WL PP/HO/D/A269.

32 Lucy Cohen, *Lady de Rothschild and
Her Daughters, 1821–1931* (London:
John Murray, 1935), 6.

33 Amalie M. and Edward H. Kass,
*Perfecting the World: The Life and
Times of Dr. Thomas Hodgkin,
1798–1866* (Boston: Harcourt
Brace Jovanovich, 1988), 120;
Thomas Hodgkin to his parents, 29

December 1823: WL PP/HO/D/
A609.

34 Kass and Kass, *Perfecting the World*,
119.

35 Green, *Moses Montefiore*, 46;
Amalie M. Kass, 'Friends and
Philanthropists: Montefiore and Dr
Hodgkin', in Lipman and Lipman,
eds., *Century of Montefiore*, 78.

36 Kass, 'Friends and Philanthropists',
78.

37 Ibid.

38 Kass and Kass, *Perfecting the World*,
121.

39 Abraham Montefiore to Thomas
Hodgkin, 8 January 1824: WL PP/
HO/D/A1051-1075.

40 While this is absent from family
testimony, it is evident from
reports on a subsequent court case
pertaining to Abraham's multiple
wills. According to the *Evening
Mail*, 19 November 1824, 'it was
between the latter end of 1823, and
the beginning of the year 1824, that
the deceased wrote the papers now
brought in and marked D, E and F.
By one of these, made at a time
when he anticipated the birth of
another child, it was certainly very
clear that he meant a departure of
some sort or other from the will of
May, 1820.' A report in the *Morning
Advertiser*, 18 November 1824,
provides some further information:
'In this document, he said, if he
should not live until the child
with which she was then pregnant
should be born, he begged that if
it proved a boy he should be called
Abraham, and in that case, 20,000l.
was to be invested for his own use,
that he might share equally with
his brothers, who had the landed
property; but if it was a girl, her
name should be Henrietta, and a
sum similar to the amount attached

to the other daughters, should be
invested for her use.'

41 Kass and Kass, *Perfecting the World*,
127.

42 *Public Ledger and Daily Advertiser*,
18 November 1824; *Evening Mail*,
19 November 1824; Kass and Kass,
Perfecting the World, 127; Green, *Moses
Montefiore*, 47.

43 Hannah [with Lionel] to Nathan
Mayer, 30 August 1824: RAL
000/848.

44 *Morning Advertiser*, 18 November
1824.

45 Ibid.

46 *Public Ledger and Daily Advertiser*,
18 November 1824; *Evening Mail*, 19
November 1824.

47 *London Courier and Evening Gazette*,
25 November 1824.

CHAPTER 7:
'Concordia, Integritas, Industria'

1 Carl to Amschel, 27 December 1816:
RAL XI/109/5A, 5B (also T33/390/2).

2 Ireland, *Plutocrats*, 57; James to
Hannah, 26 August 1815: RAL
XI/109/2/3 (also T30/49/2).

3 Carl to his brothers, 25 April [1817]:
RAL T27/149.

4 Simone Mace, 'From Frankfurt Jew
to Lord Rothschild: The Ascent
of the English Rothschilds to
the Nobility', in Heuberger, ed.,
Rothschilds, 181–2.

5 Ferguson, *World's Banker*, 216, 177;
Carl to Nathan and Salomon, 7 April
1818: RAL XI/109/9 (also T64/125/3).

6 Pückler-Muskau, *Tour in Germany,
Holland and England*, 225.

7 Mace, 'From Frankfurt Jew to Lord
Rothschild', 183.

8 Ireland, *Plutocrats*, 73.

9 Mace, 'From Frankfurt Jew to Lord
Rothschild', 183.

10 Ibid.

11 V.A.C. Gatrell, *City of Laughter: Sex
and Satire in Eighteenth-Century
London* (London: Atlantic, 2007), 9.

12 Frank Felsenstein and Sharon
Liberman Mintz, *The Jew as Other: A
Century of English Caricature, 1730–
1830* (New York: Jewish Theological
Seminary of America, 1995), 5–6.

13 British Museum, London, BM
Satires 15522, 'The Jew and the
Doctor; or, Secret Influence Behind
the Curtain!!'.

14 Ferguson, *World's Banker*, 158.

15 Salomon and James to Nathan, 22
October 1817: RAL T27/302.

16 Ferguson, *World's Banker*, 136.

17 Aspey, 'Mrs Rothschild', 66.

18 'Arrivals and Departures', *The Times*,
22 June 1824.

19 Hannah to Nathan Mayer
Rothschild, n.d.: RAL 000/10.

20 Ireland, *Plutocrats*, 59–60.

21 Dorothy Wordsworth, *The Journals
of Dorothy Wordsworth*, ed. William
Knight (London: Macmillan, 1897),
188.

22 Ireland, *Plutocrats*, 65.

23 Hannah to Nathan Mayer, n.d.:
RAL 000/10/110; ibid., 'Sunday
morning 6 o'clock': RAL 000/848.

24 Ibid., 8 July 1824: RAL 000/848.

25 Ferguson, *World's Banker*, 199.

26 Countess Harriet Granville, *Letters
of Harriet Countess Granville:
1810–1845*, ed. F. Leveson-Gower, vol.
1 (London: Longmans, Green & Co.,
1894), 243, 322.

27 Rodolphe Apponyi, *Vingt-cinq
ans à Paris, 1826–1850: journal du
comte Rodolphe Apponyi, attaché de
l'ambassade d'Autriche-Hongrie à
Paris, publié par Ernest Daudet*, vol. 1,
1826–30 (Paris: Plon-Nourrit, 1913),
6–9; Lady Sydney Morgan, *France in
1829–30*, vol. 2 (London: Saunders &
Otley, 1830), 415.

28 James to Salomon and Nathan, 11 March 1817: RAL XI/109/6 (also T27/219).

29 Ferguson, *World's Banker*, 197.

30 Carol Kennedy, *Mayfair: A Social History* (London: Hutchinson, 1986), 13, 68; Lucy Inglis, *Georgian London: Into the Streets* (London: Viking, 2013), 210.

31 Pückler-Muskau, *Tour in Germany, Holland and England*, 52–3.

32 Gerry Black, *Living Up West* (London: London Museum of Jewish Life, 1994), 15.

33 Hannah to Lionel and Anthony, 7 January 1826: RAL 000/848; Ireland, *Plutocrats*, 73.

34 *Morning Post*, 21 May 1829.

35 'Mrs de Rothschild's Ball', *Morning Post*, 4 June 1829.

36 Hannah to Charlotte, 26 August 1844: RAL 000/10/42.

37 S.M. Pennell, 'Gunter, James (bap. 1745, d. 1819), confectioner', *ODNB*, 23 September 2004.

38 Laura Mason, 'William Alexis Jarrin and the Italian Confectioner', in *The English Cookery Book: Historical Essays*, ed. E. White (Totnes: Prospect Books, 2004), 156; Pennell, 'Gunter, James'; William Jarrin, *The Italian Confectioner* (London: Ebers & Co., 1844), 43.

39 Jarrin, *Italian Confectioner*, xix, xxviii, xxix, 144.

40 *Morning Post*, 3 July 1829 and 9 July 1828.

41 'Mrs de Rothschild's Ball', *Morning Post*, 4 June 1829.

42 Mason, 'William Alexis Jarrin', 159.

43 Ireland, *Plutocrats*, 55.

44 Charlotte Moscheles, *Life of Moscheles*, ed. A.D. Coleridge, vol. 1 (London: Hurst & Blackett, 1873), 58; Ireland, *Plutocrats*, 55; Herbert Weinstock, *Rossini: A Biography*

(London: Oxford University Press, 1968), 137.

45 Moscheles, *Life of Moscheles*, 222.

46 Ibid., 224.

47 Ibid., 217.

48 Ferguson, *World's Banker*, 364–5.

49 Moscheles, *Life of Moscheles*, 219.

50 Mason, 'William Alexis Jarrin', 172.

51 *Public Ledger and Daily Advertiser*, 28 April 1824; *London Courier and Evening Gazette*, 14 February 1829; *Morning Post*, 18 April 1829; *Sligo Journal*, 1 July 1831; *Morning Post*, 7 March 1828.

52 Gerry Black, *JFS: The History of the Jews' Free School, London, since 1732* (London: Tymsder, 1998), 15.

53 Black, *JFS*, 35, 38–9.

54 Ibid., 38.

55 Ibid., 40.

56 'Donations received in aid of the fund of the Jews' Free School': London Metropolitan Archives (hereafter LMA) LMA/4046/B/04/002.

57 'Minute book': LMA LMA/4046/A/01/002; Black, *JFS*, 59.

58 Black, *JFS*, 59.

59 Tristan, *London Journal*, 142.

60 Ferguson, *World's Banker*, 158.

61 Syndicated in *Exeter and Plymouth Gazette*, 25 July 1829.

62 Ferguson, *World's Banker*, 171–2; *Allgemeine Deutsche Real-Encyklopädie für die gebildeten Stände* (Leipzig: F.A. Brockhaus, 1827).

63 Friedrich von Gentz, 'Biographische Nachrichten über das Haus Rothschild', in *Schriften von Friedrich von Gentz. Ein Denkmal. Bund 5: Ungedruckte Tagebücher, Denkschriften und Briefe*, ed. Gustav Schlesier (Mannheim: Heinrich Hoff, 1840), 119; Ferguson, *World's Banker*, 113.

CHAPTER 8:
Betrayal

1 Ferguson, *World's Banker*, 136; *The Times*, 15 January 1821.

2 Edward Royle, *Robert Owen and the Commencement of the Millennium* (Manchester: Manchester University Press, 1998), 22; Robert Owen, *Robert Owen: A New View of Society and Other Writings*, ed. Gregory Claeys (London: Penguin Classics, 1991), ix.

3 Robert Owen, *The Life of Robert Owen by Himself* (London: G. Bell & Sons, 1920), 291.

4 Robert Owen to Hannah Rothschild, 1828: RAL XI/109/11/8/64 (also in T17).

5 Roth, *History of the Jews*, 172.

6 Ibid., 215.

7 Jacob Katz, *Out of the Ghetto: The Social Background of Jewish Emancipation, 1770–1870* (New York: Schocken, 1978), 384.

8 Ian Machin, 'British Catholics', in *The Emancipation of Catholics, Jews and Protestants: Minorities and the Nation State in Nineteenth-Century Europe*, ed. Rainer Liedtke and Stephan Wendehorst (Manchester: Manchester University Press, 1999), 15.

9 Geoffrey Alderman, *The Jewish Community in British Politics* (Oxford: Clarendon Press, 1983), 18.

10 Katz, *Out of the Ghetto*, 384.

11 Green, *Moses Montefiore*, 86.

12 Ibid.

13 Montefiore and Montefiore, *Diaries*, 1: 60.

14 Ibid., 1: 62, 65.

15 Ibid., 1: 66.

16 Green, *Moses Montefiore*, 87–8; Montefiore and Montefiore, *Diaries*, 1: 61.

17 Ibid.

18 Green, *Moses Montefiore*, 91.

19 Montefiore and Montefiore, *Diaries*, 1: 71.

20 Ibid.

21 *Morning Post*, 4 June 1829 and 22 June 1829.

22 Montefiore and Montefiore, *Diaries*, 1: 78.

23 Ibid., 1: 78–9.

24 Owen, *Life of Owen*, 291; Green, *Moses Montefiore*, 92.

25 Montefiore and Montefiore, *Diaries*, 1: 79.

26 Green, *Moses Montefiore*, 92.

27 Duke of Wellington, Arthur Wellesley, Speech to the House of Lords, 1 August 1833: *Parliamentary Debates*, Lords, vol. 20, cc221–55.

28 Wolf, 'Rothschildiana', 276.

29 Souvenirs du Docteur Schlemmer, 14: RAL 000/924/2/8.

CHAPTER 9:
The Financial Prowess of Mrs Rothschild

1 Ireland, *Plutocrats*, 57.

2 Ferguson, *World's Banker*, 312–13.

3 Hannah to Lionel, n.d.: RAL 000/10/73.

4 Ibid.

5 Ibid., August 1828: RAL 000/10/72.

6 Ann M. Carlos, Karen Maguire and Larry Neal, 'Financial Acumen, Women Speculators, and the Royal African Company during the South Sea Bubble', Mark Freeman, Robin Pearson and James Taylor, '"A Doe in the City": Women Shareholders in Eighteenth- and Early Nineteenth-Century Britain', and Anne Laurence, 'Women Investors, "That Nasty South Sea Affair" and the Rage to Speculate in Early Eighteenth-Century England', *Accounting, Business and Financial*

History, 16, 2 (July 2006): 222, 268 and 245 respectively.

7 Bodleian Libraries, University of Oxford (hereafter BOD), Leopold Muller Memorial Library, Arthur Sebag-Montefiore Archive, MontA Pre422; Wolf, 'Lady Montefiore's Honeymoon', 243–4; Ferguson, *World's Banker*, 126; Salomon [& Caroline] to Nathan, Hannah and Davidson, 16 August 1816: RAL XI/109/5A, 5B (also T32/125/2).

8 Pamela Pilbeam, *The Constitutional Monarchy in France 1814–48* (London: Longman, 2000), 32–4.

9 Ireland, *Plutocrats*, 96.

10 Ibid., 97; Lionel to Nathan Mayer and Hannah, 30 July 1830: RAL XI/109/15/1/1.

11 Ireland, *Plutocrats*, 97–8; Lionel to Nathan Mayer and Hannah, 31 July 1830: RAL XI/109/27/1/1.

12 Ernest Feydeau, *Mémoires d'un coulissier* (Paris: Librairie nouvelle, 1873), 133.

13 Hannah to Nathan Mayer, 25 August 1830: RAL 000/10/119.

14 Ibid., 24 August 1830: RAL 000/10/118.

15 Ibid., 25 August 1830: RAL 000/10/119.

16 Freeman, Pearson and Taylor, '"A Doe in the City"', 281.

17 Ibid., 265.

18 Wolf, 'Lady Montefiore's Honeymoon', 243–4.

19 Hannah to Nathan Mayer, 25 August 1830: RAL 000/10/119.

20 Ibid., 24 August 1830: RAL 000/10/118; 25 August 1830: RAL 000/10/119; 27 August 1830: RAL 000/10/120; 31 August 1830: RAL 000/10/121.

21 Ibid., 24 August 1830: RAL 000/10/118.

22 David H. Pinkney, *The French Revolution of 1830* (Princeton, NJ:

Princeton University Press, 1972), 179.

23 Hannah to Nathan Mayer, 31 August 1830: RAL 000/10/121.

24 Ibid.

25 *Morning Advertiser*, 17 January 1831.

26 Ireland, *Plutocrats*, 147; Hannah, Hannah Mayer and Lionel to Nathan Mayer, 9 January 1833: RAL XI/109/1/82.

27 Hannah to Nathan Mayer, 19 January 1830: RAL 000/10/130.

28 *London Courier and Evening Gazette*, 25 February 1831.

29 Hannah to Nathan Mayer, n.d.: RAL 000/10/137.

30 Hannah to Anthony, 1831: RAL 000/10/131.

31 Ibid., 11 August 1831: RAL 000/10/133.

32 Hannah to Nathan Mayer, 11 September 1831: RAL 000/10/134.

33 Ibid., 5 September 1831: RAL 000/10/136.

CHAPTER 10:
A Wedding and a Funeral

1 Charles C.F. Greville, *The Greville Memoirs: A Journal of the Reign of Queen Victoria from 1837 to 1852*, ed. Henry Reeve, vol. 2 (London: Longmans, Green & Co., 1885), 171, 173–4; Charlotte to Louisa, 21 August 1844: British Library, London (hereafter BL), Add MS 47948, fos. 103–9.

2 Belli-Gontard, *Lebens-Erinnerungen*, 283; Elizabeth Gurney, *Elizabeth Fry's Journeys on the Continent 1840–1841 From a Diary Kept by Her Niece Elizabeth Gurney*, ed. R. Brimley Johnson (London: John Lane, 1931), 96.

3 Gutle to Salomon and Jacob, n.d.: RAL XI/82/10/18 (also in T[a]29).

4 Clara Crowninshield, *Diary: A European Tour with Longfellow, 1835–1836*, ed. Andrew Hilen (Seattle, WA: University of Washington Press, 1956), 233; Greville, *Memoirs*, 171.

5 Greville, *Memoirs*, 171, 173.

6 Gurney, *Elizabeth's Fry's Journeys*, 96.

7 Greville, *Memoirs*, 173–4.

8 Chilly to Hannah, 28 November 1831: RAL XI/109/18/1/44; Ireland, *Plutocrats*, 158.

9 Chilly to Hannah, 9 December 1831: RAL XI/109/23/1/24.

10 Henrietta to Hannah, n.d.: RAL XI/109/26/1/43 (also T22/221); Ireland, *Plutocrats*, 158.

11 Lionel to Anthony, 21 March 1835: RAL XI/109/33/1/6 (also T22/688).

12 Hannah to Charlotte, 29 September 1835: RAL 000/10/1.

13 Ibid., 24 October 1835: RAL 000/10/2.

14 Hannah to Nathaniel, 1 June 1836: RAL 000/10/54.

15 Ibid., [1836]: RAL 000/10/57.

16 Ibid.

17 Lionel to Nathaniel, 11 June 1836: RAL 000/27; Hannah to Nathaniel, 16 June 1836: RAL 000/10/62.

18 Lionel to Anthony and Nathaniel, 13 June 1836: RAL 000/27.

19 Hannah to Anthony, 14 June 1836: RAL 000/10/60.

20 Hannah to Nathaniel, 16 June 1836: RAL 000/10/62; June 1836: RAL XI/109/34/1/1 (also in T23); June 1836: RAL 000/10/61; Ireland, *Plutocrats*, 10.

21 Lionel to Anthony and Nathaniel, 15 June 1836: RAL 000/27.

22 Schlemmer to Nathaniel, 16 June 1836: RAL XI/109/34/1/6; Ireland, *Plutocrats*, 9.

23 Hannah to Nathaniel, June 1836: RAL 000/10/63; June 1836: RAL 000/10/61.

24 Ibid., June 1836: RAL 000/10/63.

25 Ibid.

26 Hannah to Anthony and Nathaniel, 1 July 1836: RAL 000/10/67.

27 Stanley Weintraub, *Charlotte and Lionel: A Rothschild Love Story* (London: Simon & Schuster, 2003), 38.

28 Hannah to Nathaniel, 27 June 1836: RAL 000/10/65.

29 *London Evening Standard*, 3 August 1836.

30 Weintraub, *Charlotte and Lionel*, 38; Ferguson, *World's Banker*, 315.

31 Ireland, *Plutocrats*, 14; Lionel to Nathaniel, 26 July 1836: RAL 000/13/149.

32 Corti, *Rise of the House of Rothschild*, 150.

33 Ferguson, *World's Banker*, 316.

34 Corti, *Rise of the House of Rothschild*, 151.

35 Ibid., 153; Ferguson, *World's Banker*, 316.

36 Montefiore and Montefiore, *Diaries*, 1: 103.

37 Weintraub, *Charlotte and Lionel*, 42; *London Courier and Evening Gazette*, 3 August 1836.

38 *Public Ledger and Daily Advertiser*, 8 August 1836.

39 *The Globe*, 1 August 1836; *Evening Standard*, 1 August 1836; *The Times*, 2 August 1836.

40 Ferguson, *World's Banker*, 317–18; *The Times*, 4 August 1836; *Bell's Life in London and Sporting Chronicle*, 7 August 1836.

41 *Souvenirs du Docteur Schlemmer*, 20: RAL 000/924/2/8; Walter Thornbury, *Old and New London: A Narrative of its History, its People, and its Places*, vol. 1 (London: Cassell, Petter & Galpin, 1879), 491.

42 '"The Rothschilds", from Mr MacGregor's New Work "My Notebook"', *Morning Herald*, 5 August 1836.

43 Anon., *The Hebrew Talisman* (London: W. Whaley, 1840).

44 Ferguson, *World's Banker*, 321; Weintraub, *Charlotte and Lionel*, 44.

45 Ferguson, *World's Banker*, 321–2.

46 'Death of Mr. Rothschild and Sketch of His Financial Life', *The Times*, 4 August 1836. Niall Ferguson suggests that this obituary, which was widely syndicated, was the work of Thomas Massa Alsager: see Ferguson, *World's Banker*, 318.

47 Rainer Erb, 'The "Damascus Affair", 1840', in Heuberger, ed., *Rothschilds*, 101.

48 *London Evening Standard*, 9 August 1836.

49 Weintraub, *Charlotte and Lionel*, 44.

50 Davis, *English Rothschilds*, 51.

51 *Morning Advertiser*, 21 September 1836.

52 This history entered family memory, albeit in a slightly hazy form: one of Hannah's granddaughters, Constance, Lady Battersea, commented that Hannah's house 'had been a royal residence, belonging to the daughter of George III [*sic*]': see Battersea, *Reminiscences*, 8.

53 Ireland, *Plutocrats*, 155.

54 Henry Harrison to Hannah Rothschild, 1 July 1835: RAL 000/848; Mr Rainy to Hannah Rothschild, 1 July 1835: RAL 000/848; Ireland, *Plutocrats*, 154–5.

55 Bridget Cherry and Nikolaus Pevsner, *Buildings of England, London 3: North West* (New Haven, CT, and London: Yale University Press, 2002), 418.

56 Ireland, *Plutocrats*, 156; Hannah to Nathaniel, 17 July 1836: RAL 000/10/68.

57 *Bell's New Weekly Messenger*, 13 November 1836.

58 Davis, *English Rothschilds*, 51.

59 Cherry and Pevsner, *Buildings of England, London 3: North West*, 419.

CHAPTER II:
'This World of Fog and Cares'

1 Weintraub, *Charlotte and Lionel*, 2.

2 Ibid., 32–3.

3 Lionel to Charlotte, 19 February 1835: RAL 000/13.

4 Ibid., 7 January 1836.

5 Schlemmer to Nathaniel, 16 June 1836: RAL XI/109/34/1/6; Ireland, *Plutocrats*, 9.

6 Ireland, *Plutocrats*, 9; Lionel to Anthony and Nathaniel, 17 June 1836: RAL, 000/27.

7 Ireland, *Plutocrats*, 9.

8 Lionel to Anthony and Nathaniel, 17 June 1836: RAL 000/27.

9 Dieter Bartetzko, 'Fairy Tales & Castles: On Rothschild Family Buildings in Frankfurt on Main', in Heuberger, ed., *Rothschilds*, 225.

10 Stanley Chapman, 'The Establishment of the Rothschilds as Bankers in London', in Heuberger, ed., *Rothschilds*, 80–1.

11 Charlotte to Leopold, 25 January 1867: RAL 000/84/4.

12 Ireland, *Plutocrats*, 104.

13 Moritz Oppenheim, *Erinnerungen*, ed. Alfred Oppenheim (Frankfurt am Main: Frankfurter Verlags-Anstalt AG, 1924), 46–7.

14 Weintraub, *Charlotte and Lionel*, 21.

15 Battersea, *Reminiscences*, 23.

16 Hannah to Nathaniel, June 1836: RAL 000/10/61; 27 June 1836: RAL 000/10/65.

17 Lionel to Charlotte, 1 March 1836: RAL 000/13.

18 Ireland, *Plutocrats*, 166.

19 Louisa Montefiore to Louise de
Rothschild, 25 March 1834: BL Add
MS 47948, fos. 69–70.

20 Weintraub, *Charlotte and Lionel*, 49.

21 Ibid., 53.

22 Davis, *English Rothschilds*, 62.

23 Weintraub, *Charlotte and Lionel*, 55.

24 Hannah to Charlotte, 1837: RAL
000/10/50; Ireland, *Plutocrats*, 167;
Weintraub, *Charlotte and Lionel*, 56.

25 Weintraub, *Charlotte and Lionel*, 58.

26 Ireland, *Plutocrats*, 167.

27 Benjamin Disraeli to Sarah Disraeli,
15 February 1838, cited in *Benjamin
Disraeli Letters, Volume III: 1838–1841*,
ed. M.G. Wiebe et al. (Toronto:
University of Toronto Press, 1987),
21–2, letter 729.

28 Aspey, 'Mrs. Rothschild', 65.

29 This process had begun several
months earlier: in May 1837, when
Charlotte was six months pregnant
with Laurie, her mother-in-law
had taken her and Lionel down to
Brighton, a place that offered, so far
as she was concerned, the perfect
mixture of restorative air and elite
sociability: see *Morning Post*, 15 May
1837.

30 Weintraub, *Charlotte and Lionel*, 60.

31 Journal of Queen Victoria, 21 June
1838: Royal Archives, Windsor
(hereafter RAW), Journal of Queen
Victoria, Lord Esher's typescripts, 6:
60–1.

32 Charles Greville, *Greville's England:
Selections from the Diaries of Charles
Greville, 1818–60*, ed. Christopher
Hibbert (London: Folio Society,
1981), 157.

33 Ireland, *Plutocrats*, 191.

CHAPTER 12:
Marrying Out

1 Battersea, *Reminiscences*, 54; Robert
Henrey, *A Century Between* (London:
W. Heinemann, 1937), 2–3; Ferguson,
World's Banker, 364.

2 Hannah to Charlotte, 24 October
1835: RAL 000/10/2.

3 Battersea, *Reminiscences*, 4.

4 Ibid., 3.

5 Benjamin Disraeli to Sarah Disraeli,
26 March 1839, cited in Wiebe et al.,
eds., *Letters: 1838–1841*, 160, letter 910.

6 Cohen, *Lady de Rothschild*, 10–11.

7 Hannah Mayer to Nathaniel, 12
June 1836: RAL XI/109/34/1/1 (also
T23/59).

8 Hannah to Anthony, 1836: RAL
000/10/64.

9 Martin Casey and Philip Salmon,
'FITZROY, Hon. Henry (1807–
1859), of 24 Chapel Street, Mdx',
History of Parliament, http://
www.historyofparliamentonline.
org/volume/1820-1832/member/
fitzroy-hon-henry-1807-1859.

10 'Mrs. Wyndham Lewis's Dejeuner',
Morning Post, 11 July 1835.

11 Henrey, *Century Between*, 6.

12 Ibid., 22.

13 Ibid., 24.

14 Ibid., 26.

15 Ibid., 36.

16 Ibid., 43.

17 Ibid., 68.

18 Ibid.

19 Ibid.

20 Ireland, *Plutocrats*, 171.

21 Ferguson, *World's Banker*, 338;
Weintraub, *Charlotte and Lionel*, 70.

22 Henrey, *Century Between*, 69;
Battersea, *Reminiscences*, 54.

23 Ferguson, *World's Banker*, 338.

24 Ibid.

25 Henrey, *Century Between*, 70–2;
Battersea, *Reminiscences*, 54.

26 Queen Victoria's Journal, Thursday, 28 March 1839, in Lord Esher's typescript, vol. 9, p. 194, www.queenvictoriasjournals.org.

27 *The Times*, 18 May 1839.

28 James to Nathaniel, 29 June 1839: RAL XI/101/2/2/34 (also T35/34).

29 Ferguson, *World's Banker*, 339.

30 Anthony to his brothers, 17 July 1839: RAL T7/9.

31 Hannah to Nathaniel, 19 May 1839: RAL 000/10/83.

CHAPTER 13:
Marrying In

1 Journal of Louisa, Lady de Rothschild, 29 July 1837: BL Add MS 47949.

2 Ibid., 2 June 1838.

3 Benjamin Disraeli to Sarah Disraeli, 28 March 1839, cited in Wiebe et al., eds., *Disraeli Letters: 1838–1841*, 160, letter 911.

4 Battersea, *Reminiscences*, 12.

5 'Pugilism in France', *Bradford Observer*, 17 January 1839.

6 Ireland, *Plutocrats*, 197, 221.

7 Ferguson, *World's Banker*, 199.

8 James to Amschel, 11 July 1839: RAL XI/101/2/2/36 (also T35/36).

9 Anthony to his brothers, 11 July: RAL XI/103/0/38 (also T25/38).

10 James to his nephews, 19 November 1839: RAL XI/101/2/6/77 (also T35/77).

11 Ireland, *Plutocrats*, 119.

12 Ibid., 175–6.

13 Cohen, *Lady de Rothschild*, 14–15.

14 Ibid., 13.

15 Anthony to Louisa, 4 January 1840: BL Add MS 47948, fos. 83–4.

16 Cohen, *Lady de Rothschild*, 17.

17 Ibid.

18 Ibid., 15.

19 Ibid., 19.

20 Ibid., 15.

21 Ibid.

22 Ibid., 20.

23 Journal of Louisa, Lady de Rothschild, 7 October 1840: BL Add MS 47949.

24 Ibid., 25 September 1841.

CHAPTER 14:
'The Management of Infancy'

1 Charlotte's 'Journal on Evelina': RAL, 000/1067.

2 Charlotte's 'Journal on Natty': RAL, 000/1067.

3 Hannah to Nathaniel, n.d.: RAL 000/10/85; Hannah to Lionel, 15 September 1842: RAL 000/10/168; Hannah to Louisa, 2 August [no year]: RAL, 000/297; Charlotte to Louisa, 10 September 1845: RAL 000/297/2/33; Henrey, *Century Between*, 92.

4 Henrey, *Century Between*, 77.

5 Louise to Louisa, 17 March 1843: RAL 000/41.

6 Ibid.

7 Hannah to Charlotte, 30 April 1843: RAL 000/10/29.

8 Battersea, *Reminiscences*, 13.

9 Louisa to Anthony, 22 April 1843: BL Add MS 47948, fos. 95–6.

10 Weintraub, *Charlotte and Lionel*, 90; Charlotte to Louisa, 10 September 1845: RAL 000/297/2/33.

11 Weintraub, *Charlotte and Lionel*, 90.

12 Charlotte to Louisa, 10 September 1845: RAL 000/297/2/33.

13 Weintraub, *Charlotte and Lionel*, 90.

CHAPTER 15:
A Muse

1 Charlotte to Lionel, n.d.: RAL XI/109/69B/2/68 (also T8/74–5).

2 P.T. Barnum, *Barnum's Own Story: The Autobiography of P.T. Barnum* (Gloucester: Peter Smith, 1972), 141; *Era*, Sunday, 28 April 1844, 6.

3 Weintraub, *Charlotte and Lionel*, 93–4.

4 K.D. Reynolds, 'Politics Without Feminism: The Victorian Political Hostess', in *Wollstonecraft's Daughters: Womanhood in England and France, 1780–1920*, ed. C.C. Orr (Manchester: Manchester University Press, 1996), 98; Weintraub, *Charlotte and Lionel*, 64.

5 Montefiore and Montefiore, *Diaries*, 1: 3–4.

6 Heidi Kaufman, *English Origins, Jewish Discourse, and the Nineteenth-Century Novel* (University Park, PA: Pennsylvania State University Press, 2009), 82.

7 Adam Kirsch, *Benjamin Disraeli* (New York: Schocken, 2008), 12.

8 Benjamin Disraeli to Sarah Disraeli, 9 December 1839, cited in Wiebe et al., eds., *Disraeli Letters: 1838–1841*, 238, letter 1013.

9 'Fete at Gunnersbury Park', *The Times*, 22 July 1843.

10 William Flavelle Monypenny, *The Life of Benjamin Disraeli, Earl of Beaconsfield*, vol. 2 (New York: Macmillan Company, 1912), 183.

11 Charlotte de Rothschild to Mary Anne Disraeli, [1846]: BOD Department of Special Collections, Dep. Hughenden 191/3, fos. 17–18.

12 Robert Blake, *Disraeli* (London: Oxford University Press, 1969), 171.

13 'Mr Disraeli's Coningsby', *Morning Post*, 21 June 1844.

14 Michael Ragussis, *Figures of Conversion: 'The Jewish Question' and English National Identity* (Durham, NC: Duke University Press, 1995), 185.

15 Benjamin Disraeli, *Coningsby, or, The New Generation*, book 7 (London: Bradenham, 1927), 98.

16 Ibid., 263.

17 'Young England Philosophy', *Morning Post*, 18 August 1845.

18 Charlotte von Rothschild to Benjamin Disraeli, [1844]: BOD Dept of Special Collections, Dep. Hughenden 233/2, fos. 33–4.

19 Charlotte to Nathaniel and Leopold, 3 January 1860; Charlotte to Leopold, 19 January 1861; Charlotte to Leonora and Leopold, 6 August 1862; Charlotte to Leonora and Leopold, 3 September 1862: all RAL 000/84/1.

20 Charlotte von Rothschild to Benjamin Disraeli, [1844]: BOD Dept of Special Collections, Dep. Hughenden 233/2, fos. 166–7.

21 John Cam Hobhouse Broughton, *Recollections of a Long Life*, ed. Lady Dorchester, vol. 6 (London: John Murray, 1909), 114–16.

22 Ibid., 114.

23 Blake, *Disraeli*, 18.

24 Ireland, *Plutocrats*, 236.

25 David Cesarani, *Disraeli: The Novel Politician* (New Haven, CT: Yale University Press, 2016), 89.

26 Battersea, *Reminiscences*, 45.

27 Charlotte to Leopold and Leonora, 8 August 1862: RAL 000/84/1; Charlotte to Leopold, 15 February 1864; Charlotte to Leopold, 26 February 1865; Charlotte to Leopold, 19 May 1865; Charlotte to Leopold, 11 December 1865: all RAL 000/84/2; Charlotte to Leopold, 7 February 1866: RAL 000/84/3.

28 Charlotte to Leopold, 11 December 1865 and 26 February 1865: RAL 000/84/2.

29 Battersea, *Reminiscences*, 45.
30 Daisy Hay, *Mr and Mrs Disraeli: A Strange Romance* (London: Chatto & Windus, 2015), 138.
31 Ibid.
32 Cohen, *Lady de Rothschild*, 30.
33 Louisa de Rothschild to Benjamin Disraeli, n.d.: BOD Dept of Special Collections, Dep. Hughenden 234/1, fos. 10–11.
34 Michal Shahaf, 'Charlotte Montefiore's Secret: The Cheap Jewish Library – An Educational Philanthropic Mission', *Nashim: A Journal of Jewish Women's Studies and Gender Issues*, 30 (Spring 2016): 49.
35 Ragussis, *Figures of Conversion*, 15; Linda Gertner Zatlin, *The Nineteenth-Century Anglo-Jewish Novel* (Boston, MA: Twayne, 1981), 21.
36 Shahaf, 'Charlotte Montefiore's Secret', 49.
37 Charlotte Montefiore to Rev. J.D.A. De Sola, n.d.: LMA LMA/4521/C/01/01/011, fo. 73.
38 Grace Aguilar to Rev. J.D.A. De Sola, n.d.: LMA LMA/4521/C/01/01/011, fo. 78.
39 *Caleb Asher*, The Jewish Miscellany series no. 1 (Philadelphia: Jewish Publication Society of America, 1845); Zatlin, *Anglo-Jewish Novel*, 58–9.
40 'America', *Jewish Chronicle*, 19 June 1846.
41 'Review: The Cheap Jewish Library', *Jewish Chronicle*, 17 August 1849.
42 Weintraub, *Charlotte and Lionel*, 98.
43 Benjamin Disraeli, *Tancred, or The New Crusade* (London: John Lane, the Bodley Head, 1927), 141–2.
44 Journal of Louisa, Lady de Rothschild, 4 July 1847: BL Add MS 47950.

CHAPTER 16:
'Surely We Do Not Deserve So Much Hatred'

1 John Thadeus Delane, *John Thadeus Delane: Editor of 'The Times'. His Life and Correspondence*, ed. Arthur Irwin Dasent (London: John Murray, 1908), 65.
2 Ibid.
3 *The Times*, 28 June 1847.
4 M.C.N. Salbstein, *The Emancipation of the Jews in Britain: The Question of the Admission of the Jews to Parliament, 1828–1860* (Rutherford, NJ: Fairleigh Dickinson University Press, 1982), 142.
5 *The Times*, 30 June 1847.
6 [Moses Margoliouth], *The Anglo-Hebrews: Their Past Wrongs and Present Grievances* (London: L. Booth, 1856), 81.
7 'Meeting of Conservative Electors', *The Times*, 9 July 1847
8 'Money Market and City Intelligence', *The Times*, 30 July 1847; Journal of Louisa, Lady de Rothschild, 7 July 1847 and 15 July 1847: BL Add MS 47950.
9 Mace, 'From Frankfurt Jew to Lord Rothschild', 185.
10 Ibid.
11 Ibid., 184.
12 Ibid., 185.
13 Ibid., 183; Weintraub, *Charlotte and Lionel*, 96.
14 Hannah to Lionel, [1846]: RAL 000/10/99.
15 Ibid., [1847]: RAL 000/10/114.
16 Ibid.
17 Journal of Louisa, Lady de Rothschild, 29 July 1847: BL Add MS 47950.
18 'Election Details', *Examiner*, 31 July 1847.
19 'The Elections', *Daily News*, 31 July 1847.

20 'The General Election', *The Times*, 31 July 1847; 'Election of Lord Mayor', *Illustrated London News*, 7 October 1843.

21 'The General Election', *The Times*, 31 July 1847.

22 Delane, *John Thadeus Delane*, 67.

23 Journal of Louisa, Lady de Rothschild, 31 July 1847: BL Add MS 47950.

24 Betty to unknown, 4 August 1847: RAL T7/128.

25 Charlotte to Lionel, n.d.: RAL T7/129.

26 Louise to Lionel, 2 August 1847: RAL T7/127.

27 Journal of Louisa, Lady de Rothschild, 16 December 1847: BL Add MS 47950.

28 Lord John Russell, Speech to the House of Commons, 16 December 1847, *Parliamentary Debates*, Commons, vol. 95, cc1234–49.

29 Sir R.H. Inglis, Speech to the House of Commons, 16 December 1847, *Parliamentary Debates*, Commons, vol. 95, cc1249–65.

30 See Benjamin Disraeli, *Benjamin Disraeli Letters: 1838–1841*, ed. M.G. Wiebe, J.B. Conacher, John Matthews, and Mary S. Millar, vol. 4 (Toronto: University of Toronto Press, 1989), 319f.

31 Cesarani, *Disraeli*, 119; Benjamin Disraeli, Speech to the House of Commons, 16 December 1847, *Parliamentary Debates*, Commons, vol. 95, cc1321–30.

32 Ferguson, *World's Banker*, 540.

33 Weintraub, *Charlotte and Lionel*, 111.

34 Bishop of Oxford, Samuel Wilberforce, Speech to the House of Commons, 25 May 1848, *Parliamentary Debates*, Lords, vol. 98, cc1370–82.

35 Judith and Sir Moses Montefiore, *Diaries of Sir Moses and Lady Montefiore*, vol. 2, ed. L. Loewe (London: Griffith, Farran, & Co., 1890), 10.

36 Journal of Louisa, Lady de Rothschild, 30 May 1848: BL Add MS 47951.

37 Ferguson, *World's Banker*, 542.

38 Montefiore and Montefiore, *Diaries*, 2: 10.

39 Ferguson, *World's Banker*, 542.

40 Journal of Louisa, Lady de Rothschild, 30 May 1848: BL Add MS 47951.

41 Nathaniel to Lionel and the London House, [1848]: RAL XI/109/65A/2/130.

CHAPTER 17:
The Great Abyss

1 Battersea, *Reminiscences*, 75.

2 Journal of Louisa, Lady de Rothschild, 28 February 1848: BL Add MS 47951.

3 Ibid.

4 Betty to Alphonse, 16 November 1848: RAL 000/930 (224).

5 Ibid., 29 November 1848.

6 Journal of Louisa, Lady de Rothschild, 28 February 1848: BL Add MS 47951.

7 Ibid., 'February 1848'.

8 Ferguson, *World's Banker*, 482.

9 Diary of Charlotte von Rothschild, 28 March 1848, quoted in Ferguson, *World's Banker*, 482.

10 David Goodway, *London Chartism, 1838–1848* (Cambridge: Cambridge University Press, 1982), 114.

11 Jonathan Sperber, *The European Revolutions, 1848–51* (Cambridge: Cambridge University Press, 1994), 122.

12 Journal of Louisa, Lady de Rothschild, 9 April 1848 and 10 April 1848: BL Add MS 47951.

13 Ireland, *Plutocrats*, 273.

14 Weintraub, *Charlotte and Lionel*, 109.

15 Davis, *English Rothschilds*, 137.

16 Weintraub, *Charlotte and Lionel*, 110.

17 Ferguson, *World's Banker*, 484.

18 Journal of Louisa, Lady de Rothschild, 6 August 1848: BL Add MS 47951.

19 Ibid., 8 August 1848.

20 Ibid., 15 August 1848.

21 William Makepeace Thackeray to Mrs Brookfield, 11 August 1848, cited in William Makepeace Thackeray, *A Collection of Letters of W.M. Thackeray, 1847–1855*, ed. William Henry Brookfield and Jane Octavia Brookfield (London: Smith & Elder, 1887), 18–21.

22 S.S. Prawer, *Israel at Vanity Fair: Jews and Judaism in the Writings of W.M. Thackeray* (Leiden: Brill, 1992), 72, 275; William Makepeace Thackeray, 'Travels in London', *Punch, or the London Charivari*, vol. 14, January–June 1848, 95.

23 Journal of Louisa, Lady de Rothschild, 15 August 1848: BL Add MS 47951.

24 Ibid., 18 December 1848.

25 Ibid., 11 October 1848, 12 February 1849, 23 February 1849 and 26 March 1849.

26 WMT to Mrs Brookfield, 1–2 February 1849: letter 563 in William Makepeace Thackeray, *The Letters and Private Papers of William Makepeace Thackeray*, ed. Gordon N. Ray (Cambridge, MA: Harvard University Press, 1946), vol. 2, 493.

27 William Makepeace Thackeray, *The History of Pendennis* (London: R.E. King, 1893), 19.

28 Hans Christian Andersen, *A Picture-Book without Pictures: and Other Stories* (New York: J.B. Alden, 1883), 105.

29 Belli-Gontard, *Lebens-Erinnerungen*, 238.

30 Ferguson, *World's Banker*, 508.

31 Journal of Louisa, Lady de Rothschild, 12 May 1849: BL Add MS 47951; Betty to Alphonse, 10 May 1849: RAL Moscow 22.

32 Betty to Alphonse, 4 April 1849: RAL 000/930 (224).

33 Charlotte to Louisa, 1 August 1849: RAL 000/297/2.

34 Ibid., 25 September 1849.

35 Ibid., 1 August 1849.

36 Ibid.

37 Ibid.

38 Ibid., 14 August 1849.

39 Ibid., 18 October 1849.

40 Hannah to Anthony, 17 October 1849: RAL 000/297/2.

41 Charlotte to Louisa, 18 October 1849: RAL 000/297/2.

42 Journal of Louisa, Lady de Rothschild, 4 September 1849: BL Add MS 47951.

43 Charlotte to Louisa, August 1849: RAL 000/297/2/42.

44 Ibid., [14] October 1849: RAL 000/297/2/45.

45 Journal of Louisa, Lady de Rothschild, 4 September 1849: BL Add MS 47951.

46 Ibid., 28 February 1850: BL Add MS 47952.

47 Ibid., 3 March 1850.

48 Ibid., 17 March 1850 and 2 June 1850.

49 Ibid., 8 April 1851.

50 Ibid.

51 Ibid., 7 July 1847: BL Add MS 47950.

52 Henrey, *Century Between*, 82–3.

53 Ibid., 89, 92, 121.

54 Ibid., 156–7.

55 'Miscellaneous', *Essex Standard and General Advertiser for the Eastern Counties*, 11 November 1859; *Evening Standard*, 23 November 1859; *Morning Post*, 29 November 1859.

56 'Death of the Right Hon. H.
FitzRoy, M.P., For Lewes', *Evening
Standard*, 20 December 1859.

57 Diary of Lady Battersea, 9
November 1858: BL Add MS 47913.

CHAPTER 18:
Loopholes and Legacies

1 Weintraub, *Charlotte and Lionel*,
115.

2 *Morning Chronicle*, 21 March 1850;
'The Parliamentary Oath', *Jewish
Chronicle*, 3 May 1850.

3 'Imperial Parliament', *Morning
Chronicle*, 27 July 1850.

4 Lionel Nathan de Rothschild,
Oath to the House of Commons,
29 July 1850, *Parliamentary Debates*,
Commons, vol. 113, cc403–4.

5 Montefiore and Montefiore, *Diaries*,
2: 21.

6 Weintraub, *Charlotte and Lionel*, 122.

7 *The Times*, 31 July 1850.

8 Weintraub, *Charlotte and Lionel*,
125.

9 Journal of Louisa, Lady de
Rothschild, 18 September 1850: BL
Add MS 47952.

10 Ibid.

11 Weintraub, *Charlotte and Lionel*, 126.

12 Journal of Louisa, Lady de
Rothschild, 2 May 1851: BL Add MS
47952.

13 *The Great Exhibition of the Works and
Industry of all Nations, 1851: Official
Descriptive and Illustrated Catalogue*,
vol. 1 (London: Spicer Bros., 1851),
173–85.

14 Journal of Louisa, Lady de
Rothschild, 22 May 1851: BL Add
MS 47952.

15 Ibid., 22 May 1851, 1 June 1851 and 14
June 1851.

16 Ibid., 26 July 1850: BL Add MS
47951.

17 Ibid., 3 July 1852: BL Add MS 47952.

18 Ibid., 5 July 1847: BL Add MS 47950.

19 Ibid., 23 February 1852 and 2 March
1852: BL Add MS 47952.

20 Ibid., 10 July 1853.

21 Ibid., 'May 1852'.

22 Black, *JFS*, 50, 72, 106–7; S.L.
Bensusan, 'The Largest School in the
World', *Windsor Magazine* (October
1896).

23 Black, *JFS*, 107.

24 Ibid., 72.

25 Journal of Louisa, Lady de
Rothschild, 19 April 1888: BL Add
MS 47958.

26 Annie Thackeray, 'Little Scholars',
Cornhill Magazine (January–June
1860); Black, *JFS*, 87.

27 Diana Gulland, 'Aston Clinton
House, Buckinghamshire', *The
Rothschild Archive Review of the Year*,
Annual Review (2002–2003): 34,
https://www.rothschildarchive.org/
materials/ar2003_aston_clinton.pdf;
Ferguson, *World's Banker*, 553.

28 Journal of Louisa, Lady de
Rothschild, 23 May 1852: BL Add
MS 47952.

29 Ibid., 23 August 1853.

30 Ibid., 11 July 1847 and 5 May 1848: BL
Add MS 47950.

31 Battersea, *Reminiscences*, 11; Journal
of Louisa, Lady de Rothschild, 23
August 1853: BL Add MS 47952.

32 Ferguson, *World's Banker*, 555.

33 Martha B. Amory, *The Domestic and
Artistic Life of John Singleton Copley*
(New York: Kennedy Galleries,
1969), 419.

34 Journal of Louisa, Lady de
Rothschild, 4 December 1853: BL
Add MS 47952.

35 Gulland, 'Aston Clinton House', 34.

36 Journal of Louisa, Lady de
Rothschild, 16 May 1853: BL Add
MS 47952.

37 Ibid., 6 June 1853.

38 Battersea, *Reminiscences*, 25; Pamela L.R. Horn, 'The Buckinghamshire Straw Plait Trade in Victorian England', *Records of Bucks*, 19, 1 (1971): 47.

39 Battersea, *Reminiscences*, 14.

40 Ibid., 25–6.

41 Ibid., 26.

42 Ibid., 16.

43 Ibid., 7.

44 Journal of Louisa, Lady de Rothschild, 18 July 1854: BL Add MS 47952.

45 Ibid., 24 September 1854.

46 Ferguson, *World's Banker*, 547.

47 'Review. The Cheap Jewish Library. Dedicated to the working classes. Evenings in Judea, Parts I and II. London: Abrahams, Solomons, and all booksellers', *Jewish Chronicle*, 17 August 1849.

48 Ireland, *Plutocrats*, 326; Adele to Constance, 16 February 1859: RAL 000/297.

49 'Addresses to young children', *Jewish Chronicle*, 26 October 1860; Charlotte's 'Journal on Evelina': RAL, 000/1067.

50 'Middlesex Election', *Standard*, 31 March 1857; 'London Correspondence', *Leeds Mercury*, 2 April 1857.

51 'Middlesex – the Nomination', *Era*, 5 April 1857; *Daily News*, 3 April 1857; 'The General Election', *Morning Post*, 3 April 1857.

52 'Election Intelligence', *Daily News*, 3 April 1857.

53 Charlotte to Viscount Chelsea (draft), undated: RAL 000/84/5 (previously RFamC/21R.38).

54 'London Correspondence', *Leeds Mercury*, 2 April 1857; 'Middlesex Election', *Morning Chronicle*, 7 April 1857.

55 Weintraub, *Charlotte and Lionel*, 139–42.

56 *Era*, 15 March 1857; Leonora to Lionel and Charlotte, 13 March 1857: RAL

000/37 (previously RFamFP/17/1); Charlotte von Rothschild to Mary Anne Disraeli, March 1857: BOD Dept of Special Collections, Dep. Hughenden 191/3, fos. 188–9.

57 Weintraub, *Charlotte and Lionel*, 146; Leonora to Charlotte, 7 May 1858: RAL 000/37 (previously RFamFP/17/5).

58 Ferguson, *World's Banker*, 548.

59 *London Evening Standard*, 27 July 1858.

CHAPTER 19:
Living in Hotels

1 A. Black, *Black's Picturesque Guide to the English Lakes*, 11th edn (Edinburgh: Adam and Charles Black, 1861), 56.

2 Harriet Martineau, *Guide to Windermere: With Tours to the Neighbouring Lakes and Other Interesting Places* (Windermere: John Garnett, 1860), 105.

3 Charlotte to Leo, August 1861: RAL 000/84/1.

4 Charlotte to Lionel and children, 5 August 1861: RAL 000/84/1; Charlotte to Leo and Evelina, 6 August 1861: RAL 000/84/1.

5 Charlotte to Leo and Evelina, 14 August 1861: RAL 000/84/1.

6 Ibid., 16 August 1861.

7 Charlotte to Leo, 16 October 1861: RAL 000/84/1.

8 Ibid.

9 Ibid., 15 October 1861.

10 Ibid., 18 October 1861.

11 Ibid., 19 October 1861.

12 Ibid., 18 October 1861.

13 Ibid., 17 October 1861.

14 Ibid.

15 Ibid., 25 October 1861.

16 Ibid., 27 October 1861.

17 Ibid., 31 October 1861.

18 Ibid., 5 November 1861.
19 Ibid., 4 November 1861.
20 Ibid., 6 November 1861.
21 Ibid.
22 Ibid., 7 November 1861.
23 Ibid.
24 Ibid. and 15 November 1861.
25 Ibid. and 10 November 1861.
26 'Death of His Royal Highness the Prince Consort', *Morning Chronicle*, 16 December 1861; 'The Death of the Prince Consort', *Morning Chronicle*, 19 December 1861.
27 Charlotte to Nathaniel and Leo, 'Xmas day 1861': RAL 000/84/1.
28 Weintraub, *Charlotte and Lionel*, 169.
29 Charlotte to Leo and Laurie, 24 August 1862: RAL 000/84/1.
30 Charlotte to Leo, Laurie, and Nathaniel, 15 September 1862: RAL 000/84/1; Charlotte to Leo and Laurie, 31 August 1862: RAL 000/84/1.
31 Charlotte to Leo and Laurie, 27 August 1862: RAL 000/84/1.
32 Ibid., 31 August 1862 and 1 September 1862.
33 Charlotte to Leonora and Leopold, 28 August 1862: RAL 000/84/1.
34 Ibid., 31 August 1862 and 1 September 1862.
35 Ibid., 3 September 1862.
36 Ibid., 6 August 1862.
37 Charlotte to Leo and Laurie, 4 September 1862: RAL 000/84/1.
38 Weintraub, *Charlotte and Lionel*, 172.
39 *Builder*, 1 November 1862.
40 Charlotte to Leopold, 27 October 1863: RAL 000/84/1.
41 Ibid., 3 November 1863: RAL 000/84/1; 5 April 1864, April 1864 and 12 April 1864: RAL 000/84/2.
42 Ibid., 3 May 1864, 8 May 1864 and 17 May 1864: RAL 000/84/2.
43 Henrey, *Century Between*, 184.
44 Charlotte to Leopold, 9 May 1864: RAL 000/84/2.

45 Ibid., 1 June 1864 and 11 February 1864.
46 Ibid., 10 May 1864.
47 Charlotte to Leonora and Leopold, Frankfurt, 29 August 1862: RAL 000/84/1.
48 Charlotte to Leopold, 12 May 1864: RAL 000/84/2.
49 Ibid., 11 May 1864.
50 *Dundee Courier & Argus*, 4 July 1864.
51 Charlotte to Leopold, 30 July 1864: RAL 000/84/2.
52 Ibid., 26 July 1864.
53 Ibid., 21 July 1864, 10 August 1864, 17 August 1864 and 18 August 1864.
54 Ibid., 4 September 1864.
55 Ibid., 16 September 1864.
56 Ibid., 3 October 1864, 12 October 1864, 14 July 1864 and 5 November 1864.
57 Ibid., 26 August 1864.
58 Ibid., 23 November 1864.
59 Ibid., 27 October 1864 and 15 November 1864.
60 Ibid., 2 December 1864.
61 Ibid., 3 December 1864.
62 Ibid.
63 Ibid., 6 December 1864.

CHAPTER 20:
A Mother's Lesson

1 Charlotte's 'Journal on Evelina': RAL, 000/1067.
2 Charlotte Rothschild to Mary Anne Disraeli, 20 January 1865: BOD Dept of Special Collections, Dep. Hughenden 191/3, fos. 318–19.
3 Diary of Constance, Lady Battersea, 'Agenda pour 1861': BL Add MS 47914.
4 Ferdinand to Charlotte, 25 December 1863: RAL, 000/26.
5 Charlotte to Leopold, 1 March 1865, 3 February 1865, 4 February 1865, 5 February 1865, 8 February 1865,

11 February 1865 and 7 March 1865: RAL 000/84/2.

6 'Marriage of Miss Rothschild', *The Times*, 8 June 1865.

7 Charlotte to Leopold, 6 May 1865: RAL 000/84/2.

8 *The Times*, 6 May 1865.

9 Charlotte to Leopold, 6 May 1865: RAL 000/84/2; *The Times*, 6 May 1865.

10 Charlotte to Leopold, 6 February 1866: RAL 000/84/3.

11 *Morning Post*, 7 February 1866.

12 Journal of Louisa, Lady de Rothschild, 20 February 1849: BL Add MS 47951.

13 Charlotte to Leopold, 29 May 1864: RAL 000/84/2.

14 Ibid., 1 June 1866: RAL 000/84/3.

15 Ibid., 24 November 1865: RAL 000/84/2.

16 Ibid., 7 February 1866: RAL 000/84/3.

17 Ibid., 19 February 1866.

18 Ibid., 21 February 1866 and 22 February 1866.

19 Ibid., 12 March 1866, 22 March 1866, 21 April 1866 and 24 March 1866.

20 Ibid., 27 April 1866.

21 Ibid., 30 April 1866.

22 Ibid., 24 March 1866.

23 Ibid., 20 July 1866.

24 Ibid., 31 July 1866 and 23 July 1866.

25 Ibid., 24 September 1866.

26 Ibid., 24 July 1866.

27 Ibid., 30 July 1866.

28 Ibid., 24 July 1866.

29 Ibid., 20 August 1866.

30 Davis, *English Rothschilds*, 127; John Cooper, *The Unexpected Story of Nathaniel Rothschild* (London: Continuum, 2015), 36–7.

31 Weintraub, *Charlotte and Lionel*, 209.

32 Emma to Charlotte and Lionel, 21 September [1866]: RAL 000/33/4.

33 Evelina to Leo, 23 September 1866: RAL 000/23/122.

34 Ibid.

35 Charlotte to Leopold, 27 November 1866 and 29 November 1866: RAL 000/84/3.

36 Ibid., 26 November 1866.

37 Weintraub, *Charlotte and Lionel*, 208; *Globe*, 15 December 1866.

38 Diary of Constance, Lady Battersea, 4 December 1866: BL Add MS 47916.

39 Ibid., 5 December 1866.

40 Ibid., 6 December 1866.

41 Ferdinand to Constance, 19 December 1866: RAL 000/26.

42 Charlotte to Leopold, 1 January 1867: RAL 000/84/4.

43 Ibid., 16 January 1867.

44 Ibid., 5 January 1867, 12 January 1867 and 16 January 1867.

45 Ibid., 16 January 1867, 12 January 1867 and 5 January 1867.

46 Ibid., 2 January 1867.

47 Ibid., 17 December 1866: RAL 000/843/4; 14 January 1867: RAL 000/84/4

48 Ibid., 4 January 1867: RAL 000/84/4.

49 Ibid., 19 January 1867.

50 Ibid., 24 January 1867.

51 Ibid., 6 January 1867.

52 Ibid., 15 January 1867 and 16 January 1867.

53 Ibid., 23 January 1867.

54 Ibid., 16 January 1867.

55 [Charlotte Rothschild], *From January to December: A Book for Children* (London: Longmans, Green & Co., 1873).

56 Ibid., 320–4.

57 Ibid., 341.

58 Ibid., 343.

59 Weintraub, *Charlotte and Lionel*, 247–8.

CHAPTER 21:
Flirtations

1 Diary of Constance, Lady Battersea, 5 February 1865: BL Add MS 47915.

2 Ibid., 5 July 1858, 17 July 1858 and 29 June 1858: BL Add MS 47913.

3 Ibid., 12 July 1858.

4 Ibid., 2 August 1858.

5 Ibid., 31 July 1858, 2 August 1858 and 7 August 1858.

6 Ibid., 10 August 1858.

7 Ibid., 28 August 1858.

8 Ibid., 6 September 1858.

9 Ibid., 14 September 1858.

10 Ibid., 21 December 1858.

11 Ibid., 25 December 1858.

12 Diary of Hon. Mrs Annie Yorke, 26 December 1858: BL Add MS 47964.

13 Diary of Constance, Lady Battersea, 26 June 1861: BL Add MS 47913.

14 Ibid., 4 September 1861, 26 August 1861 and 'Agenda pour 1865'.

15 Battersea, *Reminiscences*, 124–5.

16 Diary of Constance, Lady Battersea, 7 February 1865: BL Add MS 47915.

17 Ibid., 21 February 1865.

18 Ibid., 21 March 1865.

19 Ibid., 27 March 1865.

20 Ibid., 28 March 1865.

21 Ibid., 10 April 1865.

22 Ibid., 1 June 1865.

23 Ibid., 1 June 1865.

24 Ibid., Lady Battersea, 29 May 1865.

25 Charlotte to Leopold, 13 September 1865: RAL 000/84/2.

26 Diary of Constance, Lady Battersea, 31 July 1865 and 1 August 1865: BL Add MS 47915.

27 Ibid., 2 August 1865.

28 Ibid., 3 August 1865.

29 Ibid., 4 August 1865.

30 'The Suicide on Hampstead-Heath', *Standard*, 10 November 1865; 'Shocking Suicide on Hampstead Heath', *Lloyd's Weekly Newspaper*, 12 November 1865; Charlotte to

Leopold, 8 November 1865: RAL 000/84/2.

31 Diary of Constance, Lady Battersea, 7 November 1865: BL Add MS 47915.

32 Ibid., 22 December 1865.

33 Elizabeth Philippa Biddulph, *Charles Philip Yorke, Fourth Earl of Hardwicke. A Memoir* (London: Smith, Elder & Co., 1910), 300.

34 Diaries of Constance, Lady Battersea, 3 November 1867: BL Add MS 47917.

35 Ibid., 22 December 1867.

36 Ibid., 23 December 1867.

37 Biddulph, *Charles Philip Yorke*, 300; *The Times*, 31 December 1867.

38 Biddulph, *Charles Philip Yorke*, 300.

39 Diaries of Constance, Lady Battersea, 2 October 1870 and 6 October 1870: BL Add MS 47921.

40 Battersea, *Reminiscences*, 159–60.

41 Diaries of Constance, Lady Battersea, 30 September 1872: BL Add MS 47925.

42 Ibid., 2 October 1872.

43 Ibid., 9 October 1872, 10 October 1872 and 13 October 1872.

44 Ibid., 24 October 1872 and 26 October 1872.

45 'Marriage of Miss A. Rothschild and the Hon. E. C. Yorke', *Standard*, 13 February 1873.

46 Diaries of Constance, Lady Battersea, 10 May 1873: BL Add MS 47926.

47 Ibid., 1 June 1873.

48 Ibid., 29 August 1869.

49 Battersea, *Reminiscences*, 166.

50 Ibid.

51 Davis, *English Rothschilds*, 164.

52 Ferguson, *World's Banker*, 745 n. 39; Miriam Rothschild, *Dear Lord Rothschild: Birds, Butterflies and History* (London: Hutchinson, 1983), 15.

53 Diaries of Constance, Lady Battersea, 1 August 1872: BL Add

MS 47925; 1 February 1873: BL Add MS 47926.

54 Priscilla Metcalf, *The Park Town Estate and the Battersea Tangle: A Peculiar Piece of Victorian London Property Development and Its Background* (London: London Topographical Society, 1978), 39.

55 Ibid.

56 Diaries of Constance, Lady Battersea, 21 August 1874: BL Add MS 47929.

57 Ibid., 23 August 1874.

58 Ibid., 25 August 1874.

59 Ibid., 28 August 1874 and 29 August 1874.

60 Ibid., 29 August 1874.

61 Journal of Louisa, Lady de Rothschild, 9 September 1877: BL Add MS 47955.

62 Diaries of Constance, Lady Battersea, 15 September 1877: BL Add MS 47932.

63 'Notes of the Week: A Betrothal in High Life', *Jewish Chronicle*, 5 October 1877.

CHAPTER 22:
Heirs and Graces

1 Rothschild, *Dear Lord Rothschild*, 12.

2 Ibid., 13.

3 Charlotte to Leopold, 9 September 1869 and 18 May 1870: RAL 000/84/4.

4 Rothschild, *Dear Lord Rothschild*, 52–3.

5 Diaries of Constance, Lady Battersea, 9 January 1870: BL Add MS 47921.

6 Rothschild, *Dear Lord Rothschild*, 4.

7 Diaries of Constance, Lady Battersea, 7 May 1872: BL Add MS 47924.

8 Rothschild, *Dear Lord Rothschild*, 5; Cooper, *Unexpected Story*, 148.

9 Emma to Charlotte, [1874]: RAL 000/33/57.

10 Rothschild, *Dear Lord Rothschild*, 20–1.

11 Ibid., 20.

12 Cooper, *Unexpected Story*, 53.

13 Rothschild, *Dear Lord Rothschild*, 53.

14 Charlotte to Leonora and Leopold, 7 August 1874 and 11 August 1874: RAL 000/84/5.

15 Ibid., 7 August 1874.

16 Ibid.

17 Emma to Charlotte, n.d.: RAL 000/33/48.

18 Cooper, *Unexpected Story*, 49, 194.

19 Charlotte to Leopold, 6 May 1864: RAL 000/84/2.

20 Ferguson, *World's Banker*, 773.

21 Charlotte to Leopold, 8 March 1866: RAL 000/84/3.

22 Ferguson, *World's Banker*, 772.

23 Jane Ridley, *Bertie: A Life of Edward VII* (London: Chatto & Windus, 2012), 117.

24 Ibid., 60.

25 Juliana to Charlotte, [1868]: RAL 000/35/14; Ridley, *Bertie*, 116.

26 Juliana to Charlotte, [1868]: RAL 000/35/14.

27 Ibid.

28 Diaries of Constance, Lady Battersea, 7 January 1873: BL Add MS 47926.

29 Rothschild, *Dear Lord Rothschild*, 11n.

30 Ibid.; Davis, *English Rothschilds*, 25. This was a remarkable decision, for Alfred and Marie were welcomed by hostesses across London, albeit with Marie's husband in tow: see 'Fashionable Entertainments', *Morning Post*, 21 June 1871; 'Fashionable Entertainments', *Morning Post*, 27 June 1871; 'Hertford House', *Morning Post*, 22 June 1883.

31 Rothschild, *Dear Lord Rothschild*, 11n.

32 'Memoirs' of Charles Dilke: BL Add MS 43934.

33 Weintraub, *Charlotte and Lionel*, 264.

34 Ibid., 269, 289; Ireland, *Plutocrats*, 354.

35 Weintraub, *Charlotte and Lionel*, 269.

CHAPTER 23:
The Rose and the Lion

1 Diaries of Constance, Lady Battersea, 19 November 1890: BL Add MS 47940; Charlotte to Leopold, 4 February 1867: RAL 000/84/5.

2 Battersea, *Reminiscences*, 51.

3 Charlotte to Laurie and Leo, 29 August 1862: RAL 000/84/1.

4 Battersea, *Reminiscences*, 28; *Lady's Realm: An Illustrated Monthly Magazine*, 12 (May–October 1902).

5 Journal of Louisa, Lady de Rothschild, 18 March 1877: BL Add MS 47955.

6 Davis, *English Rothschilds*, 168.

7 Robert Rhodes James, *Rosebery: A Biography of Archibald Philip, Fifth Earl of Rosebery* (London: Weidenfeld & Nicolson, 1963), 79; Leo McKinstry, *Rosebery: Statesman in Turmoil* (London: John Murray, 2005), 67; *Daily Mail*, 16 November 1901.

8 McKinstry, *Rosebery*, 9, 11.

9 Ferguson, *World's Banker*, 765; Charles Lacaita, *An Italian Englishman, Sir James Lacaita, K.C.M.G., 1813–1895, Senator of the Kingdom of Italy* (London: G. Richards, 1933), 241; Rhodes James, *Rosebery*, 81.

10 Lewis Harcourt, *Loulou: Selected Extracts from the Journals of Lewis Harcourt (1880–1895)*, ed. Patrick Jackson (Madison, NJ: Fairleigh Dickinson University Press, 2006), 19.

11 McKinstry, *Rosebery*, 71.

12 Ibid., 72.

13 Ibid., 73.

14 Ibid., 74.

15 *Harper's Bazaar*, 2 February 1878.

16 Denis Stuart, *Millicent Duchess of Sutherland 1867–1955* (London: Victor Gollancz, 1982), 170.

17 Cohen, *Lady de Rothschild*, 175.

18 *Illustrated London News*, 30 March 1878.

19 Anthony Allfrey, *Edward VII and His Jewish Court* (London: Weidenfeld & Nicolson, 1991), 35. '[T]he one better thing he could have done', wrote a correspondent of Constance's, 'would have been to take her unto himself.' See 'L.S.P.' to Constance, 20 March 1878: BL Add MS 47911, fos. 48–51.

20 E.T. Raymond, *The Life of Lord Rosebery* (New York: George H. Doran, 1923), 60–2.

21 Henry James, *The Letters of Henry James, Volume II: 1875–1883*, ed. Leon Edel (Cambridge, MA: Harvard University Press, 1975), 318.

22 Ibid., 318; McKinstry, *Rosebery*, 70.

23 Battersea, *Reminiscences*, 263.

24 Raymond, *Life of Lord Rosebery*, 60–2.

25 Battersea, *Reminiscences*, 180–1.

26 Diaries of Constance, Lady Battersea, 20 April 1879: BL Add MS 47933.

27 McKinstry, *Rosebery*, 80.

28 Raymond, *Life of Lord Rosebery*, 64.

29 John Davis, 'Primrose, Archibald Philip, fifth earl of Rosebery and first earl of Midlothian (1847–1929), prime minister and author', *ODNB*, 23 September 2004.

30 Mary Gladstone, *Mary Gladstone (Mrs Drew): Her Diaries and Letters*, ed. Lucy Masterman (London: Methuen, 1930), 178.

31 'Mr Gladstone's visit to Scotland', *Daily News*, 24 November 1879.

32 'Essence of Midlothianism', *Punch, or the London Charivari*, 6 September 1884 (vol. 87).

33 McKinstry, *Rosebery*, 76.

34 Ibid., 88.

35 Thomas F.G. Coates, *Lord Rosebery, His Life and Speeches*, vol. 1 (London: Hutchinson, 1900), 347–8.

36 Robert Kelley, 'Midlothian: A Study
    in Politics and Ideas', *Victorian
    Studies*, 4, 2 (December 1960):
    128; George Washburn Smalley,
    *Personalities: Two Midlothian
    Campaigns* (London: Macmillan,
    1890), 444.

37 Smalley, *Personalities*, 445–6.

38 Kelley, 'Midlothian', 128.

39 McKinstry, *Rosebery*, 84.

40 'Mr Gladstone's Departure for
    Scotland', *Birmingham Daily Post*, 17
    March 1880.

41 *Leeds Mercury*, 17 March 1880.

CHAPTER 24:
Maiden Speeches

1   Constance to her mother, 23 March
    1880: BL Add MS 47910, fos. 62–3;
    Battersea, *Reminiscences*, 180–1.

2   Battersea, *Reminiscences*, 180–1.

3   Ibid., 183–4.

4   Ibid., 186.

5   Diaries of Constance, Lady
    Battersea, 30 [August] 1879: BL Add
    MS 47933.

6   Battersea, *Reminiscences*, 181–2.

7   Constance to her mother, 15 March
    1880 and 13 March 1880: BL Add
    MS 47910.

8   Battersea, *Reminiscences*, 182.

9   'You have to suffer for a beautiful
    idea'; this was a play on the more
    common phrase '*il faut souffrir pour
    être belle*' or 'You have to suffer to be
    beautiful' – Constance to her mother,
    20 March 1880: BL Add MS 47910.

10 Battersea, *Reminiscences*, 181.

11 Constance to her mother, 23 March
    1880 and 13 March 1880: BL Add
    MS 47910.

12 Cyril to Constance, 25 March 1880:
    BL Add MS 47910.

13 Constance to her mother, 23 March
    1880: BL Add MS 47910.

14 Ibid.

15 Ibid. and 15 March 1880.

16 Ibid., 15 March 1880 and 24 March 1880.

17 Battersea, *Reminiscences*, 430.

18 Diaries of Constance, Lady
    Battersea, 1 April 1880: BL Add MS
    47933.

19 Constance to her mother, 30 March
    1880: BL Add MS 47910.

20 Battersea, *Reminiscences*, 185.

21 Ibid., 186.

22 Cohen, *Lady de Rothschild*, 188–9.

23 Diaries of Constance, Lady
    Battersea, 1 April 1880: BL Add MS
    47933; Cohen, *Lady de Rothschild*,
    188–9.

24 Battersea, *Reminiscences*, 428, 171.

25 Diaries of Constance, Lady
    Battersea, 25 November 1881: BL
    Add MS 47935; 'January 1885': BL
    Add MS 47938.

26 Ibid., 3 February 1882: BL Add MS
    47935.

27 Ibid., 10 June 1884: BL Add MS 47937.

28 Ibid., 20 September 1884: BL Add
    MS 47938.

29 Ibid., 13 November 1881 and 20
    November 1881: BL Add MS 47935.

30 Ibid., 18 November 1881.

31 Ibid., 30 March 1881: BL Add MS
    47934.

32 Ibid., 1 June 1881: BL Add MS 47934;
    1 January 1882: BL Add MS 47935.

33 Ibid., 20 January 1882.

CHAPTER 25:
Blanche in Bohemia

1   Diaries of Constance, Lady
    Battersea, 24 September 1882: BL
    Add MS 47935.

2   Ibid., 2 October 1882.

3   Ibid., 3 October 1882.

4   Louise Jopling, *Twenty Years of my
    Life: 1867–1887* (London: John Lane,
    1925), 75.

5 Ibid., 74.

6 Ibid., 102, 104–5.

7 Charlotte to Leopold, 14 January 1865 and 10 February 1865: RAL 000/84/2.

8 Virginia Surtees, *Coutts Lindsay, 1824–1913* (Norwich: Michael Russell, 1993), 86.

9 Ibid., 130; Henrey, *Century Between*, 197.

10 Battersea, *Reminiscences*, 56.

11 Surtees, *Coutts Lindsay*, 133.

12 Ibid., 134.

13 Charles E. Hallé, *Notes From a Painter's Life, Including the Founding of Two Galleries* (London: John Murray, 1909), 99–100.

14 Ibid., 99.

15 Surtees, *Coutts Lindsay*, 143; Colleen Denney, 'The Grosvenor Gallery as Palace of Art: An Exhibition Model', in *The Grosvenor Gallery*, ed. Susan P. Casteras and Colleen Denney (New Haven, CT, and London: Yale University Press, 1996), 11.

16 Hallé, *Notes From a Painter's Life*, 104, 107.

17 Ibid., 107–8.

18 Ibid., 104; Christopher Newall, *The Grosvenor Gallery Exhibitions: Change and Continuity in the Victorian Art World* (Cambridge: Cambridge University Press, 1995), 16.

19 Denney, 'Grosvenor Gallery', 21.

20 Georgiana Burne-Jones, *Memorials of Edward Burne-Jones* (London: Lund Humphries, 1993), 69.

21 'The Grosvenor Gallery', *The Times*, 1 May 1877.

22 Battersea, *Reminiscences*, 56; Jopling, *Twenty Years of My Life*, 115.

23 'The Grosvenor Gallery', *The Times*, 1 May 1877.

24 Marian Adams, *The Letters of Mrs. Henry Adams 1865–1883* (Boston: Little, Brown & Co., 1936), 154; John Ruskin, *Fors Clavigera: Letters to the Workmen and Labourers of Great Britain*, vol. 7 (Orpington: George Allen, 1877), 201.

25 Hallé, *Notes From a Painter's Life*, 11.

26 Henrey, *Century Between*, 205; Hallé, *Notes From a Painter's Life*, 153.

27 Jopling, *Twenty Years of My Life*, 74; Henrey, *Century Between*, 206.

28 Newall, *Grosvenor Gallery Exhibitions*, 33; Henrey, *Century Between*, 238.

29 James, *Letters of Henry James*, 2: 249.

30 Jopling, *Twenty Years of My Life*, 158.

31 'Modern Life in London; or, *Tom and Jerry* Back Again', *Punch, or the London Charivari*, 13 May 1882; William Gilbert and Arthur Sullivan, 'Patience', in *The Annotated Gilbert and Sullivan*, ed. Ian Bradley (Oxford: Oxford University Press, 2016), 335–424.

32 Surtees, *Coutts Lindsay*, 165.

33 Diaries of Constance, Lady Battersea, 22 October 1882: BL Add MS 47935.

34 Hallé, *Notes From a Painter's Life*, 152–3; Battersea, *Reminiscences*, 56.

35 Adams, *Letters of Mrs. Henry Adams*, 403.

36 Surtees, *Coutts Lindsay*, 169–70.

37 Lady Walburga Paget, *The Linings of Life*, vol. 2 (London: Hurst & Blackett, 1928), 338.

38 Diaries of Constance, Lady Battersea, 20 January 1882: BL Add MS 47935.

39 Lady Lindsay to Robert Browning, 22 November 1882: Beinecke Rare Book and Manuscript Library, New Haven (hereafter BNH), Gen MSS 839, series I b.4.

40 Surtees, *Coutts Lindsay*, 179–80.

41 Henrey, *Century Between*, 230. Blanche's poetry collections included the following: Lady Caroline Blanche Elizabeth Lindsay, *About Robins: Songs, Facts, and Legends* (London: Routledge,

1889); Lady Caroline Blanche Elizabeth Lindsay, *Dora's Defiance* (Philadelphia: Lippincott, 1894); Lady Caroline Blanche Elizabeth Lindsay, *The Apostle of the Ardennes* (London: Paul, Trench, Trübner & Co., 1899); Lady Caroline Blanche Elizabeth Lindsay, *A Christmas Posy of Carols, Songs, and Other Pieces* (London: Paul, Trench, Trübner & Co., 1902); Lady Caroline Blanche Elizabeth Lindsay, *From a Venetian Balcony and Other Poems of Venice and the Near Lands* (London: Paul, Trench, Trübner & Co., 1903); Lady Caroline Blanche Elizabeth Lindsay, *Lyrics and Other Poems* (London: Paul, Trench, Trübner & Co., 1890).

42 Oscar Wilde (ed.), *Woman's World*, vol. 2: 1889 (London, Paris, New York and Melbourne: Cassel & Co., 1889), 167–8.

43 'New Novels', *Graphic*, 8 December 1888.

44 Hallé, *Notes From a Painter's Life*, 157.

45 Newall, *Grosvenor Gallery Exhibitions*, 35; Hallé, *Notes From a Painter's Life*, 158, 152.

CHAPTER 26:
The Royal Seal

1 *The Times*, 14 March 1884; Diary of Constance, Lady Battersea, 13 March 1884: BL Add MS 47937; Journals of Louisa, Lady de Rothschild, 22 March 1884: BL Add MS 47965.

2 *Daily Telegraph & Courier*, 17 March 1884.

3 Battersea, *Reminiscences*, 421.

4 Journal of Queen Victoria, 18 May 1885: RAW Journal of Queen Victoria, Princess Beatrice's copies, 81: 192.

5 Hannah to Edward Hamilton, 2 October 1884, BL Add MS 48613, fo. 5; 21 October 1885: BL Add MS

48613, fo. 30; 30 October 1885: BL Add MS 48613, fo. 32.

6 Diary of Constance, Lady Battersea, 19 November 1890: BL Add MS 47940.

7 Sir Edward Walter Hamilton, *The Diary of Sir Edward Walter Hamilton, 1880–1885*, ed. Dudley W. R. Bahlman, vol. 1 (Oxford: Clarendon Press, 1972), 257.

8 Hannah to Edward Hamilton, 27 January 1886: BL Add MS 48613, fo. 43.

9 Ibid., 28 January 1886: BL Add MS 48613, fo. 46.

10 Ibid.

11 McKinstry, *Rosebery*, 146.

12 Hannah to Edward Hamilton, 29 January 1886: BL Add MS 48613.

13 Ibid., 3 February 1886.

14 Hamilton, *Diary*, 1: 162.

15 McKinstry, *Rosebery*, 147, 156; Journal of Queen Victoria, 8 May 1886 and 5 July 1886: RAW Princess Beatrice's copies, 83: 146 and 234 respectively.

16 Ibid., Sunday, 9 May 1886, Tuesday, 3 August 1886 and Thursday, 19 August 1886, 83: 149, 284 and 317 respectively. Channels of communication would remain open through her private secretary, Sir Henry Ponsonby (Journal of Queen Victoria, Monday, 6 September 1886: Pss. Beatrice's copies, 84: 39).

17 Helen Rappaport, *Victoria: A Biographical Companion* (Santa Barbara, CA: ABC-CLIO, 2003), 248.

18 Cohen, *Lady de Rothschild*, 231.

19 Battersea, *Reminiscences*, 434.

20 Ibid., 110.

21 Ibid., 110–11v.

22 Ibid., 110.

23 Ibid., 111–12.

24 Ibid., 112.

25 Clement Scott, *Poppy-land: Papers Descriptive of Scenery on the East*

Coast (Norwich: Jarrold, 1894); Battersea, *Reminiscences*, 378–9.

26 Louise to Constance, [n.d.] 1889: BL Add MS 47909, fos. 18–22.

27 Diaries of Constance, Lady Battersea, 14 May 1890: BL Add MS 47939.

28 Journal of Queen Victoria, 14 May 1890: RAW, Journal of Queen Victoria, Princess Beatrice's copies, 91: 121–2.

29 Hannah to Edward Hamilton, 17 February 1889: BL Add MS 48613, fos. 75–6; 'Re-union of Deaf and Dumb People in Glasgow', *Scotsman*, 16 February 1889.

30 McKinstry, *Rosebery*, 173.

31 Hamilton, *Diary*, 1: 115.

32 Hannah to Edward Hamilton, 25 September 1890: BL Add MS 48613, fo. 99.

33 Lord Rosebery to Gladstone, 20 October 1890: BL Add MS 44288, fo. 129; Hamilton, *Diary*, 1: 125.

34 Diary of Lady Battersea, 25 October 1890: BL Add MS 47940; McKinstry, *Rosebery*, 197.

35 McKinstry, *Rosebery*, 197.

36 Hamilton, *Diary*, 1: 129.

37 'In Memoriam', Hamilton manuscript tribute for Hannah: BL Add MS 48613, fo. 104.

38 Diary of Constance, Lady Battersea, 19 November 1890 and 25 November 1890: BL Add MS 47940.

39 'Queen Victoria and her Jewish Subjects', *Jewish Chronicle*, 25 January 1901.

40 Constance to her mother, 25 March 1891: BL Add MS 47910, fo. 98.

41 Ibid., 28 March 1891: BL Add MS 47910, fos. 99–102.

42 Ibid.

43 Battersea, *Reminiscences*, 115.

44 Constance to Louisa, 31 March [1891]: BL Add MS 47910, fos. 103–5.

45 Diary of Constance, Lady Battersea, 2 April 1891: BL Add MS 47940.

46 Ibid.

47 Battersea, *Reminiscences*, 113.

48 Constance to her mother, 31 March 1891: BL Add MS 47910, fos. 103–5.

49 Constance, Grasse, to her mother, 12 April 1891: BL Add MS 47910, fos. 119–22.

50 Diaries of Constance, Lady Battersea, 17 April 1891: BL Add MS 47940.

CHAPTER 27:
Rescue and Prevention

1 Battersea, *Reminiscences*, 418–19.

2 Ibid., 418, 419–20.

3 Ibid., 419, 420.

4 Ibid., 420, 421.

5 Ibid., 421; Louise A. Jackson, *Child Sexual Abuse in Victorian England* (London and New York: Routledge, 2000), 145.

6 Eitan Bar-Yosef and Nadia Valman, 'Introduction', in *'The Jew' in Late-Victorian and Edwardian Culture: Between the East End and East Africa*, ed. Eitan Bar-Yosef and Nadia Valman (Basingstoke: Palgrave Macmillan, 2009), 12; Todd M. Endelman, *The Jews of Britain, 1656–2000* (Berkeley, CA: University of California Press, 2000), 127; Lara Marks, 'Jewish Women and Jewish Prostitution in the East End of London', *Jewish Quarterly*, 34, 126 (1987): 9; Endelman, *Jews of Britain*, 129.

7 White, *London in the Nineteenth Century*, 49.

8 Battersea, *Reminiscences*, 415.

9 'Stories for the People', *Reynolds's Newspaper*, 22 September 1889.

10 Klaus Weber, 'Transmigrants between Legal Restrictions

and Private Charity: The Jews'
Temporary Shelter in London,
1885–1939', in *Points of Passage: Jewish
Transmigrants from Eastern Europe
in Scandinavia, Germany, and Britain
1880–1914*, ed. Tobias Brinkmann
(New York and Oxford: Berghahn,
2013), 86.

11 Beatrice Potter, 'The Jewish
Community', in *Life and Labour
in London*, ed. Charles Booth
(London: Williams & Norgate,
1889–91), 582–3; Report of the Jewish
Association for the Protection
of Girls and Women for 1899
(London: Jewish Association, 1899),
18: London Library (hereafter LL),
Montefiore Pamphlet Collection,
M131.

12 Edward J. Bristow, *Prostitution and
Prejudice: The Jewish Fight against
White Slavery 1870–1939* (Oxford:
Clarendon Press, 1982), 237.

13 'Jewish Ladies' Association', *Jewish
Chronicle*, 18 June 1886.

14 Diary of Constance, Lady Battersea,
31 December 1886: BL Add MS
47938.

15 Jackson, *Child Sexual Abuse*, 146.

16 Ibid., 147–8.

17 Battersea, *Reminiscences*, 423.

18 Ibid.

19 John Joliffe, ed., *Raymond Asquith:
Life and Letters* (London: Century,
1980), 41.

20 Battersea, *Reminiscences*, 413.

21 'Montagu, Lily (1873–1963)',
*Encyclopaedia of Women Social
Reformers*, vol. 1, ed. Helen
Rappaport (Santa Barbara, CA:
ABC-CLIO, 2001), 448; Lily H.
Montagu, *My Club and I* (London:
Neville Spearman, 1954), 51–3.

22 Diary of Beatrice Webb, 16 January
1903, in *The Diary of Beatrice Webb*,
vol. 2, *1892–1905: All the Good Things
in Life* (London: Virago, 1983), 267.

23 Diary of Constance, Lady Battersea,
6 January 1886: BL Add MS 47938.

24 Anne Louise Holdorph, 'The Real
Meaning of Our Work: Religion in
Jewish Boys' and Girls' Clubs 1880–
1939', PhD dissertation, University of
Southampton, 2014, 45.

25 Montagu, *My Club and I*, 25.

26 W.T. Stead, 'The Maiden Tribute
of Modern Babylon I', *Pall Mall
Gazette*, 6 July 1885; W.T. Stead, 'The
Maiden Tribute of Modern Babylon
II', *Pall Mall Gazette*, 7 July 1885;
W.T. Stead, 'The Maiden Tribute
of Modern Babylon III', *Pall Mall
Gazette*, 8 July 1885; W.T. Stead, 'The
Maiden Tribute of Modern Babylon
IV', *Pall Mall Gazette*, 10 July 1885.

27 Journal of Louisa, Lady de
Rothschild, 22 February 1886: BL
Add MS 47957.

28 Diary of Constance, Lady Battersea,
12 August 1885: BL Add MS 47938.

29 Emilia Dilke to Cyril Flower, 29
January 1886: BL Add MS 47911, fo. 75.

30 Diary of Lady Battersea, 12 February
1886: BL Add MS 47938.

CHAPTER 28:
Elevations

1 Lady Frances Balfour, *Ne
Obliviscaris: Dinna Forget* (London:
Hodder & Stoughton, 1930), 225.

2 Journal of Louisa, Lady de
Rothschild, 3 December 1885: BL
Add MS 47957.

3 Constance to Annie, February 1886:
BL Add MS 47963, fos. 156–8.

4 Ibid., 8 February 1886: BL Add MS
47963, fos. 159–60.

5 Constance to her mother, 19 August
1892: BL Add MS 47910, fo. 131;
Diary of Constance, Lady Battersea,
21 August 1892: BL Add MS 47940.

6 Battersea, *Reminiscences*, 325.

7 Diary of Constance, Lady Battersea, 1 February 1893: BL Add MS 47940.

8 Ibid., 2 February 1893.

9 Battersea, *Reminiscences*, 325.

10 Diary of Constance, Lady Battersea, 3 February 1893: BL Add MS 47940; Battersea, *Reminiscences*, 325.

11 Diary of Constance, Lady Battersea, 4 February 1893: BL Add MS 47940.

12 Journal of Louisa, Lady de Rothschild, 9 February 1893: BL Add MS 47959.

13 Cyril to Constance, 4 February 1893: BL Add MS 47910, fos. 136–8.

14 Battersea, *Reminiscences*, 325–6.

15 Constance to Cyril, February [1893]: BL Add MS 47910, fos. 9–11.

16 Journal of Louisa, Lady de Rothschild, 16 February 1893: BL Add MS 47959.

17 Ibid.

18 Constance to Cyril, February 1893, BL Add MS 47910, fos. 9–11; Louisa to Cyril, February 1893: BL Add MS 47910, fo. 139.

19 Battersea, *Reminiscences*, 333.

20 Jane Ridley, *Edwin Lutyens: His Life, His Wife, His Work* (London: Pimlico, 2002), 102–3.

21 Battersea, *Reminiscences*, 329.

22 Diary of Constance, Lady Battersea, '1894': BL Add MS 47941.

23 'Conference of Women Workers at Bristol', *Woman's Herald*, 19 November 1892.

24 Gwen Mary Williams, *Mary Clifford* (Bristol: J.W. Arrowsmith, 1920), 185.

25 Diary of Constance, Lady Battersea, 'December 1892': BL Add MS 47940.

26 'An Old Bachelor, The Growleries, Lostbuttonbury, Singleton', 'Left to the Ladies', *Punch, or the London Charivari*, 19 November 1892.

27 Battersea, *Reminiscences*, 444.

28 Ibid., 445.

29 Diary of Constance, Lady Battersea, 'A round up of the year [1896]' and 1 January 1898: BL Add MS 47942;

Diary of Constance, Lady Battersea, 25 December 1899: BL Add MS 47943; Battersea, *Reminiscences*, 446–7.

30 'Third Day', *Woman's Signal*, 17 June 1897.

31 'Notes and Comments', *Wings*, 1 August 1899.

32 *The International Council of Women of 1899. (Report of Transactions of the Second Quinquennial Meeting [and of the International Congress of Women Connected With It], Held in London, July 1899*, ed. Countess of Aberdeen (London: T.F. Unwin, 1900), 44; 'International Congress of Women', *The Times*, 27 June 1899.

33 'Women in Council', *Weekly Standard and Express*, 24 June 1899.

34 [International Council of Women], *Women in a Changing World* (London: Routledge, 1966), 23; 'International Congress of Women', *The Times*, 27 June 1899.

35 Rosemary T. Van Arsdel, *Florence Fenwick Miller: Victorian Feminist, Journalist and Educator* (Aldershot: Ashgate, 2001), 175.

36 Ibid., 176.

37 Diary of Beatrice Webb, 3 July 1889, in Webb, *Diary*, 162.

38 Battersea, *Reminiscences*, 447–8.

39 Annie to Louisa, 9 February 1886: BL Add MS 47963, fos. 81–4.

40 Stanley Weintraub, *Victoria: Biography of a Queen* (London: Allen & Unwin, 1987), 640.

41 Henry James, *The Letters of Henry James, Volume IV: 1895–1916*, ed. Leon Edel (Cambridge, MA: Harvard University Press, 1984), 182.

42 Annie to Louisa, 3 February 1901: BL Add MS 47963, fo. 93; Battersea, *Reminiscences*, 200.

43 Battersea, *Reminiscences*, 200.

44 Tony Rennell, *Last Days of Glory: The Death of Queen Victoria* (London: Viking, 2000), 254.

45 Battersea, *Reminiscences*, 200.

46 Ibid., 200–1.

47 Diary of Constance, Lady Battersea, 2 February 1901: BL Add MS 47943.

48 Battersea, *Reminiscences*, 201.

49 Allfrey, *Edward VII*, 184; *Jewish Chronicle*, 12 June 1903.

50 'A foreshadowing of what the new reign would be,' wrote Constance in her diary. Diary of Constance, Lady Battersea, 14 February 1901: BL Add MS 47943.

51 Cooper, *Unexpected Story*, 194–5.

52 Rothschild, *Dear Lord Rothschild*, 13.

53 Diary of Constance, Lady Battersea, '1903 Overstrand': BL Add MS 47943.

CHAPTER 29:
'Big Guns Arrived during the Night'

1 Diary of Constance, Lady Battersea, 30 October 1902: BL Add MS 47943.

2 Ibid., 2 November 1902.

3 'Society Gossip. Rumoured Society Scandal A Peer's Flight', *Sunday Special*, 2 November 1902.

4 *Northern Whig*, 3 November 1902; *Gloucestershire Echo*, 3 November 1902; *Dundee Evening Telegraph*, 3 November 1902; *Bradford Daily Telegraph*, 3 November 1902; *Bournemouth Daily Echo*, 3 November 1902; *Aberdeen Press and Journal*, 3 November 1902; *Irish Times*, 3 November 1902; *Sunderland Daily Echo and Shipping Gazette*, 3 November 1902.

5 Trevor Hamilton, *Immortal Longings: FWH Myers and the Victorian Search for Life After Death* (Exeter: Imprint Academic, 2015), 23.

6 Diary of George Cecil Ives, 3 November 1902: Harry Ransom Center, University of Texas, Austin (hereafter HRC), George Cecil Ives Papers, series III, Diaries 1886–1949, vol. 61, 23–4.

7 Diaries of Constance, Lady Battersea, 1 December 1902: BL Add MS 47943.

8 Diary of Beatrice Webb, 16 January 1903, in Webb, *Diary*, 267.

9 Ibid., '1903 Overstrand'.

10 Constance's excision means that many questions about the episode remain unanswered. Is it possible that Cyril's illness caused him to withdraw from court, leading to a misunderstanding that he was running away from what was, in fact, an unrelated scandal? Or was the illness emphasised, both by Cyril and by Constance in her diaries, to diminish his responsibility for what had happened at court? Regardless, the notion that he had been implicated in the scandal would persist to his death. Cyril's obituary in the *Chicago Tribune*, written by the 'Marquise de Fontenoy' (the nom de plume of Marguerite Cunliffe-Owen), would assert: 'Some years ago he became involved in a shocking scandal. He escaped by leaving England and remaining for a considerable time in a sanitarium, the plea being successfully advanced that he was not responsible for his actions.' See 'Marquise de Fontenoy', *Chicago Tribune*, 4 December 1907.

11 Diaries of Constance, Lady Battersea, 3–6 November 1903: BL Add MS 47943.

12 'Women's Congress', *Daily Express*, 19 March 1904; 'International Congress of Women', *The Times*, 13 July 1904.

13 Diaries of Constance, Lady Battersea, 13 June 1904, 16 June 1904, 18 June 1904, 19 June 1904, 20 June 1904 and 21 June 1904: BL Add MS 47944.

14 Ibid., 'Some reflections': BL Add MS 47944, fo. 35.

15 Battersea, *Reminiscences*, 391.

16 Joliffe, ed., *Raymond Asquith*, 41–2.

17 Diaries of Constance, Lady Battersea, 4 January 1905: BL Add MS 47944.

18 Ibid.

19 Geoffrey Alderman, 'Montefiore, Claude Joseph Goldsmid- (1858–1938), scholar and founder of Liberal Judaism', *ODNB*, 23 September 2004.

20 Steven Bayme, 'Claude Montefiore, Lily Montagu and the Origins of the Jewish Religious Union – Transactions & Miscellanies', *Jewish Historical Society of England*, 27 (1978–80): 63, 65.

21 Diaries of Constance, Lady Battersea, 4 January 1905: BL Add MS 47944.

22 Ibid., 'Some reflections': BL Add MS 47944, fos. 22–3; 4 January 1905: BL Add MS 47944.

23 Ibid., 15 June 1905.

24 John Davis, 'Flower, Cyril, Baron Battersea (1843–1907), politician', *ODNB*, 23 September 2004; Journal of Louisa, Lady de Rothschild, 9 August 1905: BL Add MS 47962.

25 Diaries of Constance, Lady Battersea, 9 June 1906: BL Add MS 47944.

26 'Obituary', *The Times*, 28 November 1907; Journal of Louisa, Lady de Rothschild, 18 September 1907: BL Add MS 47962; Diaries of Constance, Lady Battersea, 5 October and 21 October 1907: BL Add MS 47944.

27 Diaries of Constance, Lady Battersea, 10 November 1907: BL Add MS 47944.

28 'Obituary', *The Times*, 28 November 1907.

29 Journal of Louisa, Lady de Rothschild, 2 December 1907: BL Add MS 47962; 'Court Circular', *The Times*, 2 December 1907.

30 Diaries of Constance, Lady Battersea, 'April 1908': BL Add MS 47944, fo. 79.

31 Ibid., 1 January 1901: BL Add MS 47943; 'April 1908': BL Add MS 47944, fo. 79.

32 Ibid., 'April 1908': BL Add MS 47944, fo. 75.

33 Ibid., 26 April 1908 and 23 July 1908: BL Add MS 47944.

34 Ibid., 23 July 1908.

35 Ibid., 27 November 1908.

36 Ibid., 'November 1910': BL Add MS 47945.

37 Ibid., 18 December 1910.

38 Battersea, *Reminiscences*, 281.

39 Ibid., 88, 282, 309; Diaries of Constance, Lady Battersea, 9 April 1895: BL Add MS 47942; Diaries of Constance, Lady Battersea, 23 April 1889: BL Add MS 47939.

40 Battersea, *Reminiscences*, 311.

41 Ibid., 310, 311.

42 Ibid., 311.

43 Isabel V. Hull, *The Entourage of Kaiser Wilhelm II 1888–1918* (Cambridge: Cambridge University Press, 1982), 20, 36.

44 Battersea, *Reminiscences*, 313.

45 Diaries of Constance, Lady Battersea, 20 July 1911: BL Add MS 47945.

46 Battersea, *Reminiscences*, 314–17.

47 Diaries of Constance, Lady Battersea, 20 July 1911: BL Add MS 47945.

48 Battersea, *Reminiscences*, 315.

49 Ibid., 317.

50 Diaries of Constance, Lady Battersea, 'Christmas 1908': BL Add MS 47944; 31 December 1910: BL Add MS 47945.

51 British Library, London: Battersea Papers, vols. V–XXXIX. Diaries of Lady Battersea; 1858–1928: Lady Battersea Diary, vol. XXXVI, June 1904–August 1910, 'Christmas 1908': BL Add MS 47944.

52 Diaries of Constance, Lady
Battersea, 28 June 1912, 11 March 1913,
15 March 1913 and 17 March 1913: BL
Add MS 47945.

53 Annie to Constance, 4 August 1914:
BL Add MS 47963, fos. 216–19.

54 Diaries of Constance, Lady
Battersea, 13 August 1914: BL Add
MS 47945.

55 Ibid., 7 August 1914.

56 Ibid. and 30 September 1914.

57 Ferguson, *World's Banker*, 973.

58 Constance to Annie, 17 November
1914: BL Add MS 47963, fos. 221–2.

59 Ibid.

CHAPTER 30:
Crossing the Border

1 Naomi Gryn, 'Dame Miriam
Rothschild', *Jewish Quarterly*, 51, 1
(2004): 53; Nat Hentoff, 'The Jazz
Baroness', *Esquire Magazine*, 1
October 1960.

2 Dorothy to James, 7 August 1914: The
Waddesdon Archive at Windmill
Hill, Waddesdon Manor, Aylesbury
(hereafter WHA) JDR2/1/325/10;
Dorothy to James, 7 August 1914:
WHA JDR2/1/325/11; 'Dame Miriam
Rothschild [Obituary]', *Daily
Telegraph*, 24 January 2005.

3 'The Rothschild Betrothal',
Jewish Chronicle, 11 January 1907;
'A Rothschild Betrothal', *Daily
Telegraph and Courier*, 29 December
1906.

4 Rothschild, *Dear Lord Rothschild*, 95.

5 'The Rothschild Betrothal',
Jewish Chronicle, 11 January 1907;
Rothschild, *Dear Lord Rothschild*,
95–6.

6 Rothschild, *Dear Lord Rothschild*, 94.

7 'The Rothschild Betrothal', *Jewish
Chronicle*, 11 January 1907; 'A
Rothschild Romance . . .', *Luton
Times and Advertiser*, 4 January
1907; 'Betrothal Romance: Sequel to
Christmas Eve Journey', *Manchester
Courier and Lancashire General
Advertiser*, 2 January 1907.

8 'Marriage of the Hon. Charles
Rothschild', *Bucks Herald*, 9 February
1907; Rothschild, *Dear Lord
Rothschild*, 97–8.

9 Rothschild, *Dear Lord Rothschild*, 98.

10 Ibid., 22.

11 Ferguson, *World's Banker*, 443n.

12 Victor Gray, '"Something in
the Genes": Walter Rothschild,
Zoological Collector Extraordinaire',
lecture delivered at the Royal
College of Surgeons, 25 October
2006, https://web.archive.org/
web/20070928061019/http://www.
rcseng.ac.uk/museums/events/Docs/
victor_gray_transcript_october06.pdf

13 Rothschild, *Dear Lord Rothschild*, 92.

14 Cooper, *Unexpected Story*, 347.

15 Rothschild, *Dear Lord Rothschild*, 96.

16 Hentoff, 'Jazz Baroness'.

17 Victor Rothschild, *Meditations of a
Broomstick* (London: Collins, 1977),
12, 18.

18 Rothschild, *Dear Lord Rothschild*, 94.

19 Hannah Rothschild, *The Baroness:
The Search for Nica, the Rebellious
Rothschild* (London: Virago, 2012),
37–40.

20 Miriam Rothschild interviewed
by Polly Toynbee for 'Miriam
Rothschild', *Women of the Century*,
BBC, London, 13 January 1989;
Kennedy Fraser, 'Fritillaries and
Hairy Violets', *New Yorker*, 12
October 1987.

21 Gryn, 'Dame Miriam Rothschild', 53.

22 Ibid., 54.

23 Ferguson, *World's Banker*, 975.

24 Miriam Rothschild interviewed
by Louise Brodie for 'Down To
Earth: An Oral History of British
Horticulture', Track 3 (Ashton,

2–4 October 2001): BL Sound
Archive; Diary of Constance, Lady
Battersea, 10 August 1915: BL Add
MS 47945.

25 Rothschild, *Dear Lord Rothschild*,
242–3.

26 Rózsika to Dorothy, 17 March 1915:
WHA JDR2/1/377/1.

CHAPTER 31:
Enlisting

1 'Dorothy de Rothschild', *Jewish
Chronicle*, 16 September 1988.

2 Dorothy de Rothschild, *The
Rothschilds at Waddesdon Manor*
(London: Collins, 1979), 94, 93.

3 'Mr James Rothschild to Marry',
Yorkshire Evening Post, 21 January
1913.

4 Rothschild, *Rothschilds at Waddesdon*,
94.

5 'A Lady's London Letter: Rothschild
Wedding', *Cheltenham Examiner*, 6
March 1913; 'Yesterday's Weddings Mr
James de Rothschild and Miss Pinto',
Yorkshire Post and Leeds Intelligencer, 28
February 1913; 'Shower of Diamonds
Gifts to Mr J De Rothschild's Bride',
*Manchester Courier and Lancashire
General Advertiser*, 26 February 1913.

6 Dorothy to James, 1 August 1914:
WHA JDR2/1/325/4.

7 Ibid. and 2 August 1914: WHA
JDR2/1/325/5.

8 Ibid., 3 August 1914: WHA
JDR2/1/325/7.

9 Ibid., 5 August 1914: WHA
JDR2/1/325/8.

10 Ibid., 9 August 1914: WHA
JDR2/1/325/13.

11 James to Dorothy, [August 1914]:
WHA JDR2/1/355/45; 11 August 1914:
WHA JDR2/1/355/53; 18 August 1914:
WHA JDR2/1/355/58; 12 September
1914: WHA JDR2/1/355/78.

12 Ibid., 29 September 1914: WHA
JDR2/1/355/88.

13 Dorothy to James, 10 August 1914:
WHA JDR2/1/325/14.

14 Chaim Weizmann, *The Letters and
Papers of Chaim Weizmann, Series
A, Letters, August 1914–November
1917*, vol. 7, ed. Leonard Stein in
collaboration with Dvorah Barzilay
and Nehama A. Chalom (Jerusalem:
Israel Universities Press, 1975), 112–13.

15 See Stuart A. Cohen, *English
Zionists and British Jews: The
Communal Politics of Anglo-Jewry,
1895–1920* (Princeton, NJ: Princeton
University Press, 1982).

16 Israel Sieff, *Memoirs* (London:
Weidenfeld & Nicolson, 1970), 67.

17 Cohen, *English Zionists and British
Jews*, 243.

18 Cooper, *Unexpected Story*, 259.

19 James to Dorothy, 12 November 1914:
WHA JDR2/1/355/115.

20 Ibid., 15 November 1914: WHA
JDR2/1/355/118.

21 Jonathan Schneer, *The Balfour
Declaration: The Origins of the Arab-
Israeli Conflict* (London: Bloomsbury,
2010), 129.

22 Weizmann, *Letters and Papers*, 51–3.

23 Schneer, *Balfour Declaration*, 130.

24 Weizmann, *Letters and Papers*, 113.

25 Chaim Weizmann, *Trial and Error*
(London: Hamish Hamilton, 1949),
161.

26 Rothschild, *Dear Lord Rothschild*,
242.

27 Sieff, *Memoirs*, 67.

28 Rózsika to Dorothy, 17 March 1915:
WHA JDR2/1/377/1.

29 Ferguson, *World's Banker*, 977–8;
Vivian D. Lipman, *A History of the
Jews in Britain since 1858* (Leicester:
Leicester University Press, 1990),
128.

30 Richard Burton Haldane, *An
Autobiography* (London: Hodder

& Stoughton, 1929), 163; Cooper,
Unexpected Story, 345–6; 'Lord
Rothschild', *Daily Telegraph*, 29
March 1915; 'Serious Operation; Baron
Rothschild Dies from Shock', *New
York Tribune*, 1 April 1915; 'Death of
Lord Rothschild', *The Times*, 1 April
1915; 'Death of Lord Rothschild', *Daily
Telegraph*, 1 April 1915.

31 Cooper, *Unexpected Story*, 347.

32 Diary of Constance, Lady Battersea,
10 August 1915: BL Add MS 47945.

33 Schneer, *Balfour Declaration*, 130.

34 Weizmann, *Letters and Papers*, 232.

35 Ibid., 202, 209; Rózsika to
Dorothy, 3 December 1915: WHA
JDR2/1/377/10.

36 James to Dorothy, 5 July 1915: WHA
JDR2/1/355/234.

37 Leonard Stein, *The Balfour
Declaration*, 2nd edn (Jerusalem:
Magnes Press, 1983), 184–5.

38 Jehuda Reinharz, *Chaim Weizmann:
The Making of a Statesman* (Oxford:
Oxford University Press, 2003), 80;
Schneer, *Balfour Declaration*, 156.

39 Simon Schama, *Two Rothschilds and
the Land of Israel* (London: Collins,
1978), 199.

40 Rothschild, *Dear Lord Rothschild*, 243.

41 Ibid., 93, 147.

42 Stein, *Balfour Declaration*, 183.

43 Rothschild, *Dear Lord Rothschild*, 245.

44 Stein, *Balfour Declaration*, 183.

45 Reinharz, *Chaim Weizmann*, 104;
Weizmann, *Letters and Papers*, 318.

46 Rothschild, *Dear Lord Rothschild*, 254.

47 Rózsika to Dorothy, n.d.: WHA
JDR2/1/377/20.

48 Schneer, *Balfour Declaration*, 195, 197.

49 'The Future of the Jews', *The Times*,
24 May 1917; Ferguson, *World's
Banker*, 978. *The Times* published the
statement while the *Jewish Chronicle*
did not: see Schneer, *Balfour
Declaration*, 310.

50 Rothschild, *Dear Lord Rothschild*, 256.

51 Diary of Constance, Lady
Battersea, 29 May 1917: BL Add
MS 47946.

52 'The Future of the Jews', *The Times*,
29 May 1917.

53 T.G. Fraser, *Chaim Weizmann: The
Zionist Dream* (London: Haus,
2009), 39.

54 Rothschild, *Dear Lord Rothschild*, 261;
Ferguson, *World's Banker*, 979.

55 *The Times*, 9 November 1917. See
also Rothschild, *Dear Lord
Rothschild*, 265; Schneer, *Balfour
Declaration*, 342.

56 Weizmann, *Trial and Error*, 161.

57 Ibid.

58 Rothschild, *Dear Lord Rothschild*,
266n.

59 Ibid., 267–8.

60 Ibid., 269.

CHAPTER 32:
Reconstruction

1 Constance to Annie, December 1915:
BL Add MS 47963, fo. 228.

2 Cohen, *Lady de Rothschild*, 302;
Constance to Annie, 12 March [1915]:
BL Add MS 47963, fos. 238–41.

3 Rózsika to Dorothy, 14 June [no
year]: WHA JDR2/1/377/8; Dorothy
to James, 14 August 1914: WHA
JDR2/1/325/15; Cohen, *Lady de
Rothschild*, 313.

4 Diary of Constance, Lady Battersea,
19 January 1915: BL Add MS 47945.

5 Constance to Annie, 15 March [1916]:
BL Add MS 47963, fo. 242.

6 Ibid., 21 February 1916: BL Add MS
47963, fos. 233–5; Cohen, *Lady de
Rothschild*, 308.

7 Cohen, *Lady de Rothschild*, 309.

8 Ibid., 312, 314.

9 Ibid., 313.

10 Annie to Constance, December
[1918]: BL Add MS 47963, fo. 286.

11 Diary of Constance, Lady Battersea, '1918': BL Add MS 47946.

12 Cohen, *Lady de Rothschild*, 327.

13 Diary of Constance, Lady Battersea, 11 November [1918]: BL Add MS 47946.

14 Rózsika to Dorothy, 9 April 1918: WHA JDR2/1/377/28.

15 Ibid., 9 March 1918: WHA JDR2/1/377/26.

16 Ibid., 21 September 1918: WHA JDR2/1/377/36.

17 Ibid.: WHA JDR2/1/377/36.

18 Ibid., 5 November 1918: WHA JDR2/1/377/39.

19 Rothschild, *Baroness*, 75.

20 Ferguson, *World's Banker*, 971.

21 Rózsika to Dorothy, 2 September 1919: WHA JDR2/1/377/42.

22 Ibid., 23 December 1919: WHA JDR2/1/377/44.

23 Ibid.

24 Ernie Trory, *Hungary 1919 and 1956: The Anatomy of Counter-Revolution* (Hove: Crabtree Press, 1981), 27.

25 Rózsika to Dorothy, 23 December 1919: WHA JDR2/1/377/44.

26 See 'Distress in Austria', House of Lords Debate, 22 December 1919, *Parliamentary Debates*, Lords, vol. 38, cc479–502; and 'Austria's Cry For Help: Famine Postponed but Urgent Need for Credits: United States to the Rescue?', *Daily Express*, 23 December 1919.

27 Rózsika to Dorothy, 30 March 1922: WHA JDR2/1/377/45; 8 April [1922]: WHA JDR2/1/377/54.

28 Ferguson, *World's Banker*, 987–8; Rothschild, *Dear Lord Rothschild*, 96, 330n.

29 Rothschild, *Baroness*, 76.

30 Diaries of Constance, Lady Battersea, 14 December 1918: BL Add MS 47946.

31 Cohen, *Lady de Rothschild*, 325.

32 Louise to Constance, 12 June [1921]: BL Add MS 47909, fo. 101.

33 Constance to Lucien Wolf, 25 October 1921: BL Add MS 47911, fos. 125–6.

34 Cohen, *Lady de Rothschild*, 330.

35 Constance to Frederick Macmillan, 21 November 1922: BL Add MS 55047, fos. 31–2; Diary of Constance, Lady Battersea, 21 November 1922: BL Add MS 47946; Constance to Frederick Macmillan, 22 November 1922 and 27 November 1922: BL Add MS 55047, fos. 35–6 and 37–8 respectively.

36 Constance to Frederick Macmillan, 5 December 1922: BL Add MS 55047, fos. 46–7.

37 Diary of Constance, Lady Battersea, 31 December 1924: BL Add MS 47946.

38 Ibid., 12 October 1923; undated entry: BL Add MS 47946, fo. 62.

39 'Hon N.C. Rothschild: Story of His Tragic Death', *The Times*, 14 October 1923.

CHAPTER 33:
Vocations

1 'Opposites', *Daily Mirror*, 13 June 1929.

2 Rothschild and Brodie, 'Down To Earth', track 4: BL Sound Archive.

3 Sue Lawley (host), 'Miriam Rothschild', *Desert Island Discs*, 28 April 1989, BBC Radio 4.

4 Miriam Rothschild, 'Homage to Wendell Krull', in *Wendell Krull: Trematodes and Naturalists*, ed. S.A. Ewing (Stillwater, OK: Oklahoma State University Press, 2001), 27.

5 Lawley, 'Miriam Rothschild'.

6 Catharine M.C. Haines, 'Rothschild, Dame Miriam Louisa (1908–2005),

naturalist, entomologist, and conservationist', *ODNB*, 8 January 2009.

7 Pannonica de Koenigswarter, *Three Wishes: An Intimate Look at Jazz Greats* (New York: Abrams Image, 2008), 14.

8 Rothschild, *Baroness*, 83.

9 Ibid.

10 David Kastin, *Nica's Dream: The Life and Legend of the Jazz Baroness* (New York: W.W. Norton, 2011), 25; Hentoff, 'Jazz Baroness'.

11 Koenigswarter, *Three Wishes*, 14; 'Opposites', *Daily Mirror*, 13 June 1929.

12 Hentoff, 'Jazz Baroness'.

13 'Diplomacy and Finance', *Sunday Times*, 26 June 1932; *Tatler*, 29 June 1932; *Bystander*, 29 June 1932.

14 Rothschild, *Baroness*, 92.

15 Rothschild and Brodie, 'Down to Earth', track 4: BL Sound Archive.

16 'Maria de Kammerer, A Portrait Painter', *New York Times*, 20 July 1970.

17 Kastin, *Nica's Dream*, 25–6; Rothschild, *Baroness*, 96; Billy Amstell, *Don't Fuss, Mr Ambrose: Memoirs of a Life Spent in Popular Music* (Staplehurst: Spellmount, 1986), 64.

18 It has previously been claimed that Nica was the first woman to earn a pilot's 'A licence', but that accolade belongs to Lady Heath, who obtained hers in 1929: see *Dundee Evening Telegraph*, 30 August 1929.

19 Rothschild, *Baroness*, 94; Robin D.G. Kelley, *Thelonious Monk: The Life and Times of an American Original* (London: JR, 2010), 175.

20 Rothschild, *Baroness*, 96; Kelley, *Thelonious Monk*, 175.

21 Kelley, *Thelonious Monk*, 175; Kastin, *Nica's Dream*, 27; *New York Times*, 16 October 1935.

22 Rothschild, *Baroness*, 100–1.

23 'Historic Chateau Figures in Sale', *New York Times*, 19 September 1937; Rothschild, *Baroness*, 107–8.

24 Rothschild, *Baroness*, 100.

25 T. Becker and D. Bennett, 'Rudolf Karl Freudenberg: From Pioneer of Insulin Treatment to Pioneering Social Psychiatrist', *History of Psychiatry*, 11, 32 (2000); Niall McCrae, '"A Violent Thunderstorm": Cardiazol Treatment in British Mental Hospitals', *History of Psychiatry*, 17, 1 (2006): 70.

CHAPTER 34:
Before the Bombs

1 'Lady Battersea – Liberal Hostess and "Grande Dame"', *The Times*, 23 November 1931.

2 'Zoology Research: Lord Rothschild's Request', *The Times*, 18 February 1938; Rothschild, *Dear Lord Rothschild*, 314–15.

3 Miriam Rothschild, 'Cercaria sinitzini n.sp., a cystophorous cercaria from Peringia ulvae (Pennant 1777)', *Novitates Zoologicae*, 41, 1 (May 1938): 42.

4 'Miriam Rothschild', *Women of the Century*.

5 Miriam Rothschild, 'Rearing Animals in Captivity for the Study of Trematode Life Histories. I. Larus ridibundus L., the Black-Headed Gull', *Journal of the Marine Biological Association of the United Kingdom*, 21, 1 (November 1936): 145.

6 Miriam Rothschild, 'Rearing Animals in Captivity for the Study of Trematode Life Histories. II', *Journal of the Marine Biological Association of the United Kingdom*, 24, 2 (August 1940): 615.

7 Ibid., 616.

8 Miriam to Dorothy, 12 September 1933: WHA JDR2/1/370/5.

9 Miriam to James, 2 October 1933: WHA JDR2/1/371/1.

10 Rothschild, *Baroness*, 110.

11 Susan Tegel, *Nazis and the Cinema* (London and New York: Hambledon Continuum, 2007), 129–32; Nicholas Reeves, *The Power of Film Propaganda: Myth or Reality?* (London and New York: Cassell, 1999), 112–13.

12 Miriam to Karl Jordan, 3 December 1938: Natural History Museum Archive, London (hereafter NHM), TM/3/11/30.

13 'Jews Urged to Help Appeal', *Western Morning News*, 12 December 1938; *The Times*, 22 June 1939. Miriam Rothschild, 'John Foster and the Jews', John Foster Memorial Lecture, University College London, 4 November 1986.

14 Rothschild and Brodie, 'Down to Earth', track 7: BL Sound Archive.

15 Miriam to Dorothy, 26 August 1939: WHA JDR2/15/7.

16 Ibid., 17 October 1939.

17 Ibid., 22 October 1939.

18 Ibid., [November 1939].

19 Ibid., 22 October 1939.

20 Miriam Rothschild, 'A Liberating Aerial Bombardment', *Scientist*, 26 July 1987.

21 Rothschild and Brodie, 'Down to Earth', track 7: BL Sound Archive.

22 'Miriam Rothschild', *Women of the Century*.

23 'Duty £201,061 Payable on Rothschild Estate', *Daily Express*, 20 August 1940.

24 Rothschild and Brodie, 'Down to Earth', track 7: BL Sound Archive.

25 Ibid.; Letter to Museum Trustees, 20 November 1940: NHM DF ZOO/205/113.

26 Rothschild and Brodie, 'Down to Earth', track 7: BL Sound Archive.

27 Miriam Rothschild, 'A Liberating Aerial Bombardment', *Scientist*, 26 July 1987.

28 'Miriam Rothschild', *Women of the Century*.

29 Ibid.

CHAPTER 35:
Sisters in Arms

1 Kastin, *Nica's Dream*, 32.

2 *Thelonious Monk: Straight, No Chaser*, dir. Charlotte Zwerin (1988; Burbank, CA: Warner Home Video, 1989), VHS.

3 Rothschild, *The Baroness*, 117.

4 Kastin, *Nica's Dream*, 32; Hentoff, 'Jazz Baroness'.

5 Rothschild, *Baroness*, 117–18.

6 Ibid., 121–2; Kelley, *Thelonious Monk*, 175; Miriam to Dorothy, n.d.: WHA JDR2/15/21.

7 Robert F. Keeler, *Newsday: A Candid History of the Respectable Tabloid* (New York: William Morrow, 1990), 99.

8 'Bulk of Renting Goes to East Side', *New York Times*, 2 August 1940.

9 Colin W. Nettelbeck, *Forever French: Exile in the United States, 1939–1945* (New York: Berg, 1991), 6; Kastin, *Nica's Dream*, 37

10 Rothschild, *Baroness*, 125; Kelley, *Thelonious Monk*, 176; Kastin, *Nica's Dream*, 37–8.

11 Hentoff, 'Jazz Baroness'.

12 'Liner Here Safely after Dodging Torpedoes', *New York Times*, 24 January 1943.

13 Gryn, 'Dame Miriam Rothschild', 56.

14 Martin Sugarman, 'Breaking the Codes: Jewish Personnel at Bletchley Park', *Jewish Historical Studies*, 40 (2005): 197.

15 Gryn, 'Dame Miriam Rothschild', 56; Sugarman, 'Breaking the Codes', 235.

16 Fraser, 'Fritillaries and Hairy Violets'. For the contemporaneous use of Mentmore as a storage facility for artworks evacuated from London, see John Martin Robinson, *Requisitioned: The British Country House in the Second World War* (London: Aurum, 2014), 129–30.

17 Gryn, 'Dame Miriam Rothschild', 56.

18 Annie Gray to Miriam, 26 December 1941: WHA JDR2/51/9.

19 Ben Macintyre, *Agent Zigzag: The True Wartime Story of Eddie Chapman* (London: Bloomsbury, 2007), 172–3; 'Miriam Rothschild', *Women of the Century*.

20 Rothschild and Brodie, 'Down to Earth', track 7: BL Sound Archive.

21 'From Fleas to Film Stars', *Jewish Chronicle*, 23 July 2004.

22 Fraser, 'Fritillaries and Hairy Violets'.

23 Gryn, 'Dame Miriam Rothschild', 56; Rothschild and Brodie, 'Down to Earth', track 7: BL Sound Archive.

24 'Churchill's Secret Commandos', *Daily Mail*, 3 April 1999.

25 Rothschild and Brodie, 'Down to Earth', track 7: BL Sound Archive; Gryn, 'Dame Miriam Rothschild', 56.

26 *The Times*, 18 August 1943; Sugarman, 'Breaking the Codes', 235; 'From Fleas to Film Stars'.

27 'From Fleas to Film Stars'; 'Dame Miriam Rothschild [Obituary]', *Daily Telegraph*, 24 January 2005; Magdolna Hargittai, *Women Scientists: Reflections, Challenges, and Breaking Boundaries* (Oxford: Oxford University Press, 2015), 157.

28 'Churchill's Secret Commandos'.

29 Edmund de Rothschild, *A Gilt-Edged Life: Memoir* (London: John Murray, 1998), 117.

30 'Churchill's Secret Commandos'.

31 Rothschild, *Dear Lord Rothschild*, 89–90.

32 Kastin, *Nica's Dream*, 46; Rothschild, *Baroness*, 125–6.

33 Rothschild, *Baroness*, 126.

34 Ibid., 128; Kastin, *Nica's Dream*, 46.

35 Kastin, *Nica's Dream*, 46–7.

36 Ibid., 49; Rothschild, *Baroness*, 127.

37 Rothschild and Brodie, 'Down to Earth', track 8: BL Sound Archive.

38 Miriam Rothschild to Alister Hinton, 28 June 1945: NHM DF ZOO/232/7/1/1/66.

39 *The Times*, 29 December 1945.

40 Rothschild and Brodie, 'Down to Earth', track 10: BL Sound Archive.

41 Fraser, 'Fritillaries and Hairy Violets'.

42 Miriam Rothschild, *John Foster and the Jews* (privately printed, 1998).

43 Ibid.

44 Ferguson, *World's Banker*, 1008; 'Miriam Rothschild', *Women of the Century*.

45 Kelley, *Thelonious Monk*, 176; Kastin, *Nica's Dream*, 51.

46 Rothschild, *Baroness*, 139–40.

47 Hentoff, 'Jazz Baroness'.

48 *Thelonious Monk: Straight, No Chaser*, dir. Zwerin.

49 Max Gordon, *Live at the Village Vanguard* (New York: Da Capo, 1980), 119.

50 Miriam to Dorothy, 26 December 1949: WHA JDR2/131/2.

51 Fraser, 'Fritillaries and Hairy Violets'.

52 Ibid.

53 Miriam Rothschild, 'My First Book', *The Author* (Spring 1994); Miriam Rothschild and Theresa Clay, *Fleas, Flukes and Cuckoos* (London: Collins, 1952).

54 Rothschild and Brodie, 'Down to Earth', track 8: BL Sound Archive.

55 Haines, 'Rothschild, Dame Miriam Louisa'.

56 'He Arrived on Wednesday!', *New Musical Express*, 18 September 1953.

57 Rothschild and Brodie, 'Down to Earth', track 8: BL Sound Archive.

58 Koenigswarter, *Three Wishes*, 17.

59 'Mulligan, Monk – and then a French Surprise', *Melody Maker*, 5 June 1954.

60 Rothschild, *Baroness*, 184.

61 Kelley, *Thelonious Monk*, 174; Rothschild, *Baroness*, 184.

CHAPTER 36:
Echoes

1 Geoffrey Lewis, *Balfour and Weizmann: The Zionist, the Zealot and the Emergence of Israel* (London: Continuum, 2009), 178.

2 Vera Weizmann, *The Impossible Takes Longer: The Memoirs of Vera Weizmann, Wife of Israel's First President, as Told to David Tutaev* (London: Hamish Hamilton, 1967), 242.

3 Isaiah Berlin to Dorothy, 1 August 1949: WHA JDR2/123/5.

4 Chaim Weizmann, to Dorothy, 8 October 1950: WHA JDR2/161/7.

5 'Mr James de Rothschild: Serious Accident', *Jewish Chronicle*, 22 August 1919; Schama, *Two Rothschilds*, 294; Rothschild, *Rothschilds at Waddesdon*, 125, 129.

6 Harry Bates to Dorothy, 12 February 1949: WHA JDR2/123/3. The Rothschilds who represented Aylesbury were Natty (between 1865 and 1885), Ferdinand (1885–99), Walter (1899–1910) and Lionel Nathan (1910–23).

7 Dorothy to Herbert Mortimer, 3 February 1950: WHA JDR2/152/5.

8 Guthrie Moir to Dorothy, 7 March 1950: WHA JDR2/132/6.

9 Miriam to Dorothy, 11 December 1952: WHA JDR2/235/1.

10 Nicola Loftus, 'Lord Rothschild: My Jewish Roots', *Jewish Chronicle*, 20 June 2019.

11 '15 Who Fled Nazis as Boys Hold a Reunion', *New York Times*, 28 July 1983.

12 H. Bodenheimer to Dorothy, 1 September 1953: WHA JDR2/226/10.

13 Loftus, 'Lord Rothschild: My Jewish Roots'.

14 Vera Weizmann to Dorothy, 27 November 1952: WHA JDR2/223/4.

15 Ibid., n.d.: WHA JDR2/242/4.

16 Dorothy to Peggy Crewe-Milne, 2 April 1954: WHA JDR2/246/14; 'Rothschild Reburial: Paris Ceremony', *Jewish Chronicle*, 2 April 1954.

17 Dorothy to Peggy Crewe-Milne, 2 April 1954: WHA JDR2/246/14.

18 Dorothy to Alexandrine de Rothschild, [1954]: WHA JDR2/259/7.

19 Dorothy to Peggy Crewe-Milne, 2 April 1954: WHA JDR2/246/14.

20 Dorothy to Alexandrine de Rothschild, [1954]: WHA JDR2/259/7; 'Baron de Rothschild's Reburial', *Jewish Chronicle*, 9 April 1954.

21 Isaiah Berlin to Dorothy, 23 March 1950: WHA JDR2/143/4.

22 Dorothy to Moshe Sharett, 17 May 1954: WHA JDR2/252/4.

23 Miriam, Wengen, to Dorothy, 11 January 1956: WHA JDR2/297/1; Miriam to Dorothy, 8 January 1957, 3 August 1957 and 27 December 1957: WHA DMR27/11/1.

24 Miriam Rothschild to F.G.A.M. Smit, 8 July 1953: NHM DF ENT/340/19/3.

25 'The Rothschild Years', Elsfield Village website, https://www.elsfield.net/history/elsfield-in-the-20th-century/the-rothschild-years/; Mary Smith, Ashton Wold, to F.G.A.M. Smit, 10 August 1953: NHM DF ENT/340/19/3.

26 Sir Reginald Franklin to Miriam Rothschild, 19 October 1953: The National Archives, Kew (hereafter TNA) MAF 131/14/17.

27 Miriam Rothschild to Sir Reginald Franklin, 20 October 1953: TNA MAF 131/14/33; 24 October 1953: TNA MAF 131/14/37.

28 Mary Smith, Ashton Wold, to F.G.A.M. Smit, 12 May 1954: NHM DF ENT/340/19/3.

29 Memo submitted by Professor C.D. Darlington, Sir Ronald Fisher and Dr Julian Huxley: TNA HO 345/8/CHP/75.

30 Jill Lloyd, *The Undiscovered Expressionist: A Life of Marie-Louise von Motesiczky* (New Haven, CT, and London: Yale University Press, 2007), 181.

31 Memo submitted by Professor C.D. Darlington, Sir Ronald Fisher and Dr Julian Huxley: TNA HO 345/8/CHP/75.

32 Rothschild and Brodie, 'Down to Earth', track 12: BL Sound Archive; 'Miriam Rothschild', *Women of the Century*.

33 Christopher Sykes, dir., 'Miriam Rothschild', *Seven Wonders of the World*, BBC, 22 March 1995.

34 Miriam to Dorothy, 9 January 1954: WHA JDR2/255/2.

35 Ibid.: WHA JDR2/255/2.

36 Miriam Rothschild to F.G.A.M. Smit, 3 December 1958: NHM DF ENT/340/19/4.

37 'Overdose of Drugs', *Oxford Times*, 13 May 1955.

38 Miriam to Dorothy, 2 January 1956: WHA JDR2/297/1.

39 Ibid., 11 January 1956; WHA JDR2/297/1.

40 Miriam Rothschild to N.D. Riley, 14 July 1955: NHM DF ENT/306/79.

41 Miriam to Dorothy, 20 January 1958: WHA DMR27/11/1.

42 R. Romilly Fedder to Dorothy, 12 November 1957: WHA JDR2/326/4; Carew Wallace to Dorothy, 13 November 1957: WHA JDR2/326/4.

43 Tess Rothschild to Dorothy, [1957]: WHA JDR2/324/22.

44 'Dorothy de Rothschild, 93, Supporter of Israel', *New York Times*, 13 December 1988; 'Court Gift', *Jewish Chronicle*, 4 January 1985; 'Trust's House Her Forte', *Guardian*, 22 December 1988; [Asher Oron and Judy Kestecher], *A Tribute to Mrs James A. De Rothschild – From PICA to Hanadiv 1957–1982* (New York: The Jerusalem Foundation, 1983).

45 Dorothy to Ben Gurion, 30 November 1958: WHA DMR28 uncatalogued [1958/Israel].

46 Dorothy to Edmond Adolphe de Rothschild, [1958]: WHA DMR27/15/9.

47 Ben Gurion to Dorothy, 26 November 1958: WHA DMR28 uncatalogued [1958/Israel].

48 Dorothy to Ben Gurion, 30 November 1958: WHA DMR28 uncatalogued [1958/Israel].

49 Imogen Taylor to Dorothy, 7 November 1958 and 27 November 1958: WHA DMR28 uncatalogued [1958/E].

50 Dorothy to Ben Gurion, 9 November 1959: WHA DMR27/27/1.

51 Dorothy to Miss Eidelberg, 27 October 1958: WHA DMR28 uncatalogued [1958/Israel(PICA)].

CHAPTER 37:
The Baroness, the Bird
and the Monk

1 Rothschild, *Baroness*, 185.

2 Gordon, *Live at the Village Vanguard*, 118.

3 Kastin, *Nica's Dream*, 123; Koenigswarter, *Three Wishes*, 18.

4 Hampton Hawes and Don Asher, *Raise Up Off Me* (New York: CM&G, 1972), 85.

5   Kastin, *Nica's Dream*, 77; Rothschild, *Baroness*, 153.

6   Robert Reisner, *Bird: The Legend of Charlie Parker* (New York: Citadel, 1962), 134.

7   Ibid., 139, 143.

8   Gary Giddins, *Celebrating Bird: The Triumph of Charlie Parker* (Minneapolis, MN: University of Minnesota Press, 2013), 141.

9   Reisner, *Bird*, 133–4.

10 'Charlie Parker, Jazz Master, Dies', *New York Times*, 15 March 1955.

11 David Kastin, 'Nica's Story: The Life and Legend of the Jazz Baroness', *Popular Music and Society*, 29, 3 (2006): 280.

12 Gordon, *Live at the Village Vanguard*, 118; Koenigswarter, *Three Wishes*, 9; Reisner, *Bird*, 132; Samantha Barbas, 'The Most Loved, Most Hated Magazine in America: The Rise and Demise of Confidential Magazine', *William & Mary Bill of Rights Journal*, 25, 121, (2016): 121; Rothschild, *Baroness*, 201.

13 Carl Woideck, *Charlie Parker: His Music and Life* (Ann Arbor, MI: University of Michigan Press, 1996), 50.

14 Julio Cortazar, 'The Pursuer', in *The Jazz Fiction Anthology*, ed. Sascha Feinstein and David Rife (Bloomington, IN: Indiana University Press, 2009), 115.

15 Kelley, *Thelonious Monk*, 185.

16 Gordon, *Live at the Village Vanguard*, 118; Kelley, *Thelonious Monk*, 185.

17 Kelley, *Thelonious Monk*, 210.

18 Kastin, *Nica's Dream*, 97; Ross Russell, *Bird Lives! The High Life and Hard Times of Charlie 'Yardbird' Parker* (London: Quartet, 1973), 314; Leslie Gourse, *Straight, No Chaser: The Life and Genius of Thelonious Monk* (New York: Schirmer, 1997), 128.

19 'Two Doctors Here Known to Users as Sources of Amphetamines', *New York Times*, 25 March 1973.

20 Kelley, *Thelonious Monk*, 268.

21 Horace Silver, *Let's Get to the Nitty Gritty: The Autobiography of Horace Silver* (Berkeley, CA: University of California Press, 2006), 86.

22 Ibid., 87.

23 'Rothschild Niece on Drug Charge', *Daily Express*, 9 March 1956.

24 Silver, *Nitty Gritty*, 88.

25 Rothschild, *Baroness*, 208–9.

26 Kastin, *Nica's Dream*, 128–9.

27 Ibid., 128–30; Kelley, *Thelonious Monk*, 240.

28 Hawes and Asher, *Raise Up Off Me*, 86–7.

29 Gordon, *Live at the Village Vanguard*, 119–20; Rothschild, *Baroness*, 223.

30 Rothschild, *Baroness*, 224; Gordon, *Live at the Village Vanguard*, 120.

31 *State of Delaware* v. *De Koenigswarter*, 177 A 2d 344 (Del. Super. Ct. 1962).

32 Kelley, *Thelonious Monk*, 282.

33 Rothschild, *Baroness*, 232.

34 Ibid.

35 Nica to Mary Lou Williams, 22 March 1960: Institute of Jazz Archive, Rutgers University, Brunswick, NJ (hereafter IJA) Mary Lou Williams Collection, series 3, 3B, MC 60 Box 8/16.

36 Rothschild, *Baroness*, 231.

37 *State of Delaware* v. *De Koenigswarter*, 177 A 2d 344 (Del. Super. Ct. 1962).

38 Miriam to Dorothy, 1 February 1962: WHA DMR27/87/10/4.

39 Kelley, *Thelonious Monk*, 335, 338–9.

40 Ibid., 376; Nica to Mary Lou, Wednesday, 2 June 1965: IJA Mary Lou Williams Collection, series 3, 3B, MC 60 Box 8/16.

41 Nica to Mary Lou Williams, 2 January 1968: IJA Mary Lou

Williams Collection, series 3, 3B, MC 60 Box 8/16.

42 Kelley, *Thelonious Monk*, 396.

43 Rothschild, *Baroness*, 251; Kelley, *Thelonious Monk*, 396.

CHAPTER 38:
The Queen of Fleas

1 David Benedictus, *Dropping Names* (London: Collins, 2005), 51.

2 Ibid., 53.

3 Ibid., 53–4.

4 Miriam to Dorothy, 27 December 1958: WHA DMR27/48/2/4.

5 Ibid., 2 January 1960: WHA DMR27/48/2/3.

6 Benedictus, *Dropping Names*, 56–7.

7 Charles Lane and Miriam Rothschild, 'Notes on Migrant Lepidoptera in Israel. 1. A Southern Movement of the Painted Lady (Vanessa cardui (L.))', *Entomologist*, 94, 1183 (December 1961): 286.

8 'Eichmann in Jerusalem', *New Yorker*, 16 February 1963.

9 Benedictus, *Dropping Names*, 58.

10 Ibid., 57.

11 Miriam to Dorothy, 5 August 1965: WHA DMR27/141/1/4.

12 Benedictus, *Dropping Names*, 51.

13 Miriam to Dorothy, 27 December 1958: WHA DMR27/30/2/5.

14 Hargittai, *Women Scientists*, 157.

15 Haines, 'Rothschild, Dame Miriam Louisa'; Anthony Tucker and Naomi Gryn, 'Dame Miriam Rothschild', *Guardian*, 22 January 2005; Peter Marren, 'Dame Miriam Rothschild', *Independent*, 22 January 2005.

16 J. Harborne, *Introduction to Ecological Biochemistry*, 4th edn (London: Elsevier, 2014), xiii.

17 Miriam Rothschild, 'Observations and Speculations Concerning the Flea Vector of Myxomatosis in

Britain', *Entomologist's Monthly Magazine*, 96, 1152 (May 1960): 106–9.

18 'Miriam Rothschild', *Women of the Century*.

19 'Problem of Schizophrenia', *The Times*, 5 May 1961.

20 Gryn, 'Dame Miriam Rothschild', 54.

21 'Rothschild Grant for Research', *Jewish Chronicle*, 18 January 1963.

22 Miriam to Dorothy, 10 January 1966: WHA DMR27/162/1. The article was 'Schizophrenia: A Chink in the Armour', *New Scientist*, November 1965.

23 Miriam to Dorothy, 9 November 1966: WHA DMR27/162/1.

24 Ibid., 11 September 1967: WHA DMR27/184/3.

25 Dorothy to Alexandrine de Rothschild, 29 December 1965: WHA DMR27/147/13/4.

26 Miranda to Dorothy, [January 1956]: WHA JDR2/303/20; Dorothy to Alexandrine de Rothschild, 2 January 1964: WHA DMR27/127/13/3.

27 Miriam (Lane) Rothschild to Marie-Louise von Motesiczky, n.d.: Tate Gallery Archive (hereafter TGA) 20129/1/1/234/13; Marie-Louise von Motesiczky to Miriam (Lane) Rothschild, n.d.: TGA 20129/1/2/35/2.

28 Miriam (Lane) Rothschild to Marie-Louise von Motesiczky, n.d.: TGA 20129/1/1/234/14.

29 Miriam (Lane) Rothschild to Marie-Louise von Motesiczky, n.d.: TGA 20129/1/1/234/15.

30 Miriam to Dorothy, 18 December 1967: WHA DMR27/184/3.

31 Lawley (host), 'Miriam Rothschild'; Sykes, dir., 'Miriam Rothschild'.

32 Miriam Rothschild and C. Neville, 'Fleas: Insects That Fly with Their Legs', *Proceedings of the Royal*

Entomological Society (London) series C, 32, 3 (June 1967): 9–10.

33 Miriam to Dorothy, 18 December 1967: WHA DMR27/184/3.

34 Charlie to Dorothy, 7 March 1969: WHA DMR27/219/2.

35 Eugene Garfield, 'A Tribute to Miriam Rothschild: Entomologist Extraordinaire', *Essays of an Information Scientist*, 7, 17 (April 1984): 121.

36 Landsborough Thomson to T.C.S. Morrison-Scott, 16 November 1968: NHM DF DIR/933/8/1.

37 Miriam (Lane) Rothschild to Marie-Louise von Motesiczky, n.d.: TGA 20129/1/1/234/15.

38 Miriam (Lane) Rothschild to Marie-Louise von Motesiczky, n.d.: TGA 20129/1/1/234/13.

39 Godfrey Samuel to Marie-Louise von Motesiczky, 30 July 1969: TGA 20129/1/1/241/55.

40 Marie-Louise von Motesiczky to Miriam (Lane) Rothschild, n.d.: TGA 20129/1/2/35/2.

41 Ibid.

42 Miriam to Dorothy, 12 August 1968: WHA DMR27/202/1/3.

43 Ibid., 10 March 1969: WHA DMR27/219/1.

CHAPTER 39:
Spare Rib and
the Subversive Stitch

1 Angela Phillips, 'Spare Rib, the Business', British Library, https://www.bl.uk/spare-rib/articles/spare-rib-the-business.

2 Pennina Barnett, 'A Tribute to Rozsika Parker (1945–2010)', *Textile*, 9, 2 (2011): 203.

3 Griselda Pollock, 'Parker [née Lane], (Mary) Rozsika [Rosie] (1945–2010), art historian and

psychotherapist', *ODNB*, 9 January 2014; 'Sidelines: Spare Rib and Tomatoes', *Guardian*, 15 June 1972.

4 Louise Kimton Nye, 'Introduction: Spare Rib – The First Nine Years', British Library, https://www.bl.uk/spare-rib/articles/introduction-spare-rib-the-first-nine-years.

5 Miriam to Dorothy, 29 August 1972: WHA DMR27/280/5.

6 Marsha Rowe, 'How and Why Does Spare Rib Work as a Collective?', *Spare Rib* (February 1975); Michele Roberts, *Paper Houses: A Memoir of the 70s and Beyond* (Virago: London, 2008), 128–9.

7 Frances Horsburgh, 'In the Front Line of Women's Lib', *Reading Evening Post*, 18 July 1974.

8 'Three Friends', *Spare Rib* (June 1973).

9 Rozsika Parker and Griselda Pollock, *Old Mistresses: Women, Art and Ideology* (London: I. B. Tauris, 2013), xxv.

10 'Woman Power', *Spare Rib* (June 1973).

11 'Women's Lib Artists at Swiss Cottage', *Guardian*, 19 April 1973; 'Police See "Women's Lib" Art Show', *The Times*, 19 April 1973.

12 'Woman Power'.

13 Barnett, 'Tribute', 202; Rozsika Parker, 'Women Artists Take Action', *Spare Rib* (July 1973); A brief history of the Women's Workshop of the Artists' Union issued by the Women's Workshop, April 1974: Goldsmiths Special Collections, University of London (hereafter GSS), WAL/2/3/3; Rozsika Parker, 'The Story of Art Groups', *Spare Rib* (June 1980).

14 Barnett, 'Tribute', 202–3.

15 Rozsika Parker, 'The Word for Embroidery Was Work', *Spare Rib* (July 1975).

16 Rozsika Parker and Griselda Pollock, *Framing Feminism: Art and

the Women's Movement 1970–1985 (London and New York: Pandora, 1987), 20; Griselda Pollock, 'The Image in Psychoanalysis and the Archaeological Metaphor', in Psychoanalysis and the Image: Transdisciplinary Perspectives, ed. Griselda Pollock (Oxford: Blackwell, 2006), 14.

17 Christopher Ward, 'Danger! These Women Are Liberated', Daily Mirror, 9 August 1974.

18 Miriam to Dorothy, 24 December 1973: WHA DMR27/300/14.

19 Ibid., 25 September 1973: WHA DMR27/300/14.

20 Ibid., 26 September 1973: WHA DMR27/300/14.

21 Ruth Petrie, 'A Day in the Life of Spare Rib', British Library, https://www.bl.uk/spare-rib/articles/a-day-in-the-life-of-spare-rib.

22 Ibid.

23 Barnett, 'Tribute', 203.

24 Parker and Pollock, Old Mistresses, xxiv.

25 Miriam (Lane) Rothschild to Marie-Louise von Motesiczky, 16 October 1981: TGA 20129/1/1/234/7.

26 Facsimile of Spare Rib Manifesto, June 1972, British Library, https://www.bl.uk/collection-items/facsimile-of-spare-rib-manifesto.

27 Natalie Thomlinson, '"Sisterhood is Plain Sailing?" Multiracial Feminist Collectives in 1980s in Britain', in The Women's Liberation Movement: Impacts and Outcomes, ed. Kristina Schulz (New York: Berghahn, 2017), 207.

28 'Jewish Sisters Under the Skin', Jewish Chronicle, 25 June 1982.

29 Rozsika Parker, 'Being Jewish: Anti-Semitism and Jewish Women', Spare Rib (February 1979).

30 Natalie Thomlinson, Race, Ethnicity and the Women's Movement in

England, 1968–1993 (Basingstoke: Palgrave Macmillan, 2016), 111.

31 'Jewish Sisters Under the Skin'.

32 Robert Fisk, Pity the Nation: Lebanon at War (Oxford: Oxford University Press, 1991), 255; Richard Gabriel, Operation Peace for Galilee: The Israeli–PLO War in Lebanon (New York: Hill & Wang, 1984), 165.

33 Roisin Boyd, 'Women Speak Out against Zionism', Spare Rib (August 1982).

34 'Dig in the Rib for Israel', Jewish Chronicle, 20 May 1983.

35 'Sisterhood . . . is Plain Sailing', Spare Rib (July 1983).

36 'Dig in the Rib for Israel'.

37 Petrie, 'Day in the Life of Spare Rib'.

38 Rozsika Parker, Subversive Stitch: Embroidery and the Making of the Feminine (London: Women's Press, 1984).

39 Barnett, 'Tribute', 209–10.

40 Miriam to Dorothy, 30 March 1984: WHA DMR27/434/1.

CHAPTER 40:
'A Glorious Indian Summer'

1 Peter Marren, 'Dame Miriam Rothschild', Independent, 22 January 2005; Rothschild and Brodie, 'Down to Earth', track 8: BL Sound Archive; Miriam Rothschild, Kate Garton and Lionel de Rothschild, The Rothschild Gardens (London: Gaia, 1996), 106; Ray Hough, dir., 'A Feast of Colour', Geoff Hamilton's Paradise Gardens, BBC, 28 January 1997.

2 Rothschild and Brodie, 'Down to Earth', track 10: BL Sound Archive.

3 Hough, dir., 'Feast of Colour'.

4 Rothschild and Brodie, 'Down to Earth', track 8: BL Sound Archive.

5 Miriam to Dorothy, 29 July 1973: WHA DMR27/300/14.

6 Rothschild and Brodie, 'Down to Earth', track 8: BL Sound Archive.

7 Rothschild, Garton and de Rothschild, *Rothschild Gardens*, 16, 18.

8 Fraser, 'Fritillaries and Hairy Violets'.

9 Miriam to Dorothy, 5 February 1970: WHA WHA DMR27/239/1.

10 Ibid., [29] April 1978: WHA DMR27/343/19.

11 Rothschild and Brodie, 'Down to Earth', track 8: BL Sound Archive; Miriam to Dorothy, 1 May 1973: WHA DMR27/300/14.

12 Miriam to Dorothy, 4 December 1973: WHA DMR27/300/14.

13 Ibid., 31 August 1974: WHA DMR27/319/14.

14 Liberty to Dorothy, 25 October 1974: WHA DMR27/319/14.

15 Fraser, 'Fritillaries and Hairy Violets'.

16 John Timlin, 'Adamson Collection', essay 2: WL PP/ADA/C/5.

17 Miriam Rothschild to Adamson, 13 December 1986: WL PP/ADA/A/4 Box 1; John Timlin, 'Adamson Collection', essay 1: WL PP/ADA/C/5.

18 John Timlin, 'Adamson Collection', essay 2: WL PP/ADA/C/5.

19 JB to Adamson, 26 October 1974: WL PP/ADA/A/4 Box 1; Janet Cook to Adamson, 6 March 1987: PP/ADA/A/4 Box 1.

20 Edward Adamson with John Timlin, *Art as Healing* (London: Conventure, 1984); Nica de Koenigswarter to Adamson, 12 April 1984: WL PP/ADA/A/1.

21 Kelley, *Thelonious Monk*, 418–19.

22 Ibid., 431–2, 411, 441.

23 Ibid., 439.

24 Ibid., 440.

25 Ibid., 442–3.

26 Ibid., 442.

27 Nica to Mary Lou Williams, 3 November 1977: IJA Mary Lou Williams Collection, series 3, 3B, correspondence with Nica Baroness Koenigswarter; Nica to Mary Lou Williams, 15 February 1979: IJA Mary Lou Williams Collection, series 3, 3B, correspondence with Nica Baroness Koenigswarter.

28 Gourse, *Straight, No Chaser*, 292.

29 Kastin, *Nica's Dream*, 204.

30 'Friends Pay Tribute to Monk with His Music', *New York Times*, 23 February 1982.

31 Miriam to Dorothy, 22 March 1984: WHA DMR27/434/1.

32 Nica de Koenigswarter to Adamson, 16 July 1984: WL PP/ADA/A/1.

33 Ibid., 19 October 1984.

34 Visitors Book, 11 May 1986: WL SA/ADC/D/1/1 Box 7.

35 Miriam to Dorothy, 20 August 1967: WHA DMR27/184/3.

36 Ibid., 6 June 1986: WHA DMR27/468/1.

37 Kastin, *Nica's Dream*, 210, 11.

38 Rothschild, *Baroness*, 272.

39 *Round Midnight*, dir. Bernard Tavernier (Burbank, CA: Warner Home Video, 1986), VHS.

40 Rothschild, *Baroness*, 272; 'Creating a Buzz: A Primer', *New York Times*, 27 June 1997.

41 Kastin, *Nica's Dream*, 217.

42 Ibid., 217–18.

43 Jessie Mangaliman, 'Baroness "Nica" de Koenigswarter', *Newsday*, 2 December 1988.

44 Kastin, *Nica's Dream*, 220–2.

45 Ibid., 220.

46 'Baroness Pannonica de Koenigswarter, 74', *New York Times*, 2 December 1988.

47 'Koenigswarter Service', *New York Times*, 10 December 1988.

48 Rothschild, *Baroness*, 272–3.

CHAPTER 41:
Mothers and Daughters

1 Handwritten note (Adamson) [1988]:
WL PP/ADA/A/4.
2 'Jerusalem Honours Mrs de
Rothschild', *Jewish Chronicle*, 2 July
1982.
3 'Philanthropist Dorothy de
Rothschild dies at 93', *Jerusalem Post*,
12 December 1988.
4 'Memorial Service', *The Times*, 12
January 1989.
5 'Rothschild Settles Old Master
Dispute', *Observer*, 18 March 1990.
6 Pollock, 'Parker [née Lane]'.
7 Miriam to Dorothy, 15 October 1985:
DMR27/468/1.
8 Melissa Benn, 'Deep Maternal
Alienation', *Guardian*, 28 October 2006.
9 Rothschild and Brodie, 'Down to
Earth', track 11: BL Sound Archive;
'A Hidden Link with Nature', *The
Times*, 16 June 1994.
10 Ashley Bruce, dir., 'Wild Flowers',
Nature Watch, Thames TV, 23 May 1988.
11 Miriam to Dorothy, 25 October 1985:
WHA DMR27/468/1.
12 Ibid., [1987]: WHA DMR27/486/5.
13 Rothschild and Brodie, 'Down to
Earth', track 12: BL Sound Archive.
14 Daniel Smith, 'It's the End of
the World as We Know it ... and
He Feels Fine', *New York Times
Magazine*, 17 April 2014.
15 Barbara Bryant, *Twyford
Down: Roads, Campaigning and
Environmental Law* (London: Spon,
1995), 42–5.
16 'Dame Miriam Rothschild
[Obituary]'; Hannah Rothschild,
'Five-Minute Memoir: Great Aunt
Miriam', *Independent Magazine*, 28
April 2012.
17 Fraser, 'Fritillaries and Hairy Violets'.
18 'Dame Miriam Rothschild
[Obituary]'.

19 Bruce, dir., 'Wild Flowers'; Chris
Tookey, dir., 'Animal Rights', *After
Dark*, Channel 4, 3 July 1988; 'Miriam
Rothschild', *Women of the Century*;
Hough, dir., 'Feast of Colour'; Sykes,
dir., 'Miriam Rothschild'.
20 Douglas Martin, 'Miriam
Rothschild, High-Spirited
Naturalist, Dies at 96', *New York
Times*, 25 January 2005.
21 Sykes, dir., 'Miriam Rothschild';
Alec Guinness, *My Name Escapes Me:
Diaries of a Retiring Actor* (London:
Hamish Hamilton, 1996), 14–15.
22 Miriam Rothschild to Sir Alec
Guinness, 31 December 1995: BL
Add MS 89015/2/7/13, fo. 75.
23 Alec Guinness, *A Positively Final
Appearance: A Journal, 1996–8* (New
York, NY: Viking, 1999), 78.
24 Ibid., 87–8; Miriam Rothschild
to Sir Alec Guinness, [1997]: BL
Add MS 89015/2/7/13, fo. 69; Sir
Alec Guinness, photograph with
description on the back: BL Add
MS 89015/2/7/13, fo. 76.
25 Helmut F. Van Emden and Sir John
Gurdon FRS, 'Dame Miriam Louisa
Rothschild CBE', *Biographical
Memoirs of Fellows of the Royal
Society*, 52 (2006): 315–30; 'Miriam
Rothschild', *The Economist*, 5
February 2005.
26 Nigel Hawkes, 'Dragonfly Dowager',
The Times, 15 July 1996.
27 'Dynastic Date', *The Times*, 28
February 1994.
28 Nadine Brozan, 'Chronicle', *New
York Times*, 1 March 1994.
29 Quoted in 'Rothschilds Celebrate
"Happy Homecoming" in Frankfurt',
Jewish Chronicle, 11 November 1994.
30 Jacob Rothschild, 'Preface', in
Heuberger, ed., *Rothschilds*, 12.
31 Miriam (Lane) Rothschild to Marie-
Louise von Motesiczky, 16 October
1981: TGA 20129/1/1/234/7.

32 Both were published in Heuberger, ed., *Rothschilds*.

33 Rothschild, 'Silent Members of the First EEC: The Women', 155; Naomi Shepherd, *A Price below Rubies: Jewish Women as Rebels and Radicals* (London: Weidenfeld & Nicolson, 1993), 17.

34 Rothschild, 'Silent Members of the First EEC', 155–6.

35 Ibid., 157.

36 Ibid., 156.

37 Ibid., 156–7.

38 Ibid., 158, 162.

39 Fraser, 'Fritillaries and Hairy Violets'.

40 'Miriam Rothschild', *The Economist*, 5 February 2005.

41 HRH The Prince of Wales and Bunny Guinness, *Highgrove: A Garden Celebrated* (London: Weidenfeld & Nicolson, 2014); 'Three Peerages among the New Year's Honours', *Jewish Chronicle*, 7 January 2000.

42 Van Emden and Gurdon, 'Dame Miriam Louisa Rothschild'.

43 Martin, 'Miriam Rothschild, High-Spirited Naturalist'; 'I Remember: Miriam Rothschild', *Globe and Mail*, 3 February 2005; Adrian Higgins, 'The Flowering of a Fertile Mind: Ecologist Miriam Rothschild Turned Her Estate into One Wild Laboratory', *Washington Post*, 10 February 2005; 'Cherish the Diaphanous Bladder Fern – And the Enthusiast Who Found It', *Country Life*, 27 January 2005; 'Miriam Rothschild', *The Economist*, 5 February 2005; 'Dame Miriam Rothschild', *Independent*, 10 February 2005; 'Dame Miriam Rothschild', *Jewish Chronicle*, 11 February 2005; 'A Tribute to Miriam Rothschild', *American Entomologist*, 51, 1 (Spring 2005): 58–63; 'Miriam Rothschild 1908–2005', *Journal of Parasitology*, 91, 6 (December 2005): 1293; Alan Burdick, 'Parasite Lover', *New York Times Magazine*, 25 December 2005.

44 Rozsika Parker, *Torn in Two: The Experience of Maternal Ambivalence* (London: Virago, 2005), xiii.

Index

Page numbers in *italic* refer to illustrations.

Aberdeen, Ishbel Hamilton-Gordon, Marchioness of 235, 236, 242
Adams, Marian 210, 211
Adamson Collection 351–2
Adamson, Edward 351–2, 354, 356, 357
Adelaide, Queen 80
Ahmed (Art Blakey's 'band boy') 322–3
Albert, Prince Consort 157, 187
Algonquin Hotel, New York 323
Alvars, Elias Parish 102
Andersen, Hans Christian 139
4 Angel Court, City of London 28, 29, 30, 119
antisemitism
    on the Continent 11, 14–15, 58, 225, 262, 264, 275, 281, 288; *see also* Holocaust
    in England 45–6, 57, 106, *131*, 132–3, 152, 187, 225, 300–1, 343–4, 344–6
Arnold, Matthew 148–9, 151, 201
Art as Healing (Adamson) 352, 354
art therapy 272, 351–2
Arundel House, 4 Palace Green, Kensington, London 256, 275
Ashkenazi Jews 45, 225
Ashton Wold, Northamptonshire
    Adamson Collection 351–2
    Charles's love of 257, 276
    Charles's suicide 278
    Liberty's death 356, 357
    Miriam and George's agricultural endeavour 299, 303

Miriam inheriting 290
Miriam returning to 332, 349
Miriam's children returning to 350–1
Miriam's daily life 359, 360, 361
Miriam's death 364–5
Nica's visits 292–3, 303, 354, 355
Rózsika's death 298
Second World War 289, 290, 295, 296
wildflower gardens 349, 359
Asquith, Raymond 227, 242, 243
Aston Clinton, Buckinghamshire 149–51, 179, 184, 185, 188–9, 201–3, 228, 231, 232, 249, 272
Austria 56–7, 59, 134, 168, 180–1, 276, 288, 331
Austria-Hungary 253, 254, 255, 257, 275
Aylesbury prison 234–5, 236

Balcarres, Fife 204–5, 207, 210
Balfour, Arthur, 1st Earl 268, 269
Balfour, Patrick 279
Balfour Declaration 4, 270–1
bank, Oppenheim 18
bank, Rothschild
    branches 6, 59
    First World War 274
    Gutle's role 19
    Hannah's role 31–2, 35, 60–1, 73, 75–6, 77, 79–80, 85–6, 89–90, 98
    Napoleonic Wars 34–5, 87

bank, Rothschild (cont.)
  Rózsika's role 258, 274–5, 276
  women, official exclusion of 2–3, 35–6
bank, Schnapper 12–13
Barent Cohen, Hannah *see*
  Rothschild, Hannah de (née
  Barent Cohen)
Barent Cohen, Levi 28, 29, 30, 32–3
Barent Cohen, Lydia 28
Barent Cohen, Solomon 32–3
Barnum, P.T. 117–18, *118*
Bayliss, Dr 290
Beaulieu, Sandgate, Folkestone 330–1
Bedford College, University of
  London 279
Begin, Menachem 346
'Being Jewish' (Parker) 343–5
Bellini, Vincenzo 64
Bellos, Linda 347
Ben-Gurion, David 306, 309, 316, 317
Benedictus, David 327, 329
Bentinck, Lord George 130, 132, 146
Berlin, Isaiah 306, 309, 316
Bexley, Nicholas Vansittart, 1st Baron
  70
'Bill for the Relief of His Majesty's
  Subjects Professing the Jewish
  Religion' (1830) 71–2
'Bird' *see* Charlie Parker ('Bird')
Bird (Eastwood) 355
Black, Henry 308
Blakey, Art 322–3
Bletchley Park, Buckinghamshire 294–5,
  296–7
Board of Deputies of British Jews
  69–70, 128
Board of Prison Visitors 234
Bodenheimer, Hans 308
Boehm, Sir Joseph Edgar 216
Bolivar (hotel), New York 321–2
Book of Snobs, The (Thackeray) 138
Booth, Mrs Alfred 235
Boyd, Roisin 346
Brassey, Maria 315, 316
Brecon, Powys 197, 198–201, 230
Brighton, Sussex 58, 77–8
British Museum 285–6, 350

Browning, Robert 211
Buderus, Carl 24, 25, 26
Burne-Jones, Edward 207, 208, 211
Butler, Josephine 223, 241

Cairo, Egypt 298
Caleb Asher (Charlotte Montefiore) 124
Canetti, Elias 335, 343
1 Carlton Gardens, St James's,
  London 259
Caroline (Blanche FitzRoy) 212
'Cat House', Weehawken, New
  Jersey 323, 326, 352–3, 355, 356
Catholic emancipation 68–70, 71
Cecil, Robert, 1st Viscount Cecil of
  Chelwood 265–6, 270
Cedars Boys 307–8
Chalet Friedheim, Wengen,
  Switzerland 310, 313, 314, 331, 332
Chambers, Lizzie 205
Charcroft House, Shepherd's Bush,
  London 226–7
Charles, Prince of Wales 364
Charles X of France 74
Chartism 135–6
Château d'Abondant, Centre-Val de
  Loire, France 283, 292, 301
Château de Suresnes, Paris 74–5
Cheap Jewish Library (CJL) 124–5, 147
Chelius, Maximilian 84–5
Chelsea, Henry Cadogan,
  Viscount 152–3
Chelsea Polytechnic 279, 280
Churchill, Winston 268, 300
circumcision 156–7
Cleveland, Wilhelmina Powlett, Duchess
  of 191
Cohen, Juliana 142, 143
Confrontation in the Forest
  (Motesiczky) 335, 336
Coningsby (Disraeli) 120–1, 123
10 Connaught Place, London 248
Crewe House, Curzon Street, Mayfair,
  London 266
Crewe-Milnes, Margaret ('Peggy') (née
  Primrose), Lady Crewe 214, 258,
  266, 268, 275

Crewe-Milnes, Robert, Lord Crewe 263–4
Cséhtelek, Austria-Hungary 254, 255, 257
Currie, Maynard Wodehouse 177, 181
17 Curzon Street, Mayfair, London 224, 272

Dalberg, Karl Theodor von, Grand Duke 24, 27
Dalmeny House, West Lothian 194–5, 204, 219
Davidson, David 179
Davis, Miles 323–4
de Sola, David Aaron 124
Dear Lord Rothschild (Miriam Rothschild) 354–5
Delane, John Thadeus 118, 127–8, 129, 132, 165, 166, 167, 170
Derby, Edward Smith-Stanley, 14th Earl 167
Dilke, Charles 228–9
Disraeli, Benjamin
    1880 general election 196
    Charlotte's beauty 100
    Delane's attacks on Russell 166
    electoral reform bill 167, 168
    Evelina and Ferdinand's wedding 165
    Gladstone's attack on 194
    Jewish Disabilities Bill 130, 132–3
    Louisa's beauty 108
    Louisa's note of caution 126
    novels 120–1, 123–4, 125
    parliamentary oath, vote on 146
    political rise 120, 122, 126
    Rothschilds, friendship with 102, 108, 119–22, 123, 125, 126, 153, 167, 191, 192
D'Israeli, Isaac 119
Disraeli, Mary Anne (née Evans, formerly Lewis) 108, 119, 122–3, 125, 126, 153
Durdans, The, Epsom, Surrey 192–3

East End Mission 223–4
Eastwood, Clint 355, 356
Edifying and Curious History of Rothschild I, King of the Jews, The 87
Edmond de Clary, Prince 104

Edward, Prince of Wales/Edward VII ('Bertie') 187–8, 190, 192, 209, 216, 238, 241, 242
Edward I 45–6
Egyptian Hall, Piccadilly 61, 211–12
Eichmann, Adolf 328
electoral reform 136, 165, 166, 167–8, 236, 242–3, 277
Elsfield Manor, Elsfield, Oxfordshire 303, 310, 313, 314, 327, 329, 332
endogamy 58–9
Entomologist 314, 328
etymology of 'Rothschild' 17
Eule (Owl), Judengasse, Frankfurt 12, 13
Eythrope, Buckinghamshire 315, 318

Fawcett, Millicent 236, 242
feminism 338–41, 343, 345, 365
Ffrwdgrech House, Ffrwdgrech, Brecon, Powys 198, 200
Firm of Nucingen, The (Balzac) 87
First World War
    armistice 273–4
    bombing raids 272
    fleeing from Continent 253–4
    Franz Ferdinand, assassination of 248
    preparations in England 248–9
    Rothschild bank, impact on 274
    Rothschild casualties 270, 273
    Rothschild homes, use of 248, 249, 258, 272
    Rothschilds enlisting 260–1
    Rothschilds under suspicion 258
    Zionist hopes 263; *see also* Zionism/anti-Zionism
Fischer, Benjamin and Jane 313, 315
Fischer, Gabrielle ('Gay') 313, 314–15
FitzRoy, Arthur Frederick 114, 143
FitzRoy, Blanche *see* **Lindsay, Caroline Blanche Elizabeth, Lady ('Blanche') (née FitzRoy)**
FitzRoy, Hannah Mayer *see* **Rothschild, Hannah Mayer de (later FitzRoy)**
FitzRoy, Henry 103–6, 114, 143

Fleas, Flukes and Cuckoos (Miriam
  Rothschild) 302–3, 360
Flower, Constance *see* **Rothschild,
  Constance de (later Constance
  Flower, Lady Battersea)**
Flower, Cyril, 1st Baron Battersea
  atheism 202
  barony offer 230
  beauty 181
  Constance, engagement to 182–3
  Constance, meeting and
    courting 181–2
  Constance, relationship with 202–3,
    228–9, 232, 243
  death and funeral 245
  Dilke, support for 228–9
  Gladstone, support for 230
  governorship of New South Wales
    offer 230–2
  illnesses 244–5
  Karlsbad, time in 244
  King Edward VII's support 241
  motoring obsession 243
  The Pleasaunce, Overstrand 233, *233*,
    240, 241–2, 243
  political ambitions 193
  political campaigns 197, 198–201
  political offices 230
  Princess Louise, hosting 216, 217
  Queen Victoria's funerary cortège
    237
  Queen Victoria's visit to
    Waddesdon 218
  sanatorium visits 241
  scandal and retreat 240–1
  sexuality 181, 240–1
Forrester, Joel 353–4, 356
Forster-Cooper, Clive 290
Foster, John 287, 288–9, 293, 299, 300,
    301, 341
France
  First World War 260–1
  Frankfurt, taking of 21
  Jules appointed diplomat 301
  Napoleonic Wars 23–4, 32, 34–5
  political disorder/unrest 74–6, 79,
    134–6

Rothschild bank, rue d'Artois,
  Paris 60, 75, 77
Second World War 292, 293, 296, 297,
  298
stock market volatility 75–6, 79
France Forever 293
Francis I of Austria 57
Frankfurt, Germany
  antisemitism 11, 14–15
  Cedars Boys 307–8
  equality of civil rights 27
  French occupation 21
  Jewish ghetto *see* Judengasse,
    Frankfurt, Germany
  Jewish Museum exhibition 362
  National Assembly 134, 135, 136–7
  'protection taxes' 27
  Prussian occupation 140, 168
  Rothschild summits 73–4
  Rothschild tourism 81–2
  Rothschild weddings 58–60, 83–4, 95,
    139–40, 141–2, 170
Franz Ferdinand, Archduke of
  Austria 248
Free French 293–4, 298
Freudenberg, Dr Rudolf 283–4, 295
Freymann, Dr Robert 320, 322
From January to December (Charlotte
  Rothschild) 170, 171

Gable, Clark 296
Garcia's Academy, Peckham 51
Garland 246, 247, 248
*General German Encyclopedia for the
  Educated Classes* (Brockhaus) 65–6
Gentz, Friedrich von 65–6
George IV 65, 78
George V 281
Germany *see* First World War; Frankfurt,
  Germany; Judengasse, Frankfurt,
  Germany; Second World War
Gladstone, Catherine 194, 195, 219
Gladstone, Mary 194, 195
Gladstone, William 165–6, 167, 187, 193,
    194–5, 196, 197, 201, 213, 214–15, 219,
    230
Glass, Frederick 164

God Giving Birth (Sjöö) 340
Goldsmid, Isaac Lyon 69, 70
Gosford, Louisa Acheson, Countess 238
Grant, Sir Robert 71
Gray, Annie 295
Great Exhibition (1851) 146–7
12 Great St Helen's, Bishopsgate,
   London 33
4 Great Stanhope Street, Mayfair,
   London 44, 48, 102, 108, 124
'Great Thanksgiving Meeting' 270–1
Greville, Charles 82
Grey, Sir Edward 265
Grosvenor Gallery, London 3, 207–9,
   209, 212
2 Grosvenor Place, Belgravia,
   London 134–6, 138, 155, 178, 248
Grünes Schild (Green Shield),
   Judengasse, Frankfurt 20–1, *21*, 22,
   23–6, 36, 59, 81, 82, 97
Gueorguieva, Veselinka Vladova 316–17
Guggenheim, Harry and Alicia 293
Guinness, Sir Alec 361
Gunnersbury Park, Gunnersbury 89–91,
   90, 99, 119, 130, 146, 152–3, 161, 168,
   169–70, 213, 261
Günthersburg Palace, Bornheim,
   Frankfurt 175
Gwynne-Holford, James 199, 200
Hallé, Charles 207, 209, 212
Hamble Cliff House, Hamble,
   Hampshire 237
Hamilton, Edward 214–15, 218, 219
Hanadiv 316
41–42 Hans Place, Knightsbridge,
   London 211, 212
Hanway Street Sabbath classes,
   London 227
Harman & Co., London 29
Harris, Barry 354, 355
Harris, Jack 281
Hawes, Hampton 319, 323–4
Herbert, Mrs 224
Herries, John Charles 34, 63, 65
Hertz, Abraham 32, 33
Herzog, Chaim 358
Hess, Michael 27

10 Hill Street, Mayfair, London 98
Hinterpfann, Judengasse, Frankfurt 17,
   18, 19, 20
Hitler, Adolf 281
Hobday, William Armfield 52, 65
Hodgkin, Thomas 53–4
Hohenzollern 247–8
Holford, May 210
Hollaender (suitor to Henriette) 37–8,
   39, 40–1
Holocaust 298, 299–300, 301, 308, 328
homosexuality 240–1, 311–13
Horthy, Miklós 276
House of Rothschild, The (film) 287
Hungary 267, 289–90; *see also*
   Austria-Hungary
Hunt, William Holman 207
Hurwitz's Academy, Highgate 51
Hutchinson, Barbara 287

Inglis, Sir Robert 130
intermarriage 58–9
International Council of Women
   (ICW) 235–6, 242
Introduction to Ecological Biochemistry
   (Harborne) 329
Ireland 68, 273, 277
Israel 306–7, 308–10, 315–17, 318, 327–8,
   332, 345–6, 357–8; *see also* Zionism/
   anti-Zionism
Ives, George 241

James, Henry 193, 210
Jarrin, William 62–3, 70
Jazz Cultural Centre, New York 355
Jewish Association for the Removal of
   Civil and Religious Disabilities 128
Jewish Chronicle 124–5, 183, 226, 268, 345,
   365
Jewish communities in England
   antisemitism 45–6, 57–8, 106, *131*,
      132–3, 152, 187, 225, 300–1, 343–4,
      344–6
   Ashkenazi Jews 42, 45, 225
   'Being Jewish' (Parker) 343–5
   Board of Deputies of British Jews
      69–70, 128

Jewish communities in England (cont.)
  Cheap Jewish Library (CJL) 124–5,
    147
  Coningsby (Disraeli) 120–1
  East End 46, 64–5, 147–9, 223–8
  emancipation campaigns 69–72, 130,
    132–3
  exclusionary legislation 46, 68, 69
  German refugees 288, 289, 307–8
  Jewish Association for the Removal of
    Civil and Religious Disabilities 128
  Jewish Ladies' Society for Preventive
    and Rescue Work 224, 225–7
  Jewish Naturalisation Act (1753) 46
  Jewish Religious Union (JRU) 243–4
  Jews' Free School, London 64–5, 67,
    147–9, 152, 225, 262
  Liberal Judaism 243–4
  Manchester 31
  medieval era 45
  Parliamentary oath 152, 153
  Piccadilly 63
  property rights 300–1
  Russian exiles 225, 262
  Sephardic Jews 42, 45, 51
  Stamford Hill 49–50
  West Central Friday Night
    Club 227–8
  Zionism/anti-Zionism 262–4, 265,
    267–8, 268–71
Jewish Museum, Frankfurt 2, 362
Jewish Naturalisation Act (1753) 46
Jewish Religious Union (JRU) 243–4
Jews' Free School, London (JFS) 64–5,
    67, 147–9, 152, 225, 262
Jews, Rothschild duty to 27, 56–7, 65, 68,
    183, 287, 315–17
Johnson, Lady Bird 359
Jopling, Louise 204, 205, 208, 210
Jordan, Karl 267, 288
*Journal of the Marine Biological
    Association* 286
Judengasse, Frankfurt, Germany *12, 13*
  confinement 11–12, 18
  defortification 22
  equality of civil rights 27
  forced resettlement in 14–15

Gutle's refusal to leave 5, 27, 59, 81–2,
    139
  house names 12, 15, 17
  living conditions 11, 15
  military assaults 21
  politics and culture 15–16
  shul and *mikveh* 15

Karlsbad, Germany 244
Kaufmann (suitor to Henriette) 37, 38–9,
    39–40
Kingston House, Kensington,
    London 154, 157
Kishinev massacre, Russian Empire 264
Koenigswarter, Berit de *304*
Koenigswarter, Janka de 292, 303, *304,*
    320, 321, 322–3
Koenigswarter, Jeanne de 292, 301
Koenigswarter, Jules de, Baron 282–3,
    292, 293–4, 298–9, 301, 303, 321
Koenigswarter, Kari de *304*
Koenigswarter, Louis de 292
Koenigswarter, Nica de see **Rothschild,
    Kathleen Annie Pannonica ('Nica')
    (later Baroness de Koenigswarter)**
Koenigswarter, Patrick de 283, 292, 293,
    326
Koenigswarter, Shaun de *304*
Kohl, Helmut 362
Kollek, Teddy 316–17

Lambert, Tony 287
Lane, Charles Daniel 299, 303, 310, *312,*
    314, 327–8, 331, 333, 350
Lane, Charlotte Theresa 303, 310, *312,* 331,
    332, 333
Lane, George (formerly György
    Lányi) 296–7, 299, 303, 310, 333
Lane, Johanna 303, *312,* 331
Lane, Mary Rozsika ('Rosie') see
    **Parker, Rozsika Mary ('Rosie')
    (née Lane)**
Lane, Miriam see **Rothschild,
    Miriam Louisa (sometimes
    'Miriam Lane')**
Lansdowne House, Mayfair,
    London 192–3, 214

Lebanon 346
Ledru-Rollin, Alexandre 135
Lennox, Lord Henry 177–8, 181
Liberal Judaism 243–4
Lindsay, Caroline Blanche
    Elizabeth, Lady ('Blanche') (née
    FitzRoy) 206
  Balcarres 204
  birth 115
  children 205
  Coutts, marriage to 160
  Coutts, separation from 211
  Coutts, unhappiness with 204, 205–6,
    210–11
  entertaining 205, 207, 208–10
  father's death 143
  Grosvenor Gallery 207–9, 209, 212
  Hans Place 212
  Looking Back (Jopling) 204
  mother's death 162
  musical composition 204–5
  outsider status 205
  painting 211–12
  patronage of the arts 207
  pregnancy 162
  self-absorption 161, 162, 163
  writing 212
Lindsay, Euphemia 205
Lindsay, Helen 205, 211
Lindsay, James 210
Lindsay, Minnie 206
Lindsay, Sir Coutts 160, 161, 204–5,
    205–6, 206, 207, 210–11
Liverpool, Robert Jenkinson, 2nd
    Earl 34, 35
Lloyd George, David 247, 268, 273,
    277
Locock, Sir Charles 115, 116
London County Council 218
Looking Back (Jopling) 204
Louis Philippe I 75, 133, 134
Louise, Princess 209, 215–16, 217, 218, 220,
    221–2, 277
Lutyens, Edwin 233
Luz, Kadish 318
Lyndhurst, John Copley, 1st Baron 69,
    70

Madley, Arthur Harris Burfield 205, 210
Madley, Kate 205
Marine Biological Association
    laboratory, Plymouth 280, 290–1
Marlborough House culture 187–8, 189
Masterman, John 129
Melbourne, William Lamb, 2nd
    Viscount 106
Mendelssohn, Felix 63, 64
Mendelssohn, Moses 27, 28
Mental Health Act (1959) 330
Mentmore Towers,
    Buckinghamshire 117, 150, 188, 190,
    191, 193, 197, 214–15, 295, 350
Metternich, Prince Klemens von 57, 60,
    134
Mile End rescue home, London 226
Millais, Effie 212
Millais, John Everett 193, 207
Milner, Alfred, 1st Viscount 268
Mitchell, Victoria 347
Mocatta, Daniel 29, 55
Mocatta, Moses 55
Monk, Nellie 323, 326, 352
Monk, Thelonious 302, 303–4, 305, 321–2,
    323–5, 326, 352–3, 354, 355–6
Monk, Toot 319, 322
Montagu, Lily 243–4
Montagu, Venetia Stanley 287
Montefiore, Abraham 42–3, 44, 45, 46–8,
    50, 53–5, 61
Montefiore, Charlotte 50, 53, 107, 109,
    124, 151
Montefiore, Claude 224, 243–4, 264
Montefiore, Henriette *see* **Rothschild,**
    Henriette de (later Montefiore)
Montefiore, Joseph Mayer 50, 53, 103,
    109, 140–1, 142
Montefiore, Judith (née Barent
    Cohen) 28, 41–2, 53, 61, 69, 74, 76,
    132
Montefiore, Louisa *see*
    Rothschild, Louisa de, Lady (née
    Montefiore)
Montefiore, Mary (née Hall) 42–3
Montefiore, Moses 41–2, 43, 47, 53, 54, 61,
    69, 70, 71, 132–3

Montefiore, Nathaniel 50, 53
Morgan, Fanny 198, 200, 234, 242–3
Moscheles, Ignaz 63, 64
Mosley Street, Manchester 31, 91
Motesiczky, Marie-Louise von 331–2,
    334, 335, 336, 342–3
Munich Academy of Fine Arts 281
Myers, Frederic William Henry 241,
    245
mythology, Rothschild 5, 87, 143–4, 277,
    287–8
myxomatosis committee 310–11

Naples 59, 97, 134, 280
Napoleonic Wars 23–4, 32, 34
National Socialist (Nazi) Party,
    Germany 281, 288, 298, 300, 301
National Trust 315
National Union of Women Workers
    (NUWW) 235–6, 238–9, 242
Natural History Museum, London 255,
    285–6, 288, 290, 302, 334
33 Neue Mainzer Straße, Frankfurt
    96–7
2 New Court, City of London
    as bank 49, 62, 79, 98, 211, 249, 256, 258,
      274, 276
    as home and bank 33, 35, 41–2
New Lanark, Scotland 67
New Scientist 330
New South Wales, Australia 231–2
New View of Society, A (Owen) 67
New York 282–3, 288–9; *see also*
    Rothschild, Kathleen Annie
    Pannonica ('Nica') (later Baroness
    de Koenigswarter)
Norway 246–7
Novitates Zoologicae 285, 286

O'Connell, Daniel 68–9, 71
Old Mistresses (Parker and Pollock)
    342–3, 347–8
Oppenheim, Jacob 18
Oppenheim, Moritz Daniel 88, 97
Ottoman Empire 263, 264
Overstrand, Norfolk *see* The Pleasaunce,
    Overstrand, Norfolk

Owen, Robert 67–8, 71
Oxford, University of 331, 334, 355, 364

Pale of Settlement, Russian Empire 225,
    262
Palestine 262, 263, 265–6, 267–8, 269–70,
    306, 315, 346
Pall Mall Gazette 228
Parker, Charlie ('Bird') 320–1, 355
Parker, Kim 332, 358
Parker, Rozsika Mary ('Rosie') (née
    Lane)
    'Being Jewish' 343–5
    birth 299
    children 358
    at Courtauld Institute 331
    Elsfield, move to 303
    embroidery 347
    feminism 338–41, 342–3, 347–8, 365
    infant sister's death 302
    Kim, meeting 332
    mother–child relationship studies 344,
      358–9, 363–4
    mother, visits to 359
    mother's view of 327
    Old Mistresses (Parker and
      Pollock) 342–3, 347–8
    Pollock, friendship with 340, 342
    psychotherapy work 358
    Samuels, relationship with 358
    Spare Rib 338–41, 341–2, 343–5, 347
    Subversive Stitch, The 347–8
    Torn in Two 364, 365
    Women's Art History Collective 340
parliamentary oath 69, 127, 145–6, 153
Pattison, Emily Francis 188–9
Paxton, Joseph 150
Peel, Sir Robert 120, 122, 130, 132
Pendennis (Thackeray) 138–9
107 Piccadilly, London 61–4, *61*, 68,
    69–70, 72, 73, 90, 91, 98, 104, 133, 145,
    190
143 Piccadilly, London 165, 167, 169
148 Piccadilly, London 99, 100, 117–18,
    121, 127, 136, 154, 159–60, 164–5, 166,
    237, 238, 265, 281
Pigott, Miss 223, 224

Pleasaunce, The, Overstrand,
   Norfolk 217–18, 227, 233, *233*, 240,
   241–2, 243, 245, 248, 249, 272–3, 285
Pollock, Griselda 340, 342
Poppyland (Scott) 217
Powell, Bud 319, 320, 355
press interest in Rothschilds
   book reviews 212, 277–8
   cartoons and satire 57–8, 65, *131*, 138,
      195, 210, 234
   entertaining 50, 70, 195
   fashion 78
   gossip and scandal 56, 240, 241, 320–1,
      323
   Grosvenor Gallery review 208
   Jewish Museum exhibition,
      Frankfurt 362
   marriages 106, 153, 183, 192
   Nathan's death 86–7
   Nathan's illness 85
   obituaries 88, 285, 356, 357, 365
   148 Piccadilly, London 159
   politics 65, 127–8, *131*
   profiles 279, 281, 361
   social reform 124–5, 149, 234, 235, 345
   Zionism/anti-Zionism 268–9
Primrose, Archibald *see* Rosebery,
   Archibald Philip Primrose, 5th Earl
Primrose, Hannah *see* **Rothschild,**
   Hannah de (later Hannah
   Primrose, Countess of Rosebery)
Primrose, Harry *see* Rosebery, Harry
   Primrose, 6th Earl
Primrose, Margaret *see* Crewe-Milnes,
   Margaret ('Peggy') (née Primrose),
   Lady Crewe
Primrose, Neil 214, 261, 270
Primrose, Sybil 194, 214, 248
*Proceedings of the Royal Entomological
   Society* 332
Prussia 21, 140, 168
Pückler-Muskau, Hermann von 51–2
Punch *131*, 195, 210, 234
'Pursuer, The' (Cortázar) 321

Qualification of Women Act (1907) 242
Quisling, Vidkun 301

racial taxonomies 121
racism, anti-black 301, 319–20, 320–1,
   322–3, 343
racism, antisemitic *see* antisemitism
Reiss, J.L. 31–2
Reminiscences (Constance de
   Rothschild) 277–8, *278*, 285
revolutions 74–6, 79, 134–6, 273, 275
Reynolds's Newspaper 225
Ricker, Bruce 355–6
Ripon, George Robinson, 1st
   Marquess 230–1, 232
*Rise and Reign of the House of Rothschild,
   The* (Corti) 1
Roehampton, London 89
Rommel, Erwin 297
Rosebery, Archibald Philip Primrose, 5th
   Earl 191–3, 194, 195, 196, 201, 214–15,
   218, 219, 234, 277
Rosebery, Hannah Primrose, Countess
   see **Rothschild, Hannah de**
   (later Hannah Primrose, Countess
   of Rosebery)
Rosebery, Harry Primrose, 6th Earl 214,
   261, 295
Rossetti, Dante Gabriel 207
Rossini, Gioachino 63, 64, 102
Rothschild, Adèle Hannah Charlotte
   von 175
Rothschild, Adelheid (Carl's wife) 82,
   84, 96–7
Rothschild, Adelheid de (Edmond's
   wife) 260, 308–9, 316
Rothschild, Albert 180–1
Rothschild, Alfred Charles de 113, 157–8,
   167, 187, 188, 248, 249, 259–60, 273
Rothschild, Alice de 169, 218, 220–1,
   222
Rothschild, Alix de 331–2
Rothschild, Alphonse *see* Rothschild,
   Mayer Alphonse James de
   ('Alphonse')
Rothschild, Amschel Mayer von
   Anthony's marriage 109
   Austrian barony 57
   birth 18–19
   civic register 27

Rothschild, Amschel Mayer von (cont.)
Henriette, relationship with 37–8, 41, 44–5, 48
hosting family 59–60, 73, 81, 84, 140
Julie, wish to marry 140–2
Nathan's appointment as Austrian consul 57
Nathan's death 86
National Assembly 137
orthodoxy 59–60
remaining in Frankfurt 59
Savagner's suspicions 25, 26
wife's death 137
Rothschild, Amschel Moses 17
Rothschild, Annie Henriette de (later Yorke)
birth 115
childhood 150, 151, 155
Cyril's New South Wales governorship offer 231, 232
Eliot, marriage to 180–1
Evelina's bridesmaid 165
First World War 248, 249, 272
flirtations 176, 179
Germany visits 175
Grosvenor Place, stripping 248
Jewish Ladies' Society for Preventive and Rescue Work 224
mother's death 246
Norway visit 246–8
Prince of Wales, dislike of 188
Queen Victoria's funerary cortège 237
temperance movement 198–9, 201
Wilhelm II, Kaiser, lunch with 247–8
Rothschild, Anselm Salomon von 58, 74–5
Rothschild, Anthony Gustav de (Leopold and Marie's son) 261
Rothschild, Anthony Nathan de ('Billy')
Annie and Eliot's marriage 180
Aston Clinton girls' school 151
Aston Clinton home 149, 150
baronetcy 128
birth 35
children 114–15
Constance, Seymour's courtship of 178

death 182, 189
Disraelis, hosting 126
education 51
Frankfurt visits 59, 73
Jewish Disabilities Bill 132–3
Jews' Free School 147–8
Lionel's honeymoon 96
Louisa, courting 110–11
Louisa, marriage to 111–12
parents' matchmaking plans 103, 109–10
in Paris 107, 109–10
Yorke family, friendship with 179–80
Rothschild, Babette 19, 38
Rothschild, Betty von 58–9, 60, 104, 130, 134, 135, 139, 141, 153
Rothschild, Carl (Mayer Amschel's brother) 18
Rothschild, Carl Mayer von 19, 20, 30, 38, 39, 40, 41, 47, 56–7, 59, 96–7
Rothschild, Caroline Julie Anselm 77
Rothschild, Caroline von (née Stern) 25, 40, 74
Rothschild, Charles see Rothschild, Nathaniel Charles ('Charles')
Rothschild, Charlotte Beatrice 161
Rothschild, Charlotte de ('Chilly') 31, 59, 74–5, 76–8, 82, 84–5, 114, 137, 140, 141
Rothschild, Charlotte Louise Adela Evelina ('Evelina') (Natty and Emma's daughter) 185
Rothschild, Charlotte von
1848 revolutions 135, 136
Alfred's illness 157–8
Amschel's wish to marry Julie 140, 141
antisemitism at court 187
beauty 83–4, 100
Blanche's engagement 160
Blanche's self-absorption 161, 162, 163
Chelsea, letter to 152–3
childbirth, fear of 115–16
childhood homes 96–7
children 98–9, 113, 116
death and funeral 213
diaries 99
Disraeli (Benjamin), friendship with 119–20, 121–2, 125

Disraeli (Mary Anne), writing about 122–3
duty, burden of 117
education 97
electoral reform 165, 166, 167, 168
Emma and Natty's engagement 168
entertaining 3, 6, 117–18, 121–2, 166, 167
Evelina and child, death of 169–70
Evelina, tribute to 170, 171
Evelina's engagement and wedding 164–5
Evelina's looks 164
Evelina's suitors 164
Folkestone visit 157–8
Frankfurt visit 140, 141–2
grandchildren 155–7, 161, 184, 186, 189
Grasmere visit 154–5
Great Exhibition 146–7
Gunnersbury Park 99, 152, 153, 161, 168, 169–70, 213, 350
Hannah Mayer's death and funeral 162–3
Hannah Mayer's illness 160–1
Hannah (mother-in-law), relationship with 97, 98–9, 99–100
illnesses in old age 189, 213
insecurities 95, 96
From January to December 170, 171
Jewish emancipation campaign 132–3, 153
Jews' Free School 152
Leonora and Alphonse's wedding 153
Lionel, marriage to 82, 83–4, 95, 96
Lionel's attempts to take Commons seat 145
Lionel's election campaign 127, 128, 129
Lionel's gout 158–9
London, arrival in 98
Louisa, relationship with 142–3, 146–7
Paris visits 155–7, 161
Piccadilly home 99, 100, 154, 159
Queen Victoria, presentation to 100
racial taxonomies 121
Tring Park purchase 185

Rothschild, Constance de (later Constance Flower, Lady Battersea)
Alice's response to Queen 220, 221
Annie and Eliot's courtship and wedding 180
Aston Clinton girls' school 151
Aston Clinton home 150, 184, 185, 249, 272
Austria visits 180–1
Aylesbury prison visits and reforms 234–5
birth 114–15
Blanche, closeness to 204, 210–11
Bristol women's work conference 234
Charles' suicide 278
Charlotte's death 213
Christianity, attraction to 202, 203
Connaught Place 248
Cyril, courtship with and engagement to 181–3
Cyril, marriage to 182–3
Cyril, memorial to 245
Cyril, relationship with 202–3, 228–9, 232, 233, 243
Cyril's barony offer 230
Cyril's death 245
Cyril's diaries and papers 245
Cyril's governorship of New South Wales offer 230–2
Cyril's illnesses 244–5
Cyril's political campaigns 193, 197, 198, 199–201
Cyril's scandal and retreat 240–1
Davidson's suicide 179
death 285
diaries 182–3, 240, *278*
Dilke court case 229
Emma and Natty's move to Tring Park 184–5
Evelina and Ferdinand's wedding 165
Evelina's death 169
family disunity 269
family letters 246
father's death 182
First World War 248–9, 272–4
flirtations 164, 176, 177–8, 181

Rothschild, Constance de (later Constance Flower, Lady Battersea) (cont.)

Frankfurt cousins, correspondence with 176
Germany visits 175–6, 244
Gladstone, opinion of 193
grandmother's death 167
Grasse visit 220–2
Grosvenor Gallery 208
Grosvenor Place 155, 178, 248
Hannah, Lady Rosebery, opinion of 193
Hannah, Lady Rosebery's death 219
Hannah Mayer's misfortunes 144
Hanway Street Sabbath classes 227
ICW conferences 235–6, 242
Jewish Ladies' Society for Preventive and Rescue Work 224, 225–7
Liberal Judaism and JRU 243–4
medium, consulting 245
Morgans, friendship with the 198, 200
mother's death 246
National Union of Women Workers 238–9, 242
Norway trip 246–7
obituary 285
Paris revolution 134
Paris visits 181
Pleasaunce, The, Overstrand 217, 227, 240, 242, 243, 244, 245, 248, 249, 272–4, 278, 285
Prince of Wales, dislike for 188
Princess Louise, friendship with 216, 217, 218, 220, 221–2
Queen Victoria's death and funerary cortège 237–8
Queen Victoria's favour 216–17, 218, 221, 222
Reminiscences 277–8, *278*
Rescue and Prevention homes 234
St Moritz visit 182
Surrey House 204, 216, 223, 230–1, 237, 244, 248
Swan coffee house, Aston Clinton 201–2
temperance movement 199, 201–2
West Central Friday Night Club 227–8
'white slavery', work against 223–4
Wilhelm II, Kaiser, lunch with 247–8
Windsor visits 216–17
women voting in 1918 election 277
women's issues campaigns 234–5, 242, 277
writing 273
Yorke's death 179

Rothschild, Dorothy Mathilde de ('Dolly') (née Pinto) *260*, *317*
background 259
Ben-Gurion, correspondence with 316–17
Cedars Boys 307–8
death 357–8
disinterment and reinterment of Edmond and Adelheid 308–9
Edmond and Veselinka's marriage 316–17
Emma's Oxford offer 331
Eythrope home 315, 318
First World War 260–1, 272
Gunnersbury Park 261
Hanadiv 316
Israel philanthropy and visits 308–10, 315–16, *317*, 318, 327–8, 357–8
Israel, State of 306–7
James's death 315
James, meeting and marrying 259–60
Liberty's sixty-fifth birthday 351
London, arrival in 261
Miriam's biography of Uncle Walter 350
political campaigning 307
Waddesdon Manor 307, 308, 315
Weizmann, coaching 266
Weizmann, correspondence with 261–2, 263–4, 266
Weizmann's death 308
will 358
Zionism 267, 268, 270
Rothschild, Edmond Adolphe Maurice Jules Jacques de 316–17

Rothschild, Edmond de, Baron 260, 262, 263, 308–9, 316

Rothschild, Élisabeth 301

Rothschild, Elizabeth Charlotte ('Liberty') 256, 278, 281, 282, 283–4, 295, 310, 330–1, 350–2, 356, 357

Rothschild, Emma Georgina 313, 331, 355

Rothschild, Emma Louisa von, Lady
children 185, 186, 189
cousins' visits 175
death 285
England visit 168
entertaining 186–7, 188, 267
family matriarch after Charlotte's death 213
intelligence 168
Jewish Ladies' Society for Preventive and Rescue Work 224
King Edward VII's favour 238
Marlborough House culture, hatred of 188
Mentmore Towers 188
Natty as MP 201
Natty made Baron Rothschild of Tring 213
Natty, meeting and marrying 168–9
Natty's affair with Lady Gosford 238
Natty's death 265
physical affection, aversion to 186
Queen Victoria's funerary cortège 237
reinventing self 184
Rózsika, friendship with 256
Tring Park 184–5, 185–6, *185*
Walter, overprotection of 255
Walter's birth and illness 184
Walter's menagerie 186
Zionism 266, 267

Rothschild, Eva von (née Hanau) 23, 25, 27, 73, 137

Rothschild, Evelina (Natty and Emma's daughter) *see* Rothschild, Charlotte Louise Adela Evelina ('Evelina') (Natty and Emma's daughter)

Rothschild, Evelina de ('Evy') (Charlotte and Lionel's daughter) 113, 123, 152, 161, 164–5, 166, 167, 169, 170, 171

Rothschild, Evelyn Achille de 261, 270, 330

Rothschild family
crest and motto 57
disunity 46–8, 104, 105–7, 188–9, 267–8, 269–70
summits 73–4
unity 35, 57, 58–9, 66, 189

Rothschild, Ferdinand James Anselm de 164–5, 166, 167, 169, 175, 176–7, 178, 218

Rothschild, Germaine Alice de 261

Rothschild, Gutle (née Schnapper) *26*
1808 police raid and questioning 23–4, 25–6
birth and childhood 11, 12, 13–14
children 18–19, 20
children leaving home 22–3
death 139
dowry 18
Grünes Schild house 20–1
Grünes Schild house, refusal to leave 5, 27, 59, 81–2, 139
Henriette's move to London 41
Hinterpfann home 18
household management 19
household staff 27
Jeannette's marriage 22
luxuries, love of 81
Mayer Amschel, marriage to 16–17, 18
Mayer Amschel's will 36
public interest in 139
registering on civic register and taking civic oath 27

Rothschild, Hannah de (later Hannah Primrose, Countess of Rosebery)
Archibald, ambitions for 214–15, 218
Archibald, meeting and marrying 191–2
childhood home 150
children 194
Dalmeny House 194–5, 219
death and funeral 219–20
Durdans 192–3
entertaining 193, 194–5
father's death 190

Rothschild, Hannah de
 (later Hannah Primrose, Countess
 of Rosebery) (cont.)
  Gladstone's admiration for 214
  Gladstone's cabinet choices 214–15
  India, trip to 218
  inheritance 190
  Lansdowne House 192, 193, 214
  mother's death 191
  personality 190
  political campaigning 194–6, 201, 214,
   218–19
  Queen Victoria's favour 215, 220
  typhoid fever 218–19
Rothschild, Hannah de (née Barent
 Cohen)
  Austrian barony 57
  baroness title 90–1
  Board of Deputies of British
   Jews 69–70
  Brighton visit 77–8
  business interests 60
  Charlotte, relationship with 97, 98–9,
   99–100
  childhood home 29
  children 31, 33, 35, 50–1
  children's education 51, 64
  Chilly's pregnancy 76–7
  death 146
  duc d'Angoulême, business with 77
  duty to Jewish community 68
  education 28
  entertaining 50, 62–4, 68, 69–70, 73,
   119
  estate, equal division of 146
  family life 52
  family portrait 52, 65
  father's death 33
  Frankfurt visits 58–9, 60, 73, 74,
   83–5
  Great St Helen's 33
  Gunnersbury Park 89, 90–1, 90, 99,
   119, 146
  Hannah Mayer's marriage 105, 106
  Henriette, closeness to 45, 54
  Henriette's wedding 43
  household management 74

  Jewish emancipation campaign 69–70,
   71–2, 145, 146
  Jews' Free School 64–5
  Judith, closeness to 41–2
  Lionel's election campaigns 128–9, 145
  Lionel's wedding 83–4
  Mosley Street home, Manchester 31
  musical patronage 64
  Nathan, marriage to 30–1
  Nathan, meeting 28
  Nathan, mourning for 89, 98
  Nathan's death 86
  Nathan's illness 84–6
  Nathan's knighthood offer 56
  Nathan's legacy 88
  Nathan's will 86
  New Court 33, 35, 41–2, 49, 62, 79, 90,
   98
  Oppenheim portraits of sons 88
  Paris visits 74–5, 75–6, 79
  philanthropy 64–5
  Piccadilly home 61–4, *61*, 69–70, 72,
   73, 90
  political lobbying 68
  press interest in 50, 58, 65
  progressive politics 67
  Queen Adelaide's party 78
  Roehampton home 89
  role in bank 31–2, 35, 60–1, 73, 75–6, 77,
   79–80, 85, 86, 89–90, 98
  Russell's emancipation resolution
   130–1, 132
  Stamford Hill House 49–50, 62, 63,
   74, 89
  stock market trading 74, 75–6, 77, 79
  Tisha B'Av incident 119
  trust fund 30
  Wellington's betrayal 71–2
 Rothschild, Hannah Mary 355
Rothschild, Hannah Mayer de (later
 FitzRoy)
  Arthur's accident and death 143
  birth 35, 50
  Blanche, ambitions for 160
  Blanche's disregard for 161, 162, 163
  Blanche's engagement 160–1
  Brighton visit 77–8

children 114, 115
conversion to Christianity 106
death and funeral 162
education 51
family relationships 106–7, 114, 139
family's marriage plans 103
Frankfurt visits 83
Henry, meeting and marrying 103–6
Henry's death 143
illness 160
misfortunes 143–4
mother's estate, share in 146
music 70, 102
post-childbirth illness 115–16
Prince Edmond's proposal 104
upbringing 102
**Rothschild, Henriette de (later
    Montefiore)** *55*
Abraham, devotion to 53–4
Abraham, marriage to 43
Abraham's death 54
Abraham's illness and trip to
    Italy 53–4
Abraham's will 54–5
birth 20
children 50
death and funeral 166–7
dowry 37, 38
entertaining 102, 108, 119
family relationships 44–5, 46–7, 47–8
father's will, impact of 37
Great Stanhope Street home 44, 48,
    102
Hannah, closeness to 45
London, move to 41
matchmaking 102, 103, 109
miscarriage 54
niece Charlotte 82
residences 102
role in Abraham's business 47, 48
Savagner's questioning 25
separation from Rothschilds 48
Stamford Hill home 50, 53, 55, 102
stock market trading 74
suitors 37–41
widowhood 102
Worth Park Farm 102

Rothschild, Isabella 19
Rothschild, Jacob, 4th Baron *see*
    Rothschild, Nathaniel Charles
    Jacob ('Jacob'), 4th Baron
Rothschild, James Armand de
    ('Jimmy') 259–61, *260*, 262, 263, 264,
    266, 270, 306, 307–10, 315, 328
Rothschild, James Mayer de
    1808 police raid and arrest 23, 25
    Amschel's wish to marry Julie 141
    Anthony's marriage 109, 110
    Austrian barony 57
    Betty, marriage to 58–9, 60
    Betty's role in bank 60
    birth 20
    caricatures 138
    civic unrest in France 75, 76
    entertaining 63
    Hannah Mayer, making peace
        with 139
    Hannah Mayer's marriage 105–6,
        106–7
    Henriette and Abraham, animosity
        towards 46, 47–8
    Henriette's suitors 37–8, 40–1
    Leonora and Alphonse's wedding 153
    Paris branch of bank 59
    political cartoons 58
    rue d'Artois home 60
Rothschild, Jeannette 17, 18, 22
Rothschild, Jimmy de *see* Rothschild,
    James Armand de ('Jimmy')
Rothschild, Juliana 117, 150, 188, 190–1
Rothschild, Julie (Chilly's daughter) 77,
    140–2
Rothschild, Julie (Gutle's daughter) 20,
    38
**Rothschild, Kathleen Annie Pannonica
    ('Nica') (later Baroness de
    Koenigswarter)** *304*
alcoholism 322
Algonquin Hotel, New York 323
Ashton Wold visits 303, 354, 355
Bird's illness and death 320–1
birth 256
Bolivar (hotel), New York 321–2
cancer 354

Rothschild, Kathleen Annie Pannonica ('Nica') (later Baroness de Koenigswarter) (cont.)
'Cat House', Weehawken, New Jersey 323, 326, 352–3, 355, 356
Château d'Abondant 283
childhood 256–7, 275
children 283, 301, *304*
children, leaving with Guggenheims 293
children, losing custody of 321
Continental tour with Liberty 281
death and scattering of ashes 356
debutante season 281
as diplomat's wife 301–2
domestic duties, hatred of 301–2
drug abuse 322
drug charge 324–6
father's suicide 278
flight from France 292–3
flying, passion for 282
France Forever work 293
at French finishing school 281
Harris, falling in love with 281
homes in Paris and London 283
honeymoon 283
illness and voyage to America 294
Janka's arrest 322–3
jazz artists, resented by younger 353
Jazz Cultural Centre 355
jazz musicians, helping 319, 320
jazz, passion for 280, 281, 282, 301–2, 303–4, 305, 355–6
Jules, breakdown of marriage with 301–2, 303
Jules, divorce from 321
Jules, meeting and marrying 282–3
Jules's call-up 292
Liberty's death 356
Monk documentary 355–6
Monk, friendship with 304, 305, 321–2, 323–5, 326, 352–3, 354
Monk's arrest in Delaware 324
Monk's death 354
mother, reunion with 292–3
mother's death 293
Munich Academy of Fine Arts 281
New York, move to 305
piano lessons 282
press attacks 320–1
Second World War honours 298
Second World War work 293–4, 298
songs inspired by 321–2
Stanhope Hotel, New York 319, 320–1, 321
Rothschild, Leonora de ('Laury') 99, 100, 152, 153, 155–6, 157, 159, 161, 182, 246
Rothschild, Leopold de ('Leo') 116, 122, 159, 181, 182, 189, 238, 264, 269, 273, 345
Rothschild, Liberty *see* Rothschild, Elizabeth Charlotte ('Liberty')
Rothschild, Lionel James Mayer René de ('René') 155–7
Rothschild, Lionel Nathan de (Hannah and Nathan's son, 1808–79)
Austrian baron title 90
banking role 84, 85–6, 98
birth 33
Blanche's engagement 160
Charlotte, courting 95
Charlotte, honeymoon with 96
Charlotte, marriage to 82–4
children 99, 113
Commons, barriers to taking seat in 130, 145–6
Commons, taking seat in 153
Constance's flirtations 178
death 213
Disraelis, friendship with 119–20, 123
education 51
election campaigns 127–9, 145, 152, 153
entertaining 118–19
Evelina, mourning for 170
Evelina's engagement and wedding 164–5
Evelina's suitors 164
father's illness 85
Frankfurt visits 59, 83, 84
Gladstone's peerage proposal 187, 213
gout 158–9, 189
Grasmere visit 154–5

Hannah Mayer's marriage 105
Jewish emancipation 132–3, 147, 152
Mayfair home 98
mother's banking role 85–6
Paris, civic unrest in 74–5
Piccadilly home 99, 100, 159
Queen Victoria's coronation
  parade 101
René, registering birth of 156
Tring Park purchase 185
Rothschild, Lionel Walter ('Walter'), 2nd
  Baron
  barony, heir to 265
  birth 184
  Charles's jealousy 255
  death 285
  frailty 184, 186
  'Great Thanksgiving Meeting' 270, 271
  illegitimate child 256
  Miriam's biography of 350, 354–5, 363
  mother's overprotection 186, 255
  natural history, interest in 186, 255
  removed from bank 256
  will 285–6
  Zionism 266, 267, 268–9, 270, 271, 363
Rothschild, Lou de see Rothschild,
  Louise de ('Lou')
**Rothschild, Louisa de, Lady (née
  Montefiore)** *148*
  Annie and Eliot's engagement and
    wedding 180
  Anthony, correspondence with 110–11
  Anthony, family's plan for match
    with 103, 107, 109–10
  Anthony, marriage to 111–12
  Anthony's death 182
  Aston Clinton 149–50, 188–9, 228,
    231–2
  beauty 108
  birth 50
  Buckinghamshire schools 150–1
  Caleb Asher (Charlotte
    Montefiore) 124
  Charlotte, relationship with 142–3,
    146–7, 155, 162
  Charlotte's death 213
  Chartism 135–6

Cheap Jewish Library (CJL) 124–5,
  147
childbirth, fear of 115
childhood 53, 108
children 114–15
Constance's engagement 182
Cyril's funeral 245
Cyril's political offices 230, 231–2
daughters' correspondence with
  cousins 176–7
death 246
Disraeli, doubts about 126
entertaining 126
family tensions 188–9
German nationalism 137
Germany visits 136–8, 139, 140, 175
Great Exhibition 146–7
Grosvenor Place 134, 138, 155, 248
Hannah Mayer, visit to 162
Hannah Mayer's funeral 163
Hannah's death 146
Henriette's death 167
house-hunting 111
Jewish Disabilities Bill 132–3
Jews' Free School 147–9
Lionel's election campaign 128, 129
Lou, friendship with 138
in Paris 114
Paris revolution (1848) 134, 135
Parliament's antisemitism 132–3
piety 108, 112
Queen Victoria's death 238
Seymour's courtship of Constance
  178
sister Charlotte's death 151
Sybil (Disraeli) 123–4
Thackeray, friendship with 137–8,
  138–9
unhappiness 108
West Central Friday Night Club
  227
Rothschild, Louise de ('Lou') 51, 77, 78,
  83, 114, 130, 138, 168, 175
Rothschild, Marie de (née Perugia) 238,
  261, 264, 267–8, 269, 270
Rothschild, Mathilde Hannah von
  139–40, 141–2, 158

Rothschild, Mayer Alphonse James de
    ('Alphonse') 153, 156, 157, 161, 169
Rothschild, Mayer Amschel de (Hannah
    and Nathan's son) 51, 77–8, 117, 130,
    133, 142, 150, 165, 188, 189, 190, 191
Rothschild, Mayer Amschel (Gutle's
    husband) 17
    1808 police raid and arrest 23–4
    apprenticeship 17–18
    Barent Cohen, relationship with 28,
        29
    birth 17
    children 18–19, 20
    coin dealing 18
    Dalberg, relationship with 24
    death 35
    Grünes Schild home 20–1, 21
    Gutle, marriage to 16–17, 18
    Henriette's dowry 37
    Hoffaktor (court agent) 18
    Jewish community, representing/
        bankrolling 27
    Nathan's business faults 29
    Nathan's marriage 30
    registering on civic register and taking
        civic oath 27
    remembered in 1994 Rothschild
        gathering 361
    textile trade 28
    will 35–6, 37
    William I, prince elector of Hesse,
        relationship with 24
    women's exclusion 2–3, 7, 35–6
Rothschild, Mayer Carl von 114, 141
**Rothschild, Miriam Louisa (sometimes
    'Miriam Lane')** 312, 360
    Adamson Collection 351–2
    America visits 288–9
    Ashton cottage 290, 295–6, 303
    Ashton Wold 289, 290, 296, 299, 332,
        349, 350–2, 354–5, 357, 359, 360, 361,
        365
    Ashton Wold, war-time use of 290,
        295–6
    atheism 302
    Benedictus' job interview 327
    birth 256

bisexuality 312–13, 332
Bletchley Park work 294–5, 296–7
bovine TB 297
cattle breeding and floriculture 299
Chalet Friedheim, Wengen,
    Switzerland 310, 313, 315, 332
Charles moving back home 350
Charlotte's skiing accident 333
childhood 253–4, 257
children 299, 303, 314, 327–8
children, loss of 299, 302
children's further education 331, 333
Confrontation in the Forest
    (Motesiczky) 335, 336
Dear Lord Rothschild 350, 354–5
death 364–5
Dolly's death 357
Eichmann trial 328
Elsfield Manor 303, 310, 313, 314, 327,
    329, 332, 334
entertaining 359, 360
environmental concerns 329, 349, 359
family history essays 362–4
father's return from sanatorium 275
father's suicide 278
fleas, cataloguing Rothschild 310, 333
Fleas, Flukes and Cuckoos 302–3
Foster, living with 289
Gay, relationship with 313
Gay's children, wardship of 315
Gay's suicide 314–15
George, meeting and marrying 296–7
George, separation from 310
George taken as POW 297
George's post-war behaviour 299
'Great Thanksgiving Meeting' 270–1
Guinness, Sir Alec, friendship
    with 361
higher education 279
Holocaust, family lost in 301
Holocaust survivors, helping 299–300
honorary doctorates 334, 364
House of Rothschild, The (film) 287
Israel visits 307, 327–8, 332
Jewish heritage 364
Jewish property rights, advocate
    for 300–1

Lady Bird Johnson, friendship
    with 359
lecture tours 333
legacy 364–5
Liberty in Ashton Wold cottage 351
Liberty's death 357
Liberty's mental illness 282, 295,
    330–1, 351
Marie-Louise, relationship with 332,
    334, 335, 342–3
Marine Biological Association
    laboratory, Plymouth 280, 290–1
modern Rothschilds, opinion of 354–5
mothering style 313–14, 327–8
mother's death and bequests 289–90
myxomatosis committee 310–11
Naples Marine Biological Station 280
Natural History Museum trustee 334
New Year Honours 2000 364
Nica, visits to 325, 354
Nica's drug charge 325–6
Nica's visits to Ashton Wold 303, 355
Old Mistresses (Parker and
    Pollock) 342–3
phone calls 360
portrait 331, 334
Prince Charles's recognition 364
Rosie's attitude to Jewish heritage 348
Rosie's feminism 341, 342–3
Rosie's visits 359
'Rothschild Women' 2, 5
Royal Free Hospital lectureship 334
Royal Society Fellowship 354
Schizophrenia Research Fund 330
Scrap Club 279
Second World War bombing 290–1
Second World War refugees 288, 289
sexism, experiences of 334
suicides, loved ones' 278, 314–15
suitors 287
television appearances 360–1, 360
Victor, relationship with 286, 336–7
Walter's bequests 285–6
wheelchair-dependency 361
Who's Who entry 336
wildflower gardens 349, 350, 359, 361
Wolfenden report 311–13

zoological studies and
    publications 279, 280, 286–7, 302–3,
    310, 327–8, 329–30, 332–4
Rothschild, Moses 18
Rothschild, Nat de see Rothschild,
    Nathaniel de ('Nat')
Rothschild, Nathan (Leopold's son) 261
Rothschild, Nathan Mayer de
    Abraham's will 55
    Anthony's romances 109
    apprenticeship 28, 29
    Austria consul appointment 56–7
    birth 19
    Austrian barony 57
    Board of Deputies of British Jews 69
    British government, banker to 34–5
    business faults 29
    caricatures 57–8, 65, 138
    children 31, 33, 35, 50–1
    children's education 51
    Cornhill office 29
    death 86–7
    death threat 58
    England, move to 22–3
    English language 29–30, 51–2
    family animosity and
        reconciliation 47–8
    family life 52
    family portrait 52, 65
    family's mourning for 98
    father-in-law's death 33
    funeral and burial 88–9
    Gunnersbury Park 89
    Hannah, marriage to 30–1
    Hannah's business role 31–2, 35, 60–1,
        73, 79–80, 85, 86, 89–90
    Henriette's alignment with 44–5
    Henriette's marriage 42–4
    illness 84–6
    James's wedding 58–9
    Jewish emancipation campaign 70–1
    knighthood offer 56
    legacy 88
    Lionel's wedding 83–4
    in Manchester 29, 31
    Montefiores, friendship with 41–2
    New Court home 33–4, 49

Rothschild, Nathan Mayer de (cont.)
 obituary 88
 Oppenheim portraits of sons 88
 Piccadilly home 6–2, 61
 Prince Edmond's proposal 104
 smuggling operations 32, 34
 Stamford Hill House 49–50
 success 29, 30, 34
 will 86, 105, 146
Rothschild, Nathaniel Charles
  ('Charles')
 banking role 255–6
 birth 189
 depression 257, 258, 267, 275–6
 family time 257
 father's bequests 265
 First World War 248, 253, 258
 jazz, interest in 280
 return from sanatorium 275
 Rózsika, meeting and marrying 255
 at sanatorium 267, 274
 suicide 278
 Walter, jealousy of 255
 Walter's Tring Museum 256
 Zionism 263, 266
 zoology, passion for 279, 302, 314
Rothschild, Nathaniel Charles Jacob
  ('Jacob'), 4th Baron 316, 358, 362
Rothschild, Nathaniel de ('Nat') 35, 51,
  59, 73, 83, 104–5, 106–7, 122, 133, 136
Rothschild, Nathaniel Mayer ('Natty'),
  1st Baron
 antisemitism experiences 187
 barony 213
 birth 113
 Charles as heir 255–6, 265
 children 184
 Constance's crush on 177
 death 265, 273
 Edward, Prince of Wales/Edward VII,
  friendship with 187, 188, 238
 electoral reform bill 167, 168
 Emma, marriage to 169–70
 father's illness 189
 First World War duties 258
 Grasmere visit 154, 155
 Lady Gosford, affair with 238

 Louisa, animosity with 189
 Member of Parliament 165, 201
 Rózsika, meeting 255
 Tring Park 184–5, 186
 Walter's removal from bank 256
 Zionism 263, 265
Rothschild, Nathaniel Mayer Victor
  ('Victor'), 3rd Baron 256–7, 278, 279,
  282, 285, 286, 287, 295, 321, 325, 336–7,
  359
Rothschild, Nathaniel Mayer von
  ('Puggy') 175, 176, 240
Rothschild, Natty, 1st Baron see
  Rothschild, Nathaniel Mayer
  ('Natty'), 1st Baron
Rothschild, Nica see Rothschild,
  Kathleen Annie Pannonica ('Nica')
  (later Baroness de Koenigswarter)
Rothschild, Puggy see Rothschild,
  Nathaniel Mayer von ('Puggy')
Rothschild, René de see Rothschild,
  Lionel James Mayer René de
  ('Rene')
Rothschild, Rózsika (née
  Wertheimstein)
 Arundel House 256, 275
 Ashton Wold 257, 276, 289
 background 254
 Balfour Declaration 269
 banking role 274–5, 276
 Charles, meeting and marrying 255
 Charles's depression 258, 267, 274,
  275–6
 Charles's return from sanatorium 275
 Charles's suicide 278
 children 256
 concerns about family on
  Continent 275
 Cséhtelek, trips home to 257
 death 289, 293
 English suspicion of 258
 Evelyn's death 270
 familial crises 267
 family duties 258, 265, 270, 275
 father's death 275
 flight from Continent 248, 253–4
 funeral 293

'Great Thanksgiving Meeting' 27–1
House of Rothschild, The (film) 287
Liberty's mental illness 282, 283–4
lobbying about Austria and
    Hungary 276
Miriam, letter given to 336
mother-in-law (Emma), friendship
    with 256
mothering instinct, lack of 256–7
Nica and Liberty on Continent 281
Nica, reunion with 292–3
Nica's debutante season 281
Rothschild eccentricities 255–6
Tisza's assassination 275
Tring Park 255–7, 258, 268, 281
war-time precautions 272
Weizmann, coaching 266
Weizmann, meeting 258, 264
Weizmann, support for 265
Weizmann's meeting with Lord
    Cecil 265–6
Zionism 265–6, 267–8, 269, 270–1, 275
Zionist memorandum 267
Rothschild, Salomon Mayer von 19, 23,
    24–5, 27, 37, 39, 46–7, 48, 57, 58, 59,
    65–6
Rothschild, Teresa Georgina ('Tess') (née
    Mayor) 313
Rothschild, Victor, 3rd Baron *see*
    Rothschild, Nathaniel Mayer Victor
    ('Victor'), 3rd Baron
Rothschild, Walter, 2nd Baron *see*
    Rothschild, Lionel Walter
    ('Walter'), 2nd Baron
Rothschild, Wilhelm Carl von
    ('Willy') 97, 139–40, 141–2
'Rothschild Women' (Miriam
    Rothschild) 2, 5
Rothschilds, Die (Waschneck) 288
''Round Midnight' (Monk) 302, 324–5
Round Midnight (Tavernier) 355
Rouse, Charlie 324
Royal Academy of Arts, London 65, 207,
    208, 211
Royal Drawing Society 281
Royal Free Hospital 334
Royal Northumberland Fusiliers 258

19 rue d'Artois (later rue Laffitte),
    Paris 60, 75, 77
rue Saint-Georges, Paris 156, 157
Ruskin, John 208
Russell, Lord John (later John Russell,
    1st Earl Russell) 127, 129, 130, 132,
    153, 165–6, 167
Russian Empire 225, 262, 264, 273

Sacramental Test Act (1828) 69
Samuel, Herbert 270
Samuels, Andrew 358
Santa Paula, SS 294
Savagner, police chief 23, 24–6
schizophrenia 330, 351
Schlemmer, Fritz 51, 72, 87
Schnapper, Bella Gans 12–13
Schnapper family 12–13; *see also*
    Rothschild, Gutle (née
    Schnapper)
Schnapper, Gutle *see* **Rothschild, Gutle**
    (née Schnapper)
Schnapper, Wolf Salomon 12–13, 13–14,
    16, 18
Second World War
    bombing raids 290
    Dunkirk evacuation 292
    German advance in France 292
    Holocaust 298, 299–300, 301, 308, 328
    Italy captured by Allies 298
    Jewish property rights 300–1
    Operation Tarbrush 297
    Rothschild contributions 293–4,
        294–5, 296–7, 298
    Rothschild homes, use of 289, 290,
        295–6
    start of 288
Sephardic Jews 42, 45, 51
sexual exploitation/trafficking 223–4,
    228–9
Seymour, Alfred 178, 181
Sharett, Moshe 306, 309, 310
Shepherd, Naomi 2, 362–3
Shepherd's Bush rescue home *see*
    Charcroft House, Shepherd's Bush,
    London
Sieff, Israel 262, 264–5

'Silent Members of the First EEC, Family Reflections II: The Women, The' (Miriam Rothschild) 362–4

Silver, Horace 322–3

smallpox 221

Smirke, Sydney 89, 90

Smit, F.G.A.M. 311

Smythe, George 123

Society of Lady Artists 211–12

Sokolow, Nahum 267

Spare Rib 338–41, 341–2, 343–5, 346, 347, 358

Stamford Hill House, Stamford Hill, London 49–50, 51, 52, 57, 60, 62, 63, 74, 89

Stanhope Hotel, New York 319–20, 320, 321, 322, 362

Stead, W.T. 228, 229

stock market 48, 74, 75–6, 78, 79, 87, 256

Stokes, George Henry 150

Subversive Stitch, The (Parker) 347–8

suicide 278, 314

Surrey House, Marble Arch, London 204, 216, 223, 230–1, 237, 244, 248

Swan coffee house, Aston Clinton, Buckinghamshire 201

Swiss Cottage Library, London 340

Sybil (Disraeli) 123–4, 194

Sydney, John Robert Townshend, 3rd Viscount 187

Sykes, Sir Mark 268, 270

Tancred (Disraeli) 125

Teleki, Countess Iska 254, 255

temperance movement 198–9, 200–1, 201–2

Test and Corporation Acts 68, 69

Thackeray, Annie 149

Thackeray, William Makepeace 137–8, 138–9, 147

Thomson, Arthur Landsborough 334

Times, The 58, 87, 88, 106, 127–8, 208, 235, 268, 277–8, 285

Tom Thumb 117–18, *118*

Torn in Two (Parker) 364, 365

Travers, Dr Benjamin 85, 86, 87

Treatise on the Physiological and Moral Management of Infancy (Combe) 114

Tring Park, Hertfordshire 184–5, *185*, 188, 255–7, 258, 265, 267, 279, 285–6, 350

Ullmann, Baron 300

United States of America 67, 282–3, 288–9, 294, 306; *see also* **Rothschild, Kathleen Annie Pannonica ('Nica') (later Baroness de Koenigswarter)**

42 Upper Grosvenor Street, Mayfair, London 160, 161, 162, 163

Victoria, Queen 100–1, 106, 166, 187, 213–14, 215, 216–17, 218, 220–2, 236–8, 278

Vienna 57, 59, 134, 255

Villa Grande, Bygdøy, Oslo 301

Villa Pignatelli, Naples 97

Villa Victoria (formerly Villa Rothschild), Grasse, France 220, 222, 245

Waddesdon Manor, Buckinghamshire 218, 307, 308, 315

Weaver, Beryl 347

Webb, Beatrice 228, 236, 241–2

Weehawken, New Jersey 323, 326, 352–3, 355, 356

Weizmann, Chaim
  background 262
  Balfour Declaration 269
  death 308
  Democratic Fraction of Zionists 262
  Dolly, correspondence with 261–2, 263, 264
  Evelyn's death 270
  'Great Thanksgiving Meeting' 270
  passionate conviction 264–5
  presidency of Israel, frustration about 306–7
  Rothschild opposition 267–8
  Rothschild support 263, 265–6, 267, 269